STATISTICS
An Introduction
FOURTH EDITION

ROGER E. KIRK
Baylor University

HARCOURT BRACE COLLEGE PUBLISHERS
Fort Worth   Philadelphia   San Diego   New York   Orlando   Austin   San Antonio
Toronto   Montreal   London   Sydney   Tokyo

Publisher	Earl McPeek
Acquisitions Editor	Lisa Hensley
Market Strategist	Kathleen Sharp
Developmental Editor	Janie Pierce-Bratcher
Project Editor	Laura Miley
Art Director	Carol Kincaid
Production Manager	Andrea Johnson

ISBN: 0-03-019337-0
Library of Congress Catalog Card Number: 98-88276

Address for Orders
Harcourt Brace College Publishers, 6277 Sea Harbor Drive, Orlando, FL 32887-6777
800-782-4479

Address for International Orders
International Customer Service
Harcourt Brace & Company, 6277 Sea Harbor Drive, Orlando, FL 32887-6777
407 345-3800
(fax) 407 345-4060
(e-mail) hbintl@harcourtbrace.com

Address for Editorial Correspondence
Harcourt Brace College Publishers, 301 Commerce Street, Suite 3700, Fort Worth, TX 76102

Web Site Address
http://www.hbcollege.com

Harcourt Brace College Publishers will provide complimentary supplements or supplement packages to those adopters qualified under our adoption policy. Please contact your sales representative to learn how you qualify. If as an adopter or potential user you receive supplements you do not need, please return them to your sales representative or send them to: Attn: Returns Department, Troy Warehouse, 465 South Lincoln Drive, Troy, MO 63379.

Printed in the United States of America

8 9 0 1 2 3 4 5 6 7   039   9 8 7 6 5 4 3 2 1

Harcourt Brace College Publishers

PREFACE

The fourth edition of *Statistics: An Introduction* reflects 39 years of experience teaching introductory statistics to more than 4000 students. I write this text for students in the behavioral sciences, health sciences, and education who are taking their first course in statistics. My goal is twofold: to provide a sound introduction to descriptive and inferential statistics and to acquaint students with computer software printouts.

During my career I have seen the profound impact that technology—computers, handheld calculators, and multimedia classrooms—has had on the way I teach statistics and the way my students learn statistics. The time-honored approach of teaching students to mechanically follow cookbook formulas is no longer appropriate. Computers have taken the drudgery out of statistics and broadened the students' statistical horizons—now students can compute the most complex statistics in a matter of seconds. Consequently, students need to understand the logic of statistical procedures, they need guidelines to help them decide when various procedures are appropriate, and they need to understand the assumptions and limitations of the various statistics. In addition, they need to become familiar with computer printouts. *Statistics* was written to meet these needs.

This fourth edition has been extensively revised in response to the 1996 recommendations of the APA Board of Scientific Affairs' Task Force on Statistical Inference. The Task Force recommended that researchers provide more extensive descriptions of data in the form of means standard deviations, sample sizes, box plots, and other graphics. Furthermore, they recommended that researchers provide enhanced characterizations of results using measures of effect size, confidence intervals, and techniques to detect anomalies in data such as outliers. Professors who are familiar with previous editions of this text will discover many changes. The most important changes are a greater emphasis on practical as opposed to statistical significance and the presentation of confidence intervals and measures of effect size alongside traditional null hypothesis significance tests in Chapters 10–15. Other changes include (1) a greater emphasis on visual approaches to understanding data such as box plots and graphs of confidence intervals; (2) discussion of procedures for detecting outliers; (3) coverage of newer, more powerful multiple comparison procedures; and (4) the inclusion of printouts from three popular microcomputer statistics packages: JMP®, SPSS®, and SYSTAT. Some of the JMP®, SPSS®, and SYSTAT printouts contain terms and statistics that are not routinely covered in introductory statistics books. To make this material accessible to students, I provide simplified discussions of selected advanced topics such as multiple regression, detecting outliers, and the use of unpooled variances in the two-sample t test for means. Also, I have included a few statistics such as the coefficient of variation that are not widely used in the behavioral sciences and education but, nevertheless, routinely appear in printouts.

Students will find this edition easier to read than previous editions. Feedback from students has enabled me to identify and simplify the difficult concepts and procedures. I remain convinced that clarity and readability can be achieved without sacrificing accuracy and depth of coverage. In this edition, I continue to rely on verbal rather than mathematical explanations. To be sure, the student will encounter the usual formulas and a few proofs, but the level of mathematics is very elementary. A familiarity with high school algebra is sufficient for understanding the text. For those whose mathematical skills are rusty, Appendix A provides a review of elementary mathematics. The diagnostic mathematics skills test in Appendix A can be used for testing one's mathematical knowledge or for identifying concepts that should be reviewed.

Statistics: An Introduction contains a number of special features that should facilitate a student's ability to learn statistics. These features include (1) chapter outlines at the beginning of chapters, (2) an expanded discussion in Chapter 1 of how to study statistics, (3) the use of color and boldface type to emphasize new terms and definitions, (4) an extensive glossary of statistical symbols (Appendix B), (5) chapter summaries, (6) an unusually complete index, (7) Check Your Understanding exercises interspersed throughout each chapter, and (8) review exercises at the end of each chapter. The review exercises indicate which concepts and procedures are most important, present interesting real-life examples from recent journal articles of the way statistics are used, and provide practice in applying what has been learned. Answers are given in Appendix C for all of the Check Your Understanding exercises. The student database in Appendix E provides an additional source of exercises. This database enables students to gain experience drawing random samples and computing statistics using real data. Students will find that selecting an appropriate statistic is easier with the help of the Selection Guide for descriptive and inferential statistics on the front endpaper. The back endpaper provides a quick reference for important formulas.

Ancillaries available for this text include an instructor's manual with test bank and a student's study guide. These supplements may be obtained through a local Harcourt Brace representative or by contacting Harcourt Brace Customer Service at 1-800-237-2665.

ACKNOWLEDGMENTS

It is a pleasure to express my appreciation to the following reviewers for reading the manuscript and providing thoughtful and helpful comments: Frank Bagrash, California State University, Fullerton; Dennis Cogan, Texas Tech University; Penny L. Fidler, California State University, Long Beach; Leslie A. Gill, Eastern New Mexico University; Michael Granaas, University of South Dakota; Carolyn Mangelsdorf, University of Washington; David Mostofsky, Boston University; John H. Neel, Georgia State University; Robert Newman, California State University, Long Beach; Linda M. Noble, Kennesaw State University; and Nancy Stone, Creighton University. Many thanks to Karen Schriefer who did an outstanding job of proofreading the manuscript. Lisa Hensley, Janie Pierce-Bratcher, Andrea Johnson, Laura Miley, and Carol Kincaid of Harcourt Brace also deserve special recognition for their efforts in making this book a reality.

I am grateful to the Literary Executor of the late Sir Ronald A. Fisher, F. R. S., to Frank Yates, R. S., and to Longman Group Ltd., London, for permission to reprint Tables D.1, D.2, D.3, D.6 and D.8 from their book *Statistical Tables for Biological, Agricultural and Medical Research* (6th edition, 1974).

I am also grateful to E. S. Pearson and H. O. Hartley, editors of *Biometrika Tables for Statisticians,* Vol. 1, and to the *Biometrika* trustees for permission to reprint Tables D.5 and D.10; and to the editor of the *Journal of The American Statistical Association* for permission to reprint Tables D.7 and D.11.

Portions of the book were written while on sabbatical from Baylor University. I am indebted to the administration of Baylor University and in particular to Robert B. Sloan, Donald D. Schmeltekopf and Wallace L. Daniel for providing an environment that encourages creative and scholarly activity.

And finally I want to express my appreciation to my statistics classes for what I trust has been a mutually rewarding learning experience. Comments about this edition and suggestions for future editions are welcome. Please direct all correspondence to my attention at the Department of Psychology and Neuroscience at Baylor University, or you may contact me via e-mail at roger_kirk@baylor.edu. My Web page

http://www.baylor.edu/~Psychology/Roger_Kirk/kirk.html

contains a list of typographical errors that is updated as they are discovered.

Roger E. Kirk

CONTENTS

Appendixes

References   **744**

Index   **749**

Chapter 1

Introduction to Statistics

1.1 INTRODUCTION

Some Misconceptions

It is widely believed that statistics can be used to prove anything—which implies, of course, that it can prove nothing. Furthermore, the word *statistics* conjures up visions of numbers piled upon numbers, uninterpretable charts, and computers cranking out gloomy predictions. To the ordinary person, besieged from all sides by advertising claims, statistics is hocus-pocus with numbers. It was Benjamin Disraeli who said, "There are three kinds of lies—lies, damned lies, and statistics."[1] In primitive cultures, exaggeration was common. One writer, with tongue in cheek, reasoned that because primitive people did not have a science of statistics, they were forced to rely on exaggeration, which is a less effective form of deception. Another writer remarked that "if all the statisticians in the world were laid end to end—it would be a good thing." Whatever its public image, statistics endures as a required course, and my students continue to refer to it, affectionately no doubt, as Sadistics 2402.

What Is Statistics?

In spite of frequent misuse, statistics can be an elegant and powerful tool for making decisions in the face of uncertainty. The word *statistics* comes from the Latin *status*, which is also the root for our modern term *state* or political unit. Statistics was a necessary tool of the state, because to levy a tax or to wage war a ruler had to know the number of subjects in the state and the amount of their wealth. Gradually the meaning of the term expanded to include any type of data.

Today the word **statistics** has four distinct meanings. Depending on the context, it can mean (1) data; (2) functions of data, such as the mean and range; (3) techniques for the collection, analysis, and interpretation of data for subsequent decision making; and (4) the science of creating and applying such techniques.

Why Study Statistics?

A knowledge of statistics yields more than the obvious benefits. For example, it generates new ways of thinking about questions and provides effective tools for an-

[1] Three recent books indicate that Disraeli's view of statistics is still with us: *How to Tell the Liars from the Statisticians* by Hooke and Liles, *Misused Statistics: Straight Talk for Twisted Numbers* by Jaffe and Spirer, and *Statistical Deception at Work* by Mauro.

swering them. It takes only a cursory examination of the professional literature in your own field to see the inroads made by statistical techniques and ways of thinking. Statistics is an indispensable tool for researchers in the behavioral sciences, health sciences, and education, but its usefulness is not limited to research. In many fields, it is virtually impossible to keep up with new developments without an understanding of elementary statistics. Also, statistics is an interesting subject—some people even find it fascinating.

In all likelihood, you are reading this book because it was assigned in your required statistics course. You have been told that the study of statistics is necessary, and there is a strong implication that it will be good for you. At this point you may be skeptical. Just what can you expect to learn by studying statistics? A quick scanning of this book will give you an idea. You will acquire a new vocabulary, because in many ways learning statistics is like learning a foreign language, and you will learn to manipulate numbers according to symbolic instructions. But more important, you will learn when and how to apply statistics to research problems in the behavioral sciences, health sciences, and education. Your study of statistics should enable you to read the literature in your field with greater understanding and make you a more critical consumer of statistical presentations in the mass media. And you should gain a greater appreciation of the probabilistic nature of scientific knowledge. Statistics involves a special way of thinking that can be used not only in research but also in one's daily life. I hope that you will add this way of thinking to your conceptual arsenal.

Kinds of Statisticians

Users of statistics fall into four categories: (1) those who must be able to understand statistical presentations of findings in their fields; (2) those who select, apply, and interpret statistical procedures in their work; (3) applied statisticians; and (4) mathematical statisticians.

This book is addressed to those in the first two categories, including psychologists, educators, sociologists, speech therapists, biologists, nurses, medical researchers, political scientists, and physical therapists, to mention only a few. In each case the person's primary interest is in his or her own field, be it sociology or city planning; he or she is interested in statistics because it is a useful tool for answering questions in that field. Such persons are both consumers and users of statistics. Their knowledge of statistics may range from meager to expert.

The applied statistician helps professionals in substantive areas to use statistics effectively.[2] He or she may work for industry or a government agency, engage in a private consulting practice, or teach in a university. Unlike individuals in the first two categories, an applied statistician usually has advanced degrees in statistics.

---

[2] Two pamphlets, "Careers in Statistics" and "Statistics as a Career: Women at Work," describe career opportunities for statisticians. These pamphlets are available from the American Statistical Association, 806 15th St. N.W., Washington, DC 20005.

The mathematical statistician is primarily interested in pure (mathematical) statistics and probability theory rather than in the application of statistics to substantive areas. Most likely this statistician teaches in a university and makes contributions to the theoretical foundations of statistics that may ultimately be used by those with applied interests.

1.2 STUDYING STATISTICS

Effective Study Techniques

Psychologists say that learning is easier when you can integrate new information into an existing knowledge base. Unfortunately, as you begin your study of statistics, your statistical knowledge base is minimal. Building a knowledge base is easier if you use effective study techniques. For example, always survey the material to be read by thumbing through the assigned pages and noting topic headings and boldfaced terms. Try to get a sense of what the material is about. Your survey will provide a general orientation to the material and help you fit facts together as you develop your statistical knowledge base.

Before you begin reading a section in the text, turn the section heading into a question. The question for this section might be, "What are some effective study techniques?" After you have formed your question, look for the answer as you read the section. Research on learning tells us that an active, searching attitude on the part of the reader promotes better learning than a passive attitude. After reading a section, try to recall the main points of the section by reciting out loud. All of us have had the experience of reading a paragraph and having no idea of what we have just read. Knowing that we will attempt to recall what we are reading develops a mental set to select and retain important facts.

Most forgetting takes place within the first 24–48 hours after learning. You can minimize the forgetting process by reviewing your assignment a day or so after reading it. Look at the major headings and boldfaced terms and see whether you can recite the main points that were covered in the section and the meaning of each boldfaced term. If the contents of some sections are hazy, reread these sections and see whether you can then recall the main points.[3]

Plan to Read More Slowly

Statistics cannot be read like assignments in history, English, or political science. Ideas and computational procedures in statistics are presented in a highly symbolic

---

[3] These study suggestions are based on the famous SQ3R study method developed by Francis P. Robinson (1946). The letters SQ3R stand for *S*urvey, *Q*uestion, *R*ead, *R*ecite, and *R*eview.

form and use a specialized vocabulary that must be learned. Consequently, a 30-page assignment may take three or four times as long to read as a comparable assignment in history. You will understand many sections of this book on a first reading; others will require two or more readings, lots of concentration, and perhaps some time between readings for the ideas to sink in.

Don't Worry If You Weren't an Ace in Math

If you're concerned about the level of mathematics required to understand statistics, stop worrying. Most statistical procedures in this book involve nothing more complicated than addition, subtraction, multiplication, and division. Although some use is made of high school algebra, the level is very elementary. For those whose skills are rusty, the essential arithmetic and algebra are reviewed in Appendix A.

Resolve to Review Often

Frequent reviews of the material are a must, or it will slip away. Don't skip the *Check Your Understanding* exercises at the end of each section and the end-of-chapter *Review Exercises.* They provide (1) feedback about what you know and what you don't, (2) an indication of which concepts and computational procedures are the most important, (3) numerous examples of how statistics are used, and (4) practice in applying what you are learning. Answers to the *Check Your Understanding* exercises are given in Appendix C. The chapter *Summaries* also are useful for reviewing because they present a condensation of the most important concepts and place the topics in perspective.

Master Foundation Concepts Before
Going On to New Material

In statistics, as in mathematics or a foreign language, the material presented first is the foundation for what follows. Each chapter should be mastered before you go on to the next. Fight the temptation to cram. Cramming can be effective for some subjects, at least as far as tests are concerned. But in statistics it inevitably results in superficial understanding of basic concepts and subsequent learning problems. Periodic reviews require discipline, but they pay off.

Strive for Understanding

This book contains hundreds of formulas. I have not memorized all of them, and neither should you. Some, such as the one for the arithmetic mean, $\overline{X} = \Sigma X/n$, appear so often that you really can't help learning them; the others aren't worth the effort. I decided a long time ago, when faced with my own inability to remember telephone numbers and addresses, that books are better repositories than my head for such things. In all likelihood you will do most of your statistical calculations with computers and calculators. These tools have phenomenal memories for formulas and can spew out statistics at the press of a key.

Instead of memorizing formulas, strive to understand the important concepts and think about ways that the concepts can be applied. In what situations is a particular statistic useful? How is the statistic interpreted? What assumptions must be fulfilled to interpret the statistic? When you read about an experiment in your field, consider how you would have designed it and how you would have analyzed the data. And check out your ideas by talking about them with your professor.

1.3 BASIC CONCEPTS

Population and Sample Defined

Many statistical terms are a legacy from the time when statistics was concerned only with the condition of the state. *Population,* for example, originally meant, and still means, the total number of inhabitants of a state. Its meaning in statistics is broader.

A **population** is the collection of all people, objects, or events having one or more specified characteristics.

The population is identified when we specify its common characteristics. All the people listed in a telephone directory constitute a population, as does the number of heads and tails obtained in tossing a coin for eternity.

A single person, object, or event is called an **element** of the population.

The population of telephone book listees contains a **finite** number of elements; the population resulting from tossing the coin contains an **infinite** number.

A population is either concrete or conceptual. For example, the population of telephone book listees is **concrete**—given sufficient time we could contact each person because the number of elements is finite and the population is well defined. The population of heads and tails is **conceptual**—try as we may, we can't record all the results of tossing a coin for eternity. This population exists as an idea rather than as a material object.

A population could consist of all the students in a university (people), their cars (objects), or their pep rallies (events).

The number or label used to represent an element of the population is called an **observation** or **datum.**

It is a measurable characteristic of the elements. The observation for students in a university might be their GPAs, their cars' gas mileage, or the number attending their pep rallies. If 362 students attended the second pep rally, the observation for this event is 362 students. The selection of an appropriate population for an experiment is determined by the nature of the research questions that a researcher wants to answer as well as by such practical matters as the availability of population elements.

A **sample** is a proper subset of a population.

That is, a sample can contain a single element or all but one of the population elements. For practical reasons, such as limited resources and time, or because the population is infinite in size, most research is carried out with samples rather than with populations. It is assumed that the study of a sample will reveal something about the population. This leap of faith often appears to be justified, as when a laboratory technician analyzes a sample of a patient's blood or when an automobile manufacturer crash tests a sample of bumpers. Occasionally, however, samples lead us astray. Later we'll see how and why.

Descriptive and Inferential Statistics

It is useful to divide statistical techniques into two categories: descriptive and inferential.

Descriptive statistics are tools for depicting or summarizing data so that they can be more readily comprehended.

When we say that a player's lifetime batting average is .420 or when we determine that 54% of voters favor a presidential candidate, we are using descriptive statistics. A computer printout listing the Scholastic Aptitude Test (SAT) scores of all college students in California would boggle our minds—not so, a statement that their mean SAT is 1054. Large masses of data are difficult to comprehend. Descriptive statistics reduce data to some form, usually a number, that is easily comprehended. We will discuss a variety of descriptive statistics in the first half of this book.

We saw that it is usually impossible for researchers to observe all the elements in a population. Instead they observe a sample of elements and generalize from the sample to all the elements—a process called **induction.**

They are aided in this process by **inferential statistics,** which are tools for inferring the properties of one or more populations from an inspection of samples drawn from the populations.

Inferential statistics were developed to improve decision making in cases where successive observations exhibit some degree of variation although they are obtained under conditions that appear to be identical. The variation may be due to (1) inherent variability in the phenomenon being observed or differences among participants, (2) errors of measurement, (3) undetected changes in conditions, or (4) a combination of these. In the behavioral sciences, health sciences, and education, differences in the past experiences and heredities of participants are the major stumbling blocks to induction. Suppose that a physiologist wants to know whether a new drug will arrest the development of cancer in humans. It is impossible to administer the drug to the population of all cancer victims, but it is possible to administer the drug to a sample. The physiologist would probably attempt to control attitudinal and other extraneous factors by administering an inert druglike substance, a *placebo,* to half the sample and the new drug to the other half. Suppose that remission of cancer occurred in 100% of the sample receiving the new drug and in only 8% of those receiving the placebo. The difference, 100% versus 8%, between the drug and placebo samples is dramatic. The physiologist would probably conclude that if the drug had been administered to the population of all cancer victims, the remission rate would have been higher than if the population had received the placebo. But what if the remission rate were 12% for the new drug and 8% for the placebo? We know that chance factors can produce a difference between two samples even though the samples are taken from the same population and receive identical treatments. Is the difference, 12% versus 8%, greater than would be expected by chance? Stated another way, if the experiment were repeated many, many times, could the physiologist predict with confidence that the difference would consistently favor the sample receiving the drug? This is the kind of question that can be answered using inferential statistics. We will describe procedures for answering such questions in the latter half of this book.

Random Sampling

Some samples provide a sound basis for drawing conclusions about populations; others do not. The difference lies in the method by which the samples are selected.

The method of drawing samples from a population such that every possible sample of a particular size has an equal chance of being selected is called **random sampling,** and the resulting samples are **random samples.**

People, when left to their own devices, find it virtually impossible to produce random samples. Consider the following experiment. One hundred people are asked to write down a random sample of four numbers from the first 20 positive integers. According to our definition of random sampling, samples containing the elements 1, 2, 3, 4 or 14, 16, 18, 20, for example, should occur as frequently as any other sample of size four. It turns out that such samples are rarely produced. People avoid writing down samples with consecutive or equally spaced integers and attempt to produce samples that span the range from 1 to 20.

Sampling methods based on haphazard or purposeless choices, such as soliciting volunteers, using students enrolled in introductory psychology, or selecting every 10th person in an alphabetical listing of names, produce **nonrandom samples.** Such samples, unlike random samples, do not provide a sound basis for deducing the properties of populations. Hence, whenever sampling is mentioned in this book, it will refer to random sampling. A detailed discussion of random sampling in Chapter 8 must await the development of other basic concepts. At this point, we will simply illustrate several characteristics of random samples.

Consider a box containing 300 balls, each identified by a number stamped on its surface. Of the balls, 200 are red *(R)*, and 100 are black *(B)*. If you didn't know the ratio of red to black balls, which is two to one (denoted by 2:1), you could estimate the ratio by drawing a random sample of balls from the box. You close your eyes, shake the box vigorously, reach in, withdraw a ball, note its color and number, and replace it. You do this six times and obtain the following sample: R_{102}, R_{75}, B_{39}, R_{62}, B_{37}, R_{50}. The subscripts — 102, 75, and so on — denote the numbers stamped on the balls. From this sample you would infer that the box contains more red than black balls — in fact, twice as many red balls. Suppose you drew four more samples, each time replacing the balls drawn, and obtained R_{154}, B_{62}, R_{35}, R_{143}, R_4, R_{29} (sample 2); R_{104}, B_{41}, B_{21}, R_{50}, R_{192}, R_{67} (sample 3); B_{28}, B_{41}, R_{150}, B_{61}, R_{88}, R_{148} (sample 4); and R_{152}, R_{120}, B_{88}, R_{33}, R_{36}, B_5 (sample 5). The results of the five random samples are summarized in Table 1.3-1.

This simple experiment illustrates several points about random samples. First, the elements obtained (and the ratio of red to black balls) differ from sample to sample. This is referred to as **sampling fluctuation** or **chance variability.** Second, the characteristics of a sample do not necessarily correspond to those in the population. It turns out, however, that the larger a random sample, the more likely it is to resemble closely the population. Hence, researchers prefer to work with large samples if it is economically feasible. Although there is no guarantee that large random samples will resemble the population, in the long run they are more likely to do so than small ones.

TABLE 1.3-1.   Outcomes of Drawing Five Random Samples

	Sample				
	1	*2*	*3*	*4*	*5*
Number of red balls	4	5	4	3	4
Number of black balls	2	1	2	3	2
Ratio of red to black	2:1	5:1	2:1	1:1	2:1

CHECK YOUR UNDERSTANDING OF SECTIONS 1.1–1.3[4]

1. Users of statistics fall into four categories.
   a. List the categories.
   b. Considering your vocational goals, into which category do you fall? Why?
2. For each of the following statements, indicate (a) the population, (b) the element, and (c) the observation to be recorded.
   a. At least 50% of white women students in this university are ambivalent about having a career.
   b. Tequila Tech students are involved in more automobile accidents than other drivers in their age group.
   c. At least 80% of the homes in Chickasha, Oklahoma, have color televisions.
   d. Students at Ginebra University who hold outside jobs have higher grade point averages than those who don't hold outside jobs.
   e. According to a recent Centers for Disease Control report, one of every 92 American men between the ages of 27 and 39 has the AIDS virus.
   f. According to the U.S. Department of Education, 49.5% of female high school students have peformed a community service during the past two years.
3. What are the lower and upper limits on the size of a sample?
4. Indicate whether each of the following procedures would produce a random sample (R) or a nonrandom sample (NR) of students in an introductory sociology class.
   a. Write each student's name on a slip of paper, place the slips in a hat, shake the hat, and draw out 10 names.
   b. Place the blindfolded instructor in the middle of a circle made up of all the class members. Have the instructor point to 10 people around the circle. The student nearest the position pointed to becomes an element of the sample.
   c. For each student, flip a fair coin. If the coin lands heads, the student is in the sample.
   d. Line up the students from the tallest to the shortest. The first, third, fifth, seventh, . . . , 21st students become members of the sample.

---

[4] Answers to the *Check Your Understanding* exercises are given in Appendix C. These exercises often contain multiple questions about a particular concept. If you have a good grasp of the concept, answering three or four questions about it may not be an efficient use of your time. If, however, your answer to a question is incorrect, reviewing the concept in the text and then answering several more questions dealing with the concept is advisable. One of the purposes of these exercises is to provide feedback about what you know and what you don't know.

5. Terms to remember
   a. Population
   b. Element
   c. Sample
   d. Observation (datum)
   e. Datum
   f. Descriptive statistics
   g. Inferential statistics
   h. Random sample
   i. Nonrandom sample
   j. Sampling fluctuation (chance variability)

1.4 DESCRIBING CHARACTERISTICS BY NUMBERS

People, objects, and events have many distinguishable characteristics. Early in the design of an experiment, two key decisions must be made: What characteristics should be measured? And how should the characteristics be measured? The answer to the first question is determined by the researcher's interests. Suppose a researcher is interested in the SAT scores of men and women college students. College students differ in many ways: gender, age, SAT scores, major, hair color, family income, and so forth, but only two characteristics are of interest in this example—gender and SAT score. These are the characteristics that are measured. The others are ignored. The second question, concerning how the characteristics should be measured, is less straightforward. The issue here is how to assign numbers to people, objects, or events so that the numbers accurately reflect the characteristic we want to measure. In the process of examining this issue, we will discuss variables and constants and see how mathematicians classify variables.

Variables and Constants

A **variable** is a characteristic that can take on different values. A variable also is a symbol, often a letter toward the end of the alphabet, such as X or Y, that is used to stand for an unspecified element of a set.

The set of elements for which the variable stands is called the **range** of the variable, and each element of the range is called a **value.** When we assign to a variable one of the elements in its range, we say that the variable "takes" this value. For example, the variable of gender might take the value women.

A **constant** is a characteristic that does not vary. A constant also is a symbol, often a letter toward the beginning of the alphabet, such as a, b, or c, whose range consists of a single element.

The ratio of the circumference of a circle to its diameter, denoted by π, is a constant because its range consists of the single value 3.1415926536. . . .

Perspectives on Numbers

We observed that selection of the characteristics to be measured is relatively straightforward and is determined by the researcher's interests. The second key decision, deciding how the characteristics should be measured or classified, isn't as simple. For example, we could measure or classify the scholastic aptitude of seniors at McKinley High by (1) assigning each student a label such as average, high average, or superior, based on his or her SAT score; (2) ranking or ordering students' SAT scores from highest to lowest and assigning each student the number of his or her rank; or (3) assigning each student her or his actual SAT score. Depending on the measuring scheme adopted, Jonathan Whiz would be designated, respectively, superior, 3, or 1480. The variable of political preference can be classified by assigning a unique symbol such as D or 1 to Democrats, I or 2 to independents, and R or 3 to Republicans.

 The assignment of numbers or labels to characteristics of people, objects, or events and the accuracy of the representation are central concerns of researchers but not of mathematicians. Only during its formative years was mathematics tied to the real world. Then it seemed perfectly natural to prove mathematical theorems by recourse to counting and measuring. But in recent times mathematics has shed its real-world ties—mathematicians are now free to manipulate symbols that are totally devoid of empirical meaning. They are interested in the formal properties of the systems they create; applications in the real world are left to other specialists. The theoretical work of mathematicians and mathematical statisticians laid the foundation for a vast collection of statistical tools. The researcher who uses these tools must decide whether a particular tool is appropriate for his or her research application and whether the numbers assigned to variables accurately represent the characteristics of interest. This division of interest between the developers and users of statistics has led to considerable confusion about the correct uses of statistical tools and also to two ways of thinking about numbers.

Classification of Variables in Mathematics

Mathematicians classify variables as qualitative or quantitative.

A **qualitative variable** is a symbol whose range consists of attributes or non-quantitative characteristics of people, objects, or events, for example, gender (men, women), race (Caucasian, African American, Asian, other), and grade in a course (A, B, C, D, F).

The categories of a qualitative variable are (1) mutually exclusive (nonoverlapping), which implies that an element cannot be in more than one category, and (2) exhaustive, which implies that an element must be in one of the categories. The categories may or may not suggest an order or rank. For example, grades in a course—A, B,

C, D, F—clearly order academic achievement from highest to lowest, but no order is suggested by the categories for gender, race, religious preference, or blood type. Course grade is an example of an **ordered qualitative variable.** Gender, race, religious preference, and blood type are examples of **unordered qualitative variables.**

A **quantitative variable** is a symbol whose range consists of a count or a numerical measurement of a characteristic.

Quantitative variables can be discrete or continuous. A variable is **discrete** if its range can assume only a finite number of values or an infinite number of values that is countable. That is, the infinite number of values can be placed in a one-to-one correspondence with the counting or natural numbers. Family size is an example of a variable with a finite range. It can assume values 1, 2, 3, 4, and so on, but not 200, 8000, or any noninteger value such as 0.5 and 4.3. The rational numbers—numbers that can be expressed as the ratio of two integers, for example, 2/2, − 2/3, 7/4— illustrate countably infinite numbers. There is no largest number and no smallest number, and between, say, 1 and 2, an infinite number of rationals can be inserted, for example, 3/2, 4/3, 5/4. . . . Other examples of discrete quantitative variables are the number of parking tickets received, the number of trials required to learn a list of nonsense syllables, and one's score on a standardized achievement test. In each of these examples, the value assigned to the variable is obtained by counting, and the counting units—family members, parking tickets, learning trials, or achievement test items—are equivalent in arriving at the total count.

By contrast, a variable is **continuous** if its range is uncountably infinite. Such a range can be likened to points on a line that have no interruptions or intervening spaces between them. Examples of continuous variables are temperature in Bangor, Maine, during January; length of fish caught off the Florida Keys; and speed of cars on the New Jersey Turnpike. Although a variable is continuous, our measurement of it is by necessity discrete because of limitations in the measuring instrument. For example, the thermometer is usually calibrated in 1° steps, the ruler in 1/16 inches, and the speedometer in 1 mile per hour. Consequently, our measurement of continuous variables is always approximate. Discrete variables, on the other hand, can be measured exactly. A husband and wife with two children are a family of exactly four, but a temperature of 80°F can be any temperature between 79.5° and 80.5°F.

The classification scheme for variables is summarized in Table 1.4-1. It is useful to mathematicians and statisticians because the nature of the variable determines which mathematical tools can be used in solving problems and doing derivations and proofs. Hence, the classification scheme is a convenience; it was not devised to mirror characteristics in the real world. When we use statistical methods to answer real-world questions, we must remember that the methods were developed to analyze numbers as numbers. If the numbers analyzed bear no relation to the characteristics in which we are interested, the statistical methods will yield answers that are meaningless.

TABLE 1.4-1.   Mathematicians' Classification of Variables

Type of Variable	Characteristics
Qualitative variable	Range consists of nonoverlapping and exhaustive categories that represent attributes or nonquantitative characteristics.
Unordered	Categories do not suggest an order or rank.
Ordered	Categories suggest an order or rank.
Quantitative variable	Range consists of a count or a numerical measurement of a characteristic.
Discrete	Range consists of only a finite number of values or an infinite number of values that is countable.
Continuous	Range consists of an uncountably infinite number of values.

Measuring Operations in the Behavioral Sciences, Health Sciences, and Education

Numbers are used for a variety of purposes, three of which are of particular interest to behavioral scientists, health scientists, and educators: (1) to serve as labels, (2) to indicate rank in a series, and (3) to represent quantity. For example, a football player is identified by the number 10 on his uniform, a team is ranked number two in the UPI poll, and the winning touchdown play covered 20 yards. Without thinking, we treat these numbers differently. It doesn't take a football fan to know that player 30 is not three times player 10 and that the number two team is not necessarily twice as good as the number four team, but a 20-yard touchdown play did indeed move the ball twice as far down the field as a 10-yard play. We intuitively treat the numbers differently because they involve different levels of measurement.

Measurement is the process of assigning numbers or labels to characteristics of people, objects, or events according to a set of rules.

We will see that the rules used to assign the numbers or labels determine the level of measurement. S. S. Stevens (1946), a behavioral scientist, identified four levels of measurement: nominal, ordinal, interval, and ratio.

Nominal Measurement

Nominal measurement is the simplest of the four levels. It consists of assigning elements to mutually exclusive and exhaustive *equivalence classes* so that those in the same class are considered to be equivalent to one another, whereas those in different classes are not equivalent. The classes are then denoted by a set of distinct labels. The set of labels constitutes a **nominal scale**.

Assignment of men to one equivalence class called "men" and women to the other called "women" is nominal measurement. The set of labels, "men" and "women," constitutes a nominal scale. Numbers can be used instead of words to identify the two classes, for example, 1 for women and 2 for men. Numbers used in this way are simply alternative labels for the equivalence classes. We could just as well have assigned the numbers 9 and 6, respectively, to women and men. The substitution of the number 9 for 1 and the number 6 for 2 is an example of a **one-to-one transformation.**[5] The numbers 9 and 6 are as useful for distinguishing between the equivalence classes as any other one-to-one transformation. The numbers in a nominal scale could be added, subtracted, averaged, and so on, but the resulting numbers would tell us nothing about the equivalence classes represented by the numbers. For example, $1 + 2 = 3$ and $9 + 6 = 15$, but neither 3 nor 15 corresponds to any characteristic of men or women. This follows because we didn't utilize the properties of size and order of numbers when we assigned them to the classes. The only property of numbers that we utilized is that 1 is distinct (different) from 2, 3. . . . Thus, the labels assigned to equivalence classes in nominal measurement only have the property of *distinctness*.

There are many examples of nominal scales in psychology and education, for example, Eysenck's four personality types (stable-extrovert, stable-introvert, unstable-extrovert, unstable-introvert), the primary taste qualities (sweet, sour, salty, bitter), and categories of psychoses (organic, functional). There is a correspondence between a nominal scale and the range of one of the mathematician's types of variables. The nominal scale corresponds to the range of an unordered qualitative variable.

Ordinal Measurement

Ordinal measurement consists of assigning elements to mutually exclusive and exhaustive equivalence classes that are ranked or ordered with respect to one another. The classes are then denoted by numbers or other ordered symbols, such as letters of the alphabet, that reflect the rank of the classes. The labels assigned to equivalence classes in ordinal measurement have the properties of *distinctness* and *order*. The set of labels constitutes an **ordinal scale.**

The labels used in ordinal measurement contain more information than those in nominal scales: both distinctness and order.

The ranking of political candidates with respect to voter appeal is an example of ordinal measurement. If candidate Jane is judged to have the greatest appeal, followed by Keith, Lewis, and then Marvin, we could assign Jane the number 1; Keith, 2; Lewis, 3; and Marvin, 4. We have no reason to believe that Keith, ranked second, is half as appealing to voters as Jane or that the difference in appeal between Jane and Keith, 1 versus 2, is the same as the difference between Keith and Lewis, 2 ver-

---

[5] A one-to-one transformation associates with each element in one set one and only one element in a second set, and vice versa. For example, if the two sets are men and women, {Jim, Chuck, Dave} {Lisa, Faith, Kristi}, each man is paired with one and only one woman, and each woman is paired with one and only one man. For example, a one-to-one transformation might result in the following pairs: Jim and Kristi, Chuck and Lisa, and Dave and Faith.

sus 3. The numbers indicate rank order but not magnitude or difference in magnitude between classes. The numbers assigned to the equivalence classes can be subjected to any monotonic transformation. A **monotonic transformation** permits one to replace the original set of numbers with new numbers as long as the new numbers have the same order as the original numbers. For example, the set of ordered numbers 2, 16, 39, 40 would serve just as well as 1, 2, 3, 4 to rank the four candidates because only the order and not the distance between any two numbers is important. Alternatively, we could assign the letter *A* to Jane, *B* to Keith, *C* to Lewis, and *D* to Marvin. The transformations that can be applied to ordinal scales are more restrictive than those that can be applied to nominal scales. This follows because the labels in ordinal scales contain more information that needs to be preserved, both distinctness and order, than do the labels in nominal scales.

Some characteristics, such as people's heights, can be measured in several ways, for example, ranking from tallest to shortest or recording actual feet and inches. The latter procedure assigns numbers that represent the magnitudes of the equivalence classes and therefore has several advantages over ordinal measurement, as we shall see later. For the moment we simply note that ordinal measurement is most often used when it is difficult or impossible to apply more refined measuring procedures. For example, it is difficult to precisely measure the tastiness of three pizzas or the leadership qualities of four political candidates. However, it is not too difficult to rank-order pizzas with respect to tastiness or candidates with respect to leadership qualities.

Numerous examples of ordinal scales can be found in the behavioral sciences, health sciences, and education, for example, classification of mentally subnormal children (borderline, educable, trainable, profoundly retarded) and professorial rank (instructor, assistant professor, associate professor, professor). Such ordinal scales correspond, in the language of the mathematician, to the range of an ordered qualitative variable.

Interval Measurement

The numbers assigned in interval measurement contain much more information than the labels used in nominal and ordinal measurement.

In **interval measurement,** the numbers assigned to equivalence classes have the properties of distinctness and order, and in addition, equal differences between numbers reflect equal magnitude differences between the corresponding classes. The measurement procedure consists of defining a unit of measurement, such as a calendar year or 1°F, and determining the number of units required to represent the difference between equivalence classes. The set of numbers assigned to the equivalence classes constitutes an **interval scale.**

In our measurement of calendar time, the same amount of time elapsed between 1970 and 1971 as between 1971 and 1972, and similarly, the temperature difference between 70° and 75°F is the same as that between 80° and 85°F. A given numerical interval, say 1 year or 5°F, represents the same difference in the characteristic measured, irrespective of the location of that interval along the measurement scale. In other words, numerically equal distances along the measurement continuum represent empirically equal differences among the corresponding equivalence classes—that is, the measured characteristic.

Because the units of measurement along interval scales are empirically equal, it is meaningful to perform most arithmetic operations on the numbers. For example, we can say that the difference between 80° and 60°F is twice as great as that between 60° and 50°F. That is, the ratio of intervals $(80° - 60°F)/(60° - 50°F) = 2$ has meaning with respect to temperature. However, not all arithmetic operations are permissible because the starting point or origin of an interval scale is always arbitrarily defined and does not correspond to an absence of the measured characteristic. In the case of the Fahrenheit scale, 0 corresponds to the temperature produced by mixing equal quantities by weight of snow and salt. This 0 does not indicate an absence of molecular action and hence an absence of heat. Therefore, although $80°F/40°F = 2$, we cannot say that 80°F is twice as hot as 40°F. The ratio $80°F/40°F = 2$ is uninterpretable because the zero point on the scale, 0°F, does not correspond to the absence of temperature. The same interpretation problem occurs for calendar time, which is measured from the birth of Christ, and altitude, which is measured from sea level.

The numbers in an interval scale can be subjected to any positive linear transformation. A **positive linear transformation** of a variable, say X, consists of multiplying X by a positive constant b and adding a constant a to the product. That is, a transformed value, X', is given by $X' = a + bX$. For example, degrees Fahrenheit, F, can be transformed into degrees Celsius, C, by means of the positive linear transformation

$$C = \frac{5}{9}(-32) + \frac{5}{9}F,$$

where $a = \frac{5}{9}(-32)$ and $b = \frac{5}{9}$. Although the variable represented by an interval scale may be continuous, our measurement of it is always discrete because measuring instruments are calibrated in discrete steps. Thus, in practice an interval scale corresponds to the range of a discrete quantitative variable.

Ratio Measurement

The numbers assigned in ratio measurement contain the most information.

> In **ratio measurement,** the numbers assigned to equivalence classes have the properties of distinctness, order, equivalence of intervals, and, in addition, the origin of the scale represents the absence of the measured characteristic. The set of numbers assigned to the equivalence classes constitutes a **ratio scale.**

Ratio scales have all the properties of interval scales plus an absolute zero. Most scales in the physical sciences are ratio scales—height in inches, weight in pounds, temperature on the Kelvin scale, and elapsed time such as the age of an object.

Not only is the difference between 5 and 6 inches the same distance as that between 10 and 11 inches, but also an object that is 10 inches long is twice as long as an object that is 5 inches long. Ratio scales permit us to make meaningful statements about the ratio of the numbers assigned to the two objects, for example, 10 in./5 in. = 2; hence 10 inches is twice as long as 5 inches. The properties of a ratio scale mentioned in the previous paragraph permit us to perform all arithmetic operations on the numbers. However, the only transformation of a ratio scale that preserves these properties is **multiplication by a positive constant:** $X' = bX$, where X' is the transformed value, b is a positive number, and X is the original value. For example, we can transform inches into centimeters by multiplying inches by the constant $b = 2.54$: 10 in. is equal to $(2.54 \times 10) = 25.4$ cm., and 5 in. is equal to $(2.54 \times 5) = 12.7$ cm. Ten inches is twice as long as 5 inches, and similarly, 25.4 centimeters is twice as long as 12.7 centimeters. As we move from measurement in which the labels contain the least information (nominal scales) to those containing more information (ordinal, interval, and ratio scales), more and more constraints are placed on the transformations that can be meaningfully applied. This occurs because the numbers in ordinal, interval, and ratio scales contain more information that can be altered or destroyed by a transformation. In practice, a ratio scale, like the interval scale, corresponds to the range of a discrete quantitative variable. The major characteristics of the four scales are summarized in Table 1.4-2.

Implications of the Two Ways of Thinking About Numbers

Two ways of thinking about numbers have been described: one reflects the concerns of mathematicians, and the other, the concerns of behavioral scientists, health scientists, and educators. Statistical methods were developed for analyzing numbers as numbers, whether or not the numbers are true measures of some characteristic. If the assumptions associated with the statistical methods are fulfilled, they will produce answers that are formally correct as numbers. And this is true regardless of the degree of correspondence between the numbers and the characteristic they represent. The problem comes in translating statistical results into statements about the real world. If numbers representing a nominal scale are manipulated arithmetically, the result will be numbers that are numerically correct but uninterpretable. If nonsense is put into the equation, nonsense indeed will come out.

Most researchers are very sensitive to the potential pitfalls associated with interpreting numbers produced by statistical procedures—and rightfully so. Some authors have even gone so far as to prescribe the statistical procedures that can be used with each measurement scale.[6] Except in the physical sciences, few scales have equal intervals, so the number of statistical techniques on the approved list is relatively small. However, this position fails to recognize that the measurement of many variables in the behavioral sciences and education lies somewhere between the ordinal and interval levels. The IQ scale is a good example. Most psychologists and educators agree that the 10-point difference between IQs of 100 and 110 represents a slightly smaller intellectual difference than the 10-point difference between IQs of 130 and 140. Although the 10-point differences do not represent identical

[6] Examples can be found in Senders (1958), Siegel (1956), and Stevens (1946, 1951).

TABLE 1.4-2.   Overview of Levels of Measurement

Level of Measurement	Characteristics
Nominal	Symbols serve as labels for mutually exclusive and exhaustive equivalence classes. The symbols have the property of distinctness. *Appropriate transformation:* any one-to-one substitution *Examples:* gender, eye color, racial origin, personality types, and primary taste qualities
Ordinal	Ordered symbols, usually numbers, indicate rank order of equivalence classes. The symbols have the properties of distinctness and order. The size of differences between ordered symbols provides no information about differences between equivalence classes. *Appropriate transformation:* monotonic *Examples:* military rank, classification of mentally retarded children, rank in high school, and a supervisor's ranking of employees.
Interval[a]	Equal differences among numbers reflect equal magnitude differences among equivalence classes, but the origin or starting point of the scale is arbitrarily determined. Numbers have the properties of distinctness, order, and equivalence of intervals. *Appropriate transformation:* positive linear *Examples:* Fahrenheit and Celsius temperature scales, calendar time, and altitude
Ratio[a]	All the properties of interval scales apply, and, in addition, the origin of the scale reflects the absence of the measured characteristic. *Appropriate transformation:* multiplication by a positive constant *Examples:* height, weight, Kelvin temperature scale, and measures of elapsed time

[a] These two levels are sometimes referred to collectively as **metric measurement** or **numerical measurement.**

intellectual differences, the intellectual differences are believed to be similar. Hence, IQ scores contain more information than ordinal scales but less than interval scales.

Another example of a measurement scale that is between the ordinal and interval levels is the attitude rating scale: strongly disagree = -2, disagree = -1, neutral = 0, agree = 1, strongly agree = 2. The numbers -2, -1, 0, 1, 2 contain ordinal information. However, it is unlikely that the actual difference in attitudes between 0 and 1, for example, is identical to the difference between 1 and 2. But, the difference in attitudes between 0 and 1 is probably similar to the difference between 1 and 2. Thus, the five numbers along the attitude scale do contain some information about the magnitude differences in attitudes.

Should we avoid performing arithmetic operations on scores when the measurement is between the ordinal and interval levels? This question has been heatedly debated.[7] We cannot look to mathematicians and statisticians for answers because the question is outside their province. The answer must come from users of statistics who are acquainted with the problems of translating numerical answers into statements about the real world. An examination of the professional literature reveals that most experts in the behavioral sciences, health sciences, and education do apply arithmetic operations to numbers even though the measurement is somewhere between the ordinal and interval levels; further, they interpret the results as if differences between the numbers reflect something about the differences in the measured characteristics. Apparently, experts prefer to utilize whatever magnitude information the numbers contain, even though differences among the numbers only approximate the true magnitude differences.

If a researcher believes that any transformation of a set of numbers that preserves the order of the original numbers adequately represents the equivalence classes, he or she should treat the scale as ordinal. If the researcher's intuition is correct, the numbers contain no magnitude information, and they should not be treated as though they do. It is the researcher, the person most familiar with the data, who must decide how much information the numbers contain.

†Some Subtle Problems in Interpreting Numbers

The preceding discussion has emphasized the importance of avoiding interpretation errors by being sensitive to the degree of correspondence between a set of numbers and the characteristic they represent. Consider now some not-so-obvious interpretation problems that occur when a test has an arbitrary zero point. Suppose that on a standardized arithmetic-achievement test, Mortimer received a score of 0, Dude, a score of 30, and Reginald, a score of 60. Can we conclude that Mortimer knows nothing about arithmetic? Obviously not; a score of 0 means that he couldn't answer any questions on the test, but easier questions may exist that he could answer. Achievement tests, as well as many other tests, have arbitrary rather than absolute zero points and therefore fall short of ratio measurement. It follows that although Reginald's score of 60 is twice as high as Dude's 30, Reginald's arithmetic achievement isn't necessarily twice Dude's.

The interpretation problem that results from lack of equal intervals is more subtle. Suppose we compare the effectiveness of two methods of teaching arithmetic. Students in a class using method A gained an average of 10 points; those in a class using method B, 7 points. The results seem straightforward—on the average, students using method A gained more points than those using method B. But suppose that at the beginning of the experiment the two classes were not equal in arithmetic achievement. Let the average score for class A be 50 and the average score for class

---

[7] The major issues in this debate have been presented by Anderson (1961), Boneau (1961), Gaito (1960), and Stevens (1968). These articles are reproduced in Kirk (1972, chap. 2) along with suggestions for further reading on the issue. Also of interest are articles by Gardner (1975), Marcus-Roberts and Roberts (1987), and Wainer (1976).

† This and similarly marked sections can be omitted without loss of continuity.

B be 80. Is it possible that a 7-point change from 80 to 87 represents more improvement in arithmetic achievement than a 10-point change from 50 to 60? Unless we know that, say, a 10-point change anywhere on the measurement scale represents the same empirical change, the interpretation of the experiment is equivocal. The greater the difference between the classes' initial average achievement scores, the greater the interpretation problem.

Consider finally the interpretation problem that occurs when a test doesn't have enough difficult items to adequately differentiate among high-scoring participants. Suppose that two individuals make the top score of 60. For one participant, this may represent maximum capability, but the other person may be capable of a much higher performance. The measuring instrument is simply incapable of showing it. Because of the limitations of the measuring instrument, it would be incorrect to conclude that the two individuals are equal in the characteristic measured.

Because numbers don't always mean what they appear to mean, they must be carefully scrutinized. The key principle that runs throughout this section is that a researcher must be guided by two sets of rules. When the tools of statistics are used, the mathematician's and statistician's rules must be followed. When the numbers are interpreted as statements about the real world, the behavioral scientist's measurement rules must be followed.

CHECK YOUR UNDERSTANDING OF SECTION 1.4

6. Ignoring for the moment limitations of measuring instruments, classify measures of the following according to the mathematician's scheme (unordered qualitative, U; ordered qualitative, O; discrete quantitative, D; continuous quantitative, C).
   a. Size of family
   b. Race
   c. Paper and pencil test of marital compatibility   *C — agree – disagree not measured exactly.*
   d. Seeding of tennis players
7. Because of the limitations of measuring instruments, measurement of some variables is of necessity approximate. Classify the variables in Exercise 6 according to whether our measurement is exact (E) or approximate (A).
8. Reclassify the variables in Exercise 6 according to the mathematician's scheme, taking into account limitations in our ability to measure some of the variables.
9. Classify the variables in Exercise 6 with respect to level of measurement, taking into account limitations in our ability to measure some of the variables.
10. For each level of measurement, indicate the appropriate transformation that can be performed on the numbers.
11. What level of measurement is most often achieved (a) in the physical sciences and (b) in the behavioral sciences and education?

12. A score of 0 on an achievement test doesn't necessarily mean that the individual knows nothing about the subject. Explain.

13. Suppose that achievement test scores for a control group increased from 62 to 65, and those for the experimental group increased from 68 to 74. What must be true to conclude unequivocally that the experimental group improved twice as much as the control group?

14. Terms to remember

   a. Variable
   b. Range of variable
   c. Value of variable
   d. Constant
   e. Qualitative variable
   f. Quantitative variable
   g. Measurement
   h. Equivalence class
   i. One-to-one transformation
   j. Monotonic transformation
   k. Positive linear transformation

†1.5 HISTORICAL DEVELOPMENT OF STATISTICS[8]

National Statistics

The science of statistics grew out of an attempt to solve practical problems associated with raising taxes, producing insurance tables, and determining the odds in games of chance. Its subject matter was shaped by three lines of development—national statistics, probability theory, and experimental statistics. The oldest of these three is **national statistics,** which were enumerative and descriptive in character; national statistics can be traced to the beginning of recorded history. David numbered his people, and the Egyptians and Romans kept detailed records of taxes and other state resources. Caesar Augustus simplified the enumerative process by ordering all citizens to report to the nearest statistician, better known as the tax collector. The descriptive use of statistics came of age in the work of an English army captain, John Graunt (1620–1674), who published in 1662 a small book of birth and death statistics for London from 1604 to 1661. Unlike earlier works, such as William the Conqueror's *Domesday Book,* which simply contained data compiled for purposes of taxation and military service, Graunt's book summarized and interpreted the data. His was the first work to shed light on the regularity of social phenomena. It marked the beginning of a theory of annuities and led to the founding of insurance societies.

Probability Theory

A second and independent line of development in statistics is **probability theory.** The earliest traces of probability, found in the Orient around 200 B.C., concerned

---

[8] The development of this section was strongly influenced by Dudycha and Dudycha (1972). Their article provides a more complete introduction to the history of statistics with special emphasis on the behavioral sciences.

† This and similarly marked sections can be omitted without loss of continuity.

whether an expected child would be a boy or girl. However, the real impetus for the development of probability came not from prospective parents but from gamblers who wanted to know the odds of winning at various games of chance. Leading mathematicians and scientists of the day—Pierre de Fermat (1601–1665), Blaise Pascal (1623–1662), Christianus Huygens (1629–1695), and James Bernoulli (1654–1705)—responded to the problem. Gradually they chiseled out the foundation of a theory of probability. A milestone in this development was the discovery of the normal curve of errors by Abraham de Moivre (1667–1754), a mathematics tutor who supplemented a meager income by calculating odds for gamblers at the coffeehouses he frequented. Apparently, de Moivre did not appreciate the significance of his discovery; it was published in 1733 only obscurely as a supplement written in Latin to a limited reprinting of a book he had published three years earlier. Therefore, it remained for others to demonstrate the pervasiveness of the *normal distribution.* For more than a century it was attributed to a later discoverer, Carl Friedrich Gauss (1777–1855), one of the greatest mathematicians of all time. It was also discovered independently by Pierre-Simon de Laplace (1749–1827), who forsook a cleric's robe for his lifework in celestial mechanics and probability. Both Laplace and Gauss used the normal distribution in investigating errors of observation in astronomy. Lambert Adolphe Jacques Quetelet (1796–1874), who is considered the father of social science, saw that the normal distribution and probability theory could be applied to all observational sciences—astronomy, anthropology, physics, the census, and the statistics of mental and moral traits. He used the normal curve, for example, to predict the number and type of crimes committed. His work integrated national statistics and probability theory and paved the way for the third line of development—experimental statistics.

Experimental Statistics

The emerging interest in the sciences in the early 1800s created a need for new statistical procedures and principles to guide the design of experiments. The result was **experimental statistics.** Its development was dominated by such intellectual giants as Sir Francis Galton (1822–1911). Terman, the developer of the Stanford-Binet intelligence test, estimated Galton's IQ at about 200. Galton, more than anyone before, used statistics in investigating problems of people and nature. His major statistical contributions were regression and correlation procedures (see Chapters 5 and 6), which he used to unravel mysteries of heredity. Karl Pearson (1857–1936) refined the mathematical theory of regression and made an astonishing number of other contributions to statistical theory and practice. Perhaps his greatest contribution was the development in 1900 of the chi-square test for goodness of fit (see Chapter 17), which is used in testing the significance of differences between observed data and those expected on the basis of some hypothesis.

The modern era in experimental statistics was ushered in by William Sealey Gosset (1876–1937), who derived the *t* distribution (see Chapter 11) in 1908. Thus began the development of exact inductive procedures appropriate for both large and small samples. Heretofore researchers had relied on large-sample statistical procedures.

Gosset, who published under the pseudonym of "Student," was a brewer for Messrs. Guiness. His discovery, like others in statistics, resulted from a practical need—in this case, the need for inductive procedures appropriate for small samples. He was involved in brewing research, where variable materials and susceptibility to temperature changes precluded the use of large samples.

The modern era matured in the work of Sir Ronald A. Fisher (1890–1962), whose contributions to statistics are legion. He is best remembered for his derivation of the F distribution, contributions to the design and analysis of experiments, and heated exchanges about statistical theory with Jerzy Neyman (1894–1981) and Egon Pearson (1895–1981). Fisher's work was a unique blend of the rigor of the mathematician with a common-sense approach; the latter was undoubtedly due to his applied work in agriculture, biology, and genetics.

Neyman and Pearson carefully consolidated the work of Fisher and others while developing their own theory of statistical inference. The bulk of the statistical arsenal of today's researcher can be traced to Fisher, Neyman, and Pearson. But in response to changing research needs, there have been many new developments. The computer has made possible the solution of problems that were heretofore intractable and has sparked new lines of inquiry. It seems unlikely, however, that a new era could be dominated to the extent that Fisher, Neyman, and Pearson dominated the one from 1920 to the present.

CHECK YOUR UNDERSTANDING OF SECTION 1.5

15. What three lines of development shaped the subject matter of contemporary statistics?
16. Briefly summarize the major characteristics of the three lines of development that shaped the subject matter of contemporary statistics.
17. What distinguishes the modern era in experimental statistics from the previous period?
18. Terms to remember
    a. National statistics   b. Probability theory
    c. Experimental statistics

1.6 SUMMARY

This book is addressed to consumers and users of statistics and, more specifically, to students in the behavioral sciences, health sciences, and education. One course doesn't make a statistician, but it can help you develop a basic understanding of and fluency in the technical jargon of statistics. This is useful because statistics is the universal language for communicating research findings.

The word *statistics* has several meanings; usually it refers either to a collection of techniques for making decisions based on data or to functions describing data, such as the mean and range. Your study of statistics should help you to (1) read the professional literature in your field, (2) design and analyze simple experiments, and (3) detect statistical fallacies in the mass media and technical reports. In addition, you should learn new, more critical and analytical ways of thinking.

Research questions usually concern characteristics of populations. For example, what do people of voting age think about an issue? Is one instructional technology for fifth graders more effective than another? Do 21-year-old women prefer smaller families than men of the same age? The populations are, respectively, the attitudes of voters on the issue, the achievement scores of fifth graders, and preferred family sizes of 21-year-old women and men. The term *population* generally refers to all the inhabitants of a city, state, or country. In statistics it refers to the collection of all people, objects, or events having one or more specified characteristics. It is rarely possible to observe all the elements of a population, either for practical reasons or because the population is infinite in size. Instead, we conduct research on a sample of elements. A sample can contain a single element or all but one of the population elements. If every sample of a particular size has an equal chance of being selected from the population, the sampling process is said to be random.

Statistics can be applied to data from samples or from populations to obtain a clearer understanding of their characteristics. If we obtained a random sample of 21-year-old women and men, we might find that on the average they prefer, respectively, 2.2 and 2.4 children. In addition, we might learn that the range for women was 0 to 14 and that for men was 0 to 8. The numbers 2.2 and 2.4 and the ranges 0–14 and 0–8 are descriptive statistics; they summarize properties of the two samples. Description is one important application of statistics. A second important application is inferring characteristics of a population by observing a sample. The sample statistics for preferred family size, for example, provide our best guess about the corresponding population values. These two uses of statistics, description and inference, are discussed in the first and second halves of this book.

Once a researcher has identified the population of interest and the characteristic to be observed, he or she must decide how the characteristic should be measured. Mathematicians and statisticians have historically classified variables as qualitative (ordered or unordered) or quantitative (discrete or continuous). This scheme evolved because different mathematical tools are used in derivations and proofs for the two kinds of variables.

Behavioral scientists, on the other hand, developed a classification scheme that reflected their concern with the degree to which numbers reflect the characteristics they represent. A four-level classification of measurement resulted: nominal, ordinal, interval, and ratio. Today we recognize that there are more than four levels of measurement and that the measurement of many variables in the behavioral sciences and education lies somewhere between the ordinal and interval levels. Much of the controversy surrounding the use of arithmetic operations with data between these levels can be resolved by adhering to two sets of rules. When the tools of statistics are used, the mathematician and statistician's rules must be followed; when the numbers are interpreted as statements about the real world, the behavioral scientist's measurement rules must be followed.

Modern statistics is the culmination of three historical lines of development: national statistics, probability theory, and experimental statistics. Its origins are in antiquity, yet most of the material in this book is the product of the 20th century. And we can expect to see an acceleration in the development of new statistical tools and theory—an acceleration made possible, in part, by the advent of the computer with its phenomenal capacity for information processing and storage.

REVIEW EXERCISES FOR CHAPTER 1[9]

1. The word *statistics* has four distinct meanings; list the four meanings.
2. Several benefits of studying statistics were mentioned; list at least three benefits.
3. How does the original meaning of the term *population* differ from today's statistical definition?
4. For each of the following statements, indicate (a) the population, (b) the element, and (c) the observation to be recorded.
   a. In the last presidential election, 36% percent of 18- to 24-year-olds voted.
   b. Approximately 16% of all children under 18 are members of families whose incomes are below the poverty level.
   c. Approximately 42% of all prison inmates are 21 to 26 years old.
   d. Approximately 32% of all high school graduates 18 to 24 years old are enrolled in college.
   e. Four out of 10 Americans are under 25 years old.
   f. According to a recent Centers for Disease Control report, one of every 1,667 American white women between the ages of 27 and 39 has the AIDS virus.
   g. According to the U.S. Department of Education, 38.4% of male high school students have peformed a community service during the past two years.
5. (a) Why is most research conducted on samples rather than populations? (b) How is sample size related to the resemblance between a random sample and the population?
6. Distinguish between descriptive and inferential statistics.
7. Mathematicians and behavioral scientists have somewhat different interests in numbers. Discuss these differences.
8. Ignoring for the moment limitations of measuring instruments, classify measures of the following according to the mathematician's scheme (unordered qualitative, U; ordered qualitative, O; discrete quantitative, D; continuous quantitative, C).
   a. Employee production on an assembly line
   b. Paper-and-pencil test of creativity

---

[9] Answers to the Review Exercises are given in the *Instructor's Manual*.

Chapter 2

Frequency Distributions and Graphs

2.1 INTRODUCTION

No two people respond exactly the same way in a situation. And even responses that have been overlearned exhibit some variability from time to time—on occasion, quarterbacks fumble the exchange from center, pianists play wrong notes, and actors muff their lines. It seems that variation in the behavior of people is inevitable. This lack of consistency is more troublesome in the behavioral sciences, health sciences, and education than in the physical sciences. A chemist can be confident that different samples of H_2O will react with another substance the same way under controlled tests. But this kind of consistency where people are involved is rare. The variability problem is usually handled by observing many people or by making many observations of the same people. The presumption is that if enough people are observed or if a person is observed enough times, errors due to variability will average out. This research strategy produces mountains of data and calls for procedures for depicting and summarizing the data so that they can be more readily comprehended. Two kinds of descriptive tools are used for this purpose: graphical methods and numerical methods. This chapter is devoted to graphical methods; numerical methods are described in Chapters 3 through 6.

2.2 FREQUENCY DISTRIBUTIONS

The first step in summarizing data is to organize the data in some logical fashion. This involves defining two or more equivalence classes and counting the number of observations in each class.

An **equivalence class** can be (1) a single score value, for example, Yale students with a 4-point GPA; (2) a collection of score values, Yale students with from five to nine traffic tickets; (3) or a qualitative category, Yale students with blue eyes. A table showing the equivalence classes and the frequency of occurrence of their elements is called a **frequency distribution.**

The equivalence classes of a frequency distribution are called **class intervals.** If each of the class intervals is a single score value, the frequency distribution is said to be **ungrouped.** If each class interval contains a collection of score values, the frequency distribution is **grouped.**

Ungrouped Frequency Distribution for Quantitative Variables

Suppose we administered a test of leadership aptitude to all high school football coaches in Punt County, Iowa. Their test scores are shown in Table 2.2-1. If we ex-

TABLE 2.2-1.   Leadership Aptitude Scores

Coach	Score	Coach	Score	Coach	Score
John Wilkins	55	William Odell	39	Frank Young	45
Holt Green	46	David Sloan	68	Dave Abbott	33
Brent Bishop	52	Bill Reynolds	52	Danny Scott	50
Charlie Seaman	51	John Kopplin	54	Ron Walbesser	51
Jim Bohannon	48	Tom Feather	48	Charles Dilday	54
John Deneve	50	Mike Bratcher	46	Winston Lamb	59
Ed Massey	30	John Achor	47	David Tobin	49
David Weaver	53	Joseph Hillis	44	Roger Harcourt	42
Jack Patton	57	Lewis Daniel	49	Robert Frish	56
Jane Benedict	62	Robert Hynan	50	Michael Barker	53

amine the table carefully, we see that the smallest score is 30 and the largest is 68 and that most of the scores are in the high 40s and low 50s. The same information can be extracted much more easily from the ungrouped frequency distribution in Table 2.2-2, which associates with each score value, X, the frequency of its occurrence, f. In constructing the frequency distribution we followed the convention of putting the largest score at the upper left of the table. In addition, each number between the largest and the smallest scores is listed in the distribution so that every possible score can be tallied and the gaps between scores easily detected.

The frequency distribution is an effective organizing device, but some information is lost. We cannot tell from Table 2.2-2 which coach made the highest score, which coach made the lowest score, or that one of the coaches is a woman. We must refer to the original data for this information.

TABLE 2.2-2.   Ungrouped Frequency Distribution for Leadership Aptitude Scores From Table 2.2-1

Score X	Frequency f	Score X	Frequency f	Score X	Frequency f	Score X	Frequency f
68	I	58	0	48	II	38	0
67	0	57	I	47	I	37	0
66	0	56	I	46	II	36	0
65	0	55	I	45	I	35	0
64	0	54	II	44	I	34	0
63	0	53	II	43	0	33	I
62	I	52	II	42	I	32	0
61	0	51	II	41	0	31	0
60	0	50	III	40	0	30	I
59	I	49	II	39	I		

TABLE 2.2-3   Grouped Frequency Distribution for Leadership Aptitude Scores From Table 2.2-1

Class Interval	Frequency, f
66–68	1
63–65	0
60–62	1
57–59	2
54–56	4
51–53	6
48–50	7
45–47	4
42–44	2
39–41	1
36–38	0
33–35	1
30–32	1
	$n^a = 30$

[a] n denotes the total number of scores in the frequency distribution.

Grouped Frequency Distribution for Quantitative Variables

If the spread of scores for a quantitative variable is large, it is useful to construct a **grouped frequency distribution** in which each class interval spans two or more score values, as shown in Table 2.2-3. Class intervals for a quantitative variable have a **nominal lower limit** and a **nominal upper limit;** for the class interval 66–68 they are, respectively, 66 and 68. However, the interval 66–68 actually includes any number *equal to or greater than* 65.5 and *less than* 68.5. The numbers 65.5 and 68.5 are called the **real limits** of the interval. They extend 0.5 below the nominal lower limit and approximately 0.5 above the nominal upper limit.[1] The nominal limits are used to denote each class interval; the real limits indicate the underlying continuity of the class intervals and are used to compute the **class interval size.** The size of a class interval, denoted by i, is given by

$$i = \text{real upper limit} - \text{real lower limit.}$$

---

[1] If our measurement were accurate to the nearest tenth, so that we had class intervals such as 6.6–6.8, the class interval nominal limits would be 6.6 and 6.8 and the real limits would be 6.55 and 6.85. These values are obtained by adding and subtracting 0.05 instead of 0.5 from the nominal limits. Similarly, if the class interval were 0.66–0.68 and our measurement were accurate to the nearest hundredth, the nominal limits would be 0.66 and 0.68 and the real limits would be 0.655 and 0.685, which differ from the nominal limits by ± 0.005.

For example, the size of the class interval 66–68, where the real lower limit = 65.5 and the real upper limit ≅ 68.5, is

$$i = 68.5 - 65.5 = 3,$$

as illustrated in the following figure.[2]

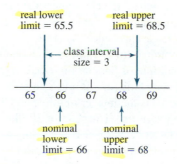

The concepts of real limits and class interval size also apply to the class intervals in ungrouped frequency distributions such as the one in Table 2.2-2. For the class interval 68, for example, the real limits are 67.5 and 68.5.[3] The class interval size is

$$i = 68.5 - 67.5 = 1,$$

as illustrated in the following figure.

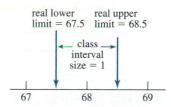

✳ Several conventions are followed in constructing a frequency distribution. They are not inviolate rules—think of them as guidelines for constructing easily interpreted tables.

1. The class intervals should be mutually exclusive; that is, the class intervals should be chosen so that a score belongs in one and only one interval.
2. For quantitative variables, there should be no gaps between the class intervals. In Table 2.2-3, even though no scores fall in the class intervals 63–65 and 36–38, the intervals are included for completeness.

---

[2] The symbol ≅ means "approximately equal."

✳ [3] Some variables do not follow this convention. A common example is age. If a person is 21, this means that the 21st birthday has passed but the 22nd has not. The real limits for the age 21 are 21.0 and 21.999.

3. All quantitative class intervals should have the same width or size.[4]

4. The distribution should have 10 to 20 class intervals unless the number of scores is very small, in which case it may be desirable to use fewer class intervals. For qualitative variables, the number of class intervals is usually dictated by the nature of the variable. For example, if the variable is gender, there may be three class intervals: men, women, and unknown.

5. For quantitative variables, one of the preferred class interval sizes should be used; these class intervals are 1, 2, 3, 5, 10, 15, 20, 25. . . .

6. The nominal lower limit of each quantitative class interval should be an integer multiple of the class interval size. In Table 2.2-5, for example, the nominal lower limit of the class interval 30–32 is 30 and is equal to 10×3, where 10 is the integer multiple and 3 is the class interval size. If the smallest score had been 31 instead of 30, the class interval still would be 30–32 and not 31–33 because 31 is not an integer multiple of 10.

7. For quantitative variables, opinion is divided as to whether the class interval containing the largest score should be at the top (top left) of the table or at the bottom (bottom left) of the table. My own preference is to put the class interval containing the largest score at the top left as in Table 2.2-2 and at the top as in Table 2.2-3. However, many statistical packages for computers (see Section 2.8) put the class interval containing the largest score at the bottom of the table.

   For qualitative variables, the order of the class intervals should reflect the order inherent in the variable. If the variable is unordered and logic does not suggest an order, the class intervals can be ordered alphabetically.

Determining the Number and Size of Class Intervals for a Quantitative Variable

The conventions for constructing a grouped frequency distribution provide general guidelines for the number and size of class intervals. We know that there should be 10 to 20 class intervals (unless there are only a few scores) and that one of the preferred class interval sizes, 1, 2, 3, 5, 10, 15, 20, 25, . . . , should be used. With

---

[4] Sometimes this is not possible or desirable. Suppose that one subject was unable to learn a list of nonsense syllables in the usual number of trials, 6–10, required by most subjects. After the 20th trial the subject was still unable to meet the learning criterion and gave up. This subject can't be given an exact score; he or she falls into the top class interval "20 or more." This interval is open because one real limit can be specified but not the other. Or, suppose that the class intervals represent family income. It might be desirable to make the bottom and top class intervals open to include the few families with extremely small or extremely large incomes.

these guidelines in mind, we can estimate the number and the size of class intervals in a trial-and-error fashion using the formula

$$\frac{\text{Range}}{\text{Preferred } i} = \text{Number of class intervals.}$$

The range is equal to the real upper limit of the largest score minus the real lower limit of the smallest score. A preferred class interval size ($i = 1$ or 2 or 3 or . . .) is selected by trial and error so that the formula yields between 10 and 20 class intervals. To illustrate, the largest and smallest scores in Table 2.2-1 are 68 and 30. The range is $68.5 - 29.5 = 39$. If a class size of 2 is tried in the formula, there will be $39/2 \cong 20$ class intervals. Because there are only 30 scores, a smaller number of class intervals would be preferable. If a class interval size of 3 is tried, the formula yields $39/3 = 13$ class intervals, the number used in Table 2.2-3. A class interval size of 5 should not be used because it would give only $39/5 \cong 8$ class intervals. For most sets of data, there will be no more than two class interval sizes that give the desired 10–20 class intervals. As a general rule, when the number of scores is small, use fewer than 15 class intervals; when the number is large, use 15–20.

Suppose that we have administered a test of reading readiness to 26 children enrolled in the first grade. The largest and smallest scores on the test are 132 and 73; the range is $132.5 - 72.5 = 60$. How many class intervals should the frequency distribution have and what should their size be? By trial and error and the formula

$$\frac{\text{Range}}{\text{Preferred } i} = \text{Number of class intervals,}$$

we see that two grouping schemes are possible: The class interval size, i, can be either 3 or 5 because both class interval sizes yield between 10 and 20 class intervals

$$\frac{60}{3} = 20 \quad \text{and} \quad \frac{60}{5} = 12.$$

The one in which $i = 5$ is preferred because there are only 26 scores. The smallest class interval, following convention 6, given earlier, would be 70–74 because 70 is an integer multiple of $i = 5$, that is, $14 \times 5 = 70$. The largest class interval would be 130–134. This grouping scheme actually results in 13 instead of 12 class intervals. The formula for estimating the number of class intervals has underestimated the required number because the smallest score (73) doesn't fall at or close to the real lower limit of its class interval (69.5), nor does the largest score (132) fall at or close to the real upper limit of its class interval (134.5). If the extreme scores had been 134 and 70 instead of 132 and 73, the formula for estimating the number of class intervals would have given 13 intervals—the number actually used. Suppose that we had tested 221 children instead of 26 in the example given earlier. In this case, a class interval size of 3 should be used. The smallest and largest class intervals would be 72–74 and 132–134 because 72 and 132 are integer multiples of 3. Even though the use of $i = 3$ results in 21 class intervals, it is preferred to

$i = 5$ because of the large number of scores. The purpose of graphical methods is to make data easier to comprehend, and sometimes this can best be done by departing from the conventions.

The Pros and Cons of Grouping Data

Grouping scores into class intervals where i is greater than 1 ($i > 1$) has several disadvantages. First, some information inevitably is lost. For example, we know from Table 2.2-3 that four scores occur in the class interval 54–56, but we don't know their individual values.

A second disadvantage is that the rules used to construct grouped frequency distributions do not always produce unique distributions. For any set of data, only one ungrouped frequency distribution can be constructed, but for grouped frequency distributions, there is often a choice between two class interval sizes. In such cases, the frequencies in the various class intervals will depend, for example, on whether the class interval size is 3 or 5.

The disadvantages of loss of information and lack of uniqueness resulting from grouping scores into class intervals where i is greater than 1 must be weighed against the simplicity achieved by grouping. If the spread of scores is large, a grouped frequency distribution is much more easily interpreted. Also, the construction of a grouped frequency distribution is necessary if a graph for a quantitative variable is to be made because the first step in making such a graph is to construct a grouped frequency distribution. Years ago grouping was used to minimize the labor required in computing statistics. The advent of calculators and computers eliminated this use for grouped frequency distributions.

Relative Frequency Distributions

To aid in the interpretation of a frequency distribution, it is often helpful to express each frequency as either a proportion or a percentage of the total number of scores. The formulas for proportionate frequency (*Prop f*) and percentage frequency (*% f*) are

$$Prop\, f = \frac{f}{n} \quad \text{and} \quad \%\, f = \frac{f}{n} \times 100,$$

where f is the frequency of a class interval and n is the total number of scores.

A distribution that shows the *Prop f* or *% f* for each class interval is called a **relative frequency distribution.**

TABLE 2.2-4. Relative Frequency Distributions for Leadership Aptitude Scores From Table 2.2-1

Class Interval	f	Prop f	% f
66–68	1	.03	3
63–65	0	0	0
60–62	1	.03	3
57–59	2	.07	7
54–56	4	.13	13
51–53	6	.20	20
48–50	7	.23	23
45–47	4	.13	13
42–44	2	.07	7
39–41	1	.03	3
36–38	0	0	0
33–35	1	.03	3
30–32	1	.03	3
	$n = 30$	Sum = .98[a]	Sum = 98[a]

[a] Due to errors introduced by rounding numbers, the sums do not equal 1.00 and 100.

Often the frequency associated with each class interval also is shown along with either *Prop f* or *% f*. For purposes of illustration, a relative frequency distribution that includes *f*, *Prop f*, and *% f* is shown in Table 2.2-4.

The transformation (conversion) of frequencies into *Prop f*'s or *% f*'s converts each frequency into a relative frequency in which the possible range of values is, respectively, 0 to 1 or 0 to 100. Relative frequencies indicate whether a frequency is "relatively large" rather than whether it is "absolutely large." For example, the class interval 48–50 in Table 2.2-4 contains only seven scores, but this is a relatively large proportion (*Prop f* = .23, almost one-fourth) of the total number of scores. Relative frequencies are particularly useful in comparing two frequency distributions with different *n*'s. Consider the history achievement scores shown in Table 2.2-5 for high school students taught by two methods. Because of the great difference in *n*'s, a comparison of percentage frequencies is more meaningful than a comparison of frequencies.

Cumulative Frequency Distributions

A **cumulative frequency distribution** shows the number, proportion, or percentage of scores that occur below the real upper limit of each class interval.

TABLE 2.2-5   History Achievement Scores for Classes Taught by Different Methods

Achievement Scores	Method A		Method B	
	f	*%f*	*f*	*%f*
150–154	1	1	1	3
145–149	0	0	2	6
140–144	2	3	2	6
135–139	4	5	4	12
130–134	6	8	6	19
125–129	8	11	8	25
120–124	9	12	5	16
115–119	10	14	2	6
110–114	8	11	1	3
105–109	8	11	0	0
100–104	6	8	1	3
95–99	5	7	0	0
90–94	3	4	0	0
85–89	2	3	0	0
80–84	1	1	0	0
	$n = 73$	Sum = 99[a]	$n = 32$	Sum = 99[a]

[a] Due to errors introduced by rounding numbers, Sum is not equal to 100.

Such a distribution is helpful in answering certain kinds of questions. For instance, if Susan's score is 62, how many students did better and how many did worse? Or, what scores divide the top 10% or the bottom 25% of students from the remainder of the class?

To construct a cumulative frequency distribution, we begin with a frequency distribution like the one in the first two columns of Table 2.2-6. A given cumulative frequency is obtained by adding the frequency in column 2 for the class interval to the cumulative frequency recorded in column 3 for the class interval below it. For example, in the class interval 30–32, $f = 1$ and there are no scores below, so the *Cum f* for that class interval is $1 + 0 = 1$. For the class interval 33–35, $f = 1$, which, added to the *Cum f* below, yields a *Cum f* of $1 + 1 = 2$. The cumulative frequency recorded for the top class interval should equal n.

Cumulative frequencies can be transformed into *Cum Prop f* and *Cum % f* by the formulas

$$Cum\ Prop\ f = Cum\ f/n$$

and

$$Cum\ \%\ f = (Cum\ f/n) \times 100.$$

These relative frequencies are shown in columns 4 and 5 of Table 2.2-6.

TABLE 2.2-6. **Cumulative Frequency Distributions for Leadership Aptitude Scores From Table 2.2-1**

(1) Class Interval	(2) f	(3) Cum f	(4) Cum prop f	(5) Cum % f
66–68	1	30	1.00	100
63–65	0	29	.97	97
60–62	1	29	.97	97
57–59	2	28	.93	93
54–56	4	26	.87	87
51–53	6	22	.73	73
48–50	7	16	.53	53
45–47	4	9	.30	30
42–44	2	5	.17	17
39–41	1	3	.10	10
36–38	0	2	.07	7
33–35	1	2	.07	7
30–32	1	1	.03	3
	n = 30			

Frequency Distributions for Qualitative Variables

The construction of frequency distributions for qualitative variables is relatively simple because no decisions about size and number of class intervals have to be made—the equivalence classes of the variable become the class intervals. Consider the unordered qualitative variable of political party affiliation: Democrat, Independent, Republican, and Unspecified or other. If we obtained a random sample of college students at Ohio State University and determined their political affiliation, we could construct a frequency distribution like the one in columns 1 and 2 of Table 2.2-7. The equivalence classes are ordered alphabetically for lack of a more logical sequence. For ordered qualitative variables, class intervals should preserve the order inherent in the original equivalence classes.

TABLE 2.2-7. **Political Affiliation of Students at Ohio State University**

(1) Political Affiliation	(2) f	(3) Prop f	(4) % f
Democrat	92	.42	42
Independent	33	.15	15
Republican	85	.38	38
Unspecified or other	11	.05	5
	n = 221	Sum = 1.00	Sum = 100

The frequencies in column 2 of Table 2.2-7 are converted to *Prop f* in column 3 and *% f* in column 4. Cumulative frequencies are not shown; they are not meaningful because the order of the class intervals was arbitrarily determined.

CHECK YOUR UNDERSTANDING OF SECTION 2.2

1. A marriage counselor asked his clients to keep a record of the number of arguments they had during the week. The following data for 23 couples were obtained. Construct an ungrouped frequency distribution for these data.

2	5	4	9	6
4	3	3	5	10
5	0	13	4	2
1	7	6	3	
4	5	4	4	

2. Assembly-line workers were asked to complete a job-satisfaction questionnaire. Construct an ungrouped frequency distribution for the following scores, where large scores correspond to high satisfaction.

7	8	4	25	9	8	4	15	11	9
6	9	7	7	10	17	5	10	5	8
3	7	11	8	13	22	7	8	7	6
10	6	7	9	4	8	6	6	8	11
15	21	5	11	6	9	5	12	10	8

3. List the guidelines for constructing an ungrouped frequency distribution.
4. For the following nominal class intervals, give the real limits and the class interval size.
   a. 50−54   b. 74   c. 18.0−19.9
5. For each of the following give (a) the number of class intervals, (b) the size of the class interval, and (c) the nominal limits of the class interval containing the smallest score.

	Largest Score	Smallest Score	Number of Scores
a.	68	22	53
b.	260	106	21
c.	254	92	91

6. A test of mechanical aptitude was given to seniors at Middlecenter High School. Construct a grouped frequency distribution for the following data.

80	73	51	81	46	85	84
75	44	84	77	95	48	88
50	35	52	93	43	59	63
47	66	55	58	62	51	75
86	82	89	51	77	73	59

7. In a traffic safety project, the reaction time of 27 participants to the onset of a light was measured in milliseconds. For the following data, (a) construct two grouped frequency distributions having different i's, and (b) discuss the relative merits of the two grouping schemes.

186	187	211	185	196	193
184	185	191	188	192	190
188	190	202	199	189	
193	186	180	205	187	
189	195	184	198	202	

8. For the data in Exercise 6, construct a relative frequency distribution using *Prop f.*

9. Thirty-two college students participated in a paired-associates learning experiment in which they were shown 12 nouns written in hiragana (a Japanese writing system) and asked to learn the corresponding English words. The number of trials each participant needed to be able to correctly anticipate the 12 English words on two consecutive trials is shown below. Construct a cumulative frequency distribution for the data.

10	9	11	12	6	14	10	12
11	10	12	10	9	11	16	8
9	7	8	11	10	8	12	12
13	10	10	9	11	13	7	11

10. For the data in Exercise 1, construct a cumulative proportionate frequency distribution.

11. A random sample of 20 students from each of the following classifications (freshman, sophomore, junior, senior, and graduate student) were asked whether they believed in extrasensory perception (ESP). The classifications of students who believed in ESP are listed below. Construct a frequency distribution for these data.

junior	senior	junior	sophomore	junior
freshman	junior	freshman	junior	sophomore
sophomore	senior	senior	senior	junior
graduate	sophomore	junior	freshman	senior
freshman	junior	junior	senior	sophomore
junior	senior	sophomore	senior	

12. Under what condition would it be meaningless to construct a cumulative frequency distribution for a qualitative variable?
13. Terms to remember
    a. Equivalence class
    b. Frequency distribution
    c. Class interval
    d. Ungrouped frequency distribution
    e. Grouped frequency distribution
    f. Nominal limits
    g. Real limits
    h. Class interval size
    i. Proportionate frequency
    j. Percentage frequency
    k. Relative frequency distribution
    l. Cumulative frequency distribution

2.3 INTRODUCTION TO GRAPHS

Frequency distributions present the main features of data succinctly, but they are still abstract numerical representations and require effort to interpret. Graphs can impart the same information and speak to us more directly. Their ease of interpretation makes them particularly useful when we want to present data to the general public.

There are many ways to graph data. In fact, whole books have been devoted to the subject.[5] Our presentation is limited to the six most common graphs: bar graphs, pie charts, histograms, frequency polygons, cumulative polygons, and stem-and-leaf displays. Qualitative variables are usually represented by bar graphs and pie charts. Quantitative variables are usually represented by histograms, frequency polygons, cumulative polygons, and stem-and-leaf displays.

2.4 GRAPHS FOR QUALITATIVE VARIABLES

Bar Graph

Once a frequency distribution has been made, most of the work of constructing a bar graph has been done. The only step remaining is to represent the data in two dimensions. This is illustrated in Figure 2.4-1 for the data in Table. 2.2-7. Class intervals are represented along the horizontal axis (**abscissa,** or *X* **axis**), and frequencies are represented along the vertical axis (**ordinate,** or *Y* **axis**). The zero point or ori-

---

[5] Several examples are Arken and Colton (1938), Cleveland (1985), and Tufte (1983).

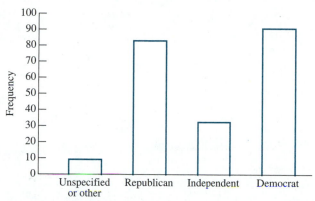

Figure 2.4-1. **Political affiliation of a random sample of $n = 221$ students at Ohio State University. (Data from Table 2.2-7)**

gin of the vertical axis is located at the *X* and *Y* **intercept**—the point where the two axes cross. A vertical bar is erected over each class interval such that its height corresponds to the number of scores in the interval. The bars can be any width, but they should not touch. A space between the bars emphasizes the discrete, qualitative character of the class intervals. By convention, the height of the graph should be 66% to 75% of its width. This results in a rectangular figure whose proportions according to the ancient Greeks are the most esthetically pleasing. Also, the *X* and *Y* axes of the graph should be labeled and a figure caption provided to help the reader interpret the graph.

The *Y* axis also can be used to represent proportionate frequency or percentage frequency, depending on the questions of interest to the researcher. We saw in Section 2.2 that these transformations are useful in determining whether a frequency is large in a relative rather than an absolute sense and in comparing frequency distributions with different total numbers of scores.

Pie Chart

Perhaps the most easily interpreted graph is a **pie chart,** which is merely a circle divided into sectors representing the proportionate frequency or percentage frequency of the class intervals.

A pie chart is illustrated in Figure 2.4-2 for the data in Table 2.2-7. To construct a pie chart, think of the chart as a circle having 60 minutes like the face of a clock. The sections corresponding to proportionate frequency or percentage frequency are marked off in minutes according to the formulas *Prop f* $\times$ 60 and (% *f*/100) $\times$ 60,

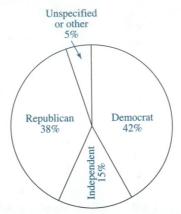

Figure 2.4-2. **Political affiliation in percentage frequency of a random sample of *n* = 221 students at Ohio State University. (Data from Table 2.2-7)**

respectively. For Figure 2.4-2, the minutes corresponding to the four percentage frequencies are

$$(42\%/100)\ 60 = 25.2 \text{ min}$$

$$(15\%/100)\ 60 = \ \ 9.0 \text{ min}$$

$$(38\%/100)\ 60 = 22.8 \text{ min}$$

$$(5\%/100)\ 60 = \ \ 3.0 \text{ min}.$$

Thus, 42% corresponds to 25.2 min after 12 o'clock; the next 15% corresponds to 25.2 + 9.0 = 34.2 min after 12 o'clock; the next 38%, to 25.2 + 9.0 + 22.8 = 57 min; and so on. The last steps in constructing a pie chart are to label the sections of the pie chart and provide an appropriate figure caption.

CHECK YOUR UNDERSTANDING OF SECTION 2.4

14. College students were asked to give their favorite leisure-time activity. The five most commonly mentioned activities were rapping with friends (RF), reading (R), watching television (TV), participating in a sport (PS), and drinking (D). Construct a bar graph for the following data.

RF	PS	D	RF	R	TV	RF	D	PS
RF	RF	R	TV	RF	D	TV	RF	TV
D	TV	RF	RF	D	RF	R	R	RF
R	R	TV	D	TV	D	D	RF	TV
TV	RF	PS	TV	RF	TV	TV	D	
D	D	TV	RF	PS	RF	RF	D	

15. A study was conducted in an Arizona nursing school to determine whether students would have a positive attitude toward research after conducting a research project of their own. After completing a required research course and project, students were asked to indicate which one of four statements best represented their attitude. Of the 230 student nurses who responded, 31 checked that they would like to be involved in research after graduation. Seventy-three checked that nurses should understand research as a part of their professional responsibility. Sixty checked that they felt confident in their ability to evaluate research in nursing. Sixty-six checked that the required project was responsible for their improved understanding of the research process. Construct a bar graph for these data. (Suggested by Van Bree, Nancee S. (1981). Undergraduate research. *Nursing Outlook, 29,* 39–41.)

16. Construct a pie chart for the data in Exercise 14.

17. Construct a pie chart for the data in Exercise 15.

18. Terms to remember
    a. Bar graph   b. Abscissa   c. *X* axis
    d. Ordinate   e. *Y* axis   f. Intercept
    g. Pie chart

2.5 GRAPHS FOR QUANTITATIVE VARIABLES

Histogram

A **histogram** is similar in appearance and construction to a bar graph, but it is used for quantitative variables rather than qualitative variables. It is constructed by erecting vertical bars over the *real limits* of each class interval, with the height of each bar corresponding to the number of scores in the interval. The bars of adjacent class intervals should touch with no space between the bars; this emphasizes the continuous, quantitative character of the class intervals.

Except for these differences, histograms and bar graphs are constructed in the same manner: (1) The class intervals are represented along the horizontal axis, and frequency is represented along the vertical axis; (2) the zero point or origin of each axis is located at the *X* and *Y* intercept; (3) the height of the graph is 66% to 75% of its width; and (4) the two axes are labeled appropriately, and a figure caption is given to help the reader interpret the graph.

A histogram for the data in Table 2.2-3 is shown in Figure 2.5-1. Note that the sides of the bars are located at the real limits of the class intervals rather than at the

Figure 2.5-1. **Histogram for leadership aptitude scores for *n* = 30 football coaches. (Data from Table 2.2-3)**

nominal limits, for example, 29.5−32.5 and not 30−32. Either frequency or relative frequency can be represented along the vertical axis. The transformation of frequencies to relative frequencies is discussed in Section 2.2.

Frequency Polygon

To construct a frequency polygon from a frequency distribution, we begin as though we were making a histogram. The horizontal axis is marked off into class intervals, and the vertical axis is divided into numbers representing frequencies. However, the frequency of a class interval is not represented by a vertical bar but by a dot placed at the proper height over the midpoint of the class interval. Finally, adjacent dots are joined by straight lines. At the extremes of the graph, two additional class intervals containing no scores are identified and lines are dropped to their midpoints so as to anchor the graph to the horizontal axis. The midpoint of a class interval is given by

$$\text{Midpoint} = \frac{\text{Upper limit of class interval} + \text{Lower limit of class interval}}{2}.$$

For example, the midpoint of the class interval 30−32 is (32 + 30)/2 = 31. A frequency polygon for the data in Table 2.2-3 is shown in Figure 2.5-2. Frequency polygons and histograms impart the same information; the choice between them is largely a matter of personal preference. The histogram is probably a little easier for the general public to interpret, but the stepwise bars tend to obscure the shape of the distribution. The frequency polygon is preferred when two or more sets of data are represented in the same graph because superimposed histograms often overlap and obscure one another.

Figure 2.5-2. **Frequency polygon for leadership aptitude scores for** $n = 30$ **football coaches. (Data from Table 2.2-3)**

Cumulative Polygon

We saw in Section 2.2 that a cumulative frequency distribution can be used to show the number, proportion, or percentage of scores that lie below the real upper limit of each class interval. This same information can be presented graphically by a cumulative polygon. Instead of placing dots over the midpoints of class intervals, we place them over the real upper limits. The vertical axis can represent *Cum f, Cum Prop f,* or *Cum % f.* A cumulative percentage frequency polygon for the data in Table 2.2-6 is shown in Figure 2.5-3. As is usually the case in the behavioral sciences and education, the cumulative polygon has the characteristic S shape. The S

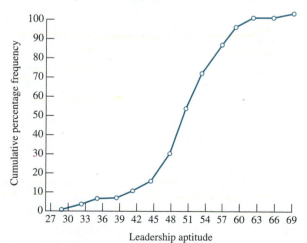

Figure 2.5-3. **Cumulative percentage frequency polygon for leadership aptitude scores for** $n = 30$ **football coaches. (Data from Table 2.2-6)**

TABLE 2.5-1.   Stem-and-Leaf Display for Data From Table 2.2-1

(1) Stem (Class Interval)	(2) Leaf (Trailing Digit)	(3) Frequency (f)
30–32	0	1
33–35	3	1
36–38		0
39–41	9	1
42–44	2 4	2
45–47	5 6 6 7	4
48–50	8 8 9 9 0 0 0	7
51–53	1 1 2 2 3 3	6
54–56	4 4 5 6	4
57–59	7 9	2
60–62	2	1
63–65		0
66–68	8	1
		n = 30

shape occurs whenever there are more scores in the middle of the frequency distribution than at the extremes. Graphs that are S shaped are called **ogives** (pronounced "oh jives").

Stem-and-Leaf Display

Another useful graphic procedure is the **stem-and-leaf display.**[6] It resembles a histogram that has been turned on its side. A stem-and-leaf display is illustrated in Table 2.5-1 for the data in Table 2.2-1. The first step in constructing the display is to specify class intervals following the procedures in Section 2.2. The class intervals become the *stems* of the display. A score is represented by its class interval, the stem, and by its trailing digit, the *leaf*. For example, the score 30 in Table 2.2-1 falls in the class interval 30–32; its trailing digit is 0. This score of 30 is represented in Table 2.5-1 by the leaf 0 on the stem 30–32. The appearance of the display can be improved by ordering the leaves on a stem from the smallest to the largest. It is customary to put the smallest class interval at the top of the display and the largest class interval at the bottom and to place a vertical line between the leaves and stems, as shown in Table 2.5-1. If these conventions are followed and the display is rotated 90° counterclockwise, the display looks like a histogram in which the vertical bars have been replaced by columns of numbers.

---

[6] The procedure was popularized by John Tukey (1977).

TABLE 2.5-2. Stem-and-Leaf Display for Job Satisfaction of First-Line Supervisors and Assembly-Line Workers (Data From Exercise 2 in Section 2.2 and Exercise 4 in Section 2.9)

Leaf First-line Supervisors	Stem	Leaf Assembly-line Workers
	2–3	3
	4–5	4 4 4 5 5 5 5
6	6–7	6 6 6 6 6 7 7 7 7 7 7 7
	8–9	8 8 8 8 8 8 8 9 9 9 9 9
	10–11	0 0 0 0 1 1 1 1
2	12–13	2 3
4 5	14–15	5 5
6 7	16–17	7
8 8 9	18–19	
0 0 1 1	20–21	1
2 3	22–23	2
4 5	24–25	5

An important advantage of a stem-and-leaf display over a histogram is that the display provides all of the information that is contained in a histogram and, in addition, preserves the value of the individual scores. If desired, the display can be supplemented with a frequency distribution, as in column 3 of Table 2.5-1. Also, two sets of data can be presented in the same table by placing one set on the left side of the stems and the other set on the right side, as in Table 2.5-2. This "back-to-back" stem-and-leaf display makes it easy to compare the two distributions.

A stem-and-leaf display can be simplified by using only the first or leading digit(s) of a stem (class interval). For example, the class interval 10–19 can be represented by the stem 1, the class interval 20–29 by the stem 2, the class interval 150–159 by the stem 15, and so on. This abbreviated representation of stems is used by most statistical packages.

CHECK YOUR UNDERSTANDING OF SECTION 2.5

19. The following data represent the number of cigarettes smoked per day by mothers whose first babies were stillborn. Construct a histogram for these data.

27	25	31	22	3	16	15
21	32	29	30	12	14	26
9	27	25	27	30	28	31
30	18	0	23	20	21	19
28	16	10	19	13		

20. Rats were shown three illuminated symbols; their task was to press the lever below the symbol that differed from the other two. The dependent measure was the number of trials required before the rat could make eight consecutive correct responses. Construct a histogram for these data.

52	34	57	47	54	56	46
60	63	42	20	50	81	41
43	51	36	73	56	77	59
50	42	58	65	42	58	63
66	55	53	63	53	54	61

21. Determine the midpoints of the following class intervals.
    a. 20–24   b. 8–11   c. 132–133   d. 15–29
22. Construct a frequency polygon for the data in Exercise 19.
23. Construct a frequency polygon for the data in Exercise 20.
24. (a) Construct a cumulative polygon for the data in Exercise 19; plot *Cum % f* on the ordinate. (b) Estimate the score above which 50% of the cases fall.
25. How can you tell from a frequency distribution whether a cumulative polygon for the data would have an **S** shape?
26. Construct a stem-and-leaf display for the data in Exercise 19.
27. Terms to remember
    a. Histogram
    c. Class interval midpoint
    e. Ogive
    b. Frequency polygon
    d. Cumulative polygon
    f. Stem-and-leaf display

2.6 SHAPES OF DISTRIBUTIONS

Graphs come in many different shapes. Some shapes occur with enough regularity that they have been given special names. These shapes are shown in Figure 2.6-1.

Bell-Shaped Distributions

The frequency polygon in Figure 2.6-1(a) approximates the shape of the normal distribution, which is discussed in Chapter 9. This important distribution is symmetrical—that is, the right half is the mirror image of the left half—and it has a particular degree of peakedness.

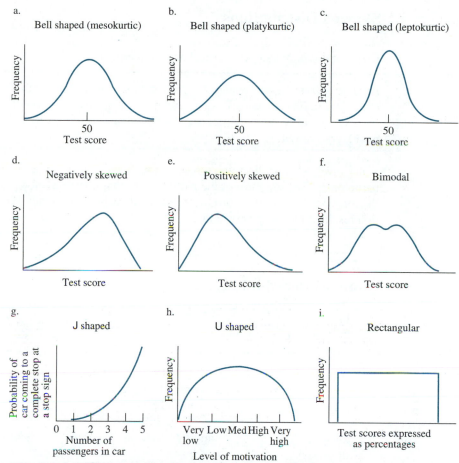

Figure 2.6-1. **Common distributions in behavioral and educational research.**

The property of being peaked, flat, or somewhere in between is referred to as **kurtosis.**

The normal distribution is **mesokurtic;** *meso-* means intermediate. Distributions that are flatter than the normal distribution are called **platykurtic;** *platy-* means flat or broad. Those that are more peaked are designated **leptokurtic;** *lepto-* meaning slender or narrow. Examples of these distributions are shown in Figure 2.6-1(b) and (c). These distributions and the one in (a) all center on the same test score, 50. The point on which a distribution centers is referred to as its **central tendency.** Another important characteristic of a distribution is its **dispersion**—the extent to which scores are spread out around a central point. The scores in Figure 2.6-1(c), for example, have less dispersion or scatter than those in (a) and (b).

Skewed Distributions

Distributions are either symmetrical or asymmetrical.

If the longer tail of an asymmetrical distribution extends toward the X and Y intercept, as in Figure 2.6-1(d), the distribution is **negatively skewed.** If the longer tail extends away from the intercept, as in Figure 2.6-1(e), the distribution is **positively skewed.**

A negatively skewed distribution results, for example, if a very easy test is given to participants. Because most of the participants score high and only a few score low, the longer tail trails off toward the X and Y intercept. A positively skewed distribution results if the test is very hard.

Bimodal Distributions

A distribution is **bimodal** if it has two humps, each having the same maximum frequency.

Bimodal distributions often result when two distinct populations are represented on a single graph. For example, a graph like Figure 2.6-1(f) would result if we plotted the masculinity scores of 50 men and 50 women.

A graph with three or more humps, each having the same maximum frequency, is **multimodal.**

Technically, a distribution is bimodal or multimodal only if its humps have the same frequency. Nevertheless, distributions with pronounced but unequal humps are commonly described as bimodal or multimodal.

J, U, and Rectangular Distributions

J and U distributions are so named because their shapes resemble those letters.

A J-shaped curve like the one in Figure 2.6-1(g) is obtained, for example, if the probability of coming to a complete stop at a stop sign is plotted on the vertical axis and the number of passengers in the car is plotted on the horizontal axis. A reversed J curve is obtained if the number of people arriving for church is plotted on the vertical axis and the number of minutes that they are late is plotted on the horizontal axis. Similar results are obtained in most studies of conforming social behavior—most people conform to social conventions and laws, so fewer and fewer people exhibit larger degrees of nonconformity.

An inverted U curve like the one in Figure 2.6-1(h) is obtained, for example, if performance on a difficult task is plotted on the vertical axis and level of motivation of the participants is plotted on the horizontal axis.

A **rectangular** or **uniform** distribution is one in which each class interval has the same frequency.

A rectangular distribution is produced when test scores are converted to percentiles (see Section 4.2) and the number of scores in the class intervals 0–10th percentile, 10th–20th percentile, . . . , 90th–100th percentile is graphed. It follows that the resulting graph will be rectangular because each of the 10 class intervals by definition must contain 10% of the scores.

In this section we have described some common distributions, and in the process we have mentioned four important characteristics of distributions: (1) central tendency, (2) dispersion, (3) symmetry or lack of symmetry, and (4) kurtosis. In Chapters 3 and 4 we will see how to compute numbers that represent each of these characteristics.

CHECK YOUR UNDERSTANDING OF SECTION 2.6

28. Indicate whether the following statements are true or false.
    a. A normal distribution is symmetrical and mesokurtic.
    b. If the upper half of a distribution is not the mirror image of the lower half, the distribution is asymmetrical.
    c. A distribution that is more peaked than the normal distribution is called platykurtic.
    d. The tail of a positively skewed distribution extends away from the X and Y intercept.
    e. A distribution with two maximum humps each having the same frequency is said to be multimodal.
29. Draw the shape of a frequency polygon that would occur in each of the following experiments. Identify each distribution.
    a. Miss America contestants take a masculinity test.
    b. An intelligence test is given to a large sample of sixth-grade children.
    c. Students at Curtis Institute of Music take a test of musical aptitude.
    d. Students are surprised with a pop quiz immediately after the Christmas vacation.

30. Terms to remember
    a. Normal distribution   b. Symmetrical distribution
    c. Kurtosis   d. Mesokurtic
    e. Platykurtic   f. Leptokurtic
    g. Central tendency   h. Dispersion
    i. Skewness (negative and   j. Bimodal
       positive)   l. J distribution
    k. Multimodal   n. Rectangular (uniform)
    m. U distribution   distribution

2.7 MISLEADING GRAPHS

Graphs should be constructed so that they accurately portray the essential characteristics of data. Not all graphs do this—some even defy correct interpretation.
Graphs of the same data can convey entirely different impressions, as shown in Figures 2.7-1(a) and (b), which report crime statistics for three similar neighborhoods.
In neighborhood A, cruising patrol cars were eliminated during a three-month trial
period; neighborhood B had five cruising cars during the period; and C was flooded
with 15 cars. Your conclusions about the effects of patrol cars would probably depend on which graph you saw. Figure 2.7-1(a) gives the impression that the presence or absence of patrol cars is associated with a dramatic difference in crime rate.
Note, however, that the largest difference—1000 versus 970—is only 3%. Such a
small difference could just as easily be attributed to chance factors or to differences
in crime reporting procedures. The graph is misleading because it violates the

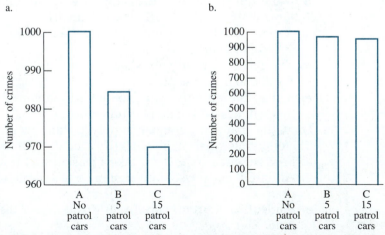

Figure 2.7-1. **Number of reported crimes in three similar neighborhoods
during a three-month test period. Note how graph (a) falsely gives the
impression of a great difference in crime rate across the three conditions.**

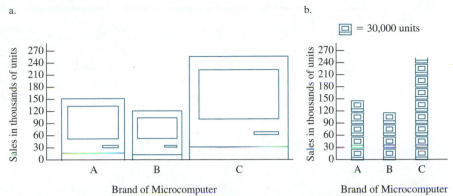

Figure 2.7-2. **Pictograms representing sales of three popular microcomputers. Pictogram (a) is misleading because our perception of sales is influenced by the heights of the pictures and by their areas, and area is an irrelevant dimension.**

66%–75% height-width rule mentioned in Section 2.4 and because the *Y* axis begins with a frequency of 960 crimes instead of 0 crimes.[7] The use of such misleading graphing procedures is contrary to the aim of statistics, which is to help the user make sense out of data.

A more subtle form of misrepresentation can occur in pictograms.

A **pictogram** represents quantity by means of pictures of the objects being compared.

Pictograms are often used in the mass media in place of bar graphs and histograms to enliven a presentation. Consider Figure 2.7-2, in which sales for three brands of microcomputers are represented by two types of pictograms. Figure 2.7-2(a) is inherently misleading because our perception of the sales of the three brands is influenced not only by the heights of the pictures but also by their areas, and area is an irrelevant dimension. For example, sales for brand C are approximately twice those for brand B, but the area of brand C's picture is 4.3 times larger than that of brand B. The pictogram in Figure 2.7-2(b) provides a more realistic representation of sales.

CHECK YOUR UNDERSTANDING OF SECTION 2.7

31. Prepare two bar graphs for the following data. Design one to deliberately suggest that government spending has been stable, and the other to suggest a dramatic increase in government spending.

---

[7] Huff (1954) and Tufte (1983) illustrate other misleading techniques and provide examples of outstanding graphs.

Month	Spending	Month	Spending
June	$29,400,000	October	$29,500,000
July	29,200,000	November	29,600,000
August	29,300,000	December	29,800,000
September	29,600,000	January	30,200,000

32. Term to remember
    a. Pictogram

†2.8 PRINTOUTS FOR THREE MICROCOMPUTER STATISTICAL PACKAGES

Computers simplify the task of analyzing data. Learning how to enter data in a statistical package and interacting with the package to obtain an analysis are important skills. These topics are beyond the scope of this book. For information about a particular package, you can consult the manual that accompanies the package. The purpose of this and similar optional sections is to acquaint you with computer printouts. Examples of printouts for three popular microcomputer statistical packages are presented: JMP®, SPSS®, and SYSTAT. One or more of these packages are probably available on the computer system at your institution. Your professor can tell you which package, if any, is used in your class.

JMP

The statistical package JMP (pronounced "jump") provides a broad range of graphical and statistical methods for analyzing data.[8] After you have accessed the package, data are entered in a data table that resembles a spreadsheet. The data table for JMP is shown in Figure 2.8-1, where the coaches' last names and leadership aptitude scores from Table 2.2-1 have been typed in columns 2 and 3, respectively. To conserve space, only data for the first seven coaches are shown.

In JMP, you can access a variety of display and optional statistical text reports. A histogram was obtained by selecting the **Analyze** command in the menu bar followed by the pull-down command **Distribution of Y.** These selections

---

† This and similarly marked sections can be omitted without loss of continuity.

[8] A student version of this package is called JMP IN®.

Leadership				
2 Cols / 30 Rows	N ☐ **Coach**	C ☐ **Score**		
1	Wilkins	55		
2	Green	46		
3	Bishop	52		
4	Seaman	51		
5	Bohannon	48		
6	Deneve	50		
7	Massey	30		
0 \ 0 Selected				

Figure 2.8-1. **JMP data table for the leadership aptitude scores in Table 2.2-1. Data for the first 7 of the 30 coaches are shown in columns 2 and 3. The N in the heading for column 2 identifies the coaches as nominal values; the C in column 3 identifies the scores as continuous values.**

brought up the dialog box in Figure 2.8-2. After **Score** was identified as the dependent variable, clicking on ▮ **OK** ▮ produced a vertical histogram. The histogram was customized using options in JMP to obtain the horizontal histogram in Figure 2.8-3. The customized histogram closely resembles the original histogram in Figure 2.5-1.

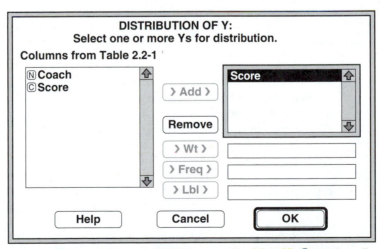

Figure 2.8-2. **This dialog box in JMP was used to identify Score as the dependent variable. Clicking on Score in the left box selected it. Then clicking on ▸ Add ▸ caused Score to appear in the right box.**

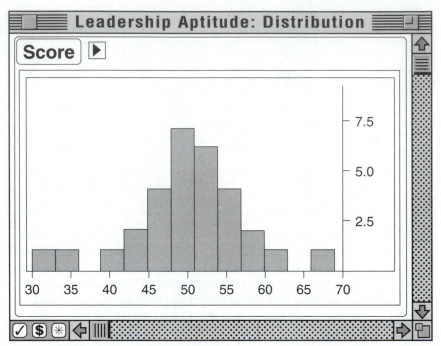

Figure 2.8-3. **Customized JMP histogram for the leadership aptitude scores in Table 2.2-1. The default histogram produced by JMP is vertical. The check (✔) box at the bottom left of the figure provides access to options that were used to produce the horizontal histogram. The hand tool from the Tools command in the menu bar was used to grab the figure and change the number of class intervals from 8 to 13.**

SPSS

The data table for SPSS is shown in Figure 2.8-4. The histogram in Figure 2.8-5 was obtained by selecting **Graph** from the menu bar and then selecting the **Histogram** option. Several options were used to change the number of class intervals from 9 to 13 and alter the proportions of the histogram so that they are similar to those in Figure 2.5-1.

SYSTAT

The data table for SYSTAT is shown in Figure 2.8-6. The histogram in Figure 2.8-7 was obtained by selecting **Graph** from the menu bar and then selecting the **Density** option followed by the **Histogram** option. Several options were used to change the number of class intervals from 8 to 13 and alter the proportions of the histogram so that they are similar to those in Figure 2.5-1.

	coach	score	var
1	Wilkins	55.00	
2	Green	46.00	
3	Bishop	52.00	
4	Seaman	51.00	
5	Bohannon	48.00	
6	Deneve	50.00	
7	Massey	30.00	

Leadership Aptitude

Figure 2.8-4 **SPSS data table for the leadership aptitude scores in Table 2.2-1. Data for the first 7 of the 30 coaches are shown in columns 1 and 2.**

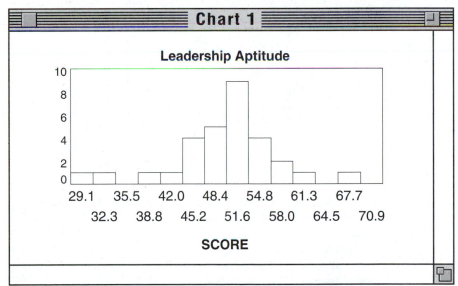

Figure 2.8-5. **Customized SPSS histogram for the leadership aptitude scores in Table 2.2-1. The default histogram produced by SPSS had 9 class intervals. The histogram was customized by clicking on Edit and double clicking on the X axis. This brought up an Interval Axis box with a Custom button. The number of class intervals was changed from 9 to 13 and the Center option in the Title Justification box was selected. The histogram was further customized by dragging the outside frame until the proportions of the histogram were similar to those in Figure 2.5-1.**

Leadership Aptitude			
	COACH$	SCORE	
1	Wilkins	55.000	
2	Green	46.000	
3	Bishop	52.000	
4	Seaman	51.000	
5	Bohannon	48.000	
6	Deneve	50.000	
7	Massey	30.000	

Figure 2.8-6. **SYSTAT data table for the leadership aptitude scores in Table 2.2-1. Data for the first 7 of the 30 coaches are shown in columns 2 and 3. The $ sign following the word COACH in column 2 identifies these data as a character variable rather than a numeric variable.**

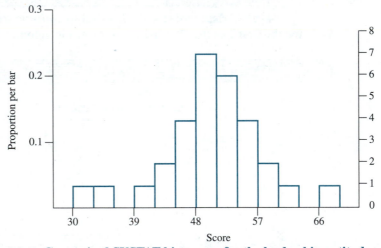

Figure 2.8-7. **Customized SYSTAT histogram for the leadership aptitude scores in Table 2.2-1. The default histogram produced by SYSTAT had 8 class intervals with a class interval size of 5. The histogram was customized by clicking on the Bwidth option and typing the number 3 in the space for bar width (class interval size). The histogram was further customized by clicking on the small resize square in the lower right corner of the graph and dragging the frame until the proportions of the histogram were similar to those in Figure 2.5-1.**

2.9 SUMMARY

This chapter presented two descriptive devices that make data easier to compre-hend: frequency distributions and graphs. As a first and sometimes final step in summarizing data, a researcher may report the various equivalence classes and the number of observations that fall into each. This results in a table called a frequency distribution. If each equivalence class is a single score value, the distribution is un-grouped; if the classes contain two or more score values, the distribution is grouped. Grouping simplifies the interpretation of data by assigning scores to a limited number of class intervals, usually between 10 and 20.

A graph is a pictorial representation of a frequency distribution and hence is much easier to interpret. The most common graphs for qualitative variables are bar graphs and pie charts. Histograms, frequency polygons, cumulative poly-gons, and stem-and-leaf displays commonly are used to represent quantitative variables.

A graph should present data accurately and unambiguously and in such a way that its main characteristics can be seen at a glance. To achieve this, certain conventions are followed: (1) plotting frequency on the Y axis and equivalence classes on the X axis; (2) placing the zero point (or origin) of the Y axis at the X and Y inter-cept; (3) making the height of the graph 66% to 75% of its width; (4) labeling the X and Y axes; and (5) providing a figure caption.

REVIEW EXERCISES FOR CHAPTER 2

1. Construct an ungrouped frequency distribution for the ages of study-abroad candidates at their last birthday. The data are as follows.

18	20	19	20
20	19	19	19
23	18	20	21
17	20	18	20

2. For the following nominal class intervals, give the real limits and the class interval size.
   a. 16   b. 60−69   c. 18.00−19.99
   d. 12.0−14.9   e. 0−0.4   f. 1.50−1.74

3. For each of the following, give (i) the number of class intervals, (ii) the size of the class interval, and (iii) the nominal limits of the class interval containing the smallest score.

	Largest Score	Smallest Score	Number of Scores
a.	37	8	106
b.	62	23	273
c.	164	126	29
d.	52	0	22

4. First-line supervisors were asked to complete a job-satisfaction questionnaire. Construct a grouped frequency distribution for the following data.

25	23	18	24	14
21	17	12	19	
15	6	22	16	
20	20	21	18	

5. What are the advantages and disadvantages of grouped and ungrouped frequency distributions?

6. For the job-satisfaction data in Exercise 4, construct a relative frequency distribution using % *f*.

7. Construct a relative frequency distribution for comparing the job satisfaction of assembly-line workers in Exercise 2 in "Check Your Understanding of Section 2.2" with that of first-line supervisors in Exercise 4.

8. Under what conditions is a relative frequency distribution more informative than an ordinary frequency distribution?

9. For the data in Exercise 6 in "Check Your Understanding of Section 2.2," construct a cumulative frequency distribution.

10. For the first-line supervisors' data in Exercise 4, construct a cumulative percentage frequency distribution.

11. Students enrolling in Introductory Sociology were randomly assigned to one of three classes: traditional lecture (TL), guided reading (GR), or lecture with multimedia supplements (LM). Following are the class assignments of the top 30 students on the final examination; construct a frequency distribution for these data.

LM	GR	LM	TL	GR	LM
LM	TL	GR	LM	LM	GR
TL	TL	TL	LM	LM	LM
GR	LM	LM	LM	TL	TL
LM	LM	TL	GR	LM	LM

12. Twenty-five physicians were asked what they felt was the main health threat to male executives. The most common responses were occupational stress (OS), obesity (OB), smoking (S), lack of exercise (LE), and other (O). Construct a frequency distribution for these data.

OB	OS	S	OB	LE
S	OB	OB	OS	O
LE	S	OS	S	OB
O	LE	O	LE	LE
OB	LE	O	O	OBF

13. Toss a die 30 times and construct a frequency distribution showing the number of times each die face occurred.
14. Contrast the procedures for constructing frequency distributions for qualitative variables with those for quantitative variables.
15. Information from a biographical inventory was used to compute a socioeconomic index for students in a university marching band. Scores above 72 were classified as very high (VH); scores from 61 to 72, as high (H); from 43 to 60, as middle (M); and below 43, as low (L). Construct a bar graph for the following data.

H	H	H	H	M	VH	VH	H	M
M	L	H	M	VH	H	H	H	VH
H	M	M	H	H	VH	H	M	
VH	H	H	M	M	VH	M	L	
H	VH	VH	H	H	M	VH	M	
M	M	VH	L	M	H	H	VH	

16. The value of psychoeducational programs as a means of preventing and relieving problems of daily living is gaining acceptance in the medical community. A health maintenance organization recently surveyed the health needs of its members by means of a questionnaire. The number of respondents who selected one of nine popular programs as the one in which they were most interested is shown in the following table. Construct a bar graph for these data. (Suggested by Burnell, George M., & Taylor, Peter H. [1982]. Psychoeducational programs for problems in living. *Health and Social Work, 7*(1), 7–13.)

Program	Number Indicating Primary Interest
Weight reduction	154
Fatigue	101
Marital and sex problems	92
Coping with physical problems	71
Stress	65
Heart disease prevention	61
Assertiveness	60
Stop smoking	48
Headaches	47

17. "Citizen contacting," in which an individual approaches government officials or other powerful persons to obtain help for themselves and others, was investigated. Among the countries surveyed were Austria, the Netherlands, and the United States. The citizens

initiating the contacts during the preceding two years were classified according to level of educational achievement. (a) Construct a bar graph for each country for the following data. (b) What conclusions can you draw from your graphs? (Suggested by Zuckerman, A. S., & West, D. M. [1985]. The political bases of citizen contacting: A cross-national analysis. The *American Political Science Review, 79,* 117–131.)

Proportion Making Contact by Level of Education

Country	1 (low)	2	3	4	5	6 (high)
Austria	.03	.07	.07	.13	.12	.25
Netherlands	.04	.09	.11	.21	.25	.23
United States	.11	.15	.21	.30	.37	.51

18. Construct a bar graph for the Introductory Sociology data in Exercise 11.
19. Construct a bar graph for the physician data in Exercise 12; plot percentage frequency on the Y axis.
20. Describe the procedure for constructing a bar graph from a frequency distribution.
21. Construct a pie chart for the Introductory Sociology data in Exercise 11.
22. Construct a pie chart for the socioeconomic data in Exercise 15.
23. Describe the procedure for constructing a pie chart from a frequency distribution.
24. Construct a histogram for the first-line supervisors' data in Exercise 4. Plot percentage frequency on the ordinate.
25. Construct a histogram for the reaction-time data in Exercise 7 in "Check Your Understanding of Section 2.2." Plot proportionate frequency on the ordinate.
26. How does the construction of histograms and bar graphs differ?
27. Determine the midpoints of the following class intervals.
    a. 1.50–1.74   b. 100–104   c. 0–2   d. 60–69
28. A study was undertaken to determine how well psychological crises resulting from traumatic events are resolved over time. The participants included 15 female cancer patients who underwent breast surgery for the first time, 15 female patients who underwent less-serious surgery (gall bladder removal, hernia repair, and so forth), and 15 physically healthy (nonsurgery) women. Each patient took the Halpern Crisis Scale at intervals of 0, 3, 7, 11, and 15 weeks. The 0 interval represented the night before surgery. The sample of healthy control participants also took the scale at the same time intervals. The following data, number of women with a Halpern Crisis

Scale score over 72, were obtained. A score above 72 is considered a high crisis score. (Suggested by Gottesman, David, & Lewis, Marc S. [1982]. Differences in crisis reactions among cancer and surgery patients. *Journal of Consulting and Clinical Psychology, 50,* 381–388.)

Group	Week Number				
	0	*3*	*7*	*11*	*15*
Cancer surgery	11	12	14	12	14
Other surgery	8	11	12	10	8
Nonsurgery	4	5	5	6	5

(a) Construct a frequency polygon for these data. Plot the data for each group on the same graph; do not anchor the polygon to the horizontal axis. (b) Write a short paragraph giving your interpretation of these data.

29. Construct a frequency polygon for the first-line supervisors' data in Exercise 4. Plot percentage frequency on the ordinate.
30. What are the relative merits of histograms and frequency polygons?
31. (a) Construct a cumulative polygon for the data in Exercise 20 in "Check Your Understanding of Section 2.5"; plot *Cum prop f* on the ordinate. (b) Estimate the score below which 50% of the cases fall and the score below which 20% of the cases fall.
32. Construct a cumulative polygon for the reaction-time data in Exercise 7 in "Check Your Understanding of Section 2.2."
33. Data on the prevalence of prostate carcinoma by age range were collected. (a) Construct a relative frequency polygon for the data listed in the following table. (b) Use your polygon to estimate the age at which 50% of men could be expected to have prostrate cancer. (c) One cannot construct a cumulative frequency polygon for these data. Explain. (Suggested by Stamey, T. A. [1982]. Cancer of the prostate: An analysis of some important contributions and dilemmas. *Monographs in Urology, 3,* 65–94.)

Age Group	Percent With Disease
90–99	61.3
80–89	38.0
70–79	29.8
60–69	20.5
50–59	11.8
40–49	6.9
30–39	2.1

34. Construct a stem-and-leaf display for the lever-pressing data in Exercise 20 in "Check Your Understanding of Section 2.5."

35. Indicate whether the following statements are true or false.
    a. A distribution that is flatter than the normal distribution is called mesokurtic.
    b. *Lepto* in leptokurtic means slender or narrow.
    c. The tail of a negatively skewed distribution extends away from the X and Y intercept.
    d. A distribution with three maximum humps each having the same frequency is bimodal.

36. Draw the shape of a frequency polygon that would occur in each of the following experiments. Identify each distribution.
    a. Students at Juilliard School of Music take a test of musical aptitude.
    b. Students are surprised with a pop quiz immediately after the Easter vacation.
    c. Participants attempt to solve 20 complex puzzles under five levels of motivation: very low, low, medium, high, and very high.
    d. Number of crimes per 1,000 inhabitants is determined for the population of five cities; it turns out that the cities have the same crime rate.
    e. Engineering majors' and business majors' scores on a test of mechanical aptitude are plotted.
    f. Strength of grip is measured for boys and men; the sample contains all ages but a preponderance of young boys, men in their early 20s, and men over 65.
    g. Arrival time is recorded for people who are late for a concert.
    h. The number of persons contracting polio in the United States from 1940 to 1970 is determined from hospital records.

37. The following data are sales figures for vacuum cleaner salespeople. Prepare graphs that suggest that (a) all the salespeople are producing at a uniformly high level, (b) Chapman should be fired, and (c) they should all be fired.

Chapman	$66,000	Hillis	$68,200
Hays	$67,300	Schmeltekopf	$71,000
Daniel	$69,900	Sloan	$71,100

38. Use a statistical software package to obtain a bar graph for the physician data in Exercise 12.

39. Use a statistical software package to obtain a bar graph for the socioeconomic data in Exercise 15.

40. Use a statistical software package to obtain a histogram for the first-line supervisors' data in Exercise 4.

41. Use a statistical software package to obtain a histogram for the mechanical-aptitude data in Exercise 6 in "Check Your Understanding of Section 2.2."

42. Use a statistical software package to obtain a histogram for the reaction-time data in Exercise 7 in "Check Your Understanding of Section 2.2."

43. Use a statistical software package to obtain a stem-and-leaf display for the learning data in Exercise 9 in "Check Your Understanding of Section 2.2."

44. Use a statistical software package to obtain a stem-and-leaf display for the first-line supervisors' data in Exercise 4.

Chapter 3

Measures of Central Tendency

3.1 INTRODUCTION

Frequency distributions and graphs summarize data, but sometimes it is desirable to summarize further by using numbers to describe interesting properties of the data. The most important property of data is usually its **central tendency,** the score value on which a distribution tends to center. This value is popularly called the *average;* it connotes what is typical, usual, representative, normal, or expected. Because of these different connotations, statisticians prefer to use the more precise terms of *mode, mean,* and *median* in referring to the central tendency of a distribution. As we will see, these terms refer to three distinct conceptions of central tendency.

Close behind central tendency in importance is **dispersion**—the extent to which scores differ from one another—that is, their scatter or heterogeneity. Several ways of describing dispersion are discussed in Chapter 4. Chapter 4 also discusses two other properties of data: *skewness* and *kurtosis.* Measures of **skewness** tell us whether a distribution is symmetrical or asymmetrical; measures of **kurtosis** tell us whether it is peaked or flat. Numbers representing these four properties of data—central tendency, dispersion, skewness, and kurtosis—provide a relatively complete summary of the information contained in frequency distributions and graphs. In many cases, a knowledge of only two of these, central tendency and dispersion, is sufficient for our purposes.

3.2 THE MODE

The simplest of the three conceptions of central tendency is the mode, denoted by *Mo.*

> The **mode** is the score or qualitative category that occurs with greatest frequency.

Consider the following scores, which represent the number of times in September that 11 college students called their parents long distance:

0   0   0   1   1   1   1   2   2   3   9.

We note that 0 occurs three times; 1, four times; 2, twice; and 3 and 9, once. The mode is 1, because it occurs with the greatest frequency. If data are tabulated in an ungrouped frequency distribution (a distribution having a class interval size of one), we can determine the mode at a glance. This can be seen for the distribution of family size of college professors shown in Table 3.2-1. The largest frequency, 10, is associated with a family size of 4; hence the mode is 4. This tells us that the most *typ-*

TABLE 3.2-1.   Frequency Distribution of Family Size of College Professors

X	f
11	1
10	0
9	0
8	1
7	1
6	2
5	4
4	10
3	8
2	8
1	5
	$n = 40$

ical family size for this sample is 4, an easy-to-understand concept. As these examples show, the mode is determined by inspection rather than by computation. The mode can be used to describe the central tendency of both qualitative and quantitative variables, but it is most often used for qualitative variables. We will see why this is true later, when we compare the relative merits of the three measures of central tendency.

The mode should be computed from an ungrouped frequency distribution if possible. If only a grouped frequency distribution (a distribution having a class interval size greater than one) is available, the midpoint of the class interval with the greatest frequency is designated as the mode. The mode in this case is imprecise because a different grouping scheme would give different class interval midpoints and hence a different mode.

As a measure of central tendency, the mode has one particularly serious limitation—it may not exist. We saw in Section 2.6 that a distribution can have two nonadjacent scores (or class intervals) with the same maximum frequency. Such distributions are called bimodal and cannot be described by a single mode. It is customary in such cases to cite the scores associated with the two maximum frequencies, but then the distribution does not have a mode or one most typical score.

CHECK YOUR UNDERSTANDING OF SECTION 3.2

1. The behavior of members of the university wine-tasting club was rated following their biweekly learn-by-doing meeting. The following scale was used: N = no change in behavior, S = slight change in verbal and/or emotional expressions, M = marked change in verbal and/or emotional expressions, C = clumsiness in locomotion, and

G = gross intoxication. (a) Determine the mode for the following data: *N, S, S, G, M, N, S, M, M, C, G, N, S, M, C, S, S, M, S, S*. (b) What type of variable do the data represent?

2. The ruling structures of 11 emerging nations were classified as 1 = premobilized authoritarian, 2 = conservative authoritarian, and 3 = premobilized democratic. (a) Determine the mode for the following data: 1, 3, 1, 1, 2, 3, 1, 3, 3, 1, 3. (b) What type of variable do the data represent?

3. Why should the mode be computed from ungrouped rather than grouped data whenever possible?

3.3 THE MEAN

The most widely used and familiar measure of central tendency is the **arithmetic mean** — the sum of scores divided by the number of scores.

The mean[1] is commonly known as the average. The usual symbol for a sample mean is $\overline{X}$ and is read "X bar."[2] The letter X identifies the variable that has been measured; the bar above $\overline{X}$ indicates a mean. Other letters toward the end of the English alphabet, for example, Y and Z, are also used as symbols for variables, and the corresponding means are denoted by $\overline{Y}$ and $\overline{Z}$.

It is customary to denote characteristics of samples by English letters and characteristics of populations by lowercase Greek letters. As we have seen, the mean of a sample is usually denoted by $\overline{X}$. The mean of a population is denoted by μ, the Greek letter mu, and is pronounced "mew." When it is necessary to distinguish among several sample means or several population means, number or letter subscripts can be used, for example, $\overline{X}_1$ and $\overline{X}_2$, $\overline{X}_A$ and $\overline{X}_B$, and μ_1 and μ_2. The distinction between samples and populations appears in another way — a descriptive measure for a sample is called a **statistic;** a descriptive measure for a population is called a **parameter.** Thus, $\overline{X}$ is a statistic, but μ is a parameter.

Summation Notation for the Mean

The mean of a sample is obtained by dividing the sum of the scores by the number of scores. At this point, we will describe a useful notation for the sum of scores. Suppose that we are interested in the frequency of movie attendance of college stu-

[1] There are several kinds of means, but only the arithmetic mean is discussed in this book.

[2] Some books in the behavioral sciences and education denote the mean by M; $\overline{X}$ or $\bar{x}$ is preferred by statisticians (Halperin, Hartley, & Hoel, 1965).

dents. We can denote this variable by the capital letter X and individual values of the variable by X and a subscript: $X_1, X_2, \ldots, X_i, \ldots, X_n$. According to this notation, X_1 is the frequency of movie attendance for person 1, X_2 is the frequency for person 2, and X_n denotes the frequency for the nth or last person in the sample. We will let i be a general subscript that designates an unspecified one of the $i = 1$, $\ldots, n$ persons (read "i equals one through n persons"). The i in X_i can be replaced by any integer between 1 and n inclusive.[3] Suppose that the following values of X_i, frequency of movie attendance, were obtained: $X_1 = 3$, $X_2 = 1$, $X_3 = 4$, and $X_4 = 2$. The mean of these $n = 4$ scores is given by

$$\overline{X} = \frac{X_1 + X_2 + X_3 + X_4}{n} = \frac{3 + 1 + 4 + 2}{4} = \frac{10}{4} = 2.5.$$

When there is a large number of scores, the formula for $\overline{X}$ is tedious to write. In this case it is customary to write the formula using the **summation symbol** Σ, the Greek capital sigma. The symbol Σ, like $+$, indicates that one should perform the operation of addition. However, $+$ indicates the addition of only two numbers, whereas $\sum\limits_{i=1}^{n}$, which is also written as $\Sigma_{i=1}^{n}$, means to perform addition until all $i = 1, \ldots, n$ numbers have been added.[4] The expression $\Sigma_{i=1}^{n} X_i$ is equivalent to $X_1 + X_2 + \cdots + X_n$. The expression $\Sigma_{i=1}^{n} X_i$ says to let the first value of X_i be X_1; add to this the second value, X_2; and continue until the X_nth value has been added. In the notation $\Sigma_{i=1}^{n}$, i is called the **index of summation,** 1 is the **initial value** of i, and n is its **terminal value.** Using summation notation, the formula for the mean movie attendance of four students is written

$$\text{mean of the sample} \rightarrow \overline{X} = \frac{\sum\limits_{i=1}^{4} X_i}{4},$$

which is equivalent to

$$\overline{X} = \frac{X_1 + X_2 + X_3 + X_4}{4}.$$

The general formula for a sample mean is written as

$$\overline{X} = \frac{\sum\limits_{i=1}^{n} X_i}{n},$$

where X_i denotes the variable of interest, $\Sigma_{i=1}^{n}$ says to sum over the $i = 1$, $\ldots, n$ scores, and n is the number of scores.

[3] The letter i is also used to denote the size of a class interval; this use is discussed in Section 2.2. Because there are only 26 letters in the alphabet, it is not surprising that they have multiple meanings.

[4] Rules of summation are described in Section 3.8.

When the initial and terminal values for the summation are clearly understood, the formula may be simplified to

$$\overline{X} = \frac{\Sigma X_i}{n} \quad \text{or} \quad \frac{\Sigma X}{n}.$$

Computing the Mean From an Ungrouped Frequency Distribution

The formula $\overline{X} = \Sigma_{i=1}^{n} X_i / n$ is appropriate for data in their original unordered state.

If the data have been ordered in an ungrouped frequency distribution, the mean can be computed from

$$\overline{X} = \frac{\displaystyle\sum_{j=1}^{k} f_j X_j}{n},$$

where X_j denotes the value of the jth class interval, f_j is the frequency of scores in the jth class interval, $\Sigma_{j=1}^{k}$ says to sum over the $j = 1, \ldots, k$ class intervals, and n is the number of scores.

The use of this formula is illustrated in Table 3.3-1. The data are scores on the Wakefield Self-Assessment Depression Inventory for a sample of 20 men facing exploratory cancer surgery.

Two formulas for computing the mean have been described:

$$\overline{X} = \frac{\displaystyle\sum_{i=1}^{n} X_i}{n},$$

where $i = 1, \ldots, n$ (n is the number of scores) and

$$\overline{X} = \frac{\displaystyle\sum_{j=1}^{k} f_j X_j}{n},$$

where $j = 1, \ldots, k$ (k is the number of class intervals). In the first formula, X_i denotes the value of the ith score. To compute the mean, the scores are summed and then divided by n, the number of scores. In the second formula, X_j denotes the value of the jth class interval, and f_j, the frequency of scores in that class interval. To compute the mean, we first obtain $f_j X_j$ for each class interval. Next we sum these products, and finally we divide the sum by n, the number of scores.

TABLE 3.3-1. **Depression Scores for Males Facing Exploratory Cancer Surgery (A Score of 25 or Above Indicates Extremely High Depression)**

(i) Data (X_j denotes the value of the jth class interval, f_j is the frequency in the jth class interval, $j = 1, \ldots, k$, and n is the number of scores)

mult. by frequencies

X_j	f_j	$f_j X_j$
28	1	$(1)(28) = 28$
27	0	$(0)(27) = 0$
26	1	$(1)(26) = 26$
25	2	$(2)(25) = 50$
24	3	$(3)(24) = 72$
23	4	$(4)(23) = 92$
22	3	$(3)(22) = 66$
21	0	$(0)(21) = 0$
20	1	$(1)(20) = 20$
19	2	$(2)(19) = 38$
18	1	$(1)(18) = 18$
17	0	$(0)(17) = 0$
16	1	$(1)(16) = 16$
15	0	$(0)(15) = 0$
14	1	$(1)(14) = 14$
$n = 20$		$\sum_{j=1}^{k} f_j X_j = 440$

(ii) Computation of $\overline{X}$ from an ungrouped frequency distribution

$$\overline{X} = \frac{\sum_{j=1}^{k} f_j X_j}{n} = \frac{440}{20} = 22$$

CHECK YOUR UNDERSTANDING OF SECTION 3.3

4. Identify the following.
   a. X_1 b. X_i c. μ_1 d. X_j
5. Write out the following, listing individual values of the variable.
   a. $\sum_{i=1}^{n} X_i$ b. $\sum_{j=1}^{k} f_j X_j / n$ c. $\sum_{\substack{i=1 \\ i \neq 3}}^{4} Z_i / n$
6. The socioeconomic level of white families in a predominantly black neighborhood was rated on the basis of income, educational attainment, physical condition of dwelling, and number of home

appliances. Compute the mean using $\sum_{i=1}^{n} X_i /n$ for the following socioeconomic scores.

5	4	9	5	3	4
4	6	7	5	3	2
6	2	5	1	7	

7. The following data represent the number of suicides per 10,000 inhabitants in predominantly rural prefectures in Japan. Compute the mean using $\sum_{i=1}^{n} X_i /n$.

22	10	12	2	10	9	16	11	8
14	11	8	13	10	9	12	0	10
12	8	11	5	7	10	7	9	9
9	8	7	8	5	14	3	10	11

8. For the data in Exercise 6, construct an ungrouped frequency distribution and compute the mean using $\overline{X} = \sum_{j=1}^{k} f_j X_j /n$.
9. For the data in Exercise 7, construct an ungrouped frequency distribution and compute the mean using $\overline{X} = \sum_{j=1}^{k} f_j X_j /n$.
10. Terms to remember
   a. Mu
   c. Parameter
   e. Terminal value of i
   g. Initial value of *i*
   b. Statistic
   d. Summation symbol, Σ
   f. Initial value of *i*

3.4 THE MEDIAN

The **median** is the point in a distribution that divides the data into two groups having equal frequency.

The median is denoted by *Mdn*. As its name suggests, the median is the middle score when scores have been arranged in order of size and *n*, the number of scores, is odd. When *n* is even, the median is the midway point between the two middle scores. The procedure for determining the median is slightly different, depending on whether *n* is odd or even and whether a frequency distribution has been constructed for the data. If the number of scores is small, the median can be determined by inspection. Consider the case in which *n* is odd, and the scores are 2, 3, 5, 8, 9, 11, 12. When the scores are ordered from smallest to largest along the number line, as in Figure 3.4-1, it is immediately apparent that the median is 8. This follows because there are three scores below the median of 8 and three scores above 8.

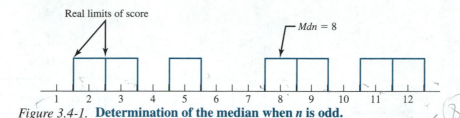

Figure 3.4-1. **Determination of the median when** *n* **is odd.**

A formal rule for determining the median is as follows.

If *n* is odd

   Mdn is the (*n* + 1)/2th score from either end of the number line.

If *n* is even

   Mdn is the midway point between the *n*/2th score and the (*n*/2) + 1th score from either end of the number line.

Consider Figure 3.4-1 again. Because *n* is odd, the median is the (*n* + 1)/2th score from either end of the number line. For example, (*n* + 1)/2 = (7 + 1)/2 = 4; hence, the median is the fourth score counting from either end. Figure 3.4-2 illustrates the location of the median along the line when *n* is even and the scores are 3, 5, 8, 9, 11, 12. Any point along the number line larger than 8 and less than 9 would qualify as the median. By convention, the median is taken as the midway point between the *n*/2th score and the (*n*/2) + 1th score. For example, 6/2 = 3 and (6/2) + 1 = 4. The midway point between the third score (8) and the fourth score (9), counting from the left, is (8 + 9)/2 = 8.5, which is the median.

Frequencies greater than 1 at the middle score value may present special problems. The median for Figure 3.4-3(a) is obviously 8, but what about Figure 3.4-3(b)? According to our definition, the median should be the (*n* + 1)/2 = (7 + 1)/2 = 4th score from either end. This score is 8, but below 8 there are three scores and above 8, only two scores. The problem is resolved by subdividing the interval—assigning half the interval 7.5–8.5 to each score. This results in two smaller subintervals, 7.5–8 and 8–8.5, as shown in the upper part of Figure 3.4-3(b). Going four scores from the lower end of the number line, we reach the score defined by 7.5–8,

Figure 3.4-2. **Determination of the median when** *n* **is even.**

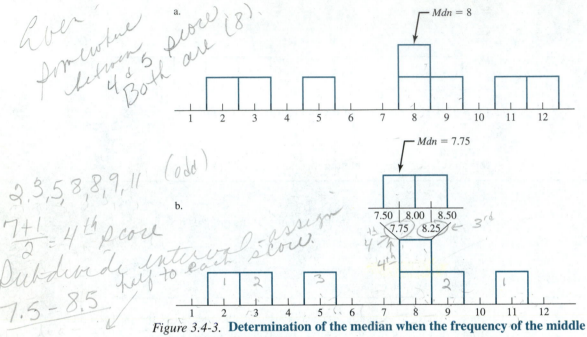

Figure 3.4-3. **Determination of the median when the frequency of the middle score value is greater than 1.**

which has a midpoint at $(7.5 + 8)/2 = 7.75$; similarly, four scores from the upper end is also the score defined by $7.5-8$. Thus, the median is 7.75, the midpoint of the score defined by the subinterval $7.5-8$. Now consider the scores in Figure 3.4-4. Again we can subdivide the interval—assigning a third of the interval $7.5-8.5$ to each score. This results in three smaller subintervals, $7.500-7.833$,

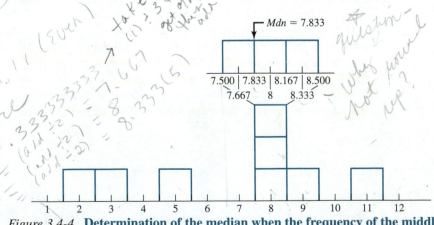

Figure 3.4-4. **Determination of the median when the frequency of the middle score value is greater than 1.**

7.833–8.167, and 8.167–8.500, as shown in the upper part of the figure. Because *n* is even, the median is the score value that is midway between the $n/2 = $ 4th and the $(n/2) + 1 = $ 5th scores. These scores are defined by the subintervals 7.500–7.833 and 7.833–8.167, respectively. The midpoints of these subintervals are 7.667 and 8.000; the median is $(7.667 + 8.000)/2 = 7.833$.

Computing the Median From an Ungrouped Frequency Distribution

We determined the median in Figures 3.4-3 and 3.4-4 by **interpolating**—dividing the class interval containing the median into subintervals and finding the point that represented the $(n + 1)/2$th score or the point that was midway between the $n/2$th and $(n/2) + 1$th scores. When data have been ordered in a frequency distribution, the interpolation can be accomplished by means of a formula. The computation is illustrated in Table 3.4-1 for the data in Figure 3.4-4.

The computational procedure illustrated in Table 3.4-1 works fine as long as the median falls in a class interval with a frequency greater than zero. For the unusual case in which the median class interval has a frequency of zero, the interpolation formula does not give the same answer as the procedure described earlier. Consider the scores 1, 2, 4, 5. We note that *n* is even; thus the median is halfway between the 2nd and 3rd scores—these scores are 2 and 4, so the median is 3. The median falls in a class interval whose frequency is zero. For these data, the interpolation formula gives

$$Mdn = 1.5 + 1\left(\frac{2-1}{1}\right) = 2.5.$$

This answer is not incorrect because any point greater than 2 and less than 4 qualifies as the median. However, by convention we consider the midway point between the 2nd score (2) and the 3rd score (4), which is $(2 + 4)/2 = 3$, to be the median rather than 2.5.

CHECK YOUR UNDERSTANDING OF SECTION 3.4

11. Determine the median for the following scores.
    a. 9, 3, 16, 5, 21
    b. 16, 19, 17, 31
    c. 3, 1, 3, 4, 5
    d. 3, 4, 4, 2, 8

TABLE 3.4-1.   Procedure for Computing the Median From a Frequency Distribution

(i) Data and computational formula

X_j	f_j	$Cum\ f^a$	
11	1	8	
10	0	7	$Mdn = X_{ll} + i\left(\dfrac{n/2 - \Sigma f_b}{f_i}\right)$
9	1	7	
8	3	6	
7	0	3	$= 7.5 + 1\left(\dfrac{8/2 - 3}{3}\right)$
6	0	3	
5	1	3	
4	0	2	$= 7.5 + 1\left(\dfrac{4 - 3}{3}\right)$
3	1	2	
2	1	1	$= 7.5 + 0.33 = 7.83$
	$n = 8$		

(ii) Definition of terms

X_j = value of jth class interval
f_j = frequency of jth class interval
X_{ll} = real lower limit of class interval containing the median
i = class interval size
n = number of scores
Σf_b = number of scores below X_{ll}
f_i = number of scores in the class interval containing the median

(iii) Computational sequence

1. Compute $n/2 = 8/2 = 4$.
2. Locate the class interval containing the $n/2 = 4$th score in the *Cum f* column. The median will fall somewhere in this class interval. The fourth score occurs in the class interval 8. This class interval contains the fourth, fifth, and sixth scores; X_{ll} for this class interval is 7.5.
3. Compute i: i = (Real upper limit of class interval − Real lower limit of class interval), for example, $i = 8.5 - 7.5 = 1$.
4. Determine Σf_b.
5. Determine f_i.

---

[a] Cumulative frequency is discussed in Section 2.2.

12. For the data in Exercise 7 in "Check Your Understanding of Section 3.3," construct an ungrouped frequency distribution and compute the median using

$$Mdn = X_{ll} + i\left(\frac{n/2 - \Sigma f_b}{f_i}\right).$$

13. The computational procedure for the median illustrated in Table 3.4-1 calculates the median from below—that is, by coming halfway through the scores, starting from the lowest class interval. Alternatively, the median can be computed by coming down halfway from above—from the highest class interval. The computational formula is

$$Mdn = X_{ul} - i\left(\frac{n/2 - \Sigma f_a}{f_i}\right).$$

By analogy with the definitions in Table 3.4-1, define each of the symbols in the alternative formula.

14. For the data in Table 3.4-1, compute the median by coming down halfway from above—from the highest class interval. The computational formula is

$$Mdn = X_{ul} - i\left(\frac{n/2 - \Sigma f_a}{f_i}\right).$$

3.5 RELATIVE MERITS OF THE MEAN, MEDIAN, AND MODE

Computation of each of the measures of central tendency is fairly simple. Which one should a researcher use for a given problem? The choice should be based on (1) the shape of the distribution, (2) the intended uses of the statistic, (3) the nature of the variable, and (4) the mathematical properties and merits of the mean, median, and mode.

Although they all are measures of central tendency, the mean, median, and mode impart somewhat different information. Consider the scores in Figure 3.5-1. By inspection, we see that the mode is 3. The median is the $(n + 1)/2 = $ 3rd score from either end of the number line. This score falls in the interval with real limits 2.5–3.5. When the interval is divided in half, the real limits of the third score are 3–3.5 and its midpoint is 3.25; hence, the median is 3.25. The mean is $\overline{X} = (2 + 3 + \cdots + 8)/5 = 4$. These three numbers—3, 3.25, and 4—represent different conceptions of the point around which scores cluster. For a unimodal set of data plotted as a histogram,

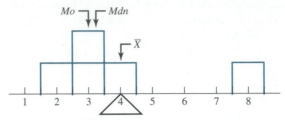

Figure 3.5-1. **Comparison of $\overline{X}$, *Mdn*, and *Mo*. The number line can be thought of as a teeter-totter whose balance point is the mean.**

1. the *mode* is the score value with the largest frequency—the most typical score;
2. the *median* is the score point that divides the ordered scores into two samples of equal size;
3. the *mean* is the score point at which the distribution balances—its center of gravity.

If a distribution is asymmetrical, as in Figure 3.5-1, the mean and the median are unequal; the value of the mode may or may not differ from the values of those for the mean and the median. If a distribution is symmetrical, the mean and the median are equal; if, in addition, the distribution is unimodal, all three measures are equal.

Merits of the Mean

The mean has a number of mathematical properties that make it the preferred measure of central tendency for relatively symmetrical distributions and for quantitative variables. One of these properties is its sampling stability. Suppose that from an extremely large population we repeatedly drew random samples of size *n*. If we computed the mean for each sample, we would expect the means to be similar but not identical. Suppose that we also computed the median and the mode for each sample. The variability from sample to sample of these statistics would be greatest for the mode and least for the mean. The better **sampling stability** of the mean is an important advantage, especially when one uses inferential statistics to draw conclusions about the central tendency of a population by observing a single sample.

Another advantage of the mean is that it is amenable to arithmetic and algebraic manipulations in ways that the median and mode are not. In other words, the mean is **mathematically tractable.** Therefore, if further statistical computations are to be performed, the mean is usually the measure of choice. This property accounts for the appearance of the mean in the formulas for many important statistics.

The mean is the only one of the three measures that reflects the value of each score. Recall that the mean is computed from the sum of all the scores, ΣX_i. The median, on the other hand, is independent of the value of each score (other than the median value itself) as long as the *number* of scores above and below the median is not altered. If, for example, the score of 8 in Figure 3.5-1 is changed to 5, the values of the median and the mode are unchanged; the value of the mean, however, is changed from 4 to 3.4.

It is no accident that the balance point of the scores in Figure 3.5-1 coincides with the mean. This fulcrum property of the mean follows from the mathematical statement $\sum_{i=1}^{n}(X_i - \overline{X}) = 0$, the sum of the deviation of the mean from each score is equal to zero. In Figure 3.5-1, for example, $\sum_{i=1}^{n}(X_i - \overline{X}) = (2 - 4) + (3 - 4) + \cdots + (8 - 4) = 0$, and this will be true for any distribution. If we think of the deviation $(X_i - \overline{X})$ as a distance, the mean is the point from which the sum of the distances to all the scores is zero. For a proof of this property, see Section 3.8.

There are three situations in which the mean is not the preferred measure of central tendency: when the distribution is very skewed, when the data are qualitative in character, and when the distribution is **open-ended**, that is, when the values of extreme scores are unknown. We will discuss the first two situations here and the third in the following section on the median.

Suppose that the following data were obtained for the number of minutes required to solve math problems: 10.1, 10.3, 10.5, 10.6, 10.7, 10.9, 56.9. The mean is $120/7 = 17.1$; the median is 10.6. Which number best represents the central tendency of the seven scores? Most readers would agree that it is 10.6, the median. The mean is unduly affected by the lone extreme score of 56.9. Any time a distribution is extremely asymmetrical, the mean is strongly affected by the extreme scores and, as a result, falls farther away from what would be considered the distribution's central area.

The mean is not the preferred measure of central tendency when the data are qualitative in character. Suppose that the dependent variable is eye color and we collect the following data: blue, brown, brown, gray, blue, brown. There is no meaningful way to represent these data by a mean; we could, however, compute the mode and say that the most typical eye color is brown.

Merits of the Median

Although the mean is usually the preferred measure of central tendency, there are several situations in which the median is preferred. As was mentioned earlier, the median is not sensitive to the values of the scores above and below it—only to the number of such scores. Unlike the mean, it is not affected by extreme scores, and thus it is a more representative measure of central tendency for very skewed distributions. Also, it can be computed when the values of the extreme scores are unknown. Suppose, for example, that we recorded the number of trials required to learn a list of paired adjectives and Japanese kana (writing) symbols. The data are as follows: 12, 17, 17, 18, 21, 24, >41. After the 41st trial, the poorest learner was still unable to learn the list and gave up; his score is some number greater than 41. The distribution is open-ended because the value of the extreme score is unknown. Although the exact value of one of the scores is unknown, the median can be computed for these data. Notice that three scores are above 18 and three are below; hence, the median is 18. The mean cannot be computed because the value of the extreme score is unknown.

The median has the added advantage of being easy to compute; when the number of scores is small, it can be determined by inspection.

 The principal disadvantages of the median relative to the mean are (1) its poorer sampling stability and (2) its poorer mathematical tractability. For these and other reasons, the median is not used as frequently as the mean in advanced descriptive and inferential statistical procedures.

Merits of the Mode

 The mode is the only measure of central tendency that can be used with unordered qualitative variables such as eye color, blood type, race, and political party affiliation. For quantitative variables that are inherently discrete, such as family size, it is sometimes a more meaningful measure of central tendency than the mean or the median. Who ever heard of an average family with 3.7 members? It makes more sense to say that the most typical family size is 3, the mode. Other than these two applications, the mode has little to recommend it except its ease of estimation.

Let us consider why the mode is called the most typical score. Because the mode is the score that occurs most frequently, the number of scores not equal to the mode is as small as it possibly can be. In Figure 3.5-1, for example, three scores differ from the mode; they are 2, 4, and 8. However, four scores differ from the mean (2, 3, 3, and 8), and five scores differ from the median (2, 3, 3, 4, and 8). Hence, the mode is the most typical score.

 The mode has a number of limitations. Its sampling stability is much poorer than that of the mean and the median, and it is also less mathematically tractable. Therefore, it is rarely used in advanced descriptive and inferential statistics. However, the mode, like the median, can be computed for an open-ended distribution if the distribution is known to be unimodal and if the unknown scores don't have the greatest frequency. However, because of the median's superior mathematical properties, it is preferred for this application.

 Consider another limitation of the mode. A mode may not exist for a set of data, as when the distribution is bi- or multimodal. In such cases, it is customary to report the two or more scores with the same maximum frequency. Because many variables in the behavioral sciences are approximately normally distributed, the existence of two scores with the same maximum frequency suggests the presence of two underlying distributions. This would occur if we administered a test of masculinity to a sample containing an equal number of men and women. To report a mean or a median for such data would be misleading without also reporting that the distribution is bimodal and revealing the values of the maximum scores.

Summary of the Properties of the Mean, Median, and Mode

The mean is

1. the balance point of a distribution, the point for which $\sum_{i=1}^{n}(X_i - \overline{X}) = 0$;
2. the preferred measure for relatively symmetrical distributions and quantitative variables;
3. the measure with the best sampling stability;
4. widely used in advanced statistical procedures;
5. mathematically tractable;
6. the only measure whose value is dependent on the value of every score in the distribution;
7. more sensitive to extreme scores than the median and the mode and, hence, is not recommended for markedly skewed distributions;
8. not appropriate for qualitative data; and
9. not appropriate for open-ended distributions.

The median is

1. the point that divides the ordered scores into two samples of equal size;
2. second to the mean in usefulness;
3. widely used for markedly skewed distributions because it is sensitive only to the number rather than to the values of scores above and below it;
4. the most stable measure that can be used with open-ended distributions;
5. more subject to sampling fluctuation than the mean;
6. less mathematically tractable than the mean; and
7. less often used in advanced statistical procedures.

The mode is

1. the score value that occurs most often and, therefore, the most typical value;
2. the only measure appropriate for unordered qualitative variables;
3. more appropriate than the mean or the median for quantitative variables that are inherently discrete; *w. family size*
4. the easiest measure to compute;
5. much more subject to sampling fluctuation than the mean and the median;
6. less mathematically tractable than the mean and the median;
7. not necessarily existent, as when a distribution has two or more scores with the same maximum frequency; and
8. rarely used in advanced statistical procedures.

CHECK YOUR UNDERSTANDING OF SECTION 3.5

15. For the following sets of data, what measures of central tendency would you compute? Justify your choices.
    a. 9, 6, 5, 7, 1, 6, 7, 8, 10, 6, 5, 4, 3, 6, 9, 7, 4, 5, 6, 8, 3, 2
    b. 6, 5, 9, 6, 7, 5, 6, 8, 3, 4, 5, 7, 5, 4, 8, 5
    c. 3, 5, 8, 5, 7, 9, 4, 2, 5, 6, 6, 23
16. Rank the three measures of central tendency with respect to the following characteristics; let 1 = most or hardest and 3 = least or easiest.
    a. Sampling stability
    b. Appropriateness for qualitative variables
17. Terms to remember
    a. Sampling stability
    b. Mathematically tractable
    c. Open-ended distribution

3.6 LOCATION OF THE MEAN, MEDIAN, AND MODE IN A DISTRIBUTION

If a distribution is unimodal and symmetrical, the mean, median, and mode have the same value. If the distribution is unimodal but skewed, usually the three measures will be arranged in a predictable order. This order is illustrated in Figure 3.6-1. In both examples, the mean is on the side of the distribution having the longest tail, and the median falls about one-third of the distance from the mean to the mode. To remember the order—mean, median, mode—note that it is alphabeti-

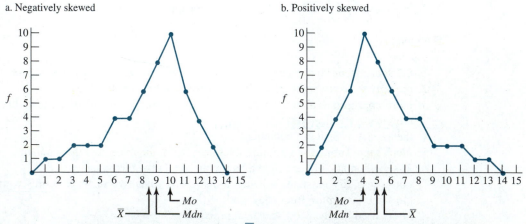

Figure 3.6-1. **Location of the $\overline{X}$, *Mdn*, and *Mo* for skewed distributions.**

cal, starting from the longer tail. This order occurs because the mean is affected by the value of extreme scores. The median is affected by the presence of extreme scores but not by their value. The mode, however, is not affected by extreme scores unless they happen to have the greatest frequency of occurrence. This ordering of the mean, median, and mode holds for most unimodal distributions.

The relative location of the mean and median can be used to determine whether a distribution is positively or negatively skewed. For negatively skewed distributions, it is virtually always true that $Mdn > \overline{X}$; for positively skewed distributions, $\overline{X} > Mdn$. If, for example, we know that the median is 25 and the mean is 20, we would strongly suspect that the distribution is negatively skewed. The greater the discrepancy between the two values, the greater the departure from symmetry.[5]

A knowledge of the relative location of the mean, median, and mode in asymmetrical distributions can be used to intentionally distort the interpretation of data and mislead consumers of statistics. If we were to graph the wages of workers in one of the construction industries, we would probably obtain a positively skewed distribution. If you were negotiating a new contract for the workers, you would want to report the modal salary in defending your request for a wage increase. However, if you were on the other side of the negotiating table, you would cite the mean, a higher figure, in arguing against the need for an increase. Even though both the mean and the mode are correct as measures of central tendency, they are misleading when the distribution is markedly skewed. The more appropriate measure for such a distribution is the median. This example illustrates one of the classic ways in which statistics can be used to mislead the unwary.

CHECK YOUR UNDERSTANDING OF SECTION 3.6

18. Determine the shape—for example, symmetrical, positively skewed, and so on—of each distribution from the following measures of central tendency.
  a. $\overline{X} = 16$, $Mdn = 10$
  b. $\overline{X} > Mdn$
  c. $\overline{X} = 34$, $Mdn = 34$, $Mo_1 = 28$, $Mo_2 = 40$
  d. $\overline{X} = 46$, $Mdn = 46$, $Mo = 46$
  f. $\overline{X} = 23$, $Mdn = 23$, $Mo_1 = 20$, $Mo_2 = 23$, $Mo_3 = 27$
  e. $Mo = 19$, $Mdn = 12$

3.7 MEAN OF TWO OR MORE MEANS

Suppose that two introductory sociology classes obtained the following mean scores on a departmental examination: 80 and 90. What is the mean of the two

---

[5] A more sophisticated measure of skewness is described in Section 4.6.

means? If each class had the same number of students, we could compute the mean of the means by $\bar{X} = (\bar{X}_1 + \bar{X}_2)/2 = (80 + 90)/2 = 85$. If, as is more likely, the classes contain different numbers of students, we must weight the means proportionally to their respective sample sizes. Assume that $\bar{X}_1 = 80$ and $n_1 = 20$ and that $\bar{X}_2 = 90$ and $n_2 = 40$. The weighted mean $\bar{X}_W$, is given by

$$\bar{X}_W = \frac{n_1\bar{X}_1 + n_2\bar{X}_2 + \cdots + n_n\bar{X}_n}{n_1 + n_2 + \cdots + n_n} = \frac{20(80) + 40(90)}{20 + 40} = \frac{5200}{60} = 86.7.$$

The weighted mean is closer to 90 than to 80; this reflects the larger n_2 associated with $\bar{X}_2 = 90$.

CHECK YOUR UNDERSTANDING OF SECTION 3.7

19. For the following data, compute weighted means.
    a. $\bar{X}_1 = 30$, $n_1 = 10$; $\bar{X}_2 = 50$, $n_2 = 20$
    b. $\bar{X}_1 = 20$, $n_1 = 10$; $\bar{X}_2 = 25$, $n_2 = 10$; $\bar{X}_3 = 30$, $n_3 = 20$

3.8   MORE ABOUT THE SUMMATION OPERATOR

The summation operator, Σ, was introduced in Section 3.3. We saw that the symbol $\Sigma_{i=1}^{n}$ tells us to perform an operation, namely, add the terms corresponding to i equals 1 through n. Many proofs in statistics involve rules for using the summation operator with variables and constants. This section describes four of these rules and illustrates their use in proving that the sum of the deviation of the mean from each score is equal to zero. Other proofs involving the summation operator are used in Exercise 22, Section 3.8, and in Exercise 21, Review Exercises for Chapter 3.

Summation Rules

The following summation rules are widely used in statistical proofs and derivations. An understanding of these rules will go far toward taking derivations out of the realm of magic.

RULE 3.8-1.   *The Sum of a Constant*
Let c be a constant; the sum over $i = 1, \ldots, n$ of the constant can be written as the product of the upper limit of the summation, n, and c. That is,

$$\sum_{i=1}^{n} c = \overbrace{c + c + \cdots + c}^{n \text{ terms}} = nc$$

For example, let $c = 2$ and $i = 1, \ldots 3$; then

$$\sum_{i=1}^{3} 2 = \overbrace{2 + 2 + 2}^{3 \text{ terms}} = 3(2) = 6$$

Thus, anytime $\sum_{i=1}^{n} c$ occurs, it can be written as nc. Similarly, $\sum_{j=1}^{k} c$ can be written as kc.

RULE 3.8-2[6]. *The Sum of a Variable*

Let V_i be a variable with values $V_1, V_2, \ldots, V_n$; the sum over $i = 1, \ldots, n$ of the variable is

$$\sum_{i=1}^{n} V_i = V_1 + V_2 + \cdots + V_n.$$

For example, let $V_1 = 2$, $V_2 = 3$, and $V_3 = 4$; then

$$\sum_{i=1}^{3} V_i = 2 + 3 + 4 = 9.$$

RULE 3.8-3. *The Sum of the Product of a Constant, c, and a Variable, V_i*

The expression $\sum_{i=1}^{n} c V_i$ can be written as the product of the constant and the sum of the variable—that is,

$$\sum_{i=1}^{n} c V_i = c \sum_{i=1}^{n} V_i.$$

For example, let $c = 2$ and $V_1 = 2$, $V_2 = 3$, and $V_3 = 4$; then

$$\sum_{i=1}^{3} cV_i = 2(2) + 2(3) + 2(4) = 18$$

$$= c \sum_{i=1}^{n} V_i = 2(2 + 3 + 4) = 2(9) = 18.$$

Similarly, the sum of a variable, V_i, divided by a constant, c,

$$\sum_{i=1}^{n} \frac{V_i}{c},$$

can be written as the reciprocal of the constant times the sum of the variable—that is,

$$\frac{1}{c} \sum_{i=1}^{n} V_i.$$

---

[6] This rule was introduced in Section 3.3.

For example, let $c = 2$ and $V_1 = 2$, $V_2 = 3$, and $V_3 = 4$; then

$$\sum_{i=1}^{3} \frac{V_i}{c} = \frac{2}{2} + \frac{3}{2} + \frac{4}{2} = 4.5$$

$$= \frac{1}{c} \sum_{i=1}^{3} V_i = \frac{1}{2} (2 + 3 + 4) = \frac{1}{2} (9) = 4.5.$$

RULE 3.8-4. *Distribution of Summation*

If the only operation to be performed before summation is addition or subtraction, the summation sign can be distributed among the separate terms of the sum. Let V and W be two variables; then

$$\sum_{i=1}^{n} (V_i + W_i) = \sum_{i=1}^{n} V_i + \sum_{i=1}^{n} W_i .$$

For example, let $V_1 = 2$, $V_2 = 3$, $V_3 = 4$, $W_1 = 5$, $W_2 = 6$, and $W_3 = 7$; then

$$\sum_{i=1}^{3} (V_i + W_i) = (2 + 5) + (3 + 6) + (4 + 7) = 27$$

$$= \sum_{i=1}^{3} V_i + \sum_{i=1}^{3} W_i$$

$$= (2 + 3 + 4) + (5 + 6 + 7) = 27.$$

This rule applies to any number of terms. For example, let V_i, W_i, and X_i be variables and a, b, and c be constants; then, according to Rules 3.8-1, 3.8-2, and 3.8-4,

$$\sum_{i=1}^{n} (V_i + W_i + X_i + a + b + c) = \sum_{i=1}^{n} V_i + \sum_{i=1}^{n} W_i + \sum_{i=1}^{n} X_i + na + nb + nc.$$

Proof That the Mean Is a Balance Point

In Section 3.5 we said that the mean is the point such that $\sum_{i=1}^{n} (X_i - \overline{X}) = 0$. We can construct a simple proof of this assertion using Rules 3.8-1, 3.8-2, and 3.8-4. In the expression $\sum_{i=1}^{n} (X_i - \overline{X})$, X_i is a variable; but for any set of scores, $\overline{X}$ is a constant. Hence,

$$\sum_{i=1}^{n} (X_i - \overline{X}) = \sum_{i=1}^{n} X_i - \sum_{i=1}^{n} \overline{X} \qquad \text{Rules 3.8-4 and 3.8-2}$$

$$= \sum_{i=1}^{n} X_i - n\overline{X} \qquad \text{Rule 3.8-1 (Note that for any set of data, } \overline{X} \text{ is a constant.)}$$

By definition, $\bar{X} = \sum_{i=1}^{n} X_i/n$. It follows that $n\bar{X} = \sum_{i=1}^{n} X_i$. Substituting $\sum_{i=1}^{n} X_i$ for $n\bar{X}$ in $\sum_{i=1}^{n} X_i - n\bar{X}$ gives

$$\sum_{i=1}^{n} X_i - \sum_{i=1}^{n} X_i = 0.$$

We have just shown that $\sum_{i=1}^{n} (X_i - \bar{X}) = 0$. Consider the following scores where $X_1 = 2$, $X_2 = 3$, $X_3 = 4$, and $\bar{X} = (2 + 3 + 4)/3 = 3$ then

$$\sum_{i=1}^{n} (X_i - \bar{X}) = (2 - 3) + (3 - 3) + (4 - 3)$$
$$= -1 + 0 + 1 = 0.$$

CHECK YOUR UNDERSTANDING OF SECTION 3.8

20. Write the following expressions as the sum of individual values of the variables X and Y or the constant a; for example, $\sum_{i=1}^{n} X_i = X_1 + X_2 + \cdots + X_n$

a. $\sum_{i=1}^{3} X_i$ b. $\sum_{i=1}^{4} Y_i$ c. $\sum_{j=1}^{3} f_j X_j$

d. $\sum_{j=1}^{k} f_j X_j$.   e. $\sum_{i=1}^{3} aX_i$ f. $\sum_{i=1}^{n} (X_i + a)$

21. Let X and Y denote variables, and let a and b denote constants. Assume that the values of the variables and the constants are as follows:

$$X_3 = 4 \qquad Y_4 = 9 \qquad a = 2$$
$$X_2 = 3 \qquad Y_3 = 4 \qquad b = 3$$
$$X_1 = 2 \qquad Y_2 = 2$$
$$\qquad\qquad Y_1 = 1$$

Determine the values of the following expressions.

a. $\sum_{i=1}^{3} a$ b. $\sum_{i=1}^{4} b$ c. $\sum_{i=1}^{n} X_i$

d. $\sum_{i=1}^{n} Y_i$ e. $\sum_{i=1}^{2} X_i$ f. $\sum_{i=1}^{n} aX_i$

g. $\sum_{i=1}^{3} (X_i + a)$ h. $\sum_{i=1}^{4} (Y_i + a - b)$ i. $\sum_{i=1}^{2} (X_i + a)$

22. The following proofs show the effect on the mean of adding a constant to each score or multiplying each score by a constant. For each proof, identify the summation rules from Section 3.8 that were used.

a. Let $\overline{X}_{X+c}$ be the mean of a distribution that has been altered by adding a constant c to each score—that is, $X_1 + c, X_2 + c, \ldots, X_n + c$. Then

$$\overline{X}_{X+c} = \frac{\sum_{i=1}^{n}(X_i + c)}{n} = \frac{\sum_{i=1}^{n}X_i + \sum_{i=1}^{n}c}{n} = \frac{\sum_{i=1}^{n}X_i + nc}{n}$$

$$= \frac{\sum_{i=1}^{n}X_i}{n} + c = \overline{X} + c.$$

Thus, the effect of adding a constant c to each score is to change $\overline{X}$, the mean of the original scores, to $\overline{X} + c$. Similarly, it can be shown that the effect of subtracting a constant from each score is to change $\overline{X}$ to $\overline{X} - c$.

b. Let $\overline{X}_{cX}$ be the mean of a distribution that has been altered by multiplying each score by a constant c—that is, $cX_1, cX_2, \ldots, cX_n$. Then

$$\overline{X}_{cX} = \frac{\sum_{i=1}^{n}(cX_i)}{n} = \frac{c\sum_{i=1}^{n}X_i}{n} = c\overline{X}.$$

Thus, the effect of multiplying each score by a constant c is to change $\overline{X}$, the mean of the original scores, to $c\overline{X}$. Similarly, it can be shown that the effect of dividing each score by a constant is to change $\overline{X}$ to $\overline{X}/c$.

†3.9 PRINTOUTS FOR THREE MICROCOMPUTER PACKAGES

JMP

Once data have been entered in a JMP data table, it is easy to obtain the median and the mean. A portion of the JMP data table for the depression scores of males facing exploratory cancer surgery in Table 3.3-1 is shown on the left side of Figure 3.9-1. The displays on the right of Figure 3.9-1, which are labeled Quantiles and Moments, were obtained by selecting **Analyze** in the menu bar followed by the pull-down command called **Distribution of Y.** The median and mean for these data are 23 and 22, respectively. The displays contain a variety of other statistics such as

---

† This and similarly marked sections can be omitted without loss of continuity.

Depression Data		
1 Cols	C	☐
21 Rows		Column 1
1		28
2		26
3		25
4		25
5		24
6		24
7		24
8		23
9		23
10		23
11		23

Quantiles

maximum	100.0%	28.000
	99.5%	28.000
	97.5%	28.000
	90.0%	25.900
quartile	75.0%	24.000
median	50.0%	23.000
quartile	25.0%	19.250
	10.0%	16.200
	2.5%	14.000
	0.5%	14.000
minimum	0.0%	14.000

Moments

Mean	22.00000
Std Dev	3.43358
Std Err Mean	0.76777
upper 95% Mean	23.60695
lower 95% Mean	20.39305
N	20.00000
Sum Wgts	20.00000

Figure 3.9-1. **The JMP data table for the depression scores in Table 3.3-1 is shown on the left. To conserve space, only the first 11 scores are shown in column 1. The median (23.000) and mean (22.000) appear in the quantiles and moments tables, respectively, along with a number of other statistics.**

the quartiles, standard deviation (Std Dev), and standard error of the mean (Std Err Mean) that are discussed in later chapters.

The label for the quantiles display in Figure 3.9-1 is appropriate because quantiles are values that divide data into a given number of equal-size subsets. Two examples of quantiles are quartiles that divide data into four equal-size subsets and the median that divides data into two equal-size subsets. The label for the moments display also is apt because most of the measures in the display are based on the mean of the sum of values raised to a power, which is the meaning of a moment. For example, the mean is obtained from the sum of values raised to the first power: $\overline{X} = \Sigma X^1/n$.

SPSS

The SPSS data table for the first seven depression scores in Table 3.3-1 is shown in Figure 3.9-2. To obtain the mean, median, and mode, **Statistics** was selected in the menu bar followed by the pull-down option called **Summarize**. This brought

Depression Scores		
	dep_scor	var
1	28.000	
2	26.000	
3	25.000	
4	25.000	
5	24.000	
6	24.000	
7	24.000	

Figure 3.9-2. **SPSS data table for the depression scores in Table 3.3-1. To conserve space, only the first seven scores are shown in the column labeled dep_scor. The dependent variable, depression score, is called dep_scor because variable names are limited to eight characters including the underscore, _, that is used to separate words.**

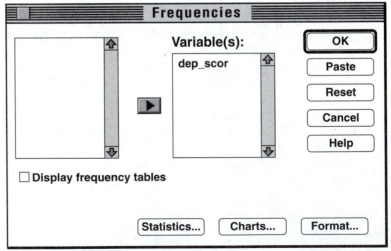

Figure 3.9-3. **This dialog box in SPSS was used to select the variables for analysis. In this example, only one variable, dep_scor, can be analyzed. The dialog box was obtained by choosing Statistics from the menu bar and then the pull-down option, Summarize. The mean, median, and mode were selected using the Statistics... option.**

DEP_SCOR					
Mean	22.000	Median	23.000	Mode	23.000
Valid cases	20	Missing cases	0		

Figure 3.9-4. **SPSS output for the depression data in Table 3.3-1.**

up the dialog box called **Frequencies** that is shown in Figure 3.9-3. The **Statistics . . .** option was selected from this dialog box, and then three measures of central tendency—mean, median, and mode—were selected from the **Frequencies: Statistics** dialog box. The output is shown in Figure 3.9-4.

SYSTAT

The SYSTAT data table, called the data editor, and the analysis window for the depression scores in Table 3.3-1 are shown in Figure 3.9-5. The mean and median were obtained by selecting **STATS** from the menu bar and then selecting the **Stats** option followed by **Statistics** in the pull-down menu. This series of choices

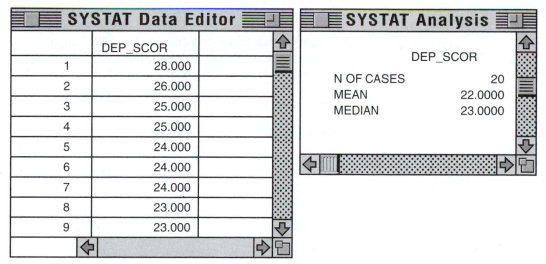

Figure 3.9-5. **A portion of the SYSTAT data table for the depression scores in Table 3.3-1 is shown on the left; the analysis window, output from SYSTAT, is shown on the right. The dependent variable, depression score, is called DEP_SCOR because variable names are limited to eight characters including the underscore, _, that is used to separate words. The number of cases, mean, and median are shown in the analysis window on the right.**

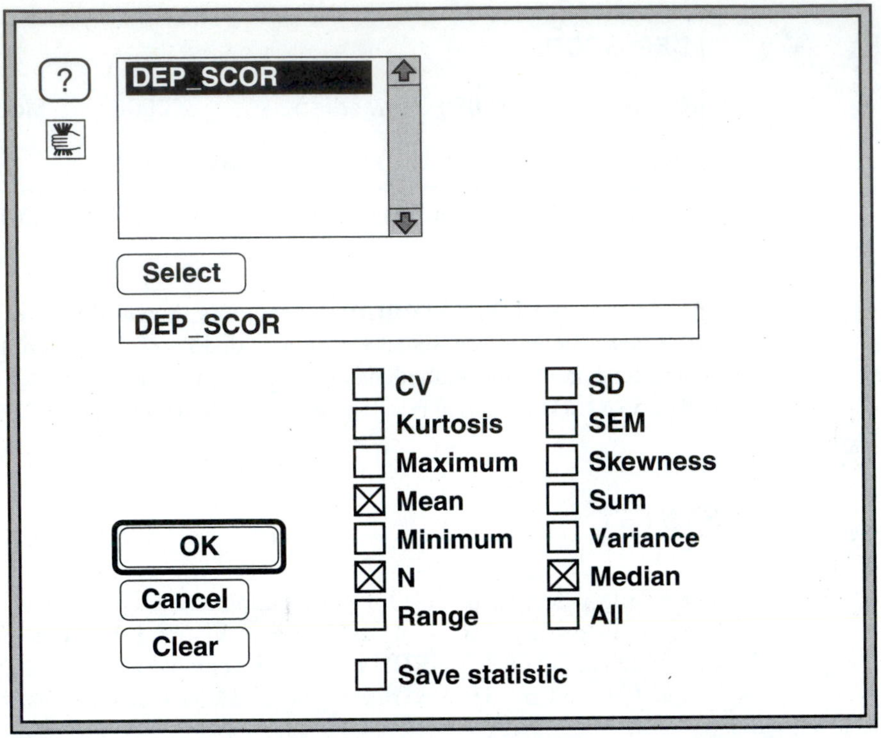

Figure 3.9-6. **This dialog box in SYSTAT was used to select the variable for analysis and the statistics to be computed. The dialog box appears when the STATS command in the menu bar is selected followed by the selection of the Stats and Statistics options in the pull-down menu. Clicking on DEP_SCOR in the top window selected the variable, and then clicking on the Select button placed the variable in the long rectangular window. A variety of statistics can be computed. In this example, only the boxes for mean, *N*, and median were checked. The output is shown on the right of Figure 3.9-5.**

brought up the dialog box shown in Figure 3.9-6. DEP_SCOR (depression score) was selected for analysis, and the mean, *N* (number of scores), and median were requested.

3.10 SUMMARY

Three measures of central tendency are described in this chapter: the mean, median, and mode. The different measures result from different ways of conceptualizing the point around which scores cluster. The mean is the point on which the distribution balances—its center of gravity; the median is the point that divides the ordered scores into two samples of equal size; and the mode is the score value with the greatest frequency—the most typical score.

The mean is the most widely used of the measures, partly because of its superior sampling stability and partly because many advanced statistical procedures are based on it. The median and the mode, by contrast, are **terminal statistics;** their usefulness in advanced descriptive and inferential procedures is limited.

There are three situations in which the mean is not the preferred measure of central tendency: when the distribution is markedly skewed, when the variable is qualitative in character, and when the distribution is open-ended. For markedly skewed distributions, the median is preferred because it is not as sensitive as the mean to the presence of extreme scores. For unordered qualitative variables, the mode is used because it is the only one of the three measures that can be computed. In addition, the mode may be more meaningful for inherently discrete ordered qualitative variables such as family size.

REVIEW EXERCISES FOR CHAPTER 3

1. In a paired-associates learning experiment, data representing the number of trials necessary to reach the criterion of three consecutive errorless trials were 10, 6, 11, 10, 9, 8, 10, 11, 14, 12, 10, 9, 11, 10, 12, 9, 8, 9. (a) Determine the mode. (b) What type of variable do the data represent?

2. The electoral systems of 11 emerging nations were classified as $N =$ noncompetitive, $P =$ partially competitive, and $C =$ competitive. (a) Determine the mode for the following data: $N, P, N, C, N, P, P, N, N, C, N$. (b) What type of variable do the data represent?

3. The mode may not exist; explain why this is so.

4. Identify
   a. $\overline{X}$ b. μ_Z c. Y_2
   d. $\overline{Y}$ e. Y_j f. Z_k
   g. Y_n h. n i. f_j
   j. k k. $\overline{Z}_3$

5. Write out the following, listing individual values of the variable.
   a. $\sum_{i=1}^{5} Y_i / n$ b. $\sum_{j=1}^{6} f_j Y_j / n$ c. $\sum_{\substack{j=1 \\ j \neq 2}}^{4} f_j Z_j$

   d. $\sum_{i=1}^{n} (n_i \overline{X}_i) / n_i$

6. The socioeconomic level of black families in a predominantly black neighborhood was rated on the basis of income, educational attainment,

physical condition of dwelling, and number of home appliances. Compute the mean using $\sum_{i=1}^{n} X_i/n$.

5	6	4	5	10	6	3	5	7	6
3	4	5	8	5	4	7	1	6	7

7. The following data represent the number of suicides per 10,000 inhabitants in predominantly urban prefectures in Japan. Compute the mean using $\overline{X} = \sum_{i=1}^{n} X_i/n$.

23	24	21	19	23	24	25	22	21	27
24	23	23	22	20	23	26	25	24	22
20	17	26	23	21	25	14	21	23	24
26	24	23	22	25	23	25	28		

8. For the socioeconomic data in Exercise 6, construct an ungrouped frequency distribution and compute the mean using $\overline{X} = \sum_{j=1}^{k} f_j X_j/n$.
9. For the suicide data in Exercise 7, construct an ungrouped frequency distribution and compute the mean using $\overline{X} = \sum_{j=1}^{k} f_j X_j/n$.
10. For a small number of scores, how is the median determined when (a) n is odd and (b) n is even?
11. Determine the median for the following scores.
    a. 2, 8, 11, 19, 3, 26, 28
    b. 3, 1, 3, 4
    c. 3, 5, 5, 4, 8
    d. 3, 5, 5, 4, 8, 5
12. For the suicide data in Exercise 7, construct an ungrouped frequency distribution and compute the median using

$$Mdn = X_{ll} + i\left(\frac{n/2 - \Sigma f_b}{f_i}\right).$$

13. For the suicide data in Exercise 7, construct an ungrouped frequency distribution and compute the median by coming down halfway from above—from the highest class interval. The computational formula is

$$Mdn = X_{ul} - i\left(\frac{n/2 - \Sigma f_a}{f_i}\right).$$

The symbols X_{ul} and f_a denote, respectively, the real upper limit of the class interval containing the median and the number of scores above X_{ul}.
14. For the following sets of data, what measures of central tendency would you compute? Justify your choices.
    a. 4, 3, 7, 5, 4, 2, 12, 6, 5, 4, 3, 3, 2, 7, 1, 6, 4, 5, 3, 5
    b. Eye color: blue, brown, brown, blue, green, brown, gray, brown, blue

c. 7, 8, 6, 7, 8, 9, 1, 6, 5, 3, 7, 8, 7, 6, 7, 8, 5, 7

d. Family size: 4, 3, 5, 4, 1, 2, 4, 6, 5

15. Rank the three measures of central tendency with respect to the following characteristics; let 1 = most or hardest and 3 = least or easiest.

   a. Suitability for advanced applications

   b. Mathematical tractability

   c. Sensitivity to value of each score

   d. Ease of computation

16. For each of the following distributions, indicate on the X axis the approximate location of $\overline{X}$, *Mdn*, and *Mo*.

a.

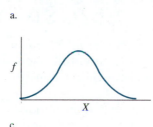

b.

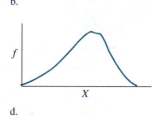

c.

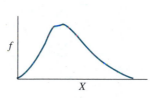

d.

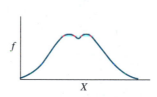

17. Determine the shape—for example, symmetrical, positively skewed, and so on—of each distribution from the following measures of central tendency. Assume a distribution similar to those in Exercise 16.

   a. $\overline{X} = 21$, *Mdn* = 21, *Mo* = 21   b. *Mdn* = 109, $\overline{X} = 116$

   c. $\overline{X} = 73$, *Mdn* = 84   d. $\overline{X} = Mdn = Mo$

   e. $\overline{X} = Mdn \neq Mo$

18. For the following data, compute weighted means.

   a. $\overline{X}_1 = 50$, $n_1 = 20$; $\overline{X}_2 = 100$, $n_2 = 30$

   b. $\overline{X}_1 = 8$, $n_1 = 10$; $\overline{X}_2 = 12$, $n_2 = 30$; $\overline{X}_3 = 18$, $n_3 = 20$

   c. $\overline{X}_1 = 100$, $n_1 = 20$; $\overline{X}_2 = 200$, $n_2 = 20$

19. Write the following expressions as the sum of individual values of the variables X and Y or the constant a; for example, $\sum_{i=1}^{n} X_i = X_1 + X_2 + \cdots + X_n$.

   a. $\sum_{i=1}^{5} X_i$ b. $\sum_{j=1}^{4} f_j Y_j$ c. $\sum_{i=1}^{4} a Y_i$

   d. $\sum_{j=1}^{3} (Y_j - a)$

20. Let X and Y denote variables, and let a and b denote constants. Assume that the values of the variables and the constants are as follows:

$$X_3 = 4 \qquad Y_4 = 9 \qquad a = 2$$
$$X_2 = 3 \qquad Y_3 = 4 \qquad b = 3$$
$$X_1 = 2 \qquad Y_2 = 2$$
$$\qquad\qquad\quad Y_1 = 1$$

Determine the values of the following expressions:

a. $\displaystyle\sum_{i=1}^{2} b$ b. $\displaystyle\sum_{i=1}^{2} a$ c. $\displaystyle\sum_{i=1}^{3} Y_i$

d. $\displaystyle\sum_{i=1}^{n} bY_i$ e. $\displaystyle\sum_{i=1}^{4} (Y_i - b)$ f. $\displaystyle\sum_{i=1}^{3} (X_i + Y_i)$

21. The following proofs show the effect on the mean of subtracting a constant from each score or dividing each score by a constant. For each proof, identify the summation rules from Section 3.8 that were used.

a. Let $\overline{X}_{X-c}$ be the mean of a distribution that has been altered by subtracting a constant c from each score—that is, $X_1 - c$, $X_2 - c$, . . . , $X_n - c$. Then

$$\overline{X}_{X-c} = \frac{\displaystyle\sum_{i=1}^{n} (X_i - c)}{n} = \frac{\displaystyle\sum_{i=1}^{n} X_i - \sum_{i=1}^{n} c}{n} = \frac{\displaystyle\sum_{i=1}^{n} X_i - nc}{n}$$

$$= \frac{\displaystyle\sum_{i=1}^{n} X_i}{n} - c = \overline{X} - c.$$

Thus, the effect of subtracting a constant c from each score is to change $\overline{X}$, the mean of the original scores, to $\overline{X} - c$.

b. Let $\overline{X}_{X/c}$ be the mean of a distribution that has been altered by dividing each score by a constant c—that is, X_1/c, X_2/c, . . . , X_n/c. Then

$$\overline{X}_{X/c} = \frac{\displaystyle\sum_{i=1}^{n} (X_i/c)}{n} = \frac{\dfrac{1}{c} \displaystyle\sum_{i=1}^{n} X_i}{n} = \frac{1}{c}\overline{X} = \overline{X}/c.$$

Thus, the effect of dividing each score by a constant c is to change $\overline{X}$, the mean of the original scores, to $\overline{X}/c$.

22. Use a statistical software package to obtain a histogram and compute the mean and median for the socioeconomic data in Exercise 6.

23. Use a statistical software package to obtain a histogram and compute the mean and median for the suicide data for urban prefectures in Exercise 7.

24. Use a statistical software package to obtain a histogram and compute the mean and median for the socioeconomic data for white families in Exercise 6 in "Check Your Understanding of Section 3.3."

25. Use a statistical software package to obtain a histogram and compute the mean and median for the suicide data for rural prefectures in Exercise 7 in "Check Your Understanding of Section 3.3."

Chapter 4

Measures of Dispersion, Skewness, and Kurtosis

4.1 INTRODUCTION TO MEASURES OF DISPERSION

Mr. Jacques and Mrs. Booker are taking a well-deserved break in the teachers' lounge. The conversation turns to Mrs. Booker's third-grade class. "I've got a bunch of little monsters this year. I can't seem to keep their interest for more than 10 minutes. I had to discipline Emerson twice this morning for flying paper airplanes during arithmetic, and Waldo is still picking fights. I just can't understand it; this class has the same average IQ as my class last year, and you remember how good those kids were." As Mrs. Booker contemplates her options—should I face the class for seven more months, quit and start a family, or go back to college and work on a master's degree in computer science—we wonder what makes one class a joy and the other a disaster. The frequency polygon in Figure 4.1-1 provides the answer. Although the two classes have almost identical mean IQs, this year's class is much more heterogeneous in learning aptitude. Last year, for example, there were no children with IQs below 90; this year there are two. That's Waldo in the class interval 75–79—moderately retarded. At the other end of the distribution in the 140–144 class interval is our paper-plane thrower—a potential genius. It is small wonder that this year's class, with its wide range of aptitude, is giving Mrs. Booker problems.

Information about central tendency is important, but central tendency tells only part of the story; the heterogeneity or dispersion of scores is often just as informative. The measures of central tendency described in Chapter 3 represent points on which a distribution tends to center. As we will see, the most widely used measures of dispersion represent the spread or scatter of scores around some central point and are expressed in terms of distance along a distribution's horizontal, or X, axis. Many measures of dispersion have been proposed. We will examine the five most

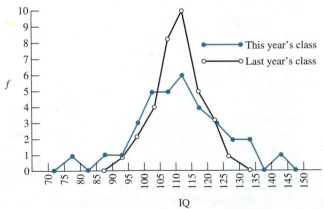

Figure 4.1-1. **Frequency polygons for two third-grade classes with the same central tendency but different dispersions.**

useful measures in the behavioral sciences, health sciences, and education; they are the range, semi-interquartile range, standard deviation, coefficient of variation, and index of dispersion.

4.2 FIVE MEASURES OF DISPERSION

Range

Intuitively, the simplest measure of dispersion is the **range**—the distance between the largest and smallest scores. The range is denoted by R and is computed from the formula

$$R = X_{ul(largest\ score)} - X_{ll(smallest\ score)},$$

where X_{ul} is the real upper limit of the largest score and X_{ll} is the real lower limit of the smallest score. Alternatively, the range can be computed from

$$R = X_{j(largest\ score)} - X_{j(smallest\ score)},$$

where $X_{j(largest\ score)}$ is the midpoint of the largest score and $X_{j(smallest\ score)}$ is the midpoint of the smallest score.

The first formula is sometimes called the **inclusive range;** we will use it throughout the book. The second formula for the **noninclusive range** is often used in computer packages.

Consider this year's class in Figure 4.1-1. If Emerson's 144 is the highest IQ and Waldo's 76 is the lowest, the range is $144.5 - 75.5 = 69$. The range of 69 IQ points is a distance that includes 100% of the scores. In general, the larger the range, the greater the spread or scatter of scores.

In spite of its simplicity, the range is not widely used. For one thing, its value is determined by the two most extreme scores, so its sampling stability—that is, its variability from one random sample to the next—is quite poor. Also, the range cannot be manipulated arithmetically and algebraically, which is another way of saying that it is not mathematically tractable. Furthermore, the range is not meaningful for unordered qualitative data. These and other disadvantages discussed in Section 4.3 limit its usefulness as a measure of dispersion.

As we will see, each measure of dispersion is typically reported with a particular measure of central tendency. For quantitative data, the range can be reported with the mode, thereby giving a more complete picture of data. However, because the mode often is used with unordered qualitative data, a different measure of dispersion is needed. The index of dispersion described later fills this need.

Semi-Interquartile Range

We have seen that the sampling stability of R is poor because it is computed from the two most extreme scores in a distribution. A second measure of dispersion, the semi-interquartile range, is based on two scores closer to the center of the distribution. Hence, it is considerably more stable than R.

> The **semi-interquartile range,** denoted by Q, is defined as one-half the distance between the first quartile point, Q_1, and the third quartile point, Q_3. These points and the median are shown in Figure 4.2-1. The formula for Q is
>
> $$Q = \frac{Q_3 - Q_1}{2}$$

The computation of Q_1 and Q_3 is similar to that for the median and is illustrated in Table 4.2-1. The data are IQ scores from Mrs. Booker's current class. The semi-interquartile range for these data is 8.4. The larger the value of Q, the greater the distance between Q_1 and Q_3, and in general, the greater the spread or scatter of scores.

The semi-interquartile range is often reported along with the median to give a more complete description of data. For a symmetrical distribution, the median plus or minus the semi-interquartile range, $Mdn \pm Q$, gives two points in the distribution such that the interval between the points contains 50% of scores. This can be seen in Figure 4.2-1. For the data in Table 4.2-1, the Mdn plus or minus Q (110.7 ± 8.5) gives the interval 102.2–119.2. The interval 102.2–119.2, however, does not contain exactly 50% of the scores because the distribution is asymmetrical.

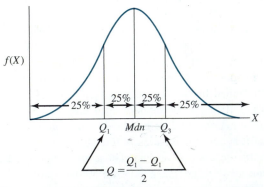

Figure 4.2-1. Q_1 **is a point below which 25% of the scores fall and above which 75% fall; Q_3 is a point below which 75% fall and above which 25% fall. The median is sometimes referred to as Q_2, because it is a point that divides the distribution of scores into two equal size subsamples. The semi-interquartile range, Q, is one-half the distance from Q_1 to Q_3.**

TABLE 4.2-1. Computational Procedures for Q_1, Q_3, and Q (Data From Figure 4.1-1, This Year's Class)

(i) Data and computational formulas

^aX_j	f_j	Cum f	
144	1		$Q_1 = X_{ll} + i\left(\dfrac{n/4 - \Sigma f_b}{f_i}\right)$
134	1		
131	1		$= 100.5 + 1\left(\dfrac{8.5 - 6}{5}\right)$
128	1		
125	1		$= 100.5 + 0.5 = 101.0$
122	3		
118	1	26	$Q_3 = X_{ll} + i\left(\dfrac{n3/4 - \Sigma f_b}{f_i}\right)$
117	3	25	
111	6	22	$= 117.5 + 1\left(\dfrac{25.5 - 25}{1}\right)$
109	2	16	
105	3	14	$= 117.5 + 0.5 = 118.0$
101	5	11	
99	2	6	$Q = \dfrac{Q_3 - Q_1}{2}$
96	1	4	
94	1	3	$= \dfrac{118.0 - 101.0}{2} = 8.5$
87	1	2	
76	1	1	
$n = 34$			

(ii) Definition of terms

X_j = value of jth class interval

f_j = frequency of jth class interval

X_{ll} = real lower limit of class interval containing Q_1 or Q_3

i = class interval size

n = number of scores

Σf_b = number of scores below X_{ll}

f_i = number of scores in class interval containing Q_1 or Q_3

(continued)

TABLE 4.2-1 *(Continued)*

(iii) Computational sequence illustrated for Q_1

1. Compute $n/4 = 34/4 = 8.5$.
2. Locate the class interval containing the $n/4 = 8.5$th score in the *Cum f* column; the 8.5th score occurs in the class interval 101. For this class interval, X_{ll} is 100.5.
3. Compute i: i = Real upper limit of class interval − Real lower limit of class interval = $101.5 - 100.5 = 1$.
4. Determine $\Sigma f_b = 6$.
5. Determine $f_i = 5$.

---

a To conserve space, class intervals with $f_j = 0$ have been omitted.

The semi-interquartile range, like the median, is a terminal statistic; by this we mean that its usefulness in advanced descriptive and inferential procedures is very limited. The semi-interquartile range shares both the advantages and the disadvantages of the median because it is computed from "medianlike" descriptive statistics, Q_1 and Q_3. We will now digress for a moment to describe another medianlike statistic—the percentile.

> A **percentile point**, also called a **percentile** or **centile** and denoted by $P_\%$, is a point on the measurement scale below which a specified percentage of scores falls. It is helpful to visualize a percentile as a *point* on the X axis of a graph. The term **percentile rank,** denoted by P_R, refers to the percentage of scores that falls below the percentile point.

Procedures for computing percentile points corresponding to the 25th, 50th, and 75th percentile ranks already have been described because these points correspond, respectively, to Q_1, *Mdn,* and Q_3. Percentiles corresponding to other percentile ranks can be computed using the formula

$$P_\% = X_{ll} + i\left(\frac{n(P_R/100) - \Sigma f_b}{f_i}\right),$$

where $P_\%$ identifies a percentile point and P_R, a percentile rank. The other symbols are defined in Table 4.2-1; $P_\%$ should be substituted for Q_1 or Q_3 where it appears.

Suppose that we wanted to determine the percentile point corresponding to the 60th percentile rank. To determine P_{60} for the data in Table 4.2-1, first compute $n(P_R/100) = 34(60/100) = 20.4$. By following the computational sequence illustrated in Table 4.2-1 for Q_1, we obtain

$$P_{60} = 110.5 + 1\left(\frac{34(60/100) - 16}{6}\right) = 110.5 + 0.7 = 111.2.$$

This tells us that the IQ score of 111.2 represents a point below which 60% of the scores in this year's class fall.

Often we have a score in mind and want to determine the percentile rank of the score. This situation is the reverse of that just described, where we had the 60th percentile rank in mind and wanted to determine the corresponding percentile point. Suppose that for the data in Table 4.2-1 we wanted to know the percentile rank of the IQ score 105.3. The percentile rank of 105.3 can be determined by using the following formula:

$$PR = \frac{100}{n}\left[\Sigma f_b + \frac{f_i(P_\% - X_{ll})}{i}\right]$$

$$PR = \frac{100}{34}\left[11 + \frac{3(105.3 - 104.5)}{1}\right] = 39.4$$

The first step in computing the percentile rank is to locate the class interval in Table 4.2-1 that contains the score 105.3. This score falls in the class interval 105; the real limits of this class interval are 104.5 and 105.5. Thus, the lower limit of the class interval containing the score 105.3 is $X_{ll} = 104.5$. We note that there are $f_i = 3$ scores in this class interval and that there are $\Sigma f_b = 11$ scores below this class interval. Inserting these values in the formula and solving for the percentile rank gives 39.4. We know from this that 39.4% of the scores in this year's class fall below a score of 105.3.

Percentiles and percentile ranks are widely used in reporting the performance of individuals on psychological tests. We will return to percentiles in Chapter 9.

Standard Deviation

The **standard deviation,** denoted by S for a sample and by σ for a population, is the most important and most widely used measure of dispersion. The formulas for S and σ are

$$S = \sqrt{\frac{\sum_{i=1}^{n}(X_i - \overline{X})^2}{n}} \quad \text{and} \quad \sigma = \sqrt{\frac{\sum_{i=1}^{n}(X_i - \mu)^2}{n}},$$

where $\overline{X}$ and μ denote the sample and population means, respectively.[1]

[1] When the population standard deviation, σ, is estimated from sample data, a better estimator is given by

$$\hat{\sigma} = \sqrt{\frac{\sum_{i=1}^{n}(X_i - \overline{X})^2}{n - 1}}$$

and is denoted by $\hat{\sigma}$. This statistic is used with inferential statistics in Chapters 11–15.

We can develop an intuitive understanding of the standard deviation by examining the formula for S. First note that, unlike R and Q, S is computed from every score in a distribution. Second, each score is expressed as a deviation from the mean, $(X_i - \overline{X})$; third, each deviation is squared; and fourth, the squared deviations are summed. What would happen if we didn't square the deviations? We know from Chapter 3 that for any distribution,[2]

$$\sum_{i=1}^{n} (X_i - \overline{X}) = 0,$$

so squaring or some other operation on the deviations is necessary for the sum to equal a value other than zero. Finally, note that the sum of the squared deviations is divided by n, which gives us the mean squared distance by which the scores deviate from the mean. To convert $\sum_{i=1}^{n} (X_i - \overline{X})^2/n$ back into deviations expressed in the original unit of measurement, we take its square root.[3]

To summarize, the standard deviation is a number that (1) is based on every score in a distribution and (2) represents the square root of the mean squared distance of scores from the mean. In general, the larger the value of S, the greater the spread or scatter of scores. Because the standard deviation is based on every score in the distribution, its sampling stability is much better than that of other measures of dispersion. For this reason and because it is mathematically tractable, the standard deviation is widely used in advanced descriptive and inferential statistics.

As we saw earlier, each measure of dispersion is typically reported with a particular measure of central tendency—R with Mo and Q with Mdn. The standard deviation is reported with the mean. One special type of distribution, called the *normal distribution,* is often approximated by behavioral science data (see Section 2.6 and Chapter 9). For this distribution, the mean plus and minus the standard deviation ($\overline{X} \pm S$) is an interval that contains 68.27% of scores, as Figure 4.2-2 illustrates. The other two dispersion measures are shown in the figure for comparison.

Computation of the standard deviation using the formula

$$S = \sqrt{\dfrac{\sum_{i=1}^{n} (X_i - \overline{X})^2}{n}}$$

---

[2] For a proof, see Section 3.8.

[3] The square of the standard deviations—S, σ, and $\hat{\sigma}$—is called *variance*. The formulas for variance are

$$S^2 = \sum_{i=1}^{n} (X_i - \overline{X})^2/n$$
$$\sigma^2 = \sum_{i=1}^{n} (X_i - \mu)^2/n$$
$$\hat{\sigma}^2 = \sum_{i=1}^{n} (X_i - \overline{X})^2/(n - 1)$$

The measures S^2 and σ^2 are, respectively, the sample variance and the population variance. The measure $\hat{\sigma}^2$ is widely used in inferential statistics. We will return to $\hat{\sigma}^2$ in Chapters 11 and 13 and in Chapters 14 and 15, when we discuss the analysis of variance.

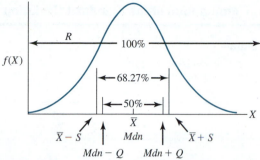

Figure 4.2-2. **A region that contains 68.27% of the area of the normal distribution is marked off by $\overline{X} \pm S$; *Mdn* $\pm$ *Q* contains 50% of the area, and the *R* contains 100% of the area.**

is illustrated in Table 4.2-2 (see columns 2 and 3 and part ii). The data represent ratings of the socioeconomic level of white families in a predominantly black neighborhood. For these data, $\overline{X} = 5$ and $S = 2.3$. If we compute $\overline{X} \pm S$, we obtain 5 ± 2.3, or the interval 2.7–7.3. It can be shown using the formula for computing a percentile rank that this interval contains 63.34% of the 12 scores because 2.7 corresponds to the 18.33rd percentile and 7.3 corresponds to the 81.67th percentile ($63.34 = 81.67 - 18.33$). The percentage 63.34 is reasonably close to the 68.27 we would find for the normal distribution, even though the example contains only 12 scores and the distribution deviates appreciably from the normal form.

The formula for S just illustrated is called the **deviation formula** because the formula involves the computation of deviations—$(X_i - \overline{X})$. If $\overline{X}$ is not an integer, the use of this formula can lead to a sizable rounding error because squaring the n deviations $(X_i - \overline{X})$ magnifies the rounding error in $\overline{X}$. An alternative formula that circumvents this problem and also is more convenient to use is

$$S = \sqrt{\dfrac{\displaystyle\sum_{i=1}^{n} X_i^2 - \dfrac{\left(\displaystyle\sum_{i=1}^{n} X_i\right)^2}{n}}{n}}.$$

This formula is called the **raw-score formula;** it is algebraically equivalent to the deviation formula.[4] Use of the raw-score formula is illustrated in Table 4.2-2 (see columns 1 and 4 and part ii). The raw-score formula looks more complicated than the deviation formula, but actually it is simpler to use. The ultimate in simplicity is a calculator with a standard deviation key. After all the scores have

---

[4] The equivalence is shown in Section 4.7.

TABLE 4.2-2.   Computation of the Standard Deviation

(i) Data

(1) X_i	(2) $X_i - \overline{X}$	(3) $(X_i - \overline{X})^2$	(4) X_i^2
5	0	0	25
9	4	16	81
2	−3	9	4
8	3	9	64
6	1	1	36
5	0	0	25
4	−1	1	16
7	2	4	49
4	−1	1	16
3	−2	4	9
1	−4	16	1
6	1	1	36
$\sum\limits_{i=1}^{n} X_i = 60$		$\sum\limits_{i=1}^{n} (X_i - \overline{X})^2 = 62$	$\sum\limits_{i=1}^{n} X_i^2 = 362$

$$\overline{X} = \frac{\sum\limits_{i=1}^{n} X_i}{n} = \frac{60}{12} = 5$$

(ii) Computational formulas

Deviation formula	Raw-score formula
$S = \sqrt{\dfrac{\sum\limits_{i=1}^{n} (X_i - \overline{X})^2}{n}}$	$S = \sqrt{\dfrac{\sum\limits_{i=1}^{n} X_i^2 - \dfrac{\left(\sum\limits_{i=1}^{n} X_i\right)^2}{n}}{n}}$
$= \sqrt{\dfrac{62}{12}}$	$= \sqrt{\dfrac{362 - \dfrac{(60)^2}{12}}{12}}$
$= 2.3$	$= \sqrt{\dfrac{362 - 300}{12}}^{a}$
	$= 2.3$

[a] The numerator of this ratio is never negative; a negative value indicates a computational error. One common error is to use the value of $\sum X_i^2$ for $(\sum X_i)^2$ and vice versa.

been entered, these calculators compute the standard deviation with the press of a key.[5]

The standard deviation also can be computed from an ungrouped frequency distribution, a distribution having a class interval size of one. For this case, the two formulas for S are modified as follows:

<table>
<tr><td>Deviation formula</td><td>Raw-score formula</td></tr>
</table>

$$S = \sqrt{\frac{\sum_{j=1}^{k} f_i (X_i - \overline{X})^2}{n}} \quad \text{and} \quad S = \sqrt{\frac{\sum_{j=1}^{k} f_j X_j - \dfrac{\left(\sum_{j=1}^{k} f_j X_j\right)^2}{n}}{n}},$$

where X_j is the value of the jth class interval, f_j is the frequency of scores in the jth class interval, and summation is performed over the $j = 1, \ldots, k$ class intervals.

Coefficient of Variation

As we have seen, the value of the standard deviation is a measure of the amount of dispersion of a set of scores. When you want to compare the dispersions of two distributions with markedly different means, it is often useful to compute a *relative measure* of dispersion called the **coefficient of variation, CV.** Consider the following distributions: distribution $A = 2, 8, 10, 12, 18$; distribution $B = 102, 108, 110, 112, 118$. The means and standard deviations of the two distributions are $\overline{X}_A = 10$, $S_A = 5.22$ and $\overline{X}_B = 110$, and $S_B = 5.22$. Notice that the standard deviations of the two distributions are identical. However, the dispersion of the scores for distribution A appears to be much greater than that for B. For example, the largest score in distribution A is 9 times the smallest score, $18/2 = 9$. Distribution B appears more homogeneous—the largest score is only 1.16 times the smallest score: $118/102 = 1.16$. The standard deviations of the distributions, $S_A = S_B = 5.22$, are not consistent with our intuition that distribution A has the greatest dispersion. When, as in this example, the means of distributions differ markedly, a clearer picture can be obtained by converting each of the standard deviations into a relative measure before attempting to compare the dispersions. This conversion can be accomplished

[5] Most statistical calculators have two keys for computing a standard deviation: one labeled $\sigma_n - 1$ and another labeled σ_n. The standard deviations produced by the two keys are defined by the formulas, respectively,

$$\hat{\sigma} = \sqrt{\frac{\sum (X_i - \overline{X})^2}{n - 1}} \quad \text{and} \quad S = \sqrt{\frac{\sum (X_i - \overline{X})^2}{n}}.$$

by computing the coefficient of variation that is given by

$$CV = 100(S/\bar{X}).$$

The larger the value of CV, the larger is the dispersion relative to the mean. Consider the two distributions again; the coefficients of variation are

$$CV_A = 100(5.22/10) = 52.2\% \qquad \text{and} \qquad CV_B = 100(5.22/110) = 4.7\%.$$

The two coefficients, 52.2% and 4.7%, are consistent with our intuition that the standard deviation of 5.22 is relatively large for distribution A but relatively small for distribution B.

The coefficient of variation also is useful for comparing standard deviations of variables that involve different units of measurement. For example, one might be interested in comparing the dispersion of income for college graduates five years after graduation with the dispersion of their Scholastic Aptitude Scores. In this example, it would be meaningless to compare a standard deviation expressed in dollars with a standard deviation expressed in test-score points. However, the comparison would be more meaningful if the two standard deviations were converted to CVs.

Index of Dispersion

The four measures of dispersion discussed thus far, R, Q, S, and CV, are distance measures and are commonly used with quantitative variables. If data do not contain distance information, as is the case for unordered qualitative variables, how can we describe dispersion? One approach is to think of dispersion as the distinguishability of observations—more precisely, as the number of pairs of observations actually distinguishable relative to the maximum possible number. Consider the example in Figure 4.2-3(a) in which there are two qualitative categories called A and B that

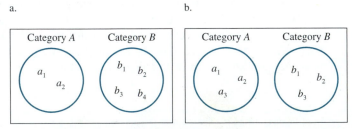

Figure 4.2-3. **In figure (a), elements are assigned to $c = 2$ qualitative categories such that those within a category are indistinguishable with respect to some characteristic. Figure (b) illustrates the case in which the number of distinguishable pairs ($a_1b_1, a_1b_2, \ldots, a_3b_3$) is maximal.**

contain a total of six elements. The elements in the *A* and *B* categories, denoted by a_i and b_j, could represent men and women students who slept through breakfast. The two elements in *A* are indistinguishable in the sense that they are both men who missed breakfast; likewise, the four elements in *B* are indistinguishable. However, the elements in *A* can be distinguished from the elements in *B*. Thus, among the six elements there are eight distinguishable pairs of elements: a_1b_1, a_1b_2, a_1b_3, a_1b_4, a_2b_1, a_2b_2, a_2b_3, a_2b_4. We will denote the observed number of distinguishable pairs by *DP*. In this example, *DP* is equal to 8. The minimum value of *DP*, which represents minimum dispersion, is zero. A value of zero occurs when all the elements are in one category and hence are indistinguishable. The maximum possible number of distinguishable pairs is denoted by DP_{max} and occurs when the elements are evenly divided among the categories, as in Figure 4.2-3(b). It can be determined from Figure 4.2-3(b) that the maximum possible number of distinguishable pairs for *c* = 2 categories and *n* = 6 observations is nine (DP_{max} = 9): a_1b_1, a_1b_2, a_1b_3, a_2b_1, a_2b_2, a_2b_3, a_3b_1, a_3b_2, a_3b_3.

The ratio DP/DP_{max}—the number of distinguishable pairs to the maximum possible number of distinguishable pairs for *c* categories—is called the **index of dispersion** and is denoted by *D*.[6]

For the data in Figure 4.2-3(a), we have seen that *DP* = 8 and that DP_{max} = 9. Hence,

$$D = \frac{DP}{DP_{max}} = \frac{8}{9} = .89,$$

which means that the observed dispersion is .89 as large as its maximum possible value.

To summarize, the minimum value of $D = DP/DP_{max}$ is 0 and occurs when *DP* = 0, which indicates that all the elements are in one category. The maximum value of *D* is 1 and occurs when $DP = DP_{max}$, which indicates that the elements are evenly divided among the *c* categories. Thus, *D* ranges over values 0–1; the larger *D*, the larger the observed number of distinguishable pairs of elements relative to the maximum number for *c* categories and, hence, the greater the dispersion.

When the number of observations *n* is large, it is tedious to determine *DP* and DP_{max} by enumerating or listing all of the possible a_ib_j pairs. A simple alternative formula for *D* that doesn't require an enumeration of the a_ib_j pairs is

$$D = \frac{c\left(n^2 - \sum_{j=1}^{c} n_j^2\right)}{n^2(c-1)},$$

---

[6] This index is also called the **index of qualitative variation**.

TABLE 4.2-3. Marital Happiness Ratings of Women With Either a High School or a College Education

(i) Data

Rating	n_j, High School Graduate	n_j, College Graduate
Very happy	15	12
Moderately happy	28	39
Neutral	16	30
Unhappy	13	12
Very unhappy	8	3
	$n = 80$	$n = 96$
	Mo = Moderately happy	Mo = Moderately happy
	$D_{HG} = .96$	$D_{CG} = .88$

(ii) Computation of D

$$D = \frac{c\left(n^2 - \sum_{j=1}^{c} n_j^2\right)}{n^2(c - 1)}$$

$$D_{HG} = \frac{5[(80)^2 - (15)^2 - (28)^2 - (16)^2 - (13)^2 - (8)^2]}{(80)^2(5 - 1)} = \frac{24,510}{25,600} = .96$$

$$D_{CG} = \frac{5[(96)^2 - (12)^2 - (39)^2 - (30)^2 - (12)^2 - (3)^2]}{(96)^2(5 - 1)} = \frac{32,490}{36,864} = .88$$

where c is the number of categories, n is the number of observations, and n_j is the number of observations in each of the $j = 1, \ldots, c$ categories.[7] For the data in Figure 4.2-3(a),

$$D = \frac{2[(6)^2 - (2)^2 - (4)^2]}{(6)^2(2 - 1)} = .89,$$

the same value obtained previously.

The index of dispersion is particularly useful for comparing the dispersions of several distributions based on the same set of c categories. Suppose that we have asked married women with either a high school or a college education to rate their marital happiness. The results of the survey along with the mode and the index of dispersion are shown in Table 4.2-3. We see that the modes are identical; however, the dispersion of the college graduates' distribution ($D_{CG} = .88$) is smaller than that for the high school graduates ($D_{HG} = .96$). It is evident from Table 4.2-3 that college grads are more likely to rate their marriage as moderately happy and less likely to use other rating categories such as very unhappy.

[7] See Kirk (1978, pp. 91–93) for the derivation of this formula.

For unordered qualitative data, the only appropriate measure of central tendency is the mode. For such data, the appropriate measure of dispersion to report with the mode is the index of dispersion. The index of dispersion has two disadvantages: (1) It is a terminal statistic (its usefulness in advanced descriptive and inferential statistics is limited) and (2) it is less familiar than R, Q, S, and CV, which are based on the concept of distance rather than on the number of distinguishable pairs of observations.

CHECK YOUR UNDERSTANDING OF SECTION 4.2

1. Compute the range for the following sets of numbers.
   a. 11, 6, 5, 2, 9, 14, 17, 4   b. 7, 1, 6, 6, 6, 7, 7, 16
   c. 12, 8, 15, 9, 7, 6, 7   d. 11, −2, 3, 7, 6, 8
2. The ranges in Exercises 1a and 1b are identical, although the first set of numbers appears to be more heterogeneous than the second. Why doesn't the range reflect this difference?
3. Data representing the length of time required to notice the onset of a warning light during the performance of a simulated driving test are listed in the following table. (a) Compute the median and the semi-interquartile range for these data. (b) Compute P_{10} and P_{90}. (c) Construct a histogram.

X_j, Time (Seconds)	f_j	X_j, Time (Seconds)	f_j
32	1	26	3
31	1	25	2
30	2	24	1
29	3	23	0
28	4	22	0
27	6	21	1

4. For the data in Exercise 3, compute the percentile rank for $X = 30$. For these data, note that $i = 1$ and that the real limits of a score, say 27, are 26.5 and 27.5.
5. Preschool children, particularly those who are very intelligent, often create imaginary companions. (a). Compute the mean and the standard deviation using $\sqrt{\Sigma(X_i - \overline{X})^2/n}$ for the following data, which represent the number of companions per child. (b) Compute the coefficient of variation.

4	2	5	3	1
3	2	1	2	3
2	4	3	2	0

6. (a) Compute S for the data in Exercise 5 using $\sqrt{[\Sigma X_i^2 - (\Sigma X_i)^2/n]/n}$.
   (b) Compute the coefficient of variation for the data in Exercises 3 and 5. Which data have the largest relative dispersion?

7. The attitudes of a random sample of white female college students toward having a career were surveyed. (a) For the data in the table, compute the mode and the index of dispersion. (b) Construct a bar graph.

Category	f
Strongly desire career	16
Moderately desire career	23
Undecided about career	19
Don't want career	10

8. The following proofs show the effect on the standard deviation of adding a constant to each score or multiplying each score by a constant. For each proof, identify the summation operations and the number of the summation rules from Section 3.8 that were used.

   a. Let S_{X+c} be the standard deviation of a distribution that has been altered by adding a constant c to each score X_i—that is, $X_1 + c$, $X_2 + c, \ldots, X_n + c$. To determine the effect on S of adding a constant, we replace X_i by $(X_i + c)$ and $\overline{X}$ by $\sum_{i=1}^{n}(X_i + c)/n$ in the formula $S = \sqrt{\sum_{i=1}^{n}(X_i - \overline{X})^2/n}$, as follows.

$$S_{X+c} = \sqrt{\frac{\sum_{i=1}^{n}\left[(X_i + c) - \sum_{i=1}^{n}(X_i + c)/n\right]^2}{n}}$$

$$= \sqrt{\frac{\sum_{i=1}^{n}\left(X_i + c - \sum_{i=1}^{n}X_i/n - nc/n\right)^2}{n}}$$

$$= \sqrt{\frac{\sum_{i=1}^{n}(X_i + c - \overline{X} - c)^2}{n}}$$

$$= \sqrt{\frac{\sum_{i=1}^{n}(X_i - \overline{X})^2}{n}}$$

$$= S$$

Because $S_{X+c} = S$, we know that adding a constant c to each score doesn't affect the value of the standard deviation. Similarly, it can be shown that subtracting a constant also doesn't affect the value of the standard deviation.

b. Let S_{cX} be the standard deviation of a distribution that has been altered by multiplying each score X by a positive constant c—that is, $cX_1, cX_2, \ldots, cX_n$. The effect of this alteration can be shown by replacing X_i by cX_i and $\overline{X}$ by $\sum_{i=1}^{n} cX_i/n$ in the formula $S = \sqrt{\sum_{i=1}^{n}(X_i - \overline{X})^2/n}$, as follows.

$$S_{cX} = \sqrt{\frac{\sum_{i=1}^{n}\left(cX_i - \sum_{i=1}^{n} cX_i/n\right)^2}{n}}$$

$$= \sqrt{\frac{\sum_{i=1}^{n}\left(cX_i - c\sum_{i=1}^{n} X_i/n\right)^2}{n}}$$

$$= \sqrt{\frac{\sum_{i=1}^{n}(cX_i - c\overline{X})^2}{n}}$$

$$= \sqrt{\frac{\sum_{i=1}^{n} c^2(X_i - \overline{X})^2}{n}}$$

$$= \sqrt{\frac{c^2\sum_{i=1}^{n}(X_i - \overline{X})^2}{n}}$$

$$= c\sqrt{\frac{\sum_{i=1}^{n}(X_i - \overline{X})^2}{n}}$$

$$= cS$$

Because $S_{cX} = cS$, we know that the effect of multiplying each score by a positive constant c is to change S, the standard deviation of the original scores, to cS. Similarly, it can be shown that the effect of dividing each score by a positive constant c is to change S to S/c.

If c is a negative constant, $S_{cX} = |c|S$. The use of $|c|$ ensures that $|c|S$ is positive and is consistent with the definition of the standard deviation as the positive square root of $\sum_{i=1}^{n}(X_i - \overline{X})^2/n$.

9. Interpret the following. (a) $\overline{X} = 100$, $S = 15$, and the distribution is approximately normal, (b) $Mdn = 70$, $Q = 12$, (c) $Mo = 16$, $R = 4$, (d) $Mo = $ Category of Pizza Inn pizza, $D = .25$.

10. Terms to remember
    a. Inclusive range
    b. Noninclusive range
    c. Semi-interquartile range
    d. Percentile point
    e. Percentile rank
    f. Standard deviation
    g. Deviation formula for S
    h. Raw-score formula for S
    i. Coefficient of variation
    j. Index of dispersion

4.3 RELATIVE MERITS OF THE MEASURES OF DISPERSION

Standard Deviation and Coefficient of Variation

The standard deviation, which is typically reported with the mean, is the most important and most widely used measure of dispersion for quantitative variables whose distributions are relatively symmetrical. Its popularity is due largely to its superior sampling stability and its mathematical tractability. There are two situations, however, in which the standard deviation is neither a preferred nor an appropriate measure of dispersion: when a distribution is very skewed and when the data are qualitative.

Consider the case of a skewed distribution. The value of the standard deviation is determined by squaring the deviation of each score from the mean. The squaring operation gives undue weight to extreme scores in the longer tail and results in a much larger standard deviation than would have been obtained in the absence of extreme scores. This is a disadvantage. For example, suppose that we wished to compare the dispersion of two distributions that are similar except that one contains several very extreme scores in the longer tail. In spite of the similarity of the two distributions, their standard deviations would be quite different, and the comparison would be misleading. A few extreme scores exert an influence that is disproportionate to their number.

Consider next the case of a qualitative variable. If the variable is ordered, the magnitude of differences between numbers on the measurement scale does not contain meaningful information about the variable. If the variable is unordered, the magnitude of differences between numbers on the measurement scale contains no information about the variable. In either case, the standard deviation is not an appropriate measure of dispersion because the measuring scale does not contain useful distance information.

The standard deviation is used to compute a relative measure of dispersion, the coefficient of variation. This statistic is useful for comparing the relative dispersion of distributions that have markedly different means or different units of measurement. The coefficient of variation, like the standard deviation, is appropriate for quantitative variables and is reported with the mean.

Semi-Interquartile Range

The semi-interquartile range, which is reported with the median, is computed from "medianlike" statistics (Q_1 and Q_3) and shares many of the median's advantages and disadvantages. For example, the semi-interquartile range is limited to descriptive applications with quantitative variables and is relatively intractable mathematically. Nevertheless, it is preferred over the standard deviation in two situations that we will now describe.

We saw in Section 3.5 that the median can be computed for open-ended distributions. This also is true of the semi-interquartile range if the unknown scores lie above Q_3 or below Q_1. Thus, the semi-interquartile range can be computed when the value of one or more extreme scores is unknown. The standard deviation also can be computed when there are unknown scores, but none of the procedures for doing so is entirely satisfactory.

The semi-interquartile range also is preferred over the standard deviation for skewed distributions. Recall that the semi-interquartile range is sensitive to the number but not to the value of scores lying above Q_3 and below Q_1. As a result, the semi-interquartile range is less influenced by the extreme scores in the longer tail of a distribution than is the standard deviation. In summary, there are only two situations in which the semi-interquartile range is preferred over the standard deviation: when a distribution is markedly skewed or when it is open-ended.

Range

The range is used for quantitative variables and may be reported with the mode. The great advantage of the range is its simplicity—it is easy to understand and to compute. As a result, it is used widely as a preliminary measure of dispersion. It also is used in deciding how to group data in a frequency distribution, an application that was described in Section 2.2.

The major deficiency of the range is its poor sampling stability. The value of the range is determined by only two scores (the largest and the smallest), which means that it is not sensitive to most of the score values.

 Another deficiency is its dependency on sample size. If scores are randomly sampled from a population, the range will tend to be larger for larger samples because large samples are more likely to include extreme scores. These deficiencies, plus its poor mathematical tractability, limit the range to descriptive applications.

Index of Dispersion

The index of dispersion, which is reported with the mode, is the only measure of dispersion that is appropriate for unordered qualitative variables. Unlike other dispersion measures, it represents not distance but the number of distinguishable pairs of observations relative to the maximum possible number in c categories. The main disadvantages of the index of dispersion are that it is less familiar than the other measures of dispersion and that it is rarely used in advanced statistical procedures.

Summary of the Properties of the Measures of Dispersion

The standard deviation is

1. a distance measure—the root-mean-squared distance by which scores deviate from the mean;
2. the preferred measure for quantitative variables whose distributions are relatively symmetrical;
3. often reported with the mean—for a normal distribution, $\overline{X} \pm S$ is an interval that contains 68.27% of scores;
4. the measure with the best sampling stability;
5. widely used, implicitly or explicitly, in advanced statistics;
6. mathematically tractable;
7. the only widely used measure whose value is affected by the value of every score in the distribution;
8. fairly sensitive to extreme scores, so it is not recommended for markedly skewed distributions;
9. not appropriate for qualitative variables; and
10. the basis for a relative measure of dispersion, the coefficient of variation.

The coefficient of variation is

1. a distance measure—the root-mean-squared distance by which scores deviate from the mean expressed relative to the size of the mean;
2. appropriate for quantitative variables whose distributions are relatively symmetrical;

3. closely related to the standard deviation because it is the ratio of the standard deviation divided by the mean;
4. may be reported with the mean although the standard deviation is generally the preferred measure to report with the mean because it is expressed in the original unit of measurement, whereas the coefficient of variation is expressed in a unit that is related to the size of the mean;
5. useful for comparing the relative dispersion of distributions that have markedly different means or different units of measurement;
6. rarely used in advanced statistical procedures;
7. fairly sensitive to extreme scores, so it is not recommended for markedly skewed distributions;

8. not appropriate for qualitative variables; and
9. less familiar than the standard deviation, range, and semi-interquartile range.

The semi-interquartile range is

1. a distance measure—one-half the distance between the first and the third quartiles;
2. often reported with the median for quantitative variables;
3. closely related to the median, because both are defined in terms of quartile points;
4. sensitive only to the number and not to the value of scores above Q_3 and below Q_1; hence, it often is used for markedly skewed distributions;
5. the only relatively stable measure that is appropriate for open-ended distributions;
6. more subject to sampling fluctuation than the standard deviation;
7. less mathematically tractable than the standard deviation; and
8. rarely used in advanced statistical procedures.

disadv

The range is

1. a distance measure—the distance between the largest and the smallest scores; *upper & lower limits*
2. often reported with the mode for quantitative variables;
3. the simplest measure of dispersion to compute and interpret;
4. used in deciding how to group data in a frequency distribution;
5. much more subject to sampling fluctuation than the other measures of dispersion;
6. dependent on sample size—the larger the sample size, the larger, on the average, the range;
7. less mathematically tractable than the standard deviation; and
8. rarely used in advanced statistical procedures.

The index of dispersion is

1. a measure of the distinguishability of observations—that is, the number of distinguishable pairs of observations relative to the number possible. The index is 0 when all observations are in one qualitative category (minimum dispersion), and it has its maximum value of 1 when the observations are evenly distributed over the categories (maximum dispersion);
2. the only measure appropriate for unordered qualitative variables;
3. reported with the mode;
4. rarely used in advanced statistical procedures; and
5. less familiar than the standard deviation, range, and semi-interquartile range, which are based on the concept of distance.

CHECK YOUR UNDERSTANDING OF SECTION 4.3

11. What measure of central tendency and dispersion would you compute for the following data? Defend your choice.

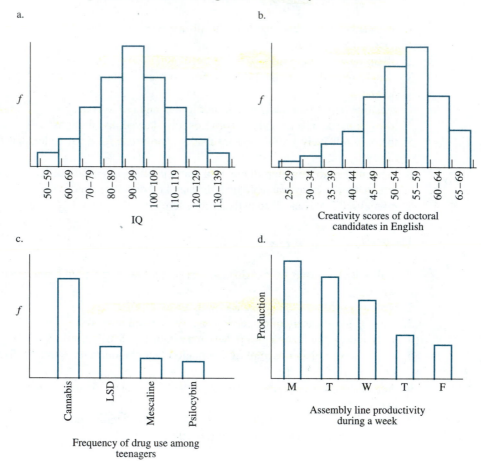

a.

f

IQ: 50–59, 60–69, 70–79, 80–89, 90–99, 100–109, 110–119, 120–129, 130–139

b.

f

Creativity scores of doctoral candidates in English: 25–29, 30–34, 35–39, 40–44, 45–49, 50–54, 55–59, 60–64, 65–69

c.

f

Cannabis, LSD, Mescaline, Psilocybin

Frequency of drug use among teenagers

d.

Production

M   T   W   T   F

Assembly line productivity during a week

4.4 DISPERSION AND THE NORMAL DISTRIBUTION

The distribution of many variables in the behavioral sciences, health sciences, and education resembles the bell-shaped normal distribution. Because this distribution is so important, its properties have been studied extensively by mathematicians. We saw in Section 4.2 that for a normal distribution the interval $\overline{X} \pm S$ includes 68.27% of scores. Suppose that we are interested in the interval $\overline{X} \pm 2S$ or $\overline{X} \pm 3S$. The percentage of scores included in these intervals is shown in Figure 4.4-1. It can be

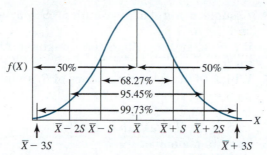

Figure 4.4-1. **Percentage of scores contained in selected intervals around the mean for a normal distribution.**

seen that an interval of six standard deviations includes almost all of the scores, 99.73%. Also, $\overline{X} \pm S$ gives the scores that mark the inflection points of the normal distribution—that is, the points where the curve changes from convex to concave or the reverse.

For samples having a close resemblance to a normally distributed population, a knowledge of S enables us to estimate Q and vice versa. For example, $Q = 0.6745S$ and $S = 1.483Q$. Computing the range from S or from Q is less accurate because the range is a function of sample size, as the following approximations illustrate.[8]

$$R \cong 3S \text{ and } S \cong R/3 \text{ when } n = 10$$

$$R \cong 4S \text{ and } S \cong R/4 \text{ when } n = 30$$

$$R \cong 5S \text{ and } S \cong R/5 \text{ when } n = 100$$

$$R \cong 6S \text{ and } S \cong R/6 \text{ when } n = 500$$

For any distribution, the minimum value of S is $S_{min} = R/\sqrt{2n}$ and the maximum is $S_{max} = R/2$.[9] This information can be used to make a quick check of the accuracy of the value computed for the standard deviation. For example, if $n = 30$, $R = 60$, and the distribution is approximately normal, the standard deviation should be close to $R/4 = 60/4 = 15$. If your computed S is 25, you should be suspicious; if it is greater than $S_{max} = R/2 = 60/2 = 30$, you know that you have made a computational error because the value of S can not exceed $R/2$.

CHECK YOUR UNDERSTANDING OF SECTION 4.4

12. For a normal distribution, what percentage of the scores falls (a) below $\overline{X} + S$? (b) between $\overline{X} - 3S$ and $\overline{X} + 3S$? (c) above $\overline{X} - 2S$? (d) below $\overline{X} - S$?

---

[8] Adapted from Tippet (1925).

[9] See Kirk (1978, pp. 90–91) for a proof.

13. Assume a normal distribution, $S = 5$, and $n = 30$. Estimate (a) Q and (b) R.
14. If $R = 30$ and $n = 50$, determine the minimum and maximum values for S.
15. Which of the following values of S are incorrect?
    a. $S = 10$, $R = 42$, $n = 30$
    b. $S = 19$, $R = 35$, $n = 10$
    c. $S = 28$, $R = 210$, $n = 100$
16. Term to remember
    a. Inflection point

4.5 DETECTING OUTLIERS

In collecting data, there are many opportunities for mistakes to occur. People misread instruments, transpose numbers, record data in the wrong place, present the wrong experimental condition or instructions, and fail to notice that equipment has malfunctioned. Often these mistakes produce scores that are indistinguishable from correct data and go undetected. However, when we find that John's IQ is 1100 and Susan's height is 56 feet, we know that something is wrong.

Scores that differ so markedly from the main body of data as to raise questions concerning their accuracy are called **outliers.**

Some outliers are obvious, an IQ of 1100 or a height of 56 feet, but not all outliers are so obvious. There are gray areas. A number of criteria have been suggested for identifying obvious and not-so-obvious outliers. According to one criterion, an outlier is any score that falls outside of the interval given by

$$Mdn \pm 2(Q_3 - Q_1).$$

Another criterion identifies an outlier as any score that falls outside of the interval

$$\overline{X} \pm 2.5S.$$

For the IQ scores in Table 4.2-1, the two criteria give the following intervals:

$$Mdn \pm 2(Q_3 - Q_1) = 110.7 \pm 2(118.0 - 101.0) = 76.7{-}144.7$$

and

$$\overline{X} \pm 2.5S = 110.35 \pm 2.5(13.53) = 76.5{-}144.2.$$

Both criteria identify one outlier—Waldo's score of 76. Of the two criteria, $Mdn \pm 2(Q_3 - Q_1)$ is preferred because the Mdn, Q_3, and Q_1 are less influenced by extreme scores than are the $\overline{X}$ and S. When a distribution is asymmetrical, a box plot, which is described in the next section, should be used to detect outliers.

Outliers should be carefully examined. Their presence suggests the possibility of some form of data contamination. Data that are obviously erroneous either must be corrected or discarded. For example, an examination of the records might reveal that John's IQ is 110 rather than 1100 and that Susan is only 5.6 feet tall, not 56 feet. However, school records might confirm that Waldo's score of 76 is correct. Outliers should be discarded only if they are impossible, for example, an IQ of 1100, or if there is ample evidence that they have resulted from some form of data contamination, for example, a participant recorded his answers in the wrong column of an answer sheet or the equipment malfunctioned.

Detecting Outliers With a Box Plot

We saw in Chapter 2 that graphs are effective ways to present data. John Tukey, who introduced the stem-and-leaf display, developed another innovative display called a **box-and-whiskers plot** or simply **box plot** (Tukey, 1977). A box plot presents important features of data and identifies outliers. There are many versions of this popular display; a simplified version for the IQ data in Table 4.2-1 is shown in Figure 4.5-1. The box plot in Figure 4.5-1 provides the following information:

1. Median ($Mdn = 110.7$). This point is represented by the vertical line in the central area of the box.
2. First quartile ($Q_1 = 101.0$) and third quartile ($Q_3 = 118.0$). These two points are represented by the ends of the box.

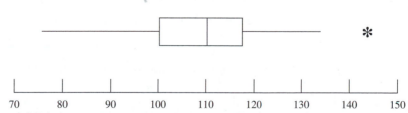

Figure 4.5-1. **Box plot for the IQ data in Table 4.2-1. The vertical line in the center of the box denotes the median. The lower and upper ends of the box denote the first and third quartiles, respectively. The whiskers are lines that extend from each end of the box to the outermost data points that fall within the distances computed as $Q_1 - 1.5(Q_3 - Q_1) = 75.5$ and $Q_3 + 1.5(Q_3 - Q_1) = 143.5$. The outermost data points that fall within these distances are 76 and 134. Data points outside the whiskers are outliers and are represented by an ∗. One data point, 144, is identified as an outlier.**

3. Lines, called **whiskers.** The two whiskers extend from each end of the box to the outermost data points that fall within the distances computed as

$$Q_1 - 1.5(Q_3 - Q_1) = 101.0 - 1.5(118.0 - 101.0) = 75.5$$

and

$$Q_3 + 1.5(Q_3 - Q_1) = 118.0 + 1.5(118.0 - 101.0) = 143.5.$$

The left whisker extends from $Q_1 = 101.0$ down to 76, the smallest score that is greater than or equal to $Q_1 - 1.5(Q_3 - Q_1) = 75.5$. The right whisker extends from $Q_3 = 118.0$ up to 134, the largest score that is less than or equal to $Q_3 + 1.5(Q_3 - Q_1) = 143.5$.

4. Outliers, which are represented by asterisks, are scores that fall outside the whiskers. One score, 144, falls above the right whisker.

The box plot identified one outlier, 144. Furthermore, it is evident that the distribution is negatively skewed because the left whisker is longer than the right whisker and the distance from Q_1 to the *Mdn* is greater than the distance from the *Mdn* to Q_3. The two criteria described earlier for detecting outliers identified a different outlier, 76. Because the distribution is skewed, the box plot rather than the other criteria should be used to identify outliers.

Box plots provide a lot of information at a glance. We will use them in later chapters to summarize the central tendency and dispersion of data and identify outliers. They are especially useful for comparing two or more sets of data. For this purpose, box plots are stacked, one above another, or turned 90° and placed side by side.

CHECK YOUR UNDERSTANDING OF SECTION 4.5

17. a. Use the criterion *Mdn* $\pm 2(Q_3 - Q_1)$ to determine whether there is reason to believe that outliers exist in the data presented in Table 4.2-2.
    b. Construct a box plot for these data. Compare the results with those obtained in (a).
18. a. Use the criterion *Mdn* $\pm 2(Q_3 - Q_1)$ to determine whether there is reason to believe that outliers exist in the reaction-time data presented in Exercise 3 in "Check Your Understanding of Section 4.2."
    b. Does the use of the criterion $\overline{X} \pm 2.5S$ lead to the same decision as *Mdn* $\pm 2(Q_3 - Q_1)$?
    c. Construct a box plot. Compare the results with those obtained in (a) and (b).
19. Term to remember
    a. Outlier

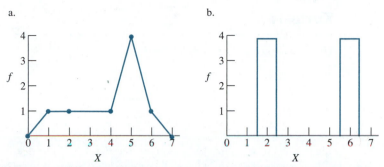

Figure 4.6-1. **(a) Frequency polygon for data in Table 4.6-1; *Sk* = −0.7 and *Kur* = −0.8. (b) Histogram for a perfectly symmetrical bimodal distribution; *Sk* = 0 and *Kur* = −2.**

4.6 SKEWNESS AND KURTOSIS

To complete our description of a distribution we need two more statistics: indexes of skewness and kurtosis. We saw in Section 2.6 that skewness refers to the asymmetry of a distribution and kurtosis, to its peakedness or flatness.

Skewness

A number of indexes of skewness have been developed; the most widely used one is

$$Sk = \frac{\displaystyle\sum_{i=1}^{n} (X_i - \overline{X})^3}{n}{S^3},$$

where S denotes the standard deviation (see Section 4.2).[10] If a distribution is **symmetrical,** $Sk = 0$; if it is **positively skewed,** $Sk > 0$; and if it is **negatively skewed,** $Sk < 0$.

Computation of Sk is illustrated in Table 4.6-1. For these data, $Sk = −0.7$, which indicates that the distribution is negatively skewed, as Figure 4.6-1 shows.

The value of Sk can be used to compare the type and the degree of skewness of two distributions independent of any differences in central tendency and dispersion. However, in practice, Sk is rarely computed because it is easy to detect asymmetry by looking at a frequency distribution or a graph of the data.

---

[10] This index, developed by Karl Pearson, is sometimes denoted by $\sqrt{\beta_1}$ and sometimes by g_1.

Kurtosis

The most common index of kurtosis is

$$Kur = \frac{\dfrac{\displaystyle\sum_{i=1}^{n} (X_i - \overline{X})^4}{n}}{S^4} - 3,$$

where S is the standard deviation (see Section 4.2).[11] If a distribution is flatter (has a broader hump and thicker tails) than the normal distribution, it is called **platykurtic,** and $Kur < 0$. If its peakedness is the same as that of the normal distribution, it is **mesokurtic,** and $kur = 0$. If it is more peaked (has a narrower hump and thinner tails) than the normal distribution, it is **leptokurtic,** and $kur > 0$.

Computation of Kur is illustrated in Table 4.6-1.

A graph for these data and one for a perfectly symmetrical bimodal distribution are given in Figure 4.6-1. In Figure 4.6-1(a), $Kur = -0.8$, and in Figure 4.6-1(b), $Kur = -2$. It follows that the interpretation of Kur is not as straightforward as that of Sk. It turns out that the value of Kur is dependent not only on the central peak of a distribution, but also on the fullness of its tails. Therefore, for distributions that deviate appreciably from the normal form, like those in Figure 4.6-1, the interpretation of Kur is ambiguous.[12] It is doubtful whether any single statistic can adequately measure the quality of peakedness.

TABLE 4.6-1. Example Illustrating Computation of Measures of Skewness and Kurtosis

(i) Data

X_i	$(X_i - \overline{X})$	$(X_i - \overline{X})^2$	$(X_i - \overline{X})^3$	$(X_i - \overline{X})^4$
6	2	4	8	16
5	1	1	1	1
5	1	1	1	1
5	1	1	1	1
5	1	1	1	1
4	0	0	0	0
3	−1	1	−1	1
2	−2	4	−8	16
1	−3	9	−27	81
$\sum_{i=1}^{n} X_i = 36$	$\sum_{i=1}^{n} (X_i - \overline{X}) = 0$	$\sum_{i=1}^{n} (X_i - \overline{X})^2 = 22$	$\sum_{i=1}^{n} (X_i - \overline{X})^3 = -24$	$\sum_{i=1}^{n} (X_i - \overline{X})^4 = 118$

(continued)

[11] This index is also denoted by g_2. As originally developed by Karl Pearson, the index was equal to $Kur + 3$ and was denoted by β_2.

[12] This point is discussed in detail by Chissom (1970) and Darlington (1970).

TABLE 4.6-1. *(Continued)*

(ii) Computation of *Sk*

$$S = \sqrt{\frac{\sum_{i=1}^{n}(X_i - \overline{X})^2}{n}} = \sqrt{\frac{22}{9}} = 1.563 \qquad Sk = \frac{\frac{\sum_{i=1}^{n}(X_i - \overline{X})^3}{n}}{S^3} = \frac{\frac{-24}{9}}{(1.563)^3} = \frac{-2.67}{3.82} = -0.7$$

(iii) Computation of *Kur*

$$Kur = \frac{\frac{\sum_{i=1}^{n}(X_i - \overline{X})^4}{n}}{S^4} - 3 = \frac{\frac{118}{9}}{(1.563)^4} - 3 = \frac{13.11}{5.97} - 3 = -0.8$$

CHECK YOUR UNDERSTANDING OF SECTION 4.6

20. Age at onset of Parkinson's disease, a degenerative brain disorder, was determined for a sample of adults between 60 and 70 years old. (a) Determine the type and degree of skewness for these data. (b) Construct a histogram. (c) Does it support your decision based on *Sk*?

67	68	60	64	68	63
68	70	63	70	68	69
70	69	69	69	69	68
62	70	70	64	66	66
66	69	67	67	70	67

21. One theory predicts that the distribution of reaction times in a paired-associates learning task will be leptokurtic. (a) Do the following learning data support the prediction? (b) Determine the type and degree of skewness for these data.

28	28	27	29	29
29	31	32	28	30
27	28	30	31	25
24	27	28	25	27
28	24	32	27	28
29	28	27	28	29

22. Determine the type and the degree of kurtosis for the Parkinson's-disease data in Exercise 20.

23. Terms to remember
    a. Symmetrical distribution
    b. Positively and negatively skewed
    c. Kurtosis
    d. Platykurtic
    e. Mesokurtic
    f. Leptokurtic

†4.7 EQUIVALENCE OF DEVIATION AND RAW-SCORE FORMULAS FOR A STANDARD DEVIATION

It is often convenient to define a statistic using a deviation formula. However, raw-score formulas are preferred for computing the statistic. Because deviation and raw-score formulas can look so different, you may wonder how it is possible for them to be equivalent. Consider, for example, the deviation and raw-score formulas for the standard deviation; they certainly don't look similar.

$$S = \sqrt{\frac{\sum_{i=1}^{n} (X_i - \overline{X})^2}{n}} \qquad \text{Deviation formula}$$

$$S = \sqrt{\frac{\sum_{i=1}^{n} X_i^2 - \frac{\left(\sum_{i=1}^{n} X_i\right)^2}{n}}{n}} \qquad \text{Raw-score formula}$$

It is easy to show by using the four summation rules in Section 3.8 and a little algebra that the formulas are equivalent. We show the equivalence by deriving the raw-score formula from the deviation formula as follows.

We begin with the deviation formula.

$$S = \sqrt{\frac{\sum_{i=1}^{n} (X_i - \overline{X})^2}{n}}$$

Then we square the term in parentheses using a rule that is taught in high school algebra: $(a - b)^2 = a^2 - 2ab + b^2$. In this example, a corresponds to X_i and b to $\overline{X}$.

$$= \sqrt{\frac{\sum_{i=1}^{n} (X_i^2 - 2X_i\overline{X} + \overline{X}^2)}{n}}$$

Next, we distribute the summation operator using the summation rules in Section 3.8. Note that X_i is a variable, but $\overline{X}$ is a constant for a set of scores.

$$= \sqrt{\frac{\sum_{i=1}^{n} X_i^2 - 2\overline{X} \sum_{i=1}^{n} X_i + n\overline{X}^2}{n}}$$

† This section, which is not essential to the text, can be omitted without loss of continuity.

We then replace the two means, $\overline{X}$ and $\overline{X}^2$, with their formulas: $\overline{X} = \sum_{i=1}^{n} X_i / n$ and $\overline{X}^2 = (\sum_{i=1}^{n} X_i)^2 / n^2$.

$$= \sqrt{\dfrac{\sum_{i=1}^{n} X_i^2 - \dfrac{2 \sum\limits_{i=1}^{n} X_i}{n} \sum\limits_{i=1}^{n} X_i + n \dfrac{\left(\sum\limits_{i=1}^{n} X_i\right)^2}{n^2}}{n}}$$

The middle term in the numerator involves the product of $2\sum_{i=1}^{n} X_i / n$ and $\sum_{i=1}^{n} X_i$. Multiplying the two terms gives $2(\sum_{i=1}^{n} X_i)^2 / n$.

$$= \sqrt{\dfrac{\sum_{i=1}^{n} X_i^2 - \dfrac{2\left(\sum\limits_{i=1}^{n} X_i\right)^2}{n} + \dfrac{\left(\sum\limits_{i=1}^{n} X_i\right)^2}{n}}{n}}$$

We then add $- \dfrac{2(\sum_{i=1}^{n} X_i)^2}{n}$ and $\dfrac{(\sum_{i=1}^{n} X_i)^2}{n}$ to obtain $- \dfrac{(\sum_{i=1}^{n} X_i)^2}{n}$. The derivation is complete.

$$= \sqrt{\dfrac{\sum_{i=1}^{n} X_i^2 - \dfrac{\left(\sum\limits_{i=1}^{n} X_i\right)^2}{n}}{n}}$$

†4.8 PRINTOUTS FOR THREE MICROCOMPUTER PACKAGES

JMP

A JMP histogram, box plot, and descriptive statistics for the socioeconomic data in Table 4.2-2 are shown in Figure 4.8-1. After the data were entered in a data table (see Figures 2.8-1 and 3.9-1 for examples), the displays in Figure 4.8-1 were obtained by selecting the **Analyze** command in the menu bar followed by the pulldown command called **Distribution of Y.** The quantiles and moments displays contain a variety of descriptive statistics: quartiles, median, mean, standard deviation (Std Dev), standard error of the mean (Std Err Mean, which is discussed in Chapter 9), and so on.

SPSS

An SPSS box plot and descriptive statistics for the socioeconomic data in Table 4.2-2 are shown in the upper and lower portions, respectively, of Figure 4.8-2. The

---

† This and similarly marked sections can be omitted without loss of continuity.

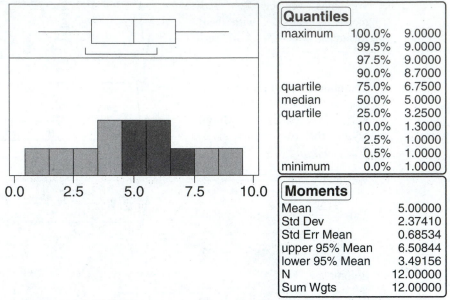

Quantiles		
maximum	100.0%	9.0000
	99.5%	9.0000
	97.5%	9.0000
	90.0%	8.7000
quartile	75.0%	6.7500
median	50.0%	5.0000
quartile	25.0%	3.2500
	10.0%	1.3000
	2.5%	1.0000
	0.5%	1.0000
minimum	0.0%	1.0000

Moments	
Mean	5.00000
Std Dev	2.37410
Std Err Mean	0.68534
upper 95% Mean	6.50844
lower 95% Mean	3.49156
N	12.00000
Sum Wgts	12.00000

Figure 4.8-1. **A JMP histogram and box plot for the socioeconomic data in Table 4.2-2 are shown on the left. The bracket below the box plot identifies the shortest most-dense 50% of the scores. A variety of descriptive statistics appear in the Quantiles and Moments displays on the right. The standard deviation was computed using the formula $\hat{\sigma} = \sqrt{\sum_{i=1}^{n}(X_i - \overline{X})/(n-1)}$, which is described in footnote 1. The sample standard deviation, S, can be obtained from $S = \hat{\sigma}\sqrt{(n-1)/n} = 2.37410\sqrt{(12-1)/12} = 2.27$.**

box plot was obtained by selecting **Graphs** from the menu bar and the pull-down option **Boxplot . . .** . The descriptive statistics were obtained by selecting **Statistics** from the menu bar and then selecting the **Summarize** and **Descriptive . . .** pull-down options.

SYSTAT

A SYSTAT box plot and descriptive statistics—number of cases, mean, and standard deviation—for the socioeconomic data in Table 4.2-2 are shown in Figure 4.8-3. The box plot was obtained by selecting **Graph** from the menu bar and then selecting the **Box** option. The number of cases, mean, and median were obtained by selecting **STATS** from the menu bar and then selecting the **Stats** option followed by **Statistics** in the pull-down menu. This series of choices brought up a dialog box like the one shown in Figure 3.9-6. SOCIOECO (socioeconomic score) was selected for analysis, and the mean, number of cases, and median were requested.

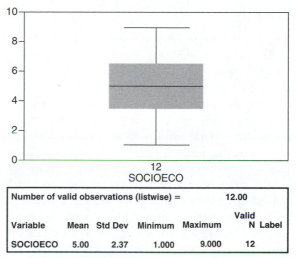

Number of valid observations (listwise) =				12.00	
Variable	Mean	Std Dev	Minimum	Maximum	Valid N Label
SOCIOECO	5.00	2.37	1.000	9.000	12

Figure 4.8-2. **An SPSS box plot for the socioeconomic data in Table 4.2-2 is shown in the top portion of the figure. The box plot gives the median, first and third quartiles, and the maximum and minimum scores. Descriptive statistics are given in the bottom portion of the figure. The standard deviation was computed using the formula $\hat{\sigma} = \sqrt{\Sigma_{i=1}^{n}(X_i - \bar{X})/(n-1)}$, which is described in footnote 1. The dependent variable is called "SOCIOECO" because variable names are limited to eight characters.**

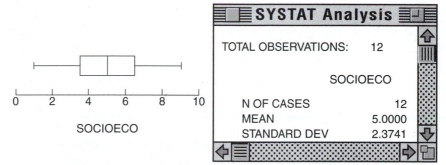

Figure 4.8-3. **A SYSTAT box plot for the socioeconomic data in Table 4.2-2 is shown on the left. If the data contain outliers, they are identified by asterisks and circles. Asterisks identify data points that lie outside the whiskers but within distances represented by $Q_1 - 1.5(Q_3 - Q_1)$ and $Q_3 + 1.5(Q_3 - Q_1)$. Circles identify data points that lie outside the distances represented by $Q_1 - 3(Q_3 - Q_1)$ and $Q_3 + 3(Q_3 - Q_1)$. No outliers were identified for these data. The analysis window is shown on the right. The dependent variable is called "SOCIOECO" because variable names are limited to eight characters. The standard deviation was computed using the formula $\hat{\sigma} = \sqrt{\Sigma_{i=1}^{n}(X_i - \bar{X})/(n-1)}$, which is described in footnote 1.**

4.9 SUMMARY

Measures of dispersion summarize the extent to which scores differ from one another, either quantitatively in terms of the spread or scatter of scores, or qualitatively in terms of their distinguishability.

Of the five measures of dispersion discussed in this chapter, four are based on the concept of distance and are appropriate for variables that contain distance information. They are the range, the semi-interquartile range, the standard deviation, and the coefficient of variation. The most important and widely used of the four is the standard deviation, which is typically reported with the mean. The standard deviation is used to compute the coefficient of variation, which is a relative measure of dispersion.

The index of dispersion, which is reported with the mode, describes the distinguishability of observations. Specifically, it indicates the number of distinguishable pairs of observations relative to the maximum possible number of distinguishable pairs in c categories. The lower bound of the index, 0, occurs when all observations are in one category; its upper bound, 1, occurs when the observations are evenly distributed over the categories. The index of dispersion is the only one of the dispersion measures that is appropriate for unordered qualitative variables.

Dispersion and central tendency are generally the most important characteristics of a distribution, and they completely describe a normal distribution, which is by definition symmetrical and mesokurtic. For nonnormal distributions, *Sk* and *Kur* provide interesting but somewhat less important information about skewness (asymmetry) and kurtosis (peakedness), respectively.

REVIEW EXERCISES FOR CHAPTER 4

1. Compute the range for the following sets of numbers.
   a. 3, 9, 5, 6, 5, 4, 5
   b. 26, 18, 30, 24, 23, 24
   c. 52, 49, 34, 53, 69, 50, 62
   d. 3, −4, 5, 2, 1, 2
2. For what kind of variable can we compute the mode but not the range?
3. The emotional stability of a random sample of encounter-group participants at Nelase Institute was measured. (a) Compute the median and the semi-interquartile range for the emotional stability scores listed in the table. (b) Compute P_{20}. (c) Construct a histogram.

X_j, Emotional Stability	f_j	X_j, Emotional Stability	f_j
30	1	18	3
27	1	17	3
25	2	16	3
23	2	15	4
22	2	13	2
21	2	12	2
20	3	10	2
19	4	8	1

4. For the data in Exercise 3, compute the percentile rank for (a) $X = 13$, (b) $X = 19$, and (c) $X = 25$.
5. Describe the nature of the distance represented by the standard deviation.
6. Infants are not as passive and undiscriminating about stimulation as we once thought; they show distinct preferences when given an opportunity to control stimuli presented to them. The following data are the number of trials required for infants to learn to control visual stimuli by varying their sucking responses. (a) Compute the mean and the standard deviation for these data. Compute S using both the deviation and the raw-score formulas. (b) Construct a frequency polygon. (c) Compute the coefficient of variation.

81	73	75	72	76	74
77	72	71	74	72	73
73	70	78	73	71	69
75	74	68	70	69	73
72	70	66	71	75	72
76	74	73	77		

7. In a concept-learning experiment, chimpanzees were taught to recognize a triangle in different orientations. (a) Compute the mean and the standard deviation for these data. Compute S using both the deviation and the raw-score formulas. (b) Compute the coefficient of variation. (c) Compare the coefficient of variation for Exercise 6 with that for Exercise 7. Which set of data has the largest relative dispersion?

X_j, Number of Trials	f_j	X_j, Number of Trials	f_j
50	1	45	6
49	3	44	4
48	4	43	2
47	6	42	1
46	8	41	1

8. For the emotional-stability data in Exercise 3, (a) compute the mean and the standard deviation. Compute S using both the deviation and the raw-score formulas for an ungrouped frequency distribution. (b) Construct a frequency polygon.
9. The attitudes of a random sample of black female high school students toward having a career were surveyed. (a) For the data in the table, compute the mode and the index of dispersion. (b) Construct a bar graph.

Category	f
Strongly desire career	38
Moderately desire career	19
Undecided about career	5
Don't want career	17

10. Approximately a million college-bound high school seniors participated in the College Board's Admissions Testing Program for
1980−81. Responses of men and women to the question "What is the
highest level of education you plan to complete beyond high
school?" follow. (Suggested by *Profiles, College-Bound Seniors,
1981*. [1982]. New York: College Entrance Examination Board.)

Category	f_{men}	f_{women}
Two-year training program	13,510	15,609
Associate in Arts degree	6,101	15,122
B.A. or B.S. degree	133,795	160,484
M.A. or M.S. degree	116,362	118,046
M.D., Ph.D., other professional degree	83,240	77,559
Undecided	82,805	100,973
	$n = 435,813$	$n = 487,793$

   a. Compute the mode and the index of dispersion for the men and
the women.

   b. Is the magnitude of the dispersion of educational plans for men
and women appreciably different?

11. The following proofs show the effect on the standard deviation of
subtracting a constant from each score or dividing each score by a
constant. For each proof, identify the summation operations from
Section 3.8 that were used.

   a. Let S_{X-c} be the standard deviation of a distribution that has been
altered by subtracting a constant c from each score X_i—that is,
$X_1 - c, X_2 - c, \ldots, X_n - c$. To determine the effect on S of subtracting a constant, we replace X_i by $(X_i - c)$ and $\overline{X}$ by
$\sum_{i=1}^{n} (X_i - c)/n$ in the formula $S = \sqrt{\sum_{i=1}^{n} (X_i - \overline{X})^2/n}$, as follows.

$$S_{X-c} = \sqrt{\frac{\sum_{i=1}^{n} \left[(X_i - c) - \sum_{i=1}^{n} (X_i - c)/n \right]^2}{n}}$$

$$= \sqrt{\frac{\sum_{i=1}^{n} \left[X_i - c - \sum_{i=1}^{n} \frac{X_i}{n} + \sum_{i=1}^{n} \frac{c}{n} \right]^2}{n}}$$

$$= \sqrt{\frac{\sum\limits_{i=1}^{n} \left[X_i - c - \sum\limits_{i=1}^{n} \dfrac{X_i}{n} + \dfrac{nc}{n} \right]^2}{n}}$$

$$= \sqrt{\frac{\sum\limits_{i=1}^{n} (X_i - c - \overline{X} + c)^2}{n}}$$

$$= \sqrt{\frac{\sum\limits_{i=1}^{n} (X_i - \overline{X})^2}{n}}$$

$$= S$$

Because $S_{X-c} = S$, we know that subtracting a constant c from each score doesn't affect the value of the standard deviation. We can also show that adding a constant does not affect it.

b. Let $S_{X/c}$ be the standard deviation of a distribution that has been altered by dividing each score X by a positive constant c—that is, $X_1/c, X_2/c, \ldots, X_n/c$. The effect of this alteration can be shown by replacing X_i by X_i/c and $\overline{X}$ by $\sum_{i=1}^{n} (X_i/c)/n$ in the formula $S = \sqrt{\sum_{i=1}^{n} (X_i - \overline{X})^2/n}$, as follows.

$$S_{X/c} = \sqrt{\frac{\sum\limits_{i=1}^{n} \left(X_i/c - \sum\limits_{i=1}^{n} (X_i/c)/n \right)^2}{n}}$$

$$= \sqrt{\frac{\sum\limits_{i=1}^{n} \left[\dfrac{X_i}{c} - \sum\limits_{i=1}^{n} \left(\dfrac{1}{c} X_i \right)/n \right]^2}{n}}$$

$$= \sqrt{\frac{\sum\limits_{i=1}^{n} \left(\dfrac{X_i}{c} - \dfrac{1}{c} \sum\limits_{i=1}^{n} \dfrac{X_i}{n} \right)^2}{n}}$$

$$= \sqrt{\frac{\sum\limits_{i=1}^{n} \dfrac{1}{c^2} (X_i - \overline{X})^2}{n}}$$

$$= \sqrt{\frac{\dfrac{1}{c^2} \sum\limits_{i=1}^{n} (X_i - \overline{X})^2}{n}}$$

$$= \frac{1}{c} \sqrt{\frac{\sum\limits_{i=1}^{n} (X_i - \overline{X})^2}{n}}$$

$$= \frac{1}{c} S = S/c$$

Because $S_{X/c} = S/c$, we know that the effect of dividing each score by a positive constant c is to change S, the standard deviation of the original scores, to S/c. Similarly, it can be shown that the effect of multiplying each score by a positive constant c is to change S to cS.

If c is a negative constant, $S_{X/c} = S/|c|$. The use of $|c|$ ensures that $S/|c|$ is positive and is consistent with the definition of the standard deviation as the positive square root of $\Sigma_{i=1}^{n} (X_i - \overline{X})^2/n$.

12. Interpret the following: (a) $Mdn = 50$, $Q = 8$, (b) $Mo = 30$, $R = 5$, (c) $\overline{X} = 70$, $S = 10$, and the distribution is approximately normal, (d) $Mo =$ Category of Ford cars, $D = .20$.

13. What measure of central tendency and dispersion would you compute for the following data? Defend your choice.

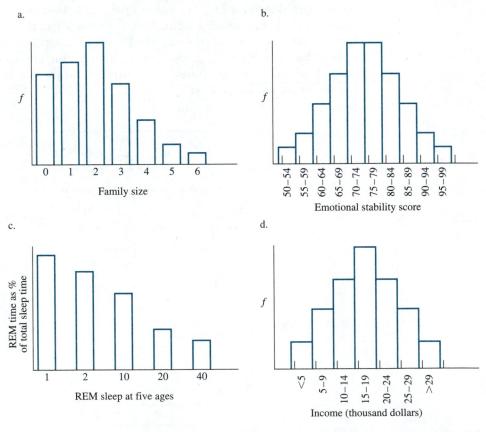

14. For a normal distribution, what percentage of the scores falls (a) above $\overline{X} - 3S$? (b) above $\overline{X} + 2S$? (c) between $\overline{X} - 2S$ and $\overline{X} + 2S$? (d) below $\overline{X} - S$?

15. Assume a normal distribution, $S = 10$, and $n = 100$. Estimate (a) Q and (b) R.

16. If $R = 40$ and $n = 32$, determine the minimum and maximum values for S.
17. Which of the following values of S are incorrect?
    a. $S = 17, R = 62, n = 30$
    b. $S = 15, R = 25, n = 10$
    c. $S = 18, R = 76, n = 50$
18. a. Use the criterion $Mdn \pm 2(Q_3 - Q_1)$ to determine whether there is reason to believe that outliers exist in the emotional-stability data presented in Exercise 3.
    b. Construct a box plot for these data. Compare the results with those obtained in (a).
19. a. Use the criterion $Mdn \pm 2(Q_3 - Q_1)$ to determine whether there is reason to believe that outliers exist in the sucking-response data presented in Exercise 6.
    b. Does the use of the criterion $\overline{X} \pm 2.5S$ lead to the same decision as $Mdn \pm 2(Q_3 - Q_1)$?
    c. Construct a box plot. Compare the results with those obtained in (a) and (b).
20. The reading readiness of preschool children in two neighborhoods was measured. (a) Determine the type and the degree of skewness for these data. (b) Which set of data has the greatest skewness? (c) Construct histograms. (d) Do the histograms support your decision based on Sk?

Neighborhood A							Neighborhood B				
30	33	32	31	35	33		29	32	28	29	29
32	29	33	30	32	28		30	31	26	30	28
31	31	29	31	26	30		28	29	29	34	30
32	30	33	32	27	32		29	27	30	31	35

21. Determine which set of data in Exercise 20 deviates most from the normal distribution in terms of kurtosis.
22. Why is *Kur* not an entirely satisfactory measure of peakedness?
23. Use a statistical software package to obtain a box plot and compute the mean and standard deviation for the emotional-stability data in Exercise 3. Determine whether the software package computed S or $\hat{\sigma}$.
24. Use a statistical software package to obtain a box plot and compute the mean and standard deviation for the sucking-response data in Exercise 6. Determine whether the software package computed S or $\hat{\sigma}$.
25. Use a statistical software package to obtain a box plot and compute the mean and standard deviation for the learning data in Exercise 7. Determine whether the software package computed S or $\hat{\sigma}$.

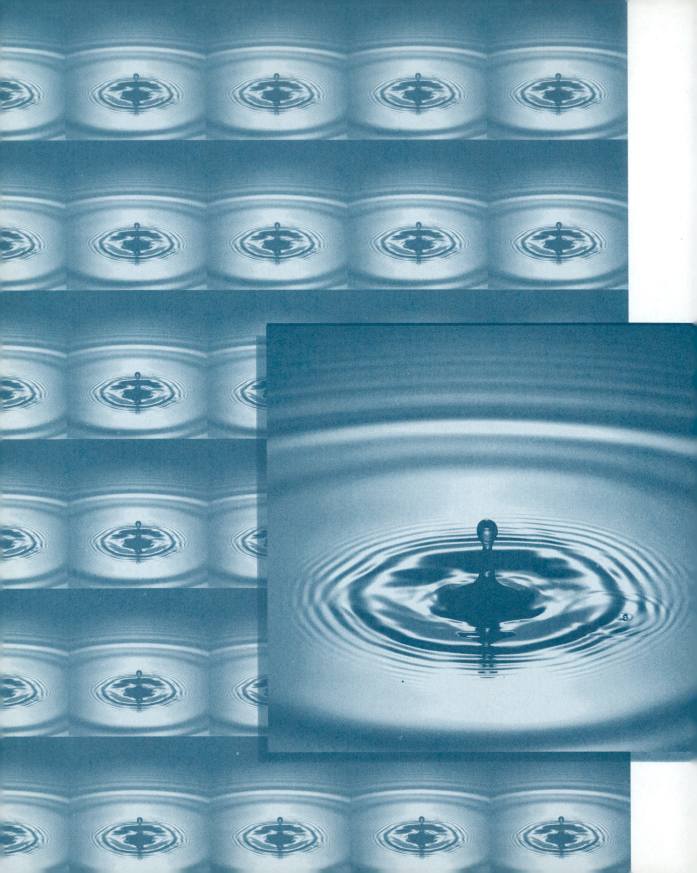

Chapter 5

Correlation

5.1 INTRODUCTION TO CORRELATION

Correlation and Regression Distinguished

Correlation and regression, which are described in this chapter and the next, are procedures for describing the relationship between two variables where the scores for one variable are paired with the scores for the other variable. The paired scores could represent salary and job satisfaction of college graduates, SAT scores and freshmen GPAs, and incidence of breast cancer and exposure to solar radiation. In each case we might be interested in predicting a score for one variable from a score for the other variable or in knowing the strength of the relationship between the two sets of scores.

Correlation and regression procedures have much in common and as a result are often confused. Perhaps the simplest way to distinguish between them is by means of examples. The classic regression situation involves one dependent variable and one or more independent variables. The **independent variable** is the variable that is controlled or manipulated by a researcher so that its effect on a **dependent variable** can be determined. Suppose we perform an experiment in which different dosages of amphetamine, the independent variable, denoted by X, are administered to children suffering from hyperkinesis, a behavioral disorder characterized by restlessness, inattention, and disruptive behavior. The dosage conditions are randomly assigned to the children. Following administration of the drug, changes in frequency of hyperkinetic behavior, the dependent variable, denoted by Y, are recorded. For each child the researcher has paired X and Y scores representing, respectively, dosage and behavior change. The researcher is interested in knowing whether the two variables are related and, if so, in predicting Y from a knowledge of X. This experiment illustrates the key features of a problem in **regression.** First, there is a clearly defined independent variable—amount of amphetamine. Second, preselected dosage levels of amphetamine are randomly assigned to the children. Third, the value of the dependent variable for a given dosage is free to vary. This is in contrast to the independent variable, whose values were selected in advance. Finally, the researcher is interested in predicting Y from a knowledge of X.

Contrast this experiment with one in which tests of reading readiness and intelligence are administered to a sample of children, yielding paired X and Y scores, respectively, for each child. The researcher is interested in knowing whether reading readiness and intelligence are related and, if so, in the strength of the association. In addition, the researcher might want to predict either variable from a knowledge of the other. This experiment illustrates a classic **correlation** situation. How does it differ from the regression situation? First, there is no obvious independent variable. Second, because the researcher did not preselect the values of either X or Y, both X

and *Y* are free to vary. Finally, the researcher is interested in assessing the strength of association between *X* and *Y* and possibly in predicting either variable from a knowledge of the other.

To summarize, both correlation and regression procedures are concerned with assessing the relationship between two variables where the scores for one variable are paired with the scores for the other variable. They differ with respect to (1) the nature of the variables—presence or absence of an independent variable; (2) use of random assignment of experimental conditions; (3) the researcher's principle interest—predicting *Y* from *X* or assessing the strength of relationship; and (4) to some extent, the kinds of conclusions that can be drawn. In practice, the distinction between regression and correlation situations often is not as clearly drawn as has been described. It is common, for example, to use correlation procedures in a regression situation and vice versa. However, it is important to be able to distinguish between the two situations because the assumptions underlying the use of regression and correlation procedures differ.

A Bit of History

The concepts of correlation and regression were developed by Sir Francis Galton during his investigations of the genetic transmission of natural characteristics. He was intrigued by the question "How is it possible for a whole population to remain alike in its features during many successive generations if the average product of each couple resembles the parents?" Data from one of his studies on the inheritance of stature are reproduced in Table 5.1-1. Parents' height is plotted on the horizontal, or *X*, axis and offspring's height on the vertical, or *Y*, axis. As a convenience in such presentations, the lengths of the *X* and *Y* axes can be made approximately equal. This representation of the joint frequency of two variables is called a **bivariate frequency distribution** or **scatterplot (scatter diagram, scattergram).** Consider the entry in the cell at the intersection of column 68.5 and row 69.2; the frequency is 48. This means that for parents whose height was 68–69, there were 48 offspring whose height was 68.7–69.7 inches. The circles in Table 5.1-1 identify the class intervals containing the median of each column as calculated by Galton. We see, as did Galton, that the relationship between height of offspring and height of parents is approximately *linear;* that is, the set of circled numbers approximates a straight line. Galton developed a procedure for finding the "straight line of best fit," thereby laying the foundation for correlation and regression.

A straight line provides a reasonably good fit for many relationships found in behavioral, health, and educational research. Even those relationships that are nonlinear are often approximately linear over some portion of their range. But let us return to the question that sparked Galton's interest. How is it that a

TABLE 5.1-1.   Scatterplot of Midparent Height and Height of Adult Offspring[a] (Female Heights Multiplied by 1.08)

Height of Adult Offspring	Midparent Height (inches)[b]										
	<64	64.5	65.5	66.5	67.5	68.5	69.5	70.5	71.5	72.5	≥73
≥73.7							5	3	2	4	
73.2						3	4	3	2	2	(3)
72.2			1		4	4	11	4	9	(7)	1
71.2			2		11	18	20	7	4	2	
70.2			5	4	19	21	25	14	(10)	1	
69.2	1	2	7	13	38	48	(33)	(18)	5	2	
68.2	1		7	14	28	(34)	20	12	3	1	
67.2	2	5	(11)	(17)	(38)	31	27	3	4		
66.2	2	(5)	11	17	36	25	17	1	3		
65.2	(1)	1	7	2	15	16	4	1	1		
64.2	4	4	5	5	14	11	16				
63.2	2	4	9	3	5	7	1				
62.2		1		3	3						
<61.7	1	1	1			1		1			

[a] Galton (1889, p. 208). I am grateful to Edward W. Minium for bringing these data to my attention.
[b] A circle marks the class interval containing the median of each column.

population remains alike? The answer is in the trend represented by the circled numbers in Table 5.1-1. We note that on the average, short parents have offspring who tend to be slightly taller than they are, whereas tall parents have offspring who tend to be slightly shorter than they. This is shown more clearly in Figure 5.1-1. Galton referred to this tendency as **regression** or **reversion toward**

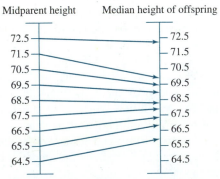

Figure 5.1-1. **Arrows relate height (in inches) of parents to median height of offspring. Tall parents tend to have slightly shorter offspring, and short parents, slightly taller offspring. Galton referred to this as reversion toward the mean.**

the mean; he called the best-fitting straight line in a scatterplot the **regression** or **reversion line.**

In the discussion that follows, we'll focus our attention on variables like those in Table 5.1-1 that appear to be linearly related.[1] Many relationships of interest in the behavioral sciences, health sciences, and education fall into this category.

CHECK YOUR UNDERSTANDING OF SECTION 5.1

1. A speech therapist interested in the relationship between two tests of articulation disorders administered the tests to 26 children. (a) Construct a scatterplot like Table 5.1-1 for the data in the following table. (b) Does the relationship appear to be linear or nonlinear?

Participant	Test A	Test B	Participant	Test A	Test B
1	26	36	14	33	39
2	28	35	15	22	33
3	25	34	16	24	32
4	21	32	17	27	35
5	25	33	18	29	36
6	26	32	19	32	39
7	26	34	20	28	36
8	31	37	21	25	36
9	27	34	22	24	34
10	20	30	23	25	34
11	23	32	24	27	36
12	30	38	25	26	34
13	29	37	26	26	35

2. Discuss the meaning of the term *regression toward the mean.*
3. Terms to remember
   a. Independent variable
   c. Regression
   e. Bivariate frequency distribution
   g. Linear relationship
   b. Dependent variable
   d. Correlation
   f. Scatterplot
   h. Regression line

[1] The nonlinear case is treated in advanced texts such as Kirk (1995, pp. 197–198).

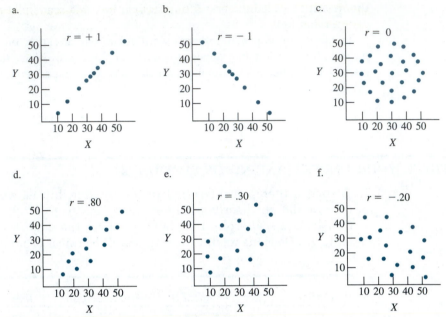

Figure 5.2-1. **Scatterplots illustrating various degrees of correlation.**

5.2 A NUMERICAL INDEX OF CORRELATION

The degree of association or strength of relationship between two variables is represented by a number called a **correlation coefficient.** The Pearson product-moment correlation coefficient is a measure of the linear relationship between two variables, X and Y, and is denoted by r_{XY} or simply r. The population correlation coefficient is denoted by the Greek letter ρ (rho).[2]

 The value of a correlation coefficient can range from -1 to $+1$. A value of $+1$ denotes a perfect **positive relationship;** this is depicted in the scatterplot in Figure 5.2-1(a). For this case, all the data points fall on a straight line such that high scores on one variable are paired with high scores on the other, and low scores are paired with low scores. A coefficient of -1 denotes a perfect **negative or inverse relationship.** For this case, the data points also fall on a straight line, but high scores on one variable are paired with low scores on the other and vice versa, resulting in a line that slopes down instead of up. This is shown in Figure 5.2-1(b). If there is no linear association between the variables, r is equal to 0. In this case, the data points tend to fall in a circle, as shown in Figure 5.2-1(c). Intermediate degrees of associa-

[2] The letter r from the word *reversion* was originally used by Galton to denote the slope of the best-fitting straight line. This line is defined in Section 6.2.

tion are represented by coefficients less than 0 ($-1 < r < 0$) or by coefficients greater than 0 ($0 < r < 1$). Some examples of intermediate degrees of association for normally distributed X and Y variables are depicted in Figures 5.2-1(d) through (f). As shown in the figures, the data points for intermediate values of r tend to form an ellipse; the lower the degree of association, the more the ellipse resembles a circle.

CHECK YOUR UNDERSTANDING OF SECTION 5.2

4. Match the r values 1, -1, 0, .4, and $-.9$ with the scatterplots shown here.

a.
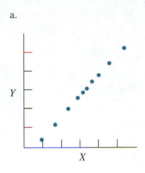

b.
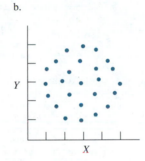

c.
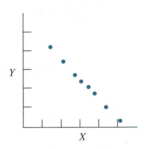

d.
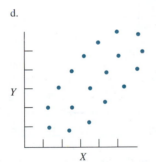

e.
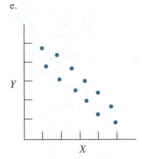

5. Would you expect the correlation between the following to be positive, negative, or essentially zero?
   a. Masculinity of fathers and sons
   b. Reaction time and number of lights in a visual discrimination task
   c. Mechanical aptitude and mother's height
   d. Verbal intelligence and percentage of words filled in on crossword puzzles

6. Terms to remember
   a. Correlation coefficient   b. Positive relationship
   c. Negative relationship

5.3 PEARSON PRODUCT-MOMENT CORRELATION COEFFICIENT

The most widely used index of correlation is called the **Pearson product-moment correlation coefficient,** after Karl Pearson (1857–1936), who contributed so much to its development. The coefficient is appropriate for describing the linear relationship between two quantitative variables.

The definitional formula for Pearson's *r* is

$$r = \frac{\dfrac{\sum\limits_{i=1}^{n} (X_i - \overline{X})(Y_i - \overline{Y})}{n}}{\sqrt{\left[\dfrac{\sum\limits_{i=1}^{n} (X_i - \overline{X})^2}{n}\right]\left[\dfrac{\sum\limits_{i=1}^{n} (Y_i - \overline{Y})^2}{n}\right]}}$$

A more convenient computational formula, called the raw-score formula,[3] is

$$r = \frac{\sum\limits_{i=1}^{n} X_i Y_i - \dfrac{\left(\sum\limits_{i=1}^{n} X_i\right)\left(\sum\limits_{i=1}^{n} Y_i\right)}{n}}{\sqrt{\left[\sum\limits_{i=1}^{n} X_i^2 - \dfrac{\left(\sum\limits_{i=1}^{n} X_i\right)^2}{n}\right]\left[\sum\limits_{i=1}^{n} Y_i^2 - \dfrac{\left(\sum\limits_{i=1}^{n} Y_i\right)^2}{n}\right]}} .$$

Calculation of *r* using the raw-score formula is illustrated in Table 5.3-1. The data are 20 paired scores of fathers and sons on a test of authoritarianism, which measures rigidity, dependency, and ethnocentrism. The coefficient is equal to .85. This tells us two things about the relationship: (1) its strength, represented by the extent to which the value of *r* differs from zero, and (2) the direction (positive or negative) of the relationship, represented by the sign of *r*. In the following discussion, we will see why *r* reflects this information. The interpretation of *r* is discussed in Section 5.4.

Information Contained in the Cross Product

A person's scores, X_i and Y_i, can be expressed as deviations from their respective means, $\overline{X}$ and $\overline{Y}$, as follows: $(X_i - \overline{X})$ and $(Y_i - \overline{Y})$. The product of the two deviations, $(X_i - \overline{X})(Y_i - \overline{Y})$, is called the **cross product.** If a person is above the mean

---

[3] The derivation of the raw-score formula is given by Kirk (1978, pp. 121–122).

TABLE 5.3-1.   Computation of *r* for Fathers' and Sons' Authoritarianism Scores

(i) Data

Family	Father's Score, X_i	Son's Score, Y_i	X_iY_i	X_i^2	Y_i^2
1	25	28	700	625	784
2	32	31	992	1,024	961
3	40	41	1,640	1,600	1,681
4	29	33	957	841	1,089
5	31	25	775	961	625
6	16	18	288	256	324
7	28	26	728	784	676
8	36	38	1,368	1,296	1,444
9	33	34	1,122	1,089	1,156
10	29	36	1,044	841	1,296
11	23	20	460	529	400
12	27	28	756	729	784
13	37	30	1,110	1,369	900
14	30	26	780	900	676
15	27	22	594	729	484
16	20	23	460	400	529
17	28	29	812	784	841
18	38	36	1,368	1,444	1,296
19	35	32	1,120	1,225	1,024
20	19	19	361	361	361
	$\Sigma X_i = 583$	$\Sigma Y_i = 575$	$\Sigma X_iY_i = 17,435$	$\Sigma X_i^2 = 17,787$	$\Sigma Y_i^2 = 17,331$

(ii) Computational procedure

$$r = \frac{\Sigma X_iY_i - \frac{(\Sigma X_i)(\Sigma Y_i)}{n}}{\sqrt{\left[\Sigma X_i^2 - \frac{(\Sigma X_i)^2}{n}\right]\left[\Sigma Y_i^2 - \frac{(\Sigma Y_i)^2}{n}\right]}} = \frac{17,435 - \frac{(583)(575)}{20}}{\sqrt{\left[17,787 - \frac{(583)^2}{20}\right]\left[17,331 - \frac{(575)^2}{20}\right]}}$$

$$= \frac{673.7500}{(28.1523)(28.2799)} = .85$$

on both variables, the algebraic sign of $(X_i - \overline{X})(Y_i - \overline{Y})$ is positive, and the associated data point falls in quadrant 1 of Figure 5.3-1(a). If a person is below the mean on both variables, the sign of $(X_i - \overline{X})(Y_i - \overline{Y})$ also is positive because it is the product of two negative numbers, but the corresponding data point falls in quadrant 3 of Figure 5.3-1(a). If a person is above the mean on one variable but below the

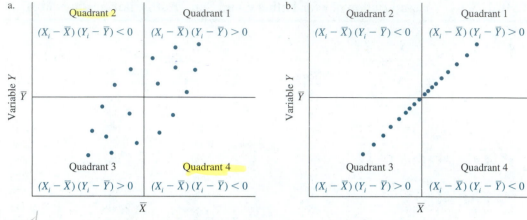

152   *Correlation*

Figure 5.3-1. **All cross products, $(X_i - \overline{X})(Y_i - \overline{Y})$ in quadrants 1 and 3 are positive; those in quadrants 2 and 4 are negative. For simplicity, the examples use data whose X and Y dispersions are equal. Such equality is rarely observed for real data.**

mean on the other, the sign of $(X_i - \overline{X})(Y_i - \overline{Y})$ is negative, and the data point falls in either quadrant 2 or quadrant 4.

In Figure 5.3-1(a), most of the data points are in quadrants 1 and 3; hence the algebraic sign of the sum $\sum_{i=1}^{n}(X_i - \overline{X})(Y_i - \overline{Y})$ is positive. When this sum is positive, the two variables are said to be positively related; that is, an increase in one variable is accompanied by an increase in the other. If an inverse relationship exists between X and Y, most of the data points fall in quadrants 2 and 4, and the sign of $\sum_{i=1}^{n}(X_i - \overline{X})(Y_i - \overline{Y})$ is negative. From the foregoing discussion, it follows that the algebraic sign of $\sum_{i=1}^{n}(X_i - \overline{X})(Y_i - \overline{Y})$ in the numerator of

$$r = \frac{\dfrac{\sum\limits_{i=1}^{n} (X_i - \overline{X})(Y_i - \overline{Y})}{n}}{\sqrt{\left[\dfrac{\sum\limits_{i=1}^{n} (X_i - \overline{X})^2}{n}\right]\left[\dfrac{\sum\limits_{i=1}^{n} (Y_i - \overline{Y})^2}{n}\right]}}$$

indicates whether X and Y are positively or inversely related. As we will see next, the numerator also indicates the strength of the association.

The greater the strength of the relationship between X and Y, the larger is the absolute value of the sum of the cross products, $\sum_{i=1}^{n}(X_i - \overline{X})(Y_i - \overline{Y})$. Consider Figure 5.1-1(b) where $r = 1$. For this case, the sum of the cross products is as large as it can be because the largest $(X_i - \overline{X})$ is paired with the largest $(Y_i - \overline{Y})$, the second largest $(X_i - \overline{X})$ with the second largest $(Y_i - \overline{Y})$, and so on. A much smaller sum of cross products occurs when some large $(X_i - \overline{X})$'s are paired with small $(Y_i - \overline{Y})$'s and vice versa, as in Figure 5.3-1(a) where $r = .65$. If the r in Figure 5.3-1(a) were equal to 0, the data points would fall within the area of a circle instead of an ellipse. In this case, positive $(X_i - \overline{X})$'s are as likely to be paired with negative $(Y_i - \overline{Y})$'s as with positive $(Y_i - \overline{Y})$'s, resulting in a sum of cross products that is equal to 0. In summary, the sign of $\sum_{i=1}^{n} (X_i - \overline{X})(Y_i - \overline{Y})$ indicates whether the relationship is positive or negative. The size of the absolute value of $\sum_{i=1}^{n} (X_i - \overline{X})(Y_i - \overline{Y})$ indicates the strength of the association.

On reflection, it also is apparent that the value of $\sum_{i=1}^{n} (X_i - \overline{X})(Y_i - \overline{Y})$ is affected by the number of paired X and Y scores: For correlations not equal to zero, the larger the number of pairs of scores, the larger the absolute value of $\sum_{i=1}^{n} (X_i - \overline{X})(Y_i - \overline{Y})$. To obtain a measure of strength of association that is independent of the number of pairs of scores, we compute the mean of the cross product sum:

$$S_{XY} = \frac{\displaystyle\sum_{i=1}^{n} (X_i - \overline{X})(Y_i - \overline{Y})}{n}$$

where n is the number of paired X and Y scores. This mean is called the **covariance** of X and Y and is denoted by S_{XY}. If we divide the covariance by the standard deviations of X and Y, S_X and S_Y, we obtain a measure of strength of association that also is independent of the dispersions of the two variables. The resulting statistic,

$$r = \frac{S_{XY}}{S_X S_Y} = \frac{\dfrac{\displaystyle\sum_{i=1}^{n} (X_i - \overline{X})(Y_i - \overline{Y})}{n}}{\sqrt{\left[\dfrac{\displaystyle\sum_{i=1}^{n} (X_i - \overline{X})^2}{n}\right]\left[\dfrac{\displaystyle\sum_{i=1}^{n} (Y_i - \overline{Y})^2}{n}\right]}},$$

was defined earlier as the definitional formula for the Pearson product-moment correlation coefficient.

To summarize, the heart of the correlation formula is the cross product sum $\sum_{i=1}^{n} (X_i - \overline{X})(Y_i - \overline{Y})$. This sum reflects both the nature of the relationship between X and Y (positive versus inverse) and the magnitude of the relationship. The cross product sum is divided by n to free it of dependence on the number of paired X and Y scores; it is divided by $S_X S_Y$ to free it of dependence on the size of the dispersions of the X and Y variables. Because of these operations and because X and Y are expressed as deviations from their respective means, the r statistic is a dimensionless index of linear relationship. This means that the value of r does not depend on the unit of measurement of either the X or Y variables or on the value that is designated as the zero point or origin of either measuring scale. To put it another way, multiplying X or Y by a positive constant and/or adding a constant (a positive linear transformation) does not affect the value of r. As stated earlier, r ranges over the interval -1 to $+1$.

In the following section we discuss ways to interpret r, but first we will make one more comment about it. If the dispersion of either X or Y is equal to zero $(S_X$ or $S_Y = 0)$, the correlation coefficient is undefined. On reflection, this seems reasonable because $r = S_{XY}/S_X S_Y$ and division by $S_X S_Y = 0$ is undefined. In words, this means that the concept of strength of association is meaningless when X or Y is a constant.

CHECK YOUR UNDERSTANDING OF SECTION 5.3

7. A reading test and an intelligence test were administered to a random sample of first-grade children. Compute r for the data in the table.

Child	Reading Readiness Score	IQ Score	Child	Reading Readiness Score	IQ Score
1	45	102	11	43	104
2	40	100	12	50	108
3	48	106	13	42	96
4	45	101	14	40	99
5	38	98	15	41	96
6	43	100	16	48	102
7	36	92	17	47	104
8	41	102	18	37	94
9	42	102	19	42	98
10	50	110	20	45	100

8. Studies have shown that music can affect mood, emotion, task performance, and cognition. It was hypothesized that the tempo of country-western music played in bars was related to the consumption of alcohol. Observers visited three bars featuring recorded country-western music on three Friday nights. They obtained permission to tape-record the music and to observe patrons at selected tables. When the music began, the rate of sipping an alcoholic beverage was recorded for each patron. The music tapes were analyzed for the tempo (beats per minute) of each song; the mean number of sips during each song was also determined. The following data were obtained. (Suggested by Bach, Paul J., and Schaefer, James M. [1979]. The tempo of country music and the rate of drinking in bars. *Journal of Studies on Alcohol, 40,* 1058–1059.)

Tempo	Mean Number of Sips	Tempo	Mean Number of Sips
35	1.150	80	0.900
38	1.150	85	0.725
44	0.400	91	0.725
48	1.075	93	0.875
51	0.950	100	0.525
64	0.975	102	0.800
68	0.950	108	0.775
68	0.925	112	0.750
72	0.875	118	0.625

    a. Construct a scatterplot for these data and decide whether the data appear to be linearly related.
    b. Compute r for these data.
    c. What does the r tell you about the relationship between tempo and sips per minute?
9. Calculate r for the data in Exercise 1 in "Check Your Understanding of Section 5.1."
10. Calculate $\sum_{i=1}^{n} (X_i - \bar{X})(Y_i - \bar{Y})$ for the following data points. In which quadrants of Figure 5.3-1 would the majority of the data points fall? Are the variables related, and if so, is the relationship positive or negative?

a. ▬▬		b. ▬▬		c. ▬▬		d. ▬▬	
X	Y	X	Y	X	Y	X	Y
9	14	9	14	9	13	6	12
11	17	11	14	10	18	9	16
13	17	11	16	12	9	14	15
7	12	9	16	9	20	11	17

11. For the data in Exercise 10, make figures like Figure 5.3-1.
12. For the data in Exercise 10, calculate r.
13. a. What does $\sum_{i=1}^{n} (X_i - \bar{X})(Y_i - \bar{Y})$ tell us about the relationship between X and Y?
    b. In computing r, why is $\sum_{i=1}^{n} (X_i - \bar{X})(Y_i - \bar{Y})$ divided by n?
14. For a set of data with $S_X = 6$ and $S_Y = 5$, what is the largest possible value that S_{XY} can be? (*Hint:* The maximum value of $r = +1$ and $r = S_{XY}/S_X S_Y$.)
15. a. If $n = 2$ and $S_X S_Y$ does not equal zero, what are the possible values of r?
    b. Make a scatterplot that supports your answer.

16. The correlation coefficient for the following data is undefined. Why is this statement true?

X	Y
8	4
8	6
8	3
8	7
8	5

17. Terms to remember
   a. Pearson product-moment correlation coefficient
   b. Cross product
   c. Covariance

5.4 INTERPRETATION OF A CORRELATION COEFFICIENT: EXPLAINED AND UNEXPLAINED VARIATION

As we have seen, a Pearson product-moment correlation coefficient reflects the nature and the strength of the linear association between two variables. However, two other statistics, both functions of r, are more useful for getting an intuitive feel for the strength of association represented by r. These statistics are the **coefficient of determination,** r^2, which is equal to the square of the correlation coefficient, and the **coefficient of nondetermination,** k^2, which is equal to $1 - r^2$.

If we examine the authoritarianism scores in Table 5.3-1, we see that there is variation among the fathers' X scores and among the sons' Y scores. How can we account for this variability? One reason why the sons' Y scores differ is that their fathers' X scores differ. Because X and Y are correlated ($r = .85$), a father who has a high score is likely to have a son who also has a high score. Thus, because of the linear relationship between X and Y, some of the variation among the Y scores can be accounted for or explained by variation among the X scores. However, not all the variation can be explained in this way because some fathers who have the same X score have sons with different Y scores. Consider, for example, families 4 and 10: $X_4 = X_{10} = 29$ but $Y_4 = 33$ and $Y_{10} = 36$.

For a given linear relationship between X and Y, we would like to know how much of the Y-score variance is accounted for by the X-score variance and how much is not accounted for. We will see that this information is given, respectively, by r^2 and k^2. Let us denote the total variance of X and of Y by S_X^2 and S_Y^2, respectively. Recall from the discussion of the standard deviation in Section 4.2 that variance is a measure of dispersion: the mean squared distance by which scores deviate from the mean. If we divide S_X^2 by itself and S_Y^2 by itself, we change both variances into proportions with values equal to 1. Each of these proportions can be partitioned into two components, as follows.[4]

$$\frac{S_X^2}{S_X^2} = r^2 + k^2$$

$$\begin{pmatrix} \text{Total } X \text{ variance} \\ \text{expressed as a} \\ \text{proportion} \end{pmatrix} = \begin{pmatrix} \text{Proportion of } X \\ \text{variance explained} \\ \text{by } Y \text{ variance} \end{pmatrix} + \begin{pmatrix} \text{Proportion of } X \\ \text{variance not explained} \\ \text{by } Y \text{ variance} \end{pmatrix}$$

$$\frac{S_Y^2}{S_Y^2} = r^2 + k^2$$

$$\begin{pmatrix} \text{Total } Y \text{ variance} \\ \text{expressed as a} \\ \text{proportion} \end{pmatrix} = \begin{pmatrix} \text{Proportion of } Y \\ \text{variance explained} \\ \text{by } X \text{ variance} \end{pmatrix} + \begin{pmatrix} \text{Proportion of } Y \\ \text{variance not explained} \\ \text{by } X \text{ variance} \end{pmatrix}$$

Thus, the total variance expressed as a proportion is equal to the coefficient of determination, r^2, plus the coefficient of nondetermination, k^2. To compute r^2 we square the correlation coefficient; k^2 is computed from $k^2 = 1 - r^2$.

For the authoritarianism data in Table 5.3-1, $r^2 = (.85)^2 = .72$ and $k^2 = 1 - .72 = .28$. This means that .72 (or .72 × 100 = 72%) of the variance of the Y scores can be explained by the linear relationship with the X scores, but .28 of the variance of the Y scores is not explained. The converse also is true; 72% of the variance of the X scores can be explained by the linear relationship with the Y scores. The linear relationship between the fathers' and sons' scores enables us to account for much of the variance in the sons' or the fathers' authoritarianism scores (72%); however, 28% of the variance is not accounted for. In all likelihood we could find other variables, such as the sons' or fathers' levels of education, that would enable us to reduce the percentage of unaccounted-for variance. The index k^2 is a measure of how much of the variance remains to be accounted for.

A visual representation of the proportion of explained and unexplained variance is presented in Figure 5.4-1, where the proportions $S_Y^2/S_Y^2 = 1$ and $S_X^2/S_X^2 = 1$ are represented by the areas of circles. The area in which the circles overlap corresponds to r^2; the nonoverlap areas correspond to k^2. If r is equal to $+1$ or -1, the circles completely overlap, as shown in Figure 5.4-1(c), and all the variance of one variable is explained by that of the other variable. If r is equal to 0, the circles do not overlap, as shown in Figure 5.4-1(d), and none of the variance of either variable is explained by that of the other variable.

Most variables of interest to behavioral scientists, health scientists, and educators are affected by a multiplicity of factors. School performance, for example, is affected by academic aptitude, scholastic motivation, health, and parental support

---

[4] The derivation of

$$S_Y^2/S_Y^2 = r^2 + k^2$$

is given by Kirk (1978, pp. 144–145).

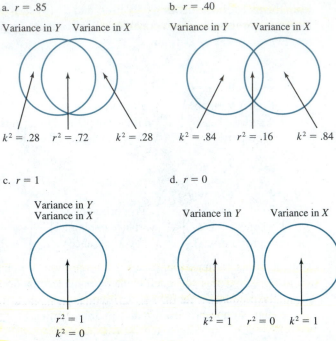

a. $r = .85$

Variance in Y Variance in X

$k^2 = .28$ $r^2 = .72$ $k^2 = .28$

b. $r = .40$

Variance in Y Variance in X

$k^2 = .84$ $r^2 = .16$ $k^2 = .84$

c. $r = 1$

Variance in Y
Variance in X

$r^2 = 1$
$k^2 = 0$

d. $r = 0$

Variance in Y Variance in X

$k^2 = 1$ $r^2 = 0$ $k^2 = 1$

Figure 5.4-1. **Visual representation of r^2, the proportion of variance of one variable that is explained by the variance of the other variable, and k^2, the proportion that is not explained by the variance of the other variable.**

for achievement, to name only a few. A correlation between performance and academic aptitude of .30, for example, tells us that we have accounted for $(.30)^2 = .09$ of performance variance and that we have to look to other variables to account for the remaining $1 - .09 = .91$ of the variance. Note that because $r^2 \leq |r|$, values of $|r|$ close to 1 are required in order to account for an appreciable proportion of variance. Not until $r = .71$ does $r^2 = .50$.

$4(.71)^2$ account for 50%.

CHECK YOUR UNDERSTANDING OF SECTION 5.4

18. For the following experiments, compute r^2 and k^2 and interpret them verbally and by means of diagrams like those in Figure 5.4-1.
    a. The correlation between freshman English grades and grades in a physical education bowling class was .22.
    b. The correlation between a self-report instrument measuring family cohesion and men's marital satisfaction was .56.
    c. The correlation between the last two digits of students' social security numbers and total fiber (vegetable, fruit, and cereal) consumed per week was .03.

19. Terms to remember
    a. Coefficient of determination   b. Coefficient of nondetermination

5.5 SOME COMMON ERRORS IN INTERPRETING A CORRELATION COEFFICIENT

Error: Interpreting *r* in Direct Proportion to Its Size

Correlation coefficients are often incorrectly interpreted. A common error is to interpret *r* as the percentage of association between two variables. For example, it is incorrect to say that an *r* of .60 means that there is a 60% association between the variables. Such a statement is meaningless. Does it mean that 60% of the elements are associated? The value of *r* does not indicate the percentage of association but rather is a measure of strength of association on a scale of −1 to +1.

A related error is concluding, for example, that an *r* of .80 represents twice the relationship indicated by an *r* of .40 or that an increase in correlation from .10 to .20 represents the same increase as that from .60 to .70. The error in such interpretations becomes apparent when we consider that an *r* equal to .80 accounts for 64% of the variance, whereas an *r* equal to .40 accounts for only 16% of the variance, and that 64% is four times larger than 16%.

Error: Interpreting *r* in Terms of Arbitrary Descriptive Labels

Various schemes have been suggested to help students interpret correlation coefficients. A common but misleading scheme is the classification of certain *r* values as "very high" (for example, $r \geq .90$), "high" ($r = .70 - .89$), "medium" ($r = .30 - .69$), or "low" ($r < .30$). The problem with such classifications is that what constitutes a high or low correlation depends on what is being correlated with what and on the use to be made of *r* once it has been computed. This will be illustrated for the concepts of *reliability* and *validity*—two desirable characteristics of psychological tests. One type of reliability, called **test-retest reliability,** is determined by administering a test to a group of participants, waiting a suitable period of time, and then readministering the test to the same participants. The test's reliability, or consistency of measurement, is the correlation between the two sets of scores. Reliability coefficients of .90 or higher are common for tests of intellectual aptitude. A test-retest reliability coefficient below .80 would raise serious questions about the reliability of an intelligence test; however, the scheme for interpreting *r* described above would classify $r = .80$ as high. Equally misleading designations result when this classification scheme is used to interpret validity coefficients. The **validity** of a test is the degree to which it measures what it is supposed to measure. To assess the validity of, say, a college aptitude test, students' aptitude scores can be correlated with their grade point averages. The best aptitude tests rarely have validity coefficients above .60. It is misleading to label a validity coefficient of .60 as medium when higher coefficients are seldom, if ever, obtained. An $r = .60$ is an extremely high validity coefficient but a very, very low reliability coefficient. As these examples illustrate, no single classification scheme for interpreting r is applicable to all situations.

Error: Inferring Causation From Correlation

Another common error in interpreting a correlation coefficient is to infer that because two variables are correlated, one causes the other.

> A nonzero correlation coefficient simply means that there is a **concomitant relationship** between X and Y; that is, variation in one variable is associated in some way with variation in the other.

It is true that if X causes Y, there must be a correlation between the variables. However, the converse of this statement is not true. A concomitant relationship is necessary but not sufficient for inferring causality. A concomitant relationship often exists because both variables are caused by a third variable. For example, it does not necessarily follow from the positive correlation between Sunday school attendance and honesty that attending Sunday school causes honesty. In all likelihood, both variables are caused by a third variable—parental reinforcement and modeling practices in the home.

It is easy to fall into the trap of inferring causality from correlation, especially when one variable occurs before the other. Consider the well-publicized positive correlation between years of formal education and income. Does such a correlation mean that going to college causes one to earn more money? Before giving an affirmative answer we would have to know how much college graduates would have earned if they hadn't gone to college. A causal relationship may in fact exist, but this can't be ascertained from the correlation. Some or all of the correlation between education and income might be explained in terms of other causal variables. For example, colleges attract two kinds of students—the bright and the rich. We know that bright individuals tend to rise to better-paying jobs whether or not they have gone to college and that few children of rich parents end up poor.

CHECK YOUR UNDERSTANDING OF SECTION 5.5

20. Which of the following are incorrect interpretations of a correlation coefficient, and why?
    a. The strength of association between test forms L and M is .96.
    b. There is a medium correlation, $r = .67$, between the age at which babies can roll over and the age at which they can sit up alone.

    c. The correlation between women's scores on the Beck Depression Inventory and a self-report questionnaire measuring marital discord is .30; this correlation is twice as high as that for men, which is $r = .15$.

    d. We can conclude from the high correlation between risk for sexual assault and alcohol consumption by female victims that victimization is caused at least in part by consuming alcohol.

21. In an attempt to help children with low IQs improve their school performance, a special perceptual awareness program was instituted. Suppose that the program was completely ineffective. The group's mean IQ before the program was 72. Would you expect it to change after the special program, and if so, in what direction? If you don't see the issue, reread Section 5.1.

22. Terms to remember
    a. Test-retest reliability   b. Validity
    c. Concomitant relationship

5.6 FACTORS THAT AFFECT THE SIZE OF A CORRELATION COEFFICIENT

Nature of the Relationship Between *X* and *Y*

There are many ways in which two variables can be related. It is sufficient for our purposes to classify them as a **linear,** straight-line, relationship, or a **nonlinear,** curved-line, relationship. Three examples showing the straight or curved lines of best fit for paired scores are presented in Figure 5.6-1. In general, the more closely data points hug the line of best fit, whether it is a straight or a curved line, the higher the correlation. We saw in Section 5.2 that when r is equal to $+1$ or -1, the data points fall on a straight line. If *X* and *Y* are normally distributed and have equal

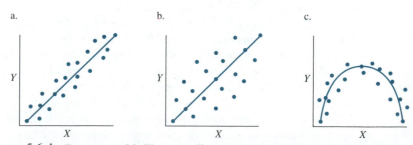

Figure 5.6-1. **Parts a and b illustrate linear relationships, and part c illustrates a nonlinear relationship. The higher the correlation, the better the data points hug the line of best fit.**

variances, as the absolute value of r decreases, the points form fatter and fatter ellipses until finally, when r is equal to 0, they tend to fall in a circle. The Pearson product-moment correlation always fits data points by a straight line. This works fine if the relationship is linear but not so well if the relationship is nonlinear, as in Figure 5.6-1(c). If a nonlinear relationship is fitted by a straight line, the data points will not hug the line as closely as they would an appropriate curved line; consequently, r underestimates the strength of association. In fact, an r equal to 0 can be obtained even though X and Y are highly correlated.

> A different correlation measure called the **correlation ratio** or **eta squared**, η^2, has been developed for determining the strength of association between nonlinearly related variables.

Eta squared fits data points by whatever line is appropriate. If the relationship is linear, a straight line is used, and $\eta^2 = r^2$. For nonlinear relationships in which the correlation is not equal to zero, η^2 fits the points by a curved line, and its value is always larger than that for r^2. A discussion of the correlation ratio can be found in more advanced texts.

How can we determine whether the relationship between X and Y is linear or nonlinear and hence whether to use r or η^2? Statistical tests can be used;[5] however, the simplest method is to examine the scatterplot for evidence of nonlinearity—the so-called eyeball test. Usually, visual inspection is adequate to detect cases in which r would underestimate strength of association.

In summary, r is a measure of the linear relationship between two quantitative variables. If the relationship is not linear, r underestimates the strength of association.

Truncated Range

The size of the Pearson product-moment correlation coefficient is affected by the range of the X and Y variables. If the range of either variable is **truncated,** that is, restricted, the size of r will be reduced. Suppose that we have administered an aptitude test to assembly-line job applicants at a new factory. Because of the large number of jobs to be filled, all the applicants were hired regardless of their scores. Six months later we construct a scatterplot like that in Figure 5.6-2, compute the correlation between aptitude scores and employee productivity, and find that r is equal to .55. This is a very respectable validity coefficient. In the future if we had a surplus of applicants, we could improve productivity by hiring only those applicants with high aptitude scores. Suppose that instead of hiring all the applicants when the plant opened, we had artificially restricted the range of aptitude scores by hiring only applicants with scores of 70 or above. For this case, the correlation between aptitude and productivity would have been .06 instead of .55, and we would have

[5] See, for example, Hays (1994, pp. 774–778).

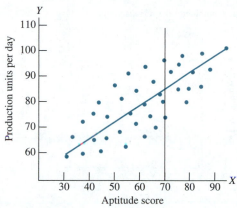

Figure 5.6-2. **Scatter diagram illustrating the effect on *r* of restricting the range of *X* to scores of 70 or above. The *r* for the unrestricted range is .55; that for the restricted range is .06.**

incorrectly concluded that the test is of little value in selecting employees. The reason the restriction or truncation of the range of the *X* variable results in a misleadingly low correlation coefficient can be seen from Figure 5.6-2. The effect would have been the same had the range of the *Y* variable been truncated.

   The truncated range problem is common in behavioral and education research because such research is often conducted with college students who have been carefully screened for intelligence and related variables and, consequently, constitute a relatively homogeneous population. It's not surprising that college aptitude scores do not correlate very highly with grades because admission offices truncate the range by admitting only students with medium to high aptitude scores.

Spurious Effects Due to Subgroups With Different Means or Standard Deviations

A substantial correlation between *X* and *Y* may occur because the sample of participants contains two or more subgroups with means that differ for both variables. Suppose that we are interested in the correlation between school achievement (*Y*) and anxiety level (*X*) as measured by the Taylor Manifest Anxiety Scale and that we obtain random samples of students from lower- and middle-class families. The correlation coefficient computed for the combined samples will be much higher than that for either sample taken alone. This occurs because the means for the two subgroups differ with respect to both *X* and *Y*. The participants from middle-class families tend to perform better in school and to be somewhat more anxious than children from lower-class families. When the subgroups are combined, the correlation between achievement and anxiety is misleadingly high because of the differing means. The reason for this is evident from Figure 5.6-3(a), where the letters *L* and

a. Combined *r* is spuriously high

b. Combined *r* is spuriously low

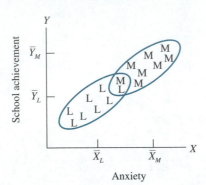

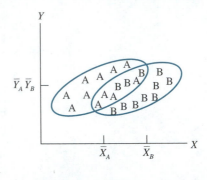

c. Combined *r* is spuriously high for B and low for A

d. Combined *r* is spuriously low

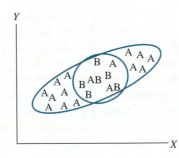

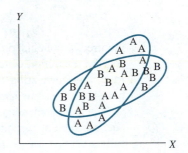

e.

f.

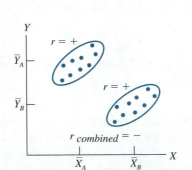

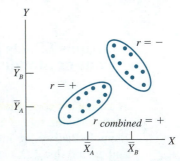

Figure 5.6-3. **These scatter diagrams illustrate the effects on *r* of subsamples with means that differ on both variables (parts a, e, and f) or on only one variable (b). Parts (c) and (d) illustrate the effects of heterogeneous standard deviations. Parts (e) and (f) show that the sign of the coefficient for the combined samples may differ from that for one or both of the subsamples.**

M denote data points for children from lower- and middle-class families, respectively. Figure 5.6-3(b) illustrates a situation in which the means of two subgroups, *A* and *B*, differ only on *X*. The correlation coefficient computed from the combined samples is lower than that for either sample taken alone.

A spurious correlation may occur when the standard deviations of the subgroups but not their means differ for one or both variables. This situation is depicted in Figure 5.6-3(c) and (d), where the letters *A* and *B* denote the subgroups. Figures 5.6-3(e) and (f) depict other ways in which subgroups can produce spurious correlations.

We conclude from the foregoing discussion that the inclusion of subgroups with different means or standard deviations on *X* and *Y* can affect the size and the sign of *r*. Unfortunately, we are not always aware that our sample contains distinct subgroups. Our first clue may come when we construct a scatterplot and note in retrospect that the scores that cluster together tend to come from participants who have some common distinguishing attribute.

Sometimes a researcher intentionally conducts research with **extreme groups**— groups at opposite ends of a continuum. The use of introverts and extraverts, high and low achievers, or normals and neurotics enhances the likelihood of detecting other variables on which the groups differ. This is a useful research strategy, but it may lead to spuriously high correlation coefficients. Frequently, the means of the groups differ on both *X* and *Y*, and the data points have the shape illustrated in Figure 5.6-4. The data were selected from Table 5.3-1 so as to contain two extreme groups: the four fathers with the highest authoritarianism scores and the four with the lowest scores. The correlation for all 20 father-son pairs in Table 5.3-1 is .85; the correlation based on the two extreme groups is .94.

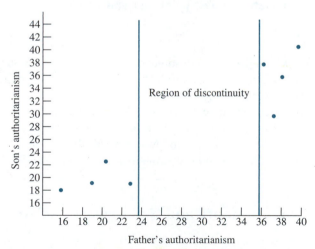

Figure 5.6-4. **This scatter diagram illustrates the effects on *r* of using extreme groups. The data are taken from Table 5.3-1, with the eight data points representing the four highest and the four lowest authoritarianism scores based on the father's data.**

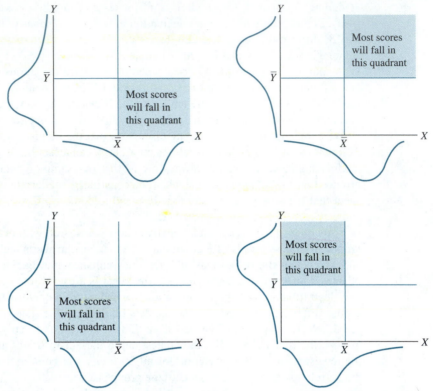

Figure 5.6-5. **Effects of markedly skewed *X* and *Y* distributions on the distribution of data points in a scatter diagram.**

Extreme groups constitute one type of **discontinuous distribution.** A discontinuous distribution also results when we restrict our sample to a relatively small number of points along a continuum or when our sample contains one or more outliers. As discussed in Section 4.5, outliers should be carefully examined. Their presence suggests errors in data recording, an equipment malfunction, or other sources of data contamination. It follows from this discussion that correlation coefficients involving discontinuous distributions should be carefully examined.

Nonnormality and Heterogeneity of Array Variances

If the distributions of *X* and *Y* are markedly skewed, the value of *r* will be less than if the variables are approximately normally distributed. The reason for this can be seen in Figure 5.6-5, which shows various combinations of skewed *X* and *Y* distributions.

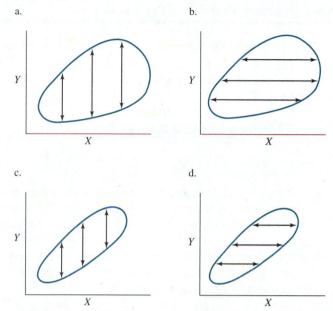

Figure 5.6-6. **Parts (a) and (b) illustrate heterogeneity of column and row dispersion, respectively; parts (c) and (d) illustrate homogeneity of dispersion.**

The presence of skewed X and Y distributions is often accompanied by unequal dispersion of the Y scores for different values of X and similarly unequal dispersion of the X scores for different values of Y. This condition is called **heterogeneity of array** (row or column) **variances** or **heteroscedasticity**.

Heteroscedasticity is illustrated in Figure 5.6-6. Earlier, we saw that r reflects the average degree to which scores hug the line of best fit. If the dispersion around the line differs for different values along the X and Y measurement scales, the correlation coefficient will not have the same meaning as when the array variances are homogeneous. For example, in Figure 5.6-6(a) and (b) the correlation coefficient will underestimate the magnitude of association for low X scores and overestimate it for high X scores.

The use of r as a descriptive measure of association requires no assumptions regarding the shape of the X and Y distributions. As we have seen, however, if X and Y are markedly skewed, the value of r will be closer to zero than if the distributions are approximately normal. Furthermore, under these conditions, the interpretation of r is altered because r no longer reflects the average degree to which the data points hug the line of best fit. Finally, the presence of skewed X and Y distributions is often accompanied by a nonlinear relationship between the variables. This condition calls for the computation of η^2 instead of r.

TABLE 5.6-1   Factors That Affect the Size of *r*

r Underestimates Magnitude of Relationship When	*r* Overestimates Magnitude of Relationship When
1. The relationship between *X* and *Y* is nonlinear.	1. The sample contains subgroups with means that differ for both variables.
2. The range of either *X* or *Y* is truncated.	2. The sample is composed of extreme groups.
3. The distributions of *X* and *Y* are skewed.	

    It is apparent from this discussion that the interpretation of *r* as a descriptive measure is simplified if *X* and *Y* are approximately normally distributed. It should be emphasized, however, that normality is not required for purely descriptive purposes because whatever the shapes of the *X* and *Y* distributions, *r* reflects the degree to which data points cluster around a straight line of best fit. We will see in Chapter 11 that normality is required when the sample correlation is used in making inferences about the population correlation.

The factors that affect the size of *r* are summarized in Table 5.6-1.

CHECK YOUR UNDERSTANDING OF SECTION 5.6

23. What effects do the following factors have on *r* as a measure of strength of association? Draw figures like Figures 5.6-1 through 5.6-5 to represent the data.

    a. The relationship between *X* and *Y* looks like an inverted U. Assume that *r* is positive.

    b. The sample contains subgroups *a* and *b* with equal standard deviations and means $\overline{X}_a = 16$, $\overline{X}_b = 22$, $\overline{Y}_a = 31$, and $\overline{Y}_b = 37$. Assume that *r* is positive for both *a* and *b*.

    c. The sample contains subgroups *a* and *b* with equal means and standard deviations $S_{X_a} = 13$, $S_{X_b} = 22$, $S_{Y_a} = 22$, and $S_{Y_b} = 13$. Assume that *r* is positive for both *a* and *b*.

    d. The distribution of the *X* variable is negatively skewed; that for the *Y* variable is positively skewed. Assume that *r* is negative.

    e. The distributions of the *X* and *Y* variables are positively skewed. Assume that *r* is positive.

    f. The sample contains subgroups *a* and *b* with equal means and standard deviations $S_{X_a} = 9$, $S_{X_b} = 9$, $S_{Y_a} = 13$, and $S_{Y_b} = 21$. Assume that *r* is positive for both *a* and *b*.

    g. The sample contains subgroups *a* and *b* with equal standard deviations and means $\overline{X}_a = 12$, $\overline{X}_b = 18$, $\overline{Y}_a = 38$, and $\overline{Y}_b = 27$. Assume that *r* is positive for both *a* and *b*.

h. The range of X is reduced by deleting participants with scores above $\overline{X}$. Assume that r is positive.

24. The correlation between IQ and ratings of the creativity of 50 highly creative individuals was .18. Can we conclude that IQ is a relatively unimportant factor in creativity? Discuss.

25. Terms to remember

a. Linear relationship

c. Correlation ratio

e. Truncated range

g. Discontinuous distribution

i. Heteroscedasticity

b. Nonlinear relationship

d. Eta squared

f. Extreme groups

h. Heterogeneity of array variance

5.7 SPEARMAN RANK CORRELATION

The **Spearman rank correlation coefficient,** denoted by r_s, is used to describe the degree of agreement between paired data that are in the form of ranks.[6]

Such data may occur as a result of ranking scores, as when grade point averages are converted to rank in graduating class, or because rank data are obtained in the original instance, as when freshman English themes are ranked on the basis of creativity. Ranking is often done when it is difficult or impossible to apply more refined measuring procedures, as in assessing creativity, attractiveness, or tastiness.

The formula for r_s is

$$r_s = 1 - \frac{6 \sum_{i=1}^{n} (R_{X_i} - R_{Y_i})^2}{n(n^2 - 1)},$$

where $R_{X_i} - R_{Y_i}$ is the difference between the ith person's ranks on X and Y and n is the number of pairs of ranks.

The computation of r_s is illustrated in Table 5.7-1, where 14 graduate school applicants have been ranked by tenured faculty (R_{X_i}) and nontenured faculty (R_{Y_i}).

The index r_s is a measure of the agreement between two sets of ranks and is interpreted in much the same way as the Pearson product-moment coefficient. The

---

[6] This coefficient was first used by Sir Francis Galton but was named for the British psychologist Charles Spearman, who made more extensive use of it.

TABLE 5.7-1   Computation of r_s for Ranks Assigned to Applicants by Tenured Faculty (R_{X_i}) and Nontenured Faculty (R_{Y_i})

(i) Data

Applicant	Rank, R_{X_i}	Rank, R_{Y_i}	$R_{X_i} - R_{Y_i}$	$(R_{X_i} - R_{Y_i})^2$
1	6	8	−2	4
2	3	2	1	1
3	4	5	−1	1
4	12	11	1	1
5	10	9	1	1
6	1	1	0	0
7	5	4	1	1
8	7	7	0	0
9	14	14	0	0
10	2	3	−1	1
11	8	10	−2	4
12	11	12	−1	1
13	9	6	3	9
14	13	13	0	0

$$\sum_{i=1}^{n} (R_{X_i} - R_{Y_i})^2 = \overline{24}$$

(ii) Computational procedure

$$r_s = 1 - \frac{6 \sum_{i=1}^{n} (R_{X_i} - R_{Y_i})^2}{n(n^2 - 1)} = 1 - \frac{6(24)}{14[(14)^2 - 1]} = 1 - \frac{144}{2730} = .95$$

range of r_s is from −1 to +1. Values of r_s greater than 0 indicate that large R_X's tend to be paired with large R_Y's. Values less than 0 indicate that large R_X's are paired with small R_Y's, and so on. The coefficient is equal to 1 if and only if each person's X and Y ranks are equal. It can be shown[7] that the formula for r_s is equivalent to that for r when two sets of consecutive untied ranks 1, . . . , n are substituted for X_i and Y_i in the Pearson formula. However, the use of ranks in place of scores alters the meaning of the correlation coefficient. This point is examined next.

Earlier we saw that r is a measure of the linear relationship between two quantitative variables; r_s is a measure of the **monotonic relationship** between two sets of ranks.

[7] See Kirk (1978, pp. 122–124) for the derivation.

A function $Y = f(X)$ is said to be **strictly monotonic increasing** if an increase in the value of X is always accompanied by an increase in Y.[8] A **strictly monotonic decreasing function** is one in which an increase in X is accompanied by a decrease in Y.

Monotonic functions include linear functions ($Y = a + bX$) as well as a number of other functions that are nonlinear ($Y = X^3$; $Y = \log X$). Thus, Spearman's rank correlation coefficient does not necessarily reflect the linear relationship between two sets of ranks. It does reflect the strength of the monotonic relationship—a more general relationship. If r_s is equal to zero, either the variables represented by ranks are not related or the form of the relationship is nonmonotonic.

The Problem of Tied Ranks

Occasionally, two or more objects or individuals are assigned the same rank, which results in **tied ranks.** The usual practice is to give them the mean of the ranks they would have received collectively if they had been distinguishable. For example, if Jane, Elaine, and Bill are considered equally gregarious, each is given the mean of the ranks they would have occupied, say, $(1 + 2 + 3)/3 = 2$. Thus, Jane, Elaine, and Bill each are assigned the same mean rank of 2. Unfortunately, the presence of tied ranks violates the assumptions underlying the derivation of the computational formula for r_s. A correction for ties can be incorporated in the formula, but the computation is tedious. The most desirable solution is to force those making ratings to discern differences among the objects or individuals, thereby eliminating tied ranks. If this is done, the uncorrected formula can be used. If raters persist in assigning tied ranks, the next best solution is to treat the sets of ranks as though they were scores and to compute a Pearson product-moment correlation coefficient. The result can be regarded as a Spearman rank correlation coefficient that has been corrected for ties.

CHECK YOUR UNDERSTANDING OF SECTION 5.7

26. A random sample of freshman psychology majors ranked various fields of psychology according to vocational attractiveness. The students again ranked the fields when they were seniors. Compute the correlation between their freshman and senior rankings.

---

[8] A strictly monotonic transformation preserves the order inherent in the original scores; it does not preserve information concerning the magnitude of differences among the original scores. Consider two scores, X_n and X_{n+1} such that X_n is less than X_{n+1}. Further, let $f(X_n)$ and $f(X_{n+1})$ be functions, respectively, of X_n and X_{n+1}. If for all $X_n < X_{n+1}$, $f(X_n) \leq f(X_{n+1})$, the function $f(X)$ is said to be monotonic increasing. If for all $X_n < X_{n+1}$, $f(X_n) < f(X_{n+1})$, the function is strictly monotonic increasing.

Field	Freshman Rank	Senior Rank
Social	5	2
Experimental	7	6
Human factors	6	7
Clinical	1	1
Statistics and measurement	8	8
Industrial	3	3
Educational	4	4
Counseling	2	5

27. The debate format can be a useful adjunct to traditional teaching methodologies for presenting complex issues. Graduate student nurses were exposed to a debate on the issue of third-party reimbursement. A questionnaire was used to evaluate pre- and post-debate knowledge of 13 affirmative and negative arguments concerning the issue. The results are listed in the following table; a rank of 1 was assigned to the argument known by the most student nurses. Compute the correlation between the two sets of ranks. (Suggested by Archold, Patricia G., and Hoeffer, Beverly. [1981]. Reframing the issue: A debate on third-party reimbursement. *Nursing Outlook,* 423–427.)

Argument	Pretest Rank	Posttest Rank
Legitimize role and service of nurses	1	7
Increase health care cost	2	7
Increase access of consumer to nursing services	3	4.5
Nursing services are undefined and dependent on physicians	4	12.5
Decrease health-care cost	6	4.5
Provide equal opportunity in a free-market system	6	11
Supports health-care delivery system not based on need	6	7
Cumbersome process for individual nurses	8	12.5
Increase accountability of nurses for their services	9	9.5
Increase power and autonomy of nursing to influence health-care delivery system	11.5	2
Supports inequitable/discriminatory health-care delivery system	11.5	1
Elitist/divisive to nursing	11.5	3
No increase in accessibility	11.5	9.5

28. Which of the following are strictly monotonic functions?
    a. $Y = 1 + 2X$ b. $Y = X^2$
    c. $Y = 2 + X^3$ d. $Y = 1/(X + 4)$
29. Terms to remember
    a. Spearman rank correlation coefficient
    b. Strictly monotonic increasing and decreasing functions
    c. Tied ranks

5.8 OTHER KINDS OF CORRELATION COEFFICIENTS

Three correlation coefficients have been mentioned thus far: r, η^2, and r_s. An extension of r to the case in which there are three or more variables is discussed in Section 6.7. This coefficient is called a multiple correlation coefficient. A fifth coefficient, Cramér's V that is appropriate for unordered qualitative variables, is discussed in Section 16.3. Other coefficients also are available, but they are beyond the scope of this book. A summary of the more widely used coefficients is given in Table 5.8-1.

†5.9 PRINTOUTS FOR THREE MICROCOMPUTER PACKAGES

JMP

A portion of the JMP data table for the father's and son's authoritarianism scores in Table 5.3-1 is shown on the left side of Figure 5.9-1. The display on the right of Figure 5.9-1 was obtained by selecting **Analyze** in the menu bar followed by the pull-down command called **Correlation of Y's.** The display gives four correlation coefficients; the coefficient of interest is that of father-son (son-father) scores, which is .8463. The coefficients of 1.000 on the main diagonal of the display are the correlation of father-father scores and son-son scores. This display of correlation coefficients is called a *correlation matrix.*

---

† This and similarly marked sections can be omitted without loss of continuity.

TABLE 5.8-1.   Summary of the Major Correlation Coefficients

Coefficient	Symbol	Characteristics	Reference[a] and pages
1. Pearson product moment	r	X and Y quantitative, linear relationship	(a) 106–117 (b) 611–622 (c) 239–240 (d) 242–243
2. Eta squared (correlation ratio)	η^2	X and Y quantitative, curvilinear relationship	(a) 180–182 (c) 331–333
3. Spearman rank coefficient	r_s	X and Y ranked, monotonic relationship	(a) 129–130 (c) 289–290 (d) 384–385
4. Kendall's tau	τ	X and Y ranked, monotonic relationship	(c) 290–291 (d) 382–384
5. Point biserial	r_{pb}	One variable quantitative, the other dichotomous[b]	(a) 133–134 (b) 336 (c) 279–282
6. Biserial	r_b	X and Y quantitative, but one variable forced into a dichotomy	(a) 134–136 (c) 287–288
7. Tetrachoric	r_t	X and Y quantitative, but both forced into dichotomies	(a) 136–137
8. Phi or fourfold	ϕ	X and Y both dichotomous	(a) 130–133 (b) 866–868 (c) 283–284
9. Cramér's measure	$\hat{V}$	X and Y both dichotomous	(b) 869 (c) 158–159

[a] (a) Glass and Hopkins (1996); (b) Hays (1994); (c) Howell (1997); (d) Wilcox (1996).
[b] Dichotomous classifications assign elements to one of two categories, for example, pass–fail, male–female, married–not married, and IQ > 100–IQ ≤ 100.

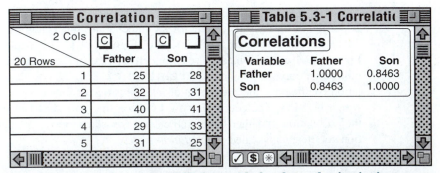

Figure 5.9-1. **A portion of the JMP data table for the authoritarianism scores in Table 5.3-1 is shown on the left side of the figure. The father-son (son-father) correlation coefficient, which is 0.8463, is shown in the display on the right.**

Correlation			
	father	son	var
1	25.000	28.000	
2	32.000	31.000	
3	40.000	41.000	
4	29.000	33.000	
5	31.000	25.000	
6	16.000	18.000	

- - Correlation Coefficients - -

	FATHER	SON
FATHER	1.0000 (20) P= .	.8463 (20) P= .000
SON	.8463 (20) P= .000	1.0000 (20) P= .

(Coefficient / (Cases) / 2-tailed Significance

"." is printed if a coefficient cannot be computed

Figure 5.9-2. **A portion of the SPSS data table for the authoritarianism scores in Table 5.3-1 is shown in the top part of the figure. The correlation coefficient for the father-son data, .8463, is shown in the bottom part. The numbers in parentheses, 20, are the numbers of fathers and sons. The meanings of "2-tailed Significance" and "$P = $" are discussed in Chapters 10 and 11, respectively.**

SPSS

The SPSS data table for the authoritarianism scores in Table 5.3-1 is shown in the top part of Figure 5.9-2. The correlation coefficients in the bottom part of Figure 5.9-2 were obtained by selecting **Statistics** in the menu bar followed by the pull-down option called **Correlate** and then **Bivariate** . . . .

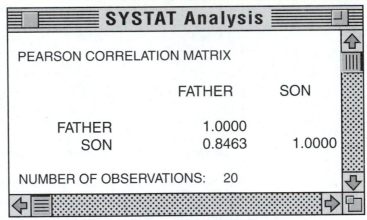

Figure 5.9-3. **A portion of the SYSTAT data table for the authoritarianism scores in Table 5.3-1 is shown on the top of the figure. The correlation coefficient for the father-son data, 0.8463, is shown in the analysis window below.**

SYSTAT

The SYSTAT data table for the authoritarianism scores in Table 5.3-1 is shown in the top part of Figure 5.9-3. The correlation coefficients in the bottom part of Figure 5.9-2 were obtained by selecting **STATS** from the menu bar and then selecting the **Corr** option followed by **Pearson** in the pull-down menu.

5.10 SUMMARY

The term *correlation* refers to the concomitance between two or more quantitative or qualitative variables. A correlation coefficient is a measure of the degree of concomitance. Concomitance does not imply causality; it does, however, imply that as one variable changes, the other variable changes.

The two most widely used correlation coefficients in the behavioral sciences and education are the Pearson product-moment correlation coefficient, r, and the Spearman rank correlation coefficient, r_s. Pearson's r reflects the strength and the direction of the linear relationship between two quantitative variables. It is a number that varies between -1 and 1, with 0 indicating the absence of a linear relationship. Negative values indicate an inverse relationship between the variables; positive values indicate a positive or direct relationship. Spearman's r_s measures the strength and the direction of the monotonic relationship between two ordered qualitative variables—that is, ranked data. It, like r, varies between -1 and 1, with 0 indicating the absence of a monotonic relationship.

Two statistics, both functions of r, are useful in interpreting a particular r value: the coefficient of determination, r^2, and the coefficient of nondetermination, $k^2 = 1 - r^2$. For a given linear relationship between X and Y, r^2 reflects the proportion of the X-score variance that can be explained by the Y-score variance and vice versa; k^2 reflects the proportion that can't be explained. If, for example, r is equal to .50, we know that, based on the linear relationship between the variables, 25% of the variance of one variable can be explained by the variance of the other variable, and 75% remains to be explained.

The Pearson product-moment correlation coefficient is appropriate for linearly related quantitative variables. For descriptive purposes, no other assumptions regarding the variables are required. However, in interpreting r, keep in mind that the size of r can be affected by such factors as the shape of the X and Y distributions, the presence of a truncated X or Y range, the presence of subgroups with standard deviations or means that differ for both variables, and the presence of a discontinuous distribution for X or Y or both.

REVIEW EXERCISES FOR CHAPTER 5

1. A job-satisfaction questionnaire was administered to a random sample of 36 men between the ages of 29 and 34. The researcher was interested in the relationship between number of years of formal education and job satisfaction. (a) Construct a scatterplot for the data in the following table. (b) Does the relationship appear to be linear or nonlinear?

Participant	Years of Education	Job Satisfaction	Participant	Years of Education	Job Satisfaction
1	14	36	19	12	43
2	11	38	20	11	46
3	10	36	21	18	53
4	15	51	22	8	30
5	7	30	23	9	35
6	8	37	24	12	40
7	12	40	25	13	40
8	13	43	26	13	41
9	16	47	27	10	32
10	12	44	28	14	50
11	12	37	29	12	33
12	11	40	30	14	47
13	9	32	31	10	38
14	12	42	32	11	37
15	13	45	33	12	40
16	11	38	34	14	50
17	12	42	35	13	42
18	11	37	36	13	45

2. Distinguish between r and ρ.

3. Match the r values 1, -1, 0, .3, and $-.8$ with the scatterplots shown here.

a.
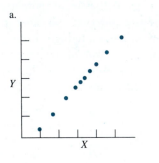

b.
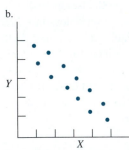

c.
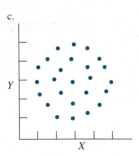

d.
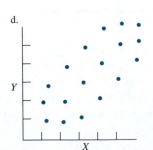

e.
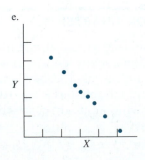

4. Would you expect the correlation between the following to be positive, negative, or essentially zero?
   a. Mechanical aptitude and birth order
   b. Verbal intelligence and number of trials to learn a list of nonsense syllables
   c. Grades in college and annual income 10 years after graduation
   d. Number of letters in last name and musical aptitude
5. The Alcohol Dependence Scale was developed to assist the World Health Organization in the classification of alcoholism. Fifteen alcoholics seeking counseling for alcohol-related disabilities took this scale and the Michigan Alcoholism Screening Test, which yields an index of problems related to drinking. The following data were obtained. (Suggested by Skinner, Harvey A., and Allen, Barbara A. [1982]. Alcohol dependence syndrome: Measurement and validation. *Journal of Abnormal Psychology, 91,* 199–209.)

Counselee	Alcohol Dependence Scale	Michigan Alcoholism Screening Test
1	89	78
2	48	57
3	74	65
4	97	86
5	59	58
6	65	75
7	46	57
8	84	95
9	78	69
10	77	86
11	67	78
12	36	47
13	83	74
14	68	77
15	96	87

   a. Construct a scatterplot for these data and decide whether the data appear to be linearly related.
   b. Compute *r* for these data.
6. Researchers have reported that lonely people often describe themselves as shy. To investigate the strength of the relationship between the two variables, a modified version of the Stanford Shyness Survey and the UCLA Loneliness Scale were given to 20 male and 20 female college students. The order of administration of the instruments was randomized independently for each student. The following data for the male students were obtained. (Experiment suggested by Maroldo,

Georgetter K. [1981]. Shyness and loneliness among college men and women. *Psychological Reports, 48,* 885–886.)

Student	Stanford Shyness Survey	UCLA Loneliness Scale	Student	Stanford Shyness Survey	UCLA Loneliness Scale
1	36	51	11	30	29
2	39	52	12	30	40
3	30	33	13	33	45
4	23	35	14	32	30
5	28	55	15	28	42
6	41	52	16	34	45
7	29	32	17	21	35
8	27	38	18	41	35
9	28	40	19	23	30
10	28	33	20	39	51

   a. Construct a scatterplot for these data and decide whether the data appear to be linearly related.

   b. Compute r for these data.

7. Calculate r for the education and job data in Exercise 1.

8. Calculate $\sum_{i=1}^{n} (X_i - \overline{X})(Y_i - \overline{Y})$ for the following data. In which quadrants of Figure 5.3-1 would the majority of the data points fall? Are the variables linearly related, and if so, is the relationship positive or negative?

a.		b.		c.		d.	
X	Y	X	Y	X	Y	X	Y
14	18	10	17	9	17	9	17
6	11	10	15	11	14	11	17
10	15	12	15	13	10	13	13
10	16	8	13	7	19	7	13

9. For the data in Exercise 8, make figures like Figure 5.3-1.

10. For the data in Exercise 8, calculate r.

11. What does the covariance S_{XY} tell us about the relationship between X and Y? In computing r, why is S_{XY} divided by $S_X S_Y$?

12. For a set of data with $S_X = 4$ and $S_Y = 5$, what is the largest possible value that S_{XY} can be? (*Hint:* The maximum value of $r = +1$ and $r = S_{XY}/S_X S_Y$.)

13. The correlation coefficient for the following data is undefined. Why is this statement true?

X	Y
13	16
16	16
11	16
17	16
12	16

14. What do r^2 and k^2 tell us about the relationship between X and Y?

15. For the following experiments, compute r^2 and k^2 and interpret them verbally and by means of diagrams like those in Figure 5.4-1.

   a. The correlation between grades in introductory psychology and introductory statistics was .32.

   b. The correlation between the number of hours that rats had been deprived of food and the time to traverse a maze with sunflower seeds in the goal box was .80.

   c. The correlation between the last two digits of students' social security numbers and the number of trials to learn nonsense syllables was .02.

16. Which of the following are incorrect interpretations of a correlation coefficient, and why?

   a. The strength of association between scores on the Attitudes Toward Disabled Persons Scale and amount of exposure to persons with disabilities is .56.

   b. The correlation between height and weight at age 6 is .40; this correlation is twice as high as that at age 16, when $r = .20$.

   c. The correlation between reaction time and number of automobile accidents is .20; 96% of the variance in frequency of accidents is unaccounted for.

   d. We can conclude from the high correlation between level of motivation and number of elective offices sought that office-seeking behavior is caused at least in part by motivation.

17. What is wrong with interpreting r

   a. in direct proportion to its size?

   b. in terms of arbitrary descriptive labels?

   c. as indicating causality?

18. Employees with the highest accident rates were required to complete a safety course. Following the course, the employees had fewer accidents. Can we conclude that the course was effective? What controls could be used in the experiment to make the outcome easier to interpret?

19. What effects do the following factors have on r as a measure of strength of association? Draw figures like Figures 5.6-1 through 5.6-5 to represent the data.

a. The relationship between X and Y looks like a U. Assume that r is positive.
b. The range of X is reduced by deleting participants with scores below $\overline{X}$.
c. The sample contains subgroups a and b with equal standard deviations and means $\overline{X}_a = 16$, $\overline{X}_b = 22$, $\overline{Y}_a = 42$, and $\overline{Y}_b = 31$. Assume that r is positive for both a and b.
d. The sample contains subgroups a and b with equal standard deviations and means $\overline{X}_a = 20$, $\overline{X}_b = 26$, $\overline{Y}_a = 35$, and $\overline{Y}_b = 41$. Assume that r is positive for both a and b.
e. The sample contains subgroups a and b with equal means and standard deviations $S_{X_a} = 15$, $S_{X_b} = 24$, $S_{Y_a} = 24$, and $S_{Y_b} = 15$. Assume that r is positive for both a and b.
f. The sample contains subgroups a and b with equal means and standard deviations $S_{X_a} = 18$, $S_{X_b} = 18$, $S_{Y_a} = 26$, and $S_{Y_b} = 34$. Assume that r is positive for both a and b.
g. The distribution of the X variable is positively skewed; that for the Y variable is negatively skewed. Assume that r is positive.
h. The distributions of the X and Y variables are negatively skewed.
20. How can we detect cases in which η^2 should be used instead of r?
21. What are the potential advantages and disadvantages of using extreme groups in research?
22. The correlation between IQ and grade point average (GPA) for high school seniors was .63. For seniors who went on to college, the correlation between IQ and college GPA was .51. Explain why this correlation is lower.
23. List the similarities and differences between r and r_s.
24. A psychiatric social worker and an occupational therapist ranked 11 Veterans Administration patients with respect to extent of recovery following 3 months of therapy. Compute the correlation between the two sets of rankings.

Patient	Social Worker	Occupational Therapist
1	7	7
2	2	1
3	1	2
4	3	5
5	8	9
6	10	10
7	4	3
8	9	8
9	11	11
10	6	6
11	5	4

25. Participants rated the attractiveness of one set of geometric shapes before smoking marijuana and a similar set after smoking marijuana. One shape in the two sets was the same. The following data are the ratings for that shape. A rating of 1 means very attractive; a rating of 20, very unattractive. Transform the ratings to ranks, and compute the correlation between the two sets of ranks.

Participant	Before Smoking	After Smoking
1	6	3
2	8	7
3	14	16
4	7	2
5	10	12
6	9	15
7	5	1
8	15	20
9	12	17

26. Suppose that for the data in Exercise 25, participant 6 had assigned a rating of 12 instead of 15 to the geometric shape after smoking marijuana. This rating results in tied ranks. How would this affect the computational procedure for the correlation coefficient?

27. Which of the following are strictly monotonic functions?
    a. $Y = 3 + 3X$ b. $Y = 1 + X^2$
    c. $Y = X^3$ d. $Y = 1/X$

28. Use a statistical software package to compute the Pearson product-moment correlation coefficient for the data in Exercise 1.

29. Use a statistical software package to compute the Pearson product-moment correlation coefficient for the data in Exercise 5.

30. Use a statistical software package to compute the Pearson product-moment correlation coefficient for the data in Exercise 6.

Chapter 6

Regression

6.1 INTRODUCTION TO REGRESSION

Jean's score on the Law School Aptitude Test (LSAT) is 69. What grade point average can she expect to make in law school? Bertha is on a 750-calorie diet. How many pounds should she be able to lose in a month? Because the variables are correlated, we can predict Jean's GPA from her LSAT score and Bertha's weight loss from her calorie intake with better than chance accuracy. The higher the correlation, the more accurate the prediction. For r equal to plus one or minus one, the dependent variable, denoted by Y, can be predicted from the independent variable, X, with perfect accuracy; but if r is equal to zero, a knowledge of X is useless in predicting Y. Although a correlation coefficient is indicative of our ability to predict, the actual prediction is made using regression analysis, the subject of this chapter.

> Strictly speaking, **regression analysis** applies to paired data (X_i, Y_i), where X is the independent variable with values X_i that are selected in advance, and Y is the dependent variable with values Y_i that are free to vary. However, regression procedures also are applicable when both X and Y are free to vary, as they are in correlation.

An Overview of Prediction

George, who is taking statistics, copies down the grades from last semester's class and constructs the scatterplot shown in Figure 6.1-1. He finds that the correlation between the midterm and the final exam was .80. His midterm grade was 82, and he wonders how he'll do on the final. According to the scatterplot, two students in last semester's class made 82; the mean of their grades—and hence George's predicted grade, assuming that the two classes are comparable—is $(74 + 84)/2 = 79$.

Although this prediction method works, it has a serious disadvantage. The prediction is based on only the two Y scores corresponding to $X_i = 82$; the other 10 paired scores are ignored. Predictions based on such small samples tend to be unstable, that is, to vary markedly from sample to sample. Prediction can be improved by utilizing all the data rather than a small subset. George notes that the relationship between the midterm and final grades appears to be linear, so he determines the best-fitting linear regression line. It is shown as a dashed line in Figure 6.1-1. To predict his final grade George draws a vertical line from $X_i = 82$ up to the regression line and then a horizontal line to the Y axis. His predicted grade is 78.

Predictions based on the regression line take into account all the sample data and hence are more stable than those based on only the mean of the Y scores corresponding to a given X score. Both procedures presuppose that the population represented by the current sample (George's statistics class) doesn't differ from that represented by the earlier sample (last semester's class). Obviously, if this assumption isn't tenable, we can have little faith in the prediction. The regression approach also

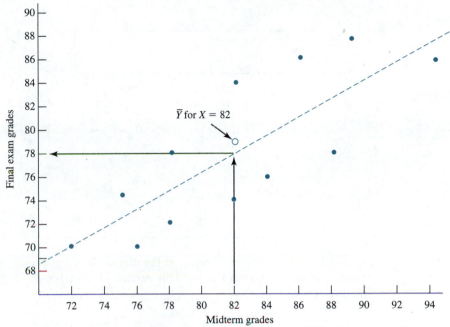

Figure 6.1-1. **Scatter diagram for paired midterm and final exam grades.**

presupposes that the data points have been fitted by the correct regression equation—in our example, the equation for a straight line. Fortunately, the tenability of this assumption is easily checked by looking at the scatterplot.

6.2 CRITERION FOR THE LINE OF BEST FIT

Predicting Y From X

We have referred several times to the line of best fit without ever defining it—what is the best-fitting line for a set of data points? Best fit can be defined in a number of ways. It seems reasonable that we should want a line that minimizes some function of the error in predicting Y_i from X_i.

A **prediction error** or **residual,** e_i, is defined as the difference between the *i*th person's actual score, Y_i, and the score predicted for that person, Y_i'—that is, $e_i = Y_i - Y_i'$.

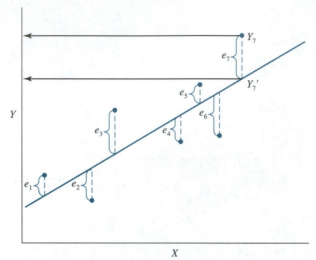

Figure 6.2-1. **A prediction error, e_i, is the discrepancy between Y_i, the actual observed score for person i, and Y_i', the predicted score based on the regression line; for example, $e_7 = Y_7 - Y_7'$.**

Prediction errors are illustrated in Figure 6.2-1 and are represented as vertical distances along the Y axis. One definition of best fit widely used by mathematicians is based on the **principle of least squares** and is as follows.

The **line of best fit** is the one that minimizes the sum of the squared prediction errors—that is, the line for which $\sum_{i=1}^{n} e_i^2 = \sum_{i=1}^{n}(Y_i - Y_i')^2$ is as small as it can be.

We will limit our discussion to linearly related data. For this case the predicted values fall on a straight line, called the **regression line.** The equation for a straight line is

$$Y_i' = a_{Y \cdot X} + b_{Y \cdot X} X_i,$$

where Y_i' is the predicted value,
$a_{Y \cdot X}$ is the point at which the line crosses the Y axis,
$b_{Y \cdot X}$ is the slope of the line, and
X_i is a value of the independent variable.

The subscript $Y \cdot X$ is read "Y given X" and indicates that we are predicting Y from X. According to the least squares criterion, we want values of the constants $a_{Y \cdot X}$ and $b_{Y \cdot X}$ such that

$$\sum_{i=1}^{n} e_i^2 = \sum_{i=1}^{n}(Y_i - Y_i')^2 = \sum_{i=1}^{n}[Y_i - (a_{Y \cdot X} + b_{Y \cdot X} X_i)]^2$$

is as small as it possibly can be.

The method of finding numerical values for $a_{Y \cdot X}$ and $b_{Y \cdot X}$ that makes $\sum_{i=1}^{n} e_i^2$ as small as it can be utilizes the differential calculus and hence is beyond the scope of this text. We shall simply report here the formulas for computing their values:[1]

$$a_{Y \cdot X} = \overline{Y} - b_{Y \cdot X}\overline{X}$$

and

$$b_{Y \cdot X} = \frac{S_{XY}}{S_X^2} = \frac{\dfrac{\sum_{i=1}^{n}(X_i - \overline{X})(Y_i - \overline{Y})}{n}}{\dfrac{\sum_{i=1}^{n}(X_i - \overline{X})^2}{n}} = \frac{\sum_{i=1}^{n}(X_i - \overline{X})(Y_i - \overline{Y})}{\sum_{i=1}^{n}(X_i - \overline{X})^2}.$$

A computational example is given in Table 6.2-1 for the data in Figure 6.1-1. The values of the constants from part ii of the table are $a_{Y \cdot X} = 12.1868$ and $b_{Y \cdot X} = 0.8026$. Hence the linear equation that minimizes the sum of the squared prediction errors is

$$Y_i' = a_{Y \cdot X} + b_{Y \cdot X} X_i$$
$$= 12.1868 + 0.8026 X_i.$$

According to the equation, the line crosses the Y axis at 12.1868 (see Figure 6.2-2). In other words, when $X = 0$, the predicted value $Y_i' = 12.1868$. The slope of the line is 0.8026, which means that as X increases 1 unit, Y increases 0.8026 unit (see Figure 6.2-2). Furthermore, the regression line goes through the point defined by the X and Y means, which is (82, 78); see the circle in Figure 6.2-3. If the regression line does not go through this point, the line is incorrect.

To determine the predicted Y value for, say, $X_i = 82$, we enter the X_i value in the regression equation and solve for Y_i'.

$$Y_i' = 12.1868 + 0.8026(82) = 78$$

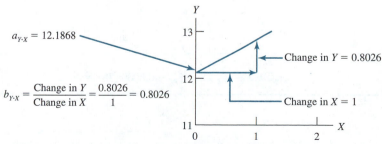

Figure 6.2-2. **Illustration of $a_{Y \cdot X}$, the point at which the regression line crosses the Y axis, and $b_{Y \cdot X}$, the slope of the regression line. The slope of the regression line is the ratio of the change in Y divided by the change in X.**

[1] A raw-score formula for $b_{Y \cdot X}$ that is simpler to use is given in Exercise 6 at the end of this section.

TABLE 6.2-1.   Computation of Least Squares Values of Constants in a Linear Equation (Data From Figure 6.1-1)

(i) Data

X_i	Y_i	$(X_i - \overline{X})$	$(Y_i - \overline{Y})$	$(X_i - \overline{X})(Y_i - \overline{Y})$	$(X_i - \overline{X})^2$	$(Y_i - \overline{Y})^2$
72	70	-10	-8	80	100	64
75	74	-7	-4	28	49	16
76	70	-6	-8	48	36	64
78	72	-4	-6	24	16	36
78	78	-4	0	0	16	0
82	74	0	-4	0	0	16
82	84	0	6	0	0	36
84	76	2	-2	-4	4	4
86	86	4	8	32	16	64
88	78	6	0	0	36	0
89	88	7	10	70	49	100
94	86	12	8	96	144	64

$\Sigma X_i = \overline{984}$ $\quad$ $\Sigma Y_i = \overline{936}$ $\qquad\qquad$ $\Sigma(X_i - \overline{X})(Y_i - \overline{Y}) = \overline{374}$ $\;$ $\Sigma(X_i - \overline{X})^2 = \overline{466}$ $\;$ $\Sigma(Y_i - \overline{Y})^2 = \overline{464}$

$\overline{X} = 82$ $\qquad$ $\overline{Y} = 78$

(ii) Computation of $a_{Y \cdot X}$ and $b_{Y \cdot X}$

$$b_{Y \cdot X} = \frac{\sum\limits_{i=1}^{n}(X_i - \overline{X})(Y_i - \overline{Y})}{\sum\limits_{i=1}^{n}(X_i - \overline{X})^2} = \frac{374}{466} = 0.8026$$

$$a_{Y \cdot X} = \overline{Y} - b_{Y \cdot X}\overline{X} = 78 - 0.8026\,(82) = 12.1868$$

(iii) Computation of $a_{X \cdot Y}$ and $b_{X \cdot Y}$

$$b_{X \cdot Y} = \frac{\sum\limits_{i=1}^{n}(X_i - \overline{X})(Y_i - \overline{Y})}{\sum\limits_{i=1}^{n}(Y_i - \overline{Y})^2} = \frac{374}{464} = 0.8060$$

$$a_{X \cdot Y} = \overline{X} - b_{X \cdot Y}\overline{Y} = 82 - 0.8060\,(78) = 19.1320$$

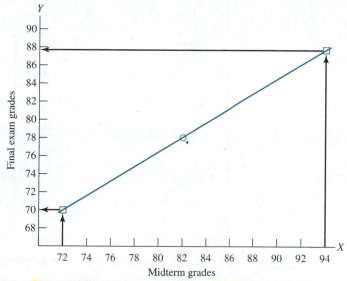

Figure 6.2-3. **To obtain the line of best fit for predicting Y from X, the smallest and largest X values (72 and 94) were inserted in the equation $Y_i' = 12.1868 + 0.8026X_i$ to obtain the predicted values 69.97 and 87.63 (see the squares). A line drawn through these two points also passes through the mean of X and Y, which is represented by the circle.**

The predicted value is 78. Alternatively, we can determine predicted values by graphic means, as we did in Figure 6.1-1. The first step is to draw the line of best fit. Because a straight line is defined by two points, we begin by solving for Y_i' when X_i is equal to 72 and when it is equal to 94 (the smallest and largest X scores, respectively). The corresponding Y_i' values are, respectively, 69.97 and 87.63. Once a line connecting the (X_i, Y_i) points (72, 69.97 and 94, 87.63) has been drawn, it can be used to obtain Y_i' for other values of X_i. The two sets of points (72, 69.97 and 94, 87.63) are represented by squares in Figure 6.2-3.

A word of caution is in order here. We should restrict our prediction of Y to the range of X values for which we have paired data points. In this example the smallest and largest X scores are, respectively, 72 and 94. Within this range of X scores we know that the relationship between X and Y is linear. However, we have no way of knowing from the data in Figure 6.2-3 whether or not our regression equation is appropriate for X scores outside the interval from 72 to 94. In the absence of such information, it is prudent to restrict our predictions to X scores between 72 and 94.

Predicting X From Y

If the value of Y_i is known, X_i can be predicted from the equation

$$X_i' = a_{X \cdot Y} + b_{X \cdot Y} Y_i.$$

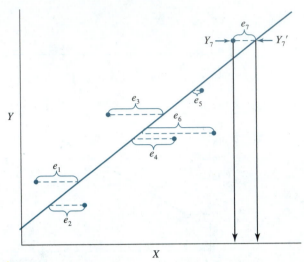

Figure 6.2-4. **The error in predicting X_i from Y_i is the discrepancy between X_i, the actual observed value for person i, and X'_i, the predicted value based on the regression line; for example, $e_7 = X_7 - X'_7$.**

The subscript $X \cdot Y$ indicates that X is predicted from Y. As we will see, $a_{X \cdot Y}$ is different from $a_{Y \cdot X}$, and $b_{X \cdot Y}$ is different from $b_{Y \cdot X}$, because they apply to different regression lines. The constants of the linear equation for predicting X from Y are given by

$$a_{X \cdot Y} = \overline{X} - b_{X \cdot Y}\overline{Y}$$

and

$$b_{X \cdot Y} = \frac{S_{XY}}{S_Y^2} = \frac{\dfrac{\sum\limits_{i=1}^{n}(X_i - \overline{X})(Y_i - \overline{Y})}{n}}{\dfrac{\sum\limits_{i=1}^{n}(Y_i - \overline{Y})^2}{n}} = \frac{\sum\limits_{i=1}^{n}(X_i - \overline{X})(Y_i - \overline{Y})}{\sum\limits_{i=1}^{n}(Y_i - \overline{Y})^2}.$$

The formulas for $a_{X \cdot Y}$ and $b_{X \cdot Y}$ were derived so as to minimize the sum of the squared prediction errors defined by $\sum_{i=1}^{n} e_i^2 = \sum_{i=1}^{n}(X_i - X'_i)^2$. These prediction errors are illustrated in Figure 6.2-4 and are represented as *horizontal distances* along the X axis. The computation of $a_{X \cdot Y}$ and $b_{X \cdot Y}$ is illustrated in Table 6.2-1. The regression equation is

$$X'_i = a_{X \cdot Y} + b_{X \cdot Y} \quad Y_i$$
$$= 19.1320 + 0.8060 \, Y_i.$$

According to the equation, the line crosses the X axis at 19.1320. In other words, when $Y = 0$, the predicted value $X' = 19.1320$. The slope of the line is 0.8060, which means that as Y increases 1 unit, X increases 0.8060 unit.

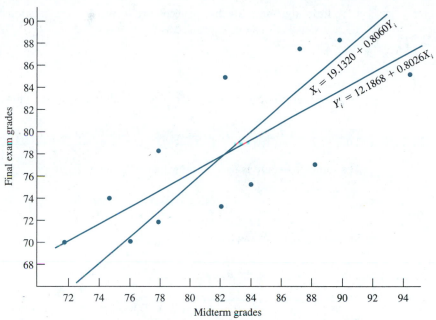

Figure 6.2-5. **Regression line for predicting Y_i from X_i and X_i from Y_i (data from Table 6.2-1). Each regression line goes through the point defined by the X and Y means. In this example that point is $\overline{X} = 82$ and $\overline{Y} = 78$.**

To summarize, for any set of paired data points we can compute two regression lines—the regression of Y on X, given by $Y'_i = a_{Y \cdot X} + b_{Y \cdot X} X_i$, and the regression of X on Y, given by $X'_i = a_{X \cdot Y} + b_{X \cdot Y} Y_i$. The two lines are shown in Figure 6.2-5 for the data in Table 6.2-1. There are two lines because in predicting Y from X we want to minimize one set of errors, $\Sigma(Y_i - Y'_i)^2$, but in predicting X from Y we minimize a different set of errors, $\Sigma(X_i - X'_i)^2$.

Relationship Between r and the Slopes of the Regression Lines

There are a number of interesting relationships between r and the two regression coefficients $b_{Y \cdot X}$ and $b_{X \cdot Y}$. It is a simple matter to show that

$$r(S_Y / S_X) = b_{Y \cdot X}$$
$$r(S_X / S_Y) = b_{X \cdot Y}$$
$$\pm \sqrt{b_{Y \cdot X} b_{X \cdot Y}} = r$$

For the latter relationship, r is positive when $b_{Y \cdot X}$ and $b_{X \cdot Y}$ are positive and negative when both coefficients are negative; $b_{Y \cdot X}$ and $b_{X \cdot Y}$ always have the same sign.

A little algebra is all that is necessary to prove these relationships. In Section 5.3, we saw that r can be expressed as

$$r = \frac{S_{XY}}{S_X S_Y}.$$

To show that $r(S_Y/S_X) = b_{Y \cdot X}$, we replace r with $S_{XY}/S_X S_Y$ as follows:

$$r \frac{S_Y}{S_X} = \frac{S_{XY}}{S_X S_Y} \frac{S_Y}{S_X} = \frac{S_{XY}}{S_X^2} = b_{Y \cdot X}.$$

The same procedure is used to show that $r(S_X/S_Y) = b_{X \cdot Y}$.

$$r \frac{S_X}{S_Y} = \frac{S_{XY}}{S_X S_Y} \frac{S_X}{S_Y} = \frac{S_{XY}}{S_Y^2} = b_{X \cdot Y}$$

Similarly, we can show that $\pm\sqrt{b_{Y \cdot X} b_{X \cdot Y}} = r$.

$$\pm\sqrt{b_{Y \cdot X} b_{X \cdot Y}} = \pm\sqrt{\frac{S_{XY}}{S_X^2} \frac{S_{XY}}{S_Y^2}} = \frac{S_{XY}}{S_X S_Y} = r$$

As we have seen, $b_{Y \cdot X} = r(S_Y/S_X)$. Thus, the linear equation for predicting Y_i from X_i can be expressed in terms of $r(S_Y/S_X)$ instead of $b_{Y \cdot X}$ as follows:

$$Y_i' = \overbrace{\overline{Y} - r \frac{S_Y}{S_X} \overline{X}}^{a_{Y \cdot X}} + \overbrace{r \frac{S_Y}{S_X} X_i}^{b_{Y \cdot X} X_i}$$

$$= \overline{Y} + r \frac{S_Y}{S_X} (X_i - \overline{X})$$

In this form we can see what happens when $r = 0$; we obtain

$$Y_i' = \overline{Y} + 0 \frac{S_Y}{S_X} (X_i - \overline{X})$$

$$= \overline{Y}.$$

This means that when r is equal to zero, the predicted value of Y is the mean of the Y scores regardless of the X value used to predict Y. In other words, knowing X_i doesn't help in predicting Y_i if r is equal to zero, because in every case the predicted Y value is $\overline{Y}$.

√ **CHECK YOUR UNDERSTANDING OF SECTIONS 6.1 AND 6.2**

1. In one sentence, state the primary purpose of a regression analysis.
2. If Y increases 2 units for every 4-unit increase in X, what is the slope of the regression line of Y on X?

3. In an experiment on gender-typed behavior, a random sample of boys ages 5 to 8 were given choices among such toys as a football, a doll carriage, a dump truck, and dishes. The number of gender-appropriate choices for boys at each age is listed in the table.

Age, X	Number of Appropriate Choices, Y	Age, X	Number of Appropriate Choices, Y
7.5	18	7.5	15
7.0	13	5.0	7
5.5	11	5.5	8
8.0	20	6.0	12
6.5	13	8.0	17
6.0	14	7.0	14
5.0	9	6.5	12
8.0	18	5.5	10
6.5	14	5.0	8
6.0	10	7.0	16
7.5	19		

a. Construct a scatterplot and decide whether the data appear to be linearly related.

b. Compute the values of $a_{Y \cdot X}$ and $b_{Y \cdot X}$ for the line of best fit, write the equation for predicting Y from X, and draw the line in the scatterplot. Compute r using the relationship $r = b_{Y \cdot X}(S_X / S_Y)$.

c. Compute the values of $a_{X \cdot Y}$ and $b_{X \cdot Y}$ for the line of best fit, write the equation for predicting X from Y, and draw the line of best fit in the scatterplot. Which slope, $b_{Y \cdot X}$ or $b_{X \cdot Y}$, is the steepest? Compute r using the relationship $r = b_{X \cdot Y}(S_Y / S_X)$.

d. Compute r using the relationship $r = \pm \sqrt{b_{Y \cdot X} b_{X \cdot Y}}$. Does your answer agree with the values you computed in parts b and c?

e. For a 6-year-old boy, estimate Y using both the regression equation and the line of best fit in the scatterplot.

4. In what sense is the regression line for predicting Y from X in Exercise 3 a best-fitting line?

5. For any set of data, there are two regression lines. Under what condition are the two lines identical?

6. The formula for $b_{Y \cdot X}$ in Table 6.2-1 is not the most convenient one for computational purposes. Show that it is algebraically equivalent to

$$b_{Y \cdot X} = \left[\Sigma X_i Y_i - \frac{\Sigma X_i \, \Sigma Y_i}{n} \right] \bigg/ \left[\Sigma X_i^2 - \frac{(\Sigma X_i)^2}{n} \right],$$

which is simpler to use.

7. If r is equal to zero, what value of Y should you predict for each value of X?

8. If $Y'_i = Y_i$ for all i, what do you know about r?
9. Terms to remember
   a. Regression analysis
   b. Prediction error (residual)
   c. Principle of least squares
   d. Line of best fit
   e. Regression line
   f. Slope of line

6.3 ANOTHER MEASURE OF ABILITY TO PREDICT: THE STANDARD ERROR OF ESTIMATE

We have seen that our ability to predict Y from X is a function of the degree of correlation between the two variables. The higher the correlation, the more closely the data points cluster around the regression line and the smaller the prediction error. A measure of the prediction error is given by the **standard error of estimate,** which is denoted by $S_{Y \cdot X}$. Don't confuse $S_{Y \cdot X}$ with covariance, which is denoted by S_{XY}. The standard error of estimate is a kind of standard deviation. For comparison purposes, the formulas for the standard error of estimate and standard deviation are given below.[2]

$$S_{Y \cdot X} = \sqrt{\frac{\Sigma(Y_i - Y'_i)^2}{n}} \qquad S_Y = \sqrt{\frac{\Sigma(Y_i - \overline{Y})^2}{n}}$$

In computing $S_{Y \cdot X}$, the deviation $(Y_i - Y'_i)$ is from the predicted value or regression line, whereas for S_Y the deviation $(Y_i - \overline{Y})$ is from the mean of Y. The two deviations are illustrated in Figure 6.3-1.

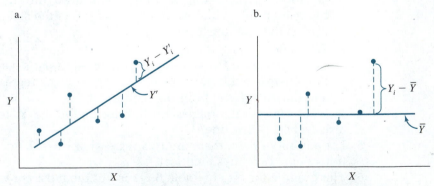

Figure 6.3-1. **Comparison of the deviation $Y_i - Y_i$ used to compute the standard error of estimate (part a) and the deviation $Y_i - \overline{Y}$ used to compute the standard deviation (part b).**

[2] When the population standard error of estimate is estimated from sample data, a better estimator is

$$\hat{\sigma}_{Y \cdot X} = \sqrt{\frac{\Sigma(Y_i - Y'_i)^2}{n - 2}}.$$

Let's look at $S_{Y \cdot X}$ more closely. The regression line denoted by Y' can be thought of as a kind of mean—a "running mean," which gives the predicted value of Y for a particular value of X. Whereas $\overline{Y}$ is the mean of all the Y's, Y' is the mean of Y for a particular value of X. Viewed in this light, $S_{Y \cdot X}$, like S_Y, is computed from the sum of squared deviations from means and hence is a standard deviation. However, $S_{Y \cdot X}$ is the standard deviation of scores around the regression line, whereas S_Y is the standard deviation of scores around the mean. As we will see, $S_{Y \cdot X}$ can be interpreted in much the same way as a regular standard deviation.

An Alternative Formula for $S_{Y \cdot X}$

The formula for the standard error of estimate described above isn't a convenient one to use. An equivalent formula[3] that is much easier to use is

$$S_{Y \cdot X} = S_Y \sqrt{1 - r^2}$$

This formula has the added advantage that it enables us to readily ascertain the maximum and minimum possible values of $S_{Y \cdot X}$. The maximum value of $S_{Y \cdot X}$ occurs when r is equal to 0, in which case $S_{Y \cdot X}$ is equal to S_Y. We can show this as follows:

$$S_{Y \cdot X} = S_Y \sqrt{1 - (0)^2} = S_Y \sqrt{1} = S_Y$$

Thus, if r is equal to 0, the dispersion of Y scores around the regression line is as large as the standard deviation of Y. In this case, knowing the X score doesn't reduce our error in predicting Y. The minimum value of $S_{Y \cdot X}$ occurs when r is equal to 1, in which case $S_{Y \cdot X}$ is equal to 0. We can show this as follows:

$$S_{Y \cdot X} = S_Y \sqrt{1 - (1)^2} = S_Y \sqrt{0} = 0$$

Thus, if r is equal to 1, there is no dispersion around the regression line and no error in predicting Y from X.

To summarize, the maximum value of $S_{Y \cdot X}$ is S_Y and occurs when r is equal to 0; the minimum value of $S_{Y \cdot X}$ is 0 and occurs when r is equal to 1. Thus, the standard error of estimate can assume a value between 0 and S_Y.

Descriptive Application of $S_{Y \cdot X}$

As we have seen, the larger $S_{Y \cdot X}$, the greater the dispersion of Y scores around the regression line and hence the larger the average prediction error. If the distribution

[3] See Kirk (1978, pp. 143–144) for the derivation of the formula. When the population standard error of estimate is estimated from sample data, a better estimator is

$$S_{Y \cdot X} = S_Y \sqrt{\frac{n}{n - 2}(1 - r^2)}.$$

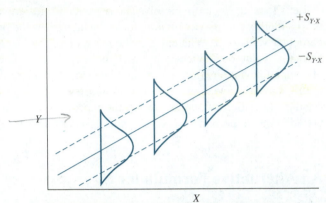

Figure 6.3-2. **Illustration of the standard error of estimate. Approximately 68.3% of the *Y* scores fall within the interval given by $Y' \pm S_{X \cdot Y}$ if the distribution of *Y* scores at every *X* score is approximately normally distributed and all the *Y*-score distributions have the same dispersion.** *See page 125.*

of *Y* scores at every *X* score is approximately normal and if all the *Y*-score distributions have the same dispersion, 68.3% of the *Y* scores will fall within the interval given by $Y' \pm S_{Y \cdot X}$. This information is illustrated in Figure 6.3-2. Similarly, 95.4% of the *Y* scores will fall within the interval given by $Y' \pm 2S_{Y \cdot X}$, and 99.7% within the interval given by $Y' \pm 3S_{Y \cdot X}$. These percentages are based on the normal distribution; see Figure 4.4-1. *Page 125.*

   Although the standard error of estimate is most often used in inferential statistics, we will briefly mention a descriptive application. Suppose an experiment was conducted to determine the relationship between *Y*, length of time (measured in hundredths of a second) necessary to reach a decision, and *X*, the number of alternative choices presented. The following data were obtained: $S_X = 1.5$, $S_Y = 12.5$, $\overline{X} = 4.5$, $\overline{Y} = 46$, $r = .78$, and $n = 100$. Assume that the distribution of *Y* scores for every *X* score is approximately normal and that all the *Y*-score distributions have the same dispersion. The predicted reaction time for a person presented with a choice from among, say, three alternatives is given by the regression equation

$$Y' = \overline{Y} + r \frac{S_Y}{S_X} (X_i - \overline{X})$$

$$Y' = 46 + .78 \frac{12.5}{1.5} (3 - 4.5)$$

$$= 46 + 6.5 (-1.5)$$

$$= 36.25. \quad \textit{predictive } y'$$

The use here of the regression equation $Y' = \overline{Y} + r(S_Y/S_X)(X_i - \overline{X})$ is convenient because of the statistics that are available. We would have arrived at the same predicted reaction time if we had used the equation $Y' = a + bX_i$. The standard error of estimate is

$$S_{Y \cdot X} = S_Y \sqrt{1 - r^2}$$
$$= 12.5\sqrt{1 - (.78)^2}$$
$$= 12.5(.6258)$$
$$= 7.82.$$

We can conclude that approximately 68.3% of the participants in the three-choice condition had reaction times between 44.07 and 28.43, as we see from

$$Y' \pm S_{Y \cdot X} = 36.25 \pm 7.82 = 44.07 \text{ and } 28.43.$$

Similarly, approximately 95.4% had reaction times between

$$Y' \pm 2S_{Y \cdot X} = 36.25 \pm 2(7.82) = 51.89 \text{ and } 20.61.$$

The percentages 68.3 and 95.4 are based on the proportion of the normal distribution that lies in the interval from $\overline{X} - S$ to $\overline{X} + S$ and from $\overline{X} - 2S$ to $\overline{X} + 2S$, respectively, as shown in Figure 4.4-1.

6.4 ASSUMPTIONS ASSOCIATED WITH REGRESSION AND THE STANDARD ERROR OF ESTIMATE

When we make predictions using the regression equation $Y'_i = a + bX_i$, we assume only that the relationship between X and Y is linear. If the assumption is tenable, the principle of least squares ensures that $Y'_i = a + bX_i$ provides the best possible fit for the data. For prediction purposes we don't have to make any assumptions regarding the shape of the X and Y distributions.

The use of the standard error of estimate involves more stringent assumptions. In addition to the linearity assumption, we must also assume that (1) for any value of X, the associated Y scores are approximately normally distributed and (2) the dispersions of Y scores for different values of X are equal. The latter assumption is referred to as the **homoscedasticity** assumption. The converse situation, heteroscedasticity, in which the dispersions of the Y scores for different values of X are unequal, was discussed in Section 5.6.

In predicting X from Y the same assumptions are required, but they must be rephrased to reflect the reversed roles of X and Y.

CHECK YOUR UNDERSTANDING OF SECTIONS 6.3 AND 6.4

10. Chimpanzees were exposed to white noise 8 hours a day for 3 months to determine whether the noise affected their hearing. The

noise levels 75 dBA, 85 dBA, 95 dBA, 105 dBA, and 115 dBA were randomly assigned to 10 animals.

Animal	Noise Level (dBA), X	Hearing Loss (dBA at 1000 Hz), Y	Animal	Noise Level (dBA), X	Hearing Loss (dBA at 1000 Hz), Y
1	105	11	6	85	9
2	85	6	7	105	13
3	95	10	8	115	11
4	115	15	9	75	5
5	75	7	10	95	8

a. Compute $S_{Y \cdot X}$ using the formula $S_{Y \cdot X} = S_Y \sqrt{1 - r^2}$.

b. Assuming a large sample in which the distribution of Y scores for every X score is approximately normal and all the distributions have the same dispersion, compute the interval that will contain 68.3% of the scores for a noise level of 115 dBA.

c. Compute the value of $S_{Y \cdot X}$ for $r = 0$ and $r = 1$. Is the $S_{Y \cdot X}$ for these data relatively large, relatively small, or somewhere in between?

11. How is $S_{Y \cdot X}$ related to the magnitude of prediction error? For the gender-typed data in Exercise 3 in "Check Your Understanding of Sections 6.1 and 6.2," what are the minimum and maximum values of $S_{Y \cdot X}$?

12. Terms to remember
   a. Standard error of estimate   b. Homoscedasticity

†6.5 MULTIPLE REGRESSION AND MULTIPLE CORRELATION

Multiple Regression

At the beginning of the chapter we talked about predicting Jean's grade point average in law school based on her LSAT score. There are other variables that also might be useful in predicting her GPA, such as freshman GPA and level of motivation for having a law career. Perhaps we could improve our prediction by using not just one, but several predictor variables.

> The simultaneous use of two or more independent variables in predicting a dependent variable is called **multiple regression.**

† This and similarly marked sections can be omitted without loss of continuity.

When there is one independent variable or predictor, the regression equation used to predict Y from X is

$$Y_i' = a + bX_i.$$

When there are two independent variables, the regression equation is

$$Y_i' = a + b_1X_{i1} + b_2X_{i2},$$

where Y_i' is the predicted value,

a is the Y intercept,

b_1 is the expected change in Y when X_1 changes one unit and X_2 remains constant,

X_1 is the value of the first independent variable,

b_2 is the expected change in Y when X_2 changes one unit and X_1 remains constant, and

X_2 is the value of the second independent variable.

The equation for two independent variables can be extended to any number of independent variables, say, k, as follows:

$$Y_i' = a + b_1X_{i1} + b_2X_{i2} + b_3X_{i3} + \cdots + b_k X_{ik}$$

In Section 6.2 we described the simplest possible regression equation—an equation with one independent variable. The line of best fit for predicting Y was defined as a straight line such that the sum of the squared prediction errors, $\sum_{i=1}^{n} e_i^2 = \sum_{i=1}^{n}(Y_i - Y_i')^2$, is as small as it possibly can be. When there is only one independent variable, the relationship between X and Y can be represented by a two-dimensional scatterplot, where Y is plotted on the vertical axis and X on the horizontal axis. When there are two independent variables, the scatterplot requires three dimensions: one for Y, one for X_1, and one for X_2. For this case, the predicted values of Y fall on a **regression plane** rather than a regression line. Furthermore, the orientation or slope of the plane is determined so that the sum of the squared prediction errors is as small as it possibly can be.

Perhaps an example will help to clarify what is meant by the slope of a plane and prediction errors around this plane. Consider the data in Table 6.5-1(i), where there are two independent variables. As can be seen from the data in the table, an observed score, Y_i, is equal to its predicted score plus its prediction error or residual, that is,

$$Y_i = Y_i' + e_i.$$

For example, the observed score for subject 1 is

$$Y_1 = Y_1' + e_1$$
$$3 = 3.90 + (-.90).$$

The multiple regression equation is shown in part (ii) of the table. Formulas for computing a, b_1, and b_2 are complex and will not be given here because the values are usually computed with the aid of a computer.[4] The data in columns 2, 3, and 4

[4] The values in Table 6.5-1 were computed using the software package JMP.

TABLE 6.5-1. Data for Multiple Regression With Two Independent Variables

(i) Data

	(1) Observed Score, Y	(2) Predictor No. One, X_1	(3) Predictor No. Two, X_2	(4) Predicted Score, Y_i'	(5) Prediction Error, e_i
Subject					
1	3	4	3	3.90	−0.90
2	1	2	6	1.02	−0.02
3	2	1	4	1.70	0.30
4	4	6	5	3.75	0.25
5	6	5	1	5.63	0.37

(ii) Multiple regression equation

$$Y_i' = a \quad + b_1 \quad X_{i1} - b_2 \quad X_{i2}$$
$$Y_i' = 3.58 + 0.53\, X_{i1} - 0.60\, X_{i2}$$

where $a = 3.58$
$b_1 = 0.53$
$b_2 = -0.60$

---

are plotted in the three-dimensional scatterplot in Figure 6.5-1(a). The predicted values of Y are shown as five solid circles on a sloped plane. In part (b) of the figure, prediction errors (see column 5 of Table 6.5-1) are shown as deviations above or below the sloped plane. The prediction errors appear to deviate little from the plane; consequently, Y can be predicted from X_1 and X_2 with considerable accuracy. A measure of just how well Y can be predicted from a knowledge of X_1 and X_2 is given by the coefficient of multiple determination, which is discussed in the next section.

Multiple Correlation

The correlation between Y and the combined predictors X_1, X_2, . . . , X_k is called the **coefficient of multiple correlation** and is denoted by $R_{Y \cdot X_1 X_2, \ldots, X_k}$ or simply R.

The dot after Y in the notation separates the dependent variable, Y, from the independent variables, X_1, X_2, . . . , X_k. For the two-predictor case, $R_{Y \cdot X_1 X_2}$ is given by

$$R_{Y \cdot X_1 X_2} = \sqrt{\frac{r_{YX_1}^2 + r_{YX_2}^2 - 2 r_{YX_1} r_{YX_2} r_{X_1 X_2}}{1 - r_{X_1 X_2}^2}},$$

where r_{YX_1}, r_{YX_2}, and $r_{X_1 X_2}$ are correlation coefficients for the respective variables.

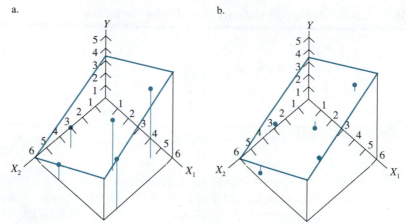

Figure 6.5-1. **(a) The five predicted Y scores in the figure on the left fall on the surface of a plane. The coefficient for X_1 is positive ($b_1 = 0.53$), hence the surface of the plane slopes up relative to the X_1 axis; the coefficient for X_2 is negative ($b_2 = -0.60$), hence the plane slopes down relative to the X_2 axis. (b) Prediction errors in the figure on the right are plotted as deviations from the plane. Recall that prediction errors are deviations of the observed scores from the predicted scores.**

The multiple regression coefficient can assume values from 0 to 1, where 0 indicates the absence of a linear multiple correlation between Y and the independent variables and 1 indicates a perfect linear multiple correlation in which all of the observed Y's fall on the regression plane.

The proportion of variance in Y accounted for by the combined predictors X_1, X_2, . . . , X_k is obtained by squaring the multiple correlation coefficient and is called the **coefficient of multiple determination,** R^2. This coefficient is an extension of the coefficient of determination for one predictor, r^2, that was discussed in Section 5.4.

A comparison of the value of R^2 with that for r^2 indicates the improvement in predicting Y that can be achieved by using a multiple regression equation instead of a one-predictor regression equation. For the data in Table 6.5-1, the correlation between Y and X_1, Y and X_2, and X_1 and X_2 is given in Table 6.5-2. This form of presentation of correlation coefficients is called a *correlation matrix*. According to Table 6.5-2, predictor variable X_2 has the highest correlation with Y ($r_{YX_2} = -.797$). This variable accounts for $r^2_{YX_2} = (-.797)^2 = .64$ of the variance in Y. The multiple correlation coefficient that reflects the contributions of both X_1 and X_2 is

$$R_{Y \cdot X_1 X_2} = \sqrt{\frac{(.777)^2 + (-.797)^2 - 2[(.777)(-.797)(-.338)]}{1 - (-.338)^2}} = .962$$

TABLE 6.5-2.   Intercorrelations Among the Variables

	Variable		
Variable	Y	X_1	X_2
Y	1.000	.777	−.797
X_1		1.000	−.338
X_2			1.000

The coefficient of multiple determination is $R^2_{Y \cdot X_1 X_2} = (.962)^2 = .93$. Thus, the inclusion of a second predictor, X_1, in the regression equation enables us to account for an additional $R^2_{Y \cdot X_1 X_2} - r^2_{YX_2} = .93 - .64 = .29$ of the variance in Y over and above the variance accounted for by the best predictor, X_2. The proportion of variance in Y that is unaccounted for by X_1 and X_2 is given by $1 - R^2_{Y \cdot X_1 X_2} = 1 - .93 = .07$.

The coefficient of multiple determination will be relatively large when the correlation of each of the predictors with Y is large and the correlations among the predictors are 0 or very small. In fact, if the independent variables are uncorrelated, $R^2_{Y \cdot X_1 X_2, \dots, X_k} = r^2_{YX_1} + r^2_{YX_2} + \cdots + r^2_{YX_k}$. If correlations exist among some or all of the independent variables, it is usually the case that $R^2_{Y \cdot X_1 X_2, \dots, X_k} < r^2_{YX_1} + r^2_{YX_2} + \cdots + r^2_{YX_k}$. The presence of nonzero correlations among the independent variables is referred to as **multicollinearity**. Extreme multicollinearity occurs when one independent variable is a linear function of other independent variables, for example, X_2 might equal $3X_1$. Or X_3 might equal $X_1 + X_2$. In the latter case, the inclusion of X_3 in the regression equation would not account for any variance in Y not already accounted for by X_1 and X_2. Ideally, one would like to have predictors that have high correlations with the dependent variable and zero correlations with each other. Unfortunately in the behavioral sciences, health sciences, and education, it is difficult to find predictors that meet these criteria. Once you have found three or four good predictors, it is often difficult to find additional predictors that are not highly correlated with at least one of the original predictors.[5]

CHECK YOUR UNDERSTANDING OF SECTION 6.5

13. a: For each of the following correlation matrices, compute the coefficient of multiple determination.

---

[5] A thorough discussion of the problems associated with multicollinearity is beyond the scope of this book; the reader is referred to Cohen and Cohen (1983); Neter, Wasserman, and Kutner (1990); and Pedhazur (1982).

(i)	Y	X_1	X_2	(ii)	Y	X_1	X_2	(iii)	Y	X_1	X_2
Y	1.00	.20	.30		1.00	.60	.50		1.00	.60	−.50
X_1		1.00	.60			1.00	.30			1.00	−.10
X_2			1.00				1.00				1.00

b. For these correlation matrices, determine the improvement in prediction that can be achieved by using a multiple regression equation instead of a one-predictor regression equation.

14. Data were obtained for 46 college students who were enrolled in an intensive French language course. The course enables students to fulfill their foreign language degree requirement (14 semester hours) in one 8-week summer session. The purpose of the research was to develop a regression equation that would assist the professor in selecting and admitting only those students most likely to succeed in the rigorous course. The dependent variable was the student's grade for the intensive course. The following grading scale was used: A = 4.0, B+ = 3.5, B = 3.0, C+ = 2.5, C = 2.0, D = 1.0, F = 0. The three most useful independent variables were found to be grade point average, X_1; professor's rating, based on an interview with the student, of his or her probable success in the course, X_2; and whether the student had previously taken a French course, X_3. The correlation matrix for these variables is as follows:

	Y	X_1	X_2	X_3
Y	1.000	.773	.681	.289
X_1		1.000	.544	.065
X_2			1.000	.083
X_3				1.000

The coefficient of multiple determination for these data is $R^2_{Y \cdot X_1 X_2 X_3} = (.862)^2 = .743$. The regression equation for predicting a student's course grade is

$$Y'_i = 1.069 + 0.742X_{i1} + 0.496X_{i2} + 0.323X_{i3}.$$

(Suggested by Currall, S. C., & Kirk, R. E. [1986]. Predicting success in intensive foreign language courses. *The Modern Language Journal, 70,* 107–113.)

a. Three two-predictor coefficients of multiple correlation can be computed for these data: $R_{Y \cdot X_1 X_2}$, $R_{Y \cdot X_1 X_3}$, and $R_{Y \cdot X_2 X_3}$. How much does the addition of a third predictor improve the prediction of Y relative to the use of the best two-predictor multiple regression equation?

b. Data for participants 3, 16, 21, and 34 are as shown in the following table. Determine the predicted letter grade for these participants. Use the following scale; ≥ 3.75 = A, 3.25−3.74 = B+, 2.75−3.24 = B, 2.25−2.74 = C+, 1.50−2.24 = C, 0.50−1.49 = D, <0.50 = F).

Participants	X_1	X_2	X_3
3	3.6	0	0
16	2.8	1	1
21	3.1	1	0
34	2.3	1	0

15. Terms to remember
   a. Multiple regression
   b. Coefficient of multiple correlation
   c. Coefficient of multiple determination
   d. Regression plane
   e. Correlation matrix
   f. Multicollinearity

†6.6 PRINTOUTS FOR THREE MICROCOMPUTER PACKAGES

JMP

A JMP scatterplot for the midterm and final exam data in Table 6.2-1 is shown in Figure 6.6-1. After the data were entered in a data table (see Figure 5.9-1 for an ex-

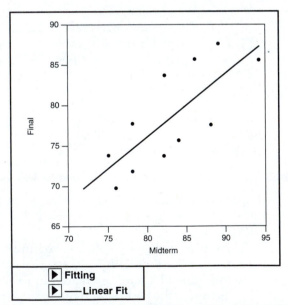

Figure 6.6-1. **JMP scatterplot for the midterm and final exam data in Table 6.2-1. It appears that the line of best fit for these data is a straight line.**

† This and similarly marked sections can be omitted without loss of continuity.

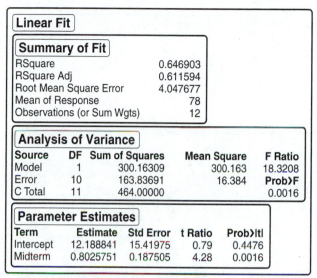

Linear Fit

Summary of Fit

RSquare	0.646903
RSquare Adj	0.611594
Root Mean Square Error	4.047677
Mean of Response	78
Observations (or Sum Wgts)	12

Analysis of Variance

Source	DF	Sum of Squares	Mean Square	F Ratio
Model	1	300.16309	300.163	18.3208
Error	10	163.83691	16.384	Prob>F
C Total	11	464.00000		0.0016

Parameter Estimates

Term	Estimate	Std Error	t Ratio	Prob>|t|
Intercept	12.188841	15.41975	0.79	0.4476
Midterm	0.8025751	0.187505	4.28	0.0016

Figure 6.6-2. **JMP statistics for the midterm and final exam data in Table 6.2-1. The meaning of some of the terms in the figure are as follows: RSquare is the coefficient of determination, RSquare Adj is the value of the coefficient of determination that we could expect if we used the regression equation for this sample of students on a new sample from the same population, Mean of Response is the mean of the final exam grades, Observations is the number of pairs of grades, Intercept Estimate (12.188841) is the $a_{Y \cdot X}$ coefficient, and Midterm Estimate (0.8025751) is the $b_{Y \cdot X}$ coefficient. The regression equation for these data is $Y_i' = a_{Y \cdot X} + b_{Y \cdot X} X_i = 12.188841 + 0.8025751 X_i$, where Y_i' denotes a predicted final examination grade for student i and X_i denotes the student's midterm grade. The meaning of Analysis of Variance is discussed in Chapter 14. Other terms in the figure are discussed in later chapters.**

ample of a similar data table), the scatterplot was obtained by selecting **Analyze** in the menu bar and then the pull-down command called **Fit Y by X.** This selection brought up a dialog box in which midterm was identified as the *X* variable and final, the *Y* variable. The regression line in Figure 6.6-1 was obtained by clicking on the box called **Fitting** in the lower left corner of Figure 6.6-1 and selecting the **Fit Line** option. Selecting the **Fit Line** option also produced the statistics in Figure 6.6-2. Some of the statistics are described in Figure 6.6-2. The statistics in the "Analysis of Variance" portion of the figure are discussed in Chapter 14.

SPSS

An SPSS scatterplot for the midterm and final exam data in Table 6.2-1 is shown in Figure 6.6-3. After the data were entered in a data table (see Figure 5.9-2 for an

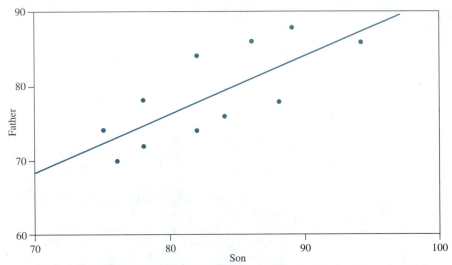

Figure 6.6-3. **SPSS scatterplot for the midterm and final exam data in Table 6.2-1.**

example of a similar data table), the scatterplot was obtained by selecting **Graphs** in the menu bar and then the pull-down command called **Scatter . . .** . This selection brought up a dialog box in which midterm was identified as the X variable and final, the Y variable. Also, the box for **Simple** regression was selected. The regression line in Figure 6.6-3 was obtained by clicking on the box called **Edit** in the scatterplot. This selection brought up the menu bar from which **Chart** was selected. Then the pull-down command **Options . . .** was selected. In the Options dialog box, the **Fit Line, Total** box was selected.

The regression statistics in Figure 6.6-4 were obtained by selecting **Statistics** in the menu bar and then the pull-down command called **Regression,** followed by **Linear . . .** . This selection brought up a dialog box in which midterm was identified as the dependent variable and final, the independent variable.

SYSTAT

A SYSTAT scatterplot for the midterm and final exam data in Table 6.2-1 is shown in Figure 6.6-5. After the data were entered in a data table (see Figure 5.9-3 for an example of a similar data table), the scatterplot was obtained by selecting **Graph** in the menu bar and then the pull-down command called **Plot.** Then the option called **Plot** was selected. This selection brought up a dialog box in which midterm was identified as the X variable and final, the Y variable. In the same dialog box, the **Axis** and **Smooth** options were selected. The **Axis** option brought up a dialog box in which the labels Midterm and Final were typed in

```
* * * * M U L T I P L E   R E G R E S S I O N * * * *

Listwise Deletion of Missing Data

Equation Number 1    Dependent Variable . .    FATHER

Block Number 1.   Method:   Enter   SON


Variable(s) Entered on Step Number

    1..   SON



    Multiple R              .80430
    R Square                .64690
    Adjusted R Square    .61159
    Standard Error      4.04768
Analysis of Variance
                        DF       Sum of Squares       Mean Square
    Regression           1          300.16309          300.16309
    Residual            10          163.83691           16.38369

F =     18.32085             Siqnif F =    .0016
```

— — — — — — — — — — — — — Variables in the Equation — — — — — — — — — — — — —

Variable	B	SE B	Beta	T	Sig T
SON	.802575	.187505	.804303	4.280	.0016
(Constant)	12.188841	15.419747		.790	.4476

End Block Number   1   All requested variables entered.

Figure 6.6-4. **SPSS statistics for the midterm and final exam data in Table 6.2-1. Because there is only one independent variable, Multiple R is the Pearson product-moment correlation coefficient. R Square is the coefficient of determination; Adjusted R Square is the value of the coefficient of determination that we could expect if we used the regression equation for this sample of students on a new sample from the same population. The SON B coefficient (.802575) is the $b_{Y \cdot X}$ coefficient, and the Constant B coefficient (12.188841) is the $a_{Y \cdot X}$ coefficient. The regression equation for these data is $Y_i' = 12.188841 + 0.802575 X_i$, where Y_i' denotes a predicted final examination grade for student i and X_i denotes the student's midterm grade.**

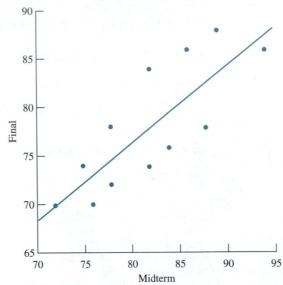

Figure 6.6-5. **SYSTAT scatterplot for the midterm and final exam data in Table 6.2-1.**

DEP VAR:	FINAL	N:	12	MULTIPLE R: 0.804	SQUARED MULTIPLE R: 0.647

ADJUSTED SQUARED MULTIPLE R: 0.612   STANDARD ERROR OF ESTIMATE: 4.0477

VARIABLE	COEFFICIENT	STD ERROR	STD COEF	TOLERANCE	T	P(2 TAIL)
CONSTANT	12.1888	15.4197	0.0000	.	0.7905	0.4476
MIDTERM	0.8026	0.1875	0.8043	1.0000	4.2803	0.0016

ANALYSIS OF VARIANCE

SOURCE	SUM-OF-SQUARES	DF	MEAN-SQUARE	F-RATIO	P
REGRESSION	300.1631	1	300.1631	18.3208	0.0016
RESIDUAL	163.8369	10	13.3837		

Figure 6.6-6. **SYSTAT statistics for the midterm and final exam data in Table 6.2-1. MULTIPLE R is the Pearson product-moment correlation coefficient; SQUARED MULTIPLE R is the coefficient of determination. The CONSTANT COEFFICIENT (12.1888) is the $a_{Y \cdot X}$ coefficient, and the MIDTERM COEFFICIENT (0.8026) is the $b_{Y \cdot X}$ coefficient. The regression equation for these data is $Y_i' = 12.1888 + 0.8026X_i$, where Y_i' denotes a predicted final examination grade for student i and X_i denotes the student's midterm grade. The meanings of other terms in the figure are discussed in later chapters.**

the label boxes for X and Y, respectively, and the axis used in Figure 6.6-5 was selected. The **Smooth** option brought up a dialog box in which the **Linear** option was selected.

The regression analysis in Figure 6.6-6 was obtained by selecting **Stats** in the menu bar followed by the pull-down command called **MGLH,** which stands for multivariate general linear hypothesis, and then the option called **Regression.** This selection brought up a dialog box in which FINAL was identified as the dependent variable and MIDTERM and CONSTANT were identified as the independent variables.

6.7 SUMMARY

The term *regression* was used first by Sir Francis Galton to refer to the tendency for short parents to have offspring who are slightly taller than they and for tall parents to have offspring who are slightly shorter than they. We still speak of regression, but today the term has a broader meaning. It refers to any analysis of paired data $(X_1, Y_1), (X_2, Y_2), \ldots, (X_n, Y_n)$, where X is the independent variable and Y, the dependent variable.

In simple linear regression analysis the line of best fit, called the regression line, is used to predict Y from a knowledge of X. The line of best fit according to the least squares principle is the one for which the sum of the squared prediction errors, the discrepancy between the observed value of Y_i and the predicted value, is as small as it possibly can be.

If r is equal to 1 or -1, the value of Y_i can be predicted perfectly from the equation $Y_i' = a + bX_i$. If the value of r is between -1 and 1, there is likely to be some discrepancy between the observed value of Y_i and the predicted value of Y_i'. The discrepancy $Y_i - Y_i'$ is called a prediction error or residual. A measure of the magnitude of the prediction error is given by the standard error of estimate, $S_{Y \cdot X}$, which is a kind of standard deviation of errors around the regression line. The maximum value of $S_{Y \cdot X}$ is the standard deviation of Y, S_Y, and occurs when r is equal to 0. The minimum value of $S_{Y \cdot X}$ is 0 and occurs when r is equal to 1.

In predicting Y from X we assume only that the relationship between the variables is linear. Interpretations involving $S_{Y \cdot X}$ also assume that the distribution of Y scores at every X score is approximately normal and that all the Y-score distributions have the same dispersion. When prediction involves different samples, as when the performance of one group of students is predicted from that of another, we also must assume that the populations represented by the two samples are identical with respect to the relevant characteristics. Of course, we should restrict our prediction of Y to the range of X values for which we have paired data points unless we are certain that the regression equation is appropriate for the additional X values.

The concepts in simple linear regression can be extended to data where there are two or more independent variables. The simultaneous use of two or more independent variables in predicting a dependent variable is called multiple regression. There is an important advantage in using multiple predictors instead of a single predictor—more accurate prediction. Prediction is most accurate when the predictors have high correlations with the dependent variable and zero correlations with each other. Unfortunately, good predictors are often highly correlated, a condition called multicollinearity. Because of multicollinearity, there is a point of diminishing returns after which adding new predictors to a multiple regression equation contributes little to the accuracy of prediction.

REVIEW EXERCISES FOR CHAPTER 6

1. If Y decreases 5 units for every 2-unit increase in X, what is the slope of the regression line of Y on X?
2. In an experiment on gender-typed behavior, a random sample of girls ages 5 to 8 was given choices among such toys as a football, a doll carriage, a dump truck, and dishes. The number of gender-appropriate choices for girls at each age is listed in the table.

Age, X	Number of Appropriate Choices, Y	Age, X	Number of Appropriate Choices, Y
7.5	10	8.0	14
6.0	11	7.0	11
5.5	10	7.5	13
8.0	15	6.5	9
7.5	14	6.5	11
5.0	6	6.0	10
6.0	8	5.5	8
7.0	12	7.0	10
8.0	12	6.5	13
5.0	7	5.0	9
5.5	9		

a. Construct a scatterplot and decide whether the data appear to be linearly related.
b. Compute the values of $a_{Y \cdot X}$ and $b_{Y \cdot X}$ for the line of best fit, write the equation for predicting Y from X, and draw the line in the scatterplot. Compute r using the relationship $r = b_{Y \cdot X}(S_X/S_Y)$.
c. Compute the values of $a_{X \cdot Y}$ and $b_{X \cdot Y}$ for the line of best fit, write the equation for predicting X from Y, and draw the line of best fit

in the scatterplot. Which slope, $b_{Y \cdot X}$ or $b_{X \cdot Y}$, is the steepest? Compute r using the relationship $r = b_{X \cdot Y}(S_Y/S_X)$.

d. Compute r using the relationship $r = \pm\sqrt{b_{Y \cdot X}b_{X \cdot Y}}$. Does your answer agree with the values you computed in parts b and c?

e. Estimate Y for a 6-year-old girl and X for a girl who made 11 "appropriate" choices using the lines of best fit in the scatter diagram.

3. In what sense are the regression lines in Exercise 2 best-fitting lines?

4. For any set of data, there are two regression lines. Explain.

5. What characteristics of the line of best fit do $a_{Y \cdot X}$ and $b_{Y \cdot X}$ describe?

6. Distinguish between $b_{Y \cdot X}$ and $b_{X \cdot Y}$.

7. In one sentence, describe a residual or prediction error. Under what conditions are all residuals equal to zero?

8. If r is equal to zero, the predicted Y score for all subjects is the mean of Y. Draw a scatter diagram that illustrates this.

9. If $Y' = a + bX_i$ for all i and $a = \overline{Y} - b\overline{X}$, prove that $\Sigma Y'_i = \Sigma Y_i$.

10. The relationship between birth order and participation in dangerous sports such as hang gliding, auto racing, and boxing was investigated. College records were screened to obtain four men who were first-born, four who were second-born, and so on. The data in the following table were obtained.

Subject	Birth Order, X	Number of Dangerous Sports, Y	Subject	Birth Order, X	Number of Dangerous Sports, Y
1	4	1	11	1	0
2	3	1	12	2	0
3	2	0	13	3	2
4	4	2	14	5	1
5	1	0	15	3	1
6	5	2	16	2	1
7	1	0	17	5	2
8	4	1	18	1	1
9	2	1	19	3	1
10	5	3	20	4	2

a. Compute $S_{Y \cdot X}$ using the formula $S_Y\sqrt{1 - r^2}$.

b. Assuming a large sample in which the distribution of Y scores for every X score is approximately normal and all the distributions have the same dispersion, compute the limits that will contain 68.3% of the scores for fourth-born men.

c. Compute the value of $S_{Y \cdot X}$ for $r = 0$ and $r = 1$. Is $S_{Y \cdot X}$ relatively large, relatively small, or somewhere in-between?

11. In what sense is Y' a mean?

12. How is $S_{Y \cdot X}$ related to the magnitude of prediction error? For the gender-typed data in Exercise 2, what are the minimum and maximum values of $S_{Y \cdot X}$?

13. Describe the effect of changes in r on the value of $S_{Y \cdot X}$.

14. Compare the assumptions associated with predictions using r, Y', and $S_{Y \cdot X}$.

15. a. For each of the following correlation matrices, compute the coefficient of multiple determination.

(i)	Y	X_1	X_2	(ii)	Y	X_1	X_2	(iii)	Y	X_1	X_2
Y	1.00	.55	.35		1.00	.80	.70		1.00	.60	$-.50$
X_1		1.00	.15			1.00	.90			1.00	$-.20$
X_2			1.00				1.00				1.00

b. For these correlation matrices, determine the improvement in prediction that can be achieved by using a multiple regression equation instead of a one-predictor regression equation.

16. It was hypothesized that there is a relationship among men's marital satisfaction and measures of gender role conflict and family environment. Data were obtained for 70 married men who completed self-report instruments measuring marital satisfaction, the dependent variable, and restrictive emotionality (X_1), conflict between work or school and family relations (X_2), and family cohesion (X_3). The correlation matrix for these variables is as follows:

	Y	X_1	X_2	X_3
Y	1.00	$-.35$	$-.37$	.56
X_1		1.00	.19	$-.28$
X_2			1.00	$-.20$
X_3				1.00

The coefficient of multiple determination for these data is $R^2_{Y \cdot X_1 X_2 X_3} = (.684)^2 = .468$. (Suggested by Campbell, J. L., & Snow, B. M. [1992]. Gender role conflict and family environment as predictors of men's marital satisfaction. *Journal of Family Psychology, 6,* 84–87.)

a. Compute the three 2-predictor coefficients of multiple correlation that can be computed for these data: $R_{Y \cdot X_1 X_2}$, $R_{Y \cdot X_1 X_3}$, and $R_{Y \cdot X_2 X_3}$.

b. How much does the addition of a third predictor improve the prediction of Y relative to the use of the best two-predictor multiple regression equation?

17. Use a statistical software package to obtain a scatterplot, regression equation, and coefficient of determination for the gender-typed data in Exercise 2.
18. Use a statistical software package to obtain a scatterplot, regression equation, and coefficient of determination for the birth-order and dangerous-sports data in Exercise 10.

Chapter 7

Probability

7.1 INTRODUCTION TO PROBABILITY

Everyone has some intuitive notion of what probability is. However, its definition is a topic for continuing debate among mathematicians. Three views of probability will be described: (1) the subjective-personalistic view, (2) the classical, or logical, view, and (3) the empirical relative-frequency view. Fortunately, the three views supplement one another.

Our interest in probability is motivated by practical considerations. As you will see, probability theory provides a set of conceptual tools for dealing with situations involving uncertainty, and that includes most research in the behavioral sciences, health sciences, and education. And probability theory provides the foundation for statistical inference, the subject of the second half of this book. This chapter on probability and the two that follow on random variables and sampling distributions introduce ideas that you will use throughout your study of statistical inference.

The Subjective-Personalistic View

According to the **subjective-personalistic view,** probability is a measure of the strength of one's expectation that an event will occur.

For example, you might assert, "Chances are I'll pass statistics," or "I think I'll go home this weekend." Such assertions express a degree of belief concerning an event whose outcome is at the moment uncertain. Subjective probabilities affect our lives because they enter into our decision-making process. For most of us the subjective probability of being struck by a car while crossing the street is low, so we proceed as if the event won't happen. But if our subjective probability of, say, being invited to a New Year's party is high enough, all suitable preparations for the event's occurrence will be made.

Although our behavior is influenced by subjective probability, there are difficulties in incorporating it into a formal decision-making process. Equally knowledgeable individuals often disagree on the probability that should be assigned to an event. We find that some people's subjective probabilities follow closely the rules of probability described later, but other people's don't. Hence, a subjective probability can't be considered apart from the person holding it. The measurement of subjective probability poses another problem, although behavioral scientists are beginning to find solutions to this problem. Despite the problems, a formal approach to decision making that utilizes subjective probability has been developed. It is popular in economics and business management and is beginning to find acceptance in behavioral research. This approach, called **Bayesian inference,**[1] enables a researcher to

---

[1] Bayesian inference is named for the Reverend Thomas Bayes (1702–1761), whose theorem laid the groundwork for the approach. For a fuller discussion see Hays (1994, pp. 45–47, 299–302), McGee (1971, chap. 10 and 11), and Novick and Jackson (1974).

make decisions about some true state of affairs using not only sample data but also any prior information that is available, either from previous samples or simply in the form of informed opinions or beliefs. Bayesian inference represents an extension of classical inferential methods that are described in Chapters 10 through 13. Bayesian methods, however, emphasize the steady accumulation and utilization of information from many sources. Furthermore, Bayesian methods lead to different ways of interpreting data, but not necessarily different conclusions about data. The body of classical statistical methods introduced in Chapters 10 through 13 is pretty well mapped out; this isn't true for Bayesian methods. The next decade will see many new developments.

The Classical, or Logical, View

Suppose that we want to know the probability of rolling a 2 with a fair die. We reason that because a fair die is symmetrical and dynamically balanced, all six faces are equally likely to appear. Of the six possible events, only one is a 2, and therefore the probability of rolling a 2, denoted by $p(2)$, is $1/6$.

> According to the **classical, or logical, view,** the probability of an event, say, A, is given by the number of events favoring A, denoted by n_A, divided by the total number of equally likely events, n_S.[2] Thus, $p(A) = n_A/n_S$.

The value of $p(A)$ is always a number between 0 and 1 inclusive because the number of events favoring A can never exceed the total number of events—that is, $n_A \leq n_S$.

The classical view of probability is based on logical analysis. We reason, for example, that when a fair coin is tossed, there are two possible outcomes—a head or a tail—and that the outcomes are equally likely. It follows that the probability of a head is $p(H) = n_H/n_S = 1/2$. The probabilities $1/2$ for a head and $1/6$ for a 2 in the die example were arrived at by logical analyses of these very simple processes. In effect, we developed a mathematical model of the processes based on a postulate and logic. We postulated that certain events are equally likely and deduced the consequences. If our logic is correct, the deductions $p(H) = 1/2$ and $p(2) = 1/6$ are formally correct. However, our deductions may not correspond to the empirical results of actually tossing a coin or rolling a die because for any particular coin or die the postulate that the outcomes are equally likely may be incorrect. For example, the coin may not be fair, or the die may be loaded. However, for fairly simple processes such as coin tossing and die rolling, where the equally likely postulate is tenable, experience has demonstrated that the classical view generates probability estimates that closely approximate empirical probabilities. Consequently, the classical view of probability is useful for practical problems.

---

[2] The letter S, which denotes a sample space, is defined in Section 7.2.

The Empirical Relative-Frequency View

A third view of probability can be adopted for processes that can be repeated without changing their characteristics, such as coin tossing and die rolling. Probability according to this view is estimated from experience—by performing an experiment and determining the ratio of the number of events of interest to the total number of events. This leads to our final definition of probability.

> According to the **empirical relative-frequency view,** the probability of event A, $p(A)$, is a number approached by the ratio n_A/n as the total number of observations, n, approaches infinity.

For example, in a simple experiment such as tossing a coin, the probability of a head can be estimated by making many tosses of the coin and recording the outcomes. If a head is obtained 12 times in 20 tosses, the best estimate of the probability of heads is $n_A/n = {}^{12}/_{20} = .6$. If a head is obtained 120 times in 200 tosses, our confidence in the estimate ${}^{120}/_{200} = .6$ is even greater. We assume that the sample estimate n_A/n moves closer and closer to some "true probability" as n approaches infinity, and thus we have greater confidence in larger samples.

Although an individual outcome of tossing a coin is uncertain, there is a pattern of outcomes that emerges in many repetitions of the toss. Many phenomena like coin tosses are random; the probabilities of their outcomes seem to approach fixed values in the long run. However, empirical probabilities are always approximations because they are based on a finite as opposed to an infinite number of trials.

The empirical view of probability is useful and intuitively simple, but it, too, has certain difficulties. It is meaningful to speak of the probability of rain tomorrow or the probability of getting an A on Tuesday's quiz; however, there is only one tomorrow and only one such quiz. The interpretation of probability as the number approached by n_A/n as the number of tomorrows approaches infinity is unconvincing.

We must conclude that none of the views of probability is completely adequate. Because they are all useful and they are not incompatible, they coexist amicably in the mathematician's bag of conceptual tools. In the discussion that follows, we will rely most on the classical and empirical views.

CHECK YOUR UNDERSTANDING OF SECTION 7.1

1. (a) According to the classical view, what is the probability of observing an odd number on the toss of a die? (b) What assumptions were required to arrive at the answer?
2. (a) What is the probability of drawing the queen of spades from a well-shuffled deck of 52 cards? (b) What assumptions were required to arrive at the answer?

3. (a) According to the relative-frequency view, what is the probability that a head will occur on the next toss of a fair coin if a head appeared on 52 of the last 100 tosses? (b) According to the classical view, what is the probability that a head will occur?
4. The English statistician Karl Pearson is reported to have tossed a coin 24,000 times and obtained 12,012 heads. (a) According to the relative-frequency view, what is the probability of a head? (b) What is the probability of a tail?

7.2 BASIC CONCEPTS

For behavioral scientists, health scientists, and educators, probability theory is a means to an end. It is the vehicle for making inferences about the characteristics of populations by observing samples drawn from the populations. Sample data are obtained by observing events in nature or experimenting in the laboratory. We will denote either procedure by the term **experiment.** In particular, we are interested in experiments whose outcomes can't be predicted with certainty. For example, will desensitization therapy result in more symptom relief than symbolic modeling therapy? Will a rat turn right or left in a T maze?

Simple and Compound Events

One of the simplest experiments we can perform is tossing a die and observing the number that appears on the upper face. Some of the possible outcomes are the following:

Event E_1—observe a 1
Event E_2—observe a 2
Event E_3—observe a 3
Event E_4—observe a 4
Event E_5—observe a 5
Event E_6—observe a 6
Event A—observe an odd number
Event B—observe an even number
Event C—observe a number less than 4

An **event** is an observable happening. Events A, B, and C are called **compound events** because they can be decomposed into simpler events. For example, event A is the occurrence of one of the simple events E_1, E_3, or E_5. Events E_1, ... , E_6

are called **simple events** because they can't be decomposed. An experiment in which two coins are tossed has four possible simple events.

	Coin 1	Coin 2
Event E_1	Head	Head
Event E_2	Head	Tail
Event E_3	Tail	Head
Event E_4	Tail	Tail

The event—observe two like coins—is a compound event because it can be decomposed into the simpler events E_1 and E_4. A single trial of an experiment will result in one and only one simple event. A list of simple events provides a breakdown of all possible outcomes of the experiment.

Graphing Simple Events

It is convenient to represent the simple events in an experiment by a graph called a Euler diagram.[3] To do this we assign to each simple event a point called a **sample point.** The symbol E_i is used to denote both the *i*th simple event and its sample point.

The set of all sample points is called the **sample space** and is denoted by the letter S.

A Euler diagram representing the sample space for the die-tossing experiment is shown in Figure 7.2-1.

Compound events are represented in the diagram by encircling the sample points for that event. For example, earlier we defined event A as observing an odd number

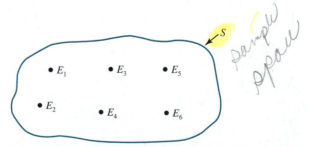

Figure 7.2-1. **Euler diagram for the die-tossing experiment. The set of all sample points $E_1, \ldots, E_6$ defines the sample space S of the experiment.**

[3] The diagram was developed by Leonhard Euler (1707–1783), a Swiss mathematician.

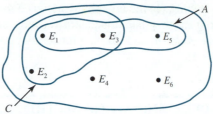

Figure 7.2-2. **Euler diagram for event *A*, observing an odd number, and event *C*, observing a number less than 4.**

on the toss of a die and event *C* as a number less than 4. The two events are represented in Figure 7.2-2 by two subsets of the sample points.

The probability of event *A* according to the classical view is $p(A) = n_A/n_S = 3/6$; the probability of event *C* is $p(C) = n_C/n_S = 3/6$. By examining the sample space, we also can determine the probability for combined events. What is the probability that when a die is tossed the outcome will be an odd number, event *A*, *and* a number less than 4, event *C?* We could observe an odd number and a number less than 4 if either E_1 or E_3 occurred—two of the six simple events in Figure 7.2-2. Hence, the probability that the outcome will represent both events *A* and *C* is $2/6 = 1/3$. We could observe an odd number *or* a number less than 4, event *A* or *C* or both *A* and *C*, in four ways: if E_1, E_2, E_3, or E_5 occurred—four of the simple events in Figure 7.2-2. Hence the probability of *A* or *C* or both *A* and *C* is $4/6 = 2/3$. We have arrived at probabilities for the combined events $p(A \text{ and } B)$ and $p(A \text{ or } B)$ by a process of deduction. In Section 7.3 we will describe formal rules for computing the probabilities of combined events, but first we will describe three properties of probabilities.

Formal Properties of Probability

Probability theory can be thought of as a system of definitions and operations pertaining to a sample space. According to the classical view described in Section 7.1, the probability of event *A* is the ratio of the number of sample points that are examples of *A* to the total number of sample points, provided all sample points are equally likely. For the die-tossing experiment represented in Figure 7.2-1, $p(E_1) = p(E_2) = \cdots = p(E_6) = n_E/n_S = 1/6$. This follows from the assumption that all six faces are equally likely—$n_{E_i} = 1$ for the $i = 1, \ldots, 6$ sample points—and the fact that there are six sample points in the sample space: $n_S = 6$. To each event defined on the sample space we can assign a number called the probability of E_i such that

1. $0 \leq p(E_i) \leq 1$ for all i,
2. $\sum_{i=1}^{n} p(E_i) = 1$, and
3. $p(S) = 1$.

In other words, (1) the probability assigned to an event is a number greater than or equal to 0 and less than or equal to 1, (2) the sum of the probabilities over the sample space equals 1, and (3) the probability of the sure event, one of the events in *S*, is always 1.

CHECK YOUR UNDERSTANDING OF SECTION 7.2

5. An experiment consists of tossing three fair coins. (a) Represent the sample space by a Euler diagram, and encircle the sample points corresponding to observing two heads, event *A*, and observing at least one head, event *B*. (b) What is the probability of event *A*? (c) What is the probability of event *B*?

6. A class contains six psychology (P) majors, one sociology (S) major, and three history (H) majors. Assume that no students have double majors. (a) Represent the sample space by an Euler diagram. (b) If a student is selected at random, what is the probability that the student will be a psychology major? (c) What is the probability that the student will be a psychology or a sociology major?

7. Determine (a) the probability that a man chosen randomly from a group of 10 men is a psychologist if the group contains three psychologists and (b) the probability that you will win a car if you buy 6 raffle tickets and 10,000 tickets are sold.

8. A package of M&M's contains the following distribution of colored chocolate candies: four green (G), five red (R), six brown (Br), one orange (O), two blue (B), and seven yellow (Y). (a) Represent the sample space of the 25 events by a Euler diagram and encircle events *G* and *B*. (b) What is the probability of reaching into the M&M bag and drawing a green or blue colored candy?

9. Terms to remember
   a. Subjective-personalistic view of probability
   b. Classical or logical view of probability
   c. Empirical-relative frequency view of probability
   d. Experiment
   e. Simple and compound events
   f. Euler diagram
   g. Sample point
   h. Sample space

7.3 PROBABILITY OF COMBINED EVENTS

This section describes rules for determining the probabilities of combined events. For example, we might want to know the probability that the outcome of an experiment will be event *A* or *B* or both *A* and *B*. We denote the probability of the event *A* or *B* or both *A* and *B* by *p(A or B)*.[4] Alternatively, we might want to know the probability that the outcome will be both *A* and *B*. We denote this probability by *p(A and B)*.[5]

The **union** of two events *A* and *B* is the set of elements that belong to *A* or to *B* or to both *A* and *B*. As we will see, the probability of the union of two events, *p(A or B)*, is computed by using the addition rule of probability. The **intersection** of two events *A* and *B* is the set of elements that belong to both *A* and *B*. We will see that the probability of the intersection of two events, *p(A and B)*, is computed by using the multiplication rule.

Addition Rule of Probability

The **addition rule** states that the probability of the union of two events *A* and *B*, *p(A or B)*, is equal to

$$p(A \text{ or } B) = p(A) + p(B) - p(A \text{ and } B).$$

For example, let event *A* be an even number when a die is tossed and event *B*, a number less than 5. The events are represented in Figure 7.3-1. Their probabilities are determined by counting sample points: $p(A) = n_A/n_S = {}^3/_6$ and $p(B) = n_B/n_S = {}^4/_6$. The probability of event *A and B* is the ratio of the number of sample points that are examples of both *A* and *B* to the total number of sample points. In

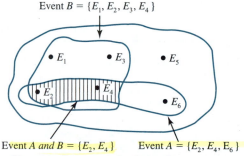

Event $B = \{E_1, E_2, E_3, E_4\}$

$\bullet E_1 \qquad \bullet E_3 \qquad \bullet E_5$

$\bullet E_2 \qquad \bullet E_4 \qquad \bullet E_6$

Event *A and B* = $\{E_2, E_4\}$ Event *A* = $\{E_2, E_4, E_6\}$

Figure 7.3-1. **Euler diagram for event *A*, observing an even number, and event *B*, observing a number less than 5. The intersection of *A and B* is the shaded area.**

[4] Some books use the Boolean algebraic symbol ∪ in place of *or*.

[5] Some books use the Boolean algebraic symbol ∩ in place of *and*.

TABLE 7.3-1.   Tabular Presentation of Information in Figure 7.3-1

		Event		
		A	*Not A*	
Event	*B*	*A and B* $= \{E_2, E_4\}$	*Not A and B* $= \{E_1, E_3\}$	$B = \{E_1, E_2, E_3, E_4\}$
	Not B	*A and Not B* $= \{E_6\}$	*Not A and Not B* $= \{E_5\}$	*Not B* $= \{E_5, E_6\}$
		$A = \{E_2, E_4, E_6\}$	*Not A* $= \{E_1, E_3, E_5\}$	

symbols, $p(A \text{ and } B) = n_{A \text{ and } B}/n_S = \frac{2}{6}$ because there are two simple events in both A and B and six in the sample space. Given this information,

$$p(A \text{ or } B) = p(A) + p(B) - p(A \text{ and } B)$$

$$= \frac{3}{6} + \frac{4}{6} - \frac{2}{6} = \frac{5}{6}.$$

Thus, the probability of observing an even number or a number less than 5 is $\frac{5}{6}$. In computing $p(A \text{ or } B)$, the value $p(A \text{ and } B) = \frac{2}{6}$ is subtracted from $p(A) + p(B)$ to avoid counting the simple events E_2 and E_4 twice, because they are contained in event A and in event B.

The information contained in Figure 7.3-1 is presented in Table 7.3-1. This mode of presentation is easier to interpret, especially when the number of events exceeds two.

The addition rule leads to another important rule: the complement rule.

For any event A, the event that A does not occur is called the **complement** of A and is written *Not A*. The probability that A does not occur, denoted by $p(Not A)$, is given by

$$p(Not A) = 1 - p(A).$$

For the sample space in Figure 7.3-1, the probability of not observing an even number, event A, or a number less than five, event B, is

$$p[Not (A \text{ or } B)] = 1 - p(A \text{ or } B) = 1 - \frac{5}{6} = \frac{1}{6}.$$

Addition Rule for Mutually Exclusive Events

Two events may contain no sample points in common, in which case the events are said to be **mutually exclusive** or **disjoint.** For example, consider the following events: observing an even number on the toss of a die, event A, and observing an

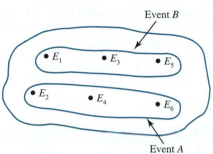

Event B

Event A

Figure 7.3-2. **Euler diagram for event *A*, observing an even number, and event *B*, observing an odd number. Since the intersection *A and B* contains no sample points, the events are mutually exclusive.**

odd number, event *B*. As shown in Figure 7.3-2, the intersection *A and B* contains no sample points, and hence *A* and *B* are mutually exclusive.

For mutually exclusive events, the addition rule is simplified because for this case $p(A \text{ and } B) = 0$. The addition rule $p(A \text{ or } B) = p(A) + p(B) - p(A \text{ and } B)$ becomes

$$p(A \text{ or } B) = p(A) + p(B).$$

The probability of observing an even number or an odd number in tossing a die is $p(A \text{ or } B) = \frac{3}{6} + \frac{3}{6} = 1$. Because the probability is 1, we know that when a die is tossed, one of the events must occur.

Events for which the probability of their union equals 1 are called **collectively exhaustive** or, simply, as is more common, **exhaustive.**

Addition Rule for Three Events

The addition rule can be extended to three or more events. For three events *A*, *B*, and *C*, the probability of *A or B or C* is given by

$$p(A \text{ or } B \text{ or } C) = p(A) + p(B) + p(C) - p(A \text{ and } B) - p(A \text{ and } C)$$
$$- p(B \text{ and } C) + p(A \text{ and } B \text{ and } C).$$

The rationale for the formula is apparent from the Euler diagram in Figure 7.3-3. If the events are mutually exclusive, the formula simplifies to

$$p(A \text{ or } B \text{ or } C) = p(A) + p(B) + p(C).$$

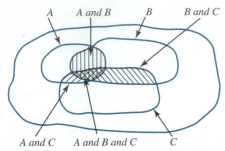

Figure 7.3-3. **Euler diagram illustrating terms in the formula *p(A or B or C)* = *p(A)* + *p(B)* + *p(C)* − *p(A and B)* − *p(A and C)* − *p(B and C)* + *p(A and B and C)*.**

Multiplication Rule of Probability

The multiplication rule is used to compute the probability of the joint occurrence, or intersection, of two or more events. For example, suppose that 100 psychology majors have been classified according to gender and class level. The number of students in each category is given in Table 7.3-2. If a student is selected by lottery, what is the probability that the student will be both a woman and a lowerclassman? As we will see, the multiplication rule lets us determine the probability that the student selected will be in the intersection *women and lowerclassmen*—that is, both a

TABLE 7.3-2. Number of Psychology Majors by Gender and Class Level

	Lowerclassmen, L	Upperclassmen, U	Marginal total
Women, W	10 $p(W \text{ and } L) = n_{W \text{ and } L} / n_S$ $= 10 / 100$ $= .10$	20	30 $p(W) = n_W / n_S$ $= 30 / 100$ $= .30$
Men, M	40	30	70 $p(M) = n_M / n_S$ $= 70 / 100$ $= .70$
Marginal total	50 $p(L) = n_L / n_S$ $= 50 / 100$ $= .50$	50 $p(U) = n_U / n_S$ $= 50 / 100$ $= .50$	100

woman and a lowerclassman. This information is different from that given by the addition rule, which tells us the probability that the student selected will be a *woman* or a *lowerclassman* or a *woman lowerclassman.*

Before presenting the multiplication rule, we need to discuss the concept of conditional probability. Two events often are related so that the probability of one event depends upon whether the other has or has not occurred. Consider these events: Your roommate reports that he feels bad, event A, and his temperature is 103, event B. The two events are obviously related because the probability of an elevated temperature, $p(B)$, is much higher if a person feels bad than if the person feels good. We refer to this type of relationship as a *conditional probability.*

The **conditional probability** of B given that A has occurred is denoted by $p(B|A)$ and is equal to

$$p(B|A) = p(A \text{ and } B)/p(A).$$

Similarly, the conditional probability of A given that B has occurred is

$$p(A|B) = p(A \text{ and } B)/p(B).$$

The vertical line $|$ in $(A|B)$ is read "given," or "given that."

The calculation of conditional probability will be illustrated using information in Table 7.3-2. The probability that a student selected by lottery is a woman, given that you know the student is a lowerclassman, is

$$p(W|L) = p(W \text{ and } L)/p(L) = (10/100)/(50/100) = .20.$$

Note that the condition of being a lowerclassman limits the outcome to the left column of Table 7.3-2, which is a smaller sample space of size 50. The probability of selecting a woman is a subset of this smaller sample space, namely, 10 events out of 50. Thus, as we saw earlier, the probability of selecting a woman if you know that the student is a lowerclassman is $.10/.50 = .20$. However, the probability of selecting a woman in the absence of information about class level is $p(W) = {}^{30}/_{100} = .30$ (see Table 7.3-2). The events W and L are related because a knowledge of one event, class level, affects the probability of the other, selecting a woman. In this example, $p(W|L) = .20$, but $p(W) = .30$.

The **multiplication rule** can be stated now. Given two events A and B, the probability of obtaining both A and B jointly is the product of the probability of obtaining one event, say A, times the conditional probability of the other event, B, given that A has occurred. Stated symbolically, the probability of the intersection of the events A and B, *p(A and B)*, is given by

$$p(A \text{ and } B) = p(A)p(B|A)$$
$$= p(B)p(A|B).$$

For the events defined in Table 7.3-2, the probability of selecting a student who is both a woman and a lowerclassman is

$$p(W \text{ and } L) = p(W)p(L \mid W) = p(W)\frac{p(W \text{ and } L)}{P(W)}$$

$$= .30\,\frac{.10}{.30} = .10$$

$$= p(L)p(W \mid L) = p(L)\frac{p(W \text{ and } L)}{P(L)}$$

$$= .50\,\frac{.10}{.50} = .10.$$

The multiplication rule may seem unnecessarily complicated because if the intersection (A *and* B) is known, the rule is not needed. However, sometimes only a **marginal probability,** $p(A)$ or $p(B)$, and a conditional probability, $p(A \mid B)$ or $p(B \mid A)$, are known. For example, suppose that we want to know the probability of drawing two aces from a 52-card deck. On the first draw, the probability of drawing an ace is $p(ace \text{ on first draw}) = \frac{4}{52}$. If an ace is drawn on the first draw and is not replaced in the deck, the conditional probability of drawing an ace on the second draw is $p(ace \text{ on second draw} \mid ace \text{ on first draw}) = \frac{3}{51}$. The probability of drawing two aces on two draws without replacement is

$$p(two\ aces) = p(ace \text{ on first draw}) \times p(ace \text{ on second draw} \mid ace \text{ on first draw})$$

$$= \left(\frac{4}{52}\right)\left(\frac{3}{51}\right) \cong .0045.$$

Multiplication Rule for Statistically Independent Events

Two events A and B are **statistically independent** if the probability of one event's occurring is unaffected by the occurrence of the other. Stated symbolically, A and B are statistically independent if and only if $p(A \mid B) = p(A)$.

If this equality holds, it must also be true that

$$p(B \mid A) = p(B).$$

The events $p(W)$ and $p(L)$ in Table 7.3-2 are not statistically independent because $p(W \mid L) = .20$ is not equal to $p(W) = .30$. We can easily construct an example in which the events are independent. Consider an experiment in which a fair coin is tossed and a fair die is rolled. Because the coin can land in one of two ways, H or T,

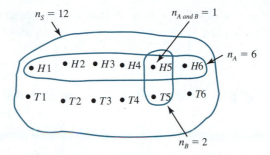

Figure 7.3-4. **Euler diagram for event A, observing a head, and event B, observing a 5, when a coin and die are tossed.**

and the die, in one of six ways, 1, . . . , 6, the possible outcomes are H1, T1, H2, T2, . . . , H6, T6. The sample space for the experiment is shown in Figure 7.3-4. Let event A be a head and B a 5. The probabilities required to demonstrate independence of A and B are

$$p(A) = n_A/n_S = {}^6\!/_{12} = {}^1\!/_2$$

and

$$p(A\,|\,B) = (n_{A\ and\ B}/n_S)/(n_B/n_S) = n_{A\ and\ B}/n_B = {}^1\!/_2.$$

Because $p(A) = p(A\,|\,B)$, the events are statistically independent; this agrees with our intuition that what happens on the roll of a die can in no way affect the outcome of tossing a coin.

For statistically independent events, the multiplication rule is simplified because

$$p(A\,|\,B) = p(A)$$

and

$$p(B\,|\,A) = p(B).$$

The multiplication rule

$$p(A \text{ and } B) = p(A)p(B\,|\,A)$$
$$= p(B)p(A\,|\,B)$$

becomes

$$p(A \text{ and } B) = p(A)p(B).$$

As we just saw, the probability of observing a head and a 5 are independent; hence, the probability of their joint occurrence is $p(A \text{ and } B) = (1/2)(1/6) = 1/12$.

Multiplication Rule for Three Events

If we want to find the joint probability of three events, the multiplication rule is

$$p(A \text{ and } B \text{ and } C) = p(A)p(B|A)p(C|A \text{ and } B).$$

To illustrate, suppose that we have a box containing five marbles, each a different color: blue, green, red, yellow, and orange. Three marbles are selected at random from the box, one at a time. Once drawn, a marble is not replaced. This procedure is called **sampling without replacement.** Consider the following events:

A—first marble is blue
B—second marble is green
C—third marble is red

According to the classical view, $p(A) = n_A/n_S = 1/5$. If a blue marble is selected first, then four remain—one of which is green. The probability of selecting a green marble given that the first is blue is $p(B|A) = 1/4$. Similarly, the probability of selecting a red marble given that a blue one and a green one have been selected is $p(C|A \text{ and } B) = 1/3$. The joint probability for A, B, and C is $p(A \text{ and } B \text{ and } C) = 1/5 \times 1/4 \times 1/3 = 1/60$.

If the marble sampled from the box is replaced after each draw (**sampling with replacement**), the multiplication rule for three events is $p(A \text{ and } B \text{ and } C) = p(A)p(B)p(C)$. This follows because the selection of the first marble does not decrease the number of sample points in the sample space, and hence $p(B|A) = p(B)$ and $p(C|A \text{ and } B) = p(C)$. If we had replaced each marble after it was drawn from the box, the joint probability for events A, B, and C would be $p(A \text{ and } B \text{ and } C) = 1/5 \times 1/5 \times 1/5 = 1/125$.

Common Errors in Applying the Rules of Probability

The probability rules described in this section often are used incorrectly. Some of the more common errors are the following:

1. Using the addition rule for mutually exclusive events, $p(A \text{ or } B) = p(A) + p(B)$, when the events are not mutually exclusive. For example, let event A be the classification "psychology major" and event B, "biology major." If $p(A) = .20$ and $p(B) = .15$, one might conclude that the probabil-

ity of a student's being either a psychology or a biology major is $p(A\ or\ B) = .20 + .15 = .35$. This is incorrect because some students have a double major, and these students have been counted twice—once in computing $p(A)$ and again in computing $p(B)$. Assume that $p(A\ and\ B) = .03$; the correct probability is given by $p(A\ or\ B) = p(A) + p(B) - p(A\ and\ B) = .20 + .15 - .03 = .32$.

2. Using the addition rule when the multiplication rule should be used, and vice versa. For example, on the toss of a die the probability of observing a 3, event A, or a 5, event B, is given by $p(A\ or\ B) = p(A) + p(B) = \frac{1}{6} + \frac{1}{6} = \frac{2}{6}$ and not by $p(A\ and\ B) = p(A)p(B) = (\frac{1}{6})(\frac{1}{6}) = \frac{1}{36}$.

3. Using the multiplication rule for statistically independent events, $p(A\ and\ B) = p(A)p(B)$, when the events are not statistically independent. Suppose the probability of seeing an advertisement for a product, event A, is .40 and the probability of buying the product, event B, is .30. If the dependency between A and B is ignored, the incorrect probability of both seeing an advertisement and buying the product is $p(A\ and\ B) = (.40)(.30) = .12$. The correct probability takes into account the conditional probability of buying the product given that the ad has been seen, $p(B\,|\,A) = .50$, so that $p(A\ and\ B) = p(A)p(B\,|\,A) = (.40)(.50) = .20$.

CHECK YOUR UNDERSTANDING OF SECTION 7.3

10. A standard deck of cards contains 52 cards: 10 number cards of each suit (counting the ace as a 1) and three face cards of each suit. If a card is drawn from the deck at random, what is the probability that it will be (a) an ace, (b) a heart, (c) an ace or a heart or both, (d) a heart or a spade, (e) a face card, (f) a card less than 5, (g) not an ace?
11. Events A, B, and C are mutually exclusive and exhaustive, each having a probability of $\frac{1}{3}$. Determine
    a. $p(A\ or\ B)$
    b. $p(A\ or\ B\ or\ C)$
    c. $p(Not\ A)$
    d. $p[Not\ (A\ or\ B)]$
12. Events A and B are independent; $p(A) = .6$ and $p(B) = .8$. What is the probability that (a) both will occur? (b) Neither will occur? (c) One or the other or both will occur?
13. Recent highway accident statistics show that 10% of all automobile accidents and half of all fatal automobile accidents are caused by drunken drivers. Four in 1,000 reported accidents are fatal. (a) Fill in the table with the appropriate probabilities. (b) What is the joint probability that a fatal accident is caused by a drunken driver?

	Fatal, F	Nonfatal, *Not F*	
Drunken Driver, D	$p(D \text{ and } F) =$	$p(D \text{ and Not } F) =$	$p(D) =$
Other Cause, O	$p(O \text{ and } F) =$	$p(O \text{ and Not } F) =$	$p(O) =$
	$p(F) =$	$p(Not\ F) =$	

14. You ask your roommate to mail a letter. The probability that she will mail it is .98. The probability that the post office will fail to deliver it, given that it was mailed, is .15. What is the probability that the letter will be mailed and the post office will fail to deliver it?

15. Exercise 8 in Section 7.2 described the color of the candies in a package of M&M's. If a candy is drawn at random from the package, what is the probability that it will be (a) green, (b) red or yellow, (c) not green, and (d) colorless? After eating the first candy, you draw another from the package. What is the probability that you have (e) eaten a blue candy and drawn an orange candy, (f) eaten a blue candy and drawn an orange or brown candy?

16. A survey of 100 students taking courses in algebra (A), history (H), and psychology (P) revealed the following enrollments: $A = 65$, $H = 37$, $P = 59$, A and $H = 17$, A and $P = 44$, H and $P = 14$, and $p(P | A \text{ and } H) = .8235$. (a) Represent the sample space by a Euler diagram. If a student is selected at random, what is the probability that he or she is taking (b) all three subjects, (c) algebra but not psychology, (d) history but not algebra, (e) psychology but not algebra or history?

17. Terms to remember

a. Union	b. Intersection
c. Addition rule	d. Addition rule for mutually exclusive events
e. Complement rule	f. Mutually exclusive events
g. Disjoint events	h. Exhaustive events
i. Conditional probability	j. Multiplication rule
k. Marginal probability	l. Statistical independence
m. Multiplication rule for mutually exclusive events	n. Sampling with (without) replacement

7.4 COUNTING SIMPLE EVENTS

Listing all the simple events in an experiment can be tedious. Even a small experiment, such as recording the outcome of tossing three dice, has a large sample

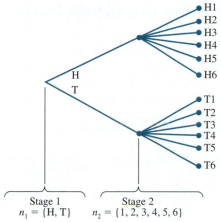

Figure 7.4-1. **Tree diagram of possible outcomes of tossing a coin and then a die.**

space—in this case $6 \times 6 \times 6 = 216$ sample points. Fortunately, it is not necessary to enumerate simple events to compute probabilities. The required information can be determined using the counting rules discussed in this section.

Fundamental Counting Rule[6]

Suppose that an event can occur in n_1 ways and a second event, in n_2 ways and that each of the first event's n_1 ways can be followed by any of the second's n_2 ways. Then, according to the **fundamental counting rule,** event 1 followed by event 2 can occur in $n_1 n_2$ ways.

To illustrate, suppose that we toss a coin and then a die. The number of possible outcomes of the experiment is

$$n_1 n_2 = (2)(6) = 12$$

because a coin can land heads or tails ($n_1 = 2$) and a die has six faces ($n_2 = 6$). The simple events are enumerated in the tree diagram of Figure 7.4-1.

The fundamental counting rule can be extended to $k > 2$ events. If there are k events (event 1 having n_1 outcomes, followed by event 2 having n_2 outcomes, and so forth), the outcome can occur in $n_1 n_2 \cdots n_k$ ways. For example, the number of possible outcomes of tossing three dice and a coin is $6 \times 6 \times 6 \times 2 = 432$.

---

[6] Also called the **multiplication principle.**

Permutation of *n* Objects Taken *n* at a Time, $_nP_n$

Suppose that we have three distinct objects and we want to find the number of different ordered sequences in which the objects can be arranged. For example, in how many ordered sequences can the letters *A*, *B*, and *C* be arranged? The answer is six: *ABC, ACB, BAC, BCA, CAB, CBA.* Arranging *n* objects in an ordered sequence is equivalent to putting them into a long box with *n* ordered compartments. The first

1	2	3	...	*n*

| *n* ways | *n* − 1 ways | *n* − 2 ways | | 1 way |

compartment can be filled in any of *n* ways, which uses up one of the objects; the second compartment can be filled in any of *n* − 1 ways, . . . , and the last compartment, in only one way. Applying the fundamental counting rule, the number of ordered arrangements of *n* objects is the product $n(n − 1)(n − 2) \cdots 1$. The quantity $n(n − 1)(n − 2) \cdots 1$ is denoted by the symbol *n*!, which is read "*n* factorial."

> An ordered sequence of *n* distinct objects taken all together is called a **permutation** of the objects. The total number of such permutations, denoted by $_nP_n$, is given by
>
> $$_nP_n = n! = n(n − 1)(n − 2) \cdots 1.$$

The symbol $_nP_n$ is read "the permutation of *n* objects taken *n* at a time."

Suppose that we are doing a taste preference experiment in which a panel of 10 experts rates five nondairy coffee creamers. We want to control for sequence effects — the effects on an expert's judgment of presenting the five coffee creamers in a particular order. One way to control for sequence effects is to present the five coffee creamers in all possible sequences to each judge. In how many ordered sequences can coffee prepared with the five creamers be presented? The answer is 5! = 5(4)(3)(2)(1) = 120. Finding 10 experts willing to sit through the 120 tasting sequences is probably impossible. We need to consider alternative designs. Another and more practical way to control for sequence effects is to present the coffee creamers in 12 of the 120 sequences to one expert, in 12 different sequences to another expert, and so on. Following this procedure, all 120 of the sequences would be used, but each of the 10 expert judges would receive only 12 sequences.

Permutation of n Objects Taken r at a Time, $_nP_r$

The number of permutations of n distinct objects taken r at a time, where $r \leq n$ is denoted[7] by $_nP_r$ and is equal to $n(n-1)(n-2) \cdots (n-r+1)$.

For example, the number of ordered sequences of five letters, *A, B, C, D, E*, taken three at a time, is $_5P_3 = 5(5-1)(5-3+1) = 5(4)(3) = 60$. The rationale behind the formula is as follows. Consider the box:

1	2	3
n ways	$n-1$ ways	$n-(r-1)$ ways

with $r = 3$ ordered compartments. The first compartment can be filled in any of $n = 5$ ways and the second, in $n - 1 = 4$ ways. When we come to the $r = 3$rd compartment, we have used $r - 1 = 2$ of the n letters so that $n - (r - 1) = n - r + 1 = 3$ letters are left to fill the last compartment. According to the fundamental counting rule, the number of ordered sequences is the product $n(n-1) \cdots (n-r+1)$. Therefore, the number of ordered sequences of the five letters taken three at a time is $5(4)(3) = 60$.

The formula for computing $_nP_r$, $n(n-1)(n-2) \cdots (n-r+1)$, is often written $n!/(n-r)!$.[8] To see why $n(n-1)(n-2) \cdots (n-r+1)$ is equal to $n!/(n-r)!$, note that the next term in the sequence $n(n-1)(n-2) \cdots (n-r+1)$ is $(n-r)$, followed by $(n-r-1) \cdots (3)(2)(1)$. The terms $(n-r)(n-r-1) \cdots (3)(2)(1)$ can be denoted by $(n-r)!$. Now—to see why the formula for $_nP_r$ can be expressed as $n!/(n-r)!$—begin by examining the following figure that shows the relationships among $n!$, $_nP_r$, and $(n-r)!$.

$$\overbrace{\underbrace{[n(n-1)(n-2) \cdots (n-r+1)]}_{_nP_r} \; \underbrace{[(n-r)(n-r-1) \cdots (3)(2)(1)]}_{(n-r)!}}^{n!}$$

If we multiply $_nP_r$ by the ratio $(n-r)!/(n-r)!$, we haven't changed the value of $_nP_r$. It follows from the relationships shown in the figure that

$$_nP_r = \frac{_nP_r(n-r)!}{(n-r)!} = \frac{n!}{(n-r)!} \, .$$

because $_nP_r \, (n-r)! = n!$.

The taste-preference experiment described earlier could be performed using the method of paired comparisons. In this method an expert sips first one and then a

---

[7] Also denoted by P^n_r, $P(n, r)$, and $(n)_r$.

[8] In computations involving $(n-r)!$, remember that $1! = 1$ and that by definition $0! = 1$.

second cup of coffee prepared with two of the creamers and indicates a preference. The procedure is repeated until each creamer has been compared twice with every other creamer, once in the first cup sipped and once in the second cup. In how many ordered sequences can five creamers be presented, two at a time? The answer is given by

$$_5P_2 = 5(5 - 2 + 1) = 5(4) = 20$$

or

$$_5P_2 = \frac{5!}{(5 - 2)!} = \frac{(5)(4)(3)(2)(1)}{(3)(2)(1)} = 20.$$

The method of paired comparisons would require each expert to make a total of 20 judgments—10 judgments in which a particular creamer in a pair is in the first cup sipped and 10 in which the creamer is in the second cup sipped.

Permutation of n Objects When Some of the Objects Are Alike, $_nP_{r_1, r_2, \ldots, r_k}$

Suppose that we have n objects that can be divided into k subsets such that each subset contains like objects, but the objects in any given subset are different from those in the other subsets. Let r_1 be the number of like objects of one kind and r_2 be the number of like objects of another kind, and so on for the k subsets, with $r_1 + r_2 + \cdots + r_k = n$.

The number of permutations of n objects in which $r_1, r_2, \ldots, r_k$ are alike is denoted by $_nP_{r_1, r_2, \ldots, r_k}$ and is equal to $n!/(r_1! \, r_2! \cdots r_k!)$.

For example, the number of ordered sequences of the 10 letters in *PSYCHOLOGY* is

$$_{10}P_{1, 1, 2, 1, 1, 2, 1, 1} = \frac{10!}{1! \, 1! \, 2! \, 1! \, 1! \, 2! \, 1! \, 1!} = 907,200.$$

Combination of n Objects Taken r at a Time, $_nC_r$

Sometimes we are not interested in the number of ordered sequences or permutations of n objects taken r at a time, but instead in the number of different combinations of r objects that can be selected from n distinct objects when order is ignored. This is referred to as the combination of n objects taken r at a time and is denoted[9] by $_nC_r$. The formula for $_nC_r$ is

$$_nC_r = \frac{n!}{r! \, (n - r)!}.$$

[9] Also denoted by C_r^n, $C(n, r)$, and $\binom{n}{r}$.

The rationale for the formula is as follows. Consider four letters A, B, C, and D taken two at a time. The number of ordered sequences is $_4P_2 = 4!/(4 - 2)! = 12$. But suppose that we don't want to distinguish AB from BA, BC from CB, and so on. We note that any sequence of $r = 2$ objects can be permuted in $r! = 2(1) = 2$ ways. If we want to ignore the order of the r objects in $_nP_r$, we can divide $_nP_r$ by $r!$, which gives

$$_nC_r = \frac{_nP_r}{r!} = \frac{\dfrac{n!}{(n - r)!}}{r!} = \frac{n!}{r!\,(n - r)!}.$$

The number of different sets of $r = 2$ letters that can be selected from $n = 4$ letters, A, B, C, D, is

$$_4C_2 = \frac{4!}{2!\,(4 - 2)!} = \frac{4(3)(2)(1)}{2(1)[2(1)]} = 6.$$

The six sets are as follows: AB, AC, AD, BC, BD, CD. Because the order of letters in a pair is of no interest, the six could just as well have been written BA, CA, AD, CB, BD, CD.

The combination of n objects taken r at a time will be used in Chapter 8 to develop the binomial distribution, which describes the possible outcomes of a particular kind of experiment.

CHECK YOUR UNDERSTANDING OF SECTION 7.4

18. Determine the number of possible outcomes for the following: (a) Three coins are tossed. (b) Four dice are rolled. (c) A coin and a die are tossed.

19. If there are three candidates for governor and five for mayor, in how many ways can the two offices be filled?

20. The four Russian novels *War and Peace, Anna Karenina, Crime and Punishment,* and *The Brothers Karamazov* are to be placed on a shelf. In how many ordered sequences can the books be arranged?

21. In how many different ways can 10 people be seated four at a time on a bench with only four seats?

22. How many ordered arrangements can be made for the letters in the word *STATISTICS*?

23. Given nine areas from which to choose, in how many ways can a student select (a) a major-minor area, (b) a major and first and second minors, (c) a major and two minors if it is not necessary to designate the order of the minors?

24. Terms to remember
     a. Fundamental counting rule   b. Permutation
     c. n factorial   d. Combination

7.5 SUMMARY

Probability is an abstract mathematical concept that can be defined in a number of ways. The three most useful views of probability are the subjective-personalistic view; the classical, or logical, view; and the empirical relative-frequency view.

Our interest in probability is pragmatic: We want to make statements about the likelihood of observing various outcomes in experiments. An experiment is any well-defined act or process that leads to an outcome. An outcome is either a compound event that can be decomposed into simple events, such as observing an even number on the toss of a die, or a simple event that can't be decomposed. If we assign to each simple event a point called a sample point, the possible outcomes of an experiment can be represented by a Euler diagram. The set of all sample points is called the sample space, S.

Whatever one's view, probability is based on a system of definitions and operations pertaining to a sample space. If S is the sample space for an experiment and n_S is the number of sample points in S, we can associate with each event E_i a real number called the probability of E_i or $p(E_i)$, satisfying the following properties:

1. $0 \leq p(E_i) \leq 1$, for all i
2. $\sum_{i=1}^{n_s} p(E_i) = 1$
3. $p(S) = 1$

These properties describe probabilities, but they don't tell us how to compute them. If we adopt the classical view, the probability of an event A is computed from the formula $p(A) = n_A/n_S$, where n_A is the number of events favoring A and n_S is the total number of equally likely events in the sample space S. This view of probability is based on logical analysis. We reason that an experiment has n_S possible outcomes, the outcomes are equally likely, and n_A of the outcomes favor A. If our reasoning is correct, the value we compute for $p(A)$ will agree closely with that based on the relative-frequency view.

According to the relative-frequency view, the probability of event A is the number approached by n_A/n as the total number of observations, n, approaches infinity. The estimate n_A/n is based on experience because it is computed for a sample from the population of possible experiments. On the average, the larger the sample, the closer the estimate is to the true probability.

Probabilities for combined events can be computed by the addition rule and the multiplication rule. The addition rule states that the probability that an event will be *A* or *B* or both is

$$p(A \text{ or } B) = p(A) + p(B) - p(A \text{ and } B).$$

For mutually exclusive events, $p(A \text{ and } B) = 0$, and the rule simplifies to

$$p(A \text{ or } B) = p(A) + p(B).$$

The multiplication rule states that the probability that an event will be both *A* and *B* is

$$p(A \text{ and } B) = p(A)p(B|A) = p(B)p(A|B).$$

For statistically independent events, $p(B|A) = p(B)$ and $p(A|B) = p(A)$, and the rule simplifies to

$$p(A \text{ and } B) = p(A)p(B).$$

The number of simple events in an experiment can be determined either by enumeration, which is the hard way, or by using counting rules, which is the easy way. The key rules are as follows:

1. Fundamental counting rule. If there are *k* events, event 1 followed by event 2, . . . , followed by the *k*th event, the outcome can occur in $n_1 n_2 \cdots n_k$ ways.
2. Permutation of *n* objects taken *n* at a time. The number of ordered sequences of *n* distinct objects taken all together is $_nP_n = n! = n(n-1)(n-2) \cdots 1$.
3. Permutation of *n* objects taken *r* at a time. The number of ordered sequences of *n* distinct objects taken *r* at a time is $_nP_r = n!/(n-r)!$.
4. Permutation of *n* objects when some of the objects are alike. The number of ordered sequences of *n* objects in which $r_1, r_2, \ldots, r_k$ are alike is $_nP_{r_1, r_2, \ldots, r_k} = n!/(r_1! \, r_2! \cdots r_k!)$.
5. Combination of *n* objects taken *r* at a time. The number of different combinations of *r* objects that can be selected from *n* distinct objects when order is ignored is $_nC_r = n!/[r! \, (n-r)!]$.

REVIEW EXERCISES FOR CHAPTER 7

1. Why is subjective probability difficult to incorporate into a formal decision-making process?
2. What distinguishes Bayesian inference from traditional classical methods?
3. (a) According to the classical view, what is the probability of observing a number less than 5 on the toss of a die? (b) What assumptions were required to arrive at the answer?

4. (a) What is the probability of drawing the king of hearts from a well-shuffled deck of 52 cards? (b) What assumptions were required to arrive at the answer?

5. (a) According to the relative-frequency view, what is the probability that a head will occur on the next toss of a fair coin if a head appeared on 54 of the last 100 tosses? (b) According to the classical view, what is the probability that a head will occur?

6. An experiment consists of tossing two dice, one green and one red, and recording the outcome. (a) Represent the sample space by a Euler diagram, and encircle the sample points corresponding to observing a 7 as the sum of the dice. (b) What is the probability that the sum of two dice is 7? (c) What is the probability that the sum of two dice is less than 5?

7. A fair die is rolled once. You win $5 if the outcome is even, event A, or if it is divisible by 3, event B. (a) Represent the sample space by a Euler diagram and encircle events A and B. (b) What is the probability of winning the $5?

8. The following are properties of probabilities. In your own words state what each property means. (a) $0 \leq p(E_i) \leq 1$ for all i. (b) $\sum_{i=1}^{n} p(E_i) = 1$. (c) $p(S) = 1$.

9. Events A, B, C, and D are mutually exclusive and exhaustive, each having a probability of $1/4$. Determine
   a. $p(A \text{ or } C)$.
   b. $p(A \text{ or } B \text{ or } C \text{ or } D)$.
   c. $p[Not(A \text{ or } C)]$.
   d. $p[Not(A \text{ or } B \text{ or } C)]$.

10. For the data in the table, determine whether the events "attend college" and "man" are statistically independent.

	Attend college		
	Yes	No	
Man	.30	.20	.50
Woman	.10	.40	.50
	.40	.60	1.00

11. Data were obtained on the incidence of rheumatic disease and the presence of grimacing in schizophrenic patients. In a sample of 1942 patients, 6% had a known history of rheumatic disease, 21.8% grimaced, and 1.8% had a history of both rheumatic disease and grimacing. (a) Fill in the table with the appropriate probabilities. (b) What is the probability of grimacing, given a history of rheumatic

disease? (c) Are grimacing and rheumatic disease statistically independent?

	Grimacing, *G*	No grimacing, *No G*
History of rheumatic disease, *D*		
No history of rheumatic disease, *No D*		

12. A smoker has 10 pipes, three of which are meerschaums. Of his six curved-stem pipes, two are meerschaums. He asks his son to bring him a curved-stem meerschaum. Because the boy doesn't know a meerschaum from other curved-stem pipes, he picks up a curved-stem pipe at random. (a) Fill in the table with the appropriate probabilities. (b) What is the probability that the son picked the right pipe?

	Meerschaum, *M*	Other Kind of Pipe, *O*	
Curved Stem, *C*	*p(C and M)* =	*p(C and O)* =	*p(C)* =
Straight Stem, *S*	*p(S and M)* =	*p(S and O)* =	*p(S)* =
	p(M) =	*p(O)* =	

13. One hundred students are enrolled in a university course. Fifty are men (*M*) and 50 are women (*W*). Of the 100 students, 60 are undergraduates (*U*) and 40 are graduate students (*G*). Of these 100 students, 20 are both men and undergraduates. For a student selected at random from the class, compute the following probabilities. [*Hint:* $p(U) = p(M \text{ and } U) + p(W \text{ and } U)$. It is helpful to construct a 2×2 table and fill in the information that is known.]
    a. $p(W \text{ and } U)$
    b. $p(W \text{ and } G)$
    c. $p(M \text{ and } G)$
    d. $p(M|U)$
    e. $p(W|G)$

14. A family of three goes to a photography studio to have a group picture made. They consider a picture good only if everyone in it looks good. Suppose the probability that any one person looks good is

$p(G_i) = 5$. Assume independence. (a) What is the probability that the picture will be good? (b) If two pictures are made, what is the probability that at least one of them will be good?

15. A drawer contains six intelligence tests (I), four personality tests (P), and five aptitude tests (A). If three tests are drawn randomly from the drawer, what is the probability that one of each test will be drawn if each test (a) is replaced in the drawer after it is drawn, (b) is not replaced after it is drawn?

16. A statistician who worked in operations research for the British Bomber Command during World War II determined that the probability that a member of a bomber crew sent on night raids over Germany would complete a standard tour of duty (30 missions) was equal to .30. (Suggested by Dyson, F. [1981]. *Disturbing the universe.* New York: Harper & Row.)

    a. What is the probability of a crewman not surviving ($p(Not\ S)$) a standard tour of duty?

    b. If successive tours of duty are treated as independent events, what is the probability of surviving two tours of duty?

    c. If successive tours of duty are treated as independent events, what is the probability of surviving the first tour of duty but not the second?

    d. If successive tours of duty are treated as independent events, what is the probability of not surviving three tours of duty?

17. A survey of 100 couples who had recently had marital counseling found that 80 of the couples reported that their relationship had improved (I). Sixty of the couples in the improved group had children (C). Assume that a couple is selected at random from the sample. Compute the following probabilities for that couple.

    a. $p(C|I)$

    b. $p(Not\ C|I)$

    c. Find two probabilities whose product gives $p(C\ and\ I)$.

18. The Greasy Spoon menu offers a choice of five appetizers, four salads, eight entrees, seven vegetables, and nine desserts. If a meal consists of one from each category, in how many ways can you select a dinner?

19. Two different psychology books, four different statistics books, and three different sociology books are to be arranged on a shelf. (a) In how many ordered sequences can the books be arranged? (b) If the books in each subject must be kept together, how many ordered sequences are possible?

20. In how many different ways can eight people be seated four at a time on a bench with only four seats?

21. How many ordered arrangements can be made for the letters in the word *DATA?*

22. If on a statistics examination consisting of 12 questions a student may omit five, in how many ways can the student select the problems to answer?

23. (a) In how many ways can six people be seated in a row at the head banquet table? (b) Suppose the people are to be seated in pairs at separate tables; in how many ways can they be seated if we consider the arrangement *AB* to be different from *BA?* (c) In how many ways if we consider *AB* to be equivalent to *BA?*

24. How many different committees of three men and four women can be formed from eight men and six women?

Chapter 8

Random Variables and Probability Distributions

8.1 RANDOM SAMPLING

Inferential statistics are used in reasoning from a sample to the population, that is, determining the characteristics of a population by observing a sample from the population. Some samples provide a sound basis for this process; others don't. The difference lies in the method by which the samples are selected.

> The method of drawing samples from a population so that every possible sample of a particular size has the same probability of being selected is called **random sampling** and the resulting sample, a **random sample.**

As the definition indicates, randomness is a property of the procedure rather than of the particular sample obtained. By the term *random sample* we mean simply a sample produced by a random sampling procedure. Any sampling method based on haphazard or purposeless choices such as enlisting volunteers, students enrolled in a psychology course, or every 10th name in an alphabetical list is called **nonrandom sampling.** The resulting samples, unlike random samples, don't provide a sound basis for determining the properties of populations.

As we will see, the inferential procedures described in subsequent chapters assume either random sampling from a population or random assignment of participants to the various conditions of an experiment.[1] If random sampling is used, there is no guarantee that a particular random sample will resemble the population, but in the long run, random samples are more likely to do so than nonrandom samples. Random assignment of experimental conditions to participants helps to ensure that systematic bias isn't introduced, as it would be, for example, if the experimental conditions that are expected to be superior were unwittingly assigned to the best participants.

Defining the Population

The first step in drawing a random sample is to identify the population. A **population** was defined in Chapter 1 as the collection of all people, objects, events, or observations having one or more specified characteristics. The population is identified when we specify the common characteristics—for example, this year's freshmen at Oregon State University or the outcomes of tossing a die for eternity. A single person, object, event, or observation is called an **element** of the population. The elements of the population can be **finite**[2] (limited) in number, as this year's freshmen

---

[1] Random assignment is discussed in Section 12.3.

[2] The probability of drawing a particular sample from a finite population is given by $1/{}_nC_r$ (see Section 7.4), where r denotes the sample size and n, the population size. For example, the probability for $r = 2$ and $n = 100$ is $1/\{100!/[2!(100 - 2)!]\} = 1/4{,}950$.

at Oregon State, or **infinite** in number, as the outcomes of tossing a die for eternity.

In practice, it is difficult to obtain a random sample from large populations like residents of a city or students at a university. There are two obstacles—obtaining an accurate list of the population elements and securing their participation once they have been selected. Some cities have lists of their residents, but unfortunately the information isn't updated frequently. Telephone directories are more current but exclude certain segments of society more often than others. The use of either list would introduce systematic bias into an experiment. A researcher faced with the choice between the two lists might prefer to redefine the population to fit the more current list. Instead of all city residents, the population is defined as all families in the telephone directory.

Sampling With or Without Replacement

After identifying the population, one must decide whether to sample with replacement or without replacement. In sampling **with replacement,** a sampled element is returned to the population so that it is available to be drawn again; in sampling **without replacement,** the element is not replaced and hence can be drawn only once.[3]

Sampling with replacement is rarely appropriate for the kinds of problems investigated in the behavioral and medical sciences and education because the sampled elements may be significantly and permanently altered by participating in the experiment. For example, once a child has learned an arithmetic unit, that child is no longer a naïve learner with respect to the unit; once tissue has been surgically removed, it can't be removed again should the organism happen to be sampled a second time.

Random Sampling Procedures

A variety of procedures can be used to draw a random sample. If the population is finite, each element can be identified on a slip of paper and the slips placed in a container, thoroughly mixed, and then drawn blindly from the container. If sampling with replacement is used, the identity of a selected element is noted and the slip is returned to the container; it is then available to be drawn again. The blind drawing-of-slips procedure seems simple enough, but it isn't always random—witness the December 1969 draft lottery for the Vietnam war. More slips containing

---

[3] The number of different samples of size r that can be drawn without replacement from a population of size n is $_nC_r$. The number of different samples with replacement is $n_1 n_2 \cdots n_r$.

birth dates in the later months of the year were drawn, much to the dismay of men with birthdays in September, October, November, and December who were sent off to fight an unpopular war. The problem with the sampling procedure was attributed to placing the slips in the bowl in chronological order and failing to shake them up thoroughly. Slips for the later months were the last ones in the bowl and the first ones drawn.

Another technique for drawing a random sample is to flip a coin or spin a roulette wheel, with the outcome of the random device determining whether an element is or isn't included in the sample. This procedure is practical for selecting a small sample but becomes tedious for larger ones.

Most researchers prefer to use a table of random numbers to draw their samples. Random number tables like the one in Appendix Table D.1 were prepared so that integers from 0 to 9 occur with about equal frequency and appear in the table in a random fashion. The digits in Appendix Table D.1 are in groups of two to make them easier to read, but the grouping has no other significance.

Using a Table of Random Numbers

Suppose that we want a random sample of 30 speech-therapy majors. A printout listing 273 majors constituting the population is obtained from the computer center, and the students are numbered serially from 001 to 273. We turn to Appendix Table D.1 and note that it has two pages with 50 rows and 25 columns each. To decide where to begin in the table we close our eyes and drop our pencil on the table. Suppose the pencil lands on the second page with the point closest to the first number in row 21 and column 13. The numbers reading from left to right are 22 00 20 35 55. . . . We let the first number, 2, identify the table page on which we begin (we had numbered the pages 1 and 2, so we were looking for a one-digit number between 1 and 2); the next two digits, 20, identify the row in which we begin (in this case we are looking for a two-digit number between 1 and 50); and the next two digits, 02, the column (here we are looking for a two-digit number between 1 and 25). Having previously decided to read the numbers from left to right, although any sequence can be used, we proceed to draw our sample. We begin on page 2, row 20, and column 2 and read numbers in groups of three until we obtain 30 numbers between 001 and 273, inclusive. The first eight numbers from the table are 644, 359, 989, 877, 876, 807, 915, 167. We ignore the first seven numbers because they are not between 001 and 273 and take as our first sample element the student identified as 167. To sample without replacement, we ignore numbers after their first appearance. The students corresponding to the 30 numbers between 001 and 273, inclusive, compose the sample.

In sampling from a list with many pages, such as a telephone directory or a student directory, it isn't necessary to number each population element if the number of names on each page is about the same. Instead of numbering each name, we number each page and each position on the page. To select a sample element, pairs of numbers are drawn from a random number table; the first number identifies the directory page and the second, the position of the element on the page. Another procedure, called **systematic sampling,** is sometimes used to sample from a list. It involves sampling every nth element, say every 20th person, in the list. Despite the simplicity of this procedure, it can't be recommended because it doesn't satisfy the definition of random sampling.

CHECK YOUR UNDERSTANDING OF SECTION 8.1

1. List the steps involved in drawing a random sample.
2. Drawing a random sample from a very large population is difficult. What are the problems?
3. (a) How many different samples of size 5 can be drawn without replacement from a population of size 50? (b) How many different samples of size 5 can be drawn with replacement from a population of size 50?
4. A sample of four supermarkets is to be selected from a total of eight in a small town. (a) How many different random samples without replacement can be drawn? (b) What is the probability that a given sample will be selected? (c) How many different random samples with replacement can be drawn?
5. (a) Use the table of random numbers in Appendix D to draw two random samples of 10 students from the following population. For one sample use sampling with replacement and for the other, sampling without replacement. (b) Describe in detail how you used the table.

Helen	Sally	Dean	Steve	Joe	Jim
Mike	Betty	David	Kris	Jack	Jane
Chuck	John	Tom	Bud	Kristina	Rita

6. Use the table of random numbers in Appendix D to draw a random sample without replacement of 30 students from the Student Database in Appendix E. (a) List the ID No., Stat Grade, and GPA for each person in your sample. Compute the mean of the variables labeled Stat Grade and GPA. (b) Compute the correlation between Stat Grade and GPA. (c) Develop a regression equation to predict Stat Grade from a knowledge of GPA. (d) If you have access to a computer and suitable software, develop a multiple regression equation for predicting Stat Grade from GPA and Math Test. How much does the addition of Math Test improve the prediction of Stat Grade?
7. Terms to remember
   a. Random and nonrandom sampling
   b. Population

   c. Element
   d. Sampling with or without replacement
   e. Random number table
   f. Systematic sampling

8.2 RANDOM VARIABLES AND THEIR DISTRIBUTIONS

Random Variables

In rolling a pair of dice we can observe the total number of dots; in tossing a coin two times, the total number of heads; in observing a naïve rat in a three-choice T maze, the total number of incorrect turns. The variable, number of dots or number of heads or number of incorrect turns, is called a **random variable** because it is quantitative and its value for a particular experiment is determined by chance. In the dice example, the random variable, number of dots, can assume values of 2, . . . , 12; in the coin example, the random variable can assume values of 0, 1, or 2 heads; in the T-maze example, the random variable can assume values of 0, 1, 2, or 3 errors. Random variables usually are denoted by a capital letter toward the end of the alphabet, for example X, Y, or Z. It helps to think of a random variable as the name for the number associated with the outcome of a random experiment before the experiment is performed. Performing the experiment converts the random variable into a specific number.

You may be wondering, why the fancy name? How does a random variable differ from just a plain old variable? We can contrast the two kinds of variables as follows:

1. The variable X is a name for any one of a set of permissible values.
2. The random variable X is a name for any one of a set of permissible numerical values of a random experiment.

Let's pursue the meaning of a random variable a bit farther. In Section 7.2 we saw that all the possible outcomes of a random experiment can be represented by points in a sample space. A random variable associates one and only one numerical value with each point; hence, in the language of the mathematician, a random variable is a **function.** To understand this, recall from your algebra course that a function consists of two sets of elements and a rule that assigns to each element in the first set one and only one element in the second set. The definition of a function is quite general; $\{(a, 1), (b, 5), (c, 6)\}$ is a function, as are $\{(Dave, tall), (Chuck, medium), (Joe, medium)\}$ and $\{(No\ errors, 0), (One\ error, 1), (Two\ errors, 2), (Three\ errors, 3)\}$. More simply stated, a function is a set of ordered pairs of elements, no two of which have the same first element. If the second element of a pair is a number, the function is said to be numerically valued. A random variable associates one and only one number with each point in a sample space; thus, it is a numerically valued function defined over a sample space. Most readers will find the following definition easier to remember: A random variable is a numerical quantity whose value is determined by the outcome of a random experiment.

Random variables are classified according to the nature of the numbers they can assume.

A random variable is **discrete** if its range can assume only a finite number of values or an infinite number of values that is countable; for example, family size, number of dates per week, or scores on a test. A random variable is **continuous** if its range is uncountably infinite; for example, temperature in Monterey, California, duration of a kiss, or height.

We must distinguish between the values the random variable can assume and those yielded by our measuring instruments. A thermometer is usually calibrated in 1° steps, a stopwatch in 0.1 second, and a ruler in $1/16$ inch. Consequently, our measurement of continuous random variables is always approximate.

Distribution of a Discrete Random Variable

We learned in Chapter 2 that a frequency distribution associates a frequency with each value or class interval of a variable.

A similar representation that associates a probability with each value of a random variable is called a **probability distribution.**

A probability distribution for an experiment of tossing a die is shown in Table 8.2-1, and a graph of the distribution is shown in Figure 8.2-1. In the table, $p(X = r)$ denotes the probability that the random variable X is equal to the value r. The

TABLE 8.2-1. Probability Distribution for Outcome of Tossing a Die

Possible Values, r, of the Random Variable X	$p(X = r)$
1	1/6
2	1/6
3	1/6
4	1/6
5	1/6
6	1/6

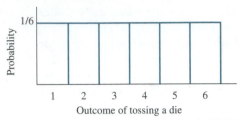

Figure 8.2-1. **Histogram for probability distribution in Table 8.2-1.**

distribution in Figure 8.2-1 is said to be uniform because each value of the random variable has the same probability. Notice that the probabilities sum to 1 because the events $X = 1, \ldots, 6$ are mutually exclusive and collectively exhaustive.

Consider next the three-choice T maze experiment mentioned earlier. Suppose that the correct series of turns is *right, left, right* (R, L, R). We know from the fundamental counting rule in Section 7.4 that a rat can traverse the maze in $2 \times 2 \times 2 = 8$ ways because three right-left choices must be made. The eight ways and the number of errors associated with each are listed in the following table.

	Number of Errors, X
R, L, R	0
R, R, R	1
R, L, L	1
L, L, R	1
R, R, L	2
L, R, R	2
L, L, L	2
L, R, L	3

The probability of making 0, 1, 2, or 3 errors—the random variable—can be computed by $p(X = r) = n_r/n_s$, where n_r is the number of events (maze routes) favoring r errors and n_s is the number of events. For example, the probability of one error is $3/8 = .375$. The probability distribution is given in Table 8.2-2 and a graph of the distribution, in Figure 8.2-2. The table and figure can be used to answer any question about the probability associated with the random variable—for instance, the probability that X is odd: $p(X = 1 \text{ or } 3) = .375 + .125 = .5$, or the probability that X is less than 3: $p(X < 3) = .125 + .375 + .375 = .875$.

A probability distribution is similar to a frequency distribution. The probability distribution associates a probability with each value of a random variable, and the frequency distribution associates a frequency with each value of a variable. A probability distribution describes data that might be observed under certain well-specified conditions; hence, it is hypothetical or theoretical. A frequency distribution describes data that actually have been observed; it is empirical. We saw in Chapter 3 that the arithmetic mean often is used to describe the central tendency of a frequency distri-

TABLE 8.2-2. **Probability Distribution for Number of Errors in a Three-Choice T Maze**

Possible Values, r, of the Random Variable X	p(X = r)
0	.125
1	.375
2	.375
3	.125

bution. A similar index of the central tendency of a probability distribution is called the **expected value**.[4] We now turn to the subject of how to compute expected values.

Expected Value of a Discrete Random Variable

If an extremely large number of naïve rats were to run the three-choice T maze, how many errors on the average would we expect them to make? Stated more formally, what is the *expected value* of that random variable?

If X is a discrete random variable that assumes values $X_1, X_2, \ldots, X_n$ with probabilities $p(X_1), p(X_2), \ldots, p(X_n)$, then the expected value of X denoted by $E(X)$ is defined as[5]

$$E(X) = p(X_1)X_1 + p(X_2)X_2 + \cdots + p(X_n)X_n$$
$$= \sum_{i=1}^{n} p(X_i)X_i,$$

where $p(X_1) + p(X_2) + \cdots + p(X_n) = 1$.

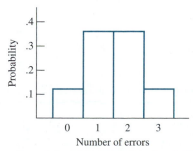

Figure 8.2-2. **Histogram for probability distribution in Table 8.2-2.**

[4] The terms *expected value* and *expectation* are synonymous.

[5] This definition of $E(X)$ doesn't commit us to a particular view of probability because the $p(X_i)$'s can be subjective, classical, or empirical.

For the T maze example, $E(X)$ for the values in Table 8.2-2 is

$$E(X) = .125(0) + .375(1) + .375(2) + .125(3) = 1.5.$$

Thus, we would expect a rat to make on the average 1.5 errors in the maze. Note the similarity between the formula for $E(X)$ and that for the mean of an ungrouped frequency distribution:

$$\overline{X} = \frac{f_1}{n}X_1 + \frac{f_2}{n}X_2 + \cdots + \frac{f_k}{n}X_k.$$

Here, X is a discrete variable that assumes values $X_1, X_2, \ldots, X_k$ with frequencies $f_1, f_2, \ldots, f_k$, where $f_1 + f_2 + \cdots + f_k = n$. The statistic $\overline{X}$ and the parameter $E(X)$ differ in that $\overline{X}$ is the mean of a sample defined by its frequency distribution; $E(X)$ is the mean of a theoretical population defined by its probability distribution. The latter mean also is denoted by μ (Greek *mu*, pronounced "mew").

Originally, the expected value concept was used in games of chance to tell a player what the long-run average loss or gain per play would be. Consider the popular casino game of roulette. A player places a bet, the roulette wheel is spun, and the ball is set in motion. The ball can drop into one of 38 slots. Thirty-six slots are numbered from 1 to 36, with half red and half black. Two green slots are numbered 0 and 00. Suppose a player places $1 on number 7. If the ball drops into the 7 slot, the player receives a $35 payoff; otherwise, the $1 bet is lost. We can calculate the player's expected winnings as shown in Table 8.2-3. According to the table, if the player keeps making $1 bets indefinitely, an average loss of 5.3¢ per bet will be incurred. On any given gamble, the player stands to either win $35 or lose only $1. What the player may choose to ignore is that on the average $35 is won in only 1 out of 38 gambles, whereas $1 is lost in 37 out of 38.

The term *expected value* is misleading in one sense because $E(X)$ is often not one of the possible outcomes of an experiment. In the T maze example, $E(X) = 1.5$, but the possible values of the random variable are 0, 1, 2, or 3 errors. Similarly, the gambler can win $35 or lose $1 on any given play, although $E(X) = -5.3$¢. In both examples, $E(X)$ is an average result, and in this respect it is like a sample mean, $\overline{X}$.

TABLE 8.2-3. Expected Value of a Bet

Possible Winnings, X_i	$p(X_i)$	$P(X_i)X_i$
+$35	$1/38$	$1/38$ ($35) = $$^{35}/_{38}$
−$1	$37/38$	$^{37}/_{38}$ (−$1) = −$$^{37}/_{38}$
		$E(X) = \sum\limits_{i=1}^{n} p(X_i)\, X_i = -\$^2/_{38} = -.053$

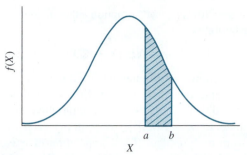

Figure 8.2-3. **The probability that X will assume a value between a and b is equal to the area under the curve between those two points. For many random variables, tables are available that simplify determining the area between two points (see Section 9.1).**

Expected Value of a Continuous Random Variable

Computing the expected value of a discrete random variable is fairly simple because we need only multiply random variable values, X_i, by probabilities, $p(X_i)$, and sum the products—that is, $E(X) = \sum_{i=1}^{n} p(X_i) X_i$. The continuous random variable case is more complicated because the variable can assume an infinite number of values. The probability that a continuous random variable X has a particular value is zero.[6] Consequently, instead of referring to the probability that X has a particular value, we refer to the probability that X lies in an interval between two values of the random variable. This notion is illustrated in Figure 8.2-3. The expected value of a continuous random variable X is the sum of the products formed by multiplying each value that X can assume by the height of the probability distribution curve above that value of X. Because X can assume an infinite number of values, its expected value is not computed by actually physically multiplying each X by the height of the curve at X but instead by means of the integral calculus.[7] As we will see, tables for most random variables of interest have been prepared; these tables simplify the calculation of the probability that X lies in an interval.

Standard Deviation of a Discrete Random Variable

In Chapter 4 we learned that the standard deviation is a useful measure of dispersion. One formula for computing a sample standard deviation is

$$S = \sqrt{\sum f_j (X_j - \overline{X})^2 / n}.$$

[6] This may not be obvious. For a discussion of this point, see Hays (1994, pp. 107–110).
[7] For those familiar with the calculus, the expected value is $E(X) = \int_{X_{min}}^{X_{max}} x f(x)\,dx$, where X_{min} is the smallest value of X and X_{max} is the largest value.

A similar formula for computing the standard deviation of a discrete probability distribution is

$$\sigma = \sqrt{E\{[X - E(X)]^2\}} = \sqrt{\Sigma p(X_i)[X_i - E(X_i)]^2}.$$

We note from the formula on the left that σ is the square root of the expected value of a squared deviation, $[X - E(X)]^2$. We compute this expected value in the same way we did for $E(X)$, where we multiplied each value of X_i by its probability. To compute $E\{[X - E(X)]^2\}$, we multiply each $[X - E(X)]^2$ by its probability $p(X_i)$ and sum the products. The computation of σ is illustrated for the T-maze data in Table 8.2-2; for these data, $E(X) = 1.5$. The standard deviation is

$$\sigma = \sqrt{.125(0 - 1.5)^2 + .375(1 - 1.5)^2 + .375(2 - 1.5)^2 + .125(3 - 1.5)^2}$$

$$= 0.866.$$

The symbol σ is used instead of S because this standard deviation is a population parameter. The value $\sigma = 0.866$ together with $E(X) = 1.5$ provides a useful summary of the theoretical population.

CHECK YOUR UNDERSTANDING OF SECTION 8.2

8. (a) Construct a probability distribution for a four-choice T maze. Assume that the correct series of turns is *right, right, left, right*. (b) Graph the probability distribution.
9. Let the random variable X be the number of cars per household. Suppose that in Waco, Texas, X has the probability distribution

X	0	1	2	3	4	5
$f(X)$	.16	.54	.23	.05	.01	.01

listed in the table. For a household selected at random, compute the following.
a. $p(X \leq 2)$ b. $p(X \geq 3)$
c. $p(1 \leq X \leq 2)$ d. $E(X)$
e. σ

10. What is the maximum you should be willing to pay to enter a game in which you can win \$30 with probability .6 and \$10 with probability .4? (*Hint:* Compute $E(X)$.)
11. The random variable X has the probability distribution listed in the table.

X	0	1	2	3	4
$f(X)$	0	$2/5$	$1/5$	$1/5$	$1/5$

a. Compute $E(X)$.   b. Compute σ.

12. Suppose that a fraternal organization plans to sell 1,000 lottery tickets for $1 each. The prize is a $750 videotape recorder. (a) If you purchase a ticket, what is the probability that you will win? (b) What is your expected gain? Remember to subtract the cost of the ticket from the value of the prize. (c) Does it make economic sense to purchase a ticket? (d) What is the maximum that you should be willing to pay for a ticket? (*Hint:* The maximum you should be willing to pay for a ticket is that amount for which $E(X) = 0$, that is, the amount for which there is no gain or loss over the long run. This amount, denoted by T, can be determined from

$$p(\text{win})(\text{gain value}) + p(\text{lose})(\text{loss value}) = 0,$$

where the gain value is equal to $[750 + (-T)]$ and the loss value is equal to $-T$.)

13. Terms to remember
    a. Discrete random variable   b. Continuous random variable
    c. Probability distribution   d. Expected value

8.3 BINOMIAL DISTRIBUTION

Bernoulli Trial

Many experiments have only two possible outcomes: a new drug is effective or it isn't, an animal takes the correct turn or the wrong turn, a job is given to an applicant or it isn't. These experiments have much in common with tossing a coin. In each case, the random variable is discrete and can assume only two values, often denoted "success" and "failure." Flipping a coin once and noting whether it landed heads or tails or randomly sampling one person from a population of former students and noting whether he or she graduated is called a **Bernoulli trial** or **Bernoulli experiment.**[8] Our interest is usually in the outcome of several Bernoulli trials. We toss a coin n times and note the number of heads, or we randomly sample n persons and note the number of graduates. The probability of observing a success on any given trial is denoted by p and the probability of a failure, by q. Because the two outcomes, success and failure, are mutually exclusive and exhaustive, $p + q = 1$. When there are n Bernoulli trials, the random variable of interest is the number of successes; its value can range from 0 to n.

The characteristics of a Bernoulli trial are as follows:

1. A trial can result in one of two outcomes.
2. The probability of a success remains constant from trial to trial.
3. The outcomes of successive trials are independent.

---

[8] After James Bernoulli (1654–1705), who discussed such trials in his *Ars Conjectandi* (1713).

Very few real-life situations perfectly satisfy the requirements. Strictly speaking, the last two are satisfied only when sampling is done with replacement or from an infinite population. In most research, sampling is done without replacement from a finite population. This practical departure from the ideal is of little consequence as long as the population is large relative to the sample size.

In the following section we describe a binomial distribution in which the random variable is a sum—the number of successes observed on *n* greater than or equal to two Bernoulli trials. A binomial distribution is a relatively simple example of an important class of theoretical distributions or models that are referred to as sampling distributions.

> The term **sampling distribution** is the special name that is given to a probability distribution where the random variable is a statistic based on the results of more than one trial.

For convenience, we will examine a simple binomial distribution here and defer discussion of the special properties of sampling distributions till Chapter 9.

The binomial distribution will be encountered repeatedly in subsequent chapters. It is the theoretical model for a variety of statistics, as we will see in Sections 11.4, 13.3, 13.4, 16.2, 16.3, and 16.4.

Binomial Distribution

> The number of successes observed on $n \geq 2$ identical Bernoulli trials is called a **binomial random variable,** and its probability distribution is called a **binomial distribution.**[9] Suppose we toss a fair coin five times. The probability of observing exactly *r* heads (successes) in *n* tosses is given by the function rule
>
> $$p(X = r) = {}_nC_r p^r q^{n-r},$$
>
> where $p(X = r)$ is the probability that the random variable X equals r heads, ${}_nC_r$ is the combination of n objects taken r at a time,[10] p is the probability of success (a head), and $q = 1 - p$.

---

[9] So named because the probabilities associated with the distribution can be obtained by raising a binomial (an algebraic expression containing two terms) to the *n*th power. For example,

$$(p + q)^n = p^n + np^{n-1}q + \frac{n(n-1)}{2(1)}p^{n-2}q^2 + \cdots + q^n,$$

where p is the probability of success, $q = 1 - p$, and n is the number of Bernoulli trials. The first term, p^n, gives the probability of n successes; the second term, $np^{n-1}q$, the probability of $n - 1$ successes; and so on.

[10] The combination of n objects taken r at a time is discussed in Section 7.4.

TABLE 8.3-1.   Binomial Distribution for $n = 5$ and $p = \frac{1}{2}$

Number of Heads, r	0	1	2	3	4	5
$p(X = r)$	$\frac{1}{32}$	$\frac{5}{32}$	$\frac{10}{32}$	$\frac{10}{32}$	$\frac{5}{32}$	$\frac{1}{32}$

For example, the probability that the random variable X equals four heads is

$$p(X = 4) = {}_5C_4\left(\frac{1}{2}\right)^4\left(\frac{1}{2}\right)^{5-4} = \frac{5!}{4!(5-4)!}\left(\frac{1}{2}\right)^4\left(\frac{1}{2}\right)^1 = \frac{5}{32}.$$

The complete probability distribution is given in Table 8.3-1 and a graph of the distribution, in Figure 8.3-1. The probability that X equals or exceeds some value or that it lies in a given interval can be obtained by combining probabilities from the table or figure. For example, the probability of obtaining four or more heads in five tosses of a fair coin is

$$p(X \geq 4) = p(X = 4) + p(X = 5) = \frac{5}{32} + \frac{1}{32} = \frac{6}{32}.$$

The probability distribution of a binomial random variable is completely specified by n, the number of trials, and the parameter p, the probability of success. When p is less than .5, a graph of the probability distribution is positively skewed; for p equal to .5, it is symmetrical; and for p greater than .5, it is negatively skewed. As n increases, the shape of the distribution approaches more and more closely that of the normal bell-shaped distribution. The binomial distribution is actually a family of distributions, one for each set of p and n values. The thread that binds the distributions into a family is their common function rule, $p(X = r) = {}_nC_r p^r q^{n-r}$.[11] The following example illustrates another member of the binomial family.

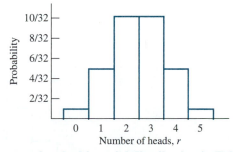

Figure 8.3-1. **Histogram for the binomial distribution in Table 8.3-1.**

[11] Other examples of families of discrete probability distributions are the uniform distribution, multinomial distribution, hypergeometric distribution, Poisson distribution, and negative binomial distribution. The first three distributions are discussed in this text. For a discussion of the latter two distributions see Hays (1994, chap. 3).

TABLE 8.3-2.   Distribution Showing Probability of Improvement Following Treatment

Number Improved, r	0	1	2	3	4	5	6
$p(X = r)$	.001	.008	.059	.185	.324	.302	.118

Suppose that we are interested in the probability that more than half of a random sample of six patients will show improvement following treatment. Let the probability of improvement, p, for any patient equal .7. The probability of observing exactly $r = 6$ successes in $n = 6$ patients is given by

$$p(X = r) = {_n}C_r p^r q^{n-r} = {_6}C_6(.7)^6(.3)^0 = \frac{6!}{6!(6 - 6)!}(.7)^6(.3)^0 = .118.$$

The complete probability distribution is given in Table 8.3-2 and graphed in Figure 8.3-2. The probability that in a random sample of six patients more than half will show improvement is given by

$$p(X \geq 4) = p(X = 4) + p(X = 5) + p(X = 6) = .324 + .302 + .118 = .744.$$

Expected Value and Standard Deviation of Binomial Distribution

The expected value of a discrete random variable always can be computed from $E(X) = \sum_{i=1}^{n} p(X_i)X_i$. For a binomial random variable, there is a simpler formula for computing the expected value of X (number of successes): [12]

$$E(X) = np,$$

where n is the number of trials and p is the probability of a success on any trial.

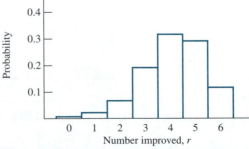

Figure 8.3-2. **Histogram for probability that patients will show improvement following treatment.**

[12] A derivation of the formula is given by Hays (1994, pp. 177–178).

For the probability distribution in Table 8.3-2, the expected number of patients showing improvement is $E(X) = 6(.7) = 4.2$. The same result is obtained using the longer formula $E(X) = \sum_{i=0}^{6} p(X_i)X_i = .001(0) + .008(1) + \cdots + .118(6) = 4.2$.

The standard deviation of a binomial distribution is given by $\sigma = \sqrt{npq}$. For the probability distribution in Table 8.3-2, the standard deviation is

$$\sigma = \sqrt{6(.7)(.3)} = 1.12.$$

Multinomial and Hypergeometric Distributions

As we have seen, the binomial distribution is the appropriate model when (1) sampling from a population whose elements belong to one of two classes, (2) the probability of obtaining an element in a class remains constant from trial to trial, as when sampling with replacement or from an infinite population, and (3) the outcomes of successive trials are independent. In subsequent chapters we will refer to two other models that apply when one or more of these conditions aren't satisfied. These models—the multinomial and the hypergeometric distributions—are described next.

Consider first an experiment in which a trial results in an outcome from one of $k \geq 2$ classes and the probabilities associated with the classes remain constant. Such an experiment is called a **multinomial experiment,** and its associated probability distribution is called a **multinomial distribution.**[13]

If n observations are made independently and at random from $k \geq 2$ mutually exclusive and exhaustive classes with probabilities $p_1, p_2, \ldots, p_k$, then the probability that exactly n_1 will be of kind 1, n_2 will be of kind 2, $\ldots$, and n_k will be of kind k, where $n_1 + n_2 + \cdots + n_k = n$, is given by the **multinomial functional rule:**

$$p(X_1 = n_1 \text{ and } X_2 = n_2 \text{ and } \cdots \text{ and } X_k = n_k) = \frac{n!}{n_1! n_2! \cdots n_k!}(p_1)^{n_1}(p_2)^{n_2} \cdots (p_k)^{n_k}.$$

When $k = 2$, this rule is the same as the binomial function rule because then $n_1 = r$, $n_2 = n - r$, $p_1 = p$, and $p_2 = 1 - p_1 = q$. A multinomial experiment is simply an extension of a binomial experiment and applies when there are two or more classes.

---

[13] So named because the probabilities associated with the distribution can be obtained by raising a multinomial (an algebraic expression containing three or more terms) to the nth power.

The computation of probabilities using the multinomial rule is not too difficult when n and the number of categories is small. Suppose that we want to know the probability of drawing two red, one white, and zero blue marbles from a box that contains four red, two white, and two blue marbles. If we randomly draw one marble at a time and replace it before drawing the next, the probability is given by

$$p(X_R = 2 \text{ and } X_W = 1 \text{ and } X_B = 0) = \frac{n!}{n_R! n_W! n_B!} (p_R)^{n_R} (p_W)^{n_W} (p_B)^{n_B}$$

$$= \frac{3!}{2! 1! 0!} (0.50)^2 (0.25)^1 (0.25)^0$$

$$= .188.$$

When n and the number of categories is large, the multinomial function rule requires a prohibitive amount of computation. As we will see in Chapter 16, this problem can be circumvented through the use of the chi-square approximation of the multinomial.

Suppose that instead of replacing marbles after they are drawn from the box, we sample without replacement. What is the probability of drawing two red, one white, and zero blue marbles? Now the probabilities associated with drawing the different colored marbles will change for each draw. This experiment is called a **hypergeometric experiment,** and its associated probability distribution is called a **hypergeometric distribution.**

If n observations are drawn at random and without replacement from a finite population containing a total of t elements that are divided into k mutually exclusive and exhaustive classes with t_1 in class 1, t_2 in class 2, . . . , t_k in class k, then the probability that exactly n_1 will be of kind 1, n_2 will be of kind 2, . . . , and n_k will be of kind k, where $n_1 + n_2 + \cdots + n_k = n$ and $t_1 + t_2 + \cdots + t_k = t$, is given by the **hypergeometric function rule:**

$$p(X_1 = n_1 \text{ and } X_2 = n_2 \text{ and } \cdots \text{ and } X_k = n_k) = \frac{({}_{t_1}C_{n_1})({}_{t_2}C_{n_2}) \cdots ({}_{t_k}C_{n_k})}{({}_{t}C_{n})}.$$

The probability for our marble experiment is given by

$$p(X_R = 2 \text{ and } X_W = 1 \text{ and } X_B = 0) = \frac{({}_4C_2)({}_2C_1)({}_2C_0)}{({}_8C_3)}$$

$$= \frac{\{4!/[2!(4-2)!]\}\{2!/[1!(2-1)!]\}\{2!/[0!(2-0)!]\}}{\{8!/[3!(8-3)!]\}}$$

$$= .214.$$

This probability is different from the .188 given by the multinomial rule. The two rules give similar results when the population is extremely large.

CHECK YOUR UNDERSTANDING OF SECTION 8.3

14. Interpret the statement $p(X = 3) = .2$.
15. What are the three characteristics of a Bernoulli trial?
16. Let the random variable X be the number of men in a random sample of size 2 taken from a population that contains 60% men and 40% women. (a) Determine the probability of the sample's containing 0, 1, or 2 men. (b) Graph the probability distribution. (c) Compute $E(X)$ and σ.
17. Thirty percent of elementary students in a school system have a reading ability below the national standard for their grade level. (a) If 10 children are selected at random, what is the probability that no more than 1 will be functioning below grade level? (b) Compute $E(X)$ and σ.
18. Of 800 families with five children each, how many would you expect to have (a) three girls, (b) five boys, (c) either two or three girls? Assume equal probabilities for girls and boys.
19. Suppose that a box contains 50% nickels, 30% dimes, and 20% quarters. If 10 coins are drawn at random and with replacement, what is the probability of drawing six nickels, three dimes, and one quarter?
20. Suppose that in Exercise 19 the box contained 20 coins and that 10 are drawn at random and without replacement. What is the probability of drawing six nickels, three dimes, and one quarter?
21. Terms to remember
    - a. Bernoulli trial
    - b. Binomial random variable
    - c. Multinomial experiment
    - d. Hypergeometric experiment

8.4 SUMMARY

Some kind of random procedure should be a part of all research with samples; most often it takes the form of random sampling from a population or random assignment of participants to experimental conditions. Randomness is a property of a procedure rather than of a sample. Any procedure for drawing samples from a population so that every possible sample of a particular size has the same probability of being selected is called random sampling, and the resulting sample is called a random sample.

A random variable is a numerical quantity whose values are determined by the outcomes of a random experiment. A table showing the possible values of a random variable and the associated probabilities is called a probability distribution. Probability distributions and the frequency distributions discussed in Chapter 2 are similar—each associates a number with the possible values of a variable. However, for a frequency distribution, the number is a frequency; for a probability distribution, it is a probability. This reflects a fundamental difference between them. A frequency distribution describes a set of data that has been observed; it is empirical. A probability distribution describes data that might be observed under certain well-specified conditions; hence, it is hypothetical or theoretical. Probability distributions are used in inferential statistics as models of how random variables are expected to behave. If empirical data deviate appreciably from the predictions of a model, doubt is cast on the correctness of the model or its assumptions. For example, if five fair coins are tossed, according to the binomial model we should observe five heads on the average once in every 32 tosses. If instead of observing five heads once we observe them in 10 of the first 32 tosses, we would begin to question the assumption that the coin is fair.

The central tendency of a theoretical population defined by its probability distribution can be described in the same way as the central tendency of a sample—by a mean. The mean of a theoretical population is called an expected value and is given by $E(X) = \sum_{i=1}^{n} p(X_i) X_i$.

An experiment is called a Bernoulli trial if (1) its random variable has only two possible outcomes, denoted "success" and "failure," (2) the probability of a success remains constant from trial to trial, and (3) the outcomes of successive trials are independent. The probability distribution of a Bernoulli random variable could hardly be simpler because it represents the possible outcomes of a single trial. The number of successes in a series of n identical Bernoulli trials is a discrete random variable that can assume integer values from zero to n. The distribution of the number of successes in n identical Bernoulli trials is called a binomial distribution. The binomial distribution is one of the more useful models of how a discrete random variable should behave. Two other useful models are the multinomial and the hypergeometric distributions. The multinomial distribution is an extension of the binomial model for the case in which a trial results in an outcome from one of $k \geq 2$ classes. If elements are sampled at random but without replacement from a finite population with $k \geq 2$ classes, the results are described by the hypergeometric distribution.

REVIEW EXERCISES FOR CHAPTER 8

1. What advantages do random samples have over nonrandom samples?

2. (a) How many different samples of size 4 can be drawn without re-placement from a population of size 30? (b) How many different samples of size 4 can be drawn with replacement from a population of size 30?

3. The probability of drawing a particular sample from a finite popula-tion is given by $1/_nC_r$. What is the probability of drawing a particular sample of size $r = 3$ from a population of size $n = 50$?

4. A sample of 5 students is to be selected from a class of 10. (a) How many different random samples without replacement can be drawn? (b) What is the probability that a given sample will be selected? (c) How many different random samples with replacement can be drawn?

5. (a) Use the table of random numbers in Appendix D to draw two ran-dom samples of 10 students from the following population. For one sample, use sampling with replacement and for the other, sampling without replacement. (b) Describe in detail how you used the table.

Don	Sonja	Jimmy	Dick	Bob	Gary
Herb	Wallace	Martha	Clyde	Sylvia	Ruben
Henry	Bill	Mike	Chuck	Richard	Milton

6. Use the table of random numbers in Appendix D to draw a random sample without replacement of 30 students from the Student Data-base in Appendix E. (a) List the ID No., Stat Grade, and GPA for each person in your sample. Compute the mean of the variables labeled Stat Grade and GPA. (b) Compute the correlation between Stat Grade and GPA. (c) Develop a regression equation to predict Stat Grade from a knowledge of GPA. (d) If you have access to a computer and suitable software, develop a multiple regression equation for predict-ing Stat Grade from GPA and Math Test. How much does the addi-tion of Math Test improve the prediction of Stat Grade?

7. Distinguish between a variable and a random variable.

8. Let the random variable X be the number of children in a family. Suppose that X has the probability distribution listed in the table.

X	0	1	2	3	4	5	6	7
$f(X)$	.40	.18	.15	.11	.09	.05	.01	.01

For a family selected at random, compute the following.

a. $p(X = 0)$ b. $p(X \geq 4)$

c. $p(X < 3)$ d. $p(2 \leq X \leq 5)$

e. $E(X)$ f. σ

9. How does an expected value differ from the mean of a frequency distribution?

10. What is the maximum you should be willing to pay to enter a game in which you can win $20 with probability .7 and $10 with probability .5? (*Hint:* Compute $E(X)$.)

11. If it rains, a fortuneteller loses $12 per day; if it is fair, she earns $110 per day. Assume that the probability of rain is .3. What are her expected earnings per day?

12. The random variable X has the probability distribution listed in the table.

X	0	1	2	3	4
f(X)	$\frac{1}{6}$	$\frac{2}{6}$	$\frac{1}{6}$	$\frac{1}{6}$	$\frac{1}{6}$

a. Compute $E(X)$.   b. Compute σ.

13. Suppose that the Lions Club plans to sell 2,000 lottery tickets for $5 each. The prize is a $4,000 trip for two to Cancun. (a) If you purchase a ticket, what is the probability that you will win? (b) What is your expected gain? Remember to subtract the cost of the ticket from the value of the prize. (c) Does it make economic sense to purchase a ticket? (d) What is the maximum that you should be willing to pay for a ticket? (*Hint:* The maximum you should be willing to pay for a ticket is that amount for which $E(X) = 0$, that is, the amount for which there is no gain or loss over the long run. This amount, denoted by T, can be determined from

$$p(\text{win})(\text{gain value}) + p(\text{lose})(\text{loss value}) = 0,$$

where the gain value is equal to $[4000 + (-T)]$ and the loss value is equal to $-T$.)

14. Interpret the statement $p(X = 5) = .4$.

15. Compare a Bernoulli random variable with a binomial random variable.

16. Suppose that 20% of eligible voters in a given city voted in the last election. A random sample of 10 eligible voters is obtained to investigate reasons for the poor turnout. (a) If X is the number of people who didn't vote, determine the probability distribution for X. (b) Compute $E(X)$ and σ.

17. Ten percent of patients fail to improve after being placed on medication. (a) If five patients are selected at random, what is the probability that two or more will not show improvement? (b) Compute $E(X)$ and σ.

18. What is the probability of guessing correctly at least 6 of 10 answers on a true-false examination?
19. A graduate admissions committee has 20 doctoral applicants, but it can admit only 10. What is the probability that the 10 selected will include the 5 most qualified applicants? (*Hint:* $t = 20$, $t_1 = 5$, and $t_2 = 15$.)

Chapter 9

Normal Distribution and Sampling Distributions

9.1 THE NORMAL DISTRIBUTION

Thus far you have seen numerous references to the normal distribution—and with good reason. The normal distribution is the most important probability distribution in statistics. One reason for the normal distribution's importance is that many variables in science and nature have probability distributions that closely resemble it. Hence, it can serve as a model for such distributions. For example, people's heights and weights are approximately normally distributed, as are intelligence, mechanical aptitude, introversion, and most other psychological attributes. The normal distribution is important also because it is a convenient model for estimating probabilities for other theoretical distributions. We will see later that it provides an excellent approximation to the binomial distribution when the number of trials is large.

Granted, the normal distribution is a useful model, but this hardly accounts for its preeminent position in statistical theory. To understand why it occupies this position, we must consider the distribution of a sample statistic such as the mean. Suppose that from a population we drew 100 random samples of size *n* (where *n* is fairly large), computed the mean of each sample, and constructed a histogram of the sample means. We would find that the resulting graph closely resembles the normal distribution. This might not surprise us if the sampled population were normally distributed, but the striking thing is that if *n* is sufficiently large, the resemblance holds regardless of the population's shape. The tendency for the distribution of a sample statistic to approximate a normal distribution as *n* (the number of observations in each random sample) increases plays a key role in inferential statistics; more will be said about this when we discuss the central limit theorem in Section 9.3.

Serendipity has produced many breakthroughs in science, and one of them is the normal distribution. Abraham de Moivre (1667–1754), a mathematics tutor, was searching for a shortcut method of computing probabilities for binomial random variables. In the process he derived the function rule for the ubiquitous normal distribution. If we toss 10 coins, it doesn't take too much effort to compute the probability of observing zero heads, one head, and so on. But suppose we toss 100 coins. The amount of work necessary to calculate the probabilities associated with 0 through 100 heads is prohibitive. We will see, as de Moivre discovered over 250 years ago, that the task is greatly simplified by using the normal distribution.

Consider the graph of the probability distribution for 16 fair coins in Figure 9.1-1. If we superimpose the graph of a normal distribution on the histogram, it provides a fairly good fit. The fit would be even better if we had graphed the distribution for 50 coins. If the number of coins were increased indefinitely, the number of bars in the histogram would increase, and their outline would eventually coincide with that of the normal distribution. De Moivre derived the function rule for determining the height of the normal distribution for any value of the random variable.

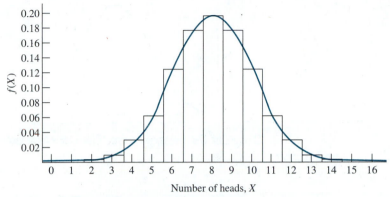

Figure 9.1-1. **Comparison of the histogram for the probability distribution of 16 fair coins and the normal curve.**

Characteristics of the Normal Distribution

A random variable X is said to be normally distributed if its probability distribution is given by the function rule for the normal distribution.

The function rule for the **normal distribution** is

$$f(X) = \frac{1}{\sigma\sqrt{2\pi}} \, e^{-(X-\mu)^2/(2\sigma^2)},$$

where $f(X)$ is the height of the distribution at X, π is approximately 3.142, e (the base of the system of natural logarithms) is approximately 2.718, and μ and σ identify a particular normal distribution in the family of normal distributions.

Fortunately, we don't have to use the rule to determine areas under the distribution between various values of X; as we will see, they can be determined from Appendix Table D.2.

   The normal distribution is shaped like a bell. Because it is unimodal and symmetrical, its mean, median, and mode have the same value, and that value corresponds to the highest point on the curve. The mean plus or minus the standard deviation, as shown in Figure 9.1-2, defines the *inflection points* of the curve—that is, the points at which the curve changes from being concave to convex or vice versa. Although not shown in the figure, the tails of the curve extend indefinitely in both directions, never quite touching the horizontal axis. The total area under the curve is equal to 1.

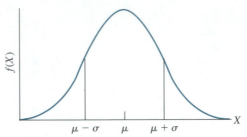

Figure 9.1-2. **Graph of the normal curve. The inflection points occur at $\mu - \sigma$ and $\mu + \sigma$.**

Converting Scores to Standard Scores

There are as many normal distributions as there are possible values of μ and σ, the parameters that identify a particular distribution. To avoid having to develop an infinite number of tables, statisticians have made one particular normal distribution the standard. It has a mean equal to 0 and a standard deviation equal to 1 ($\mu = 0$ and $\sigma = 1$) and is called the **standard normal distribution.** This is the distribution whose areas are tabulated in Appendix Table D.2. Random variable values for this distribution are called **standard scores** and are denoted by z.

If a random variable doesn't happen to have a mean of 0 and standard deviation of 1, the variable must be transformed into a standard score to use the standard normal distribution table (Appendix Table D.2). The transformation is accomplished by the formula

$$z = \frac{X - \mu}{\sigma},$$

where z is a standard score, X is a random variable value, μ is the population mean of the random variable, and σ is the population standard deviation of the random variable. A comparable formula for a sample is

$$z = \frac{X - \overline{X}}{S},$$

where $\overline{X}$ is the sample mean and S is the sample standard deviation.

If we apply this z-score transformation to each X in a distribution, will the resulting standard scores have a mean of 0 and a standard deviation of 1? The answer is yes, and the reason is as follows. It can be shown (see Exercise 21 in "Review Exercises for Chapter 3") that if a constant c is subtracted from each score in a distribution ($X_i - c$), the mean of the transformed distribution is equal to the original mean minus the constant, that is, $\overline{X}_{transformed} = \overline{X}_{original} - c$. Hence, if we subtract $c = \overline{X}_{original}$ from each score, the mean of the transformed scores will equal 0 because $\overline{X}_{transformed} = \overline{X}_{original} - \overline{X}_{original} = 0$. Also, it can be shown (see Exercise 1b in "Review Exercises for Chapter 4") that if each ($X_i - \overline{X}$) is divided by a constant c, the standard deviation of the transformed $(X_i - \overline{X})$'s is equal to the original standard deviation divided by the constant, that is, $S_{transformed} = S_{original}/c$. Hence, if we divide each $(X_i - \overline{X})$ by $c = S_{original}$, the transformed standard deviation of the $(X_i - \overline{X})$'s will equal 1 because $S_{transformed} = S_{original}/S_{original} = 1$. Thus, applying the transformation $z = (X_i - \overline{X})/S$ to each X score results in a new variable called a standard score, whose mean is 0 and whose standard deviation is 1.

Suppose that the mean of a random variable is 100 and its standard deviation is 15. The z score corresponding to an X score of 130 is $z = (130 - 100)/15 = 2$. A z score transformation alters the mean and standard deviation of a random variable, but not the relative location of scores in the distribution. For example, the X score of 130 is two standard deviations above the mean of 100 because $130 = \overline{X} + 2(S) = 100 + 2(15)$. Similarly, the corresponding z score of 2 is also two standard deviations above its mean of zero, because $2 = $ (mean of z) $+ 2$(standard deviation of z) $= 0 + 2(1) = 2$. If we were to graph the distribution of the random variable and the distribution of the z scores, we would find that they are identical in shape although they differ in central tendency and dispersion. Transforming scores to standard scores doesn't change the shape of the distribution or the relative position of scores—only the mean and the standard deviation. As we will see in Section 9.2, standard scores are particularly useful for comparing the performance of individuals on tests having different means or standard deviations.

For distributions that are approximately normal, most z scores are between -3 and $+3$. This follows from a fact we learned in Chapter 4, namely that 99.73% of the area under the normal distribution lies within ± 3 standard deviations of the mean.

Finding Areas Under the Normal Distribution

If a random variable is approximately normally distributed, the standard normal distribution in Appendix Table D.2 can be used to find the proportion of the total area falling between any two scores. The areas tabulated in Appendix Table D.2 are shown in Figures 9.1-3(a) and (b).

1. *Area between μ and a score above it [area A in Figure 9.1-3(a)].* Suppose that the distribution of college students' IQs is approximately normal with $\mu = 115$ and $\sigma = 15$ and you want to know the proportion of students with IQs between the mean and 130. The first step is to convert $X = 130$ into a standard score: $z = (X - \mu)/\sigma = (130 - 115)/15 = 1$. According to Appendix Table D.2, the proportion of the area from μ to $z = 1$ is .3413; thus, approximately 34% of students have IQs between $\mu = 115$ and $X = 130$. This area is shown as area A in Figure 9.1-3(a).

2. *Smaller area in the tail [area B in Figure 9.1-3(b)].* The proportion of students with IQs above 130, which corresponds to a standard score of 1, is shown as area B in Figure 9.1-3 (b). This area is equal to .1587.

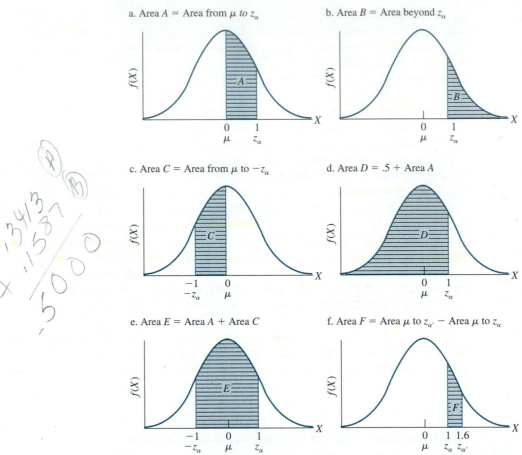

a. Area A = Area from μ to z_α

b. Area B = Area beyond z_α

c. Area C = Area from μ to $-z_\alpha$

d. Area D = .5 + Area A

e. Area E = Area A + Area C

f. Area F = Area μ to $z_{\alpha'}$ − Area μ to z_α

Figure 9.1-3. **Illustration of the areas of the standard normal distribution. Areas A and B are given in Appendix Table D.2. A standard score is denoted by z_a, where α indicates the proportion of the standard normal distribution that falls above the score. In considering area D, recall that the mean divides the total area in half, so that .5 falls above the mean and .5, below the mean.**

Because the normal distribution is symmetrical, (area A) + (area B) = .5. Standard scores are sometimes denoted by z and a subscript α that indicates the proportion of the normal distribution that lies to the right of (above) the z score. The symbol z_a denotes the standard score above which α proportion of the normal distribution falls. For example, the standard score of 1 is denoted by $z_{.1587}$ because .1587 of the area falls to the right of $z = 1$.

3. *Area between μ and a score below it [area C in Figure 9.1-3(c)].* To determine the proportion of the total area from μ to a score below the mean, say, a score of 100, we first convert the score to a z score: $z = (100 - 115)/15 = -1$. Appendix Table D.2 gives areas only for positive

z scores, but because the distribution is symmetrical, the size of the area from μ to $z = -1$ is the same as that from μ to $z = +1$. Thus, area C is obtained by ignoring the negative sign and looking up the z score in area A. The area from μ to $z = -1$ is .3413, and it is shown as area C in Figure 9.1-3(c).

4. *Larger area in the tail [area D in Figure 9.1-3(d)].* To find area D for a score of, say, 130 (z score equals 1), we find area A and add .5 to it. For example, area $D = .5 + .3413 = .8413$. A student with an IQ of 130 scores above approximately 84% of college students.

5. *Area between scores on opposite sides of the mean [area E in Figure 9.1-3(e)].* To find the proportion of the total area between two scores on opposite sides of the mean, add areas A and C. For example, if the scores are 130 and 100, the z scores are 1 and -1. The sum of areas A and C is .3413 + .3413 = .6826.

6. *Area between scores on the same side of the mean [area F in Figure 9.1-3(f)].* Suppose that we want to determine the proportion of the total area between scores of 130 and 139. We first transform the scores to z scores: $(130 - 115)/15 = 1$ and $(139 - 115)/15 = 1.6$. Area A for $z = 1$ is .3413 and for $z = 1.6$ is .4452. Area F for these z values is given by (area μ to $z = 1.6$) − (area μ to $z = 1$) = .4452 − .3413 = .1039.

Finding Scores When the Area Is Known

A different kind of problem arises when we have a percentile rank in mind or know the relative size of the area above or below a point in a distribution and we want to determine the untransformed score corresponding to that rank or point. If we know the size of the area, we can determine from Appendix Table D.2 the z score that marks the boundary of the area. In the previous examples, we knew X, μ, and σ and solved for z using the formula $z = (X - \mu)/\sigma$. If we know z, μ, and σ, it is a simple matter to solve for X. A little algebra is all that is needed to express the formula in the desired form.

$$z = \frac{X - \mu}{\sigma}$$

$$\sigma z = X - \mu$$

$$X = \mu + \sigma z$$

Suppose that we want to know the IQ score corresponding to the 80th percentile rank. We know that .80 of the area under the normal curve falls below the z score and that .20 of the area falls above the z score. To find the z score, we look in column 3 of Appendix Table D.2 until we locate .20. The corresponding z score is approximately 0.84. Knowing that $z_{.20} = 0.84$, $\mu = 115$, and $\sigma = 15$, we have all the information necessary to solve for X in the formula $X = \mu + \sigma z$. Substituting in the formula, we obtain $115 + 15(0.84) = 127.6$. Thus, a score of 127.6 corresponds to the 80th percentile rank.

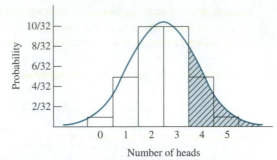

Figure 9.1-4. **Histogram for binomial distribution with *n* = 5 and *p* = .5. A normal distribution is superimposed over the histogram. The normal distribution area corresponding to the probability of observing four or more heads is represented by the shaded area.**

To take one more example, suppose that we want to know the IQ score corresponding to the 40th percentile rank. We know that the score is below the mean and that .40 of the area lies to the left of (below) the score and .60 lies above. To find the z score corresponding to the area below .40, we look in column 3 of Appendix Table D.2 until we locate .40 and find that $-z_{.60} \cong -0.25$. Remember that the sign of z scores below the mean is negative and that the subscript, .60, denotes the area above the z. Substituting in the formula $X = \mu + \sigma z$ gives $X = 115 + 15(-0.25) = 111.25$, the IQ score corresponding to the 40th percentile rank.

Normal Approximation to the Binomial Distribution

The normal distribution function rule was originally derived by de Moivre to estimate binomial distribution probabilities when the number of trials, n, is large. As we will see, the approximation is excellent even when n is small.

Consider an experiment in which a fair coin is tossed five times. The random variable of interest is the number of heads. A graph of the distribution for $n = 5$ and $p = .5$ is given in Figure 9.1-4. A normal distribution has been superimposed on the graph. The probability of observing four or more heads can be computed from the binomial distribution in Chapter 8, Table 8.3-1: $p(X \geq 4) = {}^{5}/_{32} + {}^{1}/_{32} = {}^{6}/_{32} = .1875.$

The probability of observing four or more heads can be estimated using the normal distribution table by finding the area including and to the right of four heads. Because the normal distribution is continuous, we must think of four heads as occupying the interval from 3.5 to 4.5; the lower limit of the interval is 3.5. To find the area above the lower limit of four heads, we first convert 3.5 to a z score. Recall from Section 8.3 that the mean and standard deviation of a binomial distribution are given by, respectively, $E(X) = np$ and $\sigma = \sqrt{npq}$. For our example, $E(X) = 5(.5) = 2.5$ and $\sigma = \sqrt{5(.5)(.5)} = 1.118$. The z score corresponding to observing four or more heads is

$$z = \frac{X - E(X)}{\sigma} = \frac{3.5 - 2.5}{1.118} = 0.894.$$

According to Appendix Table D.2, the area above $z = 0.894$ is .1857, which is close to the exact value of .1875 computed from the binomial distribution. So we see that although the normal distribution approximation was not intended to be used for such a small n, it yielded a value quite close to the exact probability.

CHECK YOUR UNDERSTANDING OF SECTION 9.1

1. How does a standard normal distribution differ from other normal distributions?
2. Which of the following variables do you think approximate the normal distribution? For those that you don't think are normal, sketch the form of the distribution you would expect. (a) Amount of coffee per cup dispensed by a vending machine, (b) extraversion scores of college students, (c) incomes of families in the United States, (d) time spent looking at a painting in a museum, (e) ages of residents in Normal, Ohio, and (f) the time at which students arrive for an 11 o'clock class.
3. A set of scores has a mean of 20 and a standard deviation of 5. Transform the following to z scores:
   a. 30   b. 12   c. 15   d. 27   e. 20
4. If z is a normally distributed random variable with $\mu = 0$ and $\sigma = 1$, determine the percentage of the area under the standard normal curve for the following:
   a. Above z = 1.5
   b. Below z = −2
   c. From μ to z = 3
   d. Between z = 1 and z = 2
   e. Between z = 1 and z = −3
   f. Between z = −1 and z = −3
5. Determine the percentage of the area of the standard normal distribution that falls between $\mu - k\sigma$ and $\mu + k\sigma$, where k is equal to the following:
   a. 1.0   b. 1.645   c. 1.96   d. 2.58   e. 3.30
6. Compute the score corresponding to each of the following z scores. Assume that the original distribution had a mean of 150 and a standard deviation of 20.
   a. 2.0   b. −1.5   c. 3.1   d. 0   e. 0.5

7. Find the z score such that at least the following proportion of the area under the standard normal distribution falls above it.
   a. .50   b. .05   c. .40   d. .70   e. .95
8. Junior college grade point averages (GPAs) have $\mu = 2.8$ and $\sigma = 0.24$. A university is considering raising its minimum entrance score from 2.2 to 2.5. If GPA is normally distributed, how will the proposed change affect the percentage of students eligible to enter the university from junior colleges?
9. Use the normal approximation to the binomial distribution to determine the probability of guessing correctly (a) at least 12 of 20 answers on a true-false examination and (b) at least 24 of 40 answers.
10. Suppose that 10% of physicians' diagnoses at a clinic are incorrect. Use the normal approximation to the binomial distribution to determine the probability that of 400 diagnoses (a) at most 30 will be incorrect, (b) between 30 and 50 will be incorrect, and (c) more than 50 will be incorrect.
11. Terms to remember
    a. Standard normal curve
    b. Standard score (z)

9.2 INTERPRETING SCORES IN TERMS OF z SCORES AND PERCENTILE RANKS

Your roommate announces that she got a 62 on the midterm. Not knowing whether to rejoice with her or to sympathize, you ask, "What was the class average?" "Forty-one," she replies. You press further: "What was the range?" The lowest score was 22 and the highest was 62. A celebration is in order.

This example illustrates a problem in interpreting scores. A score by itself is uninterpretable; a frame of reference is needed to know whether a score is good or bad. The frame of reference in the example was provided by the central tendency of the distribution and its dispersion. The score became interpretable when it was related to the performance of other students.

Standard Score

It would be convenient to have one number that provides all the information necessary to interpret a score instead of having to relate it to the mean and the standard deviation or perhaps the range. We have already discussed two such numbers that can be used to interpret a score: standard score and percentile.

A **standard score** is a number that expresses the value of a score relative to the mean and the standard deviation of its distribution.

For example, if $\overline{X} = 50$ and $S = 10$, a score of 70 corresponds to a z score of

$$z = \frac{X - \overline{X}}{S} = \frac{70 - 50}{10} = \frac{20}{10} = 2,$$

which is two standard deviations above the mean. A standard score tells us the location in standard deviation units of a score relative to the mean.

Percentile Rank

The second kind of number that can be used to interpret a score is percentile rank, which is discussed in Chapter 4.

The **percentile rank** of a score indicates the percentage of the scores of the distribution that fall below that score. For example, if a score has a percentile rank of 80, we know that 80% of scores fall below it and 20% fall above.

The range of the transformed scale is from the 0th percentile rank to the 100th percentile rank. The median is the 50th percentile rank. Transforming a score to a percentile rank locates it on a scale from 0 to 100 and indicates the percentage of scores below. Thus, as in the case of a standard score, a single number, the percentile rank, is sufficient for interpreting a score.

Because percentile ranks are familiar to most people, they are used widely in presenting psychological test scores. Standard scores, on the other hand, are less familiar but, as we will see, possess a number of advantages over percentiles.

Relative Advantages of z Scores and Percentile Ranks

Consider the distribution of IQ scores in Figure 9.2-1 (a); it is slightly negatively skewed. A graph of the percentile ranks corresponding to scores in Figure 9.2-1 (a) is shown in part (b) of the figure. The percentile rank graph has a rectangular shape. We can see from the figure that the transformation of scores to percentile ranks has altered four characteristics of the distribution: (1) central tendency (for example, the transformed mean is 50), (2) dispersion, (3) skewness (the percentile graph is symmetrical), and (4) kurtosis. The only characteristic that isn't changed by the transformation is the rank order of scores within the distribution. In addition, we see that the 10-point difference between, for example, the 50th and 60th percentiles corresponds to a relatively small difference between IQ scores, but a 10-point difference between the 80th and 90th percentiles corresponds to a larger difference between IQs. To put it another way, there

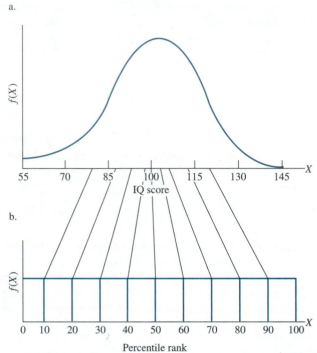

Figure 9.2-1. **(a) Graph of distribution of IQ scores. (b) Graph of distribution of percentile ranks. The transformation of scores to percentile ranks alters the shape of the distribution.**

is a greater difference in intellectual functioning between two individuals at the 80th and 90th percentiles than between individuals at the 50th and 60th percentiles. Thus, the interpretation of a 10-point difference between percentile ranks depends on where the difference is on the 0–100 scale. This problem doesn't occur with standard scores.

As we have seen, transforming scores to percentile ranks alters four characteristics of the distribution; a standard score transformation alters only two characteristics—central tendency and dispersion. Standard scores have the added advantage that they can be manipulated arithmetically. For these reasons, people who use or develop psychological tests prefer standard scores over percentile ranks even though they are less familiar to the average person.

Other Kinds of Standard Scores

The standard scores we have described range approximately from −3 to +3 and have a mean of 0 and a standard deviation of 1. It is a minor inconvenience to have to deal with negative scores, and fortunately this inconvenience can be avoided. If a sufficiently large constant is added to each *z* score, all the *z* scores will be positive,

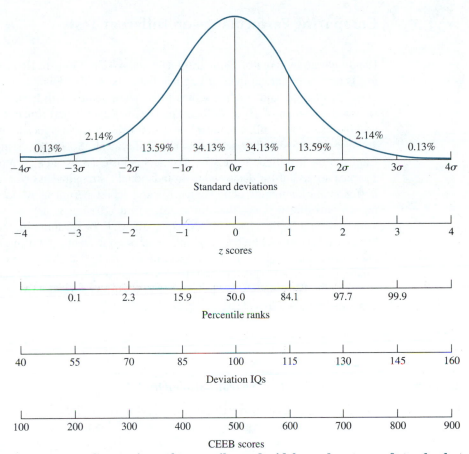

Figure 9.2-2. **Comparison of percentiles and widely used systems of standard scores.**

with a new mean equal to the constant. Similarly, if each z score is multiplied by a constant, the standard deviation is changed from 1 to the value of the constant. The formula

$$z' = \frac{X - \overline{X}}{S} S' + \overline{X}'$$

is used to change the mean and standard deviation of z scores to any desired values, where z' is the transformed standard score, S' is the value of the desired standard deviation, and $\overline{X}'$ is the value of the desired mean.

A surprising number of test scores are actually transformed z scores. Most IQ scores, for example, are really z scores that have been multiplied by 15 and then had 100 added to the product. The resulting transformed z' scores have a mean equal to 100 and a standard deviation equal to 15. Other examples of common transformed standard scores are shown in Figure 9.2-2.

Comparing Performance on Different Tests

Randy got a raw score of 68 in arithmetic and a 42 in English. He seems to be doing better in arithmetic than in English, but is he really? His teacher converts the class's arithmetic and English scores to standard scores with a mean of 50 and a standard deviation of 10. A different picture of Randy's performance emerges; his arithmetic z score is 40, 1 standard deviation below the class mean, but his English score is 65, 1.5 standard deviations above the mean. So Randy is much better in English than in arithmetic, relative to others in his class. As this example illustrates, z scores are useful for determining an individual's strengths and weaknesses—that is, for making intraindividual comparisons; z scores permit us to compare performance on different tasks that are measured on different scales, as were Randy's arithmetic and English tests. For the comparisons to be meaningful, the z scores for both variables should be based on the same or equivalent reference groups. Reference groups are equivalent with respect to a variable if their distributions have essentially the same mean, standard deviation, and shape. It wouldn't have been possible to compare Randy's z scores if he had been in an accelerated arithmetic class and a remedial English class.

CHECK YOUR UNDERSTANDING OF SECTION 9.2

12. Suppose that three tests were given in your statistics course. The class means, standard deviations, and your scores are listed in the table.

Test	μ	σ	Your Scores
1	60	11	72
2	44	17	61
3	53	8	63

On which test did you do your best, and on which did you do your worst?

13. Your statistics professor returned the midterm exam and said that the mean was 82 and the standard deviation was 14. The top 15% of the test scores received an A. Assume that the distribution is normally distributed and that your score was 99. Did you get an A?

14. Suppose that the mean of a test was 22 and the standard deviation was 5. Transform a score of 18 to standard scores with the following means and standard deviations:
    a. $\overline{X} = 100, S = 15$ b. $\overline{X} = 50, S = 10$ c. $\overline{X} = 10, S = 2$

9.3 SAMPLING DISTRIBUTIONS

Looking Ahead

So far we have covered descriptive statistics, probability, and probability distributions. These topics provide the necessary background for moving on to inferential statistics, the subject of the second half of this book. Inferential statistics are procedures for using sample data to make inferences about one or more population parameters. Two kinds of procedures are categorized under inferential statistics—estimation and hypothesis testing.

The term **estimation** is used in statistics in much the same way as it is used in everyday language. A student might estimate that the mean grade point average of members of his sailing club is 2.9 or that it is between 2.7 and 3.1. We call the first type of estimate a **point estimate** because the one number representing the estimate may be associated with a point on a number line. The second type, involving two numbers, is called an **interval estimate** because the two numbers and associated points define an interval on the real number line.

An **estimator** is a rule, usually in the form of a formula such as $\sum X_i/n$, that tells us how to calculate an estimate of a population parameter using sample information. The estimate is the numerical value that results from applying the rule to a sample.

The value of a point estimate will vary from one random sample to the next; hence the value for a particular sample is likely to differ from the population parameter. As we will see in Chapters 10–13, interval estimation is used in conjunction with point estimation to specify an interval on the real number line that has a high likelihood of containing the parameter of interest. In subsequent chapters, we will call this interval a **confidence interval.**

The other approach to statistical inference, **hypothesis testing,** is similar in many respects to the scientific method. The scientist observes nature, formulates a hypothesis, and then proceeds to test the hypothesis by comparing its predictions with data. Similarly, hypothesis testing begins with a question about nature that leads to a hypothesis regarding the value of one or more population parameters. The researcher obtains a sample from the population and compares the sample value with the hypothesized value. If the sample value is inconsistent with the hypothesized value, the hypothesis is rejected; otherwise, it isn't rejected. These procedures are discussed in Chapters 10 through 13.

In summary, estimation is concerned with getting a reasonable idea of the value of a parameter. Hypothesis testing is concerned with deciding whether a hypothesis about a parameter is or isn't tenable. In estimation, the result is a number or an interval bounded by two numbers. In hypothesis testing, the result is a decision about a hypothesis.

Before turning to hypothesis testing and confidence intervals, which are introduced in Chapter 10, we will lay a little more groundwork for statistical inference.

Introduction to Sampling Distributions

As we have learned, inferential statistics is concerned with reasoning from a sample to the population—from the particular to the general. Such reasoning is based on a knowledge of the sample-to-sample variability of a statistic—that is, on its sampling behavior. Before data have been collected we can speak of a sample statistic such as $\overline{X}$ in terms of probability. Its value is yet to be determined and will depend on which score values happen to be randomly selected from the population. Thus, at this stage of research, a sample statistic is a random variable because it is computed from score values obtained by random sampling.

Like any random variable, a sample statistic has a probability distribution that gives the probability associated with each value of the statistic over all possible samples of the same size that could be drawn from the population. The distribution of a statistic is called a **sampling distribution** to distinguish it from a probability distribution for, say, a score value.

Sampling distributions play a key role in statistical inference because they describe the sample-to-sample variability of statistics computed from random samples. In subsequent chapters we will use sampling distributions to (1) determine the tenability of the hypothesis that a population parameter is equal to a particular value and (2) specify a range of values that has a high likelihood of including the parameter.

Sampling Distribution of the Mean

Some of the important characteristics of a sampling distribution will be introduced by an example that, though obviously unrealistic, has the virtue of allowing a concrete approach to the topic. Our discussion will focus on the sampling distribution of the mean, but the ideas we will develop apply to any sampling distribution. Suppose that we have a discrete, uniform (rectangular) population consisting of N equal to four scores: 1, 2, 3, and 4. A graph of the population is shown in Figure 9.3-1. The mean of the population is

$$\mu = \frac{\sum_{i=1}^{N} X_i}{N} = \frac{1 + 2 + 3 + 4}{4} = 2.5,$$

and its standard deviation is

$$\sigma = \sqrt{\frac{\sum_{i=1}^{N}(X_i - \mu)^2}{N}}$$

$$= \sqrt{\frac{(1 - 2.5)^2 + (2 - 2.5)^2 + (3 - 2.5)^2 + (4 - 2.5)^2}{4}}$$

$$= 1.118.$$

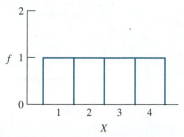

Figure 9.3-1. **Histogram of a discrete uniform population.**

If we draw all possible samples of size $n = 2$ with replacement, $k = 16$ different samples can be drawn (see Table 9.3-1). This follows because the first element can be drawn in any one of four ways and the second, in any one of four ways, making a total of $4 \times 4 = 16$ samples. The probability of drawing a particular sample is, according to the multiplication rule, $(1/4)(1/4) = 1/16$. The 16 equally likely samples and their means are given in Table 9.3-1. As shown in the table, the mean of the 16 means, denoted by $\mu_{\bar{X}}$, is equal to 2.5; the standard deviation of the means, denoted by $\sigma_{\bar{X}}$, is equal to 0.791. A chart depicting the sampling procedure along with a graph of the sampling distribution of the mean is presented in Figure 9.3-2.

TABLE 9.3-1. **Listing of All Possible Samples of Size Two From the Population in Figure 9.3-1**

(i) Data (The sample mean for each of the $j = 1, \ldots, k$ samples is given by $\bar{X}_j = \sum_{i=1}^{n} X_i / n$, where $k = 16$ and $n = 2$)

Sample Number	Sample Values	$\bar{X}_j$	Sample Number	Sample Values	$\bar{X}_j$
1	1, 1	1.0	9	2, 3	2.5
2	1, 2	1.5	10	3, 2	2.5
3	2, 1	1.5	11	2, 4	3.0
4	1, 3	2.0	12	4, 2	3.0
5	3, 1	2.0	13	3, 3	3.0
6	1, 4	2.5	14	3, 4	3.5
7	4, 1	2.5	15	4, 3	3.5
8	2, 2	2.0	16	4, 4	4.0

(ii) Mean and standard deviation of the means

$$\mu_{\bar{X}} = \frac{\sum_{j=1}^{k} \bar{X}_j}{k} = \frac{1.0 + 1.5 + \cdots + 4.0}{16} = \frac{40}{16} = 2.5$$

$$\sigma_{\bar{X}} = \sqrt{\frac{\sum_{j=1}^{k}(\bar{X}_j - \mu_{\bar{X}})^2}{k}} = \sqrt{\frac{(1.0 - 2.5)^2 + (1.5 - 2.5)^2 + \cdots + (4.0 - 2.5)^2}{16}} = 0.791$$

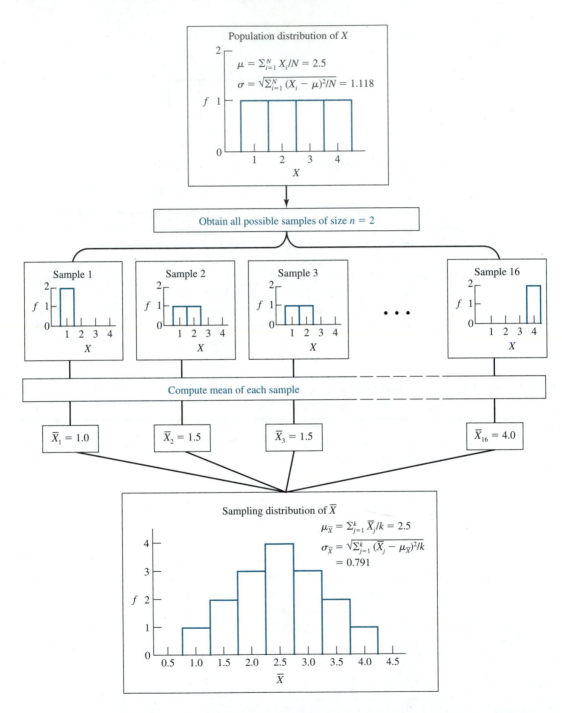

Figure 9.3-2. **Graph of the sampling procedure used to construct a sampling distribution for samples of size $n = 2$ from a discrete, uniform population.**

Three characteristics of the sampling distribution are especially significant.

1. The distribution of the sample means doesn't resemble the original population, which was rectangular in this example, but instead resembles the normal distribution. We could show that if the sample size were increased from $n = 2$ to $n = 3$, the number of possible $\overline{X}_j$ values would increase and the distribution of the $\overline{X}_j$'s would resemble more closely the normal distribution.

2. The mean of the 16 sample means, $\mu_{\overline{X}} = 2.5$, equals the mean of the four score values in the population, $\mu = 2.5$.

3. The standard deviation of the 16 sample means, $\sigma_{\overline{X}} = 0.791$, is equal to the standard deviation of the four scores in the population divided by the square root of the sample size—that is, $\sigma_{\overline{X}} = \sigma/\sqrt{n} = 1.118/\sqrt{2} = 0.791$.

Several implications of the third point are easily overlooked. It says in effect that we can compute the standard deviation of sample means in two ways—from $\sigma_{\overline{X}} = \sqrt{\sum_{j=1}^{k} (\overline{X}_j - \mu_{\overline{X}})^2/k}$ or from $\sigma_{\overline{X}} = \sigma/\sqrt{n}$. Because in practical situations the distribution of sample means isn't available, we rely on a knowledge of, or an estimate of, the population standard deviation and the formula $\sigma/\sqrt{n}$ in computing $\sigma_{\overline{X}}$. The formula $\sigma_{\overline{X}} = \sigma/\sqrt{n}$ also gives us a reason for having greater confidence in large samples. We know that the standard deviation of the population, σ, is a constant. Therefore, it follows from $\sigma_{\overline{X}} = \sigma/\sqrt{n}$ that as n (the sample size) increases, $\sigma_{\overline{X}}$ (the dispersion of sample means) decreases, and hence the closer a randomly selected sample mean is likely to be to μ. In other words, the larger the sample size, the more probable it is that the sample mean comes arbitrarily close to the population mean. This fact, referred to as the **law of large numbers,** is one justification for using random samples to learn about populations. If the sample is large enough, the sample information is likely to be very accurate.

Central Limit Theorem

The three characteristics of the sampling distribution of the mean are succinctly stated in the central limit theorem, one of the most important theorems in statistics.

In one form the **central limit theorem** states that if random samples are selected from a population with mean μ and finite standard deviation σ, as the sample size n increases, the distribution of $\overline{X}$ approaches a normal distribution with mean μ and standard deviation $\sigma/\sqrt{n}$.

Probably the most significant point is that regardless of the shape of the sampled population, the means of sufficiently large samples will be nearly normally distributed. Just how large is sufficiently large? This depends on the shape of the sampled population; the more a population departs from the normal form, the larger n must be. For most populations encountered in the behavioral sciences and education, a sample size of 100 is sufficient to produce a nearly normal sampling distribution of $\overline{X}$. The tendency for the sampling distributions of statistics to approach the normal distribution as n increases helps to explain why the normal distribution is so important in statistics.

Standard Error of a Statistic

We have used the term *standard deviation* to refer to a measure of dispersion, both for scores in a frequency distribution and statistics in a sampling distribution. To avoid confusion in the future, we will use the term **standard error** to denote the latter measure. The symbol for a standard error always includes a subscript indicating the statistic to which it applies, for example, $\sigma_{\overline{X}}$, σ_S, and σ_r. There are as many standard errors as there are sample statistics, but they are all interpreted analogously to a standard deviation.

In the future, whenever you encounter a standard error, think of it simply as a measure of the sample-to-sample variability of the values of a statistic computed from a large number of random samples. The standard error reflects the dispersion of the statistic obtained from many samples; a standard deviation reflects the dispersion of scores.

Two Properties of Good Estimators

As we have discussed, the value of sample statistics varies from one random sample to the next. Consequently, it is unlikely that a given statistic will equal the population parameter it is used to estimate. This is a little frustrating, but it is something we have to live with. However, we can require that the mean of the distribution of estimates yielded by an estimator equal the parameter it estimates and that the estimates vary from one random sample to the next as little as possible. Statistics that satisfy these two intuitively reasonable requirements are said to be unbiased estimators and minimum variance estimators, respectively.

More formally, an estimator $\hat{\theta}$ is an **unbiased estimator** of the parameter θ if $E(\hat{\theta}) = \hat{\theta}$. An estimator $\hat{\theta}$ is a **minimum variance estimator** of the parameter θ if the variance of θ, denoted by $\text{Var}(\hat{\theta})$, is smaller than that for any other unbiased estimator of θ.

The sample mean is a good estimator of μ because it satisfies both these requirements: $E(\overline{X}) = \mu$ and $\text{Var}(\overline{X})$ is a minimum. It can be shown that the sample median of normally distributed populations also is an unbiased estimator of μ, but it is not a minimum variance estimator. This can be seen by comparing the variance error (the square of the standard error) of the median with that for the mean: $\text{Var}(Mdn) = 1.57\sigma^2/n$ and is larger than $\text{Var}(\overline{X}) = \sigma^2/n$. This confirms what we stated in Section 3.5, namely, that the sample mean is more stable than the sample median—the mean varies less from sample to sample than the median. The sample variance S^2 isn't a good estimator of σ^2 because $E(S^2) \neq \sigma^2$. Instead, we use $\hat{\sigma}^2 = \Sigma(X_i - \overline{X})^2/(n - 1)$ to estimate σ^2 because $E(\hat{\sigma}^2) = \sigma^2$.[1]

Test Statistics

The statistics we have presented thus far—$\overline{X}$, *Mdn*, S, and so on—are useful for describing samples. If they are computed from a random sample, they also can be used to estimate population parameters, although, as we have seen, some are better for this purpose than others. In subsequent chapters we will introduce a new kind of statistic that is used to test hypotheses about the values of population parameters. These statistics are called **test statistics.** Consider a test statistic that is used to test a hypothesis about a population mean, μ. Its formula is

$$z = \frac{\overline{X} - \mu_0}{\sigma_{\overline{X}}},$$

where $\overline{X}$ is the mean of a random sample, μ_0 is the hypothesized value of the population mean, and $\sigma_{\overline{X}}$ is the standard error of the mean. If the sampled population is normal or the sample size is sufficiently large, it is possible to specify the sampling distribution of the z test statistic—it is the standard normal distribution whose μ is 0 and σ is 1. The similarity in appearance between this z test statistic and a z score $[z = (X - \mu)/\sigma]$ is obvious. In either case, z is obtained by subtracting the mean (μ or the hypothesized value of the mean, μ_0) from the statistic and dividing this difference by the standard deviation of the statistic (σ in the case of X, and $\sigma_{\overline{X}}$ in the case of $\overline{X}$). Other test statistics that will be introduced in later chapters include $t = (\overline{X} - \mu_0)/\sigma_{\overline{X}}$ (also used to test a hypothesis about μ), $\chi^2 = (n - 1)\hat{\sigma}^2/\sigma_0^2$ (used to test a hypothesis about σ^2), and $F = \hat{\sigma}_1^2/\hat{\sigma}_2^2$ (used to test the hypothesis that $\sigma_1^2 = \sigma_2^2$).

CHECK YOUR UNDERSTANDING OF SECTION 9.3

15. A population consists of four scores: 0, 1, 2, and 3. (a) List the $(4)(4) = 16$ samples of size two that can be drawn with replacement

---

[1] A demonstration of this is given in Section 9.5.

from the population. (b) Compute the mean and standard error of the mean using the formulas $\mu = \sum_{i=1}^{N} X_i/N$ and $\sigma_{\bar{X}} = \sigma/\sqrt{n}$, where $\sigma = \sqrt{\sum_{i=1}^{N}(X_i - \mu)^2/N}$. (c) Compute the mean and standard error of the mean using the formulas $\mu_{\bar{X}} = \sum_{j=1}^{k} \bar{X}_j/k$ and $\sigma_{\bar{X}} = \sqrt{\sum_{j=1}^{k}(\bar{X}_j - \mu_{\bar{X}})^2/k}$.

16. For the population in Exercise 15, (a) list the $_4C_2 = 6$ samples of size two that can be drawn without replacement. (b) Compute the mean and standard error of the mean using the formulas $\mu = \sum_{i=1}^{N} X_i/N$ and $\sigma_{\bar{X}} = \sigma/\sqrt{n}$, where $\sigma = \sqrt{\sum_{i=1}^{N}(X_i - \mu)^2/N}$. (c) Compute the mean and standard error of the mean using the formulas $\mu_{\bar{X}} = \sum_{j=1}^{k} \bar{X}_j/k$ and $\sigma_{\bar{X}} = \sqrt{\sum_{j=1}^{k}(\bar{X}_j - \mu_{\bar{X}})^2/k}$. The means computed from the two formulas should be equal, but the standard error computed from $\sigma/\sqrt{n}$ overestimates the true value because it assumes an infinite population and/or sampling with replacement. A correction for a finite population or when one is sampling without replacement can be made: $\sigma_{\bar{X}} = (\sigma/\sqrt{n})\sqrt{(N - n)/(N - 1)}$, where N is the number of scores in the population and n is the number in the sample. (d) Apply the correction to $\sigma/\sqrt{n}$. (e) One rule of thumb states that the finite population correction can be ignored when $n/N \le .05$. Use an example to show why this rule is reasonable.

17. How is the dispersion of the sampling distribution of $\bar{X}$ related to σ and n?

18. A sample of size n is to be drawn from a population with a mean of 100 and a standard deviation of 10. Complete the table.

	n	$\sigma_{\bar{X}}$		n	$\sigma_{\bar{X}}$
a.	2		b.	4	
c.	8		d.	16	

19. The registrar claims that the mean IQ of students at a university (μ_0) is 120, with a standard deviation (σ) of 10. You obtain a random sample of 25 students and find that their mean ($\bar{X}$) is 115. What is the probability of obtaining a mean of 115 or lower if the true mean is 120? (*Hint:* Transform $\bar{X}$ to a z score and use the standard normal distribution to find the area below 115.)

20. Terms to remember
   a. Point estimate
   b. Interval estimate
   c. Estimator
   d. Confidence interval
   e. Sampling distribution
   f. Law of large numbers
   g. Central limit theorem
   h. Standard error
   i. Unbiased estimator
   j. Minimum variance estimator
   k. Test statistic

9.4 SUMMARY

Two theoretical distributions provide a bridge between descriptive and inferential statistics: a probability distribution and its close relative, a sampling distribution. A probability distribution associates a probability with each value of a random variable. If the random variable is some function of two or more population elements, say, a mean or a standard deviation, a probability distribution is called a sampling distribution.

The normal distribution is the most widely applicable theoretical model in statistics. It provides an excellent approximation to the binomial distribution and to other theoretical distributions whose probabilities are laborious to calculate when n is large. In addition, it serves as a model for the many variables in science and nature that are approximately normally distributed. But its most important use is as a model for the sampling distribution of statistics based on large n's. According to the central limit theorem, as the sample size n increases, the distribution of $\overline{X}$'s from random samples approaches a normal distribution, with mean μ and standard deviation $\sigma/\sqrt{n}$, whatever the shape of the original population.

The normal distribution is actually a family of distributions, one for each possible combination of μ and σ. The distribution with μ equal to 0 and σ equal to 1 is called the standard normal distribution; it is the distribution whose areas are given in Appendix Table D.2. To use the standard normal distribution table, a score is transformed into a standard score (z) by the formula $z = (X - \mu)/\sigma$ or $(X - \overline{X})/S$. The transformation doesn't affect the shape of the original distribution but does change its mean and standard deviation to 0 and 1, respectively. Standard scores are widely used for reporting psychological test scores because one number contains all the information necessary to interpret a score.

An important new measure of dispersion was introduced in this chapter—the standard error, which is the standard deviation of a statistic. It is a random variable that has been computed from two or more population elements. The standard error describes the dispersion of a statistic over all possible samples of the same size. It is denoted by σ, with a subscript identifying the statistic; for example, $\sigma_{\overline{X}}$ denotes the standard error of the mean. In the following chapters we will see how the elements—standard error, sampling distribution, and test statistic—are used in inferential statistics.

† 9.5 SUPPLEMENTARY NOTE

Demonstration Showing That $\hat{\sigma}^2$ and $\hat{\sigma}^2_{est}$ Are Unbiased Estimators but S^2 Is a Biased Estimator

In Section 9.3 we drew all possible samples of size two with replacement from a finite population to show that the standard error of the mean, $\sigma_{\overline{X}}$, is equal to the

† This supplementary note can be omitted without loss of continuity.

Table 9.5-1. Computation of $\hat{\sigma}^2$, S^2, and σ^2_{est} for All Possible Samples of Size Two From the Population in Figure 9.3-1 (For This Population, $\mu = 2.5$ and $\sigma^2 = 1.25$)

(i) Data (The three variance estimators, $\hat{\sigma}^2_j$, S^2_j, and $\hat{\sigma}^2_{est\,j}$, are each computed from $i = 1, \ldots, n$ scores, where $n = 2$. There are $j = 1, \ldots, k$ variance estimates, where $k = 16$)

(1)	(2)	(3)	(4)	(5)	(6)
Sample Number	Sample Values	$\overline{X}_j$	$\hat{\sigma}^2_j = \dfrac{\sum_{i=1}^{n}(X_i - \overline{X})^2}{n-1}$	$S^2_j = \dfrac{\sum_{i=1}^{n}(X_i - \overline{X})^2}{n}$	$\hat{\sigma}^2_{est\,j} = \dfrac{\sum_{i=1}^{n}(X_i - \mu)^2}{n}$
1	1,1	1.0	0.0	0.00	2.25
2	1,2	1.5	0.5	0.25	1.25
3	2,1	1.5	0.5	0.25	1.25
4	1,3	2.0	2.0	1.00	1.25
5	3,1	2.0	2.0	1.00	1.25
6	1,4	2.5	4.5	2.25	2.25
7	4,1	2.5	4.5	2.25	2.25
8	2,2	2.0	0.0	0.00	0.25
9	2,3	2.5	0.5	0.25	0.25
10	3,2	2.5	0.5	0.25	0.25
11	2,4	3.0	2.0	1.00	1.25
12	4,2	3.0	2.0	1.00	1.25
13	3,3	3.0	0.0	0.00	0.25
14	3,4	3.5	0.5	0.25	1.25
15	4,3	3.5	0.5	0.25	1.25
16	4,4	4.0	0.0	0.00	2.25

(ii) Computation of expected value

$$p(\hat{\sigma}^2_j) = p(S^2_j) = p(\hat{\sigma}^2_{est}) = \frac{1}{16} = .0625$$

$$E(\hat{\sigma}^2) = p(\hat{\sigma}^2_1)\hat{\sigma}^2_1 + p(\hat{\sigma}^2_2)\hat{\sigma}^2_2 + \cdots + p(\hat{\sigma}^2_k)\hat{\sigma}^2_k$$
$$= .0625(0) + .0625(0.5) + \cdots + .0625(0) = 1.25$$

$$E(S^2) = p(S^2_1)S^2_1 + p(S^2_2)S^2_2 + \cdots + p(S^2_k)S^2_k$$
$$= .0625(0) + .0625(0.25) + \cdots + .0625(0) = 0.625$$

$$E(\hat{\sigma}^2_{est}) = p(\hat{\sigma}^2_{est\,1})\hat{\sigma}^2_{est\,1} + p(\hat{\sigma}^2_{est\,2})\hat{\sigma}^2_{est\,2} + \cdots + p(\hat{\sigma}^2_{est\,k})\hat{\sigma}^2_{est\,k}$$
$$= .0625(2.25) + .0625(1.25) + \cdots + .0625(2.25) = 1.25$$

(iii) Computation of variance

$$\text{Var}(\hat{\sigma}^2) = \sum_{j=1}^{k} p(\hat{\sigma}^2_j)\,[\hat{\sigma}^2_j - E(\hat{\sigma}^2)]^2$$
$$= .0625(0 - 1.25)^2 + .0625(0.5 - 1.25)^2 + \cdots + .0625(0 - 1.25)^2$$
$$= 2.0625$$

$$\text{Var}(\hat{\sigma}^2_{est}) = \sum_{j=1}^{k} p(\hat{\sigma}^2_{est\,j})[\hat{\sigma}^2_{est\,j} - E(\hat{\sigma}^2_{est})]^2$$
$$= .0625(2.25 - 1.25)^2 + .0625(1.25 - 1.25)^2 + \cdots + .0625(2.25 - 1.25)^2$$
$$= 0.5000$$

standard deviation of the population divided by the square root of the sample size, that is $\sigma_{\overline{X}} = \sigma/\sqrt{n}$. In this supplementary note we will use the same sampling procedure and data to show that $E(\hat{\sigma}^2) = \sigma^2$ and $E(S^2) \neq \sigma^2$, which means that $\hat{\sigma}^2$ is an unbiased estimator of the parameter σ^2 but S^2 is a biased estimator. The values of σ_j^2 and S_j^2 are shown in Table 9.5-1 and are based on the population in Figure 9.3-1 and the random samples in Table 9.3-1. For the moment we will ignore $\hat{\sigma}_{est\,j}^2$ in column 6 of Table 9.5-1. Because $\hat{\sigma}^2$ is a discrete random variable that assumes values $\hat{\sigma}_1^2, \hat{\sigma}_2^2, \ldots, \hat{\sigma}_k^2$ with probabilities $p(\hat{\sigma}_1^2), p(\hat{\sigma}_2^2), \ldots, p(\hat{\sigma}_k^2)$, the expected value of $\hat{\sigma}^2$ is given by $E(\hat{\sigma}^2) = \sum_{j=1}^{k} p(\hat{\sigma}_j^2)\hat{\sigma}_j^2$. Similarly, the expected value of S^2 is given by $E(S^2) = \sum_{j=1}^{k} p(S_j^2) S_j^2$. It can be seen from the computations in Table 9.5-1 (part ii) that $\hat{\sigma}^2$ is an unbiased estimator of σ^2 because $E(\hat{\sigma}^2) = 1.25 = \hat{\sigma}^2$; however, $E(S^2) = 0.625 < \sigma^2$, which means that S^2 is a biased estimator of σ^2. Thus, dividing $\sum_{i=1}^{n}(X_i - \overline{X})^2$ by $n - 1$ instead of by n provides an unbiased estimator of the population variance.

A second unbiased estimator of the population variance is $\hat{\sigma}_{est}^2$, where $\sum_{i=1}^{n}(X_i - \mu)^2$ is divided by n. According to Table 9.5-1 (part ii), $E(\hat{\sigma}_{est}^2) = 1.25 = \sigma^2$, which means that $\hat{\sigma}_{est}^2$ like $\hat{\sigma}^2$, is an unbiased estimator. It is also a better estimator of σ^2 than is $\hat{\sigma}^2$ because $\hat{\sigma}_{est}^2$ varies less from sample to sample. This is shown in part iii of the table: $Var(\hat{\sigma}_{est}^2) = 0.5000 < Var(\hat{\sigma}^2) = 2.0625$. It turns out that $\hat{\sigma}_{est}^2$ is a minimum variance estimator.

To compute $\hat{\sigma}_{est}^2$ we need to know μ, one of the parameters of the population. Because μ is rarely known in real-life situations, we rely instead on $\hat{\sigma}^2$. In computing $\hat{\sigma}^2$, we use $\overline{X}$ in place of μ; in effect, $\overline{X}$ is used to estimate the unknown population parameter. As a consequence, $\sum_{i=1}^{n}(X_i - \overline{X})^2$ must be divided by $n - 1$ (1 is the number of parameters estimated in the computation) instead of by n to obtain an unbiased estimator of σ^2.

In summary, we have just demonstrated that $\hat{\sigma}^2$ and $\hat{\sigma}_{est}^2$ are unbiased estimators of the population variance and that S^2 is a biased estimator. Furthermore, σ_{est}^2 is a minimum variance estimator. Unfortunately, $\hat{\sigma}_{est}^2$ cannot be used in practice because it requires a knowledge of the population mean, μ. Consequently, we use $\hat{\sigma}^2$ to estimate σ^2. As we have just seen, $\hat{\sigma}^2$ has the desirable property of being unbiased, although it is not a minimum variance estimator.

REVIEW EXERCISES FOR CHAPTER 9

1. Why is the normal distribution so important in statistics?
2. A set of scores has a mean of 50 and a standard deviation of 15. Transform the following to z scores:
   a. 65   b. 35   c. 50   d. 80   e. 45   f. 5
3. If z is a normally distributed random variable with $\mu = 0$ and $\sigma = 1$, determine the percentage of the area under the standard normal curve for the following:
   a. Above z = 2
   b. Below z = −3

c. From μ to $z = 2.5$

d. Between $z = 0.5$ and $z = 1$

e. Between $z = 1$ and $z = -2$

f. Between $z = -2$ and $z = -3$

g. From μ to $z = -1$

h. Between $z = -1$ and $z = 1.5$

4. Determine the percentage of the area of the standard normal distribution that falls between $\mu - k\sigma$ and $\mu + k\sigma$, where k is equal to the following:

    a. 0.5   b. 2.0   c. .67   d. 3.0   e. 2.33

5. Compute the score corresponding to each of the following z scores. Assume that the original distribution had a mean of 150 and a standard deviation of 20.

    a. 3.3   b. 2.5   c. -1.0 d. 1.8   e. 1.645

6. Find the z score such that at least the following proportion of the area under the standard normal distribution falls above it.

    a. .01   b. .16   c. .025   d. .84   e. .99

7. In the general population, Stanford-Binet IQs are nearly normally distributed, with a mean of 100 and a standard deviation of 16. (a) What is the probability that a randomly selected person will have an IQ between 100 and 124? (b) What proportion of the population will have IQs above 132?

8. Grading on the curve means assigning grades according to the normal distribution. The mean of a test is 50, with a standard deviation of 10. If 10% of the class receives A's, what is the lowest score that receives an A?

9. The time from conception to birth in humans is approximately normally distributed, with a mean of 280.5 days and a standard deviation of 8.4 days. In a paternity case it was proved that the time from the alleged conception to the birth of a 6.5-lb. baby was at least 306 days. (a) Compute the proportion of women having this or a longer gestation time. (b) Discuss the significance of the evidence.

10. Suppose that 64% of stocks recommended by a broker increase in value within six months. Use the normal approximation to the binomial distribution to determine the probability that of 372 recommendations, (a) at least 225 will increase in value and (b) more than 250 will increase in value.

11. The statement "Jane got a 29 on the quiz" is uninterpretable. Discuss.

12. Compare the relative merits of standard scores and percentile ranks for interpreting scores.

13. On a mechanical aptitude test, Bill scored 110 and Elaine scored 85. The population mean for men is 104, with a standard deviation of 20. The comparable norms for women are 70 and 30. Which of the two did better, considering the norms for their genders?

14. Suppose that the mean of a test was 30 and the standard deviation was 8. Transform a score of 18 to standard scores with the following means and standard deviations:
    a. $\bar{X} = 100$, $S = 10$ b. $\bar{X} = 500$, $S = 100$ c. $\bar{X} = 80$, $S = 10$

15. Distinguish a sampling distribution from a sample (frequency) distribution.

16. A population consists of five scores: 0, 1, 2, 3, and 4. (a) List the $(5)(5) = 25$ samples of size two that can be drawn with replacement from the population. (b) Compute the mean and standard error of the mean using the formulas $\mu = \Sigma_{i=1}^{N} X_i/N$ and $\sigma_{\bar{X}} = \sigma/\sqrt{n}$, where $\sigma = \sqrt{\Sigma_{i=1}^{N}(X_i - \mu)^2/N}$. (c) Compute the mean and standard error of the mean using the formulas $\mu_{\bar{X}} = \Sigma_{j=1}^{k} \bar{X}_j/k$ and $\sigma_{\bar{X}} = \sqrt{\Sigma_{j=1}^{k}(\bar{X}_j - \mu_{\bar{X}})^2/k}$.

17. For the population in Exercise 16, (a) list the $_5C_2 = 10$ samples of size two that can be drawn without replacement. (b) Compute the mean and standard error of the mean using the formulas $\mu = \Sigma_{i=1}^{N} X_i/N$ and $\sigma_{\bar{X}} = \sigma/\sqrt{n}$, where $\sigma = \sqrt{\Sigma_{i=1}^{N}(X_i - \mu)^2/N}$. (c) Compute the mean and standard error of the mean using the formulas $\mu_{\bar{X}} = \Sigma_{j=1}^{k} \bar{X}_j/k$ and $\sigma_{\bar{X}} = \sqrt{\Sigma_{j=1}^{k}(\bar{X}_j - \mu_{\bar{X}})^2/k}$. The means computed from the two formulas should be equal, but the standard error computed from $\sigma/\sqrt{n}$ overestimates the true value because it assumes an infinite population or sampling with replacement. A correction for a finite population or when one is sampling without replacement can be made: $\sigma_{\bar{X}} = (\sigma/\sqrt{n})\sqrt{(N - n)/(N - 1)}$, where N is the number of scores in the population and n is the number in the sample. (d) Apply the correction to $\sigma/\sqrt{n}$. (e) One rule of thumb states that the finite population correction can be ignored when $n/N \le .05$. Use an example to show why this rule is reasonable.

18. Distinguish a standard error from a standard deviation.

19. A sample of size n is to be drawn from a population with a mean of 63 and a standard deviation of 15. Complete the table.

n	$\sigma_{\bar{X}}$	n	$\sigma_{\bar{X}}$
a. 3		b. 9	
c. 27		d. 81	

20. An elevator has a maximum safe load of 1,638 pounds. If men's weights are approximately normally distributed with a mean of 165 pounds and a standard deviation of 15 pounds, what is the probability that nine men (whose weights can be assumed to be independent) will overload the elevator?

Chapter 10

Statistical Inference: One Sample

10.1 INTRODUCTION TO HYPOTHESIS TESTING

Evaluating the effectiveness of a new teaching technology or assessing attitudes toward violence on TV involves making a decision on the basis of incomplete information. The researcher's information is usually incomplete because it is impossible or impractical to observe all the people in the population of interest—for example, all schoolchildren or all TV viewers. Fortunately, there are procedures for making rational decisions about nature that use a sample containing only a small portion of the elements in the population. These procedures, called **statistical inference,** are the subject of this and subsequent chapters.

Several approaches to making decisions about a population use information from a sample, but we will limit our discussion to classical statistical inference,[1] which evolved from the work of R. A. Fisher and, more directly, Jerzy Neyman and Egon Pearson.[2] Two complementary topics fall under classical statistical inference—null hypothesis significance testing and confidence interval estimation. We will describe hypothesis testing first because the procedure is applicable to a broad range of statistical inference problems and is widely used in the behavioral sciences, health sciences, and education. Confidence interval estimation is applicable to a narrower range of inference problems. However, when the procedure can be used, it is much more informative than null hypothesis significance testing.

Scientific Hypotheses

People are by nature inquisitive. We ask questions, develop hunches, and sometimes put our hunches to the test. Over the years, a formalized procedure for testing hunches has evolved—the scientific method. It involves (1) observing nature, (2) asking questions, (3) formulating hypotheses, (4) conducting experiments, and (5) developing theories and laws. Let's examine in detail the third characteristic, formulating hypotheses.

A **scientific hypothesis** is a testable supposition that is tentatively adopted to account for certain facts and to guide in the investigation of others. It is a statement about nature that requires verification.

Some examples of scientific hypotheses are the following: The child-rearing practices of parents affect the personalities of their offspring. Students involved in student government have higher IQs than average college students. Cigarette smoking

---

[1] Other less widely used approaches are the likelihood function and Bayesian decision theory. For a discussion of these approaches, see Kirk (1972, chap. 10).

[2] The major contributions of Fisher and of Neyman and Pearson to statistical theory are summarized by Dudycha and Dudycha (1972, pp. 21–24).

is associated with high blood pressure. Children who feel insecure engage in overt aggression more frequently than children who feel secure. These hypotheses have three characteristics in common with all scientific hypotheses: (1) They are intelligent, informed guesses about phenomena of interest. (2) They can be stated in the *if-then* form of an implication, for example, "*if* John smokes, *then* he will show signs of high blood pressure." (3) Their truth or falsity can be determined by observation and experimentation.

Many interesting hypotheses don't qualify as scientific hypotheses because they aren't testable by recourse to experience. Such questions as "Can three or more angels sit on the head of a pin?" and "Does life exist in more than one galaxy in the universe?" can't be investigated because no procedures presently exist for observing angels or other galaxies. This doesn't mean that the question concerning the existence of life in other galaxies can never be investigated. Indeed, with continuing advances in space science, it is likely that this question eventually will be answered.

Why Statistical Inference?

We have said that statistical inference is a form of reasoning whereby rational decisions about states of nature can be made on the basis of incomplete information. Rational decisions often can be made without resorting to statistical inference, as when a scientific hypothesis concerns some limited phenomenon that is directly observable, for example, "This rat will run under condition *X*." The truth or falsity of the hypothesis can be determined by observing the rat under condition *X*.

Many scientific hypotheses, on the other hand, refer to phenomena that can't be directly observed—that is, to populations whose elements are so numerous that viewing them all is impossible or impractical, for example, "All rats run under condition *X*." It is impossible to observe the entire population of rats under condition *X*. Likewise, it is impossible to observe all parents rearing their children, all student leaders, all smokers, or all insecure children. If a scientific hypothesis cannot be evaluated directly by observing all members of a population, it may be possible to evaluate the hypothesis indirectly by statistical inference. Recourse to statistical inference, which involves observing a sample from the population of interest, enables a researcher to make a rational decision concerning the probable truth or falsity of the scientific hypothesis.

Statistical Hypotheses

Scientific hypotheses are statements about phenomena of nature and man and are normally stated in fairly general terms—at least in the initial stages of an inquiry. As we have said, if a scientific hypothesis can't be evaluated directly by observing all members of a population, it may be possible to evaluate the hypothesis indirectly by statistical inference. To do this, a researcher must express a scientific hypothesis in the form of a *statistical hypothesis.*

> A **statistical hypothesis** is a statement about one or more parameters of a population distribution that requires verification.

For example, $\mu > 115$ is a statistical hypothesis; it states that the population mean denoted by μ is greater than 115. Another statistical hypothesis can be formulated that states that the mean is less than or equal to 115 — that is, $\mu \leq 115$. These hypotheses, $\mu \leq 115$ and $\mu > 115$, are mutually exclusive and exhaustive; if one is true, the other must be false. They are examples, respectively, of the **null hypothesis,** denoted by H_0, and the **alternative hypothesis,** denoted by H_1. The null hypothesis is the one whose tenability is actually tested. If on the basis of this test the null hypothesis is rejected, only the alternative hypothesis remains tenable. According to convention, the alternative hypothesis is formulated so that it corresponds to the researcher's hunch.[3] The process of choosing between the null and alternative hypotheses is called **hypothesis testing.**

An example may help to clarify the nature of the null and alternative hypotheses. Consider the scientific hypothesis that student leaders are more intelligent than average college students. Let's assume that the population mean of college students' IQs, denoted by μ_0, is known to equal 115. (This information could come from college entrance examinations.) The population mean of student leaders' IQs, denoted by μ, is unknown but can be estimated from a random sample. The null hypothesis, which is contrary to what we believe to be true about μ, is $H_0: \mu \leq 115$. In words, this null hypothesis states that the population mean of student leaders' IQs is less than or equal to 115. The alternative hypothesis is $H_1: \mu > 115$. We have followed the convention of equating the alternative hypothesis with the situation we believe to be true — that student leaders have higher IQs than average college students. In this example the scientific hypothesis and its negation are expressed as two mutually exclusive and exhaustive statistical hypotheses concerning the value of μ, the population mean of student leaders.

Sometimes a researcher's scientific hypothesis as originally formulated is identical in meaning to the alternative statistical hypothesis. This is most likely to occur in research areas that have been extensively investigated. In such cases it is necessary only to formulate an appropriate null hypothesis.

Hypothesis Testing and the Method of Indirect Proof

You may marvel at the roundabout procedure whereby a researcher tests a null hypothesis that is believed to be untrue in the hope of rejecting it and thereby accept-

---

[3] The merits of this convention have been extensively debated by Binder (1963), Edwards (1965), Grant (1962), Wilson and Miller (1964), and Wilson, Miller, and Lower (1967). Articles setting forth the basic issues in the controversy are contained in Kirk (1972, chap. 4).

ing the alternative hypothesis that is believed to be true. On reflection, you may recall a similar technique that is taught in plane geometry and algebra—the method of indirect proof. This method consists of listing all possible answers or solutions to a problem and showing that all but one are contrary to known fact or lead to an absurdity. By a process of elimination, the one that isn't contrary to known fact or absurd must be true. The success of the method of indirect proof depends upon listing all possibilities and finding a contradiction for all but one. The comparable procedure in null hypothesis testing consists of formulating the null and alternative hypotheses so that they exhaust all possibilities concerning a population parameter. A sample is obtained from the population, and an appropriate statistic, such as the sample mean, is computed. If it is highly improbable that the obtained value of the sample statistic would have occurred if the null hypothesis were true, then the null hypothesis must be considered a poor prediction of the parameter and should be rejected in favor of the alternative hypothesis.

There is one important difference between the method of indirect proof and null hypothesis testing. In indirect proof, a possibility is rejected only if it is found to lead to a contradiction to known fact or is absurd. In hypothesis testing, the null hypothesis is rejected if the obtained value of a sample statistic is very unlikely if the null hypothesis is indeed true. It follows that null hypothesis testing, unlike the method of indirect proof, doesn't provide incontrovertible proof because the null hypothesis is rejected because of the occurrence of an event that is improbable but not impossible.

Rejection or Nonrejection of H_0—What Does It Mean?

If the null hypothesis isn't rejected, what conclusion can be drawn? Is the null hypothesis true? Not necessarily; there are always alternative reasons for why the null hypothesis isn't rejected:

1. The null hypothesis is true and shouldn't be rejected.
2. The null hypothesis is false and should be rejected, but the particular sample that was obtained is not representative of the population.
3. The null hypothesis is false and should be rejected, but the experimental methodology is not sufficiently sensitive to detect the true situation.

An experimental methodology can lack sensitivity for a variety of reasons: The size of the sample is too small, the measuring procedure produces large random or systematic errors, and so on. Sometimes a random sampling procedure will produce a random sample that is not representative of the population and one that is consistent with the false null hypothesis. We know, for example, that a fair coin will, on occasion, produce 10 or even 100 consecutive heads. If the null hypothesis isn't rejected, the researcher has two options: State that he or she failed to reject the null hypothesis, in which case it remains credible, or suspend judgment about the null and scientific hypotheses pending completion of a new, improved experiment.

On the other hand, if the null hypothesis is rejected, what does it mean? The researcher can conclude that the alternative hypothesis is probably true. Here, too, the possibility always exists that one's sample isn't representative, but, as we will see later, the probability of erroneously rejecting a true null hypothesis is determined by the researcher and can be made as small as desired.

The Role of Logic in Evaluating a Scientific Hypothesis

We have just dealt with the evaluation of statistical hypotheses. We turn now to the researcher's ultimate objective—evaluating a scientific hypothesis. This evaluation involves a chain of deductive and inductive logic that begins and ends with the scientific hypothesis. The chain is diagrammed in Figure 10.1-1. First, by means of deductive logic, the scientific hypothesis and its negation are expressed as two mutually exclusive and exhaustive statistical hypotheses that make predictions concerning a population parameter. These predictions, denoted by H_0 and H_1, are made about the population mean, median, variance, and so on. If, as is usually the case, all the elements in the population can't be observed, a random sample is obtained from the population. The sample provides an estimate of the unknown population parameter.

The process of deciding whether to reject the null hypothesis is called a **statistical test.** The decision is based on (1) a test statistic computed from a random sample from the population, (2) hypothesis testing conventions, and (3) a decision rule.

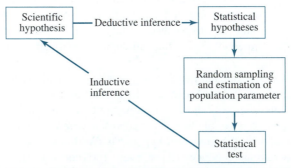

Figure 10.1-1. **The evaluation of a scientific hypothesis using deductive and inductive logic.**

These items are described in subsequent sections. The outcome of the statistical test is the basis for the final link in the chain shown in Figure 10.1-1: an inductive inference concerning the probable truth or falsity of the scientific hypothesis.

Logic therefore plays a key role in hypothesis testing. It is the basis for arriving at both the statistical hypothesis that is tested and the final decision regarding the scientific hypothesis. If errors occur in the deductive or inductive links in the chain of logic, the statistical hypothesis being tested may have little or no bearing on the original scientific hypothesis, or the inference concerning the scientific hypothesis may be incorrect, or both. Consider the scientific hypothesis that cigarette smoking is associated with high blood pressure. If this hypothesis is true, a measure of central tendency such as mean blood pressure should be higher for the population of smokers than for the population of nonsmokers. The statistical hypotheses are

$$H_0: \mu_S - \mu_N \leq 0$$
$$H_1: \mu_S - \mu_N > 0,$$

where μ_S and μ_N denote the population means for smokers and nonsmokers, respectively. The null hypothesis, H_0, states in effect that the mean blood pressure of smokers is less than or equal to that of nonsmokers; the alternative hypothesis states that the mean blood pressure of smokers is greater than that of nonsmokers. These hypotheses follow logically from the original scientific hypothesis. Suppose that the researcher formulated the statistical hypotheses in terms of population variances, for example,

$$H_0: \sigma_S^2 - \sigma_N^2 \leq 0$$
$$H_1: \sigma_S^2 - \sigma_N^2 > 0,$$

where σ_S^2 and σ_N^2 denote the population variances of smokers and nonsmokers, respectively. A statistical test of this null hypothesis, which states in effect that the variance of blood pressure for the population of smokers is less than or equal to the variance for nonsmokers, would have little bearing on the original scientific hypothesis. However, it would be relevant if the researcher were interested in determining whether the two populations differed in dispersion.

The reader should not infer that for any scientific hypothesis there is only one pertinent null hypothesis. A null hypothesis stating that the correlation between number of cigarettes smoked and blood pressure is zero bears more directly on the scientific hypothesis than does the one involving population means. If cigarette smoking is associated with high blood pressure, there should be a positive correlation, $\rho > 0$, between cigarette consumption and blood pressure. The statistical hypotheses are

$$H_0: \rho \leq 0$$
$$H_1: \rho > 0,$$

where ρ denotes the population correlation coefficient for cigarette consumption and blood pressure. So we see that both creativity and deductive skill are required to formulate pertinent statistical hypotheses.

CHECK YOUR UNDERSTANDING OF SECTION 10.1

1. Which of the following are scientific hypotheses?
    a. Right-handed people tend to be taller than left-handed people.
    b. Behavior therapy is more effective than hypnosis in helping smokers kick the habit.
    c. Most clairvoyant people are able to communicate with beings from outer space.
    d. Rats are likely to fixate an incorrect response if it is followed by an intense noxious stimulus.

2. Which of the following are examples of statistical hypotheses?
    a. $H_0: \mu = 100$
    b. $H_0: S^2 \leq 50$
    c. $H_1: \rho \neq 0$
    d. $H_0: \overline{X} > 100$
    e. $H_1: \sigma^2 > 0$
    f. $H_1: \overline{X} < 15$
    g. $H_0: \mu \geq 60$
    h. $H_0: r = 0$
    i. $H_0: \sigma^2 = 225$
    j. $H_0: \rho = 0$

3. a. According to convention, which statistical hypothesis corresponds to the researcher's scientific hunch?
    b. Which is the hypothesis that actually is tested?

4. Assume that a researcher has a hunch that insecure children engage in overt aggression more frequently than children who feel secure. Let μ and μ_0 denote the mean daily number of aggressive acts, respectively, of insecure and secure children, where it is known that $\mu_0 = 8$. Let $\alpha = .05$. State H_0 and H_1 for the research.

5. It was hypothesized that a sample of 139 women seeking treatment for marital discord at the University Marital Therapy Clinic would have a mean score above 14 on the Beck Depression Inventory (BDI). A score of 14 indicates depressive symptomatology or dysphoria. Let μ denote the BDI mean for the population of women seeking treatment and μ_0, the criterion for depressive symptomatology. Let $\alpha = .05$. State H_0 and H_1 for the research.

6. Terms to remember
    a. Statistical inference
    b. Scientific hypothesis
    c. Statistical hypothesis
    d. Null hypothesis
    e. Alternative hypothesis
    f. Hypothesis testing
    g. Statistical test

10.2 HYPOTHESIS TESTING

We will now describe the procedures for testing statistical hypotheses. For the sake of clarity, these procedures are organized around five steps and a decision rule. This should not suggest that hypothesis testing is a formal or a rigid procedure—it isn't.

However, as a researcher makes plans for doing research, each of the items in the following steps must be considered.

Step 1. State the null and alternative hypotheses.

Step 2. Specify the test statistic based on the hypothesis to be tested, information that is known about the population, and assumptions about the population that appear to be tenable.

Step 3. Specify the size n of the sample to be obtained and make assumptions that permit specification of the sampling distribution of the test statistic, given that H_0 is true.

Step 4. Specify an acceptable risk of rejecting the null hypothesis when it is true.

Step 5. Obtain a random sample of size n from the population, compute the test statistic, and make a decision about the null and alternative hypotheses and an inductive inference about the scientific hypothesis.

Decision rule:

Reject the null hypothesis if the test statistic falls in the specified region of the sampling distribution of the test statistic; otherwise, don't reject the null hypothesis. Rejection of the null hypothesis leads one to infer that the scientific hypothesis is true.

We will now examine these five steps and the decision rule in some detail.

Step 1: Stating the Statistical Hypotheses

Let's assume that we are interested in testing the scientific hypothesis that students involved in student government have higher IQs than average college students. The corresponding statistical hypothesis is $\mu > \mu_0$, where μ denotes the unknown population mean of student leaders and μ_0 denotes the population mean of college students. Assume also that μ_0 and the population standard deviation, σ, of college students are known to equal 115 and 15, respectively. We can now state the null and alternative hypotheses:

$$H_0: \mu \leq 115$$
$$H_1: \mu > 115,$$

where μ_0 has been replaced by 115, the known population mean of college students. As written, the null hypothesis is inexact because it states a whole range of possible values for the population mean—all values less than or equal to 115. However, one exact value is specified, $\mu = 115$, and that is the value actually tested. If the null hypothesis $\mu = 115$ can be rejected, then the hypothesis $\mu < 115$ is rejected automatically. Obviously, if $\mu = 115$ is considered improbable because the sample statistic exceeds 115, any population mean whose value is less than 115 would be considered even less probable.

Step 2: Specifying the Test Statistic

A relatively small number of test statistics are used to evaluate hypotheses about population parameters. The principal ones are denoted by z, t, χ^2, and F. A test statistic is called a z *statistic* if its sampling distribution is the normal distribution; a test statistic is called a t *statistic* if its sampling distribution is a t distribution; and so on. As we will see, the choice of a test statistic is determined by (1) the hypothesis to be tested, (2) the information that is known about the population, and (3) the assumptions about the population that appear to be tenable. Which test statistic should be used to test the hypothesis H_0: $\mu \leq 115$? Because the hypothesis concerns the mean of a single population, the population standard deviation is known, and the population is assumed to be approximately normal, the appropriate test statistic is

$$z = \frac{\overline{X} - \mu_0}{\sigma_{\overline{X}}} = \frac{\overline{X} - \mu_0}{\sigma/\sqrt{n}}.$$

The factors that lead a researcher to choose one test statistic over another are discussed in Chapters 11, 12, and 13 and are summarized in Tables 11.7-1, 12.7-1, and 13.5-1.

Step 3: Specifying *n* and the Sampling Distribution

In specifying the sample size, we must keep in mind that to use the standard normal distribution table, Table D.2 in Appendix D, the sampling distribution of our z test statistic must be normal. To be more precise, we should say *approximately normal*, because in practice random variables do not range from $-\infty$ to ∞ and, hence, they are never normally distributed. For simplicity, we will often omit the qualifier "approximately." The sampling distribution of the z test statistic will be normal if the sampling distribution of $\overline{X}$ is normal. This follows because the z test statistic is a linear transformation of $\overline{X}$ in which $\overline{X} - \mu_0$ is divided by $\sigma_{\overline{X}}$. The sampling distribution of $\overline{X}$ will be normal if the population distribution of X is normal or if the sample is fairly large, say, $n \geq 100$. This follows from the central limit theorem, discussed in Section 9.3. In the case of student leaders' IQs, the population distribution is probably nearly normal because college students' IQs are approximately normally distributed. To be on the safe side, we will rely on a large sample and obtain an n of 100. Later, we will describe a more rational way to determine the value of n. For practical reasons—limitations on the availability of research funds and time and the difficulty of securing participants—we don't want to specify a larger n than is needed.

We can specify the sampling distributions of the random variables $\overline{X}$ and z, given that the null hypothesis is true, on the basis of the information that (1) $\mu_0 = 115$, (2) $\sigma = 15$, and (3) $n = 100$ and the assumptions that $(1)^4$ $\mu = 115$ and (2) the population distribution of X is approximately normal. If our information and assumptions are correct, the sampling distribution of $\overline{X}$ will be normal, with mean equal to 115 and standard error equal to $\sigma/\sqrt{n} = 15/\sqrt{100} = 1.5$. This follows from the central limit theorem, discussed in Section 9.3. Because the z test statistic is simply a linear transformation of $\overline{X}$, the sampling distribution of z also will be normal, with (as we saw in Chapter 9) mean equal to 0 and standard deviation equal to 1. We now have carried out the third step in testing the null hypothesis: We have specified the sample size, n, and the sampling distribution of the z test statistic.

Step 4: Specifying α

If we decided that $\mu > 115$ when in fact $\mu \leq 115$, we would have made a decision error. The fourth step is to specify an acceptable risk of making this kind of error—that is, rejecting the null hypothesis when it is true. We will touch on this subject here and return to it later. Considering the sample-to-sample variability of random variables, we wouldn't expect the mean, $\overline{X}$, of a single random sample to exactly equal the predicted value, μ_0, even though $\mu = \mu_0$. We probably would be willing to attribute a small discrepancy between $\overline{X}$ and μ_0 to chance, but if the discrepancy is large enough, we would be inclined to believe that μ_0 is incorrect and that the null hypothesis should be rejected. According to hypothesis-testing conventions, a discrepancy between $\overline{X}$ and μ_0 that would be expected to occur five or fewer times in 100 replications of the experiment is considered to be large enough to warrant rejecting the hypothesis $\mu = \mu_0$. Stated another way, the null hypothesis $\mu = \mu_0$ should be rejected if the probability is equal to or less than .05 of observing a discrepancy between $\overline{X}$ and μ_0 as large as or larger than that observed.

A probability of .05 is by convention the largest risk a researcher is willing to take of rejecting a true null hypothesis—declaring, for example, that $\mu > 115$ when in fact $\mu \leq 115$. Such a probability, called a **level of significance,** is designated by the lowercase Greek letter alpha, α. For $\alpha = .05$ and $H_1: \mu > 115$, the region for rejecting H_0, called the **critical region,** is shown in Figure 10.2-1. The location and size of the critical region are determined, respectively, by H_1 and α.

A decision to adopt the .05, .01, or any other level of significance is based on hypothesis-testing conventions that have evolved over the past 70 years. Unfortunately, these conventions don't always lead to decisions that are optimal for a

---

^{4} Recall that this "assumption" is the null hypothesis to be tested and the hypothesis that the researcher hopes to reject.

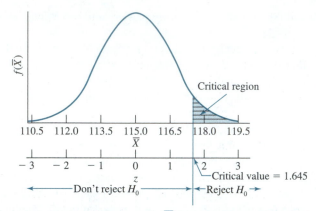

Figure 10.2-1. **Sampling distribution of $\overline{X}$ and z, given that H_0 is true. The critical region, which corresponds in this example to the upper .05 portion of the sampling distribution, defines values of $\overline{X}$ and z that are improbable if the null hypothesis $H_0\colon \mu \leq 115$ is true. Hence, if the z test statistic falls in the critical region, the null hypothesis is rejected. The value of z that cuts off the upper .05 portion of the sampling distribution is called the critical value. This value can be found in the standard normal distribution table, Appendix Table D.2, and is 1.645. It can be shown that the corresponding $\overline{X}$ value is given by $\mu_0 + z(\sigma/\sqrt{n}) = 115 + 1.645(15/\sqrt{100}) = 117.47$.**

researcher's purposes. In Section 10.4 we will return to the problem of selecting a level of significance.

Step 5: Making a Decision

The fifth step in testing a statistical hypothesis is to obtain a random sample from the population of interest, compute the test statistic, and make a decision. The **decision rule** is: Reject the null hypothesis if the test statistic falls in the critical region; otherwise, don't reject the null hypothesis. The value of z that cuts off the critical region of the sampling distribution of z is called the **critical value** (see Figure 10.2-1). In our example, this value is denoted by $z_{.05}$, where .05 represents the size of the critical region. According to the decision rule, the null hypothesis is rejected if the observed z test statistic exceeds or equals the critical value, $z_{.05}$. Otherwise, the null hypothesis is not rejected.

If the null hypothesis is rejected, a researcher can conclude that the scientific hypothesis is probably true. But what if the null hypothesis is not rejected? In such cases the researcher can either conclude that the evidence does not support the scientific hypothesis or suspend judgment pending the completion of a new, improved experiment.

CHECK YOUR UNDERSTANDING OF SECTION 10.2

7. For the past several years the mean arithmetic-achievement score for a population of ninth-grade students has been 45 with σ equal to 15. After participating in an experimental teaching program, a random sample of 100 students had a mean score of 50. (a) List the five steps you would follow in testing the hypothesis that the new program leads to better arithmetic achievement than the old program, and supply the required information. Let $\alpha = .05$. (b) State the decision rule.

8. For the data in Exercise 7 draw the sampling distribution associated with the null hypothesis, and indicate the region(s) that leads to rejection and nonrejection of the null hypothesis.

9. a. Which of the following statistical hypotheses actually is tested?

$$H_0: \mu \le 15$$

$$H_1: \mu > 15$$

   b. Which hypothesis corresponds to the researcher's scientific hypothesis?

10. What determines the size of the critical region and its location?

11. Terms to remember
    a. Level of significance   b. Critical region
    c. Critical value

10.3   ONE-SAMPLE z TEST FOR A MEAN WHEN THE VARIANCE IS KNOWN

We will now illustrate the use of

$$z = \frac{\overline{X} - \mu_0}{\sigma/\sqrt{n}}$$

in testing a hypothesis about a population mean. Recall that $\overline{X}$ is the mean of a random sample from the population of interest, μ_0 is the mean specified in the null hypothesis, σ is the standard deviation of the population, and n is the number of elements in the sample used to compute $\overline{X}$. To use this formula we must know the population standard deviation, σ. In Chapter 11 we will treat the case in which σ is unknown but can be estimated from sample data.

Let's assume that a random sample of 100 students who are leaders in student government has been obtained from the population of student leaders at the Big Ten universities and that the mean IQ of this sample is 117. The number 117 is a point estimate of μ. It is the best guess we can make concerning the unknown value of μ. The statistical hypotheses that we want to test are

$$H_0: \mu \leq 115$$
$$H_1: \mu > 115.$$

How improbable is a sample mean of 117 if the population mean is really 115? Would it occur five or fewer times in 100 by chance? Stated another way, does the sample statistic $\overline{X} = 117$ fall in the critical region, which for our example is the upper 5% of the sampling distribution? To answer this question we will transform the random variable $\overline{X}$ into a z random variable, with sampling distribution (if H_0 is true) identical to the standard normal distribution listed in Appendix Table D.2. If z falls in the upper 5% of the sampling distribution of z, we know that $\overline{X}$ also falls in the upper 5% of the sampling distribution of $\overline{X}$. Figure 10.2-1 illustrates the correspondence between the two sampling distributions. The linear transformation of $\overline{X}$ into a z test statistic is a convenience that enables us to use the standard normal distribution table.

The steps to be followed in testing the null hypothesis and the decision rule are as follows:

Step 1. State the statistical hypotheses: $H_0: \mu \leq 115$
$H_1: \mu > 115.$

Step 2. Specify the test statistic: $z = \dfrac{\overline{X} - \mu_0}{\sigma/\sqrt{n}}$ because we want to test $\mu \leq 115$, σ is known, and we assume the population distribution of X is approximately normal.

Step 3. Specify the sample size: $n = 100$;
and the sampling distribution: standard normal distribution because σ is known and the population distribution of $\overline{X}$ is approximately normal.

Step 4. Specify the level of significance: $\alpha = .05$.
Step 5. Obtain a random sample of size n, compute z, and make a decision.

Decision rule:

Reject the null hypothesis if z falls in the upper 5% of the sampling distribution of z; otherwise, don't reject the null hypothesis. If the null hypothesis is rejected, conclude that the mean IQ of student leaders at Big Ten universities is higher than that of average college students; if the null hypothesis is not rejected, do not draw this conclusion.

The z test statistic for our example is

$$z = \frac{\overline{X} - \mu_0}{\sigma/\sqrt{n}} = \frac{117 - 115}{15/\sqrt{100}} = \frac{2}{1.5} = 1.33.$$

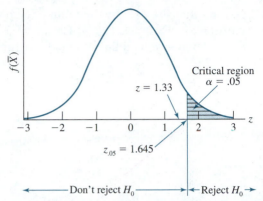

Figure 10.3-1. **Sampling distribution of z under the null hypothesis. Because z = 1.33 falls short of the critical region, the null hypothesis is not rejected.**

According to Appendix Table D.2, the value of z that cuts off the upper .05 region of the sampling distribution is 1.645. This value of z, called the critical value, is denoted by $z_{.05}$, where the subscript .05 refers to the proportion of the sampling distribution that falls above the $z = 1.645$. Because the value of the z test statistic, $z = 1.33$, is less than the critical value, $z_{.05} = 1.645$, the observed z falls short of the upper .05 critical region. This is illustrated in Figure 10.3-1. According to our decision rule, we fail to reject the null hypothesis and therefore conclude that our sample data don't indicate that the mean IQ of student leaders at the Big Ten universities is higher than that of average college students. Two points need to be emphasized. First, we haven't proven that the null hypothesis is true—only that the evidence doesn't warrant its rejection. Second, our conclusion has been restricted to the population from which we sampled, namely, the Big Ten universities.

CHECK YOUR UNDERSTANDING OF SECTION 10.3

12. Under what conditions is the sampling distribution of $z = (\overline{X} - \mu_0)/\sigma_{\overline{X}}$ the same as the standard normal distribution?
13. Assume that the Pd (Psychopathic deviate) scale of the Minnesota Multiphasic Personality Inventory has been given to a random sample of 30 men classified as habitual criminals. The researcher wants to test the hypothesis that habitual criminals have higher Pd scores than noncriminals. The latter population is known to be normally distributed, with mean and standard deviation equal to 50 and 10, respectively. (a) List the five steps you would follow in testing the scientific hypothesis. Let $\alpha = .05$. (b) State the decision rule.

14. Assume that the data in the table have been obtained for the habitual criminals in Exercise 13. (a) Compute a z statistic for these data. (b) What conclusion can be drawn about the scientific hypothesis in Exercise 13?

Participant	Pd Score	Participant	Pd Score
1	50	16	55
2	51	17	56
3	54	18	48
4	55	19	45
5	25	20	41
6	61	21	82
7	64	22	65
8	55	23	67
9	55	24	75
10	52	25	40
11	71	26	61
12	57	27	35
13	59	28	56
14	54	29	56
15	55	30	55

15. If $\alpha = .001$ in Exercise 14, what conclusion would have been drawn about the scientific hypothesis?
16. One of the prison guards confessed that for a lark he had filled out the Pd scale and used a prisoner's name, participant number 22. (a) Recompute the z statistic for the data in Exercise 14, eliminating participant 22's score. (b) What conclusion can be drawn about the scientific hypothesis?

10.4 MORE ABOUT HYPOTHESIS TESTING

In Section 10.2 we described the steps used in testing a hypothesis; we illustrated these steps in Section 10.3 by means of a one-sample z test. We now turn to several new concepts that round out our discussion of null hypothesis significance testing.

One- and Two-Tailed Tests

A statistical test for which the critical region is in either the upper tail or the lower tail of the sampling distribution is called a **one-tailed test.** If the critical region is in both the upper and lower tails of the sampling distribution, the statistical test is called a **two-tailed test.**

A one-tailed test is used whenever the researcher makes a **directional** prediction concerning the phenomenon of interest, for example, that the mean IQ of student leaders at Big Ten universities is higher than that of average college students. We know from Section 10.3 that the statistical hypotheses corresponding to this scientific hypothesis are

$$H_0: \mu \leq \mu_0$$
$$H_1: \mu > \mu_0.$$

These hypotheses are called **directional,** or **one-sided, hypotheses.** The region for rejecting the null hypothesis is shown in Figure 10.3-1. If the scientific hypothesis stated that the mean IQ of student leaders is lower than that of average college students, the following statistical hypotheses would be appropriate:

$$H_0: \mu \geq \mu_0$$
$$H_1: \mu < \mu_0.$$

The region for rejecting this null hypothesis is shown in Figure 10.4-1(a). To be significant, an observed z statistic would have to be less than or equal to the critical value $-z_{.05} = -1.645$.

Often, we don't have sufficient information to make a directional prediction about a population parameter; we simply believe that the parameter is not equal to the value specified by the null hypothesis. For example, we may believe that the mean IQ of student leaders is different from that of average college students. This situation calls for a two-tailed test. The statistical hypotheses for a two-tailed test have the following form:

$$H_0: \mu = \mu_0$$
$$H_1: \mu \neq \mu_0.$$

These hypotheses are called **nondirectional,** or **two-sided, hypotheses.** For a two-tailed test, the region for rejecting the null hypothesis lies in both the upper and lower tails of the sampling distribution. The two-tailed critical region is shown in Figure 10.4-1(b). To reject the null hypothesis at the .05 level of significance, the value of the z test statistic

$$z = \frac{\overline{X} - \mu_0}{\sigma/\sqrt{n}} = \frac{117 - 115}{15/\sqrt{100}} = \frac{2}{1.5} = 1.33$$

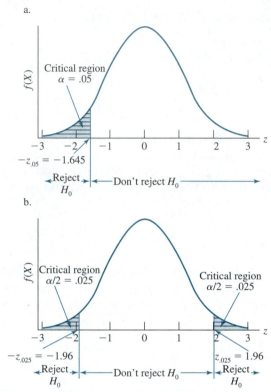

Figure 10.4-1. **(a) Critical region for one-tailed test; H_0: $\mu \geq \mu_0$; H_1: $\mu < \mu_0$; $\alpha = .05$. (b) Critical regions for two-tailed test; H_0: $\mu = \mu_0$; H_1: $\mu \neq \mu_0$; $\alpha = .025 + .025 = .05$.**

must be greater than or equal to $z_{.05/2} = 1.96$ or less than or equal to $-z_{.05/2} = -1.96$. Because $z = 1.33$ is less than $z_{.05/2} = 1.96$, the two-sided null hypothesis cannot be rejected.

In summary, a one-sided, or directional, hypothesis is called for when the researcher's original hunch is expressed in such terms as "more than," "less than," "increased," or "decreased." Such a hunch indicates that the researcher has quite a bit of knowledge about the research area. The knowledge could come from previous research, a pilot study, or perhaps theory. If the researcher is interested in determining only whether there is a difference, without specifying the direction of the difference, a two-tailed test should be used. Generally, significance tests in the behavioral sciences are two-tailed, because most researchers lack the information necessary to formulate directional hypotheses.

How does the choice of a one- or two-tailed test affect the probability of rejecting a false null hypothesis? We will answer this question by means of an illustration. Assume that $\alpha = .05$ and the following hypotheses have been advanced:

$$H_0: \mu = \mu_0$$

$$H_1: \mu \neq \mu_0.$$

If the z statistic falls in either the lower or upper .025 region of the sampling distribution, the result is said to be significant at the .05 level of significance because $.025 + .025 = .05$. The values of z that cut off the lower and upper $.05/2 = .025$ regions are $-z_{.05/2} = -1.96$ and $z_{.05/2} = 1.96$, respectively. An observed z test statistic is significant at the .05 level if its value is greater than or equal to 1.96 or less than or equal to -1.96 or, more simply, if its absolute value $|z|$ is greater than or equal to 1.96. Now consider the hypotheses

$$H_0: \mu \geq \mu_0$$

$$H_1: \mu < \mu_0;$$

again, $\alpha = .05$. If the z statistic falls in the appropriate tail of the sampling distribution, the result is said to be significant at the .05 level of significance. The critical regions and critical values for the two cases are shown in Figure 10.4-1(a and b). From an inspection of this figure it should be apparent that the size of the difference $\overline{X} - \mu_0$ necessary to reach the critical region for a two-tailed test is larger than that required for a one-tailed test. Consequently, a researcher is less likely to reject a false null hypothesis with a two-tailed test than with a one-tailed test. The term **power** refers to the probability of rejecting a false null hypothesis. A one-tailed test is more powerful than a two-tailed test if the researcher's hunch about the true difference $\mu - \mu_0$ is correct—that is, if the alternative hypothesis places the critical region in the correct tail of the sampling distribution. If the directional hunch is incorrect, the rejection region will be in the wrong tail, and the researcher will most certainly fail to reject the null hypothesis, even though it is false. A researcher is rewarded for making a correct directional prediction and is penalized for making an incorrect directional prediction. In the absence of sufficient information for using a one-tailed test, the researcher should play it safe and use a two-tailed test.

In one kind of research situation it is customary to use a one-tailed test. Consider a manufacturer who is evaluating a modified version of a product. If the modified version is better than the old product, the manufacturer will begin producing the modified version; otherwise, production of the old product will continue. In this example only one research outcome will lead to a product change—the case in which the modified version is superior. In this and similar research situations, where a researcher is interested in a change in only one direction, a one-tailed test is customarily used.[5]

---

[5] For an in-depth discussion of the issues involved in choosing between one- and two-tailed tests, see Kirk (1972, chap. 8).

Type I and Type II Errors

When the null hypothesis is tested, a researcher's decision will be either correct or incorrect.

An incorrect decision can be made in two ways. The researcher can reject the null hypothesis when it is true; this is called a **type I error.** Or the researcher can fail to reject the null hypothesis when it is false; this is called a **type II error.** Likewise, a correct decision can be made in two ways. If the null hypothesis is true and the researcher does not reject it, a **correct acceptance** has been made; if the null hypothesis is false and the researcher rejects it, a **correct rejection** has been made.

The two kinds of correct decisions and the two kinds of errors are summarized in Table 10.4-1.

The probability of making a type I error is determined by the researcher when the level of significance, α, is specified. If α is specified as .05, the probability of making a type I error is .05. The level of significance also determines the probability of a correct acceptance of a true null hypothesis because this probability is equal to $1 - \alpha$.

The probability of making a type II error, denoted by β, and the probability of making a correct rejection, denoted by $1 - \beta$, are determined by a number of variables: (1) the level of significance adopted, (2) the size of the sample, (3) the size of the population standard deviation, (4) the magnitude of the difference between μ and μ_0, and (5) whether a one- or two-tailed test is used.

The probability of making a correct rejection, $1 - \beta$, is called the **power** of a statistical test.

To compute the probability of making a type II error (β) and power ($1 - \beta$), it is necessary either to know μ, the true population mean, or to specify a value of μ

TABLE 10.4-1. Decision Outcomes Categorized

		True Situation	
		H_0 *true*	H_0 *false*
Researcher's	*Fail to reject* H_0	Correct acceptance Probability $= 1 - \alpha$	Type II error Probability $= \beta$
Decision	*Reject* H_0	Type I error Probability $= \alpha$	Correct rejection Probability $= 1 - \beta$

that is sufficiently different from μ_0 to be of practical value. We will say more about the second approach later, but first we will illustrate the computation of power.

In Section 10.3 we tested the hypothesis that student leaders have higher IQs than average college students. Let's assume for the moment that the true population mean, μ, is actually equal to 118 instead of 115 as specified by the null hypothesis. Thus, the magnitude of the difference between μ and μ_0 is $118 - 115 = 3$. Recall from the student leader example that $\alpha = .05$, $z_{.05} = 1.645$, $\sigma = 15$, and $n = 100$. To compute power, we need one more bit of information—the value of $\overline{X}$ that cuts off the upper .05 region of the standard normal distribution. Let's denote this mean by $\overline{X}_{.05}$. We can solve for $\overline{X}_{.05}$ by rearranging the terms in the formula $z_{.05} = (\overline{X}_{.05} - \mu_0)/(\sigma/\sqrt{n})$ as follows:

$$\overline{X}_{.05} = \mu_0 + z_{.05}\sigma/\sqrt{n}$$
$$= 115 + 1.645(15)/\sqrt{100}$$
$$= 117.47$$

Thus, in this example, a mean of 117.47 cuts off the upper .05 region of the standard normal distribution. To put it another way, 117.47 falls on the boundary between the rejection and nonrejection regions in Figure 10.4-2. Figure 10.4-2 shows two sampling distributions, one associated with the null hypothesis where μ_0 is equal to 115 and the other associated with the true IQ of student leaders where μ is equal to 118. The region corresponding to a type II error (labeled β) can be determined by transforming the difference $\overline{X}_{.05} - \mu$ into a z statistic. The formula is

$$z = \frac{\overline{X}_{0.5} - \mu}{\sigma/\sqrt{n}} = \frac{117.47 - 118}{15/\sqrt{100}} = \frac{-0.53}{1.50} = -0.35,$$

where $\overline{X}_{.05}$ is the mean that cuts off the upper .05 region of the standard normal distribution and μ is the true population mean. According to Appendix Table D.2, the area below a z_β of -0.35 is .36. Thus, if the true IQ of student leaders is 118, the probability of making a type II error (β) is equal to .36, and the probability of making a correct rejection (power) is equal to $1 - \beta = 1 - .36 = .64$. Figure 10.4-2 illustrates these ideas. To summarize, if μ is equal to 118, the size of the area for making a type II error is .36; the size of the area for rejecting the null hypothesis, the power of the test, is .64.

A power of .64 is considerably less than the minimum usually considered acceptable, which is .80.[6] Table 10.4-2 summarizes the probabilities associated with the possible decision outcomes when μ is equal to 115 and when μ is equal to 118. In this example, the probability of making a correct decision is larger when the null hypothesis is true (Probability $= 1 - \alpha = .95$) than when the null hypothesis is

---

[6] The selection of .80 as the minimum acceptable power is a convenient rule of thumb and reflects the view that type I errors are more serious than type II errors. Consider the value of the ratio p(type II error)/p(type I error) when the conventional .05 level of significance is adopted and power is equal to .80. Under these conditions the ratio is .20/05 = 4. The probability of a type II error is four times larger than that for a type I error. A researcher who adopts $\alpha = .05$ and $1 - \beta = .80$ is saying in effect that a type I error is considered to be four times more serious than a type II error.

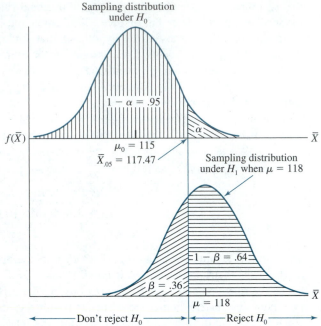

Figure 10.4-2. **Regions corresponding to probabilities of making a type I error**
(α) and a type II error (β). The mean that cuts off the upper .05 region of the
sampling distribution under H_0 is denoted by $\overline{X}_{.05}$ and is equal to 117.47. The
statistic $z = (\overline{X}_{.05} - \mu)/(\sigma/\sqrt{n}) = (117.47 - 118)/(15/\sqrt{100}) = -0.35$ along
with the standard normal distribution, Appendix Table D.2, is used to
determine the size of region corresponding to a type II error. The area that lies
below $z = -0.35$ is .36. The size and location of the region corresponding to a
type I error are determined by a and H_1, respectively. If $\mu = 118$ and the size
of the α region is made smaller, the size of the β region is increased. In other
words, if the probability of a type I error decreases, the probability of a type II
error increases.

TABLE 10.4-2.   Probabilities Associated with the Decision Process

		True Situation	
		$\mu = 115$	$\mu = 118$
Researcher's	$\mu \leq 115$	Correct acceptance $1 - \alpha = .95$	Type II error $\beta = .36$
Decision	$\mu > 115$	Type I error $\alpha = .05$	Correct rejection $1 - \beta = .64$

false (Probability $= 1 - \beta = .64$). It also is apparent that the probability of making a type I error ($\alpha = .05$) is much smaller than the probability of making a type II error ($\beta = .36$). In most research situations the researcher follows the convention of setting α equal to .05 or .01. This convention of choosing a small numerical value for α is based on the notion that a type I error is very bad and should be avoided. Unfortunately, as the probability of a type I error is made smaller and smaller, the probability of a type II error increases, and vice versa. This can be seen from an examination of Figure 10.4-2. If the vertical line cutting off the upper α region is moved to the right or to the left, the region designated β is made, respectively, larger or smaller. In our example, the decision rule, to reject the null hypothesis if z falls in the upper .05 region of the sampling distribution, is weighted in favor of deciding that the population mean is less than or equal to 115 rather than greater than 115 because the associated probabilities are .95 and .64, respectively.

Determining the *n* Required to Achieve an Acceptable α, $1 - \beta$, and $\mu - \mu_0$

On reflection, it should be apparent from Figure 10.4-2 that power can be increased by adopting a large numerical value for α, that is, increasing the size of α from .05 to .10. The effect of this increase is to shift the region for rejecting the null hypothesis to the left in Figure 10.4-2. Unfortunately, increasing α from .05 to .10 increases the probability of making a type I error and therefore may be undesirable. Often the simplest way to increase the power of a statistical test is to increase the sample size. Until now we haven't said very much about specifying n, except that it should be large enough—but not too large. There is a more rational approach to specifying sample size. The factors we have been discussing (α, $1 - \beta$, σ, n, and $\mu - \mu_0$) are interrelated; if we specify any four of them, the fifth is determined. The appropriate size of n can be estimated, therefore, if we know or specify acceptable values for α, $1 - \beta$, σ, and $\mu - \mu_0$. Again, the student leader experiment, in which $\alpha = .05$, $\sigma = 15$, and $\mu_0 = 115$, will be used to illustrate the procedure. Suppose that we want the power of the experiment to be .80, in which case $\beta = .20$. That leaves one factor, $\mu - \mu_0$, unspecified. There is no way of knowing $\mu - \mu_0$ without measuring all the student leaders in the population. However, we can specify the minimum IQ difference between μ and μ_0 that we would be interested in finding—if in fact μ is not equal to μ_0. Suppose that this difference is 3 IQ points; then $\mu - \mu_0 = 118 - 115 = 3$. By specifying that $\mu - \mu_0 = 3$, we are saying that any difference less than 3 points is too small to be of practical interest. The formula for determining the sample size[7] is

$$n = \frac{(z_\alpha - z_\beta)^2}{(\mu - \mu_0)^2 / \sigma^2},$$

[7] The derivation of the formula is given in Kirk (1978, pp. 235–236).

where z_α is the value of z that cuts off the α region of the sampling distribution of μ_0 and z_β is the value of z that cuts off the β region of the sampling distribution of μ. These regions are shown in Figure 10.4-2. If the alternative hypothesis is nondirectional, z_α is replaced by $z_\alpha/2$. For our example, the values of $z_\alpha = z_{.05} = 1.645$ and $z_\beta = -z_{.20} = -0.84$ are obtained from Appendix Table D.2. Substituting in the formula gives

$$n = \frac{[1.645 - (-0.84)]^2}{(118 - 115)^2/(15)^2} = 154.4,$$

which, when rounded to the next larger integer value, is 155. Thus, the minimum sample size required to detect a 3-point IQ difference with α equal to .05 and power $(1 - \beta)$ equal to .80 is 155. This sample size gives the researcher a fighting chance of detecting a difference considered worth finding. We can be more concrete. Suppose that we repeated the experiment 100 times using random samples of 155 student leaders. If the null hypothesis is true, we would expect to reject it five times (a type I error) and to fail to reject it 95 times (a correct acceptance). If, however, the null hypothesis is false and the true difference between μ and μ_0 is 3 IQ points, we would expect to reject the null hypothesis 80 times (a correct rejection) and to fail to reject it 20 times (a type II error).

Suppose that we consider type I and type II errors to be equally serious. If we set both errors at .05, then $z_\alpha = 1.645$ and $z_\beta = -1.645$, and the required sample size is

$$n = \frac{[1.645 - (-1.645)]^2}{(118 - 115)^2/(15)^2} \cong 271.$$

To increase the power from .80 to .95, other things being equal, we have to increase the sample size from 155 to 271—a 75% increase. Research always involves a series of tradeoffs, as this example illustrates for power and sample size. Another tradeoff, as we will see, involves n and $\mu - \mu_0$; the larger $\mu - \mu_0$ is, the smaller is the n required to reject the null hypothesis.

In many experiments the dependent variable is a new, untried measure or one with which the researcher has had little experience. For example, a researcher may have developed a new test of assertiveness for which there are no norms or a new apparatus for measuring complex reaction time. In such cases it is difficult, if not impossible, to specify the minimum difference $\mu - \mu_0$ that would be worth detecting. Fortunately, there is an alternative procedure for estimating n that doesn't require either an estimate of $\mu - \mu_0$ or a knowledge of σ. In Section 9.2 we saw that a standard score, $z = (X - \bar{X})/S$, is not expressed in the original unit of measurement but in units of the standard deviation. We can obtain a similar kind of score by dividing the absolute value of the difference we want to detect by the population standard deviation, $|\mu - \mu_0|/\sigma$. Cohen (1988, pp. 20–27), who popularized this relative measure, calls it an **effect size** and denotes it by the symbol d. It expresses the magnitude of the difference $\mu - \mu_0$ in standard deviation units. The value of d

for our student leader experiment is

$$d = \frac{|\mu - \mu_0|}{\sigma} = \frac{|118 - 115|}{15} = \frac{3}{15} = 0.2.$$

Hence, the difference we wanted to detect in that experiment was 0.2 of a standard deviation. Cohen refers to a d value of 0.2 as a small effect. A medium effect is one for which d is equal to 0.5, and a large effect is one for which d is equal to 0.8. Using Cohen's rule of thumb, a medium effect for the IQ data is one for which $\mu - \mu_0 = 122.5 - 115 = 7.5$, because

$$d = \frac{|122.5 - 115|}{15} = \frac{7.5}{15} = 0.5.$$

Similarly, a large effect corresponds to $\mu - \mu_0 = 127 - 115 = 12$, because

$$d = \frac{|127 - 115|}{15} = \frac{12}{15} = 0.8.$$

The specification of the minimum difference between μ and μ_0 that one wants to detect in terms of effect size simplifies the formula for estimating n. If d^2 is substituted for $(\mu - \mu_0)^2/\sigma^2$ in the formula for estimating n, the formula becomes

$$n = \frac{(z_\alpha - z_\beta)^2}{(\mu - \mu_0)^2/\sigma^2} = \frac{(z_\alpha - z_\beta)^2}{d^2}.$$

To compute n, all we have to specify is (1) d, (2) the probability of a type I error, and (3) power. Using Cohen's rule of thumb concerning the interpretation of $d = 0.2, 0.5,$ and 0.8, the n's necessary to detect small, medium, and large effect sizes for the student leader experiment are, respectively,

$$n = \frac{(z_\alpha - z_\beta)^2}{d^2} = \frac{[1.645 - (-0.84)]^2}{(0.2)^2} \cong 155$$

$$n = \frac{(z_\alpha - z_\beta)^2}{d^2} = \frac{[1.645 - (-0.84)]^2}{(0.5)^2} \cong 25$$

$$n = \frac{(z_\alpha - z_\beta)^2}{d^2} = \frac{[1.645 - (-0.84)]^2}{(0.8)^2} \cong 10.$$

As in the earlier computation of n, the probability of a type I error is .05 ($z_{.05} = 1.645$) and the power is equal to .80 ($-z_{.20} = -0.84$).

It is obvious that one's sample can be too small, resulting in insufficient power. But n also can be too large, resulting in wasted time and resources. A researcher can avoid these problems by using the formulas just described to make a rational choice of sample size. This procedure has two other less obvious benefits: It focuses attention on the interrelationships among n, α, $1 - \beta$, σ, and $\mu - \mu_0$, and it forces the researcher to think about the size of the difference $\mu - \mu_0$ that would be worth detecting. Critics of null hypothesis significance testing have observed that by obtaining a large enough sample virtually any null hypothesis can be rejected.[8] For this reason it is important to distinguish between **statistical significance,** which is concerned with whether a result is due to chance or sampling variability, and **practical significance,** which is concerned with whether the result is useful in the real world. By estimating the *n* required to detect a useful result, a researcher increases the chances of obtaining both statistical significance and practical significance.

More About Type I and Type II Errors

In many research situations the cost of committing a type I error can be large relative to that of a type II error. For example, falsely deciding that a new medication is more effective than conventional therapies in halting the production of cancer cells and therefore can be used in place of conventional medical procedures—a type I error—is a serious matter. On the other hand, falsely deciding that the new medication is not more effective—a type II error—would result in withholding the medication from the public and further research. Eventually, after enough research, the effectiveness of the new medication would be demonstrated. In this example, a type I error is more costly than a type II error, and is the error to be avoided. The probability of making a type I error can be reduced by using the .01 or even the .001 level of significance. However, in research situations that don't involve life and death, a type I error may be less costly than a type II error. For example, a researcher who makes a type II error may discontinue a promising line of research, whereas a type I error would lead to further exploration into a blind alley. Faced with these two alternatives, many researchers would set the level of significance equal to .05 or even .20, preferring to make a type I error rather than a type II error.

It is apparent that the costs and benefits associated with type I and type II errors must be known before a rational choice of α can be made. Unfortunately, researchers in the behavioral sciences, health sciences, and education generally are unable to specify the costs and benefits associated with the two kinds of errors, and therein lies the problem. The problem is resolved by using the conventional but arbitrary .05 or .01 level of significance.

It is hoped that this discussion has dispelled the magical aura that surrounds the .05 and .01 levels of significance—their use in hypothesis testing is simply a convention. A statistical test at the .05 level of significance addresses the question "Is chance a likely explanation for the results that have been obtained?" A null hypothesis significance test does not address the question "Are the results important or useful?" The researcher is probably the person best equipped to decide whether a statistically significant result is of any practical significance. We will say more about practical significance in Sections 10.5 and 10.6.

---

[8] For a discussion of this issue see Bakan (1966), Nunnally (1960), Rozeboom (1960), and Tukey (1991).

Reporting *p*-Values

Most research reports and computer printouts contain a statistic called a **probability value** or, simply, a ***p*-value.**

A ***p*-value** is the probability of obtaining a value of the test statistic equal to or more extreme than that observed, given that the null hypothesis is true.

Researchers usually obtain *p*-values with the aid of a computer statistical package. Alternatively, the tables in Appendix D can be used to approximate some *p*-values. Unfortunately, the range of values available in some tables is limited to .05 and .01.

In presenting the results of null hypothesis significance tests, it is customary to report, in order, the test statistic that was used, the value of the test statistic, and the *p*-value. For the student leader example, a researcher could report that "the difference between the mean IQ of student leaders and that of average college students was not statistically significant, $z = 1.33$, $p = .0918$." If the results of hypothesis tests are presented in a table, *p*-values are usually reported in a table footnote, for example, "*$p = .0918$." It is accepted practice to round *p*-values to the next larger value of .0001, .0005, .001, .005, .01, .05, .10, .20, .30, and so on. For example, $z = 1.33$, $p = .0918$ can be reported as $z = 1.33$, $p < .10$.

In Section 10.2 we formulated a hypothesis-testing decision rule in terms of a test statistic and the critical region: Reject the null hypothesis if the test statistic falls in the critical region; otherwise, do not reject the null hypothesis. A decision rule also can be formulated in terms of a *p*-value and the level of significance. The rule is as follows: Reject the null hypothesis if the *p*-value is less than or equal to the preselected level of significance; that is, reject the null hypothesis if the *p*-value is $\leq \alpha$; otherwise, do not reject the null hypothesis. The inclusion of a *p*-value in a research report provides useful information because it enables a reader to discern those significance levels for which the null hypothesis could have been rejected.

The *p*-values provided in computer printouts are usually appropriate for two-sided hypotheses. If your null hypothesis is directional, the two-tailed *p*-value given in the computer printout should be divided by 2. For example, a computer statistical package gave a *p*-value of .1835 for the data in Table 11.2-1. Because the null hypothesis is directional, the correct value is $.1835/2 = .0918$. Before leaving the subject of *p*-values, it should be emphasized that a *p*-value is related to statistical significance; it says nothing about practical significance.

CHECK YOUR UNDERSTANDING OF SECTION 10.4

17. For each of the following statistical hypotheses, (a) sketch the sampling distribution, (b) designate the critical region(s), (c) indicate their size, and (d) determine the critical value.

a. $H_0: \mu = 60$
   $H_1: \mu \neq 60$
   $\alpha = .01$

b. $H_0: \mu \leq 100$
   $H_1: \mu > 100$
   $\alpha = .05$

c. $H_0: \mu \geq 25$
   $H_1: \mu < 25$
   $\alpha = .005$

18. Which of the null hypotheses in Exercise 17 are directional?

19. Indicate the type of error or correct decision for each of the following.
    a. A true null hypothesis was rejected.
    b. The researcher failed to reject a false null hypothesis.
    c. The null hypothesis is false and the researcher rejected it.
    d. The researcher did not reject a true null hypothesis.
    e. A false null hypothesis was rejected.
    f. The researcher rejected the null hypothesis when he or she should have failed to reject it.

20. The calculation of power was illustrated in this section by means of the student leaders' IQ data. We saw that if $\overline{X}_{.05}$ is equal to 117.47, σ is equal to 15, and the student leaders' mean IQ is really equal to 118.0, the probability of correctly rejecting the null hypothesis is only .64. (a) If a sample of $n = 150$ instead of $n = 100$ had been obtained, what would the power have been? Assume that μ_0 is equal to 115 and $\overline{X}_{.05}$ is equal to $115 + 1.645(15/\sqrt{150}) = 117.01$. (b) How would the larger sample have affected the p-value? (c) How many participants would be required to achieve a power of .90 in part a? Assume that μ_0 is equal to 115.

21. Set up a table that summarizes the probabilities associated with the four possible decision outcomes in Exercise 20a.

22. Terms to remember
    a. One-tailed test
    c. One-sided (directional) hypothesis
    e. Power $(1 - \beta)$
    g. Type II error (β)
    i. Correct rejection
    k. Statistical significance
    m. p-value

    b. Two-tailed test
    d. Two-sided (nondirectional) hypothesis
    f. Type I error (α)
    h. Correct acceptance $(1 - \alpha)$
    j. Effect size
    l. Practical significance

10.5 CONFIDENCE INTERVAL FOR A MEAN

Criticisms of Null Hypothesis Significance Testing

For the past 70 years, null hypothesis significance testing has been the dominant approach to statistical inference. There is a growing awareness among researchers that this approach has some shortcomings. As we have seen, a null hypothesis significance test addresses the question "Is chance a likely explanation for the results that have been obtained?" The test does not address the question "Are the results important or useful?" There are other criticisms. For example, null hypothesis significance testing and scientific inference address different questions. In scientific inference, what we want to know is the conditional probability that the null hypothesis (H_0) is true, given that we have obtained a set of data (D); that is, $p(H_0|D)$. What null hypothesis significance testing tells us is the conditional probability of obtaining these data or more extreme data if the null hypothesis is true, $p(D|H_0)$. Unfortunately, obtaining data for which $p(D|H_0)$ is low does not imply that $p(H_0|D)$ also is low.

A third criticism of null hypothesis significance testing is that it is a trivial exercise. John Tukey (1991) observed, "It is foolish to ask 'Are the effects of A and B different?' They are always different—for some decimal place." Because the null hypothesis is always false, a decision to reject it simply indicates that the research methodology had adequate power to detect a true state of affairs, which may or may not be a large effect, $d = 0.8$, or even an effect that is useful.

A fourth criticism of null hypothesis significance testing is that by adopting a fixed level of significance such as $\alpha = .05$, a researcher turns a continuum of uncertainty into a dichotomous reject-do-not-reject decision. Researchers ordinarily react to a p-value of .06—but not p-values of .05 or smaller—with disappointment. Rosnow and Rosenthal's (1989) comment is pertinent: "Surely, God loves the .06 nearly as much as the .05." Many psychologists believe that an emphasis on null hypothesis significance tests and p-values distracts researchers from the main business of science—understanding and interpreting the outcomes of research. The next section describes an alternative approach to statistical inference.

Constructing a Confidence Interval for μ

We noted in Section 10.1 that two complementary topics are subsumed under classical statistical inference—null hypothesis significance testing and confidence interval estimation. In many inquiries, a researcher's primary interest is in obtaining an estimate of some population parameter. Because means vary from sample to sample, it is unlikely that any given sample mean will equal the population mean.

> Although we can never know the value of a population mean except by measuring all the elements in the population, a random sample can be used to specify a segment or interval on the number line such that the population mean has a high probability of lying on the segment. The segment is called a **confidence interval.**

We will now construct a confidence interval for a population mean, μ, so that the interval has a probability equal to $1 - \alpha$ of containing μ. The number $1 - \alpha$, which is usually equal to $1 - .05 = .95$, is called a **confidence coefficient** and, like

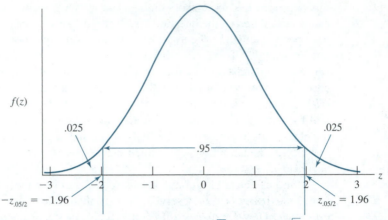

$f(z)$

.025

.025

.95

$-z_{.05/2} = -1.96$

$z_{.05/2} = 1.96$

Figure 10.5-1. **Sampling distribution of** $z = (\overline{X} - \mu_0)/(\sigma/\sqrt{n})$. **If one z statistic is randomly sampled from this population of z's, the probability is .95 that the obtained z will come from the interval** $-z_{.025/2}$ **to** $z_{.025/2}$.

the level of significance, α, is specified by the researcher. The logic underlying the construction of a confidence interval is presented in some detail because it is applicable to confidence intervals for other parameters, such as σ^2 and ρ. Consider the sampling distribution of $z = (\overline{X} - \mu)/(\sigma/\sqrt{n})$ shown in Figure 10.5-1. If one z statistic is randomly sampled from this population of z's, the probability is $1 - .05 = .95$ that the obtained z will come from the interval from $-z_{.05/2}$ to $z_{.05/2}$. We can state this more formally:

$$\text{Prob}(-z_{.05/2} < z < z_{.05/2}) = 1 - .05 = .95.$$

The next step in deriving a confidence interval for μ is to replace z with its formula, $z = (\overline{X} - \mu)/(\sigma/\sqrt{n})$, which gives

$$\text{Prob}\left(-z_{.05/2} < \frac{\overline{X} - \mu}{\sigma/\sqrt{n}} < z_{.05/2}\right) = .95.$$

Multiplying each term in the inequalities by $\sigma/\sqrt{n}$ gives[9]

$$\text{Prob}\left(\frac{-z_{.05/2}\sigma}{\sqrt{n}} < \overline{X} - \mu < \frac{z_{.05/2}\sigma}{\sqrt{n}}\right) = .95.$$

Subtracting $\overline{X}$ from each term, we obtain

$$\text{Prob}\left(-\overline{X} - \frac{z_{.05/2}\sigma}{\sqrt{n}} < -\mu < -\overline{X} + \frac{z_{.05/2}\sigma}{\sqrt{n}}\right) = .95$$

[9] A review of inequalities is given in Appendix A, Section A.6.

and multiplying by -1, which reverses the direction of the inequalities and the signs of the terms, gives

$$\text{Prob}\left(\overline{X} + \frac{z_{.05/2}\sigma}{\sqrt{n}} > \mu > +\overline{X} - \frac{z_{.05/2}\sigma}{\sqrt{n}}\right) = .95.$$

For convenience, the terms in the inequality can be rearranged to form the confidence statement

$$\text{Prob}\left(\overline{X} - \frac{z_{.05/2}\sigma}{\sqrt{n}} < \mu < +\overline{X} - \frac{z_{.05/2}\sigma}{\sqrt{n}}\right) = .95.$$

In words, this statement says that the probability is .95 that a random interval from

$$\overline{X} - z_{.05/2}\sigma/\sqrt{n} \quad \text{to} \quad \overline{X} + z_{.05/2}\sigma/\sqrt{n}$$

contains the parameter μ. The values $\overline{X} - z_{.05/2}\sigma/\sqrt{n}$ and $\overline{X} = z_{.05/2}\sigma/\sqrt{n}$ are the **lower** and **upper endpoints,** respectively, of the confidence interval; the endpoints also are called **confidence limits** and are denoted by L_1 and L_2, respectively. The value of the confidence coefficient, .95, reflects the degree of our confidence that μ does indeed lie in the specified interval.

The general form of a two-sided $100(1 - \alpha)\%$ confidence interval for μ is

$$\overline{X} - \frac{z_{\alpha/2}\sigma}{\sqrt{n}} < \mu < \overline{X} + \frac{z_{.\alpha/2}\sigma}{\sqrt{n}},$$

where $z_\alpha/2$ is the value that cuts off the upper $\alpha/2$ region of the standard normal distribution.

To summarize, it is impossible to know the value of a parameter without measuring all the elements in the population. However, for a given parameter it is possible to find two functions denoted by L_1 and L_2 of sample values such that before the sample is drawn the probability that the interval between L_1 and L_2 will contain the parameter is equal to $1 - \alpha$. That is, we can be $100(1 - \alpha)\%$ confident that this interval contains the parameter.

Computational Example of Confidence Interval for μ

In Sections 10.3 and 10.4 we used an example involving the IQs of student leaders at Big Ten universities to illustrate a one-sample z test for μ. Recall that the mean of a random sample of $n = 100$ student leaders was $\overline{X} = 117$ and the population standard deviation was $\sigma = 15$. A two-sided $100(1 - .05)\% = 95\%$ confidence interval for the population mean, μ, of student leaders at Big Ten universities is

given by

$$\overline{X} - \frac{z_{.05/2}\sigma}{\sqrt{n}} < \mu < \overline{X} + \frac{z_{.05/2}\sigma}{\sqrt{n}}$$

$$117 - \frac{1.96(15)}{\sqrt{100}} < \mu < 117 + \frac{1.96(15)}{\sqrt{100}}$$

$$117 - 2.94 < \mu < 117 + 2.94$$

$$114.06 < \mu < 119.94.$$

You may find it helpful to visualize a confidence interval as a segment of the real number line. In the following figure, the darkened segment corresponds to a 95% confidence interval.

The confidence interval $144.06 < \mu < 119.94$ is called an **open interval** as opposed to a closed interval because neither endpoint, 114.06 nor 119.94, is included in the interval.[10] We can feel quite confident that the value of μ is greater than $L_1 = 114.06$ and less than $L_2 = 119.94$. The measure of our confidence is .95 because before the sample was drawn, .95 was the probability that the interval we were going to construct would contain the population mean. If we want to feel even more confident that we have specified L_1 and L_2 so that they contain μ, we can compute a $100(1 - .01)\% = 99\%$ confidence interval. This is accomplished by substituting $z_{.01/2} = 2.576$ for $z_{.05/2} = 1.96$. The 99% confidence interval is given by

$$\overline{X} - \frac{z_{.01/2}\sigma}{\sqrt{n}} < \mu < \overline{X} + \frac{z_{.01/2}\sigma}{\sqrt{n}}$$

$$117 - \frac{2.576(15)}{\sqrt{100}} < \mu < 117 + \frac{2.576(15)}{\sqrt{100}}$$

$$117 - 3.86 < \mu < 117 + 3.86$$

$$113.14 < \mu < 120.86$$

Notice that as our confidence that we have captured μ increases, so does the size of the interval from L_1 to L_2.

---

[10] An interval in which the endpoints are included, for example, $114.06 \leq \mu \leq 119.94$, is called a **closed interval.**

Interpretation of a Confidence Interval

Earlier we stated that the probability is .95 that a random interval from $\overline{X} - z_{.05/2}\sigma\sqrt{n}$ to $\overline{X} + z_{.05/2}\sigma/\sqrt{n}$ contains the parameter μ; in symbols we wrote this confidence interval as

$$\text{Prob}\left(\overline{X} - \frac{z_{.05/2}\sigma}{\sqrt{n}} < \mu < \overline{X} + \frac{z_{.05/2}\sigma}{\sqrt{n}}\right) = .95.$$

This statement refers to the set of all confidence intervals that could be constructed. To clarify, consider obtaining an infinite number of random samples of size n from a normally distributed population and computing $\overline{X}$ for each sample. We can conceive of constructing a confidence interval based on each $\overline{X}$. Ninety-five percent of these intervals will contain μ between L_1 and L_2, and 5% will not. The probability that a randomly selected interval from this infinite set will contain μ is .95. However, once one of the $\overline{X}$'s has been computed and found to equal, say, 117, it is incorrect to state that the probability is .95 that the open interval from 114.06 to 119.94 contains μ. That is, the statement

$$\text{Prob}\left(117 - \frac{1.96(15)}{\sqrt{100}} < \mu < 117 + \frac{1.96(15)}{\sqrt{100}}\right) = .95$$

is incorrect. Such a probability statement is incorrect because 117 is not a random variable. Once a value of $\overline{X}$ has been inserted in the confidence statement, the interval either does or doesn't contain μ. Hence, one should not say that the probability is .95 that μ lies in the open interval from 114.06 to 119.94. It is correct to say that a 95% confidence interval for μ is from 114.06 to 119.94, or that the degree of one's confidence that μ lies in the open interval from 114.06 to 119.94 is .95, or, more simply, "I am 95% confident that μ is greater than 114.06 and less than 119.94."

One-Sided Confidence Interval

The confidence interval

$$114.06 < \mu < 119.94$$

is two-sided. Such an interval is used when the researcher is interested in the possibility that the mean IQ of student leaders is either higher than or lower than that of other students. In a sense, this interval is analogous to the two-sided hypotheses:

$$H_0: \mu = 115$$
$$H_1: \mu \neq 115.$$

Suppose that the researcher is interested in only the possibility that the mean IQ is higher than that of other students,

$$H_0: \mu \leq 115$$
$$H_1: \mu > 115.$$

The analogous **one-sided confidence limit,** L_1, for this hypothesis with confidence coefficient equal to $100(1 - .05)\% = 95\%$ is

$$\overline{X} - \frac{z_{.05}\sigma}{\sqrt{n}} < \mu$$

$$117 - \frac{1.645(15)}{\sqrt{100}} < \mu$$

$$117 - 2.47 < \mu$$

$$114.53 < \mu,$$

where $z_{05} = 1.645$ is the value of z that cuts off the upper $\alpha = .05$ region of the sampling distribution of the standard normal distribution. The researcher can be fairly confident that μ is greater than 114.53. The confidence interval corresponds to the colored segment of the real number line in the following figure.

$L_1 = 114.53$

113 114 115 116 117 118 119 120 121
μ

If the researcher is interested in only the possibility that the mean IQ of student leaders is lower than that of other students, the one-sided confidence limit, L_2, with confidence coefficient equal to $100(1 - .05)\% = .95\%$ is

$$\mu < \overline{X} + \frac{z_{.05}\sigma}{\sqrt{n}}$$

$$\mu < 117 + \frac{1.645(15)}{\sqrt{100}}$$

$$\mu < 117 + 2.47$$

$$\mu < 119.47.$$

This confidence interval corresponds to the darker segment of the real number line in the following figure.

$L_2 = 119.47$

113 114 115 116 117 118 119 120 121
μ

Interval Estimation Versus Hypothesis Testing

In Sections 10.3 and 10.4 we saw that the z test statistic for the student leader IQ data was not significant. In such cases, we have the option of suspending judgment regarding the null hypothesis or concluding that the null hypothesis remains tenable. If we had rejected the null hypothesis, we would have concluded that μ is not equal to 115. In either case, our best guess regarding the value of μ is that it is equal to $\overline{X} = 117$. What additional information does a confidence interval provide? From the two-sided 95% confidence interval,

$$114.06 < \mu < 119.94,$$

we can conclude that μ is probably between 114.06 and 119.94. This information is much more useful than simply concluding that the hypothesis $\mu = 115$ remains tenable.

A confidence interval also can be used to test any null hypothesis for μ simply by looking at the interval. For example, we know that the null hypothesis $\mu = 115$ would not be rejected at the .05 level of significance because 115 is included in the $100(1 - .05)\% = 95\%$ confidence interval. However, the null hypothesis $\mu = 113$ would be rejected because 113 is not included in the 95% confidence interval. Considering the advantages of confidence intervals, you may wonder why null hypothesis significance tests have been given a prominent place in this book. There are two reasons. For the past 70 years, significance tests have been the dominant approach to statistical inference. Hence, an understanding of this approach is necessary to read the literature in the behavioral sciences, health sciences, and education. Second, there are some statistical inference questions that cannot be addressed using confidence intervals. In such cases, a researcher must resort to null hypothesis significance tests.

To summarize, a sample mean and confidence interval provide an estimate of the population parameter and a range of values—the error variation—qualifying that estimate. A $100(1 - \alpha)\%$ confidence interval for μ contains all the values of μ_0 for which the null hypothesis would not be rejected at a level of significance. All values of μ_0 outside the confidence interval would be rejected. Researchers routinely report the results of null hypothesis significance tests. Whenever confidence intervals can be computed, they should be reported along with a measure of effect magnitude. In addition, research reports also should contain descriptive measures of central tendency and dispersion, sample size, and, where appropriate, graphs such as box plots.

10.6 PRACTICAL SIGNIFICANCE

The point has been made repeatedly that statistically significant results are not necessarily important, large, or even useful. What is needed is a measure of the practical significance of results. Unfortunately, such a measure does not exist. However, measures of effect magnitude can assist a researcher in deciding whether results are practically significant. Most measures of **effect magnitude** fall into one of two categories: measures of effect size and measures of strength of association.[11] The use of Cohen's (1988) effect size, d, is described here. A measure of strength of association for experiments with three or more samples is described in Chapter 14. It is recommended that researchers always supplement reports of null hypothesis significance tests and confidence intervals with a measure of effect magnitude.

Cohen's effect size parameter, d, which was introduced in Section 10.4, is

$$d = \frac{|\mu - \mu_0|}{\sigma}.$$

This parameter expresses the difference that a researcher considers worth detecting in units of the population standard deviation. According to Cohen, a d value of 0.2 is a small effect, 0.5 is a medium effect, and 0.8 is a large effect. Several surveys have found that 0.5 approximates the average size of observed effects in various fields.

Cohen's d also can be used to represent the size of a difference that has been obtained. The formula is

$$d = \frac{|\overline{X} - \mu_0|}{\sigma}.$$

For the student leader IQ data in Sections 10.3 and 10.4, d is

$$d = \frac{|117 - 115|}{15} = 0.13,$$

which is considerably smaller than 0.2, Cohen's definition of a small effect. I believe that most researchers would consider an IQ difference that is only $^{13}/_{100}$ of the size of the population standard deviation to be of little practical value. Thus, even if the null hypothesis $\mu \leq 115$ had been rejected, the statistically significant difference would have been of little practical significance.

CHECK YOUR UNDERSTANDING OF SECTIONS 10.5 AND 10.6

23. What assumptions are associated with the following statement?

$$\text{Prob}\left(\overline{X} - \frac{z_{\alpha/2}\sigma}{\sqrt{n}} < \mu < \overline{X} + \frac{z_{\alpha/2}\sigma}{\sqrt{n}}\right) = 1 - \alpha$$

24. What are the advantages of confidence-interval procedures over null hypothesis–testing procedures?
25. a. For the arithmetic-achievement data in "Check Your Understanding of Section 10.2," Exercise 7, construct a 95% confidence interval.

---

[11] See Kirk (1996) for a summary of 40 measures of effect magnitude that have been recommended since 1925.

    b. Based on the confidence interval, specify all null hypotheses that could be rejected using a null hypothesis significance test.

    c. Compute *d* and interpret.

26. a. For the Minnesota Multiphasic Personality Inventory data in "Check Your Understanding of Section 10.3," Exercise 14, construct a 95% confidence interval.

    b. Based on the confidence interval, list all null hypotheses that could be rejected using a null hypothesis significance test.

    c. Compute *d* and interpret.

    d. Construct a box plot. Do the data contain outliers? Does the sample distribution appear to be relatively symmetrical?

27. a. A soft-drink machine is designed to dispense a measured amount of a popular drink. Construct a 99% confidence interval for μ if a random sample of 29 drinks has $\overline{X} = 7.2$ oz. Assume that the distribution is approximately normal, with $\sigma = 0.42$ oz.

    b. Machines of the same design are supposed to have a mean of 8 oz. Does this machine need to be repaired?

    c. Compute *d* and interpret.

28. If $23 < \mu < 36$ is a 95% confidence interval for μ, indicate which of the following statements are correct (C) and which are incorrect (I).

    a. The probability is .95 that the open interval from 23 to 36 contains the population mean.

    b. The probability that the open interval $\overline{X} \pm 1.96\sigma\sqrt{n}$ contains μ is .95.

    c. Prob $(23 < \mu < 36)$ is .95.

    d. A researcher can be 95% confident that the open interval from 23 to 36 contains μ.

    e. A 95% confidence interval for μ is $23-36$.

    f. Prob$(\overline{X} - 1.96\sigma\sqrt{n} < \mu < \overline{X} + 1.96\sigma\sqrt{n}) = .95$, where $\overline{X} = 29.5$ and $\sigma = 6.1$.

29. How is the size of a confidence interval related to the following?

    a. Size of population standard deviation

    b. Sample size

    c. Confidence coefficient

30. Use the table of random numbers in Appendix D.1 to draw a random sample without replacement of 25 women from the Student Database in Appendix E. (a) List the Subject Number and Stat Grade for each woman in your sample. (b) Compute the mean of the variable labeled Stat Grade. (c) Summarize the data by means of a box plot. Do the data contain outliers? (d) Construct a 95% confidence interval for μ. Assume that the population standard deviation is 1.019. Is it reasonable to believe that the population mean is 2.805?

31. Terms to remember

    a. Confidence interval   b. Confidence coefficient

    c. Lower and upper endpoints   d. Confidence limits

    e. Open interval   f. One-sided confidence limit

    g. Effect magnitude

10.7 SUMMARY

Hypothesis-testing procedures, one form of statistical inference, use sample data in making a decision about a scientific hypothesis when it is impossible or impractical to observe all the elements in the population. The main features of hypothesis testing are as follows: A researcher formulates from a scientific hypothesis two mutually exclusive and exhaustive statistical hypotheses—the null hypothesis, H_0, and the alternative hypothesis, H_1—that make predictions about one or more parameters of a population distribution. The alternative hypothesis is formulated so that it is in agreement with the researcher's scientific hypothesis. The null hypothesis is contrary to the researcher's scientific hypothesis. A test of the null hypothesis consists of determining whether the obtained value of a sample statistic would be improbable if the null hypothesis is true. If the value would be improbable, then the null hypothesis is a poor prediction and should be rejected in favor of the alternative hypothesis.

The test of the null hypothesis is actually performed using a test statistic. It is a simple matter to transform a sample mean into a z test statistic using the formula $z = (\bar{X} - \mu_0)/(\sigma/\sqrt{n})$. The criterion for what constitutes improbable values of the test statistic is expressed in terms of a probability called a level of significance and denoted by α. By convention, a researcher usually sets this probability equal to or less than .05. The level of significance along with the alternative hypothesis identify a range of values of the test statistic that would be improbable if the null hypothesis is true. This range of improbable values is called the critical region. If a test statistic falls in the critical region, the test statistic is said to be statistically significant, in which case the researcher rejects the null hypothesis and concludes that the scientific hypothesis is probably true. If a test statistic doesn't fall in the critical region, the null hypothesis remains tenable.

How does one determine whether the test statistic falls in the critical region? This can be determined with the aid of a table that gives values of the test statistic that cut off various regions of the sampling distribution of the test statistic. For example, according to Appendix Table D.2, a z value of 1.645 cuts off the upper .05 region of the z sampling distribution. The value of z that cuts off a critical region of size α is called a critical value and is denoted by z_α. Now to answer the question posed a moment ago. We can determine whether the test statistic falls in the critical region by determining whether the test statistic is greater than or equal to the critical value, that is, whether $z \geq z_\alpha$. Alternatively, if a statistical software package is used to obtain the value of the test statistic, the p-value provided by the package can be compared with the researcher's level of significance. If the p-value is less than or equal to the level of significance, p-value $\leq \alpha$, the test statistic falls in the critical region.

It is helpful to think of hypothesis testing as a series of steps that culminate in a decision about the scientific hypothesis. The steps can be summarized as follows:

Step 1.   State the null and alternative hypotheses.
Step 2.   Specify the test statistic based on the hypothesis to be tested, informa-

tion that is known about the population, and assumptions about the population that appear to be tenable.

Step 3. Specify the size *n* of the sample to be obtained and make assumptions that permit specification of the sampling distribution of the test statistic, given that the null hypothesis is true.

Step 4. Specify an acceptable risk of rejecting the null hypothesis when it is true.

Step 5. Obtain a random sample of size *n* from the population, compute the test statistic, and make a decision about the null and alternative hypotheses and an inductive inference about the scientific hypothesis.

Decision rule:

Reject the null hypothesis if the test statistic falls in the critical region of the sampling distribution of the test statistic; otherwise, don't reject the null hypothesis. Rejection of the null hypothesis leads to the inductive inference that the scientific hypothesis is true, in which case the statistic is said to be statistically significant.

There is a tendency among researchers to impart surplus meaning to the term *statistical significance.* All the term really means is that a result has been obtained that is improbable if the null hypothesis is true. Statistical significance doesn't connote importance or usefulness, and it shouldn't be confused with practical significance. In the simplest terms, a statistically significant result is one for which chance is an unlikely explanation.

An alternative approach to statistical inference, the confidence interval, provides more information about one's data than a null hypothesis significance test. In many research situations, we want to know the value of a population mean. If, as is usually the case, it is not possible to observe all of the population elements, a researcher must resort to obtaining a random sample and computing the sample mean. The sample mean is the best guess that a researcher can make concerning the value of the population mean. Because of sampling variability, it is unlikely that the sample mean will equal the population mean. This is frustrating, but it is possible to find two functions L_1 and L_2 of the sample data such that before the sample is drawn, the probability that the open interval from L_1 to L_2 will contain μ is equal to $1 - \alpha$. The open interval from L_1 to L_2 is called a confidence interval for μ with a confidence coefficient equal to $1 - \alpha$. The researcher can be $100(1 - \alpha)\%$ confident that μ is contained in the confidence limits from L_1 and L_2.

The size of a confidence interval is determined by (1) the confidence coefficient that the researcher specifies, (2) the size of the sample, and (3) the size of the population standard deviation. The construction of a confidence interval involves the same assumptions as a null hypothesis significance test. However, a confidence interval has some important advantages: (1) It provides a range of values that are likely to contain the population mean and (2) any null hypothesis can be tested by looking at the confidence interval. By comparison, a null hypothesis significance test is less informative. Rejection of a null hypothesis, for example, indicates that μ

is probably not equal to μ_0; nonrejection of the hypothesis indicates that μ_0 remains as a possible value of μ.

Regardless of which statistical inference approach one uses, it is important also to assess the practical significance of one's results. Although a measure of practical significance does not exist, several statistics can help a researcher make this kind of assessment. The statistics are called measures of effect magnitude. The one that is described in this chapter is Cohen's $d = |\overline{X} - \mu_0|/\sigma$. His guidelines for small, 0.2, medium, 0.5, and large effects, 0.8, are helpful. However, the determination of practical significance should not be ritualized. Ultimately, the researcher who collected and analyzed a set of data is in the best position to decide whether the results are useful or important.

REVIEW EXERCISES FOR CHAPTER 10

1. Which of the following are scientific hypotheses?
   a. Wives in unhappy marriages have lower problem-solving ability than wives in happy marriages.
   b. Office workers who listen to music with stereo headsets while working exhibit lower job turnover.
   c. Dominant chimpanzees in a colony have a better self-image than chimpanzees who are less dominant.
   d. Mice prefer the music of Mozart over that of Schönberg because Mozart's music is less dissonant.
2. Why is it often necessary to use the techniques of statistical inference in evaluating a scientific hypothesis?
3. Which of the following are examples of null hypotheses?
   a. $\mu = 22$ b. $r = 0$
   c. $\rho > 0$ d. $\mu < 50$
   e. $\sigma^2 < 0$ f. $\overline{X} = 15$
   g. $\mu \geq 60$ h. $S^2 \leq 16$
   i. $\sigma^2 = 100$ j. $\rho = .30$
4. Why might a researcher fail to reject a null hypothesis?
5. If a null hypothesis is correctly rejected, what does this imply about the experimental methodology?
6. It was hypothesized that a random sample of 28 drug abusers who were clients of the Narcotics Service Council, Inc., in St. Louis would rate the credibility of drug information provided by social workers below that of ex-addicts. Let μ denote the mean rating assigned to social workers. The known rating assigned to ex-addicts is $\mu_0 = 72.8$ with $\sigma = 18$. (a) List the five steps you would follow in testing the hypothesis that the credibility rating of social workers is lower than that of ex-addicts, and supply the required information. Let $\alpha = .05$. (b) State the decision rule.

7. For the data in Exercise 6, sketch the sampling distribution associated with the null hypothesis, and indicate the region(s) that lead to rejection and nonrejection of the null hypothesis.

8. For the data in Exercise 6, suppose that the mean credibility rating assigned to social workers is $\overline{X} = 58.2$. (a) Compute a z statistic for these data. (b) What conclusion can be drawn about the scientific hypothesis?

9. If $\alpha = .01$ in Exercise 6, what conclusion would have been drawn about the scientific hypothesis?

10. For the data in Exercises 6 and 8, assess the practical significance of the difference $\overline{X} - \mu_0$.

11. Can you think of some reasons why a researcher should always specify H_0, H_1, α, and n before collecting data?

12. For each of the following statistical hypotheses, sketch the sampling distribution associated with the null hypothesis, designate the critical region(s), and indicate their size.

a. $H_0: \mu \leq 50$ b. $H_0: \mu = 20$
   $H_1: \mu > 50$ $H_1: \mu \neq 20$
   $\alpha = .05$ $\alpha = .01$

c. $H_0: \mu \geq 65$
   $H_1: \mu < 65$
   $\alpha = .005$

13. Which of the null hypotheses in Exercise 12 are directional?

14. Under what condition is a one-tailed test less powerful than a two-tailed test?

15. Indicate the type of error or correct decision for each of the following:

a. A false null hypothesis was rejected.

b. The researcher did not reject a true null hypothesis.

c. The null hypothesis is false and the researcher failed to reject it.

d. The researcher rejected a true null hypothesis.

e. A false null hypothesis was not rejected.

f. The researcher rejected the null hypothesis when he or she should have rejected it.

16. The calculation of power was illustrated in Section 10.4 by means of the student leaders' IQ data. We saw that if $\overline{X}_{.05}$ is equal to 117.47, σ is equal to 15, n is equal to 100, and the student leaders' mean IQ is really equal to 118.0, the probability of correctly rejecting the null hypothesis is only .64. (a) If $\mu = 118.5$ instead of 118.0, what would the power have been? Assume that μ_0 is equal to 115. (b) How would the larger population mean, $\mu = 118.5$, have affected the p-value? (c) How many participants would be required to achieve a power of .80 in part a? Assume that μ_0 is equal to 115.

17. Set up a table that summarizes the probabilities associated with the four possible decision outcomes in Exercise 16a.

18. For the credibility data in Exercises 6 and 8, suppose that the population mean credibility rating of social workers is $\mu = 60.1$. (a) Compute the power of the z test. (b) How large a sample of drug abusers would be required to achieve a power of .80?

19. Set up a table that summarizes the probabilities associated with the four possible decision outcomes in Exercise 18.

20. List the ways in which a researcher can increase the power of an experimental methodology. What are their relative merits?

21. List four shortcomings of null hypothesis significance tests.

22. Ordinarily, $L_1 < L_2$. Can you think of a condition under which L_1 and L_2 would be equal?

23. a. For the credibility data in Exercises 6 and 8, construct a 95% confidence interval.

    b. Based on the confidence interval, specify all null hypotheses that could be rejected.

24. Students desiring to enter graduate school at Kandykane Technical Institute (KTI) are required to submit Graduate Record Examination (GRE) scores with their applications. The verbal scores for the first 20 applications received this year are given in the table. The population standard deviation of applicants is known to equal 18.

GRE Scores for Verbal Section of Test			
402	390	429	391
381	407	410	403
430	413	406	398
376	424	382	410
395	360	410	404

a. If the first 20 applicants can be considered a random sample of applicants who will apply, what is the best estimate of the mean for this year's applicants?

b. Construct a 95% confidence interval for μ for these data.

c. Based on the confidence interval, list all null hypotheses that could be rejected.

d. Last year the mean GRE verbal score of all KTI applicants was 428. Is the mean verbal aptitude for this year's applicants different from that for last year?

e. Let $\mu_0 = 428$ and $\sigma = 18$. Compute d and interpret.

f. Construct a box plot for the data. Do the data contain outliers?

25. Use the table of random numbers in Appendix D.1 to draw a random sample without replacement of 25 men from the Student Database in Appendix E. (a) List the Subject Number and Stat Grade for each

man in your sample. (b) Compute the mean of the variable labeled Statistics Grade. (c) Summarize the data by means of a box plot. Do the data contain outliers? (d) Construct a 95% confidence interval for μ. Assume that the population standard deviation is 1.053. Is it reasonable to believe that the population mean is 2.662?

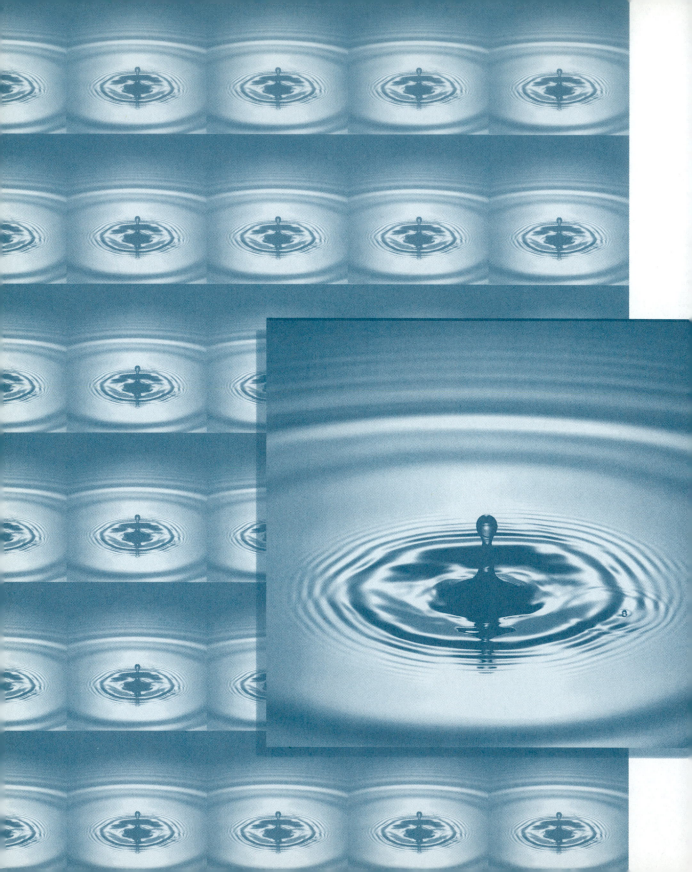

Chapter 11

Statistical Inference: Other One-Sample Test Statistics

11.1 INTRODUCTION TO OTHER ONE-SAMPLE TEST STATISTICS

This chapter could be entitled "Theme With Variations"—it applies the five-step null hypothesis-testing format and the confidence interval procedures introduced in the previous chapter to six new test statistics. In the preceding chapter we described procedures for drawing inferences about μ when σ is known. The same procedures, with slight modifications, are used to make decisions about μ when σ is unknown. And the procedures can be used in making decisions about other population parameters such as a variance (σ^2), proportion (p), and correlation (ρ). Two new test statistics, t and χ^2 (Greek chi square), and their sampling distributions are introduced.

11.2 ONE-SAMPLE t TEST AND CONFIDENCE INTERVAL FOR A MEAN

When a researcher tests a hypothesis about μ, the value of σ rarely is known, and, as we have seen, σ is required to compute the z test statistic. The t test statistic that we will describe now does not require a knowledge of σ. Instead, it requires only an estimate of σ computed from a random sample and the assumption that the population distribution of X is approximately normal.

The formula for the one-sample t statistic is

$$t = \frac{\overline{X} - \mu_0}{\hat{\sigma}_{\overline{X}}} = \frac{\overline{X} - \mu_0}{\hat{\sigma}/\sqrt{n}},$$

where $\overline{X}$ is the mean of a random sample, μ_0 is the mean specified in the null hypothesis, $\hat{\sigma}_{\overline{X}}$ is an estimator of the population standard error of the mean, $\hat{\sigma}$ is an estimator of the population standard deviation, and n is the size of the sample from a normal population used to compute $\overline{X}$.

The estimator $\hat{\sigma}$ is given by

$$\hat{\sigma} = \sqrt{\frac{\Sigma(X_i - \overline{X})^2}{n - 1}} \quad \text{or} \quad \sqrt{\frac{\Sigma X_i^2 - \dfrac{(\Sigma X_i)^2}{n}}{n - 1}}$$

A caret (or hat—⌃) over σ indicates that the statistic is a sample estimator of the population parameter.

The sampling distribution of t was derived by William Sealey Gossett, who published under the pseudonym *Student;* hence, the distribution is often referred to as

Student's *t* distribution. The shape of the *t* sampling distribution is similar to that of the *z* sampling distribution in that it is symmetrical and centered over a mean of zero. However, the variance of the *t* sampling distribution depends on sample size, or, more specifically, degrees of freedom. Before going any further, we need to discuss the concept of degrees of freedom, abbreviated *df* or ν (Greek nu, pronounced "new"). The term comes from the physical sciences, where it refers to the number of planes or directions in which an object is free to move. In statistics, the term **degrees of freedom** refers to the number of scores whose values are free to vary, as we will now see.

Consider a sample of size $n = 3$, with mean $= 5$, that is, $\overline{X} = (X_1 + X_2 + X_3)/3 = 5$. If we arbitrarily specify that X_1 is equal to 4 and X_2 is equal to 5, then X_3 must equal 6, because $(4 + 5 + 6)/3 = 15/3 = 5$. Given the statement that $\overline{X} = 5$, we are free to assign any values to $n - 1 = 2$ of the scores, but having done so, the value of the *n*th score is determined. Thus, the number of degrees of freedom associated with $\overline{X}$ is $n - 1$. Let us consider another example, one that is particularly relevant to the *t* statistic. The number of degrees of freedom associated with $\hat{\sigma} = \sqrt{\Sigma(X_i - \overline{X})^2/(n - 1)}$ is $n - 1$. This follows because once $n - 1$ of the *n* deviations $(X_i - \overline{X})$ have been arbitrarily specified, the *n*th deviation is not free to vary because $\Sigma(X_i - \overline{X})$ must equal 0 (as shown in Section 3.8 under "Proof That the Mean Is a Balance Point"). The number of degrees of freedom for the one-sample *t* statistic is $n - 1$, the number of degrees of freedom of $\hat{\sigma}$ in the denominator of *t*.

Now that we have introduced the concept of degrees of freedom, we are ready to describe the dispersion of the *t* sampling distribution and to compare its dispersion with that of the *z* sampling distribution. It can be shown that when *n* is greater than 3, the variance of the *t* sampling distribution, or, more simply, the *t* distribution, is

$$\text{Var}(t) = \frac{\nu}{\nu - 2},$$

where ν, the degrees of freedom, is equal to $n - 1$. According to the formula, if random samples of size $n = 5$ are obtained from a population, the variance of the resulting *t* distribution is

$$\text{Var}(t) = \frac{\nu}{\nu - 2} = \frac{4}{2} = 2.$$

When *n* is equal to 5, the variance of the *t* distribution is 2, which is twice as large as the variance of the *z* distribution. Recall from Section 9.3 that the variance of the *z* sampling distribution is equal to 1. As the number of degrees of freedom increases, the variance of the *t* distribution approaches more and more closely that of *z*. For example, when *n* is equal to 30,

$$\text{Var}(t) = \frac{29}{29 - 2} = 1.07,$$

which differs only slightly from the variance of *z*. When ν is equal to ∞, the two sampling distributions are identical. Because the two sampling distributions are so similar for samples equal to or larger than 30, an n of 30 is often taken as the dividing point between large and small samples.

The t distribution is actually a family of distributions whose shapes depend on the associated number of degrees of freedom. A comparison of three members of the t family and the z distribution is shown in Figure 11.2-1. As this figure illustrates, the t and z sampling distributions are alike in that both have a mean of 0, are symmetrical, and are unimodal. The distributions differ when ν is less than ∞—the distribution of t is more leptokurtic and has a larger variance.

At first glance the t and z test statistics look alike, but a difference can be seen on close inspection.

$$z = \frac{\bar{X} - \mu_0}{\sigma/\sqrt{n}} = \frac{\text{(Random variable)} - \text{(Constant)}}{\text{(Constant)}}$$

$$t = \frac{\bar{X} - \mu_0}{\hat{\sigma}/\sqrt{n}} = \frac{\text{(Random variable)} - \text{(Constant)}}{\text{(Random variable)}}$$

The z statistic is the ratio of a random variable to a constant; t is the ratio of two random variables. This follows because when ν is less than ∞, both $\bar{X}$ and $\hat{\sigma}$ in the t statistic vary from sample to sample and hence are random variables. The difference in the nature of the z and t denominators has an important ramification, which we will now examine.

Earlier we saw that the sampling distribution of the z test statistic is the standard normal distribution when the null hypothesis is true and the population distribution of X is normal in form or n is sufficiently large. Note that the normality assumption is not required if n is sufficiently large. The normality assumption, however, is required for the t test statistic. It serves two purposes. First, it permits us to specify the sampling distribution of the numerator of the t statistic without regard to sample size: It is the normal distribution. Second, it is a necessary condition for the numerator and denominator (both random variables) of the t statistic to be statistically

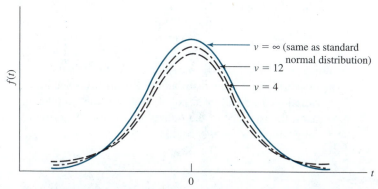

Figure 11.2-1. **Graph of the distribution of t for 4, 12, and ∞ degrees of freedom. The t distribution for $\nu = \infty$ is identical to the z distribution.**

"independent," which means that the information contained in $\overline{X}$ does not affect the value of $\hat{\sigma}$, and vice versa. Independence was a simplifying assumption that Gossett made when he originally derived the sampling distribution of t. If the numerator and denominator of the t statistic are not independent, specifying the exact sampling distribution of t is extremely difficult. This problem does not occur with the z test statistic because its denominator is a constant rather than a random variable. The important point is that the normality assumption plays a more important role in the derivation and use of t than in z.[1]

The t test statistic can be used to test null hypotheses of the form

$$H_0: \mu \geq \mu_0 \qquad H_0: \mu \leq \mu_0 \qquad H_0: \mu = \mu_0$$
$$H_1: \mu < \mu_0 \qquad H_1: \mu > \mu_0 \qquad H_1: \mu \neq \mu_0,$$

where μ denotes the unknown population mean and μ_0 denotes the hypothesized value of the population mean. The assumptions associated with using t to test these hypotheses are that (1) the population distribution of X is normally distributed, (2) the X's are a random sample from the population of interest, (3) the population variance isn't known, and (4) the null hypothesis is true, which is the hypothesis the researcher hopes to reject.

The null hypothesis is rejected if an observed t falls in the critical region of the t sampling distribution. The critical value of t that cuts off the upper α region of the sampling distribution for ν degrees of freedom is given in Appendix Table D.3 and is denoted by $t_{\alpha,\nu}$; the value that cuts off the lower α region is denoted by $-t_{\alpha,\nu}$. If α is to be divided equally between the two tails, as in performing a two-tailed test, the critical values are denoted by $t_{\alpha/2,\nu}$ and $-t_{\alpha/2,\nu}$. To illustrate, suppose that a researcher wants to test the one-sided hypothesis $H_0: \mu \leq 50$ versus $H_1: \mu > 50$, and suppose that α is set at .05 and ν is equal to 30. According to Appendix Table D.3, the value of t that cuts off the upper .05 region is $t_{.05,30} = 1.697$. The null hypothesis would be rejected if $t \geq 1.697$. The critical value for a two-sided hypothesis is $t_{.05/2,30} = 2.042$, in which case the null hypothesis would be rejected if the absolute value of t is greater than or equal to 2.042, that is, if $|t| \geq 2.042$. In reporting the computed value of t, say, 2.351 with 30 degrees of freedom, it is customary to write $t(30) = 2.351$. The number in parentheses, 30, is the degrees of freedom for the computed t statistic.

Computational Example for *t* Test for a Mean

Consider the scientific hypothesis that a new class registration procedure at Idle-On-In College will reduce the time required for a student to register. Over the past

---

[1] You should always examine a plot of your sample distribution for signs that the population might be markedly nonnormal. Research by Micceri (1989) suggests that extreme nonnormality in behavioral science data is more common than was once thought. Wilcox (1996) provides an excellent discussion of procedures for dealing with normality.

several years, the mean time required to register has been 3.1 hours. A trial run to test the new procedure was conducted with a random sample of 21 undergraduates. The decision rule and the steps to be followed in testing the null hypothesis are as follows.

Step 1. State the statistical hypotheses:

$H_0: \mu \geq 3.1$
$H_1: \mu < 3.1$.

Step 2. Specify the test statistic:

$t = \dfrac{\bar{X} - \mu_0}{\hat{\sigma}/\sqrt{n}}$ because we want to test $\mu \geq 3.1$, σ is unknown, the sample is random, and we assume the population distribution of X is approximately normal.

Step 3. Specify the sample size:
specify the sampling distribution:

$n = 21$;
t distribution with $\nu = n - 1$, because σ is unknown and must be estimated, and we assume the population distribution of X is approximately normal.

Step 4. Specify the significance level:

$\alpha = .05$.

Step 5. Obtain a random sample of size n, compute t, and make a decision.

Decision rule:

Reject the null hypothesis if t falls in the lower 5% of the sampling distribution of t; otherwise, don't reject the null hypothesis. If the null hypothesis is rejected, conclude that the new class registration procedure reduces the time required to register; if the null hypothesis is not rejected, do not draw this conclusion.

The data for the trial run are shown in Table 11.2-1. According to Appendix Table D.3, a t of -1.725 with $n - 1 = 20$ degrees of freedom cuts off the lower .05 region of the sampling distribution—that is, $-t_{.05,20}$ is equal to -1.725. Because the computed $t(20) = -5.797$ in Table 11.2-1 is less than $-t_{.05,20} = -1.725$, the null hypothesis is rejected and the school administrators conclude that registration can be completed in less time with the new procedure than with the old procedure.

Some Experimental Design Considerations

Let's digress for a moment and explore some experimental design issues concerning the registration experiment at Idle-On-In College. The school administrators would like to believe that the new registration procedure is extremely efficient and,

TABLE 11.2-1.   Registration-Time Data

(i) Data

Student	Registration Time, X_i (hours)	X_i^2	Student	Registration Time, X_i (hours)	X_i^2
1	2.9	8.41	12	3.0	9.00
2	2.7	7.29	13	2.8	7.84
3	2.8	7.84	14	3.1	9.61
4	3.0	9.00	15	2.9	8.41
5	2.6	6.76	16	2.7	7.29
6	2.9	8.41	17	3.2	10.24
7	3.1	9.61	18	2.8	7.84
8	2.9	8.41	19	2.8	7.84
9	3.0	9.00	20	3.1	9.61
10	2.7	7.29	21	3.0	9.00
11	2.9	8.41		$\Sigma X_i = 60.9$	$\Sigma X_i^2 = 177.11$

(ii) Computation

$$\bar{X} = \frac{\Sigma X_i}{n} = \frac{60.9}{21} = 2.9$$

$$\hat{\sigma} = \sqrt{\frac{\Sigma X_i^2 - \frac{(\Sigma X_i)^2}{n}}{n-1}} = \sqrt{\frac{177.11 - \frac{(60.9)^2}{21}}{21-1}} = \sqrt{\frac{0.50}{20}} = 0.1581$$

$$t = \frac{\bar{X} - \mu_0}{\hat{\sigma}/\sqrt{n}} = \frac{2.9 - 3.1}{0.1581/\sqrt{21}} = \frac{-0.2}{0.0345} = -5.797$$

$$\nu = n - 1 = 21 - 1 = 20$$

$$-t_{.05,20} = -1.725$$

if adopted for all students, would shorten registration time. But can we think of some alternative explanations for the apparent greater efficiency of the new procedure? Because the 21 students were selected for the trial run, they may have felt that they should make a special effort to complete registration quickly—an effort they wouldn't make once the new procedure was adopted and they were no longer under scrutiny. It is also possible that the personnel assisting in registration were more alert and tried to expedite the registration because they, too, were under scrutiny and because the procedure was a break from the usual routine. It is common for people to put forth special effort when they know that they are under scrutiny. The phenomenon even has a name—it is called the **John Henry effect** in honor of the steel driver who, when he learned that his performance was being compared with that of a steam drill, worked so hard that he outperformed the drill and died of overexertion.

Other explanations for the apparent greater efficiency of the new procedure could be advanced, and unless these explanations can be ruled out, the administrators may be disappointed if they adopt the new procedure. Once the novelty wears off, the new procedure may be no better, or may be even poorer, than the old one.

Designing an experiment whose outcome can be unambiguously interpreted requires careful planning.

> It is customary in behavioral science research to use one or more **control groups.** These groups contain subjects who do not receive the treatment. The purpose of control groups is to provide data on the effects of extraneous variables that affect the interpretation of the experiment.[2]

For example, the design of our registration experiment could be improved by drawing a sample of 42 students, with half the students assigned to use the new procedure and the other half, the old procedure. This change in the design of the experiment would provide data on the effects of being specially selected to participate in the trial run. If this design modification were adopted, the appropriate test statistic is the two-sample *t* statistic for independent samples discussed in Section 12.4.

Practical Significance

Let us assume for purposes of discussion that the results obtained in the trial run would also be obtained if the new registration procedure were adopted for all students. The difference in registration time between the new and old procedures was $2.9 - 3.1 = -0.2$ hours, or -12 minutes. Before adopting the new procedure, the school administrators would have to decide whether the statistically significant difference in class registration time is significant from a practical point of view. Is an average saving of 12 minutes per student worth the cost of changing the registration procedures? If the change involves hiring new personnel, scrapping costly registration forms, or extensively modifying physical facilities, the administrators might decide the change isn't cost effective. On the other hand, a 12-minute reduction per student might be achievable without costly changes and could result in substantial savings in personnel costs for registration. In this example, the school administrators would, in all likelihood, rely on a cost-benefit analysis to assist them in making a decision.

In general, researchers in the behavioral sciences, health sciences, and education are unable to assign a dollar value to research results. In Sections 10.4 and 10.6, we described Cohen's measure of effect size, $d = |\overline{X} - \mu_0|/\sigma$. This measure can help a researcher assess the practical significance of results. Recall that a *d* value of 0.2 is a small effect, 0.5 is a medium effect, and 0.8 is a large effect. If, as is usually the

---

[2] For an excellent discussion of these procedures, see Campbell (1957). This article is reprinted in Kirk (1972).

case, the researcher doesn't know the population standard deviation, a d-like measure of effect size can be computed by replacing σ with $\hat{\sigma}$, a sample estimator of the unknown population standard deviation. The effect size for the registration example is

$$d = \frac{|\overline{X} - \mu_0|}{\hat{\sigma}} = \frac{|2.9 - 3.1|}{0.1581} = 1.3.$$

According to Cohen's criteria, the reduction in class registration time represents a large effect. As discussed in Chapter 10, a result that is statistically significant may or may not be practically significant. Statistical significance is concerned with whether a result could have occurred by chance if the null hypothesis is true. Practical significance is concerned with whether the result is useful or beneficial and is based on a researcher's informed judgment. Cohen's d and the confidence interval for μ that is described later in this section can help a researcher make that judgment.

Determining the Required Sample Size

Procedures for making a rational choice of n were discussed in Section 10.4. Similar procedures can be used with t, but the computations are difficult to perform. If the difference you are interested in detecting is expressed as an effect size, d, the required n can be looked up in Appendix Table D.9.[3] To use the table, it is necessary to specify d, α, $1 - \beta$, and whether the test is directional or nondirectional. In the class registration experiment, suppose that we wanted to detect a large effect ($d = 0.8$) and that we wanted α to equal .05 and $1 - \beta$ to equal .80. The required sample size according to Appendix Table D.9 is 12, which is approximately half the number used in the experiment. The answer to the question "Will the new procedure reduce the time required for students to register?" could have been answered with a much smaller expenditure of time and effort.

More About the Normality Assumption

One of the assumptions of the t test is that the population distribution of X is normal in form, in which case the sampling distribution of $\overline{X}$ is normal for any size n and the numerator and denominator of t are statistically independent. What are the consequences when X is not normal? Research has suggested that when n is fairly large, and provided that the population distribution of X is unimodal and symmetrical, the t distribution still gives an adequate approximation to the exact probability of a type I error (Boneau, 1960). We can find comfort in the fact that when n is

---

[3] More extensive tables are provided by Cohen (1988) and Kraemer and Thiemann (1987).

large, the t test is not very sensitive to departures from normality; that is, it is **robust** with respect to nonnormality. If, however, n is small and the population distribution of X deviates appreciably from normality, the approximation yielded by t can be seriously in error. For less marked deviations from normality, the actual probability of a type I error generally will be fairly close to the nominal or specified probability of a type I error, even when n is small. Unfortunately, research indicates that large departures from normality in behavioral science data are more common than was once believed (Micceri, 1989).

Research also has indicated that power and the probability of a type II error are not significantly affected by lack of normality of the population, provided n is large. However, when n is small, a researcher may fail to reject a false null hypothesis due to lack of power resulting from nonnormality of the population.

Confidence Interval for a Mean

The advantages of confidence interval estimation over null hypothesis significance tests were discussed in detail in Section 10.5. The confidence interval procedures described in Section 10.5 can, with slight modification, be used to construct a confidence interval for μ when the population standard deviation is unknown.

A two-sided $100(1 - \alpha)\%$ confidence interval for μ is

$$\overline{X} - \frac{t_{\alpha/2,\nu}\hat{\sigma}}{\sqrt{n}} < \mu < \overline{X} + \frac{t_{\alpha/2,\nu}\hat{\sigma}}{\sqrt{n}},$$

where n is the number of elements in a random sample from a normally distributed population used to compute $\overline{X}$, $t_{\alpha/2,\nu}$ is the value that cuts off the upper $\alpha/2$ region of Student's t distribution for $\nu = n - 1$ degrees of freedom, and $\hat{\sigma} = \sqrt{\Sigma(X_i - \overline{X})^2/(n - 1)}$ is an estimator of the unknown population standard deviation.

A one-sided $100(1 - \alpha)\%$ confidence interval for μ is

$$\overline{X} - \frac{t_{\alpha,\nu}\hat{\sigma}}{\sqrt{n}} < \mu \qquad \text{or} \qquad \mu < \overline{X} + \frac{t_{\alpha,\nu}\hat{\sigma}}{\sqrt{n}},$$

where $t_{\alpha,\nu}$ is the value that cuts off the upper α region of Student's t distribution for $n - 1$ degrees of freedom.

The researcher's hypotheses for the new class registration procedure at Idle-On-In College were directional:

$$H_0: \mu \geq 3.1$$

$$H_1: \mu < 3.1.$$

An analogous one-sided $100(1 - .05)\% = 95\%$ confidence interval for these data where $\overline{X} = 2.9$, $\hat{\sigma} = 0.1581$, $n = 21$, and $t_{.05,20} = 1.725$ is

$$\mu < \overline{X} + \frac{t_{.05,20}\,\hat{\sigma}}{\sqrt{n}}$$

$$\mu < 2.9 + \frac{1.725(0.1581)}{\sqrt{21}}$$

$$\mu < 2.9 + 0.0595$$

$$\mu < 2.96.$$

This 95% confidence interval corresponds to the darkened portion of the real number line as follows.

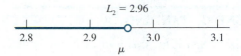

Earlier we saw that the difference between the registration times for the new and old procedures, 2.9 versus 3.1 hours, is a large effect, $d = 1.3$. Based on the confidence interval, the researcher can be 95% confident that registration time for the new procedure is less than 2.96 hours. The best guess that can be made concerning the population mean is that it is equal to $\overline{X} = 2.9$. In making a decision as to whether or not to adopt the new procedure, the school administrators would want to consider both the expected savings in registration time—$2.9 - 3.1 = -0.2$ hour—and the worst-case scenario based on the upper bound for μ—$2.96 - 3.1 = -0.14$ hour.

As discussed in Section 10.45, a confidence interval provides more information about the outcome of the experiment than a null hypothesis significance test. Furthermore, a confidence interval for μ contains all the values of μ_0 for which the null hypothesis would *not* be rejected at α level of significance. That is, the null hypothesis $\mu \geq \mu_0$ would not be rejected if μ_0 lies in the $100(1 - \alpha)\%$ confidence interval. Only if μ_0 lies outside the $100(1 - \alpha)\%$ confidence interval would the null hypothesis be rejected at α level of significance. For example, the null hypothesis for the new egistration procedure at Idle-On-In College would be rejected only if μ_0 is greater than or equal to 2.96.

For purposes of illustration, we will construct a two-sided confidence interval for the new registration procedure at Idle-On-In College. A $100(1 - .05)\% = 95\%$ confidence interval for these data where $\overline{X} = 2.9$, $\hat{\sigma} = 0.1581$, $n = 21$, and $t_{.05/2,20} = 2.086$ is given by

$$\overline{X} - \frac{t_{.05/2,20}\,\hat{\sigma}}{\sqrt{n}} < \mu < \overline{X} + \frac{t_{.05/2,20}\,\hat{\sigma}}{\sqrt{n}}$$

$$2.9 - \frac{2.086(0.1581)}{\sqrt{21}} < \mu < 2.9 + \frac{2.086(0.1581)}{\sqrt{21}}$$

$$2.9 - 0.072 < \mu < 2.9 + 0.072$$

$$2.83 < \mu < 2.97.$$

We can be 95% confident that μ for the new registration procedure is greater than 2.83 hours and less than 2.97 hours. This confidence interval corresponds to the colored portion of the real number line as follows:

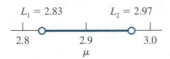

$$L_1 = 2.83 \qquad\qquad L_2 = 2.97$$

2.8   2.9   3.0

μ

CHECK YOUR UNDERSTANDING OF SECTION 11.2

1. List the similarities and differences between the t and z sampling distributions.
2. A random sample of 65 freshman college students was selected to participate in a new look-say teaching program designed to increase reading speed in French. The final exam consisted of a French passage that the students translated. The time required for each student to complete the translation was recorded. The sample statistics were $\overline{X} = 302$ sec and $\hat{\sigma} = 56$ sec. According to departmental records, the mean for students in conventional classes was 320 sec. Let $\alpha = .05$.
   a. List the steps you would use in testing the scientific hypothesis that the look-say program resulted in a decrease in time required to translate the French passage.
   b. Compute a t statistic and make a decision about the scientific hypothesis.
   c. What is the p-value of the t statistic?
   d. How could the design of the experiment be improved?
   e. Use Appendix Table D.9 to determine whether the sample size is adequate to detect a medium-size effect if a power of .95 is desired.
   f. Compute a $100(1 - .05)\% = 95\%$ confidence interval for μ; assume that $t_{.05,64} = 1.669$. Locate the confidence interval on the real number line.
   g. Specify all null hypotheses that could be rejected.
   h. Compute the effect size and interpret the result.
3. Derive a $100(1 - \alpha)\%$ confidence interval for μ from
$$\text{Prob}(-t_{\alpha/2,\nu} < t < t_{\alpha/2,\nu}) = 1 - \alpha,$$
   where $t = (\overline{X} - \mu)/(\hat{\sigma}/\sqrt{n})$. (Hint: See a similar derivation in Section 10.5.)
4. Terms to remember
   a. Student's t distribution   b. Degrees of freedom
   c. John Henry effect   d. Control group
   e. Robust statistic

11.3 ONE-SAMPLE CHI-SQUARE TEST AND CONFIDENCE INTERVAL FOR A VARIANCE

Most scientific hypotheses are concerned with central tendency, but hypotheses concerning a population variance, proportion, and correlation also can be of interest. In this section, we describe a chi-square (χ^2) statistic for evaluating a hypothesis about a single population variance. Recall from Section 4.2 that variance is a measure of dispersion—the square of the standard deviation.

The chi-square test statistic is

$$\chi^2 = \frac{(n-1)\hat{\sigma}^2}{\sigma_0^2},$$

where n is the size of a random sample from a normally distributed population used to compute $\hat{\sigma}^2$, $\hat{\sigma}^2 = \Sigma(X_i - \bar{X})^2/(n-1)$ is an unbiased estimator of the population variance, and σ_0^2 is the value of the population variance specified in the null hypothesis.

The chi-square statistic can be used to test null hypotheses of the form

$$H_0: \sigma^2 = \sigma_0^2 \qquad H_0: \sigma^2 \le \sigma_0^2 \qquad H_0: \sigma^2 \ge \sigma_0^2$$
$$H_1: \sigma^2 \ne \sigma_0^2 \qquad H_1: \sigma^2 > \sigma_0^2 \qquad H_1: \sigma^2 < \sigma_0^2.$$

The assumptions associated with using the chi-square statistic to test these hypotheses are that (1) the population distribution of X is normal, (2) the X's are a random sample from the population of interest, and (3) the null hypothesis is true, which is the hypothesis that the researcher hopes to reject.

The sampling distribution of chi square was derived by F. R. Helmert in 1876. Karl Pearson first used the distribution to test hypotheses in 1900. The chi-square distribution, like the t distribution, is actually a family of distributions whose shapes depend on the associated degrees of freedom. The number of degrees of freedom, ν, for χ^2 is equal to $n-1$. Unlike the z and t distributions, the chi-square distribution is positively skewed for small degrees of freedom, but as ν increases, the distribution approaches a normal distribution with mean and variance, respectively,

$$E(\chi_\nu^2) = \nu \qquad \text{and} \qquad \text{Var}(\chi_\nu^2) = 2\nu.$$

Because χ^2 is a squared quantity, it can range over only nonnegative numbers, zero to positive infinity, whereas t and z can range over all real numbers. The chi-square distributions for several different degrees of freedom are shown in Figure 11.3-1. The critical value of χ^2 that cuts off the upper α region of the sampling distribution for ν degrees of freedom is given in Appendix Table D.4 and is denoted by $\chi_{\alpha,\nu}^2$; the value that cuts off the lower α region is denoted by $\chi_{1-\alpha,\nu}^2$. If α is to be divided equally between the two tails—a two-tailed test—the critical values are denoted by $\chi_{\alpha/2,\nu}^2$ and $\chi_{1-\alpha/2,\nu}^2$. A null hypothesis is rejected if χ^2 falls in the critical region of the chi square sampling distribution given in Appendix Table D.4.

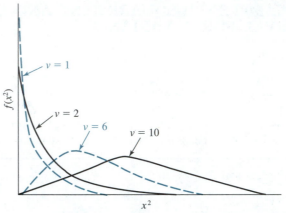

Figure 11.3-1. **Chi-square distributions for different degrees of freedom.**

Computational Example for Chi-Square Test for a Variance

It has been shown that students who take a driver education course in high school receive, on the average, higher scores on the state licensing test than do students who haven't taken the course. One might also expect less variability among the scores of students who have taken driver education than among students who haven't.

We can determine whether the latter scientific hypothesis is tenable by means of the one-sample chi-square test. Let's assume that the variance of the license test scores for high school seniors who haven't taken the driver education course is known to equal 324. The decision rule and the steps to be followed in testing the null hypothesis are as follows.

Step 1. State the statistical hypotheses: $H_0 \colon \sigma^2 \geq 324$
$H_1 \colon \sigma^2 < 324$.

Step 2. Specify the test statistic: $\chi^2 = \dfrac{(n-1)\hat{\sigma}^2}{\sigma_0^2}$ because we want to test $\sigma^2 \geq 324$, the sample is random, and we assume the population distribution of X is approximately normal.

Step 3. Specify the sample size: $n = 16$;
specify the sampling distribution: chi-square distribution with $\nu = n - 1$, because the population distribution of X is assumed to be normal.

Step 4. Specify the significance level: $\alpha = .05$.

Step 5. Obtain a random sample of size n, compute χ^2, and make a decision.

Decision rule:

Reject the null hypothesis if χ^2 falls in the lower 5% of the sampling distribution of χ^2; otherwise, don't reject H_0. If the null hypothesis is rejected, conclude that there is less variability among the scores of students who have taken a driver education course in high school than among the scores of students who haven't taken the course; if the null hypothesis is not rejected, do not draw this conclusion.

Assume that driver's license scores for a random sample of 16 high-school seniors who have taken the driving course have been obtained from the Bureaucracy of Motor Vehicles. The data are given in Table 11.3-1. For this sample, the variance is equal to 150.7. Is this sample variance small enough to warrant the conclusion that the population parameter is not greater than or equal to 324?

TABLE 11.3-1. Driver's License Test Scores for a Random Sample of High-School Seniors Who Have Completed a Driving Course

(i) Data

Student Number	Score, X_i	X_i^2	Student Number	Score, X_i	X_i^2
1	70	4900	9	57	3249
2	68	4624	10	61	3721
3	81	6561	11	72	5184
4	95	9025	12	78	6084
5	63	3969	13	71	5041
6	69	4761	14	82	6724
7	47	2209	15	87	7569
8	79	6241	16	59	3481
				$\Sigma X_i = 1139$	$\Sigma X_i^2 = 83{,}343$

(ii) Computation

$$\hat{\sigma} = \frac{\Sigma X_i^2 - \frac{(\Sigma X_i)^2}{n}}{n-1} = \frac{83{,}343 - \frac{(1139)^2}{16}}{16-1} = 150.6958$$

$$\chi^2 = \frac{(n-1)\hat{\sigma}^2}{\sigma_0^2} = \frac{(16-1)150.6958}{324} = \frac{2260.4370}{324} = 6.977$$

$$\nu = n - 1 = 16 - 1 = 15$$

$$\chi^2_{1-.05,15} = 7.261$$

According to the chi-square table, Appendix Table D.4, a χ^2 of 7.261 cuts off the lower .05 region of the sampling distribution—that is, $\chi^2_{1-.05,15}$ is equal to 7.261. Because the computed $\chi^2(15) = 6.977$ is less than $\chi^2_{1-.05,15} = 7.261$, the null hypothesis is rejected and the researcher concludes that the population variance of driver's license scores is smaller for students who have taken a driving course in high school than for students who haven't taken a course.

More About the Normality Assumption for the Chi-Square Test

How important is the assumption that the population distribution of X is approximately normal? In Section 11.2 we learned that the t test is robust with respect to departures from normality. Unfortunately, this isn't true for this chi-square test. If the sampling distribution of χ^2 is to have the same form as the chi-square distribution, the population distribution of X must be approximately normal. Deviations from normality can result in large discrepancies between the actual and nominal type I and II errors.

Confidence Interval for a Variance

A two-sided $100(1 - \alpha)\%$ confidence interval for σ^2 is

$$\frac{(n-1)\hat{\sigma}^2}{\chi^2_{\alpha/2,\nu}} < \sigma^2 < \frac{(n-1)\hat{\sigma}^2}{\chi^2_{1-\alpha/2,\nu}},$$

where n is the size of the sample from a normally distributed population used to compute $\hat{\sigma}^2$; $\hat{\sigma}^2$ is an unbiased estimator of the population variance, $\hat{\sigma}^2 = \Sigma(X_i - \overline{X})^2/(n-1)$; σ^2 is the unknown population variance; and $\chi^2_{1-\alpha/2,\nu}$

and $\chi^2_{\alpha/2,\nu}$ are the values of the chi-square distribution for $\nu = n - 1$ degrees of freedom that cut off the lower and upper $\alpha/2$ regions, respectively,
   A one-sided $100(1 - \alpha)\%$ confidence interval for σ^2 is given by

$$\frac{(n-1)\hat{\sigma}^2}{\chi^2_{\alpha,\nu}} < \sigma^2 \quad \text{or} \quad \sigma^2 < \frac{(n-1)\hat{\sigma}^2}{\chi^2_{1-\alpha,\nu}},$$

where $\chi^2_{1-\alpha,\nu}$ and $\chi^2_{\alpha,\nu}$ are the values of the chi-square distribution for $\nu = n - 1$ degrees of freedom that cut off the lower and upper α regions, respectively.

The assumptions associated with these intervals are that (1) the population distribution of X is normal and (2) the X's are a random sample from the population of interest.

Computational Example of Confidence Interval for a Variance

To illustrate the construction of a confidence interval for σ^2, we will use the driver's license test-score data presented in Table 11.3-1 where $\hat{\sigma}^2$, the variance of the test scores, is equal to 150.696 and n is equal to 16. Recall that the statistical hypotheses were

$$H_0: \sigma^2 \geq 324$$
$$H_1: \sigma^2 < 324.$$

An analogous $100(1 - .05)\% = 95\%$ confidence interval for these data is

$$\sigma^2 < \frac{(n - 1)\hat{\sigma}^2}{\chi^2_{1 - .05, 15}}$$

$$\sigma^2 < \frac{(16 - 1)150.696}{7.261}$$

$$\sigma^2 < 311.3.$$

This confidence interval corresponds to the darkened portion of the real number line as follows.

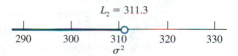

The best guess that we can make about the unknown population variance is that it is equal to $\hat{\sigma}^2 = 150.696$. We can be 95% confident that the population variance is less than 311.3.

CHECK YOUR UNDERSTANDING OF SECTION 11.3

5. Students desiring to enter graduate school at Kandykane Technical Institute (KTI) are required to submit Graduate Record Examination (GRE) scores with their applications. The verbal scores for the first 20 applications received this year are given in the table.

GRE Scores for Verbal Section of Test

402	390	429	391
381	407	410	403
430	413	406	398
376	424	382	410
395	360	410	404

    a. If the first 20 applicants can be considered a random sample of applicants who will apply, what is the best estimate of the variance for this year's applicants?

    b. List the steps you would follow in testing the hypothesis that $\sigma^2 = 306.1$, the variance for last year's applicants. Let $\alpha = .05$.

    c. Compute a χ^2 statistic for these data and make a decision about the scientific hypothesis.

    d. What is the p-value of the χ^2 statistic?

    e. Compute a $100(1 - .05)\% = 95\%$ confidence interval for σ^2. Locate the confidence interval on the real number line.

    f. Specify all null hypotheses that could be rejected.

6. The mean number of movies attended per month by 14-year-old boys in the United States is 4.8, with a standard deviation of 1.3. According to juvenile court records in Houston, Texas, the corresponding statistics for a random sample of 31 boys who appeared in court are $\overline{X} = 4.9$ and $\hat{\sigma} = 1.6$.

    a. List the steps you would follow in testing the scientific hypothesis that the dispersion of the movie attendance distribution for boys appearing in the Houston juvenile court is different from that for the nation at large. Let $\alpha = .05$.

    b. Compute a χ^2 statistic for these data and make a decision about the scientific hypothesis.

    c. What is the p-value of the χ^2 statistic?

    d. Compute a $100(1 - .05)\% = 95\%$ confidence interval for σ^2. Locate the confidence interval on the real number line.

    e. Specify all null hypotheses that could be rejected.

11.4 ONE-SAMPLE z TEST AND CONFIDENCE INTERVAL FOR A PROPORTION

A researcher is often interested in testing a hypothesis about a population proportion. For example, an opinion pollster may want to know whether a majority of the voters favor a certain candidate, an automobile manufacturer may want to know whether at least .70 of new car buyers are willing to pay \$150 for a safety device, or the United States Marine Corps may want to know whether at least .35 of its volunteers plan to re-enlist. Each of these examples has a large number of occasions, or independent trials, in which one of two outcomes can occur, and the probabilities associated with the two outcomes remain constant from trial to trial. For convenience, the outcomes are designated "success" and "failure," with probabilities p and $1 - p = q$, respectively. What we have just summarized are the characteristics of a Bernoulli trial, which is discussed in Section 8.3. Recall that the number of successes on $n \geq 2$ Bernoulli trials is a binomial random variable. The probability of exactly r successes in n independent trials for the binomial random variable X is given by the function rule

$$p(X = r) = {}_nC_r p^r q^{n-r}.$$

If n is very small, we can use this binomial function rule to determine the probability associated with values of the random variable X—that is, the probability that various numbers of successes will occur. However, if n is large, this procedure is not computationally feasible. In this case, the normal distribution approximation to the binomial distribution can be used. This approximation is excellent if n is large and p is equal to .5; as n becomes smaller or as p approaches either 0 or 1, the approximation becomes poorer. As a rule of thumb, if np_0 (the sample size multiplied by the population proportion specified in the null hypothesis) and $n(1 - p_0)$ are both greater than 5, the normal approximation is satisfactory.

> The z statistic for testing the null hypothesis about a population proportion is given by
>
> $$z = \frac{\hat{p} - p_0}{\sqrt{p_0 q_0 / n}} \quad \text{or} \quad z = \frac{X - np_0}{\sqrt{np_0 q_0}},$$
>
> where $\hat{p}$ is the sample estimator of the population proportion, p_0 is the value of the population proportion specified in the null hypothesis, q_0 is equal to $1 - p_0$, n is the size of the random sample used to compute $\hat{p}$, and X is equal to $n\hat{p}$ (the number of elements in the success category).[4]

The z statistic can be used to test null hypotheses such as the following:

$$H_0: p = p_0 \qquad H_0: p \leq p_0 \qquad H_0: p \geq p_0$$
$$H_1: p \neq p_0 \qquad H_1: p > p_0 \qquad H_1: p < p_0$$

Here, p denotes the unknown population proportion. The assumptions associated with using the z statistic to test these hypotheses are (1) random sampling from the population of interest, (2) binomial population, and (3) $n\hat{p}$ and $n(1 - \hat{p})$ are both greater than 5. A null hypothesis is rejected if z falls in the critical region of the sampling distribution of the standard normal distribution given in Appendix Table D.2. The values of z that cut off the upper and lower critical regions for a two-sided null hypothesis are denoted by $z_\alpha/2$ and $-z_\alpha/2$, respectively. For a one-sided null hypothesis, the critical regions are denoted by z_α and $-z_\alpha$.

Computational Example for z Test for a Proportion

Suppose the League for Better Housing has conducted a survey to determine whether the proportion of substandard dwelling units in a large city has changed since the previous census five years ago. At that time, .30 of the dwelling units were

---

[4] An alternative statistic that provides a test of the same null hypothesis is described in Section 16.7.

classified as substandard. A random sample of 900 dwelling units is surveyed. The steps to be followed in testing the null hypothesis are as follows:

Step 1. State the statistical hypotheses: $H_0: p = .30$
$H_1: p \neq .30.$

Step 2. Specify the test statistic: $z = \dfrac{\hat{p} - p_0}{\sqrt{p_0 q_0 / n}}$ because we want to test $p = .30$, the sample is random, and both $np_0 = 270$ and $n(1 - p_0) = 630$ are greater than 5.

Step 3. Specify the sample size:[5] $n = 900;$
specify the sampling distribution: standard normal distribution, because z is a satisfactory approximation to the binomial distribution when both $np_0 = 270$ and $n(1 - p_0) = 630$ are greater than 5.

Step 4. Specify the significance level: $\alpha = .05.$
Step 5. Obtain a random sample of size n, compute z, and make a decision.

Decision rule:

Reject the null hypothesis if z falls in either the lower 2.5% or the upper 2.5% of the sampling distribution of z; otherwise, don't reject the null hypothesis. If the null hypothesis is rejected, conclude that the proportion of substandard dwelling units in the city has changed since the previous census; if the null hypothesis is not rejected, do not draw this conclusion.

For $\hat{p} = .34$, the sample proportion of substandard dwelling units in the recent survey, the z statistic is

$$z = \frac{\hat{p} - p_0}{\sqrt{p_0 q_0 / n}} = \frac{.34 - .30}{\sqrt{(.30)(.70)/900}} = \frac{.04}{0.0153} = 2.62.$$

According to Appendix Table D.2, $z_{.05/2} = 1.96$ and $-z_{.05/2} = -1.96$, respectively, cut off the upper and lower .025 regions of the sampling distribution. Because the computed $z = 2.62$ is greater than $z_{.05/2} = 1.96$, the null hypothesis is rejected, and it is concluded that the proportion of substandard dwelling units has changed. In fact, data for the recent survey, $\hat{p} = .34$, suggest that the housing situation has deteriorated.

---

[5] Cohen (1988, chap. 6) and Kraemer and Thiemann (1987, chap. 8) provide tables for estimating the sample size required for various values of α, $1 - \beta$, and effect size.

Correction for Continuity

Many variables, such as the number of substandard dwelling units, are discrete and have a discrete probability distribution. For example, the number of dwelling units is either 1 or 2 or 3 and so on. The number can't be 2.6.

When the continuous normal distribution is used to estimate probabilities for a discrete distribution and n is small, it is desirable to apply a **correction for continuity.** In making a correction for continuity, we treat a number, say $X = 6$, as representing the interval 5.5–6.5; that is, a number is considered to have an actual lower limit equal to $X - c$, $(6 - .5 = 5.5)$, and an actual upper limit equal to $X + c$, $(6 + .5 = 6.5)$, where $c = $ (unit of measurement)$/2 = 1/2 = .5$. The correction for continuity consists of making the appropriate addition or subtraction.

The rule for applying the correction is simple. If $\hat{p} < p_0$; add $c/n = 1/2n$ to $\hat{p}$ in the formula

$$z = \frac{(\hat{p} \pm c/n) - p_0}{\sqrt{(p_0 q_0)/n}};$$

if $\hat{p} > p_0$, subtract $c/n = 1/2n$ from $\hat{p}$. The correction for continuity also can be incorporated in the formula $z = (X - np_0)/\sqrt{np_0 q_0}$. If $X < np_0$, add $c = 1/2$ to X in the formula

$$z = \frac{(X \pm c) - np_0}{\sqrt{np_0 q_0}};$$

if $X > np_0$, subtract $c = 1/2$ from X.

If n is large, the use of the continuity correction has little effect on the z statistic and can be dispensed with. The correction has little effect on the z statistic for the housing survey data, as the following computation shows.

$$z = \frac{(\hat{p} - 1/2n) - p_0}{\sqrt{(p_0 q_0)/n}} = \frac{[.34 - 1/2(900)] - .30}{\sqrt{(.30)(.70)/900}} = \frac{.03944}{.01528} = 2.58$$

The difference between the corrected and uncorrected z statistics, $2.58 - 2.62 = -.04$, is negligible.

Computational Procedure When the Sample Size Is Equal to or Greater Than 10% of the Population

If the population is finite and if sampling is carried out without replacement, the random variable X is distributed as the hypergeometric distribution (see Section

8.3) rather than as the binomial distribution. For this situation, the z statistic should be modified if the ratio $n/n_{Pop} \geq .10$, where n is the number of elements in the sample and n_{Pop} is the number of elements in the population. The modified z statistic is

$$z = \frac{\hat{p} - p_0}{\sqrt{(p_0 q_0/n)[(n_{Pop} - n)/(n_{Pop} - 1)]}}.$$

The denominator adjustment $(n_{Pop} - n)/(n_{Pop} - 1)$ can be ignored if $n/n_{Pop} < .10$.

Confidence Interval for a Proportion

A two-sided $100(1 - \alpha)\%$ confidence interval for p is given by

$$\left(\hat{p} - \frac{1}{2n}\right) - z_{\alpha/2}\sqrt{\frac{\hat{p}\hat{q}}{n}} < p < \left(\hat{p} + \frac{1}{2n}\right) + z_{\alpha/2}\sqrt{\frac{\hat{p}\hat{q}}{n}},$$

where $\hat{p}$ is an estimator of the population proportion, $\hat{q} = 1 - \hat{p}$, n is the number of elements in a random sample used to compute $\hat{p}$, $1/2n$ is the correction for continuity, and $z_{\alpha/2}$ is the value of the standard normal distribution that cuts off the upper $\alpha/2$ region.

A one-sided $100(1 - \alpha)\%$ confidence interval for p is

$$\left(\hat{p} - \frac{1}{2n}\right) - z_{\alpha}\sqrt{\frac{\hat{p}\hat{q}}{n}} < p \qquad \text{or} \qquad p < \left(\hat{p} + \frac{1}{2n}\right) + z_{\alpha}\sqrt{\frac{\hat{p}\hat{q}}{n}},$$

where z_{α} is the value of the standard normal distribution that cuts off the upper α region.

When n is large, the correction for continuity, $1/2n$, can be dispensed with. The assumptions associated with these interval are (1) random sampling from the population of interest, (2) binomial population, and (3) $n\hat{p}$ and $n(1 - \hat{p})$ are both greater than 5.

Computational Example of Confidence Interval for a Proportion

To illustrate the construction of a confidence interval for p, we will use the League for Better Housing data described earlier. Recall that the sample proportion of substandard dwelling units was $\hat{p} = .34$ and $n = 900$. The statistical hypotheses were

$$H_0: p = .30$$
$$H_1: p \neq .30.$$

An analogous two-sided $100(1 - .05)\% = 95\%$ confidence interval for these data is

$$\hat{p} - z_{.05/2}\sqrt{\frac{\hat{p}\hat{q}}{n}} < p < \hat{p} + z_{.05/2}\sqrt{\frac{\hat{p}\hat{q}}{n}}$$

$$.34 - 1.96\sqrt{\frac{(.34)(.66)}{900}} < p < .34 + 1.96\sqrt{\frac{(.34)(.66)}{900}}$$

$$.34 - .031 < p < .34 + .031$$

$$.31 < p < .37$$

This confidence interval corresponds to the colored portion of the real number line as follows:

A researcher can be 95% confident that p is greater than .31 and less than .37.

CHECK YOUR UNDERSTANDING OF SECTION 11.4

7. If $p_0 = .20$, how large should n be to use the normal approximation to the binomial distribution?

8. The election is only days away, and the latest Giddyup poll gives Mr. Jerry Mander 55% of the vote. Between periods of euphoria, Mr. Jerry Mander ponders the question of whether he should or should not cancel the expensive political advertisement planned for election eve. Is it possible that he doesn't have a majority, although the highly respected poll of $n = 1,000$ randomly selected potential voters says he will win? Now, Mr. Mander is no statistician, but he knows that polls are subject to sampling error. With anxiety mounting, he decides to forego a vacation to Hawaii and use the campaign funds for their intended purpose.

   a. List the steps you would follow in testing the scientific hypothesis that the population proportion is not equal to .50. Let $\alpha = .01$.
   b. Test the null hypothesis that $p = .50$.
   c. What does the use of the .01 instead of the .05 level of significance tell you about the relative importance that Mr. Mander assigned to type I and II errors?
   d. What is the p-value of the z statistic?
   e. Compute a $100(1 - .01)\% = 99\%$ confidence interval for p.

Locate the confidence interval on the real number line. Was Mr. Mander's decision to forego the Hawaii vacation a good one?

f. Specify all null hypotheses that could be rejected.

9. Suppose that you are interested in testing babies' color preferences. On each of $n = 20$ trials you offer a baby a choice between two balls—one red and one green. The baby chooses a red ball on 12 of the 20 trials.

   a. List the steps you would follow in testing the scientific hypothesis that the babies have a preference for one of the two colors. Use the correction for continuity. Let $\alpha = .05$.

   b. Can you conclude that the babies have a color preference?

   c. What is the p-value of the test statistic?

   d. Compute a $100(1 - .05)\% = 95\%$ confidence interval for p. Use the correction for continuity. Locate the confidence interval on the real number line.

   e. Specify all null hypotheses that could be rejected.

10. A national survey of 300 unmarried women between the ages of 15 and 19 found that 46% of the 19-year-olds had experienced sexual intercourse.

    a. List the steps you would follow in testing the scientific hypothesis that the population proportion has changed from an earlier survey in which $p = .37$. Let $\alpha = .01$.

    b. Test the null hypothesis that $p = .37$.

    c. What is the p-value of the z statistic?

    d. Compute a $100(1 - .01)\% = 99\%$ confidence interval for p. Locate the confidence interval on the real number line.

    e. Specify all null hypotheses that could be rejected.

11. One hundred men who had suffered one heart attack participated in a supervised physical fitness program. Only seven of the men had a second attack during the 12 months after beginning the program. According to national statistics, the chances of a man having a second heart attack are 1 in 10 each year after the first seizure.

    a. List the steps you would follow in testing the scientific hypothesis that the supervised physical fitness program affected the chances of a man having a second heart attack. Use a correction for continuity and let $\alpha = .05$.

    b. Test the null hypothesis. Was the physical fitness program effective? Why?

    c. What is the p-value of the z statistic?

    d. Compute a $100(1 - .05)\% = 95\%$ confidence interval for p. Locate the confidence interval on the real number line.

    e. Specify all null hypotheses that could be rejected.

12. Term to remember

    a. Correction for continuity

11.5 ONE-SAMPLE t AND z TESTS AND CONFIDENCE INTERVAL FOR A CORRELATION

t Test for Correlations Equal to Zero

Many research questions are concerned with whether two variables, say X and Y, are correlated. The hypotheses of interest are

$$H_0: \rho = 0$$

$$H_1: \rho \neq 0,$$

where ρ denotes the population correlation between the variables. A sample correlation coefficient, r, can differ from 0 due to chance sampling variability, even though $\rho = 0$. In this section, we describe a t test that helps a researcher decide on the basis of a random sample whether the population correlation is different from 0.

The one-sample t test statistic is

$$t = \frac{r\sqrt{n-2}}{\sqrt{1 - r^2}},$$

where n is the number of paired X and Y scores in the random sample used to compute r and r is an estimator of the population correlation coefficient. This t statistic has $\nu = n - 2$ degrees of freedom.

The null hypothesis is rejected if t falls in the critical region of the sampling distribution of t given in Appendix Table D.3. An important assumption underlying the use of the t statistic is that the population of paired X and Y scores is *bivariate normal* in form.

A **bivariate normal population** is one for which the distributions of X and Y are normal, the relationship between X and Y is linear, and the distribution of Y for any value of X is normal with variance that does not depend on the X value selected and vice versa.

The t statistic is appropriate only for testing the null hypothesis that $H_0: \rho = 0$. The sampling distribution of r can be regarded as approximately normal when ρ is close to 0; for other values of ρ, the sampling distribution of r tends to be very skewed, and the z statistic described later should be used instead of the t statistic.

Computational Example for t Test for a Correlation

Consider a researcher who is interested in determining whether a correlation exists between college grades and income 10 years after graduation. Assume that grade point averages and income for a random sample of 62 male graduates of Boston Central College have been obtained. The product-moment correlation between grade point average and income for this sample is .16. How likely is it that a sample correlation coefficient of this size would have been obtained if the correlation between income and grades really is equal to 0? The steps to be followed in testing the null hypothesis are as follows:

Step 1. State the statistical hypotheses: $H_0: \rho = 0$
                                                $H_1: \rho \neq 0.$

Step 2. Specify the test statistic: $t = \dfrac{r\sqrt{n-2}}{\sqrt{1-r^2}}$ because we want to

test $\rho = 0$, the sample is random, and the population is assumed to be bivariate normal.

Step 3. Specify the sample size:[6] $n = 62;$
          specify the sampling distribution: t distribution with $\nu = n - 2$, because the population is assumed to be bivariate normal.

Step 4. Specify the significance level: $\alpha = .05.$

Step 5. Obtain a random sample of size n, compute t, and make a decision.

Decision rule:

Reject the null hypothesis if t falls in either the lower 2.5% or the upper 2.5% of the sampling distribution of t; otherwise, don't reject the null hypothesis. If the null hypothesis is rejected, conclude that a correlation exists between college grades and income 10 years after graduation; if the null hypothesis is not rejected, do not draw this conclusion.

The t statistic for the correlation between college grades and income 10 years after graduation is

$$t = \frac{.16\sqrt{62-2}}{\sqrt{1-(.16)^2}} = \frac{1.239}{0.987} = 1.26,$$

where $r = .16$, $n = 62$, and $\nu = n - 2 = 62 - 2 = 60$. According to Appendix Table D.3, the value of t that cuts off the upper .05/2 region of the sampling distribution is $t_{.05/2, 60} = 2.00$. Because the computed $t(60) = 1.26$ is less than $t_{.05/2, 60} = 2.00$, the null hypothesis isn't rejected. The data do not warrant the conclusion that the population correlation coefficient is not equal to zero.

---

[6] Cohen (1988, chap. 6) and Kraemer and Thiemann (1987, chap. 8) provide tables for estimating the sample size required for various values of α, $1 - \beta$, and effect size.

Because researchers are often interested in testing the null hypothesis that $\rho = 0$, special tables have been developed that simplify the test. The critical values of r and r_s (r_s is the Spearman rank correlation coefficient) necessary to reject the null hypothesis that $\rho = 0$ or $\rho_s = 0$ are tabulated in Appendix Tables D.6 and D.7, respectively. If the absolute value of r, $|r|$, is greater than or equal to the critical value in the table, the hypothesis that ρ is equal to 0 can be rejected. According to Appendix Table D.6, the critical value of r for $\alpha = .05$ and $\nu = 60$ is .25. The use of Appendix Table D.6 leads to the same decision we reached using the t statistic and Appendix Table D.3.

z Test for Correlations Other Than Zero

The t statistic or the table of critical values of r can be used to test the null hypothesis that the population correlation is equal to 0. But what if the researcher wants to test a hypothesis in which the population correlation of interest is equal to some number other than 0, for example, $\rho = .50$? A procedure developed by R. A. Fisher can be used in such cases. It uses a particular function of r, rather than r; the function is called the **Fisher r-to-Z' transformation.** The transformation of r into Z' is easily accomplished by means of Appendix Table D.8. This table gives for each value of r the corresponding Fisher Z' statistic. For example, if r is equal to .50, the value of Z' is 0.549. Fisher showed that the sampling distribution of Z' is approximately normal if (1) ρ is not too close to 1 or -1, (2) the population is bivariate normal, and (3) the sample is moderately large, say n greater than 10.

The one-sample z statistic that is used to test hypotheses about ρ when $\rho_0 \neq 0$ is

$$z = \frac{Z' - Z'_0}{\sqrt{1/(n-3)}},$$

where Z' is the transformed sample r, Z'_0 is the transformed value of ρ_0 specified by the null hypothesis, and n is the size of the random sample used to compute r.

This test statistic assumes that (1) r was computed for a random sample from the population of interest, (2) the population is bivariate normal, and (3) the sample is greater than or equal to 10. The null hypothesis is rejected if z falls in the critical region of the standard normal sampling distribution given in Appendix Table D.2.

Computational Example for z Test for a Correlation

Assume that a researcher believes on the basis of previous research that the correlation between scores on the Coping Mastery Scale and the Self-Esteem Scale of parents of severely mentally ill children is greater than .25. A random sample of 83 parents from the population of interest has been obtained, and r is found to equal .47. The decision rule and the steps to be followed in testing the null hypothesis are as follows:

Step 1. State the statistical hypotheses: $H_0: \rho \leq .25$
$H_1: \rho > .25$.

Step 2. Specify the test statistic: $z = \dfrac{Z' - Z'_0}{\sqrt{1/(n - 3)}}$ because we want to test $\rho \leq .25$, the sample is random, the sample n is moderately large, and the population is assumed to be bivariate normal.

Step 3. Specify the sample size: $n = 83$;
specify the sampling distribution: z distribution, because the population is assumed to be bivariate normal and the parameter specified in the null hypothesis is not 0.

Step 4. Specify the significance level: $\alpha = .05$.

Step 5. Obtain a random sample of size n, compute z, and make a decision.

Decision rule:

Reject the null hypothesis if z falls in the upper 5% of the sampling distribution of z; otherwise, don't reject the null hypothesis. If the null hypothesis is rejected, conclude that the population correlation between coping mastery ability and self-esteem is greater than .25; if the null hypothesis is not rejected, do not draw this conclusion.

The z test statistic is given by

$$z = \frac{Z' - Z'_0}{\sqrt{1/(n - 3)}} = \frac{0.510 - 0.255}{\sqrt{1/(83 - 3)}} = \frac{0.255}{\sqrt{0.0125}} = 2.28.$$

According to Appendix Table D.2, a z of 1.645 cuts off the upper .05 region of the sampling distribution of z—that is, $z_{.05} = 1.645$. Because the computed $z = 2.28$ is greater than $z_{.05} = 1.645$, we reject the null hypothesis and conclude that the population correlation coefficient is greater than .25.

Confidence Interval for a Correlation

The Fisher r-to-Z' transformation described earlier is used to construct a confidence interval for a population correlation coefficient ρ. The confidence interval is constructed for Z', and then the interval is converted into a confidence interval for ρ.

A two-sided $100(1 - \alpha)\%$ confidence interval for Z'_{Pop} is given by

$$Z' - z_{\alpha/2}\sqrt{\frac{1}{n-3}} < Z'_{Pop} < Z' + z_{\alpha/2}\sqrt{\frac{1}{n-3}},$$

where Z' is the transformed sample r, $z_{\alpha/2}$ is the value of z that cuts off the upper $\alpha/2$ region of the sampling distribution of z, n is the size of the sample used to estimate ρ, and Z'_{Pop} is the transformed population correlation coefficient.
  A one-sided $100(1 - \alpha)\%$ confidence interval for Z'_{Pop} is

$$Z' - z_{\alpha}\sqrt{\frac{1}{n-3}} < Z'_{Pop} \quad \text{or} \quad Z'_{Pop} < Z' + z_{\alpha}\sqrt{\frac{1}{n-3}},$$

where z_{α} is the value of z that cuts off the upper α region of the sampling distribution of z.

Once the confidence limits of Z'_{Pop} have been determined, they are then transformed into confidence limits for ρ by means of Appendix Table D.8. The confidence intervals assume that (1) r was computed for a random sample from the population of interest, (2) the population is bivariate normal, and (3) the sample is moderately large, say, n greater than 50.

Computational Example of Confidence Interval for a Correlation

Earlier, we tested the null hypothesis that the correlation between college grades and income 10 years after graduation for a random sample of 62 graduates of Boston Central College is equal to 0. The sample estimate of the population correlation coefficient was .16. According to Appendix Table D.8, the corresponding value of Z' is 0.161. A two-sided $100(1 - .05)\% = 95\%$ confidence interval is given by

$$Z' - z_{.05/2}\sqrt{\frac{1}{n-3}} < Z'_{Pop} < Z' + z_{.05/2}\sqrt{\frac{1}{n-3}}$$

$$0.161 - 1.96\sqrt{\frac{1}{62-3}} < Z'_{Pop} < 0.161 + 1.96\sqrt{\frac{1}{62-3}}$$

$$0.161 - 0.255 < Z'_{Pop} < 0.161 + 0.255$$

$$-0.094 < Z'_{Pop} < 0.416.$$

Transforming the lower and upper limits of Z' into correlation coefficients yields the 95% confidence interval for ρ, which is $-.09 < \rho < .39$. Because the confidence interval includes 0, it is apparent that a test of the null hypothesis that ρ is equal to 0 or any other null hypothesis in which ρ_0 is greater than $-.09$ and less than .39 could not be rejected. This confidence interval corresponds to the colored portion of the real number line as follows:

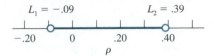

The researcher's best guess concerning the value of ρ is that it is equal to .16—the value of the sample correlation coefficient. The researcher can be 95% confident that ρ is greater than $-.09$ and less than 39.

Practical Significance of a Correlation

As discussed in Section 10.6, most measures of effect magnitude fall into one of two categories: measures of effect size such as d and measures of strength of association. Cohen (1988, pp. 77–83) has suggested using r, a measure of the linear strength of association between two variables, to assess effect magnitude. According to Cohen, $r = .10$ is a small strength of association, $r = .30$ is a medium strength of association, and $r = .50$ is a large strength of association. He has shown that the strengths of association represented by .10, .30, and .50 are roughly equivalent to the effect sizes represented by d values of .2, .5, and .8, respectively. Hence, the terms *small, medium,* and *large* mean about the same thing whether we are talking about strength of association or effect size.

Using Cohen's guidelines, the correlation ($r = .47$) between parents' scores on the Coping Mastery Scale and the Self-Esteem Scale discussed earlier represents a medium strength of association.

CHECK YOUR UNDERSTANDING OF SECTION 11.5

13. Convert r into Z'.
    a. $r = .46$ b. $r = -.23$
    c. $r = -.96$ d. $r = .15$
14. Convert Z' into r.
    a. $Z' = 0.549$ b. $Z' = -0.192$
    c. $Z' = 0.245$ d. $Z' = -1.256$
15. It was hypothesized that the correlation between the scores of truck drivers on the realistic and artistic scales of the Career Assessment Inventory (CAI) is negligible. Assume that $r = .09$ has been computed for a random sample of 26 drivers.
    a. List the steps you would follow in testing the hypothesis that $\rho = 0$. Let $\alpha = .05$.

b. Test the null hypothesis using $t = (r\sqrt{n-2})/\sqrt{1-r^2}$.
c. What is the *p*-value of the test statistic?
d. Test the null hypothesis using the critical value from Appendix Table D.6.
e. Compute a $100(1 - .05)\% = 95\%$ confidence interval for ρ. Locate the confidence interval on the real number line.
f. Specify all null hypotheses that could be rejected.
g. Interpret the effect size.

16. The correlation between scores on the TAC (a college entrance test) and grade point averages for a random sample of $n = 100$ freshmen was .54. Last year, the correlation for the freshman class was .61.
    a. List the steps you would follow in testing the scientific hypothesis that the correlation for this year's class is different from that for last year. Let $\alpha = .05$.
    b. Test the null hypothesis using $z = (Z' - Z'_0)/\sqrt{1/(n-3)}$.
    c. What is the *p*-value of the test statistic?
    d. Compute a $100(1 - .05)\% = 95\%$ confidence interval for ρ. Locate the confidence interval on the real number line.
    e. Specify all null hypotheses that could be rejected.

17. Terms to remember
    a. Bivariate normal population   b. Fisher *r*-to-Z' transformation

†11.6 PRINTOUTS FOR THREE MICROCOMPUTER PACKAGES

JMP

JMP was used to compute a one-sample *t* statistic and two-sided confidence interval for the registration-time data in Table 11.2-1. After the data were entered in a data table (see Figures 2.8-1 and 3.9-1 for examples), the selection of the **Analysis** command in the menu bar followed by the pull-down command called **Distribution of Y** produced a box plot and Quantiles and Moments displays. The dialog box in Figure 11.6-1 was obtained by clicking on the ▶ button above the box plot and selecting the **Test Mean=value . . .** option. After the null hypothesis value $\mu_0 = 3.1$ was entered and **OK** was checked, a **Test Mean=value** display was added to the Box plot, Quantiles, and Moments displays. Only the **Moments** and **Test mean=value** displays are shown in Figure 11.6-2. The latter display also includes the Wilcoxon signed-ranks statistic that is discussed in Chapter 17.

† This and similarly marked sections can be omitted without loss of continuity.

> **Specify Hypothesized Value for Mean:**
>
> 3.1
>
> [Cancel]   [OK]

Figure 11.6-1. **The JMP dialog box lets the user specify the null hypothesis value, μ_0, for the one-sample t test. The value 3.1 has been entered for the registration-time data in Table 11.2-1.**

SPSS

SPSS was used to compute a one-sample t statistic and two-sided confidence interval for the registration-time data in Table 11.2-1. The selection of the **Statistics** command in the menu bar followed by the pull-down command called **Compare Means** and the selection of **One-Sample T Test . . .** produced the dialog box called **One-Sample T Test** shown in Figure 11.6-3. After the variable Reg_Time and the null hypothesis value 3.1 were entered in the dialog boxes, the descriptive statistics, two-sided confidence interval, and one-sample t statistic in Figure 11.6-4 were obtained.

Moments	
Mean	2.9000
Std Dev	0.1581
Std Err Mean	0.0345
upper 95% Mean	2.9720
lower 95% Mean	2.8280
N	21.0000
Sum Wgts	21.0000

Test Mean=value		
Hypothesized Value	3.1	
Actual Estimate	2.9	
	t Test	Signed-Rank
Test Statistic	−5.7966	−82.500
Prob > |t|	0.0000	0.000
Prob > t	1.0000	1.000
Prob < t	0.0000	0.000

Figure 11.6-2. **The JMP Moments and Test Mean = value displays provide descriptive statistics, a one-sample t statistic, and a two-sided confidence interval for the registration-time data in Table 11.2-1. In the Test Mean = value display, the p-value, 0.000, in the "Prob > $|t|$" row is appropriate for the two-sided null hypothesis $\mu = 3.1$. The other two p-values, 1.000 and 0.000, are appropriate for the one-sided null hypotheses $\mu \geq 3.1$ and $\mu \leq 3.1$, respectively. The actual p-value for $\mu \leq 3.1$ is .0000057. The Moments display gives a two-sided $100(1 - .05)\%$ confidence interval for μ. The "upper 95% Mean" corresponds to the upper end point, L_2, of the confidence interval; the "lower 95% Mean" corresponds to the lower end point, L_1. The column labeled Signed-Ranks contains p-values for the Wilcoxon test that is discussed in Chapter 17.**

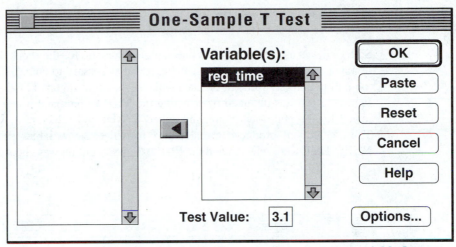

Figure 11.6-3. **This dialog box in SPSS was used to select the variable for analysis and specify the null hypothesis value, called the Test Value, for the one-sample *t* test. The null hypothesis value 3.1 has been entered for the registration-time data in Table 11.2-1.**

SPSS for Macintosh Release 6.1

One Sample t-tests

Variable	Number of Cases	Mean	SD	SE of Mean
REG_TIME	21	2.9000	.158	.035

Test Value = 3.1

Mean Difference	95% CI Lower	95% CI Upper		t-value	df	2-Tail Sig
						.000
−.20	−.272	−.128		−5.80	20	

Figure 11.6-4. **The SPSS output provides descriptive statistics, one-sample *t* statistic, and two-sided confidence interval for the registration-time data in Table 11.2-1. The *t* test gives a two-tailed *p*-value. The $100(1 - .05)\%$ two-sided confidence interval, $-.272 < \mu - \mu_0 < -.128$, is for the difference between μ and μ_0. The sample estimator of this difference is $\overline{X} - \mu_0 = 2.9 - 3.1 = -.20$.**

SYSTAT

SYSTAT was used to compute a one-sample t statistic for the registration-time data in Table 11.2-1. To obtain the t statistic, it was necessary to enter both the data and the null hypothesis value in the data table as shown in Figure 11.6-5. The output in Figure 11.6-6 was obtained by selecting the **Stats** command in the menu bar followed by the pull-down command called **Stats** and selecting **t tests . . . .** These selections produced a dialog box in which the variables REG_TIME and NULL_HYP were selected and the **Paired** option button was checked.

	REG_TIME	NULL_HYP	
SYSTAT Data Editor			
1	2.900	3.100	
2	2.700	3.100	
3	2.800	3.100	
4	3.000	3.100	
5	2.600	3.100	
6	2.900	3.100	
7	3.100	3.100	

Figure 11.6-5. **This SYSTAT data table shows a portion of the registration-time data from Table 11.2-1. To obtain a one-sample t statistic, it is necessary to enter both the data and the null hypothesis value in the data table. The null hypothesis value, 3.1, is shown in column 3.**

```
PAIRED SAMPLES T-TEST ON REG_TIME    VS NULL_HYP   WITH   21 CASES

MEAN DIFFERENCE =       −0.2000
SD DIFFERENCE =         0.1581
T =       −5.7966 DF =     20 PROB =      0.0000
```

Figure 11.6-6. **The SYSTAT output gives a one-sample t test for the registration-time data in Table 11.2-1. SYSTAT uses the formula for a paired samples t test, which is discussed in Chapter 12, to compute a one-sample t test. The user must enter both the data and the null hypothesis value in the data table (see Table 11.6-5). The p-value is for a two-tailed test.**

11.7 SUMMARY

We have covered much ground in Chapters 10 and 11—the basic concepts of statistical inference and a variety of null hypothesis significance tests and confidence intervals for the one-sample case. Although the null hypothesis test statistics have different formulas and are used to test hypotheses about different parameters, they all use the same five-step format in arriving at a decision about a hypothesis. Similarly, the construction of confidence intervals follows the same pattern regardless of the parameter of interest. We will see that the logic underlying null hypothesis significance tests and confidence intervals described in Chapters 10 and 11 generalizes to the two-sample case and to more complex decision-making situations.

The test statistics and confidence intervals for the one-sample case are summarized in Tables 11.7-1 and 11.7-2, respectively. As shown in the tables, the assumptions of the test statistics and analogous confidence intervals are the same.

REVIEW EXERCISES FOR CHAPTER 11

1. List the similarities and differences between the t and z test statistics.
2. Suppose that several first-grade teachers have complained that their classes this year are unusually slow in learning to read. The school principal has asked you to determine whether the children are below average in intelligence, that is, have a mean IQ below 100. Because there are 362 first-grade children, giving each of them an individual intelligence test is not feasible. Instead, you administer the Wechsler Intelligence Scale for Children–Revised (WISC–R) to a random sample of 16 children. Assume that the data in the following table have been obtained. Let $\alpha = .05$.
    a. List the steps you would follow in testing the scientific hypothesis.
    b. Compute a t statistic for these data and make a decision about the scientific hypothesis.
    c. Use Appendix Table D.9 to estimate the sample size needed to detect a large effect for $\alpha = .05$ and $1 - \beta = .80$.
    d. What is the p-value of the t statistic?
    e. Construct a box plot for the data. Do the data contain outliers? Does the sample distribution appear to be relatively symmetrical?

TABLE 11.7-1.   Summary of One-Sample Test Statistics

Chapter Section	Statistical Hypotheses	Test Statistic	Assumptions
10.3	$H_0: \mu = \mu_0$	$z = \dfrac{\bar{X} - \mu_0}{\sigma/\sqrt{n}}$	1. Random sampling
	$H_1: \mu \neq \mu_0$		2. Normality or large sample
			3. Variance is known
11.2	$H_0: \mu = \mu_0$	$t = \dfrac{\bar{X} - \mu_0}{\hat{\sigma}/\sqrt{n}}$	1. Random sampling
	$H_1: \mu \neq \mu_0$	$v = n - 1$	2. Normality
			3. Variance is unknown
11.3	$H_0: \sigma^2 = \sigma_0^2$	$\chi^2 = \dfrac{(n-1)\hat{\sigma}^2}{\sigma_0^2}$	1. Random sampling
	$H_1: \sigma^2 \neq \sigma_0^2$	$v = n - 1$	2. Normality
11.4	$H_0: p = p_0$	$z = \dfrac{\hat{p} - p_0}{\sqrt{p_0 q_0/n}}$	1. Random sampling
	$H_1: p \neq p_0$	$z = \dfrac{X - np_0}{\sqrt{np_0 q_0}}$	2. Binomial distribution
			3. $np_0 > 5, n(1 - p_0) > 5$
11.4	$H_0: p = p_0$	$z = \dfrac{\hat{p} - p_0}{\sqrt{\dfrac{p_0 q_0}{n}\left(\dfrac{n_{Pop} - n}{n_{Pop} - 1}\right)}}$	1. Random sampling
	$H_1: p \neq p_0$		2. Hypergeometric distribution
			3. $np_0 > 5, n(1 - p_0) > 5$
			4. $n/n_{Pop} \geq 0.10$
11.5	$H_0: \rho = 0$	$t = \dfrac{r\sqrt{n - 2}}{\sqrt{1 - r^2}}$	1. Random sampling
	$H_1: \rho \neq 0$	$v = n - 2$	2. Bivariate normality
11.5	$H_0: \rho = \rho_0$	$z = \dfrac{Z' - Z_0'}{\sqrt{1/(n - 3)}}$	1. Random sampling
	$H_1: \rho \neq \rho_0$		2. Bivariate normality
			3. Moderately large sample

f. Compute a $100(1 - .05)\% = 95\%$ confidence interval for μ. Locate the confidence interval on the real number line.

g. Specify all null hypotheses that could be rejected.

h. Compute the effect size and interpret the result.

TABLE 11.7-2.   Summary of One-Sample Confidence Intervals

Chapter Section	Parameter	Confidence Interval	Assumptions
10.5	μ	$\bar{X} - \dfrac{z_{\alpha/2}\sigma}{\sqrt{n}} < \mu < \bar{X} + \dfrac{z_{\alpha/2}\sigma}{\sqrt{n}}$	1. Random sampling 2. Normality or large sample 3. Variance is known
11.2	μ	$\bar{X} - \dfrac{t_{\alpha/2,v}\hat{\sigma}}{\sqrt{n}} < \mu < \bar{X} + \dfrac{t_{\alpha/2,v}\hat{\sigma}}{\sqrt{n}}$	1. Random sampling 2. Normality 3. Variance is unknown
11.3	σ^2	$\dfrac{(n-1)\hat{\sigma}^2}{\chi^2_{\alpha/2,v}} < \sigma^2 < \dfrac{(n-1)\hat{\sigma}^2}{\chi^2_{1-\alpha/2,v}}$	1. Random sampling 2. Normality
11.4	ρ	$\hat{p} - z_{\alpha/2}\sqrt{\dfrac{\hat{p}\hat{q}}{n}} < p < \hat{p} + z_{\alpha/2}\sqrt{\dfrac{\hat{p}\hat{q}}{n}}$	1. Random sampling 2. Binomial distribution 3. $np_0 > 5,\ n(1-p_0) > 5$
11.5	ρ	$Z' - z_{\alpha/2}\sqrt{\dfrac{1}{n-3}} < Z'_{Pop} < Z' + z_{\alpha/2}\sqrt{\dfrac{1}{n-3}}$	1. Random sampling 2. Bivariate normality 3. Moderately large sample

Child	IQ	Child	IQ
1	89	9	86
2	96	10	88
3	86	11	92
4	92	12	101
5	78	13	87
6	110	14	93
7	82	15	97
8	69	16	74

3. (a) Make a frequency distribution for the data in Exercise 2. Use 10 class intervals, with a class interval size of five. (b) From a visual inspection of the frequency distribution, is it reasonable to assume that the population distribution is normal in form?

4. Use the table of random numbers in Appendix Table D.1 to draw a random sample without replacement of 31 students from the Student Database in Appendix E.
   a. List the steps you would follow in testing the scientific hypothesis that the population mean is different from that for last year, $\mu = 2.7$. Let $\alpha = .05$.
   b. List the Participant Number and GPA for each person in your sample. Compute the mean and standard deviation of the variable labeled GPA.
   c. Test the null hypothesis that $\mu = 2.7$, where 2.7 is the mean population GPA of students who enrolled in the statistics course last year.
   d. Use Appendix Table D.9 to estimate the sample size needed to detect a large effect for $\alpha = .05$ and $1 - \beta = .80$.
   e. What is the p-value of the t statistic?
   f. Construct a box plot for the data. Do the data contain outliers? Does the sample distribution appear to be relatively symmetrical?
   g. Compute a $100(1 - .05)\% = 95\%$ confidence interval for μ. Locate the confidence interval on the real number line.
   h. Specify all null hypotheses that could be rejected.
   i. Compute the effect size and interpret the result.
5. List the similarities and differences between the χ^2 and t sampling distributions.
6. a. For the IQ data in Exercise 2, list the steps you would follow in testing the hypothesis $H_0: \sigma^2 \geq 225$, where 15 is the standard deviation of the WISC–R. Let $\alpha = .05$.
   b. Compute a χ^2 statistic for these data and make a decision about the scientific hypothesis.
   c. What is the p-value of the χ^2 statistic?
   d. Compute a $100(1 - .05)\% = 95\%$ confidence interval for σ^2. Locate the confidence interval on the real number line.
   e. Specify all null hypotheses that could be rejected.
7. Use the table of random numbers in Appendix Table D.1 to draw a random sample without replacement of 31 students from the Student Database in Appendix E.
   a. List the steps you would follow in testing the scientific hypothesis that the population variance of the variable labeled GPA is different from that for last year, $\sigma^2 = 0.26$. Let $\alpha = .05$.
   b. List the Participant Number and GPA for each person in your sample. Compute the mean and standard deviation of the variable labeled GPA.
   c. Test the null hypothesis that $\sigma^2 = 0.26$, where 0.26 is the population variance of GPAs of students who enrolled in the statistics course last year.

    d. What is the p-value of the χ^2 statistic?

    e. Construct a box plot for the data. Do the data contain outliers? Does the sample distribution appear to be relatively symmetrical?

    f. Compute a $100(1 - .05)\% = 95\%$ confidence interval for σ^2. Locate the confidence interval on the real number line.

    g. Specify all null hypotheses that could be rejected.

8. List the assumptions associated with using the chi-square statistic to test a null hypothesis or construct a confidence interval.

9. If $p_0 = .40$, how large should n be to use the normal approximation to the binomial distribution?

10. The probability of recovery for schizophrenic patients after receiving six months of conventional therapy at Happyfarm Hospital was .60. A token economy program was introduced for a random sample of 30 schizophrenic patients. At the end of the six-month trial period, 21 patients had recovered.

    a. List the steps you would follow in testing the scientific hypothesis that if the token economy program was used for all patients, the recovery probability would be higher than that for the conventional therapy. Use the correction for continuity. Let $\alpha = .05$.

    b. Can you conclude that the token economy program would result in a higher recovery probability than the conventional therapy?

    c. What is the p-value of the test statistic?

    d. Compute a $100(1 - .05)\% = 95\%$ confidence interval for p. Use the correction for continuity. Locate the confidence interval on the real number line.

    e. Specify all null hypotheses that could be rejected.

11. Sketch the sampling distribution for z in Exercise 10 and label the critical region.

12. a. Assume that in Exercise 10 there were only 90 schizophrenic patients in the hospital. Test the null hypothesis using the z statistic for the finite population case. Use the correction for continuity.

    b. What is the p-value of the test statistic?

    c. Compute a $100(1 - .05)\% = 95\%$ confidence interval for p. Use the correction for the finite population case and the correction for continuity.

    d. Specify all null hypotheses that could be rejected.

13. In a random sample of 75 homes in Junction City, Oklahoma, it was found that 63 have VCRs.

    a. List the steps you would follow in testing the scientific hypothesis that the proportion in Junction City differs from that in a nearby community where the proportion of homes with VCRs is known to be .71. Use a correction for continuity and let $\alpha = .05$.

    b. Test the null hypothesis. Does the proportion in Junction City differ from the other community?

    c. What is the *p*-value of the *z* statistic?

    d. Compute a $100(1 - .05)\% = 95\%$ confidence interval for *p*. Locate the confidence interval on the real number line.

    e. Specify all null hypotheses that could be rejected.

14. Convert *r* into Z'.

    a. $r = .39$ b. $r = -.19$

    c. $r = -.84$ d. $r = .11$

15. Convert Z' into *r*.

    a. $Z' = 0.576$ b. $Z' = -0.198$

    c. $Z' = 0.250$ d. $Z' = -1.499$

16. It was hypothesized that the correlation between the scores of accountants on the learning strategy and discriminability factors of the California Verbal Learning Test (CVLT) is negligible. Assume that $r = .12$ has been computed for a random sample of 29 accountants.

    a. List the steps you would follow in testing the hypothesis that $\rho = 0$. Let $\alpha = .05$.

    b. Test the null hypothesis using $t = (r\sqrt{n - 2})/\sqrt{1 - r^2}$.

    c. What is the *p*-value of the test statistic?

    d. Test the null hypothesis using the critical value from Appendix Table D.6.

    e. Compute a $100(1 - .05)\% = 95\%$ confidence interval for ρ. Locate the confidence interval on the real number line.

    f. Specify all null hypotheses that could be rejected.

    g. Interpret the effect size.

17. Psychological Associates, a consulting firm, has revised a test that is used to select managers for a large chain of hamburger restaurants. The revised test was given to a random sample of 170 managers. The correlation between their test scores and a measure of their stores' net incomes was .31. The correlation for the old test was .19.

    a. List the steps you would follow in testing the scientific hypothesis that the correlation for the new test is higher than that for the old test. Let $\alpha = .05$.

    b. Test the null hypothesis using $z = (Z' - Z'_0)/\sqrt{1/(n - 3)}$.

    c. What is the *p*-value of the test statistic?

    d. Compute a $100(1 - .05)\% = 95\%$ confidence interval for ρ. Locate the confidence interval on the real number line.

    e. Specify all null hypotheses that could be rejected.

    f. Should the revised test be used in selecting future managers for the chain? Why?

18. The correlation between the recreational interests of a random sample of $n = 67$ pairs of husbands and wives who had contacted a large travel agency was .52.

    a. Compute a $100(1 - .01)\% = 99\%$ confidence interval for ρ. Locate the confidence interval on the real number line.

    b. Specify all null hypotheses that could be rejected.

19. The sampling distribution of r is not likely to be normal when ρ deviates appreciably from 0. From what you know about r, why is this true?

Chapter 12

Statistical Inference: Two Samples

12.1 INTRODUCTION TO HYPOTHESIS TESTING FOR TWO SAMPLES

Are men able to withstand weightlessness better than women? Do disadvantaged children learn more quickly in a contingency management classroom than in a traditional classroom? Do people who jog have fewer heart attacks than those who don't? Is one antilitter slogan more effective than another? Each of these questions involves a comparison of two population distributions. Population distributions can differ in central tendency, dispersion, skewness, and kurtosis. Most questions in the behavioral sciences, health sciences, and education are concerned with central tendency and, more specifically, with whether the means of two populations differ.

We learned in Chapter 10 that scientific hypotheses often involve predictions (1) about populations whose elements are so numerous that viewing them all is impossible (all men and women in a weightless environment, all disadvantaged school children, all joggers and nonjoggers) or (2) about phenomena that can't be directly observed (the effectiveness of two antilitter slogans). In such cases we can use random samples from the populations to make inferences as to whether the means, variances, and so on of the populations differ. Our inferences are based on null hypothesis-testing and confidence-interval procedures that are straightforward extensions of those for the one-sample case described in Chapters 10 and 11.

12.2 TWO-SAMPLE z TEST FOR MEANS USING INDEPENDENT SAMPLES

We now will describe a z test statistic for determining whether the means of two populations differ. The statistic can be used to test any of the following null hypotheses:

$$H_0: \mu_1 - \mu_2 = \delta_0 \qquad H_0: \mu_1 - \mu_2 \leq \delta_0 \qquad H_0: \mu_1 - \mu_2 \geq \delta_0$$
$$H_1: \mu_1 - \mu_2 \neq \delta_0 \qquad H_1: \mu_1 - \mu_2 > \delta_0 \qquad H_1: \mu_1 - \mu_2 < \delta_0$$

Here, δ_0 is the predicted difference between the population means. Usually, a researcher is interested in testing the hypothesis that two population means are equal, in which case δ_0 is equal to 0.

Consider two populations with unknown means μ_1 and μ_2. Assume that the variances of the populations, σ_1^2 and σ_2^2, are known but are not necessarily equal and that random samples of size n_1 and n_2 have been obtained from the respective populations. If the population distributions of X_1 and X_2 are normally distributed or if the samples are sufficiently large, the sampling distribution of the difference between sample, the means $\overline{X}_1 - \overline{X}_2$, is normal. It can be shown that the expectation of the difference between sample means, $E(\overline{X}_1 - \overline{X}_2)$, is equal to $\mu_1 - \mu_2$. Furthermore, the variance of the difference between sample means, $\sigma^2_{\bar{X}_1 - \bar{X}_2}$, for the case in which the selection of elements in one sample is not affected by (is independent of) the selection of elements in the other sample, is given by

$$\sigma^2_{\bar{X}_1 - \bar{X}_2} = \frac{\sigma^2_1}{n_1} + \frac{\sigma^2_2}{n_2}.$$

We will consider the dependent-samples case in Section 12.5. The square root of $\sigma^2_{\bar{X}_1 - \bar{X}_2}$ is called the **standard error of the difference between two means.**

The z statistic for testing the null hypothesis when the scores in the two samples are independent is given by

$$z = \frac{(\bar{X}_1 - \bar{X}_2) - \delta_0}{\sigma_{\bar{X}_1 - \bar{X}_2}} = \frac{(\bar{X}_1 - \bar{X}_2) - \delta_0}{\sqrt{\sigma^2_1/n_1 + \sigma^2_2/n_2}}.$$

If the null hypothesis specifies that δ_0 is equal to 0, the z formula simplifies to

$$z = \frac{(\bar{X}_1 - \bar{X}_2)}{\sqrt{\sigma^2_1/n_1 + \sigma^2_2/n_2}}.$$

When the null hypothesis is true, the sampling distribution of z is approximately normal with mean equal to 0, that is, $E(z) = 0$, and variance equal to 1, that is, $\sigma^2_z = 1$. Hence, the sampling distribution of z has approximately the same shape, mean, and standard deviation as the standard normal distribution represented in Appendix Table D.2. These similarities enable us to use the standard normal distribution as the theoretical model for determining whether an obtained z, our transformed difference between sample means, lies in the critical region of the sampling distribution of z.

In the preceding discussion we assumed that σ^2_1 and σ^2_2 were somehow known so that we could compute the standard error of the difference between means. In the real world, such knowledge is rare; the fact of the matter is that population variances are seldom known. We can, however, compute unbiased estimates of the population variances from the samples used to estimate the population means. When the population variances are estimated from samples, the appropriate test statistic is t. But before describing this statistic, we will turn briefly in the next section to an issue concerning the design of experiments: deciding on an appropriate randomization strategy.

CHECK YOUR UNDERSTANDING OF SECTION 12.2

1. The null hypothesis is sometimes written $H_0: \mu_1 = \mu_2$. What does this indicate about δ_0?
2. A researcher is interested in testing the hypothesis that members of fraternities have higher GPAs than nonmembers. Random samples of

$n_1 = 50$ members and $n_2 = 52$ nonmembers are obtained from the respective populations. The populations are known to be normally distributed with $\sigma_1 = 0.4$ and $\sigma_2 = 0.5$. List the five steps you would follow in testing the null hypothesis and state the decision rule. Let $\alpha = .05$.

3. (a) Suppose that in Exercise 2, $\overline{X}_1 = 2.91$ and $\overline{X}_2 = 2.72$. Compute the test statistic and make a decision. (b) What is the *p*-value of the test statistic?

4. Term to remember
   a. Standard error of the difference between two means $(\sigma_{\overline{X}_1 - \overline{X}_2})$

12.3 TWO RANDOMIZATION STRATEGIES: RANDOM SAMPLING AND RANDOM ASSIGNMENT

Two randomization strategies can be used in investigating scientific hypotheses. A researcher can obtain random samples from two existing populations of interest or randomly assign elements of a sample to experimental and control conditions. In rare cases, the two methods can be combined—that is, the researcher can obtain a random sample and randomly assign the sample elements to the experimental and control conditions.

The choice of a randomization strategy affects a researcher's conclusions, as we will now see.

The Strategy of Random Sampling

Consider the scientific hypothesis that men who jog have fewer heart attacks than those who don't. The statistical hypotheses are

$$H_0: \mu_1 - \mu_2 \geq 0$$
$$H_1: \mu_1 - \mu_2 < 0,$$

where μ_1 and μ_2 designate the mean number of heart attacks of the populations of joggers and nonjoggers, respectively. The alternative hypothesis, which corresponds to the researcher's hunch, states that the mean number of heart attacks is smaller for joggers than for nonjoggers. To test the null hypothesis, a researcher could obtain a random sample of 70-year-old men who have jogged regularly since they were 40 and a second sample of men the same age who have never jogged. Suppose that the mean number of heart attacks is 0.2 for the joggers and 1.1 for the nonjoggers and that the difference between the means, $0.2 - 1.1 = -0.9$, is significant at the .01 level. It can be concluded that the population of joggers has fewer heart attacks than the nonjoggers, and hence the scientific hypothesis is supported.

Can the researcher conclude that the difference between population means is due to jogging per se? Unfortunately, the answer is no, because in all likelihood the two populations of men differ in other ways besides jogging. More than likely, men who jog are concerned about their health and about staying in good physical shape. Joggers are probably less obese, have better muscle tone, and have more healthful diets than nonjoggers. If our researcher had sampled from populations of obese and nonobese men, or from men with good and poor muscle tone, or from men who are and aren't diet conscious, a significant difference in mean number of heart attacks would probably also have been found.

The Strategy of Random Assignment

Suppose that a population of 40-year-old prisoners at Oops Penitentiary is available and that it is possible to exercise some control over their lives for a period of 30 years. The prisoners are randomly assigned to one of two groups, which we will call the experimental and control groups. Those assigned to the experimental group participate in a jogging program for 30 years; those in the control group don't participate in the jogging program. Suppose that at the end of 30 years, the mean numbers of heart attacks for those in the experimental and control groups are, respectively, 0.3 and 1.4, and that the difference, $0.3 - 1.4 = -1.1$, is significant at the .01 level. As in the previous experiment, the scientific hypothesis is supported.

Can the researcher conclude that the difference between the experimental and control groups is due to jogging per se? Again the answer is no. What have we accomplished by using random assignment? The use of random assignment makes it very likely that idiosyncratic characteristics of the participants, such as their interest in staying in shape, their tendency toward obesity, the adequacy of their diets, and so forth, will be randomly distributed over the two groups. Hence, these idiosyncratic characteristics will not selectively bias the dependent measure, number of heart attacks, for either group. Stated another way, random assignment helps to make the experimental and control groups comparable on all extraneous variables because prior to the experiment the two groups should differ no more than would be expected by chance. If at the conclusion of the experiment a significant difference exists between the groups in the incidence of heart attacks, the researcher can be confident that the difference is due to events that occurred after the experiment began rather than to idiosyncratic characteristics of the participants that existed prior to the experiment. And if during the experiment all conditions except the independent variable of jogging are held constant, differences between the groups in number of heart attacks must be due to jogging per se. Unfortunately, it is often difficult and sometimes impossible to verify that all conditions except the independent variable have been held constant. This difficulty would certainly exist in a 30-year experiment.

Advantages and Disadvantages of the Two Research Strategies

Most experiments in the behavioral sciences and education are designed to establish **concomitant relationships** rather than **causal relationships.** To establish that an independent variable X causes an effect Y, it is necessary to demonstrate that X is both necessary and sufficient for the occurrence of Y. To establish a concomitant relationship, it is necessary to demonstrate only that the occurrence or nonoccurrence of one event is accompanied by the occurrence or nonoccurrence of the other event.

The distinction between causal and concomitant relationships is important because the type of relationship that is established affects the way in which a researcher interprets his or her results. Neither the random-sampling nor the random-assignment experiments just described have established that jogging per se results in fewer heart attacks—a causal relationship—but they have established that men who jog have, on the average, fewer heart attacks than nonjoggers—a concomitant relationship.

The strategy of drawing random samples from two existing populations that are known to differ in X can't be used to establish causality because the two populations also may differ on other variables. One or more of the other variables could be responsible for the observed difference. A researcher obtains random samples from two existing populations so that conclusions can be generalized to the populations. In many research situations, most notably opinion polling, the discovery of a concomitant relationship is sufficient for the researcher's purposes.

In the behavioral sciences, health sciences, and education, most researchers have neither the time nor the resources to obtain random samples. In the rare cases in which random samples are obtained, the populations are often so narrowly defined that they are of little interest. For example, human participants frequently are randomly sampled from a population of students enrolled in a college course, or from volunteers, and so forth. And researchers who work with animal subjects rarely attempt to obtain random samples.

The second strategy of randomly assigning participants to the experimental and control conditions can be used to establish the existence of a causal relationship if all conditions except the independent variable can be held constant. This is a big *if* because the requirement is difficult to satisfy.

Random assignment of participants to the experimental and control groups helps to distribute the effects of extraneous variables equally across the two groups. Hence, any differences between the groups at the conclusion of the experiment are not likely to be due to the extraneous variables. This is obviously an important advantage of the random-assignment research strategy. A disadvantage is that the conclusions apply only to the sample of participants used in the experiment—in our example, prisoners at Oops Penitentiary. To the extent that these prisoners resemble men in the United States, the findings logically can be generalized to the larger population. It should be emphasized that any generalization to populations not actually sampled is an exercise in logic rather than statistical inference.[1] In this example it seems unlikely that the resemblance between prisoners at Oops Penitentiary and men in the general population is great enough to permit such a generalization.

If a researcher wants to generalize findings to some population and also to obtain experimental and control groups that are comparable, the two research strategies can be combined. A random sample of participants from the population of interest can be obtained and then the participants can be randomly assigned to the two conditions. This combined strategy obviously cannot be used when a researcher samples from two populations that differ with respect to the independent variable, for example, populations of joggers and nonjoggers. Such populations are referred to as **intact populations.**

A final point: If a researcher wants to use statistical inference, the experimental design must include some form of randomization. Which randomization procedure is appropriate will depend upon the objectives of the experiment.

CHECK YOUR UNDERSTANDING OF SECTION 12.3

5. Researchers investigated the effects of stereo headset use among office workers in a large retail organization on measures of employee performance and job satisfaction. Two hundred fifty-six employees were assigned to headset and nonheadset groups on the basis of their stated preference for using a stereo headset at work. The researchers found that the headset group exhibited significant improvements in performance, organizational satisfaction, and mood states relative to the nonheadset group. All of the *t* tests were significant beyond the .001 level. The researchers recommended that all employees be required to use stereo headsets. (a) Comment on the appropriateness of the researchers' conclusion. (b) List some alternative explanations for the observed difference in performance and job satisfaction.

6. In Exercise 5, what does the fact that the test statistic was significant at the .001 level tell you about the magnitude of the difference between the population means?

7. What condition in the random assignment strategy must be satisfied to establish a causal relationship between the independent and dependent variables?

8. For each of the following research topics, indicate the research strategy that seems most appropriate. Justify your choice.
   a. Relative resistance to extinction of a bar-pressing response acquired under 100% reinforcement versus 50% reinforcement

---

[1] This point is thoroughly discussed by Edgington (1966). This article is reprinted in Kirk (1972).

      b. Difference between adult men and women in the incidence of alcohol use

      c. Relationship between grades in college and number of hours studied per week

      d. Difference in reaction time to the onset of a light versus the onset of a tone

9. Terms to remember

      a. Concomitant relationship   b. Causal relationship

      c. Intact populations

12.4 TWO-SAMPLE t TEST AND CONFIDENCE INTERVAL FOR MEANS USING INDEPENDENT SAMPLES

If a researcher wants to test the null hypothesis that the difference between two population means is equal to some value, say, 0, in all likelihood the population variances, σ_1^2 and σ_2^2, will not be known. Hence, the z test statistic described in Section 12.2 can't be computed. The solution to this problem is to estimate the population variances from sample data and use a t statistic instead of the z statistic. For the t statistic, one assumes that the population variances are unknown but equal and that random samples of size n_1 and n_2 have been obtained from the respective populations. If the X_1 and X_2 populations are normally distributed or if the samples are sufficiently large, the sampling distribution of the differences between sample means is normally distributed. It can be shown that the expectation of the difference between sample means, $E(\overline{X}_1 - \overline{X}_2)$, is equal to $\mu_1 - \mu_2$. Furthermore, an unbiased estimator of the variance of the difference between population means for the case in which the selection of elements in one sample is independent of the selection of elements in the other sample is given by

$$\hat{\sigma}_{\overline{X}_1 - \overline{X}_2}^2 = \frac{\hat{\sigma}_{Pooled}^2}{n_1} + \frac{\hat{\sigma}_{Pooled}^2}{n_2} = \hat{\sigma}_{Pooled}^2 \left(\frac{1}{n_1} + \frac{1}{n_2} \right),$$

where

$$\hat{\sigma}_{Pooled}^2 = \frac{(n_1 - 1)\hat{\sigma}_1^2 + (n_2 - 1)\hat{\sigma}_2^2}{(n_1 - 1) + (n_2 - 1)}.$$

The t test statistic is given by

$$t = \frac{(\overline{X}_1 - \overline{X}_2) - \delta_0}{\hat{\sigma}_{\overline{X}_1 - \overline{X}_2}^2} = \frac{(\overline{X}_1 - \overline{X}_2) - \delta_0}{\sqrt{\hat{\sigma}_{Pooled}^2(1/n_1 + 1/n_2)}},$$

where δ_0 is the predicted difference between the population means, which is usually equal to zero, and $\hat{\sigma}_{\overline{X}_1 - \overline{X}_2}$ is an estimator of the standard error of the difference between two population means.

The number of degrees of freedom, ν, for the t statistic is equal to $n_1 + n_2 - 2$. Sample 1 contributes $n_1 - 1$ degrees of freedom, the number of degrees of freedom associated with $\hat{\sigma}_1^2$ and, likewise, sample 2 contributes $n_2 - 1$ degrees of freedom, the number of degrees of freedom associated with $\hat{\sigma}_2^2$.[2]

The use of $\hat{\sigma}_{Pooled}^2$ in the formula for t requires a word of explanation. We assumed that the variances of populations 1 and 2 are equal; hence, $\hat{\sigma}_1^2$ and $\hat{\sigma}_2^2$ both estimate the same parameter, σ^2. Whenever two independent estimators of σ^2 are available, a pooled estimator is likely to provide a better estimate than either of the sample estimators taken alone. The estimator $\hat{\sigma}_{Pooled}^2$ is simply a weighted mean of $\hat{\sigma}_1^2$ and $\hat{\sigma}_2^2$ where the weights are the respective degrees of freedom. This can be seen from the equation

$$\hat{\sigma}_{Pooled}^2 = \frac{(n_1 - 1)\hat{\sigma}_1^2 + (n_2 - 1)\hat{\sigma}_2^2}{(n_1 - 1) + (n_2 - 1)}.$$

But what if the variances of populations 1 and 2 are unequal? It has been shown that the two-sample t test for independent samples is robust with respect to violation of the assumption of equal population variances, provided that the sample n's are equal. This is an excellent reason for always using equal sample sizes. If the population variances are unequal and the sample n's are markedly different, the sample variances should not be pooled in computing a t statistic. Several approximate solutions have been proposed for this situation; the interested reader is referred to Hays (1994, p. 328), Howell (1997, pp. 197–198), or Kirk (1995, pp. 133–134). Some computer packages compute two t statistics: one based on the use of pooled variances and the other, an approximate t statistic, based on separate (unpooled) variances. Usually computer packages that provide the two t statistics also provide a test of the assumption that the two population variances are equal, that is, $H_0: \sigma_1^2 = \sigma_2^2$.[3] Researchers then can choose the t statistic that appears to be most appropriate for their data. Computer printouts showing the two t statistics are given in Section 12.6.

As in the case of the two-sample z test statistic, t can be used to test any of the following null hypotheses:

$$H_0: \mu_1 - \mu_2 = \delta_0 \qquad H_0: \mu_1 - \mu_2 \leq \delta_0 \qquad H_0: \mu_1 - \mu_2 \geq \delta_0$$
$$H_1: \mu_1 - \mu_2 \neq \delta_0 \qquad H_1: \mu_1 - \mu_2 > \delta_0 \qquad H_1: \mu_1 - \mu_2 < \delta_0$$

Computational Example for t Test for Two Means (Independent Samples)

Let's suppose that a student in an experimental psychology course is investigating the hypothesis that distributed practice is superior to massed practice in developing

---

[2] The degrees of freedom associated with $\hat{\sigma}$ is discussed in Section 11.2.

[3] This test is described in Section 13.1.

skill on a mirror-tracing task. The task requires participants to trace a star pattern on a sheet of paper with their nonpreferred hand; they can see themselves tracing the pattern only by looking in a mirror. Forty students, an entire introductory psychology class, are randomly assigned to the two practice conditions with the restriction that an equal number of students are assigned to each condition. Participants in the distributed condition have a 3-minute rest period at the end of each practice trial. Participants in the massed condition have only a 5-second pause at the end of each trial—just long enough to permit the researcher to place a new sheet of paper in the tracing apparatus. Both groups receive 15 practice trials. Because the groups may differ in amount of fatigue at the conclusion of practice, the dependent variable is measured the following day. The participants are given two warm-up trials; the dependent variable is the time required to trace the star pattern on the next three trials. The decision rule and the steps to be followed in testing the null hypothesis are as follows:

Step 1. State the statistical hypotheses:

$H_0: \mu_1 - \mu_2 \geq 0$
$H_1: \mu_1 - \mu_2 < 0$,
where μ_1 and μ_2 denote the population means, respectively, for the distributed and massed conditions.

Step 2. Specify the test statistic:

$t = \dfrac{(\bar{X}_1 - \bar{X}_2)}{\hat{\sigma}^2_{\bar{X}_1 - \bar{X}_2}}$ because we want to test $\mu_1 - \mu_2 \geq 0$, σ_1^2 and σ_2^2 are unknown, the samples are independent, random assignment was used, and we assume the population distributions of X_1 and X_2 are approximately normal.

Step 3. Specify the sample sizes:[4] specify the sampling distribution:

$n_1 = 20$ and $n_2 = 20$;
t distribution, because the population variances are estimated from sample data, the X_1 and X_2 populations are approximately normal, and there is no reason to believe that σ_1^2 does not equal σ_2^2.

Step 4. Specify the significance level: $\alpha = .05$.

Step 5. Obtain random samples of size n_1 and n_2, compute t, and make a decision.

Decision Rule:

Reject the null hypothesis if t falls in the lower .05 portion of the sampling distribution of t; otherwise, don't reject the null hypothesis. If the

---

[4] The use of Appendix Table D.9 to estimate the required sample size is discussed later in this section.

null hypothesis is rejected, conclude that distributed practice is superior to massed practice in developing skill on a mirror-tracing task; if the null hypothesis is not rejected, do not draw this conclusion.

The data for the experiment are shown in the top portion of Table 12.4-1. Before testing the null hypothesis, it is good statistical practice to examine a descriptive summary of the data for outliers and look for evidence of nonnormality and unequal dispersions in the populations. The box plot introduced in Section 4.5 is particularly useful for this purpose. Stacked box plots for the data in Table 12.4-1 are shown in Figure 12.4-1. It is apparent from the figure that the sample distributions are negatively skewed and have different dispersions. Fortunately, the t test is relatively unaffected by this degree of population nonnormality and variance heterogeneity when the sample n's are equal. We also note that the distributed-practice

TABLE 12.4-1.   Mirror-Tracing Data

(i) Data

	Distributed Practice		Massed Practice	
Student	Time, X_1 (Seconds)		Student	Time, X_2 (Seconds)
1	17		21	19
2	18		22	20
3	16		23	22
4	18		24	24
5	12		25	10
6	20		26	25
7	18		27	20
8	20		28	22
9	20		29	21
10	22		30	23
11	20		31	20
12	10		32	10
13	8		33	12
14	12		34	14
15	16		35	12
16	16		36	20
17	18		37	22
18	20		38	24
19	18		39	23
20	21		40	17
$n_1 - 20$	$\Sigma X_1 = 340$		$n_2 - 20$	$\Sigma X_2 = 380$
	$\Sigma X_1^2 = 6054$			$\Sigma X_2^2 = 7662$

TABLE 12.4-1. Mirror-Tracing Data *(continued)*

(ii) Computation of preliminary statistics

$$\overline{X}_1 = \frac{\Sigma X_i}{n_1} = \frac{340}{20} = 17 \qquad\qquad \overline{X}_2 = \frac{\Sigma X_i}{n_2} = \frac{380}{20} = 19$$

$$\hat{\sigma}_1^2 = \frac{\Sigma X_1^2 - (\Sigma X_1)^2/n_1}{n_1 - 1} \qquad\qquad \hat{\sigma}_2^2 = \frac{\Sigma X_2^2 - (\Sigma X_2)^2/n_2}{n_2 - 1}$$

$$= \frac{6054 - (340)^2/20}{20 - 1} \qquad\qquad = \frac{7662 - (380)^2/20}{20 - 1}$$

$$= 14.421 \qquad\qquad\qquad = 23.263$$

$$\hat{\sigma}_{Pooled}^2 = \frac{(n_1 - 1)\hat{\sigma}_1^2 + (n_2 - 1)\hat{\sigma}_2^2}{(n_1 - 1) + (n_2 - 1)} = \frac{(20 - 1)(14.421) + (20 - 1)23.263}{(20 - 1) + (20 - 1)}$$

$$= 18.842$$

(iii) Computation of t

$$t = \frac{\overline{X}_1 - \overline{X}_2}{\sqrt{\hat{\sigma}_{Pooled}^2(1/n_1 + 1/n_2)}} = \frac{17 - 19}{\sqrt{18.842(1/20 + 1/20)}}$$

$$= \frac{-2}{1.373} = -1.457$$

$$-t_{.05,38} = -1.686$$

data contain one outlier, 8. We will assume that a careful examination of the data collection and recording procedures gives no reason to question the accuracy of this datum. The next step in analyzing the data is to compute a t statistic as shown in the lower portion of Table 12.4-1. The value of t is -1.457. According to Appendix Table D.3, a t of -1.686 with 38 degrees of freedom cuts off the lower .05 region

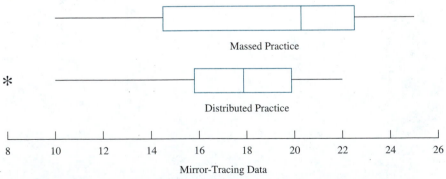

Figure 12.4-1. **Stacked box plots for the mirror-tracing data in Table 12.4-1. The lower and upper ends of each box identify the first and third quartiles, respectively. The vertical center line is the median. The asterisk identifies an outlier.**

of the sampling distribution—that is, $-t_{.05,38}$ is equal to -1.686. Because the computed $t(38) = -1.457$ is not less than or equal to $t_{.05,38} = -1.686$, the null hypothesis is not rejected. The test doesn't warrant the inference that distributed practice leads to better performance on the tracing task than massed practice.

Practical Significance

In Section 11.2, we computed a d-like measure of effect size, $d = |\overline{X} - \mu_0|/\hat{\sigma}$, by replacing the unknown population standard deviation with $\hat{\sigma}$. For the two-sample case, Hedges (1981) has popularized a similar d-like measure of effect size:

$$g = \frac{|\overline{X}_1 - \overline{X}_2|}{\hat{\sigma}_{Pooled}},$$

where

$$\hat{\sigma}_{Pooled} = \sqrt{\frac{(n_1 - 1)\hat{\sigma}_1^2 + (n_2 - 1)\hat{\sigma}_2^2}{(n_1 - 1) + (n_2 - 1)}}.$$

Hedges' g, which uses a pooled estimator of the population standard deviation, is interpreted like Cohen's d. A g value of 0.2 is a small effect, 0.5 is a medium effect, and 0.8 is a large effect.

For purposes of illustration, we will compute g for the mirror-tracing data in Table 12.4-1. Ordinarily, you would not compute g when the null hypothesis is not rejected. The effect size for the mirror-tracing data is

$$g = \frac{|\overline{X}_1 - \overline{X}_2|}{\hat{\sigma}_{Pooled}} = \frac{|17 - 19|}{4.341} = 0.46,$$

where

$$\hat{\sigma}_{Pooled} = \sqrt{\frac{(n_1 - 1)\hat{\sigma}_1^2 + (n_2 - 1)\hat{\sigma}_2^2}{(n_1 - 1) + (n_2 - 1)}}$$

$$= \sqrt{\frac{(20 - 1)(14.421) + (20 - 1)(23.263)}{(20 - 1) + (20 - 1)}} = 4.341.$$

According to Cohen's guidelines, the difference in tracing time between the distributed and massed practice conditions is a small effect.

Determining the Required Sample Size (Independent Samples)

In the previous chapter (Section 11.2) we saw how to use Appendix Table D.9 to make a rational choice of sample size for the one-sample t test. Appendix Table D.9 also can be used to choose a sample size for the two-sample t test. To estimate n, it is necessary to specify α, $1 - \beta$, and Hedges' g. Recall that g is a d-like measure of effect size that is interpreted in the same way as Cohen's d: $g = 0.2$, 0.5, and 0.8 correspond, respectively, to small, medium, and large effects. Consider the mirror-tracing task described earlier. Suppose that we wanted to detect a medium-size effect ($g = 0.5$) and we wanted α to equal .05 and $1 - \beta$ to equal .80. According to Appendix Table D.9, we should use 50 participants in each sample. The n actually used was only 20.

Confidence Interval for Two Means (Independent Samples)

Confidence-interval procedures for the one-sample case described in Chapters 10 and 11 generalize to the two-sample case.

A two-sided $100(1 - \alpha)\%$ confidence interval for $\mu_1 - \mu_2$ for independent samples is

$$(\overline{X}_1 - \overline{X}_2) - t_{\alpha/2,\nu} \sqrt{\hat{\sigma}^2_{Pooled}\left(\frac{1}{n_1} + \frac{1}{n_2}\right)} < \mu_1 - \mu_2$$

$$< (\overline{X}_1 - \overline{X}_2) + t_{\alpha/2,\nu} \sqrt{\hat{\sigma}^2_{Pooled}\left(\frac{1}{n_1} + \frac{1}{n_2}\right)} \,,$$

where $t_{\alpha/2,\nu}$ is the value that cuts off the upper $\alpha/2$ region of the sampling distribution of t for $\nu = n_1 + n_2 - 2$ and

$$\hat{\sigma}^2_{Pooled} = \frac{(n_1 - 1)\hat{\sigma}^2_1 + (n_2 - 1)\hat{\sigma}^2_2}{(n_1 - 1) + (n_2 - 1)}.$$

A one-sided $100(1 - \alpha)\%$ confidence interval for $\mu_1 - \mu_2$ for independent samples is

$$(\overline{X}_1 - \overline{X}_2) - t_{\alpha,\nu} \sqrt{\hat{\sigma}^2_{Pooled}\left(\frac{1}{n_1} + \frac{1}{n_2}\right)} < \mu_1 - \mu_2$$

or

$$\mu_1 - \mu_2 < (\overline{X}_1 - \overline{X}_2) + t_{\alpha,\nu} \sqrt{\hat{\sigma}^2_{Pooled}\left(\frac{1}{n_1} + \frac{1}{n_2}\right)} \,,$$

where $t_{\alpha,\nu}$ is the value that cuts off the upper α region of the sampling distribution of t for $\nu = n_1 + n_2 - 2$.

We will use the data in Table 12.4-1 ($\overline{X}_1 = 17$, $\overline{X}_2 = 19$, $\hat{\sigma}^2_{Pooled} = 18.842$, and $n_1 = n_2 = 20$) to illustrate a one-sided confidence interval. The researcher's hypotheses for the mirror-tracing experiment were directional:

$$H_0: \mu_1 - \mu_2 \geq 0$$
$$H_1: \mu_1 - \mu_2 < 0.$$

An analogous one-sided $100(1 - .05)\% = .95\%$ confidence interval for the difference $\mu_1 - \mu_2$ is

$$\mu_1 - \mu_2 < (\overline{X}_1 - \overline{X}_2) + t_{.05,38} \sqrt{\hat{\sigma}^2_{Pooled}\left(\frac{1}{n_1} + \frac{1}{n_2}\right)}$$

$$\mu_1 - \mu_2 < (17 - 19) + 1.686\sqrt{18.842\left(\frac{1}{20} + \frac{1}{20}\right)}$$

$$\mu_1 - \mu_2 < 0.31.$$

This 95% confidence interval corresponds to the colored portion of the real number line as follows:

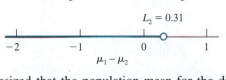

The researcher hypothesized that the population mean for the distributed practice condition would be less than that for the massed condition, that is, $\mu_1 < \mu_2$. However, it is apparent from the confidence interval that the population mean for the distributed practice condition, μ_1, could be less than that for the massed practice condition, μ_2, or it could be equal to it or even larger.

CHECK YOUR UNDERSTANDING OF SECTION 12.4

10. Under what condition is it appropriate to pool $\hat{\sigma}_1^2$ and $\hat{\sigma}_2^2$ in estimating $\sigma_{\bar{X}_1 - \bar{X}_2}^2$?

11. It has been reported that employment interviewers spend more time talking to applicants who are hired than to applicants who are rejected. To determine whether this is true for college students seeking summer employment through a university placement center, a researcher posing as an applicant accompanied a random sample of referees to their job interviews. A record of the duration and outcome of $n = 49$ interviews was kept.

Duration of Interview
(minutes)

Hired		Rejected	
30	23	19	17
21	24	18	18
24	26	22	19
25	27	13	22
29	24	15	15
24	22	18	19
23	25	17	17
24	26	20	20
28	23	18	18
25	24	19	17
24	27	23	
19	26	12	
25	25	18	

a. Construct box plots for the hired and rejected applicants and stack the plots one above the other. Do the data contain outliers? Do the sample distributions appear to be relatively symmetrical?

b. Compute a t test statistic and make a decision about the researcher's hypothesis. Let $\alpha = .05$.

c. What is the p-value of the t statistic?

d. Compute a measure of effect size.

e. Use Appendix Table D.9 to determine whether the sample size is adequate to detect a large-size effect if a power of .80 is desired. What is the minimum number of subjects that is required?

f. Compute a $100(1 - .05)\% = 95\%$ confidence interval for $\mu_1 - \mu_2$; assume that $t_{.05,47} = 1.678$. Locate the confidence interval on the real number line.

g. Specify all null hypotheses that could be rejected.

12. The effect of early language experience on the discrimination of speech sounds was investigated. Twenty-eight 6- to 8-month-old infants raised in English- or Spanish-speaking homes were trained to turn their heads when they detected a change in a sound stimulus. Following the discrimination training, Spanish contrasts involving a tapped and a trilled "r" were presented. The dependent measure was the number of head turns to stimuli involving a change minus the number of head turns on control trials divided by the number of experimental trials. The following data were obtained. (Suggested by Eilers, Rebecca E., Gavin, William J., and Oller, D. Kimbrough. [1981]. Cross-linguistic perception in infancy: Early effects of linguistic experience. *Journal of Child Language, 9*, 289–302.)

English-Speaking Home	Spanish-Speaking Home
.0421	.1081
.0941	.0986
.1064	.1566
.0242	.1961
.1331	.1125
.0773	.1942
.0243	.1079
.0815	.1021
.1186	.1583
.0356	.1673
.0728	.1675
.0999	.1856
.0614	.1688
.0479	.1512

a. Construct box plots for English-speaking and Spanish-speaking homes and stack the plots one above the other. Assume that for the English-speaking homes $Mdn = 0.07285$, $Q_1 = 0.0421$, and $Q_3 = 0.0999$. Assume that for the Spanish-speaking homes $Mdn = 0.15665$, $Q_1 = 0.1081$, and $Q_3 = 0.1688$. Do the data contain outliers? Do the sample distributions appear to be relatively symmetrical?

b. Use a t statistic to test the null hypothesis that $\mu_1 - \mu_2 = 0$, where μ_1 and μ_2 denote, respectively, the population means for infants raised in English- and Spanish-speaking homes. Let $\alpha = .001$. What decision should the researcher make?

c. What is the p-value of the t statistic?

d. Compute a measure of effect size.

e. Compute a $100(1 - .001)\% = 99.9\%$ confidence interval for $\mu_1 - \mu_2$; assume that $t_{.001/2, 26} = 3.707$. Locate the confidence interval on the real number line.

f. Specify all null hypotheses that could be rejected.

13. Use the table of random numbers in Appendix Table D.1 to draw random samples without replacement of 25 men and 25 women from the Student Database in Appendix E.

a. List the Participant Number, Gender, and Stat Grade for each person in your sample. For each gender, construct a box plot and stack the plots one above the other. Do the data contain outliers? Do the sample distributions appear to be relatively symmetrical?

b. Test the null hypothesis that $\mu_1 - \mu_2 = 0$, where μ_1 and μ_2 denote, respectively, the population mean of men's and women's Stat Grade. Let $\alpha = .05$.

c. What is the p-value of the t statistic?

d. Compute a measure of effect size.

e. Use Appendix Table D.9 to determine whether the sample size is adequate to detect a large-size effect if a power of .80 is desired.

f. What is the minimum number of subjects that is required?

g. Compute a $100(1 - .05)\% = 95\%$ confidence interval for $\mu_1 - \mu_2$. Locate the confidence interval on the real number line.

h. Specify all null hypotheses that could be rejected.

i. Write a paragraph summarizing your results and conclusions.

12.5 TWO-SAMPLE z AND t TESTS AND CONFIDENCE INTERVAL FOR MEANS USING DEPENDENT SAMPLES

Introduction to Dependent Samples

The significance tests and confidence intervals described earlier require the use of **independent samples** in which the selection of elements in one sample is not affected by the selection of elements in the other. Samples are independent if, for example, a researcher samples randomly from two populations or uses a random procedure to assign elements to two samples. As we will see, a researcher can obtain a more powerful test of a false null hypothesis and a shorter confidence interval by using dependent samples. **Dependent samples** can be obtained by any of the following research procedures:

1. Observing participants under both the experimental condition and the control condition—that is, obtaining **repeated measures** on each of the participants.
2. Matching each participant in the experimental condition with a participant in the control condition on some variable that is correlated with the dependent variable. This is called **participant matching.**
3. Obtaining sets of identical twins or littermates and assigning one member of the pair randomly to the experimental condition and the other member to the control condition.
4. Obtaining pairs of participants who are matched by mutual selection, for example, husband-and-wife pairs or business partners.

Let us consider these procedures in more detail. The first procedure, observing a set of participants under both the experimental and control conditions, can be used only with independent variables that have relatively short-duration effects. The nature of the independent variable should be such that the effects of one condition dissipate before the participant is observed under the other condition. Otherwise, the second dependent measure will reflect the cumulative effects of two conditions rather than only the effects of the second condition. There is no such restriction, of course, when carry-over effects such as learning or fatigue are the principal interest of the researcher. If repeated measures are obtained, the order of presentation of the two conditions should be randomized independently for each participant if possible. It is customary to randomize with the restriction that half the participants receive one condition first, while the other half receive the other condition first.

The remaining three procedures for obtaining dependent samples involve forming pairs of participants who are matched on some basis. In participant matching, a matching variable is used to pair up otherwise unrelated participants; the matching variable should be highly correlated with the dependent variable. For example, IQ and ability to learn verbal material are highly correlated; hence, participants can be assigned to pairs so that members of each pair have similar IQs and therefore similar verbal learning abilities. The higher the correlation between the matching variable and the dependent variable, the more effective the matching. If identical twins or littermates are used, it can be assumed that participants within a pair are matched with respect to genetic characteristics. The aptitudes and abilities of identical twins, fraternal twins to some extent, and even siblings are more similar than those of unrelated participants. When participants are matched by mutual selection, the researcher always must ascertain that the participants within pairs are in fact more similar with respect to the dependent variable than are unmatched participants. Knowing a husband's attitudes about abortion and legalization of marijuana, for example, may provide considerable information about his wife's attitudes on the issues, and vice versa. However, knowing the husband's mechanical aptitude may provide no information about his wife's mechanical aptitude.

z Test for Dependent Samples

You probably wonder what difference it makes whether samples are dependent or independent. If the same participants are observed twice or if participants in one sample are paired with participants in another sample, the outcomes of X_1 and X_2 for each pair are not statistically independent. This doesn't affect the expectation of the difference between sample means; the expectation of $E(\overline{X}_1 - \overline{X}_2)$ is equal to $\mu_1 - \mu_2$. However, dependence within pairs affects the variance of the difference between means. Let us consider first the case in which σ_1^2, σ_2^2, and ρ_{12} are known. The variance of $\overline{X}_1 - \overline{X}_2$ when samples are dependent is

$$\sigma_{\overline{X}_1 - \overline{X}_2}^2 = \sigma_{\overline{X}_1}^2 + \sigma_{\overline{X}_2}^2 - 2\rho_{12}\sigma_{\overline{X}_1}\sigma_{\overline{X}_2},$$

where $\sigma_{\overline{X}_1}^2 = \sigma_1^2/n_1$, $\sigma_{\overline{X}_2}^2 = \sigma_2^2/n_2$, and ρ_{12} is the Pearson product-moment correlation between the dependent populations. The corresponding formula for independent samples given in Section 12.2 is

$$\sigma_{\overline{X}_1 - \overline{X}_2}^2 = \sigma_{\overline{X}_1}^2 + \sigma_{\overline{X}_2}^2.$$

A comparison of these formulas reveals that the larger the positive correlation, ρ_{12}, the smaller is $\sigma_{\overline{X}_1 - \overline{X}_2}^2$ for dependent samples relative to that for independent samples. Hence, if ρ_{12} is greater than 0, a researcher will underestimate z by using

$$z = \frac{(\overline{X}_1 - \overline{X}_2) - \delta_0}{\sqrt{\sigma_{\overline{X}_1}^2 + \sigma_{\overline{X}_2}^2}}$$

instead of

$$z = \frac{(\overline{X}_1 - \overline{X}_2) - \delta_0}{\sqrt{\sigma_{\overline{X}_1}^2 + \sigma_{\overline{X}_2}^2 - 2\rho_{12}\sigma_{\overline{X}_1}\sigma_{\overline{X}_2}}}.$$

The computational procedures for the dependent-samples z test will not be illustrated because in practice, we rarely know the values of σ_1^2, σ_2^2, and ρ_{12}. When these parameters are unknown, researchers use the t statistic that is discussed next instead of z.

t Test for Dependent Samples

We will now consider the more usual case, in which σ_1^2, σ_2^2, and ρ_{12} are unknown. If the population distributions are normally distributed or if the samples are sufficiently large, a t statistic for dependent samples can be used to test any of the following null hypotheses:

$$H_0: \mu_1 - \mu_2 = \delta_0 \qquad H_0: \mu_1 - \mu_2 \leq \delta_0 \qquad H_0: \mu_1 - \mu_2 \geq \delta_0$$

$$H_1: \mu_1 - \mu_2 \neq \delta_0 \qquad H_1: \mu_1 - \mu_2 > \delta_0 \qquad H_1: \mu_1 - \mu_2 < \delta_0$$

One form of the t statistic is

$$t = \frac{(\overline{X}_1 - \overline{X}_2) - \delta_0}{\sqrt{\hat{\sigma}_{\overline{X}_1}^2 + \hat{\sigma}_{\overline{X}_2}^2 - 2r_{12}\hat{\sigma}_{\overline{X}_1}\hat{\sigma}_{\overline{X}_2}}}.$$

This formula is not used because a simpler computational formula—one that doesn't require the computation of a correlation coefficient, r_{12}—is available. The formula to be described is simpler because it replaces each pair of scores X_1 and X_2 with one difference score D_i, where $D_i = X_{i1} - X_{i2}$, for each of the $i = 1, \ldots, n$ pairs of scores. In effect, this converts the two-sample dependent t test for μ_1 and μ_2 into a one-sample t test. The null hypothesis for this analysis is

$$H_0: \mu_D = \delta_0,$$

where μ_D is the population mean of differences between paired scores. This null hypothesis is equivalent to $H_0: \mu_1 - \mu_2 = \delta_0$.

The t test statistic for dependent samples using the difference-score approach is

$$t = \frac{\overline{X}_D}{\hat{\sigma}_{\overline{X}_D}} = \frac{\dfrac{\sum\limits_{i=1}^{n} D_i}{n}}{\dfrac{\sqrt{\dfrac{\sum\limits_{i=1}^{n} D_i^2 - \left(\sum\limits_{i=1}^{n} D_i\right)^2 / n}{n}}}{\sqrt{n-1}}},$$

where $\overline{X}_D$ is the sample mean of difference scores, $\hat{\sigma}_{\overline{X}_D}$ is used to estimate the standard error of the mean of difference scores, D_i is equal to $X_{i1} - X_{i2}$ for the ith pair of scores, and n is the number of pairs of scores.

The number of degrees of freedom, ν, for this test statistic is equal to $n - 1$, the degrees of freedom associated with $\hat{\sigma}_{\overline{X}_D}$. The following example should help to clarify the meaning of the terms in this t test statistic.

Computational Example for t Test for Two Means (Dependent Samples)

The scientific hypothesis that the population mean for the distributed practice condition is smaller than that for the massed condition for the mirror-tracing task described in Section 12.4 could have been investigated using matched participants. Suppose that participants are tested on the mirror-tracing task using their preferred hand. The time required to trace the star pattern on the last three of five trials is used to form pairs of participants having comparable tracing times and hence similar motor skills. The participants in each pair are randomly assigned to the distributed and massed practice conditions. Then the experiment is carried out as described previously. Data for the experiment are shown in Table 12.5-1. According to Appendix Table D.3, a t of -1.729 with $\nu = 20 - 1 = 19$ cuts off the lower .05 region of the sampling distribution, that is, $-t_{.05,19} = -1.729$. The computed $t(19) = -3.044$ in Table 12.5-1 is less than $-t_{.05,19} = -1.729$. Hence, the null hypothesis is rejected, and it is concluded that distributed practice leads to better performance on the task than massed practice. Of course, this inference applies only to the population represented by the participants in the experiment and to the particular practice conditions and task that were used.

Has the researcher gained anything by using matched participants? To answer this question, we can compare the results using independent samples with those for dependent samples. This comparison can be made from Tables 12.4-1 and 12.5-1, which illustrate the t computational procedures for the same set of data. The null hypothesis is rejected for the dependent-samples analysis, $t(19) = -3.044$, $p < .004$, but not for the independent-samples analysis, $t(38) = -1.457$, $p < .08$. Clearly, the use of matched participants has resulted in a more powerful test of the false null hypothesis.

An examination of the data for the two practice conditions suggests that they are positively correlated; the Pearson product-moment correlation coefficient, r, is actually .79. This example illustrates an important principle: Whenever the correlation between samples is positive, the t statistic for dependent samples will be larger than the t statistic for independent samples. As noted earlier, the use of dependent samples results in a more powerful test of a false null hypothesis. This statement must be qualified. The number of degrees of freedom for the independent t statistic, $n_1 + n_2 - 2 = 38$, is larger than that for the dependent t statistic, $n - 1 = 19$. The values of t that cut off the critical region for the independent and dependent samples are, respectively, $-t_{.05,38} = -1.686$ and $-t_{.05,19} = -1.729$. Now for the qualification: For a t test with dependent samples to be more powerful than a t test with independent samples, the correlation between the dependent samples must be large enough to more than compensate for the smaller degrees of freedom and for the larger absolute value of t required for significance.

Several assumptions are associated with the t statistic for dependent samples.

1. The population of differences, D_i, is approximately normally distributed. These differences will be normally distributed if X_1 and X_2 are normally distributed.
2. The population variance of the mean of the difference scores, $\sigma^2_{\bar{X}_D}$, is unknown.
3. If repeated measures are obtained, the participants are a random sample from the population of interest. The order in which the conditions are presented should be randomized for each participant. If pairs of matched participants are used, the participants in each pair are randomly assigned to the experimental and control conditions.

TABLE 12.5-1. Mirror-Tracing Data (Dependent Samples)

(i) Data

Student Pair	Distributed Practice Time, X_1 (Seconds)	Massed Practice Time, X_2 (Seconds)	Difference, $D_i = X_{i1} - X_{i2+}$
1	17	19	−2
2	18	20	−2
3	16	22	−6
4	18	24	−6
5	12	10	2
6	20	25	−5
7	18	20	−2
8	20	22	−2
9	20	21	−1
10	22	23	−1
11	20	20	0
12	10	10	0
13	8	12	−4
14	12	14	−2
15	16	12	4
16	16	20	−4
17	18	22	−4
18	20	24	−4
19	18	23	−5
20	21	17	4
$n = 20$	$\overline{X}_1 = 17$	$\overline{X}_2 = 19$	$\Sigma D_i = -40$
			$\Sigma D_i^2 = 244$

(ii) Computation of preliminary statistics

$$\overline{X}_D = \frac{\Sigma D_i}{n} = \frac{-40}{20} = -2$$

$$\hat{\sigma}_{\overline{x}_D} = \frac{\sqrt{\dfrac{\Sigma D_i^2 - (\Sigma D_i)^2/n}{n}}}{\sqrt{n-1}} = \frac{\sqrt{\dfrac{244 - (-40)^2/20}{20}}}{\sqrt{20-1}} = \frac{2.8636}{4.3589} = 0.657$$

Computational check

$$\overline{X}_1 - \overline{X}_2 = \overline{X}_D = 17 - 19 = -2$$

(iii) Computation of t

$$t = \frac{\overline{X}_D}{\hat{\sigma}_{\overline{x}_D}} = \frac{-2}{0.657} = -3.044$$

$$-t_{.05,19} = -1.729$$

Determining the Required Sample Size (Dependent Samples)

We have repeatedly emphasized the importance of making a rational choice of sample size. We don't want to use a sample that is too small and possibly fail to reject a false null hypothesis because of low power. Alternatively, we don't want to use a sample that is too large and waste the time of participants and other research resources. Appendix Table D.9 can be used to make a rational choice of sample size for the two-sample *t* test with dependent samples. To estimate *n*, it is necessary to specify α, $1 - \beta$, Hedges' *g*, and ρ, the correlation between the two populations. Because ρ is rarely known, its estimation must be based on previous research or informed judgment. Consider the mirror-tracing task with repeated measures on each subject described in this section. Suppose that we wanted to detect a medium-size effect ($g = 0.5$) and we wanted α to equal .05 and $1 - \beta$ to equal .80. If we estimate that the population correlation between the distributed and massed practice times is at least .70, the required *n* according to Appendix Table D.9 is 16.

If we are not confident of our estimate of ρ, we can use conservative and optimistic estimates to bracket the required sample size. For example, we might believe that the population correlation is not less than .60 nor higher than .80. According to Appendix Table D.9, we should use at least 11 subjects but not more than 21. The sample correlation between the distributed and massed practice times in Table 12.5-1 is .79. This sample correlation suggests that our estimate of the population correlation, .70, is reasonably good.

Confidence Interval for Two Means (Dependent Samples)

A two-sided $100(1 - \alpha)\%$ confidence interval for $\mu_1 - \mu_2$ for dependent samples is

$$\overline{X}_D - t_{\alpha/2,\nu}\,\hat{\sigma}_{\overline{X}_D} < \mu_1 - \mu_2 < \overline{X}_D + t_{\alpha/2,\nu}\,\hat{\sigma}_{\overline{X}_D},$$

where $\overline{X}_D = \sum_{i=1}^{n} D_i/n$, $t_{\alpha/2,\nu}$ is the value that cuts off the upper $\alpha/2$ region of the sampling distribution of *t* for $\nu = n - 1$, and

$$\hat{\sigma}_{\overline{X}_D} = \frac{\sqrt{\dfrac{\sum_{i=1}^{n} D_i^2 - \left(\sum_{i=1}^{n} D_i\right)^2/n}{n}}}{\sqrt{n - 1}}.$$

A one-sided $100(1 - \alpha)\%$ confidence interval for $\mu_1 - \mu_2$ is

$$\overline{X}_D - t_{\alpha,\nu}\hat{\sigma}_{\overline{X}_D} < \mu_1 - \mu_2 \qquad \text{or} \qquad \mu_1 - \mu_2 < \overline{X}_D + t_{\alpha,\nu}\hat{\sigma}_{\overline{X}_D},$$

where $t_{\alpha,\nu}$ is the value that cuts off the upper α region of the sampling distribution of *t* for $\nu = n - 1$.

We will use the data in Table 12.5-1 ($\overline{X}_D = -2$, $\hat{\sigma}_{\overline{X}_D} = 0.657$, and $n = 20$) to illustrate a one-sided confidence interval. The researcher's hypotheses for the mirror-tracing experiment were directional:

$$H_0: \mu_1 - \mu_2 \geq 0$$
$$H_1: \mu_1 - \mu_2 < 0.$$

An analogous one-sided $100(1 - .05)\% = 95\%$ confidence interval for the difference $\mu_1 - \mu_2$ is

$$\mu_1 - \mu_2 < \overline{X}_D + t_{.05,19}\hat{\sigma}_{\overline{X}_D}$$
$$\mu_1 - \mu_2 < -2 + (1.729)(0.657)$$
$$\mu_1 - \mu_2 < -0.86.$$

This 95% confidence interval corresponds to the darkened portion of the real number line as follows:

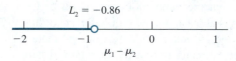

The researcher can be 95% confident that the difference $\mu_1 - \mu_2$ is less than -0.86, which is consistent with the scientific hypothesis. Furthermore, it is reasonable to conclude that the small size effect, $g = |\overline{X}_1 - \overline{X}_2|/\hat{\sigma}_{Pooled} = |17 - 19|/4.341 = .46$, is not attributable to chance (see "Practical Significance" in Section 12.4-1 for the computation). The confidence interval for dependent samples is shorter than that for the case in which independent samples were used. For comparison purposes, the confidence interval for the independent samples case is shown below.

Group Matching: A Research Strategy to Be Avoided

A procedure called **group matching** is sometimes seen in the literature. It involves matching samples on one or more relevant characteristics so that the means and the variances of the samples are approximately equal. No attempt is made to match individuals in one sample with those in another sample.

Group matching instead of individual matching is often used in ex post facto experiments. In an **ex post facto experiment** the independent variable has occurred prior to the experiment. Thus, the independent variable is not under a researcher's control; rather, records or other information are used to construct two samples that differ with respect to the independent variable. For example, a researcher might be interested in determining whether the amount of community service (the dependent variable) of women who participated in Girl Scouting is greater than that for women who didn't participate (participation-nonparticipation is the independent variable). Scout records can be used to identify those women who were Girl Scouts. In all likelihood the samples of former Scouts and non-Scouts differ on a variety of variables besides the independent variable. Group matching consists of adjusting the membership of each sample so that the samples' means and variances are identical on a select set of extraneous variables. For example, high-school records could be used to adjust the composition of the samples so as to equate the sample means and variances on school achievement, number of extracurricular activities, and socioeconomic background.

One might anticipate that the use of group matching would result in a more powerful test than the use of independent samples. This is not the case. Unfortunately, there are several problems inherent in using group matching.[5] Although the procedure results in dependent samples, the *t* statistic for dependent samples can't be used because individual participants aren't matched. The data have to be analyzed using the *t* statistic for independent samples. This is not a good research strategy because (1) group matching restricts the ordinary variation between sample means that is expected on the basis of random sampling and (2) the denominator of the *t* statistic for independent samples overestimates the standard error of the difference between means when the samples are dependent. Hence, the *t* statistic for independent samples gives a less powerful test than would have been obtained if group matching had not been used. An important experimental design principle emerges from this discussion—the sampling, randomization, and control procedures used in an experiment must be reflected in the statistical analysis and interpretation of data. If this is not possible, presumed refinements such as group matching should not be used.

CHECK YOUR UNDERSTANDING OF SECTION 12.5

14. If repeated measures are obtained, what restriction customarily is placed on the order of presentation of the conditions in the experiment?
15. (a) How is the size of the correlation between dependent samples related to the size of the standard error of the difference between means? (b) How is the size of the correlation between dependent samples related to the probability of rejecting a false null hypothesis?
16. Before and after seeing a film about marijuana, 16 participants

---

[5] For an in-depth discussion of these problems, see Boneau and Pennypacker (1961). This article is reproduced in Kirk (1972).

completed a questionnaire designed to assess their attitudes toward legalization of the drug. The following data were obtained.

		Favorableness of Attitude			
Participant	*Before*	*After*	*Participant*	*Before*	*After*
1	13	16	9	19	20
2	16	18	10	16	18
3	10	12	11	15	18
4	14	18	12	14	15
5	15	18	13	12	12
6	12	15	14	13	17
7	11	12	15	14	16
8	18	20	16	15	17

a. Construct box plots for the before and after attitudes and stack the plots one above the other. Do the data contain outliers? Do the sample distributions appear to be relatively symmetrical?

b. Use a t statistic to test the null hypothesis that $\mu_1 - \mu_2 \geq 0$, where μ_1 and μ_2 denote, respectively, the population means for the before and after attitudes. Let $\alpha = .05$. What decision should the researcher make?

c. What is the p-value of the t statistic?

d. Compute a measure of effect size.

e. Use Appendix Table D.9 to determine whether the sample size is adequate to detect a large size effect for $\alpha = .05$, $1 - \beta = .95$, and $\rho = .70$. What is the minimum number of subjects that is required?

f. Compute a $100(1 - .05)\% = 95\%$ confidence interval for $\mu_1 - \mu_2$. Locate the confidence interval on the real number line.

g. Specify all null hypotheses that could be rejected.

17. Expanding technology and the growth of knowledge in medicine require that nurses continually upgrade their skills. One way to accomplish this upgrading is through continuing-education workshops. The present study investigated the impact of a 60-hour workshop on a measure of the participants' cognitive knowledge. Twenty-two staff nurses took a paper-and-pencil pretest to evaluate their basic knowledge of cancer and cancer nursing prior to the 10-day workshop. The following data were obtained. (Suggested by Donovan, Marilee, Wolpert, Patricia, and Yasko, Joyce. [1981]. Gaps and contracts. *Nursing Outlook*, 467–471.)

		Knowledge Score	
Participant	Pretest Score	Posttest Score
1	29	35
2	20	41
3	24	33
4	32	41
5	33	39
6	19	20
7	17	29
8	32	42
9	16	36
10	28	37
11	35	36
12	19	27
13	31	50
14	28	33
15	23	23
16	18	35
17	24	34
18	25	30
19	28	39
20	32	45
21	25	36
22	27	29

a. Construct box plots for the pretest and posttest scores and stack the plots one above the other. Do the data contain outliers? Do the sample distributions appear to be relatively symmetrical?

b. Use a t statistic to test the null hypothesis that $\mu_1 - \mu_2 = 0$, where μ_1 and μ_2 denote, respectively, the population means for the pretest and posttest scores. Let $\alpha = .01$. What decision should the researcher make?

c. What is the p-value of the t statistic?

d. Compute a measure of effect size.

e. Use Appendix Table D.9 to determine whether the sample size is adequate to detect a large size effect for $\alpha = .01$, $1 - \beta = .80$, and $\rho = .50$. What is the minimum number of subjects that is required?

f. Compute a $100(1 - .01)\% = 99\%$ confidence interval for $\mu_1 - \mu_2$. Locate the confidence interval on the real number line.

g. Specify all null hypotheses that could be rejected.

h. For purposes of comparison, compute a t statistic for independent samples. Compare the result with the t statistic for dependent samples. Was the use of repeated measures an effective experimental design strategy?

i. In this experiment the order of presentation of the pretest and the posttest obviously could not be randomized. Describe how a control group could be used in the experiment. How could the use of a control group help to clarify the interpretation of the results of the experiment?

18. Assume that a t statistic will be used to test the following null hypotheses. For (a), (b), and (c), estimate the total number of participants required; for (d), (e), and (f), estimate the number of pairs of dependent participants required.

a. $H_0: \mu_1 - \mu_2 \geq 0$
$\alpha = .05$
$1 - \beta = .80$
$d = 0.5$

b. $H_0: \mu_1 - \mu_2 = 0$
$\alpha = .01$
$1 - \beta = .90$
$d = 0.2$

c. $H_0: \mu_1 - \mu_2 = 0$
$\alpha = .05$
$1 - \beta = .95$
$d = 0.8$

d. $H_0: \mu_1 - \mu_2 \geq 0$
$\alpha = .05$
$1 - \beta = .80$
$d = 0.5$
$\rho = .6$

e. $H_0: \mu_1 - \mu_2 = 0$
$\alpha = .01$
$1 - \beta = .90$
$d = 0.2$
$\rho = .7$

f. $H_0: \mu_1 - \mu_2 = 0$
$\alpha = .05$
$1 - \beta = .95$
$d = 0.8$
$\rho = .5$

19. Terms to remember
   a. Independent samples
   b. Dependent samples
   c. Repeated measures
   d. Participant matching
   e. Group matching
   f. Ex post facto experiment

†12.6 PRINTOUTS FOR THREE MICROCOMPUTER PACKAGES

JMP

JMP was used to compute an independent-samples t statistic for the mirror-tracing data in Table 12.4-1. After the data were entered in the data table shown in Figure 12.6-1, the selection of the **Analyze** command in the menu bar followed by the pull-down command **Fit Y by X** produced Figure 12.6-2. The **Analysis** and **Display** boxes, ▶, at the bottom of the figure, provide access to a variety of op-

† This and similarly marked sections can be omitted without loss of continuity.

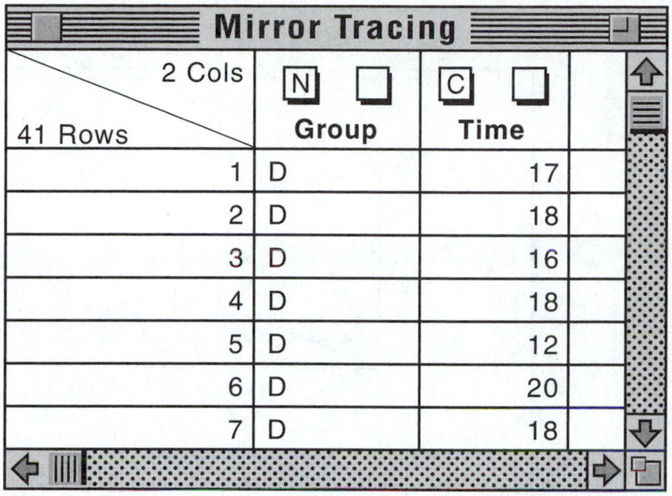

Mirror Tracing

2 Cols / 41 Rows	N Group	C Time
1	D	17
2	D	18
3	D	16
4	D	18
5	D	12
6	D	20
7	D	18

Figure 12.6-1. **JMP data table for the mirror-tracing data in table 12.4-1. To conserve space, only the first seven of the 40 scores are shown. Column 2 is a grouping (independent) variable in which the letters D and M are used to identify, respectively, the distributed and massed practice conditions. Column 3 contains the dependent variable, time required to trace the star pattern on three consective trials. The first 20 scores are for the distributed practice condition. The last 20 scores are for the massed practice condition.**

tions. The **Analysis** box was used to select the **Means, Anova/t-Test** option. After selecting this option, diamonds appeared on the figure along with new displays. The relevant displays for the independent-samples *t* test are shown in Figure 12.6-3.

SPSS

SPSS was used to compute an independent-samples *t* statistic and 100(1 − .05)% = 95% confidence interval for the mirror-tracing data in Table 12.4-1. The data were entered in a data table like that in Figure 12.6-4. The selection of the **Statistics** command in the menu bar followed by the pull-down command called **Compare Means** and the selection of **Independent-Samples T Test . . .** brought up a dialog box in which the letters *D* for distributed practice and *M* for massed practice were identified as the values of the grouping variable. The output is shown in Figure 12.6-5. The SPSS output provides two *t* statistics—one

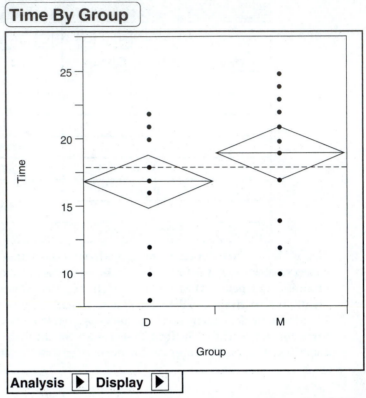

Figure 12.6-2. **The dots in the JMP figure represent score values for the distributed (D) and massed (M) practice conditions. The horizontal lines in the diamonds denote the means of the two conditions. The top and bottom of the diamonds represent two-sided, upper and lower boundaries, respectively, of $100(1 - .05)\% = 95\%$ confidence intervals. A variety of analysis and display options including tests of the assumption that the population variances are equal can be obtained by clicking on the Analysis and Display boxes, ▶.**

appropriate for the case in which the population variances can be assumed to be equal and the other for the case in which they cannot be assumed to be equal. Which statistic should one use? SPSS provides some assistance here in the form of Levene's F test of the hypothesis that the population variances are equal, $H_0 : \sigma_1^2 = \sigma_2^2$.

When a test is used to decide whether an assumption such as equality of variances is tenable, the test is referred to as a **preliminary test** on the model.

Means for Oneway Anova			
Level	Number	Mean	Std Error
D	20	17.0000	0.97062
M	20	19.0000	0.97062
Std Error uses a pooled estimate of error variance			

t-Test		
t-Test	DF	Prob>ltl
1.45701923	38	0.1533
Assuming equal variances		

Figure 12.6-3. **The JMP output on the left of the figure gives means and standard errors, $\hat{\sigma}_{\overline{X}} = \hat{\sigma}_{Pooled}/\sqrt{n}$, for the mirror-tracing data in Table 12.4-1. The acronym ᴀɴoᴠa stands for *analysis of variance,* a procedure discussed in Chapters 14 and 15 for determining if two or more population means are unequal. A nondirectional, independent-samples *t* test is shown on the right. An approximate *t* test based on separate (unpooled) variances also can be obtained if the assumption of equality of population variances is not tenable. A one-tailed *p*-value can be obtained by dividing the observed *p*-value by 2, for example, $p = .1533/2 = .077$.**

untitled data		
40:time		17
	group	time
1	D	17.00
2	D	18.00
3	D	16.00
4	D	18.00
5	D	12.00
6	D	20.00
7	D	18.00

Figure 12.6-4. **SPSS data table for the mirror-tracing data in Table 12.4-1. To conserve space, only the first seven of the 40 scores are shown. Column 1 is a grouping (independent) variable in which the letters D and M are used to identify, respectively, the distributed and massed practice conditions. The dependent variable, reaction time, is shown in column 2.**

t-tests for Independent Samples of GROUP				
Variable	Number of Cases	Mean	SD	SE of Mean
TIME				
GROUP D	20	17.0000	3.798	.849
GROUP M	20	19.0000	4.823	1.078

Mean Difference = −2.0000

Levene's Test for Equality of Variances: F = 1.560 P = .219

t-test for Equality of Means Variances	t-value	df	2- Tail Sig	SE of Diff	95% CI for Diff
Equal	−1.46	38	.153	1.373	(−4.779, .779)
Unequal	−1.46	36.02	.154	1.373	(−4.784, .784)

Figure 12.6-5. **The SPSS output for the mirror-tracing data in Table 12.4-1 provides means, standard deviations, and standard errors for the distributed (D) and massed (M) practice conditions. A test of the assumption that the population variances for the two practice conditions are equal is provided by Levene's *F* test. Because the assumption of equality of population variances is not rejected (see the text for the α level), the *t* test with equal variances, $t(38) = -1.46, p = .153$, should be used. A one-tailed *p*-value can be obtained by dividing the observed *p*-value by 2, for example, $p = .153/2 = .077$. A two-sided 95% confidence interval for the difference between the population means is $-4.779 < \mu_1 - \mu_2 < 0.779$.**

For such tests, it is customary to adopt a low level of significance, for example, α equal to .15 or .20. The adoption of a low level of significance increases the probability of rejecting a false null hypothesis. The *p*-value of the *F* test in Figure 12.6-5 is .219. Hence there is no reason for believing that the population variances are not equal. Thus, the *t* statistic for equal variance should be used.

SYSTAT

SYSTAT was used to compute an independent-samples *t* statistic for the mirror-tracing data in Table 12.4-1. To obtain the *t* statistic, two variables were defined in the data table shown in Figure 12.6-6: GROUP$ and TIME. The $ sign after the word GROUP indicates that this is a character variable. The two values of the character variable are *D* for distributed practice and *M* for massed practice. The output in Figure 12.6-7 was obtained by selecting the **Stats** command in the menu bar followed by the pull-down command called **Stats** and selecting **t test . . .** . These selections produced a dialog box in which the variables GROUP$ and TIME were selected

SYSTAT Data Editor		
	GROUP$	TIME
1	D	17.000
2	D	18.000
3	D	16.000
4	D	18.000
5	D	12.000
6	D	20.000
7	D	18.000

Figure 12.6-6. **SYSTAT data table for the mirror-tracing data in Table 12.4-1. To conserve space, only the first seven of the 40 scores are shown. The $ sign after the word GROUP indicates that this is a character variable. The two values of the character variable are *D* for distributed practice and *M* for massed practice.**

INDEPENDENT SAMPLES T-TEST ON	TIME	GROUPED BY	GROUP$

GROUP	N	MEAN	SD
D	20	17.0000	3.7975
M	20	19.0000	4.8232

SEPARATE VARIANCES T =	−1.4570 DF =	36.0 PROB =	0.1538
POOLED VARIANCES T =	−1.4570 DF =	38 PROB =	0.1533

Figure 12.6-7. **The SYSTAT output gives means, standard deviations, and nondirectional, independent-samples *t* tests for the mirror-tracing data in Table 12.4-1. The pooled variances *t* should be used if it is reasonable to believe that the population variances are equal. If this assumption is not tenable, the separate variances *t* should be used. A one-tailed *p*-value can be obtained by dividing the observed *p*-value by 2, for example, $p = .1533/2 = .077$.**

and the **Independent** option button was checked. SYSTAT provides nondirectional *t* statistics for the case in which the population variances are assumed to be equal and for the case in which the variances are not assumed to be equal.

12.7 SUMMARY

Two-sample z and t null hypothesis significance tests and confidence intervals for means are described in this chapter. The tests are presented within the now-familiar five-step hypothesis testing format.

TABLE 12.7-1.   Summary of Two-Sample Test Statistics

Chapter Section	Statistical Hypotheses	Test Statistic	Assumptions
12.2	$H_0: \mu_1 - \mu_2 = \delta_0$ $H_1: \mu_1 - \mu_2 \neq \delta_0$	$z = \dfrac{(\overline{X}_1 - \overline{X}_2) - \delta_0}{\sqrt{\sigma_1^2/n_1 + \sigma_2^2/n_2}}$	1. Random sampling or random assignment 2. Normality or large samples 3. Population variances are known but not necessarily equal. 4. Independent samples
12.4	$H_0: \mu_1 - \mu_2 = \delta_0$ $H_1: \mu_1 - \mu_2 \neq \delta_0$	$t = \dfrac{(\overline{X}_1 - \overline{X}_2) - \delta_0}{\sqrt{\hat{\sigma}_{Pooled}^2 \, (1/n_1 + 1/n_2)}}$ $\nu = n_1 + n_2 - 2$	1. Random sampling or random assignment 2. Normality 3. Population variances are unknown but assumed equal. 4. Independent samples
12.5	$H_0: \mu_1 - \mu_2 = \delta_0$ $H_1: \mu_1 - \mu_2 \neq \delta_0$	$z = \dfrac{(\overline{X}_1 - \overline{X}_2) - \delta_0}{\sqrt{\sigma_{\overline{X}_1}^2 + \sigma_{\overline{X}_2}^2 - 2\rho_{12}\sigma_{\overline{X}_1}\sigma_{\overline{X}_2}}}$	1. Random sampling or random assignment 2. Normality or large samples 3. Population variances and correlation are known. Variances are not necessarily equal. 4. Dependent samples
12.5	$H_0: \mu_1 - \mu_2 = \delta_0$ $H_1: \mu_1 - \mu_2 \neq \delta_0$	$t = \dfrac{\Sigma D_i/n}{\dfrac{\sqrt{\dfrac{\Sigma D_i^2 - (\Sigma D_i)^2/n}{n}}}{\sqrt{n-1}}}$ $\nu = n - 1$	1. Random sampling or random assignment 2. Normality 3. Population variances and correlation are unknown. 4. Dependent samples

Two important topics related to the design of experiments also are discussed. The first concerns the relative merits of two randomization strategies—random sampling of elements from two populations versus random assignment of elements to the experimental and control conditions. A researcher's research objectives determine whether one or the other procedure is sufficient or whether both procedures are required. Remember that an experiment should contain some randomization procedure to justify using statistical inference.

The other topic related to the design of experiments concerns the use of independent samples versus dependent samples. It is to a researcher's advantage to use dependent samples whenever the nature of the independent variable permits it. Matching participants on some variable that correlates positively with the dependent variable or observing the same participants under both the experimental and control conditions results in a more powerful test of a false null hypothesis than using independent samples. However, the use of group matching instead of individual matching is not recommended because the presumed refinement cannot be taken into account in the statistical analysis. This suggests an important general principle—the sampling, randomization, and control procedures used in an experiment must be reflected in the statistical analysis and interpretation.

The test statistics and confidence intervals that we have described in this chapter are summarized in Tables 12.7-1 and 12.7-2, respectively. As shown in the tables, the assumptions of the test statistics and analogous confidence intervals are the same.

TABLE 12.7-2.   Summary of Two-Sample Confidence Intervals

Chapter Section	*Parameters*	*Confidence Interval*	*Assumptions*
12.4	$\mu_1 - \mu_2$	$(\overline{X}_1 - \overline{X}_2) - t_{\alpha/2,v}\,\hat{\sigma}_{\overline{X}_1-\overline{X}_2}$ $< \mu_1 - \mu_2 < (\overline{X}_1 - \overline{X}_2) + t_{\alpha/2,v}\,\hat{\sigma}_{\overline{X}_1-\overline{X}_2}$ where $\hat{\sigma}_{\overline{X}_1-\overline{X}_2} = \sqrt{\hat{\sigma}_{Pooled}^2\,(1/n_1 + 1/n_2)}$	1. Random sampling or random assignment 2. Normality 3. Population variances are unknown but assumed equal. 4. Independent sample
12.5	$\mu_1 - \mu_2$	$\overline{X}_D - t_{\alpha/2,v}\,\hat{\sigma}_{\overline{X}_D}$ $< \mu_1 - \mu_2 < \overline{X}_D + t_{\alpha/2,v}\,\hat{\sigma}_{\overline{X}_D}$ where $\overline{X}_D = \sum_{i=1}^{n}D_i/n$ $\hat{\sigma}_{\overline{X}_D} = \dfrac{\sqrt{\dfrac{\sum D_i^2 - (\sum D_i)^2/n}{n}}}{\sqrt{n-1}}$	1. Random sampling or Random assignment 2. Normality 3. Population variances and correlation are unknown. 4. Dependence between samples

REVIEW EXERCISES FOR CHAPTER 12

1. Under what conditions does the sampling distribution of $z = [(\overline{X}_1 - \overline{X}_2) - \delta_0]/\sigma_{\overline{X}_1 - \overline{X}_2}$ approximate the standard normal distribution?

2. A researcher is interested in testing the hypothesis that college freshmen who are on probation have lower academic aptitude scores than those not on probation. Random samples of $n_1 = 50$ probationers and $n_2 = 50$ nonprobationers are obtained from the respective populations. The populations are known to be normally distributed with $\sigma_1 = 15$ and $\sigma_2 = 15$. List the five steps you would follow in testing the null hypothesis and state the decision rule. Let $\alpha = .05$.

3. (a) Suppose that in Exercise 2, $\overline{X}_1 = 112$, $\overline{X}_2 = 116$, and α has been set at .05. Compute the test statistic and make a decision. (b) What is the *p*-value of the test statistic?

4. Discuss the statement "The absolute magnitude of the *z* test statistic is indicative of the importance or practical significance of the difference between two sample means."

5. A researcher in Conception, Iowa, wished to determine whether there is a relationship between children's IQs and their mothers' ages when they were born. Using school records, a list was compiled of 10-year-olds whose mothers were over 35 at parturition, and a second list was compiled of 10-year-olds whose mothers were 20 or under at parturition. The researcher randomly sampled 50 children from each list and administered the Stanford-Binet intelligence test to them. The IQs were found to be considerably higher for the children of older mothers, and the difference was significant beyond the .001 level. The researcher concluded that a woman should postpone childbearing until later in life to ensure a high IQ for her offspring. (a) Comment on the appropriateness of the researcher's conclusion. (b) List some alternative explanations for the observed difference in IQs.

6. a. In Exercise 5, which sampling strategy was used?
   b. Would this strategy enable the researcher to establish a causal relationship between the IQs of children and the ages of their mothers at parturition?

7. In Exercise 5, what does the fact that the test statistic was significant at the .001 level tell you about the magnitude of the difference between the population means?

8. What are the advantages and disadvantages of random sampling and random assignment?

9. For each of the following research topics, indicate the research strategy that seems most appropriate. Justify your choice.
   a. Effects of two levels of feedback in acquiring a complex motor skill

    b. Classical music preferences of teenage boys and girls

    c. Relationship between freshmen grades and size of high school graduation class

    d. Effects of 12 and 24 hours of food deprivation on the problem solving of chimpanzees

10. Discuss the meaning of the following statement:

$t = (\bar{X}_1 - \bar{X}_2)/\sqrt{\hat{\sigma}^2_{Pooled}(1/n_1 + 1/n_2)}$ is the ratio of two random variables, but $z = (\bar{X}_1 - \bar{X}_2)/\sqrt{\sigma^2_1/n_1 + \sigma^2_2/n_2}$ is the ratio of a random variable to a constant.

11. A college dean believed that car ownership among students leads to lower grades. To test this hypothesis, she obtained a random sample of student car owners and non-owners and looked up their grades. Let $\alpha = .05$.

Grade Point Averages

Students Owning Cars			Students Not Owning Cars		
2.6	2.5	2.4	2.7	2.9	3.0
2.4	2.6	2.5	2.9	2.5	2.9
2.9	2.8	2.8	2.6	3.1	2.7
2.6	2.7	2.6	2.8	2.8	3.2
2.7	3.0	2.5	3.0	2.9	2.9
2.2	2.3	2.6	2.8	3.0	3.0

    a. Construct box plots for car owners and non-owners and stack the plots one above the other. Do the data contain outliers? Do the sample distributions appear to be relatively symmetrical?

    b. Compute a t test statistic and make a decision about the researcher's hypothesis. Let $\alpha = .05$.

    c. What is the p-value of the t statistic?

    d. Compute a measure of effect size.

    e. Use Appendix Table D.9 to determine whether the sample size is adequate to detect a large size effect if a power of .80 is desired. What is the minimum number of subjects that is required?

    f. Construct a $100(1 - .05)\% = 95\%$ confidence interval for $\mu_1 - \mu_2$; assume that $t_{.05,34} = 1.691$. Locate the confidence interval on the real number line.

    g. Specify all null hypotheses that could be rejected.

12. In Exercise 11, the dean decided to prohibit freshmen from bringing cars to campus. (a) Do you think this action was justified by the data? (b) What other kinds of data about car owners and non-owners would be useful in helping the dean arrive at a rational car policy?

13. For children having problems in school, it was hypothesized that the mean IQ of those diagnosed as being depressed would be different from the IQ of those not diagnosed as being depressed. IQ data for 25

children who were referred to an educational diagnostic center because of problems in school are as follows. (Suggested by Brumback, R. A., Jackson, M. K., & Weinberg, W. A. [1980]. Relation of intelligence to childhood depression in children referred to an educational diagnostic center. *Perceptual and Motor Skills, 50*, 11–17).

Full-Scale IQ		
Depressed Children	*Nondepressed Children*	
117	110	106
102	112	85
104	100	105
89	97	106
84	106	105
128	92	
107	127	
102	121	
98	108	
92	108	

a. Construct box plots for the depressed and nondepressed children and stack the plots one above the other. Do the data contain outliers? Do the sample distributions appear to be relatively symmetrical?

b. Use a t statistic to test the null hypothesis that $\mu_1 - \mu_2 = 0$, where μ_1 and μ_2 denote, respectively, the population means for depressed and nondepressed children. Let $\alpha = .05$. What decision should the researcher make?

c. What is the p-value of the t statistic?

d. Compute a measure of effect size.

e. Compute a $100(1 - .05)\% = 95\%$ confidence interval for $\mu_1 - \mu_2$. Locate the confidence interval on the real number line.

f. Specify all null hypotheses that could be rejected.

14. Use the table of random numbers in Appendix D to draw random samples without replacement of 25 men and 25 women from the Student Database in Appendix E.

a. List the Participant Number, Gender, and Math Test score for each person in your sample. For each gender, construct a box plot and stack the plots one above the other. Do the data contain outliers? Do the sample distributions appear to be relatively symmetrical?

b. Test the null hypothesis that $\mu_1 - \mu_2 = 0$, where μ_1 and μ_2 denote, respectively, the population mean of men's and women's Statistics Grade. Let $\alpha = .05$.

c. What is the p-value of the t statistic?

d. Compute a measure of effect size.

e. Use Appendix Table D.9 to determine whether the sample size is adequate to detect a large size effect if a power of .80 is desired. What is the minimum number of subjects that is required?

f. Compute a $100(1 - .05)\% = 95\%$ confidence interval for $\mu_1 - \mu_2$. Locate the confidence interval on the real number line.

g. Specify all null hypotheses that could be rejected.

h. Write a paragraph summarizing your results and conclusions.

15. (a) List three matching variables that you believe could be used to form pairs of participants in a learning experiment using nonsense syllables. (b) Which matching variable do you think would have the highest correlation with number of trials required to learn nonsense syllables?

16. It is well known that increasing room illumination up to some level increases reading speed. A random sample of 14 sixth-grade students read standardized passages under two levels of ambient room illumination: 5 foot-candles and 15 foot-candles. The order in which the conditions were presented was randomized independently for each participant, with the restriction that the conditions were presented first or second equally often. The reading sessions were separated by an interval of 2 hours.

	Reading Speed (Words/Minute)				
Participant	5 Foot-Candles	15 Foot-Candles	Participant	5 Foot-Candles	15 Foot-Candles
1	88	92	8	90	92
2	92	91	9	84	88
3	86	88	10	82	88
4	84	89	11	86	84
5	90	95	12	84	87
6	86	86	13	86	89
7	88	95	14	86	87

a. Construct box plots for the 5- and 15-foot-candle conditions and stack the plots one above the other. Do the data contain outliers? Do the sample distributions appear to be relatively symmetrical?

b. Use a t statistic to test the null hypothesis that $\mu_1 - \mu_2 \leq 0$, where μ_1 and μ_2 denote, respectively, the population means for the 5- and 15-foot-candle conditions. Let $\alpha = .05$. What decision should the researcher make?

c. What is the p-value of the t statistic?

d. Compute a measure of effect size.

e. Use Appendix Table D.9 to determine whether the sample size is adequate to detect a large-size effect for $\alpha = .05$, $1 - \beta = .80$, and $\rho = .60$. What is the minimum number of subjects that is required?

f. Compute a $100(1 - .05)\% = 95\%$ confidence interval for $\mu_1 - \mu_2$. Locate the confidence interval on the real number line.

g. Specify all null hypotheses that could be rejected.

17. The effect of a curriculum designed to develop children's critical viewing attitudes toward television programs was investigated. Eighteen second-grade children participated in the curriculum that dealt with such topics as the portrayal of violence on TV, commercials, stereotypes about gender and race, and the comprehension of magical effects on TV. The curriculum was presented in six 30- to 45-minute lessons and used brief videotape excerpts, class play activities, and homework assignments. A specially developed TV Comprehension Test was administered prior to the introduction of the curriculum and at its conclusion. The following data on the "impossible" characters subtest were obtained. (Suggested by Rapaczynski, Wanda, and Singer, Dorothy G. [1982]. Teaching television: A curriculum for young children. *Journal of Communication, 32* (2), 46–55.)

	Score on "Impossible" Characters Subtest	
Participant	Pretest Score	Posttest Score
1	1	1
2	3	3
3	0	3
4	2	4
5	1	2
6	2	4
7	3	3
8	3	2
9	2	4
10	2	3
11	1	4
12	3	3
13	1	2
14	2	2
15	3	4
16	3	4
17	1	2
18	2	4

a. Construct box plots for the pretest and posttest scores and stack the plots one above the other. Do the data contain outliers? Do the sample distributions appear to be relatively symmetrical?

b. Use a t statistic to test the null hypothesis that $\mu_1 - \mu_2 \geq 0$, where μ_1 and μ_2 denote, respectively, the population means for the pretest and posttest scores. Let $\alpha = .01$. What decision should the researcher make?

c. What is the p-value of the t statistic?

d. Compute a measure of effect size.

e. Use Appendix Table D.9 to determine whether the sample is adequate to detect a large effect for $\alpha = .01$, $1 - \beta = .80$, and $\rho = .40$. What is the minimum number of subjects that is required?

f. Compute a $100(1 - .01)\% = 99\%$ confidence interval for $\mu_1 - \mu_2$. Locate the confidence interval on the real number line.

g. Specify all null hypotheses that could be rejected.

h. For purposes of comparison, compute a t statistic for independent samples. Compare the result with the t statistic for dependent samples. Was the use of repeated measures an effective experimental design strategy?

18. Assume that a t statistic will be used to test the following null hypotheses. For (a), (b), and (c), estimate the total number of participants required; for (d), (e), and (f), estimate the number of pairs of dependent participants required.

   a. H_0: $\mu_1 - \mu_2 \geq 0$
   $\alpha = .05$
   $1 - \beta = .90$
   $d = 0.5$

   b. H_0: $\mu_1 - \mu_2 = 0$
   $\alpha = .01$
   $1 - \beta = .80$
   $d = 0.2$

   c. H_0: $\mu_1 - \mu_2 = 0$
   $\alpha = .05$
   $1 - \beta = .80$
   $d = 0.8$

   d. H_0: $\mu_1 - \mu_2 = 0$
   $\alpha = .05$
   $1 - \beta = .90$
   $d = 0.5$
   $\rho = .6$

   e. H_0: $\mu_1 - \mu_2 = 0$
   $\alpha = .01$
   $1 - \beta = .80$
   $d = 0.2$
   $\rho = .7$

   f. H_0: $\mu_1 - \mu_2 = 0$
   $\alpha = .05$
   $1 - \beta = .80$
   $d = 0.8$
   $\rho = .5$

19. If the correlation between matched samples equals 0, the t test for dependent samples will be less powerful than the t test for independent samples. Explain why this assertion is true.

20. Use the table of random numbers in Appendix Table D.1 to draw random samples without replacement of 25 men and 25 women students from the Student Database in Appendix E. Use the variable of GPA to form 25 man-woman pairs of matched participants. The

GPAs of men and women in a matched pair do not have to be equal, but the GPAs should be similar.

a. List the Participant Number, Gender, and Stat Grade for each matched pair in your sample. For each gender, construct a box plot and stack the plots one above the other. Do the data contain outliers? Do the sample distributions appear to be relatively symmetrical?

b. Test the null hypothesis that $\mu_1 - \mu_2 = 0$, where μ_1 and μ_2 denote, respectively, the population mean of men's and women's Stat Grade. Let $\alpha = .05$.

c. What is the p-value of the t statistic?

d. Compute a measure of effect size.

e. Use Appendix Table D.9 to determine whether the sample size is adequate to detect a large-size effect if $\rho = .70$ and a power of .80 is desired. What is the minimum number of subjects that is required?

f. Compute a $100(1 - .05)\% = 95\%$ confidence interval for $\mu_1 - \mu_2$. Locate the confidence interval on the real number line. Specify all null hypotheses that could be rejected.

g. Write a paragraph summarizing your results and conclusions.

h. If you did Exercise 13 in Section 12.4, compare the t statistic for independent samples with the t statistic for dependent samples. Was GPA an effective matching variable? Compute the correlation between Stat Grade and GPA. Does the correlation shed any light on why the use of the dependent samples t statistic was or was not an effective research strategy?

21. Use the table of random numbers in Appendix Table D.1 to draw random samples without replacement of 30 men and 30 women students from the Student Database in Appendix E. Use the variable of GPA to form 30 man-woman pairs of matched participants. The GPAs of men and women in a matched pair do not have to be equal, but the GPAs should be similar.

a. List the Participant Number, Gender, and Number of Math Courses for each matched pair in your sample. For each gender, construct a box plot and stack the plots one above the other. Do the data contain outliers? Do the sample distributions appear to be relatively symmetrical?

b. Test the null hypothesis that $\mu_1 - \mu_2 = 0$, where μ_1 and μ_2 denote, respectively, the population mean of men's and women's Number of Math Courses. Let $\alpha = .05$.

c. What is the p-value of the t statistic?

d. Compute a measure of effect size.

e. Use Appendix Table D.9 to determine whether the sample size is adequate to detect a large-size effect if $\rho = .40$ and a power of .80

is desired. What is the minimum number of subjects that is required?

f. Compute a $100(1 - .05)\% = 95\%$ confidence interval for $\mu_1 - \mu_2$. Locate the confidence interval on the real number line. Specify all null hypotheses that could be rejected.

g. Write a paragraph summarizing your results and conclusions.

h. Analyze the data using a t statistic for independent samples. Compare the results with the t statistic for dependent samples. Was GPA an effective matching variable? Compute the correlation between Number of Math Courses and GPA. Does the correlation shed any light on why the use of the dependent samples t statistic was or was not an effective research strategy?

22. Why should group matching be avoided?

Chapter 13

Statistical Inference: Other Two-Sample Test Statistics

13.1 TWO-SAMPLE *F* TEST AND CONFIDENCE INTERVAL FOR VARIANCES USING INDEPENDENT SAMPLES

F Test for Two Variances (Independent Samples)

Frequently, a researcher's interest focuses on whether two populations differ in dispersion. For example, a researcher might want to know whether placing disadvantaged children in a contingency management classroom results in less variability in their English-achievement scores than does placing them in a traditional classroom. Or the researcher might want to test one of the assumptions of the *t* test for independent samples—that two unknown population variances are equal.[1]

An *F* statistic for testing the null hypothesis

$$H_0: \sigma_1^2 = \sigma_2^2$$

$$H_1: \sigma_1^2 \neq \sigma_2^2$$

is

$$F = \frac{\hat{\sigma}_1^2}{\hat{\sigma}_2^2},$$

where $\hat{\sigma}_1^2$ and $\hat{\sigma}_2^2$ are unbiased estimators of the population variances.[2] The degrees of freedom for the numerator and denominator are, respectively, $\nu_1 = n_1 - 1$ and $\nu_2 = n_2 - 1$.

The sampling distribution of the *F* statistic was derived by R. A. Fisher in 1924 and given the name *F* in his honor by G. W. Snedecor. The *F* distribution, like the *t* and chi-square distributions, is actually a family of distributions whose shape is dependent on its degrees of freedom. The *F* distribution is positively skewed, as we will see in the next section. The shape of the *F* distribution approaches the normal distribution for very large values of ν_1 and ν_2. Because *F* is a ratio of nonnegative numbers, it can take values only from 0 to ∞; *F* values around 1 are expected if the null hypothesis that $\sigma_1^2 = \sigma_2^2$ is true. The assumptions associated with using the *F*

---

[1] Some books recommend always testing the assumption of equality of variances before performing a *t* test for $\mu_1 - \mu_2 = \delta_0$. If this advice is followed, it should be noted that the *t* test is robust with respect to violation of the assumption of normalcy. However, the *F* test for $\sigma_1^2 = \sigma_2^2$ described in this section is almost as sensitive to nonnormality as it is to nonequality of variances. Hence, a researcher may be dissuaded from using a *t* test when it is actually appropriate.

[2] This statistic is based on the definition of *F* as the ratio of two independent chi-square random variables, each divided by its degrees of freedom: $F = \chi_{\nu_1}^2/\nu_1 / \chi_{\nu_2}^2/\nu_2$. According to Section 11.3, $\chi_{\nu_1}^2 = \nu_1 \hat{\sigma}_1^2/\sigma_1^2$ and $\chi_{\nu_2}^2 = \nu_2 \hat{\sigma}_2^2/\sigma_2^2$. Hence,

$$F = (\hat{\sigma}_1^2/\sigma_1^2)/(\hat{\sigma}_2^2/\sigma_2^2) = \sigma_2^2 \hat{\sigma}_1^2/\sigma_1^2 \hat{\sigma}_2^2.$$

If the null hypothesis that σ_1^2 is equal to σ_2^2 is true, then $F = \hat{\sigma}_1^2/\hat{\sigma}_2^2$.

statistic to test this null hypothesis are that (1) the population distributions of X_1 and X_2 are independent and normal, (2) the two collections of X's are random samples from the populations of interest, and (3) the population variances are equal, which is the null hypothesis that the researcher hopes to reject. The F test, unlike the t test, is not robust with respect to violation of the normality assumption. Hence, unless the assumption is fulfilled, the probability of making a type I error will not equal the preselected value of α.

The critical value of F that cuts off the upper α region of the sampling distribution for ν_1 and ν_2 degrees of freedom is given in Appendix Table D.5 and is denoted by $F_{\alpha;\nu_1,\nu_2}$. To use the table, we locate the column corresponding to the numerator degrees of freedom (ν_1) along the top of the table and the row corresponding to the denominator degrees of freedom (ν_2) along the side. The column-row intersection gives the critical values of F. The critical value that cuts off the lower α region is denoted by $F_{1-\alpha;\nu_1,\nu_2}$. These values are not given in the table, but they can be determined from $F_{\alpha;\nu_2,\nu_1}$ because

$$F_{1-\alpha;\nu_1,\nu_2} = \frac{1}{F_{\alpha;\nu_2,\nu_1}}.$$

That is, the value of F in the lower region of the F distribution can be found by computing the reciprocal of the corresponding value in the upper region, with degrees of freedom for numerator and denominator reversed. An example illustrating the computation of $F_{1-\alpha;\nu_1,\nu_2}$ is given in the next section.

In testing the one-sided null hypothesis

$$H_0: \sigma_1^2 \leq \sigma_2^2$$
$$H_1: \sigma_1^2 > \sigma_2^2,$$

the hypothesis is rejected if F is greater than or equal to $F_{\alpha;\nu_1,\nu_2}$. For

$$H_0: \sigma_1^2 \geq \sigma_2^2$$
$$H_1: \sigma_1^2 < \sigma_2^2,$$

the null hypothesis is rejected if F is less than or equal to $F_{1-\alpha;\nu_1,\nu_2}$. Consider next the two-sided null hypothesis

$$H_0: \sigma_1^2 = \sigma_2^2$$
$$H_1: \sigma_1^2 \neq \sigma_2^2$$

in which α is divided equally between the two tails of the F distribution. The critical values that cut off the upper and lower $\alpha/2$ regions are denoted by $F_{\alpha/2;\nu_1,\nu_2}$ and $F_{1-\alpha/2;\nu_1,\nu_2}$, respectively. For these critical values, the null hypothesis is rejected if F is greater than or equal to $F_{\alpha/2;\nu_1,\nu_2}$ or less than or equal to $F_{1-\alpha/2;\nu_1,\nu_2}$. A researcher can avoid having to compute the critical values in the lower tail, $F_{\alpha/2;\nu_1,\nu_2}$ and $F_{1-\alpha/2;\nu_1,\nu_2}$, by always placing the larger variance in the numerator of $F = \hat{\sigma}_1^2/\hat{\sigma}_2^2$. This is illustrated for $F_{1-\alpha;\nu_1,\nu_2}$ at the end of the following computational example.

Computational Example for *F* Test for Two Variances (Independent Samples)

Suppose that 46 disadvantaged children were randomly assigned to contingency management and traditional classrooms: 25 children were placed in the contingency management classroom and 21 in the traditional classroom. At the end of the school year, an English-achievement test was administered to the two samples. The researcher believed that the children in the contingency management classroom would be more homogeneous in English achievement than the children in the traditional classroom. The steps to be followed in testing the null hypothesis are as follows:

Step 1. State the statistical hypotheses:

$H_0: \sigma_1^2 \geq \sigma_2^2$
$H_1: \sigma_1^2 < \sigma_2^2$,
where σ_1^2 and σ_2^2 denote the population variances, respectively, for the contingency management and traditional classrooms.

Step 2. Specify the test statistic:

$F = \dfrac{\hat{\sigma}_1^2}{\hat{\sigma}_2^2}$ because we want to test $\sigma_1^2 \geq \sigma_2^2$, the samples are random and independent, and we assume the populations are approximately normal.

Step 3. Specify the sample sizes: specify the sampling distribution:

$n_1 = 25$ and $n_2 = 21$; F distribution, because the X_1 and X_2 populations are independent and approximately normal.

Step 4. Specify the significance level:

$\alpha = .05$.

Step 5. Obtain random samples of size n_1 and n_2, compute F, and make a decision.

Decision rule:

Reject the null hypothesis if F falls in the lower .05 portion of the sampling distribution of F; otherwise, don't reject the null hypothesis. If the null hypothesis is rejected, conclude that the population dispersion is smaller for children in the contingency management classroom than for those in the traditional classroom; if the null hypothesis is not rejected, do not draw this conclusion.

Assume that unbiased estimates of the population variances are $\hat{\sigma}_1^2 = 64$ and $\hat{\sigma}_2^2 = 196$, where $\hat{\sigma}_1^2$ and $\hat{\sigma}_2^2$ are computed from

$$\hat{\sigma}^2 = \frac{\sum X_i^2 - \dfrac{(\sum X_i)^2}{n}}{n - 1}.$$

The *F* test statistic is

$$F = \frac{\hat{\sigma}_1^2}{\hat{\sigma}_2^2} = \frac{64}{196} = 0.33.$$

Because the critical region is in the lower tail of the sampling distribution, we need to know the value of *F* that cuts off the lower .05 region—that is, $F_{1-.05;24,20}$. This value can be determined from the *F* table by means of the relation $F_{1-.05;24,20} = 1/F_{.05;20,24}$. According to Appendix Table D.5, $F_{.05;20,24} = 2.03$ cuts off the upper .05 region of the sampling distribution. Thus, $F_{1-.05;24,20} = 1/2.03 = 0.49$. The critical region for rejecting the null hypothesis is shown in Figure 13.1-1. Because the computed $F(24, 20) = 0.33$ is less than $F_{1-.05;24,20} = 0.49$, the null hypothesis is rejected, and the researcher concludes that placing disadvantaged children in a contingency management classroom results in smaller variance in English-achievement scores than placing them in a traditional classroom.

We could have avoided having to compute $F_{1-.05;24,20}$, the critical value in the lower region of the *F* sampling distribution, by placing the larger variance estimate ($\hat{\sigma}_2^2 = 196$) in the numerator of the *F* statistic and determining whether *F* is greater than or equal to $F_{\alpha;\nu_2,\nu_1}$, where ν_2 and ν_1 now denote the *F* numerator and denominator degrees of freedom, respectively. For this case

$$F = \frac{\hat{\sigma}_2^2}{\hat{\sigma}_1^2} = \frac{196}{64} = 3.06.$$

The critical value of *F* is $F_{.05;20,24} = 2.03$. The one-sided null hypothesis can be rejected because $F(20, 24) = 3.06$ is greater than $F_{.05;20,24} = 2.03$ and the relative size of $\hat{\sigma}_1^2$ and $\hat{\sigma}_2^2$ is consistent with the alternative hypothesis; that is, $\hat{\sigma}_1^2$ is less than $\hat{\sigma}_2^2$ as specified in the alternative hypothesis.

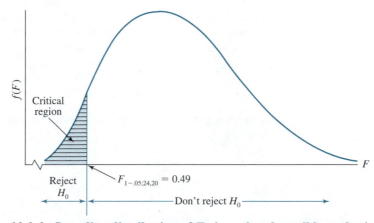

Figure 13.1-1. **Sampling distribution of *F* given that the null hypothesis is true. Since the observed *F* = .33 falls in the critical region, the null hypothesis is rejected.**

Confidence Interval for Two Variances (Independent Samples)

Let $\hat{\sigma}_1^2$ and $\hat{\sigma}_2^2$ be sample variances from independent, normal populations. We can construct a confidence interval for the ratio σ_1^2/σ_2^2 by using the F statistic defined in footnote 2.

A two-sided $100(1 - \alpha)\%$ confidence interval for σ_1^2/σ_2^2 for independent samples is

$$\frac{\hat{\sigma}_1^2}{\hat{\sigma}_2^2} \frac{1}{F_{\alpha/2;\nu_1,\nu_2}} < \frac{\sigma_1^2}{\sigma_2^2} < \frac{\hat{\sigma}_1^2}{\hat{\sigma}_2^2} F_{\alpha/2;\nu_2,\nu_1},$$

where $F_{\alpha/2;\nu_1,\nu_2}$ and $F_{\alpha/2;\nu_2,\nu_1}$ are the values of F that cut off the upper $\alpha/2$ region of the sampling distribution of F for $\nu_1 = n_1 - 1$ and $\nu_2 = n_2 - 1$. To find the critical value of $F_{\alpha/2;\nu_2,\nu_1}$ in Appendix Table D.5, the roles of ν_1 and ν_2 are reversed: ν_2 is the numerator degrees of freedom, and ν_1 is the denominator degrees of freedom.

Upper and lower one-sided $100(1 - \alpha)\%$ confidence intervals for σ_1^2/σ_2^2 are, respectively,

$$\frac{\sigma_1^2}{\sigma_2^2} < \frac{\hat{\sigma}_1^2}{\hat{\sigma}_2^2} F_{\alpha;\nu_2,\nu_1} \quad \text{and} \quad \frac{\hat{\sigma}_1^2}{\hat{\sigma}_2^2} F_{\alpha;\nu_1,\nu_2} < \frac{\sigma_1^2}{\sigma_2^2}.$$

Computational Example of Confidence Interval for Two Variances (Independent Samples)

We will illustrate the computation of a one-sided confidence interval using the English-achievement test data of the 46 children who were randomly assigned to contingency management and traditional classrooms. The statistical hypotheses were

$$H_0: \sigma_1^2 \geq \sigma_2^2$$
$$H_1: \sigma_1^2 < \sigma_2^2.$$

An analogous one-sided $100(1 - .05)\% = .95$ confidence interval for the data is

$$\frac{\sigma_1^2}{\sigma_2^2} < \frac{\hat{\sigma}_1^2}{\hat{\sigma}_2^2} F_{.05;\nu_2,\nu_1}$$

$$\frac{\sigma_1^2}{\sigma_2^2} < \frac{64}{196} 2.03$$

$$\frac{\sigma_1^2}{\sigma_2^2} < 0.66.$$

This confidence interval corresponds to the colored portion of the real number line as follows:

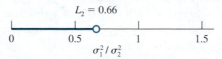

Because the interval doesn't include 1, the researcher can be confident that σ_1^2 is less than σ_2^2. The best guess the researcher can make regarding the ratio σ_1^2/σ_2^2 is that it is equal to $\hat{\sigma}_1^2/\hat{\sigma}_2^2 = 0.33$. The researcher can be 95% confident that the ratio is less than $L_2 = 0.66$.

CHECK YOUR UNDERSTANDING OF SECTION 13.1

1. Can $F = \hat{\sigma}_1^2/\hat{\sigma}_2^2$ be used to test hypotheses of the form H_0: $\sigma_1^2 - \sigma_2^2 = \delta_0$ where $\delta_0 \neq 0$? Explain.
2. In testing the tenability of the assumption $\sigma_1^2 = \sigma_2^2$ prior to testing H_0: $\mu_1 - \mu_2 = \delta_0$, it is common practice to set $\alpha = .15$ or $.20$. What justification for this practice can you offer?
3. Exercise 11 in "Check Your Understanding of Section 12.4" described a study to determine whether interviewers spent more time talking to applicants who were hired than to applicants who were rejected. The data from the study are reproduced in the following table.

Duration of Interview (Minutes)

Hired		Rejected	
30	23	19	17
21	24	18	18
24	26	22	19
25	27	13	22
29	24	15	15
24	22	18	19
23	25	17	17
24	26	20	20
28	23	18	18
25	24	19	17
24	27	23	
19	26	12	
25	25	18	

a. Construct box plots for the hired and rejected applicants and stack the plots one above the other. Do the data contain outliers? Do the sample distributions appear to be relatively symmetrical?

b. Test the null hypothesis that $\sigma_1^2 = \sigma_2^2$ using the statistic $F = \hat{\sigma}_2^2/\hat{\sigma}_1^2$. Let $\alpha = .05$. Assume that $F_{.05/2;22,25} = 2.269$.

c. Compute a $100(1 - .05)\% = 95\%$ confidence interval for σ_2^2/σ_1^2 Assume that $F_{.05/2;25,22} = 2.320$. Locate the confidence interval on the real number line.

d. Is the confidence interval consistent with the null hypothesis significance test? Why?

4. Exercise 12 in "Check Your Understanding of Section 12.4" presented data on the discrimination of speech sounds for infants raised in English- or Spanish-speaking homes. The data from the study are reproduced in the following table.

English-Speaking Home	Spanish-Speaking Home
.0421	.1081
.0941	.0986
.1064	.1566
.0242	.1961
.1331	.1125
.0773	.1942
.0243	.1079
.0815	.1021
.1186	.1583
.0356	.1673
.0728	.1675
.0999	.1856
.0614	.1688
.0479	.1512

a. Construct box plots for English-speaking and Spanish-speaking homes and stack the plots one above the other. Assume that for the English-speaking homes, $Mdn = 0.07285$, $Q_1 = 0.0421$, and $Q_3 = 0.0999$. Assume that for the Spanish-speaking homes, $Mdn = 0.15665$, $Q_1 = 0.1081$, and $Q_3 = 0.1688$. Do the data contain outliers? Do the sample distributions appear to be relatively symmetrical?

b. Test the null hypothesis that $\sigma_1^2 \geq \sigma_2^2$ using the statistic $F = \hat{\sigma}_1^2/\hat{\sigma}_2^2$. Let $\alpha = .05$. Assume that $F_{.05;13,13} = 2.577$.

c. Compute a $100(1 - .05)\% = 95\%$ confidence interval for σ_1^2/σ_2^2. Locate the confidence interval on the real number line.

d. Is the confidence consistent with the null hypothesis significance test? Why?

5. The nicotine content of random samples of two brands of cigarettes, denoted by 1 and 2, was measured. The following data were obtained: $\bar{X}_1 = 18.6$ milligrams, $\bar{X}_2 = 16.1$ milligrams, $\hat{\sigma}_1 = 2.8$, $\hat{\sigma}_2 = 1.9$, $n_1 = 38$, and $n_2 = 35$.

a. Test the null hypothesis that $\sigma_1^2 = \sigma_2^2$ using the statistic $F = \hat{\sigma}_1^2/\hat{\sigma}_2^2$. Let $\alpha = .05$. Assume that $F_{.05/2;37,34} = 1.962$.

b. Compute a $100(1 - .05)\% = 95\%$ confidence interval for σ_1^2/σ_2^2. Assume that $F_{.05/2;34,37} = 1.943$. Locate the confidence interval on the real number line.

c. Is the confidence interval consistent with the null hypothesis significance test? Why?

d. Specify all null hypotheses that could be rejected.

†13.2 TWO-SAMPLE *t* TEST AND CONFIDENCE INTERVAL FOR VARIANCES USING DEPENDENT SAMPLES

t Test for Two Variances (Dependent Samples)

When the variances to be compared arise from dependent samples, for example, participants who are matched or observed on two occasions, the appropriate statistic for testing a null hypothesis about σ_1^2 and σ_2^2 is t rather than F.

The t statistic is

$$t = \frac{\hat{\sigma}_1^2 - \hat{\sigma}_2^2}{\sqrt{[4\hat{\sigma}_1^2\hat{\sigma}_2^2/(n - 2)](1 - r_{12}^2)}}$$

with degrees of freedom equal to $n - 2$, where n is the number of pairs of scores and r_{12} is the Pearson-product moment correlation coefficient.

To illustrate, suppose that 32 freshmen college students enrolled in a psychology course entitled Effective Personal Adjustment took the College Life Adjustment and Stress Survey. The survey is an interactive, computerized inventory designed to assess situation-specific stress, psychological distress, and satisfaction with support from family and friends. The test was administered on the first and last day of class. We will assume that the sample of students enrolled in the course is representative of the population of freshmen at the college. The college administrators want to know, among other things, whether taking the course would affect the population dispersion of scores on the support from family and friends scale. Suppose that the following data for students enrolled in the course were obtained: pretest dispersion $\hat{\sigma}_1^2 = 256$, posttest dispersion $\hat{\sigma}_2^2 = 121$, $r = .60$, and $n = 32$. A test of the null hypothesis

$$H_0: \sigma_1^2 = \sigma_2^2$$
$$H_1: \sigma_1^2 \neq \sigma_2^2$$

---

† This section can be omitted without loss of continuity.

is given by

$$t = \frac{\hat{\sigma}_1^2 - \hat{\sigma}_2^2}{\sqrt{[4\hat{\sigma}_1^2\hat{\sigma}_2^2/(n-2)](1-r_{12}^2)}}$$

$$t = \frac{256 - 121}{\sqrt{[4(256)(121)/(32-2)][1-(.60)^2]}} = \frac{135}{51.4129} = 2.626,$$

with $\nu = 32 - 2 = 30$. According to Appendix Table D.3, a t of 2.042 cuts off the upper .025 region of the sampling distribution, that is, $t_{.05/2, 30} = 2.042$. The computed $t(30) = 2.626$ is greater than $t_{.05/2, 30} = 2.042$. Hence, the null hypothesis is rejected, and the college administrators conclude that the dispersion of freshmen scores on the support scale would be smaller if all freshmen at the college took the psychology course.

Confidence Interval for Two Variances (Dependent Samples)

A two-sided $100(1 - \alpha)\%$ confidence interval for $\sigma_1^2 - \sigma_2^2$ for dependent samples is

$$(\hat{\sigma}_1^2 - \hat{\sigma}_2^2) - t_{\alpha/2,\nu}\sqrt{[4\hat{\sigma}_1^2\hat{\sigma}_2^2/(n-2)](1-r_{12}^2)} < \sigma_1^2 - \sigma_2^2$$
$$< (\hat{\sigma}_1^2 - \hat{\sigma}_2^2) + t_{\alpha/2,\nu}\sqrt{[4\hat{\sigma}_1^2\hat{\sigma}_2^2/(n-2)](1-r_{12}^2)},$$

where $t_{\alpha/2,\nu}$ is the value that cuts off the upper $\alpha/2$ region of the sampling distribution of t for $\nu = n - 2$.

A one-sided $100(1 - \alpha)\%$ confidence interval for $\sigma_1^2 - \sigma_2^2$ is

$$(\hat{\sigma}_1^2 - \hat{\sigma}_2^2) - t_{\alpha,\nu}\sqrt{[4\hat{\sigma}_1^2\hat{\sigma}_2^2/(n-2)](1-r_{12}^2)} < \sigma_1^2 - \sigma_2^2,$$

or

$$\sigma_1^2 - \sigma_2^2 < (\hat{\sigma}_1^2 - \hat{\sigma}_2^2) + t_{\alpha,\nu}\sqrt{[4\hat{\sigma}_1^2\hat{\sigma}_2^2/(n-2)](1-r_{12}^2)},$$

where $t_{\alpha,\nu}$ is the value that cuts off the upper α region of the sampling distribution of t for $\nu = n - 2$.

We will use the data from the psychology class described earlier to illustrate the confidence interval. The college administrator's hypotheses for these data were nondirectional:

$$H_0: \sigma_1^2 = \sigma_2^2$$
$$H_1: \sigma_1^2 \neq \sigma_2^2.$$

An analogous two-sided $100(1 - .05)\% = 95\%$ confidence interval for the difference $\sigma_1^2 - \sigma_2^2$ is

$$(\hat{\sigma}_1^2 - \hat{\sigma}_2^2) - t_{\alpha/2,\nu}\sqrt{\left(\frac{4\hat{\sigma}_1^2\hat{\sigma}_2^2}{n-2}\right)(1-r_{12}^2)} < \sigma_1^2 - \sigma_2^2$$

$$(256 - 121) - 2.042 \sqrt{\left[\frac{4(256)(121)}{32 - 2}\right][1 - (.60)^2]} < \sigma_1^2 - \sigma_2^2$$

$$< (\hat{\sigma}_1^2 - \hat{\sigma}_2^2) + t_{\alpha/2,\nu} \sqrt{\left(\frac{4\hat{\sigma}_1^2\hat{\sigma}_2^2}{n - 2}\right)(1 - r_{12}^2)}$$

$$< (256 - 121) + 2.042 \sqrt{\left[\frac{4(256)(121)}{32 - 2}\right][1 - (.60)^2]}$$

$$135 - 104.9851 < \sigma_1^2 - \sigma_2^2 < 135 + 104.9851$$

$$30.01 < \sigma_1^2 - \sigma_2^2 < 239.99.$$

This 95% confidence interval corresponds to the colored portion of the real number line as follows:

Because the interval doesn't include 0, the researcher can be confident that σ_1^2 is greater than σ_2^2. The best guess the college administrators can make regarding the difference $\sigma_1^2 - \sigma_2^2$ is that it is equal to $\hat{\sigma}_1^2 - \hat{\sigma}_2^2 = 135$. The administrators can be 95% confident that the difference is greater than $L_1 = 30.01$ and less than $L_2 = 239.99$.

CHECK YOUR UNDERSTANDING OF SECTION 13.2

6. Exercise 16 in "Check Your Understanding of Section 12.5" described a study to determine the effect of seeing a film about marijuana on attitudes toward legalization of the drug. The participants' attitudes were measured before and after seeing the film. The data from the study are reproduced in the following table.

Favorableness of Attitude

Participant	Before	After	Participant	Before	After
1	13	16	9	19	20
2	16	18	10	16	18
3	10	12	11	15	18
4	14	18	12	14	15
5	15	18	13	12	12
6	12	15	14	13	17
7	11	12	15	14	16
8	18	20	16	15	17

a. Construct box plots for the before and after attitudes and stack the plots one above the other. Do the data contain outliers? Do the sample distributions appear to be relatively symmetrical?
b. Test the hypothesis that the population variances are equal versus the alternative that they are not equal. Let $\alpha = .05$.
c. Compute a $100(1 - .05)\% = 95\%$ confidence interval for $\sigma_1^2 - \sigma_2^2$. Locate the confidence interval on the real number line.
d. Is the confidence interval consistent with the null hypothesis significance test? Why?

7. Exercise 17 in "Check Your Understanding of Section 12.5" described a study to investigate the impact of a 60-hour workshop on nurses' knowledge of cancer and cancer nursing. The data from the study are reproduced in the following table.

	Knowledge Score	
Participant	Pretest Score	Posttest Score
1	29	35
2	20	41
3	24	33
4	32	41
5	33	39
6	19	20
7	17	29
8	32	42
9	16	36
10	28	37
11	35	36
12	19	27
13	31	50
14	28	33
15	23	23
16	18	35
17	24	34
18	25	30
19	28	39
20	32	45
21	25	36
22	27	29

a. Construct box plots for the pretest and posttest scores and stack the plots one above the other. Do the data contain outliers? Do the sample distributions appear to be relatively symmetrical?
b. Test the hypothesis that $\sigma_1^2 \geq \sigma_2^2$, where σ_1^2 and σ_2^2 denote the pretest and posttest population variances, respectively. Let $\alpha = .05$.

c. Compute a $100(1 - .05)\% = 95\%$ confidence interval for $\sigma_1^2 - \sigma_2^2$. Locate the confidence interval on the real number line.

d. Is the confidence interval consistent with the null hypothesis significance test? Why?

†13.3 TWO-SAMPLE z TEST AND CONFIDENCE INTERVAL FOR PROPORTIONS USING INDEPENDENT SAMPLES

z Test for Two Proportions (Independent Samples)

Many variables in the behavioral sciences, health sciences, and education can be partitioned into two nonoverlapping and exhaustive classes and are qualitative in character, for example, men or women, cigarette smokers or nonsmokers, and pass or fail. In such cases p, the proportion in one class, and $q = 1 - p$, the proportion in the other class, are useful descriptive measures. In Section 11.4 we described a z statistic for testing hypotheses about a single population proportion, p. The procedures described there can be extended to testing any of the following null hypotheses about two independent population proportions, p_1 and p_2.

$$H_0: p_1 = p_2 \qquad H_0: p_1 \leq p_2 \qquad H_0: p_1 \geq p_2$$
$$H_1: p_1 \neq p_2 \qquad H_1: p_1 > p_2 \qquad H_1: p_1 < p_2$$

The z statistic is

$$z = \frac{\hat{p}_1 - \hat{p}_2}{\sqrt{\hat{p}_{Pd}\hat{q}_{Pd}/n_1 + \hat{p}_{Pd}\hat{q}_{Pd}/n_2}}.$$

Here, $\hat{p}_1$ and $\hat{p}_2$ are the sample estimators of the population proportions, n_1 and n_2 are the sizes of the samples used to estimate the population proportions, and $\hat{p}_{Pd}$ and $\hat{q}_{Pd}$ are pooled estimators: $\hat{p}_{Pd} = (n_1\hat{p}_1 + n_2\hat{p}_2)/(n_1 + n_2)$ and $\hat{q}_{Pd} = (n_1\hat{q}_1 + n_2\hat{q}_2)/(n_1 + n_2)$, where $\hat{q}_1$ is equal to $1 - \hat{p}_1$ and $\hat{q}_2$ is equal to $1 - \hat{p}_2$.

The sampling distribution of the z test statistic approaches a standard normal distribution if all the products $n_1\hat{p}_{Pd}$, $n_1\hat{q}_{Pd}$, $n_2\hat{p}_{Pd}$, and $n_2\hat{q}_{Pd}$ are greater than 5. If any of these products is between 5 and 10, it is desirable to apply a correction for continuity. As discussed in Section 11.4, the correction should be applied when the continuous normal distribution is used to estimate probabilities for a discrete distribution and n is small. The correction consists of subtracting the quantity

---

† This section can be omitted without loss of continuity.

$(1/2)(1/n_1 + 1/n_2)$ from the absolute value of the z numerator, that is, $|\hat{p}_1 - \hat{p}_2| - (1/2)(1/n_1 + 1/n_2)$.

z Test for Two Proportions, Where $\delta_0 \neq 0$ (Independent Samples)

On occasion, a researcher might want to test a null hypothesis of the form $p_1 - p_2 = \delta_0$, where δ_0 is not equal to 0. In such cases it is not assumed that the sample proportions $\hat{p}_1$ and $\hat{p}_2$ are estimators of the same population parameter p. Hence, the sample proportions should not be pooled as was done earlier.

The z statistic for testing one of the null hypotheses

$$H_0\text{: } p_1 - p_2 = \delta_0 \qquad H_0\text{: } p_1 - p_2 \leq \delta_0 \qquad H_0\text{: } p_1 - p_2 \geq \delta_0,$$

where δ_0 is not equal to 0, is

$$z = \frac{(\hat{p}_1 - \hat{p}_2) - \delta_0}{\sqrt{\hat{p}_1\hat{q}_1/n_1 + \hat{p}_1\hat{q}_2/n_2}}.$$

The sampling distribution of z approaches a standard normal distribution if all the products $n_1\hat{p}_1$, $n_1\hat{q}_1$, $n_2\hat{p}_2$, and $n_2\hat{q}_2$ are greater than 5. If any of the products is between 5 and 10, it is desirable to apply a correction for continuity. A correction for continuity can be applied to the z statistic by subtracting the quantity $(1/2)(1/n_1 + 1/n_2)$ from the absolute value of the z numerator, that is, $|(\hat{p}_1 - \hat{p}_2) - \delta_0| - (1/2)(1/n_1 + 1/n_2)$.

Confidence Interval for Two Proportions (Independent Samples)

A two-sided $100(1 - \alpha)\%$ confidence interval for $p_1 - p_2$ for independent samples is

$$(\hat{p}_1 - \hat{p}_2) - z_{\alpha/2}\sqrt{\frac{\hat{p}_1\hat{q}_1}{n_1} + \frac{\hat{p}_2\hat{q}_2}{n_2}} < p_1 - p_2$$

$$< (\hat{p}_1 - \hat{p}_2) + z_{\alpha/2}\sqrt{\frac{\hat{p}_1\hat{q}_1}{n_1} + \frac{\hat{p}_2\hat{q}_2}{n_2}},$$

where $z_{\alpha/2}$ is the value that cuts off the upper $\alpha/2$ region of the sampling distribution of z.

A one-sided $100(1 - \alpha)\%$ confidence interval for $p_1 - p_2$ is

$$(\hat{p}_1 - \hat{p}_2) - z_\alpha \sqrt{\frac{\hat{p}_1\hat{q}_1}{n_1} + \frac{\hat{p}_2\hat{q}_2}{n_2}} < p_1 - p_2$$

or

$$p_1 - p_2 < (\hat{p}_1 - \hat{p}_2) + z_\alpha \sqrt{\frac{\hat{p}_1\hat{q}_1}{n_1} + \frac{\hat{p}_2\hat{q}_2}{n_2}},$$

where z_α is the value that cuts off the upper α region of the sampling distribution of z.

This confidence interval, like that for p, is approximate because the standard error of $p_1 - p_2$ depends on a knowledge of the parameters p_1 and p_2. Because p_1 and p_2 are unknown, sample estimates of the parameters must be used in the confidence interval. The use of $\hat{p}_1$ and $\hat{p}_2$ in place of p_1 and p_2 is satisfactory for all practical purposes if $n_1\hat{p}_1$ $n_1\hat{q}_1$, $n_2\hat{p}_2$, and $n_2\hat{q}_2$ are all greater than 5. If any of the products is between 5 and 10, it is desirable to incorporate a correction for continuity in the confidence interval as follows:

$$\left[(\hat{p}_1 - \hat{p}_2) \pm \left(\frac{1}{2}\right)\left(\frac{1}{n_1} + \frac{1}{n_2}\right)\right] - z_{\alpha/2} \sqrt{\frac{\hat{p}_1\hat{q}_1}{n_1} + \frac{\hat{p}_2\hat{q}_2}{n_2}} < p_1 - p_2$$

$$< \left[(\hat{p}_1 - \hat{p}_2) \pm \left(\frac{1}{2}\right)\left(\frac{1}{n_1} + \frac{1}{n_2}\right)\right] + z_{\alpha/2} \sqrt{\frac{\hat{p}_1\hat{q}_1}{n_1} + \frac{\hat{p}_2\hat{q}_2}{n_2}}.$$

You should subtract the correction $\pm (1/2)(1/n_1 + n_2)$ if $\hat{p}_1 - \hat{p}_2$ is positive; add the correction if $\hat{p}_1 - \hat{p}_2$ is negative.

CHECK YOUR UNDERSTANDING OF SECTION 13.3

8. In a 1996 Shuffle Poll of $n_2 = 500$ Americans over 18 years old, 29% said they had smoked pot. In 1986, the figure for a sample of $n_1 = 600$ was 22%.
   a. Test the null hypothesis that $p_1 = p_2$. Let $\alpha = .05$.
   b. Compute a $100(1 - .05)\% = 95\%$ confidence interval for $p_1 = p_2$. Locate the confidence interval on the real number line.
   c. Is the confidence interval consistent with the null hypothesis significance test? Why?
   d. Specify all null hypotheses that could be rejected.
9. In the 1996 survey cited in Exercise 8, 76% of the interviewees opposed legalization of marijuana. The figure in 1986 was 84%.
   a. Test the null hypothesis that $p_1 = p_2$. Let $\alpha = .05$.
   b. Compute a $100(1 - .05)\% = 95\%$ confidence interval for $p_1 = p_2$. Locate the confidence interval on the real number line.

    c. Is the confidence interval consistent with the null hypothesis significance test? Why?

    d. Specify all null hypotheses that could be rejected.

10. According to the 1986 survey cited in Exercise 8, 8% more men than women had tried marijuana. In the 1996 survey, 11% of the $n_1 = 300$ men and 8% of the $n_2 = 200$ women reported that they had smoked pot.

    a. Test the null hypothesis that the difference between the proportion of pot smokers among men and women in 1996 is 8%. Let $\alpha = .05$.

    b. Compute a $100(1 - .05)\% = 95\%$ confidence interval for the difference between the proportion of pot smokers among men and women in 1996. Locate the confidence interval on the real number line.

    c. Is the confidence interval consistent with the null hypothesis significance test? Why?

†13.4 TWO-SAMPLE z TEST AND CONFIDENCE INTERVAL FOR PROPORTIONS USING DEPENDENT SAMPLES

z Test for Two Proportions (Dependent Samples)

If two samples are dependent, a statistic developed by McNemar (1947) should be used to test any of the following null hypotheses:

$$H_0\text{: } p_1 = p_2 \qquad H_0\text{: } p_1 \leq p_2 \qquad H_0\text{: } p_1 \geq p_2$$
$$H_1\text{: } p_1 \neq p_2 \qquad H_1\text{: } p_1 > p_2 \qquad H_1\text{: } p_1 < p_2$$

To test one of these hypotheses, the data are placed into a 2×2 table, as shown.

		Sample 2		
		Category 0	Category 1	
Sample 1	Category 1	a	b	$a + b$
	Category 0	c	d	$c + d$
		$a + c$	$b + d$	n

The cell entry a denotes the number of elements classified in category 1 for sample 1 and in category 0 for sample 2; b denotes the number of elements that is classified

---

† This section can be omitted without loss of continuity.

in category 1 for both samples; and so on. The number of elements in each sample is n.

An estimator of the population proportion of individuals in category 1 for sample 1 is $\hat{p}_1 = (a + b)/n$. Similarly, the proportion in category 1 for sample 2 is $\hat{p}_2 = (b + d)/n$. The difference between the two populations can be expressed either as a proportion, $p_1 - p_2$, or as a frequency, $a - d$. With a little algebra, it can be shown that $n(\hat{p}_1 - \hat{p}_2) = a - d$.

$$\hat{p}_1 - \hat{p}_2 = \frac{a + b}{n} - \frac{b + d}{n} \qquad \text{by definition}$$

$$= \frac{1}{n}(a + b - b - d)$$

$$n(\hat{p}_1 - \hat{p}_2) = a - d.$$

The use of frequencies instead of proportions results in a simpler z test statistic. If the null hypothesis is true, the z test statistic

$$z = \frac{a - d}{\sqrt{a + d}}$$

is approximately distributed as the standard normal distribution, provided that $(a + d) \geq 10$. If $(a + d)$ is between 10 and 20, a correction for continuity should be used. The z statistic with the correction is as follows:

$$z = \frac{|a - d| - 1}{\sqrt{a + d}}$$

Computational Example for z Test for Two Proportions (Dependent Samples)

Suppose that a random sample of 100 students at Thanatos University are polled about whether they approve or disapprove of capital punishment. Following the survey, the students are shown a film depicting the effects of crime and acts of violence on the victims and their families. The 100 students are again polled about capital punishment. It is hypothesized that the proportion of students who approve of capital punishment will be higher after seeing the film than before. The statistical hypotheses are

$$H_0: p_1 \geq p_2$$
$$H_1: p_1 < p_2,$$

where p_1 and p_2 denote, respectively, the before and after population proportions. The data, number of students who approve or disapprove of capital punishment before and after seeing the film, are shown in Table 13.4-1. The z statistic is positive

---

TABLE 13.4-1.   Capital Punishment Data

(i) Data

Sample 2

		Disapprove	Approve	
Sample 1	Approve	$a = 2$	$b = 12$	$a + b = 14$
	Disapprove	$c = 76$	$d = 10$	$c + d = 86$

$a + c = 78 \quad b + d = 22 \qquad n = 100$

(ii) Computation

$$z = \frac{|a - d| - 1}{\sqrt{a + d}} = \frac{|2 - 10| - 1}{\sqrt{2 + 10}} = \frac{7}{3.464} = 2.021$$

$$z_{.05} = 1.645$$

$$\hat{p}_1 = \frac{a + b}{n} = \frac{14}{100} = .14$$

$$\hat{p}_2 = \frac{b + d}{n} = \frac{22}{100} = .22$$

---

because we applied the correction for continuity to the absolute value of the difference, $a - d$. It is apparent that the difference $a - d = -8$ is consistent with the alternative hypothesis. According to Appendix Table D.2, $z_{.05} = 1.645$ cuts off the upper .05 region of the sampling distribution. Because the computed $z = 2.021$ is greater than $z_{.05} = 1.645$, the null hypothesis is rejected. It is concluded that if the population of students were polled, a higher proportion of them would approve of capital punishment after seeing the film than before seeing the film.

Confidence Interval for Two Proportions (Dependent Samples)

A two-sided $100(1 - \alpha)\%$ confidence interval for $p_1 - p_2$ for dependent samples is

$$\frac{a - d}{n} - z_{\alpha/2} \sqrt{\frac{(a + d)(b + c) + 4ad}{n^3}} < p_1 - p_2$$

$$< \frac{a - d}{n} - z_{\alpha/2} \sqrt{\frac{(a + d)(b + c) + 4ad}{n^3}},$$

where a, b, c, and d denote cell frequencies as defined in Table 13.4-1, n is the number of elements in each sample, and $z_{\alpha/2}$ is the value that cuts off the upper $\alpha/2$ region of the sampling distribution of z.

A one-sided $100(1 - \alpha)\%$ confidence interval for $p_1 - p_2$ is

$$\frac{a - d}{n} - z_\alpha \sqrt{\frac{(a + d)(b + c) + 4ad}{n^3}} < p_1 - p_2$$

or

$$p_1 - p_2 < \frac{a - d}{n} + z_\alpha \sqrt{\frac{(a + d)(b + c) + 4ad}{n^3}},$$

where z_α is the value that cuts off the upper α region of the sampling distribution of z.

This confidence interval, like that for the independent samples case, is approximate. The approximation is satisfactory if $(a + d) \geq 10$. If $(a + d)$ is between 10 and 20, it is desirable to apply a correction for continuity. The correction, $\pm(1/n)$, is applied to $(a - d)$ as follows:

$$\frac{(a - d) \pm (1/n)}{n}$$

You should subtract the correction, $\pm(1/n)$, if $(a - d)$ is positive; add the correction if $(a - d)$ is negative.

Computational Example of Confidence Interval for Two Proportions (Dependent Samples)

We will use the experiment on attitudes toward capital punishment of Thanatos University students to illustrate the dependent-samples confidence interval for $p_1 - p_2$. The researcher's hypotheses were

$$H_0: p_1 \geq p_2$$

$$H_1: p_1 < p_2.$$

An analogous one-sided $100(1 - .05)\% = 95\%$ confidence interval is

$$p_1 - p_2 < \frac{(a - d) \pm (1/n)}{n} + z_\alpha \sqrt{\frac{(a + d)(b + c) + 4ad}{n^3}}$$

$$p_1 - p_2 < \frac{(2 - 10) + 1/100}{100} + 1.45 \sqrt{\frac{(2 + 10)(12 + 76) + 4(2)(10)}{(100)^3}}$$

$$p_1 - p_2 < -.015$$

The correction for continuity, $\pm(1/n)$, was added to $(a - d)$ because $(a - d)$ is negative. The 95% confidence interval corresponds to the darkened portion of the real number line as follows:

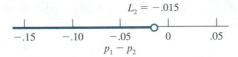

The researcher can be 95% confident that $p_1 - p_2$ is less than $-.015$. Although the difference between p_1 and p_2 could be quite small, it is reasonable to believe that after seeing the film, the population proportion of students who favor capital punishment would be larger than before seeing the film. The best guess the researcher can make regarding the difference between $p_1 - p_2$ is that it is equal to $\hat{p}_1 - \hat{p}_2 = .14 - .22 = -.08$.

CHECK YOUR UNDERSTANDING OF SECTION 13.4

11. Attitudes of a sample of college students toward taking a required course in music appreciation were measured prior to taking the course and after completing the course. The following data were obtained:

		Postcourse Attitude		
		Unfavorable	Favorable	
Precourse	Favorable	13	24	37
Attitude	Unfavorable	19	27	46
		32	51	83

   a. Compute p_1 and p_2, where the subscripts 1 and 2 denote, respectively, the pre- and postcourse attitudes.
   b. Test the null hypothesis that $p_1 = p_2$. Let $\alpha = .05$.
   c. Compute a $100(1 - .01)\% = 95\%$ confidence interval for $p_1 - p_2$. Locate the confidence interval on the real number line.
   d. Is the confidence interval consistent with the null hypothesis significance test? Why?
   e. Specify all null hypotheses that could be rejected.

13.5 SUMMARY

This chapter described null hypothesis significance tests and confidence intervals for two variances and two proportions. The chapter also introduced the important F statistic and its sampling distribution.

TABLE 13.5-1. Summary of Two-Sample Test Statistics

Chapter Section	Statistical Hypotheses	Test Statistic	Assumptions
13.1	$H_0: \sigma_1^2 = \sigma_2^2$ $H_1: \sigma_1^2 \neq \sigma_2^2$	$F = \dfrac{\hat{\sigma}_1^2}{\hat{\sigma}_2^2}$ $\nu_1 = n_1 - 1, \nu_2 = n_2 - 1$	1. Random sampling or random assignment 2. Normality 3. Independent samples
13.2	$H_0: \sigma_1^2 = \sigma_2^2$ $H_1: \sigma_1^2 \neq \sigma_2^2$	$t = \dfrac{\hat{\sigma}_1^2 - \hat{\sigma}_2^2}{\sqrt{[4\hat{\sigma}_1^2\hat{\sigma}_2^2/(n-2)](1 - r_{12}^2)}}$ $\nu = n - 2$	1. Random sampling or random assignment 2. Normality 3. Dependent samples
13.3	$H_0: p_1 = p_2$ $H_1: p_1 \neq p_2$	$z = \dfrac{\hat{p}_1 - \hat{p}_2}{\sqrt{\hat{p}_{Pd}\hat{q}_{Pd}/n_1 + \hat{p}_{Pd}\hat{q}_{Pd}/n_2}}$	1. Random sampling or random assignment 2. Binomial distributions 3. Independent samples 4. $n_1\hat{p}_{Pd} > 5, n_1\hat{q}_{Pd} > 5$ $n_2\hat{p}_{Pd} > 5, n_2\hat{q}_{Pd} > 5$
13.3	$H_0: p_1 - p_2 = \delta_0$ $H_1: p_1 - p_2 \neq \delta_0,$ where $\delta_0 \neq 0$	$z = \dfrac{(\hat{p}_1 - \hat{p}_2) - \delta_0}{\sqrt{\hat{p}_1\hat{q}_1/n_1 + \hat{p}_2\hat{q}_2/n_2}}$	1. Random sampling or random assignment 2. Binomial distributions 3. Independent samples 4. $n_1\hat{p}_1 > 5, n_1\hat{q}_1 > 5$ $n_2\hat{p}_2 > 5, n_2\hat{q}_2 > 5$
13.4	$H_0: p_1 = p_2$ $H_1: p_1 \neq p_2$	$z = \dfrac{a - d}{\sqrt{a + d}}$	1. Random sampling or random assignment 2. Binomial distributions 3. Dependent samples 4. $a + d \geq 10$

The z, t, χ^2, and F statistics presented in Chapters 10 through 13 have a number of common characteristics that might be overlooked because of differences in their formulas. Each statistic (1) assumes random sampling or random assignment of participants, (2) is used to test null hypotheses or construct confidence intervals for one or two parameters of the sampled populations, and (3) assumes, with the exception of proportions, that the sampled population is normally distributed. The z statistic that is used with proportions assumes that the sampled population is binomially distributed.

The test statistics and confidence intervals are summarized in Tables 13.5-1 and 13.5-2, respectively. As shown in the tables, the assumptions of the test statistics and analogous confidence intervals are the same.

TABLE 13.5-2. Summary of Two-Sample Confidence Intervals

Chapter Section	Parameters	Confidence Interval	Assumptions
13.1	$\dfrac{\sigma_1^2}{\sigma_2^2}$	$\dfrac{\hat{\sigma}_1^2}{\hat{\sigma}_2^2}\dfrac{1}{F_{\alpha/2;\nu_1,\nu_2}} < \dfrac{\sigma_1^2}{\sigma_2^2} < \dfrac{\hat{\sigma}_1^2}{\hat{\sigma}_2^2} F_{\alpha/2;\nu_2,\nu_1}$	1. Random sampling or random assignment 2. Normality 3. Independent samples
13.2	$\sigma_1^2 - \sigma_2^2$	$(\hat{\sigma}_1^2 - \hat{\sigma}_2^2) - t_{\alpha/2,\nu}\sqrt{\left[\dfrac{4\hat{\sigma}_1^2\hat{\sigma}_2^2}{n-2}\right](1 - r_{12}^2)} < \sigma_1^2 - \sigma_2^2$ $< (\hat{\sigma}_1^2 - \hat{\sigma}_2^2) + t_{\alpha/2,\nu}\sqrt{\left[\dfrac{4\hat{\sigma}_1^2\hat{\sigma}_2^2}{n-2}\right](1 - r_{12}^2)}$	1. Random sampling or random assignment 2. Normality 3. Dependent samples
13.3	$p_1 - p_2$	$(\hat{p}_1 - \hat{p}_2) - z_{\alpha/2}\sqrt{\dfrac{\hat{p}_1\hat{q}_1}{n_1} + \dfrac{\hat{p}_2\hat{q}_2}{n_2}} < p_1 - p_2$ $< (\hat{p}_1 - \hat{p}_2) + z_{\alpha/2}\sqrt{\dfrac{\hat{p}_1\hat{q}_1}{n_1} + \dfrac{\hat{p}_2\hat{q}_2}{n_2}}$	1. Random sampling or random assignment 2. Binomial distributions 3. Independent samples 4. $n_1\hat{p}_{Pd} > 5, n_1\hat{q}_{Pd} > 5$ $n_2\hat{p}_{Pd} > 5, n_2\hat{q}_{Pd} > 5$
13.4	$p_1 - p_2$	$\dfrac{a-d}{n} - z_{\alpha/2}\sqrt{\dfrac{(a+d)(b+c)+4ad}{n^3}} < p_1 - p_2$ $< \dfrac{a-d}{n} + z_{\alpha/2}\sqrt{\dfrac{(a+d)(b+c)+4ad}{n^3}}$	1. Random sampling or random assignment 2. Binomial distributions 3. Dependent samples 4. $a + d \geq 10$

REVIEW EXERCISES FOR CHAPTER 13

1. What are the main factors a researcher should keep in mind when using an F test to determine the tenability of the assumption $\sigma_1^2 = \sigma_2^2$ prior to testing H_0: $\mu_1 - \mu_2 = \delta_0$?
2. A 95% confidence interval for σ_1^2/σ_2^2 is 0.6 to 2.7. Do you think that the population variances are unequal? Why?
3. An experiment was performed to compare disjunctive and simple reaction times. In the latter condition, a participant responded to a single light by pressing a button below the light; the disjunctive condition required a participant to press the right button if the right light was illuminated and the left button if the left light was illuminated. Twenty-four participants were randomly assigned to the two conditions with the restriction that an equal number of participants participated under each condition. One participant in the simple reaction condition became ill during the experiment and had to withdraw. This reduced the sample size from 12 to 11.

Reaction Time (Hundredths of a Second)

Disjunctive			Simple		
27	34	35	24	24	24
31	32	31	27	26	22
28	30	32	23	24	25
37	30	31	25	23	

a. Construct box plots for the disjunctive and simple reaction time (RT) data and stack the plots one above the other. Do the data contain outliers? Do the sample distributions appear to be relatively symmetrical? Is it reasonable to believe that the populations are normally distributed?

b. Test the hypothesis that $\sigma_1^2 = \sigma_2^2$ using the statistic $F = \hat{\sigma}_1^2/\hat{\sigma}_2^2$. Let $\alpha = .05$. Assume that $F_{.05/2;11,10} = 3.665$.

c. Compute a $100(1 - .05)\% = 95\%$ confidence interval for σ_1^2/σ_2^2. Locate the confidence interval on the real number line. Assume that $F_{.05/2;10,11} = 3.526$.

d. Is the confidence interval consistent with the null hypothesis significance test? Why?

e. Specify all null hypotheses that could be rejected.

4. Use the table of random numbers in Appendix Table D.1 to draw random samples without replacement of 31 men and 41 women from the Student Database in Appendix E.

a. List the Participant Number, Gender, and Stat Grade for each person in your sample. For each gender, construct a box plot and stack the plots one above the other. Do the data contain outliers? Do the sample distributions appear to be relatively symmetrical?

b. Test the null hypothesis that $\sigma_1^2 = \sigma_2^2$, where σ_1^2 and σ_2^2 denote, respectively, the population variances of men's and women's Stat Grade. Let $\alpha = .05$. Assume that $F_{.05/2;30,40} = 1.943$ and $F_{.05/2;40,30} = 2.009$.

c. Compute a $100(1 - .05)\% = 95\%$ confidence interval for σ_1^2/σ_2^2. Locate the confidence interval on the real number line.

d. Is the confidence interval consistent with the null hypothesis significance test? Why?

e. Write a paragraph summarizing your results and conclusions.

5. (a) For the data in Chapter 12, Table 12.4-1, test the tenability of the t test assumption that $\sigma_1^2 = \sigma_2^2$. Let $\alpha = .20$. (b) Explain why one would use $\alpha = .20$ for this test instead of, say, $\alpha = .05$.

6. It is reasonable to expect 13-year-old boys to exceed 12-year-old boys in strength of grip. In all likelihood, the dispersion of strength of grip is greater for 13-year-olds than for 12-year-olds. To test this hypothesis, strength of grip was measured by means of a hand dynamometer for a random sample of 42 boys who had just turned 12. One year

later the same boys were remeasured. The variances for the first and second sets of measurements are 196 and 289, respectively. The correlation between the two sets of measurements is .83.

a. Test the null hypothesis that $\sigma_1^2 \geq \sigma_2^2$. Let $\alpha = .05$.

b. Compute a $100(1 - .05)\% = 95\%$ confidence interval for $\sigma_1^2 - \sigma_2^2$. Locate the confidence interval on the real number line.

c. Is the confidence interval consistent with the null hypothesis significance test? Why?

d. Specify all null hypotheses that could be rejected.

7. Use the table of random numbers in Appendix Table D.1 to draw random samples without replacement of 32 male and 32 female students from the Student Database in Appendix E. Use the variable of GPA to form 32 men-women pairs of matched participants. The GPAs of men and women in a matched pair do not have to be equal, but the GPAs should be similar.

a. List the Participant Number, Gender, and Stat Grade for each matched pair in your sample. For each gender, construct a box plot and stack the plots one above the other. Do the data contain outliers? Do the sample distributions appear to be relatively symmetrical?

b. Test the null hypothesis that $\sigma_1^2 = \sigma_2^2$, where σ_1^2 and σ_2^2 denote, respectively, the population variances of men's and women's Stat Grade. Let $\alpha = .05$.

c. Compute a $100(1 - .05)\% = 95\%$ confidence interval for $\sigma_1^2 - \sigma_2^2$. Locate the confidence interval on the real number line.

d. Is the confidence interval consistent with the null hypothesis significance test? Why?

e. Write a paragraph summarizing your results and conclusions.

f. Compute the correlation between Stat Grade and GPA. Was GPA an effective matching variable? Does the correlation shed any light on why the use of the dependent samples t statistic was or was not an effective research strategy?

8. A national survey of 3,000 college and university students conducted by the American Council of Day-Care Centers found that 78% of West Coast freshmen return to college for their second year. The comparable figure for freshmen at southern schools is 85%. The percentages are based on $n_1 = 1800$ and $n_2 = 1200$ students, respectively.

a. Test the null hypothesis that $p_1 = p_2$. Let $\alpha = .001$.

b. Compute a $100(1 - .001)\% = 99.9\%$ confidence interval for $p_1 - p_2$. Locate the confidence interval on the real number line.

c. Is the confidence interval consistent with the null hypothesis significance test? Why?

d. Specify all null hypotheses that could be rejected.

9. A national survey of 1,000 unmarried women between the ages of 15 and 19 found that 46% of 19-year-olds and 26.6% of 17-year-olds had experienced sexual intercourse. The sample contained $n_1 = 200$ 19-year-olds and $n_2 = 150$ 17-year-olds.

a. Test the null hypothesis that $p_1 = p_2$. Let $\alpha = .01$.

b. Compute a $100(1 - .01)\% = 99\%$ confidence interval for $p_1 - p_2$. Locate the confidence interval on the real number line.

c. Is the confidence interval consistent with the null hypothesis significance test? Why?

d. Specify all null hypotheses that could be rejected.

10. A test comparing the detectability of two hues of stoplights under simulated fog conditions found that the relative frequencies of detection for red and yellow lights were $p_1 = .56$ and $p_2 = .62$, respectively. The subjects were randomly assigned to view one or the other condition: 321 viewed the red light, and 315 viewed the yellow light.

a. Test the null hypothesis that $p_1 = p_2$. Let $\alpha = .05$.

b. Compute a $100(1 - .01)\% = 95\%$ confidence interval for $p_1 - p_2$. Locate the confidence interval on the real number line.

c. Is the confidence interval consistent with the null hypothesis significance test? Why?

11. Learning one task often enhances the learning of a similar task; this phenomenon is called *learning to learn.* To investigate this phenomenon, a researcher asked students to learn 20 lists of nonsense syllables. For the data in the table, test the hypothesis that p_1, the population proportion for students who learned lists 2 to 6 in fewer than 25 trials, and p_2, the population proportion for students who learned lists 16 to 20 in fewer than 25 trials, are equal. Let $\alpha = .05$. (b) What is the p-value of the test statistic?

		Number of Students Who Learned Lists 16 to 20		
		In 25 Trials or More	In Fewer Than 25 Trials	
Number of Students Who Learned Lists 2 to 6	In Fewer Than 25 trials	3	7	10
	In 25 Trials or More	13	13	26
		16	20	36

a. Compute p_1 and p_2, where the subscripts 1 and 2 denote, respectively, the students who learned lists 2 to 6 and lists 16 to 20.

b. Test the null hypothesis that $p_1 = p_2$. Let $\alpha = .05$.

c. Compute a $100(1 - .01)\% = 95\%$ confidence interval for $p_1 - p_2$. Locate the confidence interval on the real number line.

d. Is the confidence interval consistent with the null hypothesis significance test? Why?

e. Specify all null hypotheses that could be rejected.

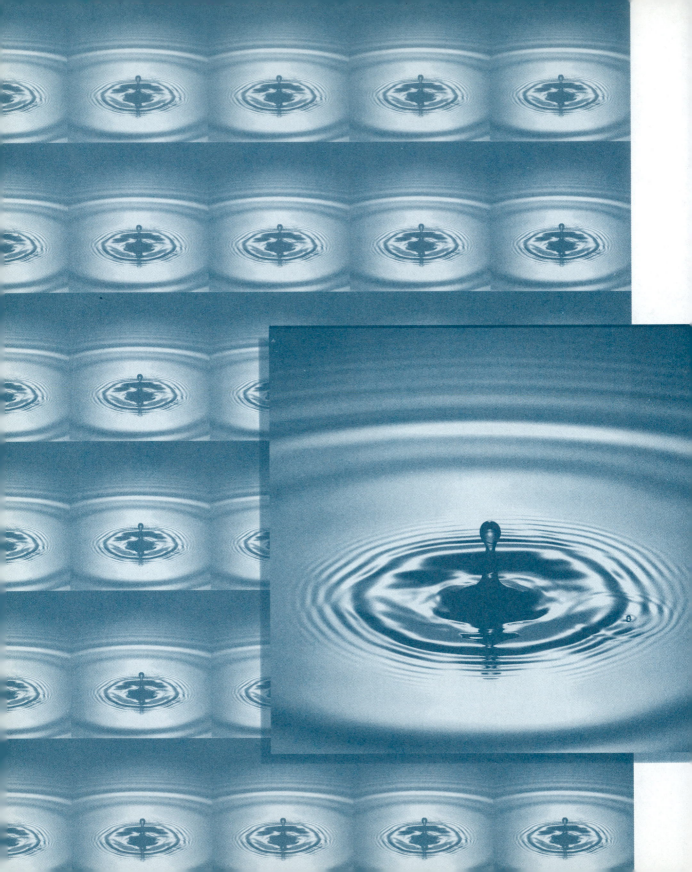

Chapter 14

Introduction to the Analysis of Variance

14.1 INTRODUCTION TO ANALYSIS OF VARIANCE

The Omnibus Null Hypothesis

One of the most frequently used statistical procedures in the behavioral sciences is analysis of variance, often referred to as ANOVA (pronounced an-noh-va). The procedure was developed by R. A. Fisher in the early 1920s to test null hypotheses of the form

$$H_0: \mu_1 = \mu_2 = \cdots = \mu_p,$$

where $\mu_1, \mu_2, \ldots, \mu_p$ denote the means of $p \geq 2$ populations. If the null hypothesis is rejected, the alternative hypothesis that at least two of the population means are not equal is tenable. That is, $\mu_j \neq \mu_{j'}$ for some pair of population means, where the subscripts j and j' denote different populations. If the null hypothesis is not rejected, it remains tenable. It is helpful to think of the null hypothesis as an omnibus or overall hypothesis because it states that all of the $j = 1, \ldots, p$ population means are equal.

Answering General Versus Specific Research Questions

Often when samples from three or more populations are obtained, the researcher is interested in answering the general question: Are there any differences among the population means? This is the kind of research question that analysis of variance was developed to answer. Alternatively, samples may be obtained to answer more specific research questions, for example: Are the means of populations 1 and 2 different and are the means of populations 3 and 4 different, or does the control-group mean differ from each of the experimental-group means? As we will see in Section 14.5, such specific research questions can be answered by using a multiple comparison procedure.

Let's pursue the distinction between ANOVA and multiple comparison procedures a bit more. Suppose that we perform an ANOVA and reject the null hypothesis that $\mu_1 = \mu_2 = \mu_3 = \mu_4$. What do we know? We know that one or more of the following alternative hypotheses is probably true:[1]

$$H_1: \mu_j \neq \mu_{j'} \qquad \qquad \text{for some } j\text{'s}$$

$$H_1: \mu_j \neq \frac{\mu_{j'} + \mu_{j''}}{2} \qquad \qquad \text{for some } j\text{'s}$$

$$H_1: \mu_j \neq \frac{\mu_{j'} + \mu_{j''} + \mu_{j'''}}{3} \qquad \qquad \text{for some } j\text{'s}$$

$$H_1: \frac{\mu_j + \mu_{j'}}{2} \neq \frac{\mu_{j''} + \mu_{j'''}}{2} \qquad \text{for some } j\text{'s}$$

---

[1] These hypotheses are described in Section 14.5.

What we don't know when we reject the null hypothesis in ANOVA is which one or ones of the alternative hypotheses is tenable. We can answer this question concerning the tenability of the various alternative hypotheses by using one of the multiple comparison procedures described in Section 14.5.

To summarize, analysis of variance is the appropriate procedure for answering the general question: Are there any differences among a set of population means? If you are interested in more specific research questions, one of the multiple comparison procedures described in Section 14.5 can be used.

Analysis of Variance Versus Multiple t Tests

In Chapter 12 you learned how to test a null hypothesis for two population means: $H_0: \mu_1 = \mu_2$. You may wonder why we don't test the ANOVA null hypothesis

$$H_0: \mu_1 = \mu_2 = \mu_3,$$

for example, by performing three t tests on the following null hypotheses.

$$H_0: \mu_1 = \mu_2 \qquad H_0: \mu_1 = \mu_3 \qquad H_0: \mu_2 = \mu_3$$

It is obvious that if $\mu_1 = \mu_2$, $\mu_1 = \mu_3$, and $\mu_2 = \mu_3$, then it must be true that $\mu_1 = \mu_2 = \mu_3$. Although this research strategy seems reasonable, we will see that it has a flaw.

If there are p population means, we can test $p(p - 1)/2$ null hypotheses of the form $\mu_j = \mu_{j'}$. For p equal to 3, we have already listed the $3(3 - 1)/2 = 3$ null hypotheses. When p is equal to 4, there are $4(4 - 1)/2 = 6$ null hypotheses that can be tested; when p is equal to 5, there are 10 null hypotheses, and so on.

Now let's examine the flaw in the multiple-t testing strategy. To test the null hypothesis

$$H_0: \mu_1 = \mu_2 = \mu_3 = \mu_4 = \mu_5,$$

we would have to perform $C = p(p - 1)/2 = 5(5 - 1)/2 = 10$ t tests. If we tested each of the 10 t statistics at $\alpha = .05$ level of significance, it can be shown[2] that the probability of making one or more type I errors is less than but not too different from

$$1 - (1 - \alpha)^C = 1 - (1 - .05)^{10} = .40.$$

Because in most research situations we would like the probability of making one or more type I errors to not exceed $\alpha = .05$, a probability approaching .40 is unacceptable. Notice also that the probability of making one or more type I errors increases as the number of population means increases. For six means, the probability is less than $1 - (1 - .05)^{15} = .54$; for seven means, the probability is less than $1 - (1 - .05)^{21} = .66$; and so on. The advantage of using an analysis of variance to test the omnibus null hypothesis is that whatever the number of population means, the probability of making a type I error is equal to α.

---

[2] See Kirk (1995, pp. 119–122).

The principal difference between the analysis of variance approach and the multiple t approach can be summarized as follows. For ANOVA, the probability of making a type I error is equal to α for the omnibus null hypothesis $\mu_1 = \mu_2 = \dots = \mu_p$. For the multiple t approach, the probability of making a type I error for the collection of tests is greater than α. In the multiple t approach, although a researcher tests each null hypothesis at α level of significance, the probability of making a type I error increases as the number of hypotheses that are tested increases. Thus, a persistent researcher who performs enough t tests, each at α level of significance, will certainly reject too many true null hypotheses.

For the special case in which an experiment contains only two experimental conditions and the null hypothesis is $\mu_j = \mu_{j'}$, the ANOVA and t approaches have the same probability of making a type I error because in this case, only one null hypothesis is tested.

CHECK YOUR UNDERSTANDING OF SECTION 14.1

1. Suppose that four methods of teaching foreign-language vocabulary are compared in an experiment. The dependent variable is performance on a 25-item vocabulary test. (a) State the null hypothesis. (b) How many t tests would be required to test hypotheses of the form $\mu_j = \mu_{j'}$? (c) If $\alpha = .01$, what is the probability of making one or more type I errors using ANOVA? What is the probability when using multiple t tests? (d) If the omnibus null hypothesis is rejected by means of an ANOVA F test, what does this tell the researcher?
2. For experiments in which the number of experimental conditions is greater than two, what advantage does the ANOVA approach have over the multiple t approach?

14.2 BASIC CONCEPTS IN ANOVA

The material in this section provides a glimpse of some of the basic concepts associated with a completely randomized ANOVA, the simplest of all the ANOVA designs. The rationale underlying ANOVA is somewhat involved, although the computations are straightforward. It should be helpful to review Section 14.2 after working through one of the ANOVA problems in Section 14.3.

The Composite Nature of a Score

The value of a score in an experiment is determined by a variety of variables. We will now examine this idea in some detail because it is an important concept. A score can be thought of as a composite, reflecting, for example, the effects of the (1) independent variable, (2) individual characteristics of the participant or experimental unit, (3) chance fluctuations in the participant's performance, and (4) environmental and other uncontrolled conditions. Similarly, the variability among scores also is a composite that reflects the effects of the same variables.

ANOVA is a procedure for determining how much of the total variability among scores to attribute to various sources of variation and for testing hypotheses concerning some of the sources.

The composite nature of a score will be illustrated by an example. Consider an experiment to determine the effectiveness of three diets for obese teenage girls. Thirty girls who want to lose weight are randomly assigned to the three diets with the restriction that 10 girls are assigned to each diet. The independent variable is type of diet; the dependent variable is weight loss in pounds after being on a diet for one month.

For notational convenience, the diets are called **treatment A.** The levels of treatment A, corresponding to the specific diets, are designated by the lowercase letter a and numeric subscripts—a_1, a_2, and a_3. A particular but unspecified score is denoted by X_{ij}, where the first subscript designates one of the $i = 1, \ldots, n$ participants in a treatment level and the second subscript designates one of the $j = 1, \ldots, p$ levels of treatment A.

Let X_{72} denote Bella Ablipid's score in the diet experiment. From X_{72}, we know that she is participant seven and that she used diet a_2. What factors have affected the value of her score? If she stuck to her diet, one major factor is the efficacy of diet a_2. Other factors are her degree of obesity, day-to-day fluctuations in her eating and exercise habits, time of day that her weight loss was measured, and so on. In summary, Bella's weight loss, X_{72}, reflects (1) the effect of treatment level a_2, (2) effects unique to her, (3) effects attributable to chance fluctuations in her behavior, and (4) effects attributable to environmental and other uncontrolled conditions.

The Linear Model Equation for a Score

Our conjectures about X_{72} or any other score can be expressed more formally by a **linear model equation.** We assume that each of the 30 scores is the sum of three parameters in the equation

$$X_{ij} = \mu + \alpha_j + \epsilon_{ij},$$

where

X_{ij} is the score for participant i in treatment level j.

μ is the grand mean of μ_1, μ_2, and μ_3, the mean of the three treatment populations. We can think of μ as the average value around which the treatment means and scores vary.

α_j is the **treatment effect** of population j and is equal to $\mu_j - \mu$, the deviation of the jth population mean from the grand mean. α_j reflects the effects of using the jth diet.

ϵ_{ij} is the **error effect** associated with X_{ij} and is equal to $X_{ij} - \mu - \alpha_j$. The error effect is that portion of a participant's score that remains after the grand mean and jth treatment effect have been subtracted from it. ϵ_{ij} represents effects unique to participant i, effects attributable to chance fluctuations in participant i, and effects attributable to environmental and other uncontrolled conditions—in other words, all effects not attributable to treatment level j.

The values of the parameters μ, α_j, and ϵ_{ij} are unknown, but, as we will see, they can be estimated from sample data. Furthermore, analysis of variance lets us partition the variance of the scores so as to test the null hypothesis $\mu_1 = \mu_2 = \cdots = \mu_p$.

The null hypothesis in ANOVA also can be expressed as $\alpha_1 = \alpha_2 = \cdots = \alpha_p = 0$. This follows because if $\mu_1 = \mu_2 = \cdots = \mu_p = \mu$, then $\mu_1 - \mu = \alpha_1 = 0$, $\mu_2 - \mu = \alpha_2 = 0$, and so on. Thus, a test of $\mu_1 = \mu_2 = \cdots = \mu_p$ is equivalent to testing the hypothesis that all population treatment effects, α_j's, are equal to 0.

Estimating the Parameters of the Linear Model Equation

Suppose that the data in Table 14.2-1 have been obtained in our diet experiment. The treatment means, $\overline{X}_{.1}$, $\overline{X}_{.2}$, $\overline{X}_{.3}$, and the grand mean, $\overline{X}_{..}$, are shown in the table. The use of a dot in the notation indicates that the mean was obtained by averaging over the subscript replaced by the dot. For example, treatment means are obtained from

$$\overline{X}_{.1} = \frac{\sum_{i=1}^{n} X_{i1}}{n} = \frac{X_{11} + X_{21} + X_{31} + \cdots + X_{10,1}}{n} = \frac{80}{10} = 8$$

$$\overline{X}_{.2} = \frac{\sum_{i=1}^{n} X_{i2}}{n} = \frac{X_{12} + X_{22} + X_{32} + \cdots + X_{10,2}}{n} = \frac{90}{10} = 9$$

$$\overline{X}_{.3} = \frac{\sum_{i=1}^{n} X_{i3}}{n} = \frac{X_{13} + X_{23} + X_{33} + \cdots + X_{10,3}}{n} = \frac{120}{10} = 12$$

TABLE 14.2-1. One-Month Weight Losses Measured to the Nearest Pound

(i) Data and notation (X_{ij} denotes a score for participant i in treatment level j; $i = 1, \ldots, n$ participants; $j = 1, \ldots, p$ levels of treatment A)

Treatment Levels (Diets)

	a_1	a_2	a_3
	7	10	12
	9	13	11
	8	9	15
	12	11	7
	8	5	14
	7	9	10
	4	8	12
	10	10	12
	9	8	13
	6	7	14

Sum of $i = 1, \ldots, n$ scores in each treatment level
$$\sum_{i=1}^{n} X_{i1} = 80 \qquad \sum_{i=1}^{n} X_{i2} = 90 \qquad \sum_{i=1}^{n} X_{i3} = 120$$

Sum of all scores $\longmapsto \displaystyle\sum_{j=1}^{p}\sum_{i=1}^{n} X_{ij} = 290$

Mean of each treatment level
$$\bar{X}_{\cdot 1} = 8 \qquad \bar{X}_{\cdot 2} = 9 \qquad \bar{X}_{\cdot 3} = 12$$

Grand mean $\longmapsto \bar{X}_{\cdot\cdot} = 9.67$

The grand mean is obtained by summing all the np scores and dividing by np.

$$\bar{X}_{\cdot\cdot} = \frac{\displaystyle\sum_{j=1}^{p}\sum_{i=1}^{n} X_{ij}}{np}$$

$$= \frac{(X_{11} + \cdots + X_{10,1}) + (X_{12} + \cdots + X_{10,2}) + (X_{13} + \cdots + X_{10,3})}{np}$$

$$= \frac{80 + 90 + 120}{(10)(3)} = 9.67$$

The grand mean subscript has two dots because we averaged over both i and j.

Table 14.2-1 contains scores and means, but the values of the parameters μ, α_j, and ϵ_{ij} in the linear model equation are unknown. However, unbiased estimators of the parameters can be obtained from the sample data as shown in Table 14.2-2. We

TABLE 14.2-2. Estimators of Parameters of the Linear Model

Statistic	Parameter Estimated	Interpretation of Parameter
$\overline{X}_{..}$	μ	Average value around which the treatment means and scores vary
$\overline{X}_{.j} - \overline{X}_{..}$	α_j	Effect attributable to the *j*th treatment level
$X_{ij} - \overline{X}_{.j}$	ϵ_{ij}	Error effect unique to participant *i* in treatment level *j*

can rewrite the linear model equation $X_{ij} = \mu + \alpha_j + \epsilon_{ij}$ using these estimators, as follows.

Parameters of the linear model equation

$$X_{ij} = \quad \mu \quad + \quad \alpha_j \quad + \quad \epsilon_{ij}$$

Estimators of the parameters

$$X_{ij} = \quad \overline{X}_{..} \quad + (\overline{X}_{.j} - \overline{X}_{..}) + (X_{ij} - \overline{X}_{.j})$$

Score	Grand Mean	Treatment Effect	Error Effect

Perhaps an example using Bella's score, X_{72}, will help to clarify the meaning of these estimators. According to Table 14.2-1, Bella lost 8 pounds ($X_{72} = 8$), which is 1.67 pounds less than the average weight loss for the 30 girls ($\overline{X}_{..} = 9.67$). Her weight loss can be expressed as follows:

$$
\begin{aligned}
X_{72} &= \overline{X}_{..} &+\ & (\overline{X}_{.2} - \overline{X}_{..}) &+\ & (X_{72} - \overline{X}_{.2}) \\
8 &= 9.67 &+\ & (9 - 9.67) &+\ & (8 - 9) \\
8 &= 9.67 &+\ & (-0.67) &+\ & (-1)
\end{aligned}
$$

Bella's Score	Grand Mean	α_2 Treatment Effect	Bella's Error Effect

This model equation gives us a bit more insight into why Bella's weight loss, $X_{72} = 8$ pounds, was 1.67 pounds less than the average weight loss. She used a less effective diet, $\overline{X}_{.2} - \overline{X}_{..} = -0.67$ pound, and in addition, the diet was not as effective for her as it was for the average of the 10 girls who used it, $X_{72} - \overline{X}_{.2} = -1$ pound.

The sample data allow us to estimate three parameters that account for Bella's weight loss: the population average weight loss, estimated by $\overline{X}_{..} = 9.67$ pounds, the effect of diet a_2, estimated by $\overline{X}_{.2} - \overline{X}_{..} = 9 - 9.67 = -0.67$; and the error effect unique to Bella, estimated by $X_{72} - \overline{X}_{.2} = 8 - 9 = -1$. This error effect estimates that part of X_{72} not due to μ and α_2, in other words, $\epsilon_{72} = X_{72} - \mu - \alpha_2$. In fact, the estimator for ϵ_{72}, denoted by $\hat{\epsilon}_{72}$, is obtained by replacing the parameters in $X_{72} - \mu - \alpha_2$ with statistics, as follows.

$$\epsilon_{72} = X_{72} - \mu - \alpha_2$$
$$\hat{\epsilon}_{72} = X_{72} - \overline{X}.. - (\overline{X}._2 - \overline{X}..)$$
$$= X_{72} - \overline{X}._2$$
$$= 8 - 9 = -1$$

The error effect $\hat{\epsilon}_{72}$ reflects all of the characteristics peculiar to Bella, such as her degree of obesity and her day-to-day fluctuations in eating and exercise habits, as well as those characteristics peculiar to the testing conditions, such as the time of day that her weight loss was measured. The name *error effect* is an apt one because an error effect represents all of the effects not otherwise estimated in the experiment.

We have illustrated the composite nature of a score and procedures for estimating the parameters of the model equation. Our ultimate purpose is to develop procedures for testing the null hypothesis that all of the treatment effects, α_j's, are equal to 0. To accomplish this purpose, several more concepts must be introduced.

Partition of the Total Sum of Squares

Earlier, we saw that a score, X_{ij}, is a composite. The total variability among scores in the diet experiment,

$$SSTO = \sum_{j=1}^{p}\sum_{i=1}^{n}(X_{ij} - \overline{X})^2,$$

called the **total sum of squares (SSTO),** also is a composite. It can be shown (see "Check Your Understanding of Section 14.2," Exercise 5) that the total sum of squares can be partitioned into two parts: variability between the treatment levels, called the **between-groups sum of squares (SSBG),**

$$SSBG = n\sum_{j=1}^{p}(\overline{X}._j - \overline{X})^2,$$

and variability within the treatment levels, called the **within-groups sum of squares (SSWG),**

$$SSWG = \sum_{j=1}^{p}\sum_{i=1}^{n}(X_{ij} - \overline{X}._j)^2.$$

That is,

$$SSTO \quad = \quad SSBG \quad + \quad SSWG$$

$$\sum_{j=1}^{p}\sum_{i=1}^{n}(X_{ij} - \overline{X}..)^2 = n\sum_{j=1}^{p}(\overline{X}._j - \overline{X}..)^2 + \sum_{j=1}^{p}\sum_{i=1}^{n}(X_{ij} - \overline{X}._j)^2.$$

Now we need to show what the partition of *SSTO* into *SSBG* and *SSWG* has to do with testing the hypothesis that $\mu_1 = \mu_2 = \cdots = \mu_p$ or the equivalent hypothesis that $\alpha_1 = \alpha_2 = \cdots = \alpha_p = 0$. But before we can do this, we must discuss the degrees of freedom associated with each of the sums of squares.

Degrees of Freedom

The term *degrees of freedom* refers to the number of observations whose values can be assigned arbitrarily, as we saw in Section 11.2. We now will determine the degrees of freedom associated with *SSBG*, *SSWG*, and *SSTO*. Consider $SSBG = n\sum_{j=1}^{p}(\overline{X}_{\cdot j} - \overline{X}_{\cdot\cdot})^2$ and let n be the same for each of the sample means. If we have, say, $p = 4$ sample means, they are related to the grand mean by the equation

$$\frac{\overline{X}_{\cdot 1} + \overline{X}_{\cdot 2} + \overline{X}_{\cdot 3} + \overline{X}_{\cdot 4}}{4} = \overline{X}_{\cdot\cdot\cdot}$$

If $\overline{X}_{\cdot\cdot} = 6$ and we arbitrarily specify that $\overline{X}_{\cdot 1} = 6$, $\overline{X}_{\cdot 2} = 8$, and $\overline{X}_{\cdot 3} = 7$, then $\overline{X}_{\cdot 4}$ must equal 3 because $(6 + 8 + 7 + 3)/4 = 6$. Alternatively, if we specify that $\overline{X}_{\cdot 1} = 5$, $\overline{X}_{\cdot 2} = 7$, and $\overline{X}_{\cdot 3} = 4$, then $\overline{X}_{\cdot 4}$ must equal 8 because $(5 + 7 + 4 + 8)/4 = 6$. Given the value of the grand mean, we are free to assign any values to three of the four treatment means, but having done so, the fourth mean is determined.

The number of degrees of freedom associated with *SSBG* is $p - 1$, one less than the number of treatment means.

The number of degrees of freedom associated with *SSWG* is $p(n - 1)$. To see why this is true, consider $SSWG = \sum_{j=1}^{p} \sum_{i=1}^{n} (X_{ij} - \overline{X}_{\cdot j})^2$ and let $p = 4$ and $n = 8$. The eight scores in the jth treatment level are related to the jth mean by

$$\frac{X_{1j} + X_{2j} + \cdots + X_{8j}}{8} = \overline{X}_{\cdot j}.$$

Seven of the scores can take any value, but the eighth is determined because the sum of the scores divided by eight must equal $\overline{X}_{\cdot j}$. Hence, there are $n - 1 = 8 - 1 = 7$ degrees of freedom associated with the jth treatment level, and this is true for each of the $j = 4$ treatment levels. Thus, there are $p(n - 1) = 4(8 - 1) = 28$ degrees of freedom associated with *SSWG*.

In the general case, if $n_1 = n_2 = \cdots = n_p$, each of the p treatment levels has $n - 1$ degrees of freedom. Thus, there are $p(n - 1)$ degrees of freedom associated with *SSWG*. If the n_j's are not equal, the degrees of freedom for *SSWG* are $(n_1 - 1) + (n_2 - 1) + \cdots + (n_p - 1) = N - p$, where N is the total number of scores.

The same line of reasoning can be used to show that when $n_1 = n_2 = \cdots = n_p$, the total sum of squares has $pn - 1$ degrees of freedom.

This follows because the $pn = 4(8) = 32$ scores are related to the grand mean by

$$\frac{X_{11} + X_{21} + \cdots + X_{84}}{32} = \bar{X}...$$

Hence, $np - 1 = 31$ of the scores can take any value, but the 32nd score must be assigned so that the mean of the scores equals $\bar{X}...$ If the n_j's are not equal, the number of degrees of freedom for the total sum of squares is $n_1 + n_2 + \cdots + n_p - 1 = N - 1$.

Mean Squares and the *F* Statistic

The term *mean square* (*MS*) is new, but the concept isn't; mean square is simply another name for variance.

A **mean square** (*MS*) is obtained by dividing a sum of squares (*SS*) by its degrees of freedom (*df*). Thus,

$$MSTO = SSTO/(np - 1) \text{ or } SSTO/(N - 1)$$

$$MSBG = SSBG/(p - 1)$$

$$MSWG = SSWG/[p(n - 1)] \text{ or } SSWG/[(N - p)].$$

The *F* statistic and *F* sampling distribution were introduced in Section 13.1. We saw that the *F* statistic could be used to test the null hypothesis that two population variances are equal. The *F* statistic also is used in ANOVA to test the omnibus null hypothesis for population means.

The null hypothesis $\mu_1 = \mu_2 = \cdots = \mu_p$ is tested by means of an *F* test statistic, which is the ratio of the between-groups variance to the within-groups variance:

$$F = MSBG/MSWG.$$

The degrees of freedom for the numerator and denominator of the *F* statistic are, respectively, $v_1 = p - 1$ and $v_2 = p(n - 1)$.

The *F* statistic is referred to the sampling distribution of *F*, which is tabled in Appendix Table D.5. If the *F* statistic is greater than or equal to the tabled value, $F_{\alpha; v_1, v_2}$, the null hypothesis is rejected.

The Nature of *MSBG* and *MSWG*

It may seem paradoxical to test a hypothesis about population means by using the ratio of two sample variances, $F = =MSBG/MSWG$. To show that this procedure is reasonable, we need to consider the nature of the population variances estimated by *MSWG* and *MSBG*. It is helpful to think of analysis of variance as a statistical method for deciding which of two model equations best describes the scores in an experiment. We will refer to the two equations as the **full model** and the **reduced model:**

$$X_{ij} = \mu + \alpha_j + \epsilon_{ij} \qquad \text{Full model}$$
$$X_{ij} = \mu + \epsilon_{ij} \qquad\qquad \text{Reduced model}$$

The two model equations differ with respect to the inclusion of α_j, the treatment effect. The reduced model says that the inclusion of α_j is not necessary to adequately describe a score; the full model says that all three terms are needed. Recall that the null hypothesis in ANOVA can be expressed as $\alpha_1 = \alpha_2 = \cdots = \alpha_p = 0$. If the null hypothesis is true, the reduced model provides an adequate description of a score. However, if the null hypothesis is false, the full model is required to provide an adequate description. What does all of this have to do with $F = MSBG/MSWG$? We will examine the connection after reviewing the concept of expected value.

We learned in Section 9.3 that $E(\overline{X}) = \mu$. This means that if we draw many, many random samples from a population and compute a mean for each sample, the long-run average of the sample means is μ. We call μ the expected value of $\overline{X}$. It can be shown that for (1) random samples from (2) normally distributed populations having (3) equal means and (4) equal variances, the expected value of both *MSBG* and *MSWG* is σ_ϵ^2, that is

$$E(MSBG) = E(MSWG) = \sigma_\epsilon^2,$$

where σ_ϵ^2 is the **population error variance.**[3] When the population means are all equal, the ratio $F = MSBG/MSWG$ should be close to 1 because both mean squares estimate σ_ϵ^2. Thus, F ratios close to 1 provide support for the null hypothesis—support for believing that the reduced model equation $X_{ij} = \mu + \epsilon_{ij}$ provides an adequate description of each of the scores. When the populations have different means, the expected values of *MSWG* and *MSBG* differ:

$$E(MSWG) = \sigma_\epsilon^2,$$

but

$$E(MSBG) = \sigma_\epsilon^2 + n \sum_{j=1}^{p} (\mu_j - \mu)^2/(p - 1)$$
$$= \sigma_\epsilon^2 + n \sum_{j=1}^{p} \alpha_j^2/(p - 1).$$

When two or more of the population means are unequal, the statistic $F = MSBG/MSWG$ should be larger than 1 because *MSBG* estimates σ_ϵ^2 plus $n\sum_{j=1}^{p} \alpha_j^2/(p - 1)$. If any of the treatment effects, $\alpha_j = \mu_j - \mu$, are not equal to 0,

---

[3] The proof is given by Kirk (1995, pp. 86–94).

the term $\sum_{j=1}^{p} \alpha_j^2$ will be greater than 0. Thus, F statistics larger than 1 provide evidence against the null hypothesis and support for believing that the full model $X_{ij} = \mu + \alpha_j + \epsilon_{ij}$ provides a better description of some scores than does the reduced model $X_{ij} = \mu + \epsilon_{ij}$.

How much larger than 1 should $F = MSBG/MSWG$ be for a researcher to feel confident in rejecting the null hypothesis that $\alpha_1 = \alpha_2 = \cdots = \alpha_p = 0$? The usual practice is to reject the null hypothesis of zero treatment effects if F falls in the upper .05 region of the sampling distribution of F.

Before concluding this section, let us reexamine the nature of $MSWG$ and $MSBG$. Our discussion has focused on the expected values of these mean squares. Unfortunately, the derivation of these expected values is beyond the scope of this book. However, it would be nice if you came away from this discussion with an intuitive feel for the sources of variation that are being tapped by the two mean squares. An examination of the $MSWG$ formula $\sum_{j=1}^{p}\sum_{i=1}^{n}(X_{ij} - \overline{X}_{\cdot j})^2/[p(n-1)]$ and Figure 14.2-1 suggests that $MSWG$ estimates the variation among participants who have been treated alike. This follows because the deviations of the scores in the formula are taken from their respective treatment means. On the other hand, $MSBG$ estimates the variation among participants who have been treated differently, that is, assigned to different treatment levels. This follows because the deviations of the treatment means in the formula $n\sum_{j=1}^{p}(\overline{X}_{\cdot j} - \overline{X}_{\cdot\cdot})^2/(p-1)$ are taken from the grand mean. If, in Figure 14.2-1, the three treatment conditions really had no effect on the dependent variable, the variation among the treatment means reflects nothing more than chance variation and should be about the same size as the variation among the scores within each treatment condition. In this case, the F statistic should be close to 1. If, however, the treatment conditions do affect the dependent variable, the variation among the means should be larger than the variation among the scores within each treatment condition. In this case, the F statistic should be larger than 1. The labels "within groups" and "between groups" are appropriate because they describe the deviations that are used in computing the two mean squares.

CHECK YOUR UNDERSTANDING OF SECTION 14.2

3. Suppose that an experiment has been performed over a period of six months to evaluate the effectiveness of three exercise programs denoted by a_1, a_2, a_3 for developing muscle mass. Sixty 21-year-old men have been randomly assigned to the three programs, with 20 in each program. Let X_{42} denote the change in muscle mass of participant 4 who was assigned to exercise program a_2. What specific factors do you think affected the value of his score?
4. Identify the following:
   a. a_2 b. X_{24}
   c. $\overline{X}_{16,1}$ d. $\overline{X}_{\cdot 4}$
   e. $\overline{X}_{\cdot\cdot}$ f. $X_{73} = \mu + \alpha_3 + \epsilon_{73}$
   g. $\mu_2 - \mu$ h. $X_{13} - \mu - \alpha_3$

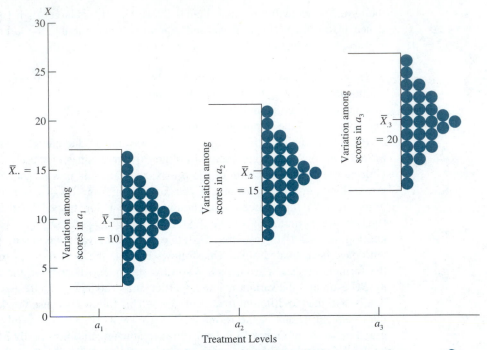

Figure 14.2-1. **As shown in the figure, there is variation among the scores, ●, and among the three sample means. The within-groups mean square, $MSWG = \sum \sum (X_{ij} - \overline{X}_{.j})^2/[p(n-1)]$, reflects the variation among the scores of participants who receive the same treatment level. This source of variation is not affected by differences among the sample means. The between-groups mean square, $MSBG = n\sum (\overline{X}_{.j} - \overline{X}_{..})^2/(p-1)$, reflects the variation among the means of participants who receive different treatment levels. This source of variation is affected by differences among the sample means. If the three treatment conditions have no affect on the dependent variable, $F = MSBG/MSWG$ should be close to 1. If, however, one or more of the treatment conditions affects the dependent variable, $F = MSBG/MSWG$ should be greater than 1.**

5. The total sum of squares, $\sum_{j=1}^{p}\sum_{i=1}^{n}(X_{ij} - \overline{X}_{..})^2$, can be partitioned into sum of squares between groups, $n\sum_{j=1}^{p}(\overline{X}_{.j} - \overline{X}_{..})^2$, and sum of squares within groups, $\sum_{j=1}^{p}\sum_{i=1}^{n}(X_{ij} - \overline{X}_{.j})^2$. Describe in words the operation that was performed for each equation that has a letter in front of it. We begin the derivation with the sample model equation for the completely randomized design.

$$X_{ij} = \overline{X}.. + (\overline{X}._j - \overline{X}..) + (X_{ij} - \overline{X}._j)$$

a.
$$X_{ij} - \overline{X}.. = \overline{X}.. + (\overline{X}._j - \overline{X}..) + (X_{ij} - \overline{X}._j) - \overline{X}..$$
$$= (\overline{X}._j - \overline{X}..) + (X_{ij} - \overline{X}._j)$$

b.
$$(X_{ij} - \overline{X}..)^2 = [(\overline{X}._j - \overline{X}..) + (X_{ij} - \overline{X}._j)]^2$$

c.
$$\sum_{j=1}^{p}\sum_{i=1}^{n}(X_{ij} - \overline{X}..)^2 = \sum_{j=1}^{p}\sum_{i=1}^{n}[(\overline{X}._j - \overline{X}..) + (X_{ij} - \overline{X}._j)]^2$$

d.
$$= \sum_{j=1}^{p}\sum_{i=1}^{n}[(\overline{X}._j - \overline{X}..)^2 + 2(\overline{X}._j - \overline{X}..)(X_{ij} - \overline{X}._j)$$
$$+ (X_{ij} - \overline{X}._j)^2]$$

e.
$$= n\sum_{j=1}^{p}(\overline{X}._j - \overline{X}..)^2 + 2\sum_{j=1}^{p}(\overline{X}._j - \overline{X}..)\sum_{i=1}^{n}(X_{ij} - \overline{X}._j)$$
$$+ \sum_{j=1}^{p}\sum_{i=1}^{n}(X_{ij} - \overline{X}._j)^2$$

f.
$$\sum_{j=1}^{p}\sum_{i=1}^{n}(X_{ij} - \overline{X}..)^2 = n\sum_{j=1}^{p}(\overline{X}._j - \overline{X}..)^2 + \sum_{j=1}^{p}\sum_{i=1}^{n}(X_{ij} - \overline{X}._j)^2$$
$$\text{SSTO} \quad = \quad \text{SSBG} \quad + \quad \text{SSWG}$$

6. For each of the following alternative hypotheses in ANOVA, indicate whether it is correctly or incorrectly stated.
   a. $\mu_j - \mu_{j'} \neq 0$ for some j and j'
   b. $\mu_1 \neq \mu_2 \neq \mu_3$
   c. $\sum_{j=1}^{p}(\mu_j - \mu) \neq 0$
   d. $\alpha_1 \neq 0, \alpha_2 \neq 0, \alpha_3 \neq 0$
   e. $\alpha_j \neq 0$ for some j.
7. Express the following scores in terms of estimates of the parameters of the full linear model equation: (a) X_{83}, (b) X_{52}, (c) X_{24}.
8. Calculate the degrees of freedom for *MSTO, MSBG,* and *MSWG* for the following conditions.
   a. $p = 4, n = 21$
   b. $p = 5, n = 11$
   c. $p = 4, n = 8$
   d. $p = 3, n_1 = 6, n_2 = 5, n_3 = 6$
   e. $p = 4, n_1 = 10, n_2 = 10, n_3 = 9, n_4 = 8$
9. a. Under what conditions do both *MSBG* and *MSWG* estimate only the population error variance, σ_ϵ^2?
   b. Under what condition would you expect *MSBG* to be bigger than *MSWG*?
10. Terms to remember
    a. ANOVA
    b. Treatment *A*
    c. Linear model equation
    d. Treatment effect

e. Error effect
g. Between-groups sum
   of squares
i. Mean square
k. Reduced model

f. Total sum of squares
h. Within-groups sum of squares
j. Full model
l. Population error variance

14.3 COMPLETELY RANDOMIZED DESIGN

This section presents the computational procedures associated with the simplest of all ANOVA designs—the *completely randomized design*. Here you will see how nicely some of the complex ideas presented previously fit together to produce a decision about the null hypothesis. In fact, after pondering over the next two tables, you will see that the computational procedures for ANOVA are tedious but not difficult to carry out. Fortunately, a variety of computer packages are available for doing the number crunching. Three packages are described in Section 14.7.

The completely randomized design is appropriate for experiments with one treatment (independent variable) with $p \geq 2$ treatment levels. The N participants in an experiment should be randomly assigned to the p treatment levels. As we will see, it is desirable but not necessary to assign the same number of participants to each treatment level.

The **completely randomized design** is so named because the assignment of participants to the treatment levels is completely random. Each participant is assigned to only one level. For convenience, the design is referred to as a **CR-p design**,[4] where p denotes the number of levels of treatment A.

A CR-p design with more than two treatment levels can be thought of as an extension of a t test for independent samples. A comparison of the layouts for a t test and a CR-3 design is shown in Figure 14.3-1. When a CR-p design has two treatment levels, the layouts are identical. For this case, it can be shown that the value of the t statistic is equal to $\sqrt{F}$ for the CR-p design.

Computational Formulas

In Section 14.2 we introduced deviation formulas for computing *SSTO, SSBG,* and *SSWG*. These deviation formulas are useful for understanding the nature of the three sums of squares, but they are not the most convenient for computational purposes. It can be shown (see "Check Your Understanding of Section 14.3," Exercise

---

[4] For a comprehensive design classification system and nomenclature, see Kirk (1995, pp. 43–46).

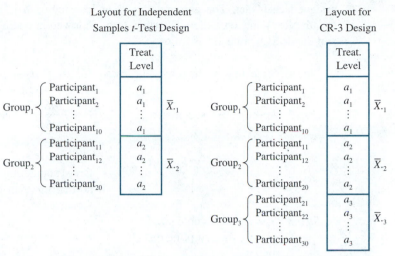

Figure 14.3-1. **Comparison of layouts for *t*-test design for independent samples shown on the left and completely randomized ANOVA design on the right. For the *t*-test design, 20 participants were randomly assigned to the two levels of treatment *A*; for the CR-3 design, 30 participants were randomly assigned to the three levels of treatment *A*.**

11, and "Review Exercises for Chapter 14," Exercise 11) that raw-score formulas for computing these sums of squares are as follows:

$$SSTO = \sum_{j=1}^{p}\sum_{i=1}^{n} X_{ij}^2 - \frac{\left(\sum_{j=1}^{p}\sum_{i=1}^{n} X_{ij}\right)^2}{np}$$

$$SSBG = \sum_{j=1}^{p} \frac{\left(\sum_{i=1}^{n} X_{ij}\right)^2}{n} - \frac{\left(\sum_{j=1}^{p}\sum_{i=1}^{n} X_{ij}\right)^2}{np}$$

$$SSWG = \sum_{j=1}^{p}\sum_{i=1}^{n} X_{ij}^2 - \sum_{j=1}^{p} \frac{\left(\sum_{i=1}^{n} X_{ij}\right)^2}{n}$$

The use of these raw-score formulas is illustrated in Table 14.3-2.

Computational Procedures for CR-3 Design

The computational procedures associated with a completely randomized design will be illustrated for the data from the diet experiment. You will recall that 30 girls were randomly assigned to three diets, with the restriction that 10 girls were assigned each diet. The amount of weight loss for each girl was measured one month after going on a diet. The steps to be followed in testing the null hypothesis and the decision rule are as follows:

Step 1. State the statistical hypotheses:

$H_0: \mu_1 = \mu_2 = \mu_3$
$H_1: \mu_j \neq \mu_{j'}$ for some j and j'.

Step 2. Specify the test statistic:

$F = \dfrac{MSBG}{MSWG}$ because we want to test $\mu_1 = \mu_2 = \mu_3$, random sampling was used, and we assume that the three populations are approximately normally distributed with equal variances.

Step 3. Specify the sample size:[5] specify the sampling distribution:

$np = 30$;
F distribution with $v_1 = p - 1$ and $v_2 = p(n - 1)$ because we assume that the three populations are approximately normally distributed.

Step 4. Specify the significance level:

$\alpha = .05$.

Step 5. Obtain a random sample of np participants or randomly assign np participants to p treatment levels, compute F, and make a decision.

Decision rule:

Reject the null hypothesis if F falls in the upper 5% of the sampling distribution of F; otherwise, don't reject the null hypothesis. If the null hypothesis is rejected, conclude that the weight loss population means for the three diets are not equal; if the null hypothesis is not rejected, do not draw this conclusion.

Before testing the null hypothesis, it is good statistical practice to first compute descriptive statistics for one's data. The stacked box plots in Figure 14.3-2 indicate that the weight-loss data do not contain outliers and are relatively symmetrical. The symmetry of the sample distributions suggests that the populations also are probably symmetrical. This is useful information because, as we will see in Section 14.4, the ANOVA F test is robust to nonnormality if the populations are relatively symmetrical. The sample means and standard deviations for the

---

[5] A discussion of procedures for making a rational specification of sample size for a completely randomized design is beyond the scope of this book. The interested reader is referred to Cohen (1988, chap. 8) and Kirk (1995, pp. 182–188).

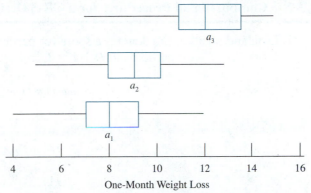

Figure 14.3-2. **Stacked box plots for the weight-loss data in Table 14.2-1. The sample distributions are relatively symmetrical and have about the same amount of dispersion. There are no outliers.**

weight-loss data are shown in Table 14.3-1. It appears that there are sizable differences among several of the weight-loss sample means. For example, diet a_3 resulted in a much greater weight loss than the other two diets. If the differences are statistically significant, that is, cannot be attributed to chance, they would be practically significant. If the three sample means had been 8.00, 8.25, and 8.75, there would be little point in testing the null hypothesis because a weight loss difference of only 0.75 pounds after one month of dieting is of no practical value. We also note from Table 14.3-1 that the three sample standard deviations are very similar. The researcher can conclude that the population variances are probably homogeneous. Homogeneity of population variances is one of the assumptions of ANOVA discussed in Section 14.4. After examining Figure 14.3-1 and Table 14.3-1, a researcher would probably feel comfortable proceeding to test the ANOVA null hypothesis.

Table 14.3-2 presents the details of the computational procedures. The results of the analysis are summarized in the ANOVA table shown in Table 14.3-3. The sums of squares (*SS*) in Table 14.3-3 were obtained from Table 14.3-2. The mean squares (*MS*) were obtained by dividing the sums of squares by their respective degrees of

TABLE 14.3-1.   Descriptive Statistics for Weight-Loss Data

		Diet	
	a_1	a_2	a_3
$\overline{X}_{\cdot j}$	8.00	9.00	12.00
$\hat{\sigma}_j$	2.21	2.21	2.31

TABLE 14.3-2.   Computational Procedures for a CR-3 Design

(i) Data and notation [X_{ij} denotes a score for participant i in treatment level j; $i = 1, \ldots, n$ participants (s_i); $j = 1, \ldots, p$ treatment levels (a_j)]

AS Summary Table[a]

	a_1	a_2	a_3
	7	10	12
	9	13	11
	8	9	15
	12	11	7
	8	5	14
	7	9	10
	4	8	12
	10	10	12
	9	8	13
	6	7	14
$\sum\limits_{i=1}^{n} X_{ij} =$	80	90	120
$\overline{X}._{j} =$	8	9	12

(ii) Computational symbols[b]

$$\sum_{j=1}^{p} \sum_{i=1}^{n} X_{ij} = 7 + 9 + 8 + \cdots + 14 = 290.000$$

$$\sum_{j=1}^{p} \sum_{i=1}^{n} X_{ij}^2 = [AS] = (7)^2 + (9)^2 + (8)^2 + \cdots + (14)^2 = 3026.000$$

$$\frac{\left(\sum\limits_{j=1}^{p} \sum\limits_{i=1}^{n} X_{ij}\right)^2}{np} = [X] = \frac{(290)^2}{(3)(10)} = 2803.333$$

$$\sum_{j=1}^{p} \frac{\left(\sum\limits_{i=1}^{n} X_{ij}\right)^2}{n} = [A] = \frac{(80)^2}{10} + \cdots + \frac{(120)^2}{10} = 2890.000$$

(iii) Computational formulas

$$SSTO = [AS] - [X] = 3026.000 - 2803.333 = 222.667$$

$$SSBG = [A] - [X] = 2890.000 - 2803.333 = 86.667$$

$$SSWG = [AS] - [A] = 3026.000 - 2890.000 = 136.000$$

[a] A denotes treatment A, and S denotes participants; the table is so named because it reflects variation attributable to treatment levels (A) and participants (S).
[b] The symbols $[AS]$, $[X]$, and $[A]$ are used to simplify the computational formulas in part (iii).

TABLE 14.3-3. ANOVA Table for a CR-3 Design

Source	SS	df	MS	F
1. Between groups (*BG*) (three diets)	86.667	$p - 1 = 3 - 1 = 2$	43.334	[$^1/_2$] 8.60*
2. Within groups (*WG*)	136.000	$p(n - 1) = 3(10 - 1) = 27$	5.037	
3. Total	222.667	$np - 1 = (3)(10) - 1 = 29$		

[$^1/_2$] indicates that *F* was obtained by dividing the value of the *MS* in row 1 by the value of the *MS* in row 2.

* $p < .002$; see footnote 7.

freedom. The *F* statistic was obtained by dividing *MSBG* in row 1 by *MSWG* in row 2; this operation is indicated in the table by the symbol [$^1/_2$].

According to Appendix Table D.5, an *F* of 3.36 for 2 and 27 degrees of freedom cuts off the upper .05 region of the sampling distribution—that is, $F_{.05;2,27}$ is equal to 3.36.[6] Because the computed $F(2, 27) = 8.60$ is greater than $F_{.05;2,27} = 3.36$, the null hypothesis is rejected, and we conclude that at least two of the diets aren't equally effective.

The results of the *F* test can be presented either by means of a table, as in Table 14.3-3, or as a statement in the text. Using the latter method of presentation, one might say, "We can infer from the analysis of variance that the weight-loss population means for the three diets are not all equal, $F(2, 27) = 8.60$, $p < .002$."[7] When the results are presented in the text, it is customary to identify (1) the test statistic, (2) degrees of freedom (in parentheses) associated with the test statistic, (3) value of the statistic, and (4) *p*-value. A decision to reject the null hypothesis should always be based on the researcher's preselected level of significance, .05 in our example. The inclusion of the *p*-value in the text or in a footnote to the ANOVA table permits a reader to, in effect, set his or her own level of significance.

If the omnibus null hypothesis $\mu_1 = \mu_2 = \cdots = \mu_p$ is rejected in ANOVA, we know that at least one difference among the population means is not equal to 0. The next question is, "Which difference(s) isn't equal to 0?" Procedures for answering this question are described in Section 14.5. But before turning to that topic, we will examine the assumptions underlying the *F* test for a completely randomized design.

[6] *F* values for 2, 26 and 2, 28 degrees of freedom are given in Appendix Table D.5. The value for $F_{.05;2,27}$ was obtained by interpolation.

[7] The *p*-value, which was obtained with the aid of a computer, is .00129 and was rounded up to .002.

CHECK YOUR UNDERSTANDING OF SECTION 14.3

11. Deviation formulas are less convenient than raw-score formulas for computing sums of squares. The raw-score formula for *SSBG* can be derived from the deviation formula. Describe in words the operation(s) that was performed for each equation.

a. $\displaystyle n \sum_{j=1}^{p} (\overline{X}_{\cdot j} - \overline{X}_{\cdot\cdot})^2 = n \sum_{j=1}^{p} (\overline{X}_{\cdot j}^2 - 2\overline{X}_{\cdot\cdot}\overline{X}_{\cdot j} + \overline{X}_{\cdot\cdot}^2)$

b. $\displaystyle = n \sum_{j=1}^{p} \overline{X}_{\cdot j}^2 - 2n\overline{X}_{\cdot\cdot} \sum_{j=1}^{p} \overline{X}_{\cdot j} + np\overline{X}_{\cdot\cdot}^2$

c. $\displaystyle = n \sum_{j=1}^{p} \frac{\left(\sum_{i=1}^{n} X_{ij}\right)^2}{n^2} - 2n \frac{\sum_{j=1}^{p}\sum_{i=1}^{n} X_{ij}}{np} \frac{\sum_{j=1}^{p}\sum_{i=1}^{n} X_{ij}}{n}$
$\displaystyle + np \frac{\left(\sum_{j=1}^{p}\sum_{i=1}^{n} X_{ij}\right)^2}{n^2 p^2}$

d. $\displaystyle = \sum_{j=1}^{p} \frac{\left(\sum_{i=1}^{n} X_{ij}\right)^2}{n} - 2 \frac{\left(\sum_{j=1}^{p}\sum_{i=1}^{n} X_{ij}\right)^2}{np} + \frac{\left(\sum_{j=1}^{p}\sum_{i=1}^{n} X_{ij}\right)^2}{np}$

e. $\displaystyle = \sum_{j=1}^{p} \frac{\left(\sum_{i=1}^{n} X_{ij}\right)^2}{n} - \frac{\left(\sum_{j=1}^{p}\sum_{i=1}^{n} X_{ij}\right)^2}{np}$

12. a. Fill in the blanks in the following ANOVA table.

Source	SS	df	MS	F
Between groups	168.000	( )	( )	( )
Within groups	( )	76	( )	
Total	1384.000	79		

b. What is the approximate *p*-value of the F statistic?

13. An experiment was performed to investigate the effects of meaningfulness, or association value, of nonsense syllables on learning. Thirty-two participants were randomly assigned to four treatment levels, with the restriction that eight were assigned to each level. The nonsense syllables were selected from the list compiled by C. E. Noble. The association values of the lists were 25% for a_1, 50% for a_2, 75% for a_3, and 100% for a_4. The dependent variable was time (in minutes) needed to learn the list well enough to recite it correctly twice. The following data were obtained:

a_1	a_2	a_3	a_4
22	22	18	18
21	20	20	17
20	18	17	16
21	21	16	18
22	20	18	19
24	19	19	15
22	21	18	16
23	19	17	17

a. Construct stacked box plots for the data. Are the sample distributions relatively symmetrical? Do the data contain outliers?
b. Compute descriptive statistics, $\overline{X}_{.j}$'s and $\hat{\sigma}_j$'s, for the data, and construct a table similar to Table 14.3-1.
c. Are the sample data consistent with the researcher's hypothesis that $\mu_j \neq \mu_{j'}$, for some j and j'?
d. Test the hypothesis $\mu_1 = \mu_2 = \mu_3 = \mu_4$. Let $\alpha = .05$. Construct an ANOVA summary table; include the p-value.
e. Summarize the results of the ANOVA in a sentence or two.

14. List the steps used in testing the null hypothesis in Exercise 13, and state the decision rule.
15. Reaction time to red, green, and yellow instrument-panel warning lights was investigated. Thirty-one participants were randomly assigned to the three colors of warning lights. The participants pressed a microswitch as soon as they noticed the onset of the warning light. The dependent variable was reaction time in hundredths of a second. The following data were obtained; decimal points have been omitted.

a_1 (Yellow)	a_2 (Red)	a_3 (Green)
20	23	21
20	20	21
21	21	20
22	21	23
21	23	22
20	22	20
19	22	21
21	21	22
19	22	22
20	22	20
		19

  a. Construct stacked box plots for the data. Are the sample distributions relatively symmetrical? Do the data contain outliers?

  b. Compute descriptive statistics, $\overline{X}_{.j}$'s and $\hat{\sigma}_j$'s, for the data, and construct a table similar to Table 14.3-1.

  c. Are the sample data consistent with the researcher's hypothesis that $\mu_j \neq \mu_{j'}$ for some j and j'?

  d. Test the hypothesis $\mu_1 = \mu_2 = \mu_3$. Let $\alpha = .05$. Construct an ANOVA summary table; include the p-value.

  e. Summarize the results of the ANOVA in a sentence or two.

16. List the steps used in testing the null hypothesis in Exercise 15, and state the decision rule.

14.4 ASSUMPTIONS ASSOCIATED WITH A CR-p DESIGN

As with all statistical tests, the F test of the omnibus null hypothesis in analysis of variance involves assumptions. We will list the assumptions and then describe the effects of violating them.

1. The model equation $X_{ij} = \mu + \alpha_j + \epsilon_{ij}$ reflects all the sources of variation that affect X_{ij}.
2. Participants are random samples from the respective populations, or the participants have been randomly assigned to the treatment levels.
3. The $j = 1, \ldots, p$ populations are normally distributed.
4. The variances of the $j = 1, \ldots, p$ populations are equal.

At the outset it should be noted that for real data, some of the assumptions will always be violated. For example, the underlying populations from which samples are drawn are never exactly normally distributed. The important question, then, is not whether the assumptions are violated but rather whether minor violations seriously affect the significance level and power of the F test. Fortunately, as we will see, the F test in ANOVA is robust with respect to violation of a number of assumptions. That is, the test is not very sensitive to departures from some of its assumptions. Unfortunately, the F test is not as robust to violation of certain assumptions as was once thought.

Assumption That $X_{ij} = \mu + \alpha_j + \epsilon_{ij}$

Assumption 1 states that a score, X_{ij}, is the sum of three components: μ, the grand mean; α_j, the treatment effect of population j; and ϵ_{ij}, the error effect associated with participant i. The latter effect includes all effects not attributable to treatment level j, such as chance fluctuations in the participant's behavior, variations in the administration of the treatment condition, and any other conditions that are not held constant.

A completely randomized design is appropriate for experiments with one treatment in which the participants are randomly assigned to only one treatment level. If, for example, an experiment contains two or more treatments, say, treatment A with p levels and treatment B with q levels, or if a researcher wants to observe the participants under more than one treatment level, a different ANOVA design must be used. Designs appropriate for these situations are described in Chapter 15. The choice of an incorrect design can seriously affect the probability of a type I error and the power of the F test.

Assumption of Random Sampling or Random Assignment

Assumption 2 states that the participants in an experiment have been randomly sampled from populations of interest or have been randomly assigned to treatment levels. This is an important assumption. The use of random sampling or random assignment helps to distribute idiosyncratic characteristics of participants randomly over the treatment levels so that the characteristics do not selectively bias the outcome of an experiment.[8] In the absence of randomization, there is always the possibility that some variable other than the treatment produced the observed differences among the sample means. Hence, the interpretation of the results of experiments that do not use randomization involves some ambiguity.

Assumption of Normally Distributed Populations

Assumption 3 states that the populations are normally distributed. In the real world, this assumption is never satisfied because, for example, observations do not take values from $-\infty$ to $+\infty$. Fortunately, the F test in ANOVA, like the t test, is robust with respect to departures from normality. This is especially true when the populations are symmetrical and the sample sizes are equal and are greater than 12 (Clinch & Keselman, 1982; Tan, 1982). Studies indicate that even if the treatment populations are asymmetrical or are flatter or more peaked than normal, the actual probability of making a type I error will be fairly close to the nominal or specified probability if all of the populations have the same shape.

---

[8] Sometimes factors beyond the researcher's control preclude the random assignment of participants to treatment levels and the control of important extraneous variables. Cook and Campbell (1979) refer to such experiments as "quasi-experimental designs." Campbell (1957) examines potential sources of bias inherent in these designs. His paper is reprinted in Kirk (1972).

A rough check on the normality assumption can be made by constructing a frequency distribution for the scores in each treatment level and inspecting the distributions for evidence of skewness and kurtosis. Box plots also are useful for detecting marked departures from symmetry. Marked departures from normality in the samples raise questions concerning normality of the populations.

Assumption of Homogeneity of Variance

Assumption 4 states that the $j = 1, \ldots, p$ population variances are equal to σ_ϵ^2, that is, $\sigma_1^2 = \sigma_2^2 = \cdots = \sigma_p^2 = \sigma_\epsilon^2$. This assumption is referred to as the **homogeneity of variance assumption.**

Box (1954) reported that the ANOVA F test is robust with respect to violation of the homogeneity of variance assumption provided (1) there is an equal number of observations in each of the treatment levels, (2) the populations are normal, and (3) the ratio of the largest variance to the smallest variance does not exceed 3. Considering these restrictions and the fact that it is not unusual for the ratio of the largest to smallest sample variance to exceed 3, it seems prudent to question the reputed robustness of ANOVA with respect to unequal (heterogeneous) variances. Indeed, numerous investigators have shown that even when sample sizes are equal, the ANOVA F test is not robust with respect to the variance heterogeneity often encountered in behavioral and educational research. In the face of this evidence, it is clear that researchers should not ignore violations of the homogeneity of variance assumption. Fortunately, there are robust alternatives to the ANOVA F test statistic that can be used when heterogeneous population variances are suspected. The interested reader is referred to Clinch and Keselman (1982) and Wilcox (1996).

CHECK YOUR UNDERSTANDING OF SECTION 14.4

17. Qualify the statement "The F test in ANOVA is robust with respect to departures from normality."
18. A rough but adequate check on the tenability of the normality assumption consists of making a frequency distribution of the scores in each treatment level and inspecting them for evidence of skewness and kurtosis. Decide on the tenability of this assumption for the data in Exercises (a) 13 and (b) 15 in "Check Your Understanding of Section 14.3."
19. In words, what is the assumption of homogeneity of variance?
20. Term to remember
    a. Homogeneity of variance

14.5 MULTIPLE COMPARISON PROCEDURES

As we have seen, the ANOVA F test is used to determine the tenability of the omnibus null hypothesis $\mu_1 = \mu_2 = \cdots = \mu_p$. If this hypothesis is rejected, usually the next question is, Which population means are not equal? A number of test statistics have been developed for answering this question, that is, for ferreting out significant differences among population means, or, as it is often called, **data snooping.** Because the tests are performed after observing one's sample data, the tests also are referred to as **a posteriori** or **post hoc tests.**

In Section 14.1 we observed that researchers may have little interest in testing the omnibus null hypothesis that all population means are equal. Instead, they may be interested in testing only a specific set of null hypotheses. If this is the case, it would be pointless to use ANOVA to test the omnibus null hypothesis. When a researcher wishes to test a specific set of null hypotheses prior to observing the sample data, the tests are referred to as a **priori tests.** Statisticians have developed a variety of statistics called **multiple-comparison statistics** for performing both a posteriori and a priori tests. In the following paragraphs we will describe four multiple-comparison statistics. But first we will define a contrast among means.

Contrasts Among Means

A **contrast** or **comparison** among means is a difference among the means, with appropriate algebraic signs. We will use the symbols ψ_i and $\hat{\psi}_i$ to denote, respectively, the ith contrast among population means and a sample estimate of the ith contrast. For example, the population contrast $\mu_1 - \mu_2$ is denoted by the symbol ψ_1; the sample contrast $\overline{X}_1 - \overline{X}_2$, by $\hat{\psi}_1$. If an experiment contains $p = 3$ means, contrasts involving two and three population means may be of interest, for example,

$$\psi_1 = \mu_1 - \mu_2 \qquad \psi_4 = \frac{\mu_1 + \mu_2}{2} - \mu_3$$

$$\psi_2 = \mu_1 - \mu_3 \qquad \psi_5 = \frac{\mu_1 + \mu_3}{2} - \mu_2$$

$$\psi_3 = \mu_2 - \mu_3 \qquad \psi_6 = \frac{\mu_2 + \mu_3}{2} - \mu_1.$$

The contrasts on the left involve a difference between two means. Those on the right involve the average of two means versus a third mean. Contrast $\psi_4 = (\mu_1 + \mu_2)/2 - \mu_3$, for example, could represent the average of two experimental conditions versus a control condition.

All contrasts have a set of underlying coefficients, denoted by $c_1, c_2, \ldots, c_p$ that define the contrast. For example,

$$\psi_i = (c_1)\mu_1 + (c_2)\mu_2 + (c_3)\mu_3$$
$$\psi_1 = (1)\mu_1 + (-1)\mu_2 + (0)\mu_3 = \mu_1 - \mu_2, \text{ where } c_1 = 1, c_2 = -1, \text{ and } c_3 = 0$$

$$\psi_4 = (\tfrac{1}{2})\mu_1 + (\tfrac{1}{2})\mu_2 + (-1)\mu_3 = \frac{\mu_1 + \mu_2}{2} - \mu_3,$$
$$\text{where } c_1 = c_2 = \tfrac{1}{2} \text{ and } c_3 = -1.$$

Earlier, we wrote ψ_1, contrast 1, as $\mu_1 - \mu_2$; it was understood that the coefficients of the contrast were 1, −1, and 0. Ordinarily, we don't bother to write the coefficients unless they are numbers other than 1, −1, and 0. Notice that we couldn't express ψ_4, contrast 4, without using the coefficients $c_1 = c_2 = \tfrac{1}{2}$.

The difference $(\mu_1 + \mu_2)/2 - \mu_3$ is a contrast, but $(\mu_1 + \mu_2) - \mu_3$ is not. Why? For a difference among means to be a contrast, the coefficients must satisfy the following condition.

The **coefficients of a contrast,** $c_1, c_2, \ldots, c_p$, must be numbers such that the coefficients sum to 0. That is, $\Sigma_{j=1}^{p} c_j = c_1 + c_2 + \cdots + c_p = 0$.

The coefficients of the difference $(\mu_1 - \mu_2)/2 - \mu_3$ sum to zero: $\tfrac{1}{2} + \tfrac{1}{2} + (-1) = 0$. Hence, this difference is a contrast. However, the difference $(\mu_1 + \mu_2) - \mu_3$ is not a contrast because the coefficients do not sum to zero: $1 + 1 + (-1) = 1$.

For convenience, coefficients of contrasts usually are chosen so that the sum of their absolute values is equal to 2. That is,

$$\sum_{j=1}^{p} |c_j| = 2,$$

where $|c_j|$ indicates that the sign of c_j is always taken to be positive. All six of the contrasts described earlier satisfy this property. For example, the sum of the absolute value of the coefficients for ψ_1 and ψ_4 are, respectively,

$$|c_1| + |c_2| + |c_3| = |1| + |-1| + |0| = 1 + 1 + 0 = 2$$
$$|c_1| + |c_2| + |c_3| = |\tfrac{1}{2}| + |\tfrac{1}{2}| + |-1| = \tfrac{1}{2} + \tfrac{1}{2} + 1 = 2.$$

When all of the coefficients of a contrast except two are equal to 0, the contrast is called a **pairwise contrast.** Otherwise, the contrast is a nonpairwise contrast. For example, contrast

$$\psi_1 = (1)\mu_1 + (-1)\mu_2 + (0)\mu_3 = \mu_1 - \mu_2$$

is a pairwise contrast. However, contrast

$$\psi_4 = (\tfrac{1}{2})\mu_1 + (\tfrac{1}{2})\mu_2 + (-1)\mu_3 = (\mu_1 + \mu_2)/2 - \mu_3$$

is a nonpairwise contrast.

A Posteriori Multiple Comparison Tests

A variety of multiple comparison tests have been developed to help researchers decide which population contrasts are not equal to 0.[9] Three a posteriori multiple comparison tests are described in this section: Tukey's HSD test, the Fisher-Hayter test, and Scheffé's (pronounced Shef-fay) test. The Tukey and Fisher-Hayter tests are appropriate for testing all pairwise contrasts among p means. Scheffé's test can be used for making pairwise and nonpairwise tests. All three tests control the probability of making one or more type I errors for the collection of tests at or less than α.

Tukey's Multiple Comparison Test and Confidence Interval

Tukey's HSD test (HSD stands for *Honestly Significant Difference*) is the best known and most widely used of the a posteriori tests.

The formula for **Tukey's HSD test statistic,** denoted by q, is

$$q = \frac{\overline{X}_{.j} - \overline{X}_{.j'}}{\sqrt{\dfrac{MSWG}{n}}},$$

where $\overline{X}_{.j}$ and $\overline{X}_{.j'}$ are means of random samples from normal populations, *MSWG* is the denominator of the F statistic as computed in ANOVA, and n is the size of each sample used to compute the sample means.

MSWG can be obtained from an ANOVA or computed from sample estimators of the population standard deviations, $\hat{\sigma}_1, \hat{\sigma}_2, \ldots \hat{\sigma}_p$, as follows:

$$MSWG = \frac{(n_1 - 1)\hat{\sigma}_1^2 + (n_2 - 1)\hat{\sigma}_2^2 + \cdots + (n_p - 1)\hat{\sigma}_p^2}{(n_1 - 1) + (n_2 - 1) + \cdots + (n_p - 1)}$$

A test of the omnibus null hypothesis, $\mu_1 = \mu_1 = \cdots = \mu_p$, prior to testing all pairwise contrasts with Tukey's statistic is not required and would be superfluous. A pairwise, nondirectional null hypothesis, $\mu_j = \mu_{j'}$, is rejected if the absolute value of Tukey's q statistic exceeds or equals the critical value $q_{\alpha;p,\nu}$, where $q_{\alpha;p,\nu}$ is obtained from the distribution of the Studentized Range in Appendix Table D.10. The meaning of the subscripts in $q_{\alpha;p,\nu}$ is as follows: α is the two-tailed probability of

[9] Kirk (1994) describes 22 multiple comparison tests and provides guidelines for deciding when to use each test.

making one or more type I errors for the collection of all pairwise contrasts, p is the number of means in the experiment, and v is the degrees of freedom associated with *MSWG,* which is equal to $p(n - 1)$ for the completely randomized ANOVA design. Ordinarily, we would use $\alpha/2$ instead of α to denote a two-tailed probability. It is common to depart from this convention when a statistic is appropriate for performing only two-tailed tests. None of the three a posteriori tests is appropriate for one-tailed tests because they are performed after examining the sample means. Tukey's test has another limitation: It requires equal sample n's. If the sample n's are not equal, the Fisher-Hayter test described later can be used to test all pairwise contrasts.

We will use the weight-loss data in Tables 14.3-1 and 14.3-3 to illustrate the computational procedures for Tukey's test. The sample means in Table 14.3-1 are $\overline{X}_{.1} = 8.00$, $\overline{X}_{.2} = 9.00$, $\overline{X}_{.3} = 12.00$; $MSWG = 5.037$ from Table 14.3-3, and $n = 10$. The .05 level of significance is adopted. Hence, the probability of making one or more type I errors for the collection of all a posteriori, pairwise contrasts will not exceed .05. The three q statistics, $q = (\overline{X}_{.j} - \overline{X}_{.j'})/\sqrt{MSWG/n}$, are as follows:

$$q = \frac{8.00 - 9.00}{\sqrt{\dfrac{5.037}{10}}} = -1.41 \qquad (\overline{X}_{.1} \text{ versus } \overline{X}_{.2})$$

$$q = \frac{8.00 - 12.00}{\sqrt{\dfrac{5.037}{10}}} = -5.64 \qquad (\overline{X}_{.1} \text{ versus } \overline{X}_{.3})$$

$$q = \frac{9.00 - 12.00}{\sqrt{\dfrac{5.037}{10}}} = -4.23 \qquad (\overline{X}_{.2} \text{ versus } \overline{X}_{.3})$$

To reject a null hypothesis, the absolute value $|q|$ must exceed or equal $q_{.05;3,27} \cong 3.51$. Because $|q(27)| = 5.64$ and 4.23 are greater than $q_{.05;3,27} \cong 3.51$, the null hypotheses $\mu_1 = \mu_3$ and $\mu_2 = \mu_3$ can be rejected. We can conclude that for the population of girls represented in the experiment, diet a_3 would produce a greater weight loss than diets a_1 and a_2. Based on the sample data, our best guess is that the use of diet a_3 would result in losing 4 more pounds than diet a_1 and 3 more than diet a_2.

Tukey's statistic also can be used to construct confidence intervals for all a posteriori, pairwise contrasts.

A two-sided $100(1 - \alpha)\%$ confidence interval for the contrast $\psi_i = \mu_j - \mu_{j'}$ is

$$(\overline{X}_{.j} - \overline{X}_{.j'}) - \frac{q_{\alpha;p,v}\sqrt{MSWG}}{\sqrt{n}} < \mu_j - \mu_{j'} < (\overline{X}_{.j} - \overline{X}_{.j'}) + \frac{q_{\alpha;p,v}\sqrt{MSWG}}{\sqrt{n}},$$

where $\overline{X}_{.j}$ and $\overline{X}_{.j'}$ are means of random samples from normal populations; $q_{\alpha;p,v}$ is the value that cuts off the upper $\alpha/2$ region from Appendix Table D.10; p is the number of means in the experiment; ν is the degrees of freedom associated with *MSWG*, which is equal to $p(n - 1)$ for the completely randomized ANOVA design; and n is the size of each sample used to compute the sample means.

MSWG can be obtained from an ANOVA or computed from sample estimators of the population standard deviations, $\hat{\sigma}_1, \hat{\sigma}_2, \ldots, \hat{\sigma}_p$, as follows:

$$MSWG = \frac{(n_1 - 1)\hat{\sigma}_1^2 + (n_2 - 1)\hat{\sigma}_2^2 + \cdots + (n_p - 1)\hat{\sigma}_p^2}{(n_1 - 1) + (n_2 - 1) + \cdots + (n_p - 1)}$$

Two-sided $100(1 - .05)\% = 95\%$ confidence intervals for all pairwise contrasts among the weight-loss means, where $\overline{X}_{.1} = 8.00$, $\overline{X}_{.2} = 9.00$, $\overline{X}_{.3} = 12.00$, $MSWG = 5.037$, $q_{.05;3,27} = 3.51$, and $n = 10$, are as follows:

$$(\overline{X}_{.j} - \overline{X}_{.j'}) - \frac{q_{.05;3,27}\sqrt{MSWG}}{\sqrt{n}} < \mu_j - \mu_{j'} < \overline{X}_{.j} - \overline{X}_{.j'}) + \frac{q_{.05;3,27}\sqrt{MSWG}}{\sqrt{n}}$$

$$(8.00 - 9.00) - \frac{3.51\sqrt{5.037}}{\sqrt{10}} < \mu_1 - \mu_2 < (8.00 - 9.00) + \frac{3.51\sqrt{5.037}}{\sqrt{10}}$$

$$-3.49 < \mu_1 - \mu_2 < 1.49$$

$$(8.00 - 12.00) - \frac{3.51\sqrt{5.073}}{\sqrt{10}} < \mu_1 - \mu_3 < (8.00 - 12.00) + \frac{3.51\sqrt{5.037}}{\sqrt{10}}$$

$$-6.49 < \mu_1 - \mu_3 < -1.51$$

$$(9.00 - 12.00) - \frac{3.51\sqrt{5.073}}{\sqrt{10}} < \mu_2 - \mu_3 < (9.00 - 12.00) + \frac{3.51\sqrt{5.037}}{\sqrt{10}}$$

$$-5.49 < \mu_2 - \mu_3 < -0.51$$

These 95% confidence intervals correspond to the colored portion of the real number line as follows:

Because the confidence intervals for $\mu_1 - \mu_3$ and $\mu_2 - \mu_3$ do not include 0, we can be 95% confident that the contrasts are not equal to 0. Furthermore, for the population of girls represented in the experiment, we can be 95% confident that the mean weight loss difference between girls who use diets a_1 and a_3 is -1.51 to -6.49 pounds. The mean weight loss difference between girls who use diets a_2 and a_3 is -0.51 to -5.49 pounds. Diet a_3 is the clear choice.

The assumptions associated with Tukey's statistic and confidence interval are as follows.

1. Random sampling or random assignment of participants.
2. The $j = 1, \ldots, p$ populations are normally distributed.
3. The variances of the $j = 1, \ldots, p$ populations are equal.
4. The sample n's are equal.

Robust alternative tests that can be used when the population variances are unequal (assumption 3) are described by Kirk (1995, pp. 146–148) and Wilcox (1996). If the sample n's are unequal (assumption 4), the Fisher-Hayter test described in the next section can be used to test null hypotheses for all pairwise contrasts.

Fisher-Hayter Multiple Comparison Test

The Fisher-Hayter multiple comparison test is a two-step procedure. The first step consists of testing the omnibus null hypothesis, $\mu_1 = \mu_2 = \cdots = \mu_p$, at α level of significance. If the ANOVA F test is not significant, the omnibus null hypothesis is not rejected, and it is concluded that none of the pairwise contrasts differs from 0. If the omnibus null hypothesis is rejected, each of the pairwise contrasts is tested using the Fisher-Hayter test statistic.

The formula for the **Fisher-Hayter test statistic,** denoted by *qFH*, is

$$qFH = \frac{\overline{X}_{\cdot j} - \overline{X}_{\cdot j'}}{\sqrt{\dfrac{MSWG}{2}\left(\dfrac{1}{n_j} + \dfrac{1}{n_{j'}}\right)}},$$

where $\overline{X}_{\cdot j}$ and $\overline{X}_{\cdot j'}$ are means of random samples from normal populations, *MSWG* is the denominator of the F statistic as computed in ANOVA, and n_j and $n_{j'}$ are the sizes of the samples used to compute the sample means.

A pairwise, nondirectional null hypothesis, $\mu_j = \mu_{j'}$, is rejected if the absolute value of the Fisher-Hayter qFH statistic exceeds or equals the critical value $q_{\alpha; p-1, \nu}$, where $q_{\alpha; p-1, \nu}$, is obtained from the distribution of the Studentized Range in Appendix Table D.10. Notice that Appendix Table D.10 is entered for $p - 1$

means instead of the actual number of means in the experiment. The meaning of the other subscripts in $q_{\alpha;p-1,\nu}$, is as follows: α is the two-tailed probability of making one or more type I errors for the collection of all possible pairwise contrasts, and ν is the degrees of freedom associated with *MSWG*, which is equal to $p(n-1)$ for the completely randomized ANOVA design.

The Fisher-Hayter test has two important advantages relative to Tukey's test: (1) It can be used when the sample sizes are not equal and (2) it is more powerful than Tukey's test for most data. Hence, researchers who use the Fisher-Hayter test are more likely to reject false null hypotheses. The test has one major limitation: Because of the two-step nature of the procedure, it cannot be used to construct confidence intervals. If a researcher's only interest is in testing null hypotheses, the Fisher-Hayter test is preferred over Tukey's test because of its superior power.

The weight-loss data in Tables 14.3-1 and 14.3-3 will be used to illustrate the computational procedures for the Fisher-Hayter test. The first step is to test the omnibus null hypothesis using an ANOVA F test. The F test is summarized in Table 14.3-3 and is significant. Because the F test is significant, the next step is to compute

$$qFH = \frac{\overline{X}_{\cdot j} - \overline{X}_{\cdot j'}}{\sqrt{\dfrac{MSWG}{2}\left(\dfrac{1}{n_j} + \dfrac{1}{n_{j'}}\right)}}$$

for each pairwise contrast.

$$qFH = \frac{8.00 - 9.00}{\sqrt{\dfrac{5.037}{2}\left(\dfrac{1}{10} + \dfrac{1}{10}\right)}} = -1.41 \qquad (\overline{X}_{\cdot 1} \text{ versus } \overline{X}_{\cdot 2})$$

$$qFH = \frac{8.00 - 12.00}{\sqrt{\dfrac{5.037}{2}\left(\dfrac{1}{10} + \dfrac{1}{10}\right)}} = -5.64 \qquad (\overline{X}_{\cdot 1} \text{ versus } \overline{X}_{\cdot 3})$$

$$qFH = \frac{9.00 - 12.00}{\sqrt{\dfrac{5.037}{2}\left(\dfrac{1}{10} + \dfrac{1}{10}\right)}} = -4.23 \qquad (\overline{X}_{\cdot 2} \text{ versus } \overline{X}_{\cdot 3})$$

To reject a null hypothesis, the absolute value $|qFH|$ must exceed or equal $q_{.05;3-1,27} \cong 2.90$. Because $|qFH(27)| = 5.64$ and 4.23 are greater than $q_{.05;3-1,27} \cong 2.90$, the null hypotheses for $\mu_1 = \mu_3$ and $\mu_2 = \mu_3$ are rejected. We reached the same decision using Tukey's test. When the sample n's are equal, as in the present example, the formulas for Tukey's q statistic and the Fisher-Hayter qFH statistic are equivalent. The Fisher-Hayter test is more likely to reject false null hypotheses because its critical value is less than that for Tukey's test. In the present example, $q_{.05;3-1,27} \cong 2.90$ for the Fisher-Hayter test versus $q_{.05;3,27} \cong 3.51$ for Tukey's test.

The assumptions associated with the Fisher-Hayter statistic are as follows:

1. Random sampling or random assignment of participants.
2. The $j = 1, \ldots, p$ populations are normally distributed.
3. The variances of the $j = 1, \ldots, p$ populations are equal.

Scheffé's Multiple Comparison Test and Confidence Interval

We turn now to Scheffé's test—one of the more versatile of the a posteriori tests. The test should be used if any of the null hypotheses involves a nonpairwise contrast, that is, a contrast of the form

$$\psi_i = c_1\mu_1 + c_2\mu_2 + \cdots + c_p\mu_p,$$

where three or more of the c_j coefficients are not 0. As noted earlier, if a researcher is interested only in hypotheses involving pairwise contrasts, Tukey's test or the Fisher-Hayter test should be used because of their greater power.

After examining the weight-loss data in Table 14.3-1, a researcher might be interested in the following nondirectional null hypotheses: $\mu_1 - \mu_3 = 0$, $\mu_2 - \mu_3 = 0$, and $(\mu_1 + \mu_2)/2 - \mu_3 = 0$.

The formula for **Scheffé's test statistic,** denoted by *FS*, is

$$FS = \frac{(c_1\overline{X}_{.1} + c_2\overline{X}_{.2} + \cdots + c_p\overline{X}_{.p})^2}{MSWG\left(\dfrac{c_1^2}{n_1} + \dfrac{c_2^2}{n_2} + \cdots + \dfrac{c_p^2}{n_p}\right)},$$

where $c_1, c_2, \ldots, c_p$ are coefficients that define a contrast, $\overline{X}_{.1}, \overline{X}_{.2}, \ldots, \overline{X}_{.p}$ are means of random samples from normal populations, *MSWG* is the denominator of the F statistic as computed in ANOVA, and $n_1, n_2, \ldots, n_p$ are the sizes of the samples used to compute the sample means.

A test of the omnibus null hypothesis, $\mu_1 = \mu_1 = \cdots = \mu_p$, prior to testing contrasts with Scheffé's statistic is not required and would be superfluous. A nondirectional null hypothesis for $\psi_i = c_1\mu_1 + c_2\mu_2 + \cdots + c_p\mu_p = 0$ is rejected if the absolute value of Scheffé's *FS* statistic exceeds or equals the critical value $(p-1)F_{\alpha;\nu_1,\nu_2}$, where p is the number of means in the experiment and $F_{\alpha;\nu_1,\nu_2}$ is obtained from Appendix Table D.5. The meaning of the subscripts in $F_{\alpha;\nu_1,\nu_2}$ is as follows: α is the value that cuts off the upper α region from Appendix Table D.5, ν_1 is equal to $p - 1$, and ν_2 is the degrees of freedom associated with the *MSWG* error term, which is equal to $p(n-1)$ for the completely randomized ANOVA design.

The Scheffé *FS* statistics for the weight-loss data in Tables 14.3-1 and 14.3-3 are as follows:

$$FS = \frac{[(1)8.00 + (0)9.00 + (-1)12.00]^2}{5.037\left(\dfrac{(1)^2}{10} + \dfrac{(0)^2}{10} + \dfrac{(-1)^2}{10}\right)} = 15.88 \qquad (\overline{X}_{.1} \text{ versus } \overline{X}_{.3})$$

$$FS = \frac{[(0)8.00 + (1)9.00 + (-1)12.00]^2}{5.037\left(\dfrac{(0)^2}{10} + \dfrac{(1)^2}{10} + \dfrac{(-1)^2}{10}\right)} = 8.93 \qquad (\overline{X}_{.2} \text{ versus } \overline{X}_{.3})$$

$$FS = \frac{\left[\left(\dfrac{1}{2}\right)8.00 + \left(\dfrac{1}{2}\right)9.00 + (-1)12.00\right]^2}{5.037\left[\dfrac{\left(\dfrac{1}{2}\right)^2}{10} + \dfrac{\left(\dfrac{1}{2}\right)^2}{10} + \dfrac{(-1)^2}{10}\right]} \qquad \left(\dfrac{\overline{X}_{.1} + \overline{X}_{.2}}{2} \text{ versus } \overline{X}_{.3}\right)$$

$$= 16.21$$

To reject a null hypothesis, the absolute value $|FS|$ must exceed or equal $(3 - 1)F_{.05;2,27} = (2)(3.35) = 6.70$. Because $|FS(2, 27)| = 15.88$, 8.93 and 16.21 are greater than 6.70, the null hypotheses $\mu_1 = \mu_3$, $\mu_2 = \mu_3$ and $(\mu_1 + \mu_2)/2 = \mu_3$ can be rejected.

Scheffé's statistic also can be used to construct confidence intervals for all a posteriori contrasts of interest.

A two-sided $100(1 - \alpha)\%$ confidence interval for $\psi_i = c_1\mu_1 + c_2\mu_2 + \cdots + c_p\mu_p$ is

$$\hat{\psi}_i - \sqrt{(p - 1)F_{\alpha;v_1,v_2}}\sqrt{MSWG \sum_{j=1}^{p} \frac{c_j^2}{n_j}} < \psi_i$$

$$< \hat{\psi}_i + \sqrt{(p - 1)F_{\alpha;v_1,v_2}}\sqrt{MSWG \sum_{j=1}^{p} \frac{c_j^2}{n_j}},$$

where $\hat{\psi} = c_1\overline{X}_{.1} + c_2\overline{X}_{.2} + \cdots + c_p\overline{X}_{.p}$, $c_1, c_2, \ldots, c_p$ are coefficients that define a contrast, $\overline{X}_{.1}, \overline{X}_{.2}, \ldots, \overline{X}_{.p}$ are means of random samples from normal populations, p is the number of means in the experiment, $F_{\alpha;v_1,v_2}$ is the value that cuts off the upper α region from Appendix Table D.5, $v_1 = p - 1$, v_2 is the degrees of freedom associated with *MSWG*, which is equal to $p(n - 1)$ for the completely randomized ANOVA design, *MSWG* is the denominator of the F statistic as computed in ANOVA, and $n_1, n_2, \ldots, n_p$ are the sizes of the samples used to compute the sample means.

MSWG can be obtained from an ANOVA or computed from sample estimators of the population standard deviations, $\hat{\sigma}_1, \hat{\sigma}_2, \ldots, \hat{\sigma}_p$, as follows.

$$MSWG = \frac{(n_1 - 1)\hat{\sigma}_1^2 + (n_2 - 1)\hat{\sigma}_2^2 + \cdots + (n_p - 1)\hat{\sigma}_p^2}{(n_1 - 1) + (n_2 - 1) + \cdots + (n_p - 1)}$$

We will use the data from the diet experiment to illustrate a two-sided $100(1 - .05)\% = 95\%$ confidence interval for $\psi = (\frac{1}{2})\mu_1 + (\frac{1}{2})\mu_2 + (-1)\mu_3$. Recall that the weight-loss means were $\overline{X}_{.1} = 8.0,\ \ \overline{X}_{.2} = 9.0,\ \overline{X}_{.3} = 12.0;\ MSWG = 5.037,\ (3 - 1)F_{.05;2,27} = (2)(3.35) = 6.70$, and $n_1 = n_2 = n_3 = 10$.

$$[(\tfrac{1}{2})8.0 + (\tfrac{1}{2})9.0 + (-1)12.0] - \sqrt{(2)(3.35)(5.037)\left[\frac{(\tfrac{1}{2})^2 + (\tfrac{1}{2})^2 + (-1)^2}{10 + 10 + 10}\right]}$$

$$< \psi < [(\tfrac{1}{2})8.0 + (\tfrac{1}{2})9.0 + (-1)12.0]$$

$$+ \sqrt{(2)(3.35)(5.037)\left[\frac{(\tfrac{1}{2})^2 + (\tfrac{1}{2})^2 + (-1)^2}{10 + 10 + 10}\right]}$$

$$-5.45 < \psi < -1.55$$

Because the 95% confidence interval does not include 0, a test of the null hypothesis that the contrast $\psi = (\mu_1 - \mu_2)/2 - \mu_3$ is equal to 0 would be rejected. For the population of girls represented in the experiment, the researcher can be 95% confident that the mean of the mean weight losses for girls who use diets a_1 and a_2 versus the mean for those who use a_3 is between -5.46 and -1.55 pounds. The 95% confidence interval corresponds to the colored portion of the real number line as follows:

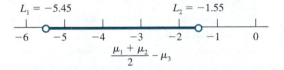

The assumptions associated with Scheffé's statistic and confidence interval are as follows:

1. Random sampling or random assignment of participants.
2. The $j = 1, \ldots, p$ populations are normally distributed.
3. The variances of each of the $j = 1, \ldots, p$ populations are equal.

A robust alternative test that can be used when the population variances are unequal (assumption 3) is described by Kirk (1995, p. 155).

A Priori Multiple Comparison Test and Confidence Interval

If an experiment has been designed to answer a specific set of research questions, there usually is little interest in the omnibus ANOVA null hypothesis. Suppose, for example, that the diet experiment in Section 14.2 had been designed to compare the standard diet, a_1, with two new diets, a_2 and a_3. The researcher is interested in the following null hypotheses, where the dependent variable is amount of weight lost.

$$H_0: \mu_1 - \mu_2 \geq 0 \qquad H_0: \mu_1 - \mu_3 \geq 0 \qquad H_0: \mu_2 - \mu_3 = 0$$
$$H_1: \mu_1 - \mu_2 < 0 \qquad H_1: \mu_1 - \mu_3 < 0 \qquad H_1: \mu_2 - \mu_3 \neq 0$$

The first two hypotheses are directional; the third is nondirectional. In words, these hypotheses express the researcher's belief that the new diets, a_2 and a_3, will result in larger weight losses than the standard diet, a_1, but the researcher is unable to predict which of the new diets will be the most effective.

A number of tests have been developed for testing a priori hypotheses. The one that is described here is the Dunn-Šidàk test.[10] The test enables you to test $C \geq 3$ a priori, pairwise or nonpairwise, one- or two-sided null hypotheses and maintain the probability of making one or more type I errors at or less than α for the collection of tests. The procedure consists of dividing the level of significance, α, equally among a set of C tests. For example, if you wanted to perform three nondirectional tests and control the probability of making one or more erroneous decisions at $\alpha = .05$ for the collection of tests, you could perform each of the $i = 1, \ldots, C$ tests at $\alpha_i = 1 - (1 - .05)^{1/C} = .01695$. If this is done, the probability of making one or more erroneous decisions for the collection of three tests is

$$\text{Prob. of one or more type I errors } \leq 1 - (1 - \alpha_i)^C$$
$$\leq 1 - (1 - .01695)^3$$
$$\leq .05.$$

The table of critical values for the Dunn-Šidàk test in Appendix Table D.11 is based on dividing a level of significance, α, equally among C tests.

The formula for the **Dunn-Šidàk test statistic,** denoted by tDS, is

$$tDS = \frac{c_1\overline{X}_{.1} + c_2\overline{X}_{.2} + \cdots + c_p\overline{X}_{.p}}{\sqrt{MSWG\left(\frac{c_1^2}{n_1} + \frac{c_2^2}{n_2} + \cdots + \frac{c_p^2}{n_p}\right)}},$$

where $c_1, c_2, \ldots, c_p$ are coefficients that define a contrast, $\overline{X}_{.1}, \overline{X}_{.2}, \ldots, \overline{X}_{.p}$, are means of random samples from normal populations, $MSWG$ is the denominator of the F statistic as computed in ANOVA, and $n_1, n_2, \ldots, n_p$ are the sizes of the samples used to compute the sample means.

A nondirectional null hypothesis, $c_1\mu_1 = c_2\mu_2 = \cdots = c_p\mu_p = 0$, is rejected if the absolute value of the Dunn-Šidàk tDS statistic exceeds or equals the critical value $tDS_{\alpha/2;C,\nu}$, where $tDS_{\alpha/2;C,\nu}$ is obtained from Appendix Table D.11. If a null hypothesis is directional, the absolute value of tDS must exceed or equal $tDS_{\alpha;C,\nu}$ and the difference among the means must be consistent with the alternative hypothesis. The meaning of the subscripts in $tDS_{\alpha/2;C,\nu}$ is as follows: $\alpha/2$ is the two-tailed probability of making one or more type I errors for C a priori contrasts, C is the number of a

[10] Some computer software packages refer to this test as the Šidàk test.

priori contrasts to be tested, and ν is the degrees of freedom associated with *MSWG*, which is equal to $p(n - 1)$ for the completely randomized ANOVA design. The critical value $tDS_{\alpha;C,\nu}$ denotes the one-tailed probability of making one or more type I errors for C a priori contrasts.

Tests of the null hypotheses

$$H_0: \mu_1 - \mu_2 \geq 0 \qquad H_0: \mu_1 - \mu_3 \geq 0 \qquad H_0: \mu_2 - \mu_3 = 0$$

for the weight-loss data are as follows:

$$tDS = \frac{(1)8.00 + (-1)9.00 + (0)12.000}{\sqrt{5.037\left[\frac{(1)^2}{10} + \frac{(-1)^2}{10} + \frac{(0)^2}{10}\right]}} = -1.00 \qquad (\overline{X}_{.1} \text{ versus } \overline{X}_{.2})$$

$$tDS = \frac{(1)8.00 + (0)9.00 + (-1)12.000}{\sqrt{5.037\left[\frac{(1)^2}{10} + \frac{(0)^2}{10} + \frac{(-1)^2}{10}\right]}} = -3.99 \qquad (\overline{X}_{.1} \text{ versus } \overline{X}_{.3})$$

$$tDS = \frac{(0)8.00 + (1)9.00 + (-1)12.000}{\sqrt{5.037\left[\frac{(0)^2}{10} + \frac{(1)^2}{10} + \frac{(-1)^2}{10}\right]}} = -2.99 \qquad (\overline{X}_{.2} \text{ versus } \overline{X}_{.3})$$

According to Appendix Table D.11, the one-tailed critical value for the first two statistics is $tDS_{.05;3,27} \cong 2.23$. The two-tailed critical value for the third statistic is $tDS_{.05/2;3,27} \cong 2.55$. The null hypothesis $\mu_1 - \mu_3 \geq 0$ can be rejected because the absolute value $|tDS(27)| = 3.99$ is greater than $tDS_{.05;3,27} \cong 2.23$ and the difference $\overline{X}_{.1} - \overline{X}_{.3} = -3.99$ is consistent with the alternative hypothesis; similarly, $\mu_2 - \mu_3 = 0$ can be rejected because the absolute value $|tDS(27)| = 2.99$ is greater than $tDS_{.05/2;3,27} \cong 2.55$.

The Dunn-Šidàk statistic also can be used to construct confidence intervals for C a priori contrasts.

A two-sided $100(1 - \alpha)\%$ confidence interval for the contrast $\psi_i = c_1\mu_1 + c_2\mu_2 + \cdots + c_p\mu_p$ is

$$\hat{\psi}_i - qDS_{\alpha/2,C,\nu}\sqrt{MSWG\sum_{j=1}^{p}\frac{c_j^2}{n_j}} < \psi_i < \hat{\psi}_i + qDS_{\alpha/2,C,\nu}\sqrt{MSWG\sum_{j=1}^{p}\frac{c_j^2}{n_j}},$$

where $\hat{\psi}_i = c_1\overline{X}_{.1} + c_2\overline{X}_{.2} + \cdots + c_p\overline{X}_{.p}, c_1, c_2, \ldots, c_p$ are coefficients that define a contrast, $\overline{X}_{.1}, \overline{X}_{.2}, \ldots, \overline{X}_{.p}$ are means of random samples from normal populations, p is the number of means in the experiment, $qDS_{\alpha/2,C,\nu}$ is the value that cuts off the upper $\alpha/2$ region from Appendix Table D.11, C is the number of a priori contrast, ν is the degrees of freedom associated with *MSWG*, which is equal to $p(n - 1)$ for the completely randomized ANOVA design, *MSWG* is the denominator of the F statistic as computed in ANOVA, and $n_1, n_2, \ldots, n_p$ are the sizes of the samples used to compute the sample means.

A one-sided $100(1 - \alpha)\%$ confidence interval is

$$\hat{\psi}_i - qDS_{\alpha,C,\nu} \sqrt{MSWG \sum_{j=1}^{p} \frac{c_j^2}{n_j}} < \psi_i \quad \text{or} \quad \psi_i < \hat{\psi} + qDS_{\alpha,C,\nu} \sqrt{MSWG \sum_{j=1}^{p} \frac{c_j^2}{n_j}},$$

where $qDS_{\alpha,C,\nu}$ is the value that cuts off the upper α region from Appendix Table D.11.

Earlier we used the Dunn-Šidàk statistic to test the one-sided null hypothesis

$$H_0\text{: } \mu_1 - \mu_2 \geq 0$$

for the weight-loss data. An analogous $100(1 - .05)\% = 95\%$ confidence interval is

$$\mu_1 - \mu_2 < [(c_1)\overline{X}_{.1} + (c_2)\overline{X}_{.2} + (c_3)\overline{X}_{.3}] + qDS_{\alpha,C,\nu} \sqrt{MSWG \sum_{j=1}^{p} \frac{c_j^2}{n_j}}$$

$$< [(1)8.0 + (-1)9.0 + (0)12.0] + 2.23\sqrt{5.037 \left[\frac{(1)^2}{10} + \frac{(-1)^2}{10} + \frac{(0)^2}{10} \right]}$$

$$< 1.24$$

The researcher can be 95% confident that the population contrast $\psi = \mu_1 - \mu_2$ is less than 1.24. The interval includes 0 and is consistent with the nonsignificant test of the null hypothesis. The 95% confidence interval corresponds to the colored portion of the real number line as follows:

The assumptions associated with the Dunn-Šidàk statistic and confidence interval are as follows:

1. Random sampling or random assignment of participants.
2. The $j = 1, \ldots, p$ populations are normally distributed.
3. The variances of each of the $j = 1, \ldots, p$ populations are equal.

Comparison of the Multiple Comparison Tests

Four multiple comparison tests have been described. Each of the tests controls the probability of making one or more type I errors at or less than α for a collection of tests, but they differ in the nature of the collection.

1. The Tukey and the Fisher-Hayter tests control the type I error for the collection of all pairwise, a posteriori contrasts.
2. The Scheffé test controls the type I error for the collection of all pairwise and nonpairwise, a posteriori contrasts.
3. The Dunn-Šidàk test controls the type I error for the collection of C pairwise and nonpairwise, a priori contrasts.

Other similarities and differences among the tests are summarized in Table 14.5-1.

As noted earlier, the three a posteriori tests differ in power. The Fisher-Hayter test is the most powerful. Scheffé's test is the least powerful. We can get a feeling for the relative power of the three tests by determining the value of the smallest difference between two means that would be significant at, say, the .05 level of significance. We will make the comparisons comparable by assuming that we want to test all pairwise comparisons among the weight-loss means. The smallest difference between two means that would be significant for the three tests is as follows:

Fisher-Hayter $\quad qFH_{.05;3-1,27} \sqrt{\dfrac{MSWG}{2}\left(\dfrac{1}{n_j}+\dfrac{1}{n_{j'}}\right)} = 2.90(.07097) = 2.06$

Tukey $\quad q_{.05;3,27} \sqrt{\dfrac{MSWG}{n}} = 3.51(.07097) = 2.49$

Scheffé $\quad \sqrt{(p-1)F_{.05;2,27}} \sqrt{MSWG\left(\dfrac{1}{n_j}+\dfrac{1}{n_{j'}}\right)} = 2.59(1.0037) = 2.60$

Assuming that the ANOVA F test for the Fisher-Hayter procedure is significant, it is the most powerful because it will reject the null hypothesis $\mu_j = \mu_{j'}$ for differences among sample means as small as 2.06.

TABLE 14.5-1.   Comparison of Multiple-Comparison Tests

	Tukey	Fisher-Hayter	Scheffé	Dunn-Šidàk
Type of hypothesis	a posteriori	a posteriori	a posteriori	a priori
Type of contrast	pairwise	pairwise	pairwise and nonpairwise	pairwise and nonpairwise
Confidence intervals available	yes	no	yes	yes
Two-tailed test only	yes	yes	yes	no
Requires equal n's	yes	no	no	no
Must be preceded by a significant ANOVA	no	yes	no	no
Assumes random sampling or random assignment, normal populations, and equal variances	yes	yes	yes	yes

14.6 PRACTICAL SIGNIFICANCE

In Section 10.6, we observed that most measures of effect magnitude fall into one of two categories: measures of effect size and measures of strength of association. A measure of strength of association that can be used with the ANOVA F test is **omega squared,** denoted by $\hat{\omega}^2$. The formula for $\hat{\omega}^2$ is

$$\hat{\omega}^2 = \frac{SSBG - (p - 1)MSWG}{SSTO + MSWG}.$$

Omega squared estimates the proportion of the population variance in the dependent variable that is accounted for by the p treatments levels. Cohen (1988, pp. 284–288) has suggested the following guidelines for interpreting strength of association:

$\omega^2 = .010$ is a small association.
$\omega^2 = .059$ is a medium association.
$\omega^2 = .138$ or larger is a large association.

For the diet data in Table 14.3-3, an estimate of the proportion of the population weight-loss variance accounted for by the three diets is

$$\hat{\omega}^2 = \frac{86.667 - (3 - 1)5.037}{222.667 + 5.037} = .34.$$

According to Cohen's guidelines, the strength of association between the diets and weight loss is large—34% of the variance in weight loss is associated with the diets; $100 - 34\% = 66\%$ is associated with factors other than the diets.

Hedges's g statistic, described in Section 12.4, can be used to measure the effect size of contrasts among the diets. The g statistic is

$$g = \frac{|\bar{X}_{.j} - \bar{X}_{.j'}|}{\hat{\sigma}_{Pooled}},$$

where

$$\hat{\sigma}_{Pooled} = \sqrt{MSWG}.$$

For the weight-loss data in Table 14.3-1, Tukey's multiple comparison procedure as well as the Fisher-Hayter procedure identified two significant pairwise contrasts, $\mu_1 - \mu_3$ and $\mu_2 - \mu_3$. The effect sizes for these two contrasts are, respectively,

$$g = \frac{|8 - 12|}{2.244} = 1.8$$

$$g = \frac{|9 - 12|}{2.244} = 1.3,$$

where $\hat{\sigma}_{Pooled} = \sqrt{MSWG} = \sqrt{5.037} = 2.244$. According to Cohen's guidelines for interpreting d-like measures of effect size in Section 10.6, both of the contrasts represent large effects. This suggests that the difference between diets a_1 and a_3 and between diets a_2 and a_3 is large enough to be of practical value. Indeed, what dieter wouldn't want to use diet a_3 that produced a one-month weight loss of 4 pounds more than diet a_1 and 3 pounds more than diet a_2?

CHECK YOUR UNDERSTANDING OF SECTIONS 14.5 AND 14.6

21. For an experiment with $p = 4$ treatment levels, list the coefficients, c_j, for the following population contrasts:
    a. μ_1 versus μ_2
    b. μ_2 versus μ_4
    c. μ_1 versus the mean of μ_2 and μ_3
    d. μ_1 versus the mean of μ_2, μ_3, and μ_4
    e. mean of μ_1 and μ_2 versus the mean of μ_3 and μ_4
    f. μ_1 versus the weighted mean of μ_2 and μ_3, where μ_2 is weighted twice as much as μ_3
22. Which of the following are contrasts?
    a. $\mu_1 - \mu_2$
    b. $2\mu_1 - \mu_2 - \mu_3$
    c. $(1)\mu_1 + (-\frac{1}{3})\mu_2 + (-\frac{1}{3})\mu_3$
    d. $(1\frac{1}{2})\mu_1 + (-\frac{1}{2})\mu_2 + (-1)\mu_3$
    e. $(3)\mu_1 + (-3)\mu_2 + (0)\mu_3$
    f. $(\frac{1}{2})\mu_1 + (\frac{1}{2})\mu_2 + (-\frac{1}{2})\mu_3 + (-\frac{1}{2})\mu_4$
23. Which of the sets of means in Exercise 22 above satisfy $|c_1| + |c_2| + \cdots + |c_p| = 2$?
24. Determine the value of $q_{\alpha;p,\nu}$ for Tukey's test for (a) $p = 4$, $n = 11$, $\alpha = .01$; (b) $p = 5$, $n = 13$, $\alpha = .05$; (c) $p = 3$, $n = 6$, $\alpha = .05$.
25. Determine the value of $q_{\alpha;p-1,\nu}$ for the Fisher-Hayter test for (a) $p = 4$, $n = 11$, $\alpha = .01$; (b) $p = 5$, $n = 13$, $\alpha = .05$; (c) $p = 3$, $n = 6$, $\alpha = .05$.
26. Determine the value of $(p - 1)F_{\alpha;\nu_1,\nu_2}$ for Scheffé's test for (a) $p = 4$, $n = 11$, $\alpha = .01$; (b) $p = 5$, $n = 13$, $\alpha = .05$; (c) $p = 3$, $n_1 = 6$, $n_2 = 7$, $n_3 = 8$, $\alpha = .05$.
27. Determine the value of $tDS_{\alpha/2;C,\nu}$ for the Dunn-Šidàk test for (a) $p = 4$, $n = 11$, $C = 6$, $\alpha = .01$; (b) $p = 4$, $n = 11$, $C = 4$, $\alpha = .01$; (c) $p = 5$, $n = 13$, $C = 10$, $\alpha = .05$.
28. Determine the value of $tDS_{\alpha;C,\nu}$ for the Dunn-Šidàk test for (a) $p = 4$, $n = 11$, $C = 2$, $\alpha = .05$; (b) $p = 3$, $n = 11$, $C = 3$, $\alpha = .05$; (c) $p = 5$, $n = 13$, $C = 4$, $\alpha = .05$.
29. The effects of three dosages of ethylene glycol on the reaction time of chimpanzees was investigated. The animals were randomly assigned to the dosage levels so that five animals received 2 cc of the

drug, treatment level a_1; five received 4 cc, a_2; and five received 6 cc, a_3. The sample means were $\overline{X}_{.1} = 0.29$ sec, $\overline{X}_{.2} = 0.31$ sec, and $\overline{X}_{.3} = 0.39$ sec; $MSWG = .002$ and $\nu_2 = 3(5 - 1) = 12$. The hypothesis that $\mu_1 = \mu_2 = \mu_3$ was rejected at the .05 level of significance using a CR-3 design.

a. Perform all pairwise contrasts using the Fisher-Hayter test.

b. Use Hedges's g statistic to measure the effect size of those contrasts for which the null hypothesis was rejected and interpret the results.

30. The effectiveness of three approaches to drug education in junior high school was investigated. The approaches were scare tactics, treatment level a_1; providing objective scientific information about physiological and psychological effects, a_2; and examining the psychology of drug use, a_3. Forty-one students who didn't use drugs were randomly assigned to each treatment level. At the conclusion of an educational program, the students evaluated its effectiveness; a high score signified effectiveness. The sample means were $\overline{X}_{.1} = 23.1$, $\overline{X}_{.2} = 23.8$, and $\overline{X}_{.3} = 26.7$; $MSWG = 16.4$ and $\nu_2 = 3(41 - 1) = 120$.

a. After examining the data, the researcher decided to use Scheffé's statistic to determine which of the following contrasts are not equal to 0: $\psi_1 = \mu_1 - \mu_2$, $\psi_2 = \mu_1 - \mu_3$, $\psi_3 = \mu_2 - \mu_3$, and $\psi_4 = (\mu_1 + \mu_2)/2 - \mu_3$. Test the null hypotheses for these contrasts; let $\alpha = .01$.

b. Construct confidence intervals for each of the contrasts and locate the confidence intervals on the real number line.

c. Use Hedges's g statistic to assess the effect size of those contrasts for which the confidence interval does not include 0 and interpret the results.

d. Suppose that the hypotheses in (a) had been a priori. Test the hypotheses using the Dunn-Šidàk test; use two-tailed tests. Compare the results with those obtained with Scheffé's test.

31. Exercise 13 in "Check Your Understanding of Section 14.3" described an experiment to investigate the effects of meaningfulness of nonsense syllables on learning.

a. Estimate the proportion of the population variance in the dependent variable that is accounted for by the four treatments levels and interpret the result.

b. Use the Fisher-Hayter test to determine which pairwise contrasts among means are not equal to zero. Let $\alpha = .05$.

32. Terms to remember

a. Data snooping   b. A posteriori (post hoc) test

c. A priori test   d. Multiple comparison statistic

e. Contrast (comparison)   f. Coefficients of a contrast

g. Pairwise contrast   h. Omega squared

†14.7 PRINTOUTS FOR THREE MICROCOMPUTER PACKAGES

JMP

Performing the computations associated with an analysis of variance is tedious. Fortunately, computer programs can do most of the work for you. The weight-loss data in Table 14.2-1 were entered into the JMP data table shown in Figure 14.7-1. The display in Figure 14.7-2 was obtained by selecting **Analyze** in the menu bar followed by the pull-down command called **Fit Y by X.** The display shows the different values that the data assume. When the **Analysis** ▶ button in this display was selected, a number of options appeared. The selection of the **Means,**

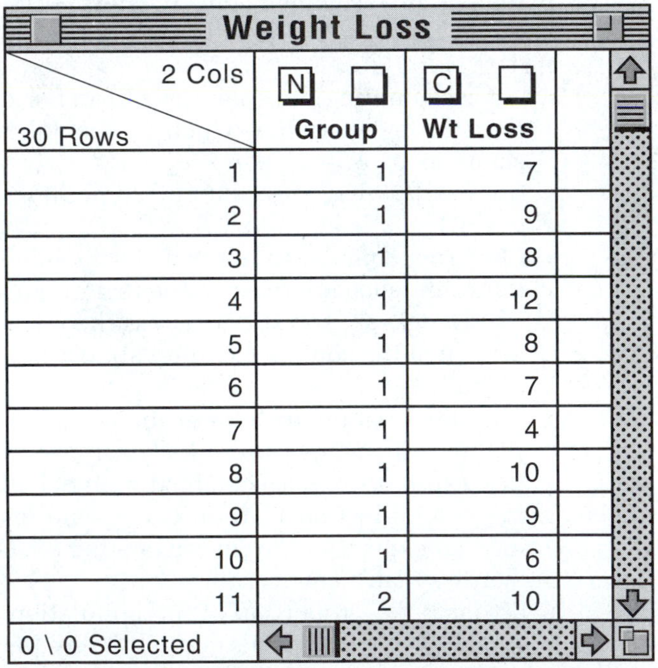

Weight Loss		
2 Cols / 30 Rows	N Group	C Wt Loss
1	1	7
2	1	9
3	1	8
4	1	12
5	1	8
6	1	7
7	1	4
8	1	10
9	1	9
10	1	6
11	2	10

0 \ 0 Selected

Figure 14.7-1. **JMP data table for the weight-loss data in Table 14.2-1. To conserve space, only the first 11 of the 30 scores are shown. Column 2 is a grouping variable; the numbers 1, 2, and 3 are used to identify the three treatment levels. The first 10 scores are in treatment level a_1, the next 10 are in a_2, and the last 10 are in a_3.**

---

† This and similarly marked sections can be omitted without loss of continuity.

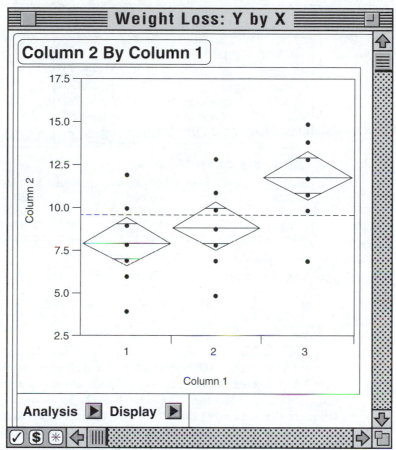

Figure 14.7-2. **The dots in the JMP figure represent scores for the three treatment levels. The horizontal line in the center of the diamonds denotes the means of the treatment levels. The tops and bottoms of the diamonds represent two-sided, upper and lower boundaries, respectively, of $100(1 - .05)\% = 95\%$ confidence intervals. A variety of analysis and display options including tests of the assumption that the population variances are equal can be obtained by clicking on the Analysis ▶ button.**

Anova/t-test option caused three diamonds to appear in Figure 14.7-2 along with a new display entitled **Oneway Anova** that is shown in Figure 14.7-3. A comparison of the JMP **Analysis of Variance** table with Table 14.3-3 reveals that they provide the same information, although the labels in the ANOVA source column are different.

> **Oneway Anova** ▶
>
> **Summary of Fit**
>
> | | |
> |---|---|
> | RSquare | 0.389222 |
> | RSquare Adj | 0.343979 |
> | Root Mean Square Error | 2.244334 |
> | Mean of Response | 9.666667 |
> | Observations (or Sum Wgts) | 30 |
>
> **Analysis of Variance**
>
> | Source | DF | Sum of Squares | Mean Square | F Ratio |
> |---|---|---|---|---|
> | Model | 2 | 86.66667 | 43.3333 | 8.6029 |
> | Error | 27 | 136.00000 | 5.0370 | **Prob>F** |
> | C Total | 29 | 222.66667 | 7.6782 | 0.0013 |
>
> **Means for Oneway Anova**
>
> | Level | Number | Mean | Std Error |
> |---|---|---|---|
> | 1 | 10 | 8.0000 | 0.70972 |
> | 2 | 10 | 9.0000 | 0.70972 |
> | 3 | 10 | 12.0000 | 0.70972 |
>
> Std Error uses a pooled estimate of error variance

Figure 14.7-3. **The JMP Summary of Fit display shows that the full ANOVA model accounted for 39% of the variation in weight loss (RSquare = $SS_{\text{Model}}/SS_{\text{C Total}}$ = 86.6667/222.6667 = 0.3892). RSquare Adj is the value of RSquare that we could expect if we used the full model equation for this sample of dieters on a new sample from the same population. Root Mean Square Error is the square root of the denominator of the F statistic ($\sqrt{MS_{\text{Error}}} = \sqrt{5.0370} = 2.2443$). Mean of Response, 9.9667, is the grand mean of the 30 weight-loss scores. Observations is the number of participants in the experiment. The Analysis of Variance display duplicates the information in Table 14.3-3. The sources in the first column, Model, Error, and C Total, denote, respectively, Between Groups, Within Groups, and Total. The Means for Oneway Anova display contains sample sizes, means, and standard errors ($\hat{\sigma}_{\overline{X}} = \sqrt{MS_{\text{Error}}}/\sqrt{n}$) for the three weight-loss treatment levels.**

SPSS

SPSS was used to perform an analysis of variance for the weight-loss data in Table 14.2-1. The data were entered in an SPSS data table like that in Figure 14.7-4. The selection of the **Statistics** command in the menu bar followed by the pull-down command called **Compare Means** and the selection of **One-Way ANOVA . . .** brought up a dialog box in which **group** was identified as the

Diet Data			
	group	**wt_loss**	v
1	1	7.00	
2	1	9.00	
3	1	8.00	
4	1	12.00	
5	1	8.00	
6	1	7.00	
7	1	4.00	

Figure 14.7-4. **SPSS data table for the weight-loss data in Table 14.2-1. To conserve space, only the first 7 of the 30 scores are shown. Column 1 is a grouping variable; the numbers 1, 2, and 3 are used to identify the three treatment levels. The first seven weight-loss scores are shown in column 2.**

grouping (factor) variable with a range of 1 to 3 and **wt_loss** was identified as the dependent variable. The dialog box also had an option for selecting from among seven multiple comparison tests, including Tukey's HSD test and Scheffé's test. The ANOVA output is shown in Figure 14.7-5.

```
----- O N E W A Y -----

     Variable   WT_LOSS
  By Variable   GROUP

                      Analysis of Variance

                         Sum of      Mean       F        F
           Source   D.F.  Squares   Squares    Ratio    Prob.

Between Groups        2   86.6667   43.3333   8.6029   .0013
Within Groups        27  136.0000    5.0370
Total                29  222.6667
```

Figure 14.7-5. **The SPSS analysis of variance output for the weight-loss data provides the same information as that in Table 14.3-3.**

SYSTAT Data Editor		
	GROUP	WT_LOSS
1	1.000	7.000
2	1.000	9.000
3	1.000	8.000
4	1.000	12.000
5	1.000	8.000
6	1.000	7.000
7	1.000	4.000
8	1.000	10.000
9	1.000	9.000
10	1.000	6.000
11	2.000	10.000

Figure 14.7-6.   **SYSTAT data table for the weight-loss data in Table 14.2-1. To conserve space, only the first 11 of the 30 scores are shown. Column 2 is a grouping variable; the numbers 1, 2, and 3 are used to identify the three treatment levels. The first eleven weight-loss scores are shown in column 3.**

SYSTAT

SYSTAT was used to perform an analysis of variance for the data in Table 14.2-1. The data were entered in a SYSTAT data table like that in Table 14.7-3. The output in Figure 14.7-4 was obtained by selecting the **Stats** command in the menu bar followed by the pull-down command called **MGLH,** which stands for Multivariate

```
LEVELS ENCOUNTERED DURING PROCESSING ARE:
GROUP
        1.0000        2.0000        3.0000
```

| DEP VAR: WT_LOSS | N 30 MULTIPLE R: 0.624 | SQUARED MULTIPLE R: 0.389 |

ANALYSIS OF VARIANCE

SOURCE	SUM-OF-SQUARES	DF	MEAN-SQUARE	F-RATIO	P
GROUP	86.6667	2	43.3333	8.6029	0.0013
ERROR	136.0000	27	5.0370		

Figure 14.7-7.   **SYSTAT analysis of variance output for the weight-loss data in Table 14.2-1. The Squared Multiple R shows that the full ANOVA model accounted for 39% of the variation in weight loss [Squared Multiple R = $SS_{GROUP}/(SS_{GROUP} + SS_{ERROR}) = 0.389$]. The sources in the first column, GROUP and ERROR, denote, respectively, Between Groups and Within Groups.**

General Linear Hypothesis, and selecting **Fully Factorial (M)ANOVA . . . .** These selections produced a dialog box in which the variables GROUP and WT_LOSS were identified, respectively, as the grouping (factor) variable and dependent variable. An alternative selection under the **MGLH** pull-down command gives access to five multiple comparison procedures, including Tukey's HSD test and Scheffé's test.

14.8 SUMMARY

Analysis of variance, ANOVA, is a statistical procedure for (1) determining how much of the total variability among scores to attribute to each source of variation in an experiment and for (2) testing hypotheses about some of these sources. The principal application of ANOVA is testing the omnibus null hypothesis that two or more population means are equal. A completely randomized design (CR-p), the simplest ANOVA design, is described in this chapter. It is appropriate for experiments that meet the following conditions:

1. One treatment or independent variable with two or more treatment levels. The levels of the treatment can differ either quantitatively or qualitatively. When the treatment has two levels, an F statistic for a completely randomized design is equivalent to Student's t statistic for independent samples. In fact, for this case, t^2 is equal to F.
2. Random assignment of participants to treatment levels, with each participant designated to receive only one level. If the treatment levels are of equal interest, it is advantageous to assign the same number of participants to each level, although this is not necessary. Actually, flexibility in this respect is one of the advantages of the design.

Although ANOVA appears to be a complicated procedure, the basic notions are relatively simple. A score X_{ij} in a completely randomized design is a composite. It is equal to the sum of three parameters in the model equation

$$X_{ij} = \mu + \alpha_j + \epsilon_{ij},$$

where μ is a constant that reflects the average value around which the treatment means and scores vary; α_j is the treatment effect of the jth population; and ϵ_{ij} reflects all other effects that affect X_{ij}, which is apparent when the terms in the model are rearranged as follows: $\epsilon_{ij} = X_{ij} - \mu - \alpha_j$.

The total variation among the scores, designated by *SSTO,* also is a composite and can be partitioned into two parts: the sum of squares between groups, *SSBG,* and the sum of squares within groups, *SSWG.* A variance, or mean square, is obtained by dividing a sum of squares by its degrees of freedom, for example, $SSBG/df_{BG} = MSBG$ and $SSWG/df_{WG} = MSWG$. The statistic for testing the omnibus null hypothesis, $\mu_1 = \mu_2 = \cdots = \mu_p$, is $F = MSBG/MSWG$. To use the ratio of two variances to test a hypothesis about means may seem a bit strange. It does make sense if you consider the expected values of $MSBG$ and $MSWG$ for the case in which the null hypothesis is true and the case in which it is false. If the null hypothesis is true, all the squared treatment effects equal 0, $\alpha_1{}^2 = \alpha_2{}^2 = \cdots = \alpha_p{}^2 = 0$, in which case

$$\frac{E(MSBG)}{E(MSWG)} = \frac{\sigma_\epsilon^2}{\sigma_\epsilon^2}$$

If the null hypothesis is false, at least two of the squared treatment effects are greater than 0, $\alpha_j{}^2 \neq 0$ and $\alpha_{j'}{}^2 \neq 0$ for some j and j', in which case

$$\frac{E(MSBG)}{E(MSWG)} = \frac{\sigma_\epsilon^2 + n \sum_{j=1}^{p} \alpha_j^2/(p-1)}{\sigma_\epsilon^2}.$$

The larger the ratio $F = MSBG/MSWG$, the more likely it is that two or more α_j's are not equal to 0. How large should the F statistic be to reject the null hypothesis? According to hypothesis-testing conventions, the null hypothesis is rejected if F falls in at least the upper 5% region of the sampling distribution of F.

If the omnibus null hypothesis is rejected, the researcher must still decide which means are not equal. Multiple comparison tests are used for this purpose. Four of the more popular multiple comparison tests are the Tukey, Fisher-Hayter, Scheffé, and Dunn-Šidàk tests. The Tukey and Fisher-Hayter tests are used for testing hypotheses about all a posteriori, pairwise contrasts. Scheffé's test is used for testing hypotheses about a posteriori contrasts when at least one of the contrasts is a non-pairwise contrast. The Dunn-Šidàk test is used for testing hypotheses about C a priori hypotheses involving pairwise or nonpairwise contrasts.

Typically, a posteriori tests are used following rejection of the omnibus ANOVA null hypothesis. However, a test of the omnibus null hypothesis is not necessary prior to using the Tukey or Scheffé test. What many researchers don't understand is that it is entirely appropriate to examine a set of means and decide to forego an omnibus ANOVA test in favor of testing contrasts suggested by an inspection of the means using either the Tukey or Scheffé test. The Fisher-Hayter test, on the other hand, is used only if the omnibus null hypothesis is rejected. The use of the Dunn-Sidàk test, an a priori procedure, requires a researcher to decide prior to seeing the data which of C contrasts to test. Obviously, this procedure is used when an experiment has been designed to answer C specific research questions.

The four multiple comparison tests share an important advantage over Student's t test. They control the probability of making one or more type I errors at or less than α for a collection of tests. To put it another way, when these multiple comparison tests are used, the probability of erroneously rejecting one or more null hypotheses doesn't increase as a function of the number of hypotheses tested, which is a problem with Student's t test.

It is not enough to perform a null hypothesis significance test or construct a confidence interval. Researchers should routinely provide measures that can be used to assess the practical significance of data. Such a measure for the omnibus null hypothesis is omega squared. Omega squared estimates the proportion of variance in the dependent variable that is accounted for by the independent variable. If multiple comparisons have been performed, Hedges's g, which measures the size of an effect relative to a pooled estimate of the population standard deviation, can help a researcher decide whether statistically significant contrasts are practically significant.

REVIEW EXERCISES FOR CHAPTER 14

1. Five colors of warning lights on an automobile instrument panel were compared. The dependent measure was reaction time to the onset of a light. (a) State the null hypothesis. (b) How many t tests would be required to test hypotheses of the form $\mu_j = \mu_{j'}$? (c) If $\alpha = .01$, what is the probability of making one or more type I errors using ANOVA? What is the probability when using multiple t tests? (d) If the overall null hypothesis is rejected, what does this tell the researcher?

2. Under what conditions do the ANOVA and t approaches lead to the same probability of making a type I error?

3. (a) Give two examples of independent variables for which the ANOVA and multiple t approaches would lead to identical conclusions. (b) What characteristic do the examples have in common?

4. Identify the following:
   a. a_3 b. $\overline{X}_{44}$
   c. $X_{12,2}$ d. $\overline{X}_{.3}$
   e. $\hat{\epsilon}_{61}$ f. $X_{42} = \mu + \alpha_4 + \epsilon_{42}$
   g. $\mu_4 - \mu$ h. $\overline{X}_{.j}$

5. For each of the following null hypotheses, indicate whether it is correctly or incorrectly stated.
   a. $\mu_j - \mu_{j'} = 0$ for all j and j'
   b. $\mu_1 = \mu_2 = \mu_3$
   c. $\sum_{j=1}^{p} (\mu_j - \mu) = 0$
   d. $\sum_{j=1}^{p} \alpha_j = 0$
   e. $\alpha_j = 0$ for all j.

6. Express the following scores in terms of estimates of the parameters of the full linear model equation: (a) X_{31}, (b) X_{35}, (c) $X_{11,4}$.

7. Express the hypothesis $\mu_1 = \mu_2 = \mu_3 = \mu_4$ in terms of treatment effects (α_j's).

8. Calculate the degrees of freedom for *MSTO, MSBG,* and *MSWG* for the following conditions:
   a. $p = 5, n = 15$
   b. $p = 4, n = 22$

c. $p = 3$, $n = 24$

d. $p = 4$, $n_1 = 8$, $n_2 = 8$, $n_3 = 6$, $n_4 = 6$

9. Under what conditions does $F = MSBG/MSWG$ tend to be larger than 1?

10. Under what conditions is a completely randomized design appropriate?

11. Deviation formulas are less convenient than raw-score formulas for computing sums of squares. The raw-score formula for $SSWG$ can be derived from the deviation formula. Describe in words the operation(s) that was performed for each equation.

a. $\displaystyle\sum_{j=1}^{p} \sum_{i=1}^{n} (X_{ij} - \overline{X}_{.j})^2 = \sum_{j=1}^{p} \sum_{i=1}^{n} (X_{ij}^2 - 2\overline{X}_{.j} X_{ij} + \overline{X}_{.j}^2)$

b. $\displaystyle = \sum_{j=1}^{p} \sum_{i=1}^{n} X_{ij}^2 - 2\sum_{j=1}^{p} \overline{X}_{.j} \sum_{i=1}^{n} X_{ij} + n \sum_{j=1}^{p} \overline{X}_{.j}^2$

c. $\displaystyle = \sum_{j=1}^{p} \sum_{i=1}^{n} X_{ij}^2 - 2\sum_{j=1}^{p} \frac{\displaystyle\sum_{i=1}^{n} X_{ij}}{n} \sum_{i=1}^{n} X_{ij} + n \sum_{j=1}^{p} \frac{\left(\displaystyle\sum_{i=1}^{n} X_{ij}\right)^2}{n^2}$

d. $\displaystyle = \sum_{j=1}^{p} \sum_{i=1}^{n} X_{ij}^2 - 2\sum_{j=1}^{p} \frac{\left(\displaystyle\sum_{i=1}^{n} X_{ij}\right)^2}{n} + \sum_{j=1}^{p} \frac{\left(\displaystyle\sum_{i=1}^{n} X_{ij}\right)^2}{n}$

e. $\displaystyle = \sum_{j=1}^{p} \sum_{i=1}^{n} X_{ij}^2 - \sum_{j=1}^{p} \frac{\left(\displaystyle\sum_{i=1}^{n} X_{ij}\right)^2}{n}$

12. a. Fill in the blanks in the following ANOVA table.

Source	SS	df	MS	F
Between groups	36.000	3	( )	( )
Within groups	( )	( )	( )	
Total	164.000	35		

b. What is the approximate p-value of the F statistic?

13. The learning of one task enhances the learning of different but similar tasks. To investigate this phenomenon (called *learning to learn*), 30 participants were randomly assigned to three conditions subject to the restriction that an equal number were assigned to each condition. Participants in condition a_1 learned 2 lists of nonsense syllables, those in a_2 learned 8 lists, and those in a_3 learned 14 lists. The next day all the participants learned another list. The dependent variable was the number of trials required to learn this list. The following data were obtained:

a_1	a_2	a_3
7	6	3
9	5	2
5	7	3
7	3	6
8	4	3
7	5	4
6	6	5
8	5	5
7	4	4
6	5	4

a. Construct stacked box plots for the data. Are the sample distributions relatively symmetrical? Do the data contain outliers?
b. Compute descriptive statistics, $\overline{X}_j$ and $\hat{\sigma}_j$'s, for the data, and construct a table similar to Table 14.3-1.
c. Are the sample data consistent with the researcher's hypothesis that $\mu_j \neq \mu_{j'}$ for some j and j'?
d. Test the hypothesis $\mu_1 = \mu_2 = \mu_3$. Let $\alpha = .05$. Construct an ANOVA summary table; include the p-value.
e. Summarize the results of the ANOVA in a sentence or two.

14. List the steps used in testing the null hypothesis in Exercise 13, and state the decision rule.

15. Presidents of companies employing between 5,000 and 8,000 employees were randomly sampled from five geographic areas: $a_1 =$ southeast, $a_2 =$ east, $a_3 =$ midwest, $a_4 =$ southwest, and $a_5 =$ west. Use ANOVA to test the null hypothesis that mean income for the presidents is the same in different areas of the country. The following data, representing thousands of dollars, were obtained.

a_1	a_2	a_3	a_4	a_5
40	42	37	36	46
31	40	46	40	40
32	46	45	34	45
35	45	42	34	48
37	37	42	33	46
38	43	43	39	47
35	43	40	38	
33	44	39	37	
35	42		34	
37	39			

a. Construct stacked box plots for the data. Are the sample distributions relatively symmetrical? Do the data contain outliers?

b. Compute descriptive statistics, $\overline{X}_j$'s and $\hat{\sigma}_j$'s, for the data, and construct a table similar to Table 14.3-1.

c. Are the sample data consistent with the researcher's hypothesis that $\mu_j \neq \mu_{j'}$ for some j and j'?

d. Test the hypothesis $\mu_1 = \mu_2 = \mu_3 = \mu_4 = \mu_5$. Let $\alpha = .05$. Construct an ANOVA summary table; include the p-value.

e. Summarize the results of the ANOVA in a sentence or two.

16. List the steps used in testing the null hypothesis in Exercise 15, and state the decision rule.

17. What does the use of random sampling or random assignment in an experiment accomplish?

18. A rough but adequate check on the tenability of the normality assumption consists of making a frequency distribution of the scores in each treatment level and inspecting them for evidence of skewness and kurtosis. Decide on the tenability of this assumption for the data in Exercise 13 above.

19. Comment on the statement "The F test in ANOVA is robust with respect to heterogeneity of variance."

20. For an experiment with $p = 5$ treatment levels, list the coefficients, c_j, for the following population contrasts:

a. μ_1 versus μ_2

b. μ_1 versus μ_3

c. μ_2 versus μ_3

d. μ_1 versus the mean of μ_2 and μ_4

e. mean of μ_1 and μ_2 versus the mean of μ_3, μ_4, and μ_5

f. weighted mean of μ_1 and μ_2 versus the weighted mean of μ_3 and μ_4, where μ_1 and μ_3 are weighted twice as much as μ_2 and μ_4

21. Which of the following are contrasts?

a. $(2)\mu_1 + (-1)\mu_2 + (0)\mu_3$

b. $(5)\mu_1 + (-2)\mu_2 + (-3)\mu_3$

c. $\left(\dfrac{1}{2}\right)\mu_1 + (-1)\mu_2 + \left(\dfrac{1}{2}\right)\mu_3$

d. $\left(\dfrac{1}{2}\right)\mu_1 + \left(-\dfrac{1}{4}\right)\mu_2 + \left(-\dfrac{1}{4}\right)\mu_3$

e. $(2)\mu_1 + (0)\mu_2 + (0)\mu_3$

f. $\left(\dfrac{3}{5}\right)\mu_1 + \left(\dfrac{2}{5}\right)\mu_2 + \left(-\dfrac{1}{2}\right)\mu_3 + \left(-\dfrac{1}{2}\right)\mu_4$

22. Which of the sets of means in Exercise 21 above satisfy $|c_1| + |c_2| + \cdots + |c_p| = 2$?

23. Determine the value of $q_{\alpha;p,\nu}$ for Tukey's test for (a) $p = 3$, $n = 9$, $\alpha = .05$; (b) $p = 6$, $n = 11$, $\alpha = .05$; (c) $p = 4$, $n = 6$, $\alpha = .01$.

24. Determine the value of $q_{\alpha;p-1,\nu}$ for the Fisher-Hayter test for (a) $p = 3$, $n = 9$, $\alpha = .05$; (b) $p = 6$, $n = 11$, $\alpha = .05$; (c) $p = 4$, $n = 6$, $\alpha = .01$.

25. Determine the value of $(p - 1) F_{\alpha;\nu_1,\nu_2}$ for Scheffé's test for (a) $p = 3$, $n = 7$, $\alpha = .01$; (b) $p = 5$, $n = 25$, $\alpha = .05$; (c) $p = 4$, $n_1 = 5$, $n_2 = 5$, $n_3 = 6$, $n_4 = 8$, $\alpha = .05$.

26. Determine the value of $tDS_{\alpha/2;C,\nu}$ for the Dunn-Šidàk test for (a) $p = 5$, $n = 13$, $C = 5$, $\alpha = .05$; (b) $p = 3$, $n_1 = 6$, $n_2 = 7$, $n_3 = 8$, $C = 3$, $\alpha = .05$; (c) $p = 3$, $n_1 = 6$, $n_2 = 9$, $n_3 = 6$, $C = 2$, $\alpha = .05$.

27. Determine the value of $tDS_{\alpha;C,\nu}$ for (a) $p = 5$, $n = 13$, $C = 5$, $\alpha = .05$; (b) $p = 3$, $n = 21$, $C = 3$, $\alpha = .05$; (c) $p = 4$, $n = 6$, $C = 5$, $\alpha = .05$.

28. Exercise 13 above described an experiment to investigate the phenomenon called *learning to learn*.
    a. Estimate the proportion of the population variance in the dependent variable that is accounted for by the three treatment levels.
    b. Use the Fisher-Hayter test to determine which pairwise contrasts among means are not equal to zero. Let $\alpha = .05$.
    c. Compare the results of using the Fisher-Hayter test with those for the Tukey test.

29. Exercise 15 described an experiment to investigate mean income of company presidents from five geographic areas.
    a. Estimate the proportion of the population variance in the dependent variable that is accounted for by the five treatment levels.
    b. Use the Scheffé statistic to test the following a posteriori null hypotheses: $\psi_1 = \mu_1 - \mu_4 = 0$, $\psi_2 = \mu_3 - \mu_4 = 0$, and $\psi_3 = (\mu_2 + \mu_5) - (\mu_1 + \mu_4) = 0$. Let $\alpha = .05$.
    c. Use Hedges's g statistic to measure the effect size of those contrasts for which the null hypothesis was rejected, and interpret the results.
    d. Construct confidence intervals for each of the contrasts and locate the confidence intervals on the real number line.

30. The religious dogmatism of four church denominations in a large midwestern city was investigated. A random sample of 31 members from each denomination took a paper-and-pencil test of dogmatism. The sample means were $\overline{X}_{.1} = 64$, $\overline{X}_{.2} = 73$, $\overline{X}_{.3} = 61$, and $\overline{X}_{.4} = 49$; $MSWG = 120$, and $\nu_2 = 4(31 - 1) = 120$.
    a. Use the Dunn-Šidàk test to evaluate the following a priori hypotheses at the .05 level of significance:

    $$H_0 : \mu_2 - \mu_3 = 0$$

    $$H_0 : \left(-\frac{1}{2}\right)\mu_1 + (1)\mu_2 + \left(-\frac{1}{2}\right)\mu_3 = 0$$

    $$H_0 : \left(\frac{1}{2}\right)\mu_1 + \left(\frac{1}{2}\right)\mu_3 + (-1)\mu_4 = 0$$

    b. Use Hedges's g statistic to measure the effect size of those contrasts for which the null hypothesis was rejected, and interpret the results.
    c. Construct confidence intervals for each of the contrasts and locate the confidence intervals on the real number line.

31. List the requirements for using the four multiple comparison tests.

Chapter 15

Other Analysis of Variance Designs

15.1 BASIC EXPERIMENTAL DESIGN CONCEPTS

Definition of Experimental Design

> The term **experimental design** refers to a randomization plan for assigning participants to experimental conditions and the statistical analysis associated with the plan.

The simplest experimental design is the randomization and analysis plan used with a *t* test for independent samples. This plan was discussed in Section 12.4. A *t* test for dependent samples uses a more complex randomization and analysis plan, but the added complexity is usually accompanied by greater power. This point was discussed in Section 12.5. The next level of design complexity is the randomization and analysis plan used with a completely randomized ANOVA design (CR-*p* design). As we saw in Chapter 14, this design is appropriate for an experiment having one treatment with *p* equal to two or more levels.

Two more ANOVA designs are described in this chapter: a randomized block design and a completely randomized factorial design. A **randomized block design,** like the completely randomized design, is appropriate for experiments having one treatment with two or more levels. The randomized block design is usually more powerful than a completely randomized design because it uses dependent samples, a feature the design shares with the *t* test for dependent samples. A **completely randomized factorial design,** which is described in Section 15.3, is appropriate for experiments having two or more treatments, with each treatment having two or more levels.

Controlling Nuisance Variables

A randomized block design with *p* treatment levels, denoted by the letters RB-*p*, uses a blocking procedure to reduce the variance of the error effects, ϵ_{ij}, and thereby obtain a more powerful test of a false null hypothesis. Recall from Section 14.2 that error effects are effects that are unique to a particular participant, effects attributable to chance fluctuations in the participant's performance, and effects attributable to environmental and other uncontrolled conditions. Recall also that the variance of error effects is the denominator of an ANOVA *F* statistic—the smaller this variance, the larger the *F* statistic.

In the behavioral sciences, health sciences, and education, differences among participants or experimental units may make a significant contribution to the variance of error effects and thereby mask or obscure the effects of a treatment. Similarly, administering the levels of a treatment under different environmental conditions—say, at different times of day, locations, and seasons of the year—also may mask treatment effects. Variation in the dependent variable attributable to such sources is called **nuisance variation.** There are three experimental approaches to controlling or minimizing these undesired sources of variation.

1. Hold the potential nuisance variables constant, for example, use only 19-year-old women participants, and administer all treatment levels at the same time of day and in the same room.
2. Assign the treatment levels randomly to the experimental units so that known and unsuspected sources of variation among the units are distributed over the entire experiment and thus do not affect only one or a limited number of treatment levels. If the treatment levels must be administered at different times of day or in different locations, randomize the assignment of treatment levels to times and locations. This research strategy, along with the strategy of holding some variables constant, is used in the completely randomized design.
3. Include the nuisance variable as one of the factors in the experiment. The randomized block design uses this research strategy in conjunction with the two just described.

To include a nuisance variable as one of the factors in an experiment, it is necessary to form **blocks** of participants so that the participants within a block are more homogeneous with respect to the nuisance variable than those in different blocks. Perhaps an example will help to clarify the procedure. In Chapter 14 we described an experiment to determine the effectiveness of three diets for obese teenage girls. In that example, 30 girls who wanted to lose weight were randomly assigned to three diets with the restriction that 10 girls were assigned to each diet. Because of random assignment, one would expect that nuisance variables such as average initial weight of the girls assigned to each diet would be approximately the same. Initial weight is an important nuisance variable because it is positively correlated with the dependent variable of weight loss. The more overweight a girl is, the easier it is for her to lose weight.

When samples are small, as in the diet experiment, random assignment of participants to treatment levels doesn't always distribute the nuisance variables evenly over the levels. One treatment level may have a disproportionately large number of very obese girls. We can minimize the likelihood of this occurring by assigning participants to blocks so that those assigned to the same block are similar with respect to the nuisance variable. A simple way to form the blocks is to rank the girls from heaviest to lightest. The three heaviest girls become block 1, the next three heaviest girls become block 2, and so on. The matching procedure continues until all 30 girls have been assigned to 1 of 10 blocks. The three girls in a block are then randomly assigned to the diets. The layout for this RB-3 design is shown in Figure 15.1-1(a). For comparison purposes, the layout for the

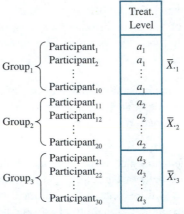

a. Layout for randomized block design

	Treat. Level	Treat. Level	Treat. Level	
Block$_1$	a_1	a_2	a_3	$\bar{X}_1.$
Block$_2$	a_1	a_2	a_3	$\bar{X}_2.$
Block$_3$	a_1	a_2	a_3	$\bar{X}_3.$
⋮	⋮	⋮	⋮	
Block$_{10}$	a_1	a_2	a_3	$\bar{X}_{10}.$
	$\bar{X}._1$	$\bar{X}._2$	$\bar{X}._3$	

b. Layout for completely randomized block design

		Treat. Level	
Group$_1$	Participant$_1$	a_1	
	Participant$_2$	a_1	$\bar{X}._1$
	⋮	⋮	
	Participant$_{10}$	a_1	
Group$_2$	Participant$_{11}$	a_2	
	Participant$_{12}$	a_2	$\bar{X}._2$
	⋮	⋮	
	Participant$_{20}$	a_2	
Group$_3$	Participant$_{21}$	a_3	
	Participant$_{22}$	a_3	$\bar{X}._3$
	⋮	⋮	
	Participant$_{30}$	a_3	

Figure 15.1-1. **Comparison of layouts for RB-3 and CR-3 designs. In the RB-3 design, each of the ten blocks contains three matched participants who are randomly assigned the treatment levels within a block. In the CR-3 design, thirty participants are randomly assigned to the three treatment levels.**

completely randomized design described in Chapter 14 also is shown. An advantage of the RB-3 design, as we will see, is that it removes the effects of the nuisance variable from the denominator of the F statistic. This results in a more powerful test of a false null hypothesis.

Another approach to minimizing the effect of nuisance variables that was mentioned earlier is to hold them constant. For example, measure each girl's weight loss using the same scale and at the same time of day. Some variables are not easy to hold constant, such as genetic predisposition to obesity and amount of daily exercise. These and other unsuspected nuisance variables are usually controlled by random assignment. The larger the sample, the more confident a researcher can be that the effects of nuisance variables have been evenly distributed across the treatment conditions. The randomized block design enables a researcher to use all three strategies for controlling nuisance variables.

Criteria for Blocking

Any variable that is positively correlated with the dependent variable other than the independent variable is a candidate for becoming a blocking variable.

In forming blocks it is important to assign participants to blocks so that those in a given block are as similar as possible with respect to the dependent variable, with those in different blocks being less similar. Any one of the four procedures described in Section 12.5 for obtaining dependent samples can be used to form blocks. These procedures are as follows:

1. Observing participants under all of the conditions in the experiment — that is, obtaining repeated measures on each participant.
2. Forming blocks of participants who are similar with respect to a nuisance variable that is positively correlated with the dependent variable. This is called participant matching.
3. Obtaining blocks of identical twins or littermates and assigning members of a pair or a litter randomly to the conditions in the experiment.
4. Obtaining blocks of participants who are matched by mutual selection, for example, a husband and wife or business partners.

In the diet experiment, the use of participant matching appears to be the most appropriate blocking strategy for controlling the nuisance variable of initial weight. In general, however, participant matching is used less often than observing each participant under all of the conditions in the experiment. When each block consists of one participant who is observed p times, it is desirable if possible to randomize the order in which the p treatment levels are administered. The effects of some treatments such as medications remain in a participant's system for some time. In such cases, it is desirable to provide a "washout period" between administrations of the medications to allow the effects of the previous medication to dissipate.

When researchers consider potential blocking variables, they often overlook characteristics of the environmental setting such as time of day. For example, if a researcher plans to test participants from 1:00 to 6:00 P.M. in an experiment with three treatment levels, the blocks might represent the following afternoon time periods:

Block 1	1:00–1:10	1:15–1:25	1:30–1:40
Block 2	1:45–1:55	2:00–2:10	2:15–2:25
⋮	⋮	⋮	⋮
Block 8	5:15–5:25	5:30–5:40	5:45–5:55

The time periods within a block are randomly assigned to the three treatment levels. This blocking procedure ensures that the administration of treatment levels is evenly distributed over the testing period from 1:00 to 6:00 P.M. Time of day is a particularly effective blocking variable because it often isolates a number of additional sources of variability: fluctuation in daily body cycles, fatigue, changes in weather conditions, and drifts in the calibration of electronic equipment, to mention only a few. The use of time of day or other blocking variables such as day of the week, season, room location, and experimental apparatus can significantly decrease the **variance of the error effects** (also called **error variance** and **experimental error**).

CHECK YOUR UNDERSTANDING OF SECTION 15.1

1. Describe the character of nuisance variables and three ways to control or minimize them.
2. In selecting a blocking variable, what should a researcher look for?
3. The effects of three kinds of instruction on first-grade students' tendency to help another child were investigated. Forty-two boys were randomly assigned to one of three kinds of instructions, denoted by a_1, a_2, and a_3, with the restriction that 14 boys were assigned to each kind of instruction. Boys in the α_1 group (indirect responsibility group) were told that there was another boy alone in an adjoining room who had been told not to climb on a chair. Boys in the a_2 group were told the same story and, in addition, were told that they were being left in charge and to take care of anything that happened (direct responsibility group 1). All of the boys were given a simple task to perform. Shortly after the researcher left the room, there was a loud crash in the adjoining room followed by a minute of crying and sobbing. Boys in the a_3 group were given the same instructions as those in group a_2, but the sounds from the adjoining room included calls for help (direct responsibility group 2). The behavior of the boys was observed from behind a one-way mirror and rated in terms of the amount of help offered: 1 = no help, . . . , 5 = went to the adjoining room. (Experiment suggested by Staub, E. [1970]. A child in distress: The effect of focusing of responsibility on children on their attempts to help. *Developmental Psychology, 2,* 152−153.)
   a. Identify the independent and dependent variables.
   b. Identify nuisance variables that were held constant.
   c. Can you think of some nuisance variables that were controlled by randomization?
   d. Suppose that scores on the Conforming-Compulsive scale of the Millon Clinical Multiaxial Inventory are available for each of the 42 children and that the scale is known to be positively correlated

with the dependent variable. Describe in detail how you could use this information.

4. Terms to remember
   a. Experimental design
   b. Randomized block design
   c. Completely randomized factorial design
   d. Nuisance variation
   e. Block
   f. Variance of error effects (error variance or experimental error)

15.2 RANDOMIZED BLOCK DESIGN

Linear Model Equation for a Score

A score, X_{ij}, in a randomized block design is a composite that reflects all of the sources of variation that affect the score. We saw in Section 14.2-2 that a score for a completely randomized ANOVA design is the sum of three parameters in the linear model equation $X_{ij} = \mu + \alpha_j + \epsilon_{ij}$. In a randomized block design, a score is the sum of four parameters. The values of the parameters are unknown, but they can be estimated as follows:

Parameters of the linear model equation

$$X_{ij} \quad = \quad \mu \quad + \quad \alpha_j \quad + \quad \pi_i \quad + \quad \epsilon_{ij}$$

Estimators of the parameters

$$X_{ij} \quad = \quad \overline{X}_{..} \;\; + \;(\overline{X}_{.j} - \overline{X}_{..}) + (\overline{X}_{i.} - \overline{X}_{..}) + (X_{ij} - \overline{X}_{i.} - \overline{X}_{.j} + \overline{X}_{..})$$

Score	Grand Mean	Treatment Effect	Block Effect	Error Effect

Notice that the model equation for a randomized block design enables a researcher to estimate one more effect than the completely randomized design—the block effect. The model equation for a randomized block design allows us to partition the total sum of squares and total degrees of freedom $(np - 1)$ into three parts as follows:

SS TOTAL = SS TREATMENT A + SS BLOCKS + SS RESIDUAL

$$SSTO \quad = \quad SSA \quad + \quad SSBL \quad + \quad SSRES$$

$$np - 1 \quad = \quad p - 1 \quad + \quad n - 1 \quad + (n - 1)(p - 1)$$

A test of the null hypothesis that population means for treatment A are equal is given by

$$F = \frac{SSA/(p - 1)}{SSRES/[(n - 1)(p - 1)]} = \frac{MSA}{MSRES}.$$

It also is possible to test the null hypothesis that the population block means are equal by using the F statistic

$$F = \frac{SSBL/(n-1)}{SSRES/[(n-1)(p-1)]} = \frac{MSBL}{MSRES}.$$

Ordinarily, a test of this hypothesis is of little interest because the blocks represent a nuisance variable whose means are expected to differ. In the following section we will see how to compute the required mean squares and F statistics.

Computational Procedures for RB-3 Design

For purposes of comparison, we will reanalyze the weight-loss data in Table 14.2-1 as if the randomization plan appropriate for a randomized block design had been used. We want to form 10 blocks of girls who are matched in terms of initial weight. Earlier, we described a simple way to accomplish this. The 30 girls are ranked from heaviest to lightest. The three heaviest girls become block 1, the next three heaviest girls become block 2, and so on. The matching procedure continues until all 30 girls have been assigned to one of 10 blocks. The three girls in each block are then randomly assigned to the diets.

As discussed in Section 14.3, it is good statistical practice to compute descriptive statistics for one's data prior to testing the omnibus null hypothesis. A descriptive summary in the form of stacked box plots and a table of means and standard deviations for the weight-loss data is given in Figure 14.3-1 and Table 14.3-1, respectively. As discussed in Section 14.3, there is nothing in the descriptive summary that dissuades us from proceeding to test the omnibus null hypothesis. The data and computational procedures are shown in Table 15.2-1. The .05 level of significance is adopted. The results of the analysis are summarized in Table 15.2-2. It is apparent from Table 15.2-2 that the null hypotheses for treatment A and blocks can be rejected.

You are probably wondering, "What, if anything, has been gained by using a randomized block design instead of a completely randomized design?" The answer is greater power. A comparison of Tables 14.3-3 and 15.2-2 shows that the F statistics for testing treatment A are

$$\text{Completely randomized design} \qquad F = \frac{43.334}{5.037} = 8.60$$

$$\text{Randomized block design} \qquad F = \frac{43.334}{2.815} = 15.39$$

The F statistic for the randomized block design is larger because its error term ($MSRES = 2.815$) is about half as large as the error term for the completely randomized design ($MSWG = 5.037$). The reduction in the error term has been accomplished by isolating the nuisance variable of the girls' initial weight. Consequently,

TABLE 15.2-1. Computational Procedures for RB-3 Design

(i) Data and notation [X_{ij} denotes a score for the participant in block i and treatment level j; $i = 1, \ldots, n$ blocks (s_i); $j = 1, \ldots, p$ treatment levels (a_j)]

AS Summary Table[a]

	a_1	a_2	a_3	$\sum_{j=1}^{p} X_{ij}$
s_1	7	13	14	34
s_2	9	9	10	28
s_3	8	8	12	28
s_4	12	10	12	34
s_5	8	9	15	32
s_6	7	8	14	29
s_7	4	7	7	18
s_8	10	10	12	32
s_9	9	11	13	33
s_{10}	6	5	11	22
$\sum_{i=1}^{n} X_{ij} =$	80	90	120	

(ii) Computational symbols[b]

$$\sum_{j=1}^{p} \sum_{i=1}^{n} X_{ij} = 7 + 9 + 8 + \cdots + 11 = 290.000$$

$$\sum_{j=1}^{p} \sum_{i=1}^{n} X_{ij}^2 = [AS] = (7)^2 + (9)^2 + (8)^2 + \cdots + (11)^2 = 3026.000$$

$$\frac{\left(\sum_{j=1}^{p} \sum_{i=1}^{n} X_{ij}\right)^2}{np} = [X] = \frac{(290)^2}{(10)(3)} = 2803.333$$

$$\sum_{j=1}^{p} \frac{\left(\sum_{i=1}^{n} X_{ij}\right)^2}{n} = [A] = \frac{(80)^2}{10} + \cdots + \frac{(120)^2}{10} = 2890.000$$

$$\sum_{i=1}^{n} \frac{\left(\sum_{j=1}^{p} X_{ij}\right)^2}{p} = [S] = \frac{(34)^2}{3} + \cdots + \frac{(22)^2}{3} = 2888.667$$

(continued)

TABLE 15.2-1.   Computational Procedures for RB-3 Design *(Continued)*

(iii) Computational formulas

$$SSTO = [AS] - [X] = 3026.000 - 2803.333 = 222.667$$

$$SSA = [A] - [X] = 2890.000 - 2803.333 = 86.667$$

$$SSBL = [S] - [X] = 2888.667 - 2803.333 = 85.333$$

$$SSRES = [AS] - [A] - [S] + [X] = 3026.000 - 2890.000 - 2888.667 + 2803.333$$

[a] *A* denotes treatment *A*, and *S* denotes subjects or blocks; the table is so named because it reflects variation attributable to treatment levels (*A*) and subjects (*S*).

[b] The symbols [*AS*], [*X*], [*A*], and [*S*] are used to simplify the computational formulas.

this nuisance variable doesn't contribute to the randomized block design's error term. This point is graphically illustrated in Figure 15.2-1, where the partition of the total sum of squares for the two designs is shown. As this figure suggests, all sources of variation not specifically identified in the linear model equation contribute to the error term.

The effectiveness of the blocking procedure is determined by how well participants in each block are matched. The better the matching, the higher the mean correlation between all pairs of treatment levels, and the more powerful the randomized block design relative to a completely randomized design.

The weight-loss data in Table 15.2-1 will be used to illustrate what we mean. For these data, the correlations among the three treatment levels are $r_{12} = .477$ for a_1 and a_2, $r_{13} = .370$ for a_1 and a_3, and $r_{23} = .479$ for a_2 and a_3. The mean correlation, $\bar{r}$, is

$$\bar{r} = \frac{.477 + .370 + .479}{3} = .442.$$

TABLE 15.2-2.   ANOVA Table for RB-3 Design

Source	SS	df	MS	F
1. Treatment *A* (three diets)	86.667	$p - 1 = 2$	43.334	[1/3] 15.39**
2. Blocks (initial weight)	85.333	$n - 1 = 9$	9.481	[2/3] 3.37*
3. Residual	50.667	$(n - 1)(p - 1) = 18$	2.815	
4. Total	222.667	$np - 1 = 29$		

**p < .01, *p < .05; [1/3] indicates that the *F* statistic was obtained by dividing *MSA* in row 1 by *MSRES* in row 3; [2/3] indicates that the *F* statistic was obtained by dividing *MSBL* in row 2 by *MSRES* in row 3.

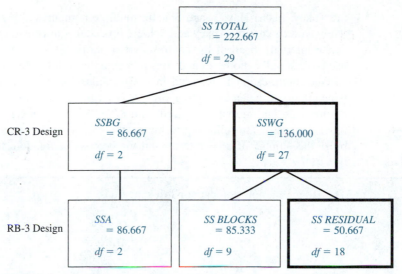

Figure 15.2-1. **Partition of the total sum of squares and degrees of freedom for a type CR-3 design and a type RB-3 design. The error term for each design is indicated by the rectangle with the thicker lines. Note that for the type RB-3 design, the nuisance variable represented by blocks has been isolated and thus removed from the error term. In other words,** *SSRESIDUAL = SSWG − SSBLOCKS*

The error term for the randomized block design, *MSRES,* is equal to

$$MSRES = MSWG(1 - \bar{r}),$$

where *MSWG* is the error term for a completely randomized design. The value of *MSWG* from Table 14.3-3 is 5.037. For our weight-loss data, $MSWG(1 - \bar{r}) = 5.037(1 - .442) = 2.811$, which, within rounding error, is equal to *MSRES.* From an examination of the equation for *MSRES,* it can be seen that the larger the mean correlation among treatment levels, $\bar{r}$, the smaller is *MSRES.* What this means is that by carefully matching the participants in each of the blocks, a researcher can greatly increase the power of the randomized block design relative to that of a completely randomized design.

Multiple Comparison Procedures

After rejecting the omnibus null hypothesis for treatment *A,* a researcher would probably want to determine which contrasts are not equal to 0. The multiple comparison procedures described in Section 14.5 are used for this purpose. As discussed in Section 14.5, you can test null hypotheses for a posteriori contrasts with the Tukey, Fisher-Hayter, and Scheffé multiple comparison test statistics. Alternatively, you can use the Tukey and Scheffé procedures to construct a posteriori confidence intervals. If all of the contrasts are a priori, the Dunn-Šidàk statistic can be used to test null hypotheses and construct confidence intervals.

One modification is required in the formulas for the test statistics and confidence intervals given in Section 14.5: *MSWG,* the error term for a completely randomized design, must be replaced with *MSRES,* the error term for a randomized block design. In the following formulas, the number of treatment levels is denoted by p, the number of blocks by n, and the degrees of freedom for *MSRES* by $\nu = (n - 1)(p - 1)$.

The Tukey multiple comparison test statistic is

$$q = \frac{\overline{X}_{\cdot j} - \overline{X}_{\cdot j'}}{\sqrt{\dfrac{MSRES}{n}}}.$$

The critical value, $q_{\alpha;p,\nu}$, for Tukey's test is obtained from Appendix Table D.10.

A two-sided $100(1 - \alpha)\%$ confidence interval is

$$(\overline{X}_{\cdot j} - \overline{X}_{\cdot j'}) - \frac{q_{\alpha;p,\nu}\sqrt{MSRES}}{\sqrt{n}} < \mu_j - \mu_{j'} < (\overline{X}_{\cdot j} - \overline{X}_{\cdot j'}) + \frac{q_{\alpha;p,\nu}\sqrt{MSRES}}{\sqrt{n}}.$$

The Fisher-Hayter multiple comparison test statistic is

$$qFH = \frac{\overline{X}_{\cdot j} - \overline{X}_{\cdot j'}}{\sqrt{\dfrac{MSRES}{n}}}.$$

The critical value, $q_{\alpha;p-1,\nu}$, for the Fisher-Hayter test is obtained from Appendix Table D.10.

The Scheffé multiple comparison test statistic is

$$FS = \frac{(c_1\overline{X}_{\cdot 1} + c_2\overline{X}_{\cdot 2} + \cdots + c_p\overline{X}_{\cdot p})^2}{MSRES\left(\dfrac{c_1^2}{n} + \dfrac{c_2^2}{n} + \cdots + \dfrac{c_p^2}{n}\right)}.$$

The $F_{\alpha;\nu_1,\nu_2}$ portion of the critical value $(p - 1)F_{\alpha;\nu_1,\nu_2}$ is obtained from Appendix Table D.5; $\nu_1 = (p - 1)$ and $\nu_2 = (n - 1)(p - 1)$.

A two-sided $100(1 - \alpha)\%$ confidence interval is

$$\hat{\psi}_i - \sqrt{(p-1)F_{\alpha;\nu_1,\nu_2}}\sqrt{MSRES\sum_{j=1}^{p}\frac{c_j^2}{n}} < \psi_i < \hat{\psi}_i + \sqrt{(p-1)F_{\alpha;\nu_1,\nu_2}}\sqrt{MSRES\sum_{j=1}^{p}\frac{c_j^2}{n}},$$

where $\psi_i = c_1\mu_1 + c_2\mu_2 + \cdots + c_p\mu_p$ and $\hat{\psi}_i = c_1\overline{X}_{.1} + c_2\overline{X}_{.2} + \cdots + c_p\overline{X}_{.p}$.

The Dunn-Šidàk multiple comparison test statistic is

$$tDS = \frac{c_1\overline{X}_{.1} + c_2\overline{X}_{.2} + \cdots + c_p\overline{X}_{.p}}{\sqrt{MSRES\left(\dfrac{c_1^2}{n} + \dfrac{c_2^2}{n} + \cdots + \dfrac{c_p^2}{n}\right)}}.$$

The critical value, $tDS_{\alpha/2;C,\nu}$, for the Dunn-Šidàk test is obtained from Appendix Table D.11; C is the number of a priori contrasts.

A two-sided $100(1 - \alpha)\%$ confidence interval is

$$\hat{\psi}_i - qDS_{\alpha/2;C,\nu}\sqrt{MSRES\sum_{j=1}^{p}\frac{c_j^2}{n}} < \psi_i < \hat{\psi}_i + qDS_{\alpha/2;C,\nu}\sqrt{MSRES\sum_{j=1}^{p}\frac{c_j^2}{n}},$$

where $\psi_i = c_1\mu_1 + c_2\mu_2 + \cdots + c_p\mu_p$ and $\hat{\psi}_i = c_1\overline{X}_{.1} + c_2\overline{X}_{.2} + \cdots + c_p\overline{X}_{.p}$. A one-sided $100(1 - \alpha)\%$ confidence interval is

$$\hat{\psi}_i - qDS_{\alpha;C,\nu}\sqrt{MSRES\sum_{j=1}^{p}\frac{c_j^2}{n}} < \psi_i \text{ or } \psi_i < \hat{\psi} + qDS_{\alpha;C,\nu}\sqrt{MSRES\sum_{j=1}^{p}\frac{c_j^2}{n}}.$$

Computational Example for the Fisher-Hayter Multiple Comparison Procedure

The omnibus null hypothesis for the weight-loss data in Tables 15.2-1 and 15.2-2 was rejected. After examining the sample means, the researcher decided to use the Fisher-Hayter multiple comparison statistic to test the null hypotheses $\mu_{.1} = \mu_{.2}$, $\mu_{.1} = \mu_{.3}$, and $\mu_{.2} = \mu_{.3}$. The weight-loss sample means are $\overline{X}_{.1} = 8.00$, $\overline{X}_{.2} = 9.00$, $\overline{X}_{.3} = 12.00$; $MSRES = 2.815$, and $n = 10$. Because the ANOVA F test was significant, the next step is to test the three pairwise contrasts using

$$qFH = \frac{\overline{X}_{.j} - \overline{X}_{.j'}}{\sqrt{\dfrac{MSWG}{n}}}.$$

The test statistics are

$$qFH = \frac{8.00 - 9.00}{\sqrt{\dfrac{2.815}{10}}} = -1.88 \qquad (\overline{X}_{.1} \text{ versus } \overline{X}_{.2})$$

$$qFH = \frac{8.00 - 12.00}{\sqrt{\dfrac{2.815}{10}}} = -7.54 \qquad (\overline{X}_{.1} \text{ versus } \overline{X}_{.3})$$

$$qFH = \frac{9.00 - 12.00}{\sqrt{\dfrac{2.815}{10}}} = -5.65 \qquad (\overline{X}_{.2} \text{ versus } \overline{X}_{.3})$$

To reject a null hypothesis, the absolute value $|qFH|$ must exceed or equal $q_{.05;3-1,18} = 2.97$. Because $|qFH(18)| = 7.54$ and 5.65 are greater than $q_{.05;3-1,18} = 2.97$, the null hypotheses for $\mu_1 = \mu_3$ and $\mu_2 = \mu_3$ are rejected. We can conclude that for the population of girls represented in the experiment, diet a_3 would produce a greater weight loss than diets a_1 and a_2. Based on the sample data, our best guess is that the use of diet a_3 would result in losing 4 more pounds than diet a_1 and 3 more than diet a_2.

As discussed in Section 14.5, computation of the Fisher-Hayter statistics is the second step of a two-step procedure. The first step is a test of the omnibus null hypothesis using an ANOVA F test. If the omnibus null hypothesis is not rejected, the second step—using the Fisher-Hayter statistic—is not performed. In contrast, the procedures of Tukey, Scheffé, and Dunn-Šidàk do not have to be preceded by a significant ANOVA F test. All four of the multiple comparison procedures control the probability of making one or more type I errors for a collection of tests at or less than α. As discussed in Section 14.5, however, the tests differ markedly in their power: the ability to correctly detect population contrasts that are not equal to 0. The Fisher-Hayter procedure is the most powerful; Scheffé's procedure is the least powerful.

Practical Significance

In Section 14.6, we described omega squared, a measure of strength of association, that can be used with the ANOVA F test. Omega squared estimates the proportion of variance in the dependent variable that is accounted for by the p treatment levels. For a randomized block design, we want to estimate the proportion of variance in the dependent variable that is accounted for by the p treatment levels while ignoring the nuisance variable of blocks. The appropriate measure of strength of association between the dependent variable X and treatment A is **partial omega squared,** denoted by $\hat{\omega}^2_{X|A \cdot BL}$. The subscript $X|A \cdot BL$ indicates that the association is between the dependent variable X and treatment A; the dot indicates that the effects of blocks are ignored. The formula for is $\hat{\omega}^2_{X|A \cdot BL}$ is

$$\hat{\omega}^2_{X|A \cdot BL} = \frac{(p - 1)(F_A - 1)}{(p - 1)(F_A - 1) + np},$$

where F_A is the F statistic for treatment A ($F_A = MSA/MSRES$). For the weight-loss data in Table 15.2-2, an estimate of the proportion of the population weight-loss variance accounted for by the three diets is

$$\hat{\omega}_{X|A \cdot BL}^2 = \frac{(3-1)(15.394-1)}{(3-1)(15.394-1)+(10)(3)} = .49.$$

According to Cohen's guidelines for interpreting omega squared in Section 14.6, the strength of association between the diets and weight loss is large—49% of the variance in weight loss is associated with the diets; $100 - 49\% = 51\%$ is associated with factors other than the diets.

Hedges's g statistic, described in Section 12.4, can be used to assess the effect size of contrasts among the diet means. The g statistic is

$$g = \frac{|\overline{X}_{\cdot j} - \overline{X}_{\cdot j'}|}{\hat{\sigma}_{Pooled}},$$

where

$$\hat{\sigma}_{Pooled} = \sqrt{\frac{(n_1-1)\,\hat{\sigma}_1^2 + (n_2-1)\,\hat{\sigma}_2^2 + \cdots + (n_p-1)\hat{\sigma}_p^2}{(n_1-1) + (n_2-1) + \cdots + (n_p-1)}}.$$

For a randomized block design, a simpler formula for computing $\hat{\sigma}_{Pooled}$ is

$$\hat{\sigma}_{Pooled} = \sqrt{\frac{SSBL + SSRES}{p(n-1)}},$$

where $SSBL$ and $SSRES$ are obtained from a randomized block ANOVA table. For the weight-loss data in Tables 15.2-1 and 15.2-2, the Fisher-Hayter multiple comparison procedure identified two significant pairwise contrasts, $\mu_1 - \mu_3$ and $\mu_2 - \mu_3$. The effect sizes for these two contrasts are, respectively,

$$g = \frac{|\overline{X}_{\cdot j} - \overline{X}_{\cdot j'}|}{\hat{\sigma}_{Pooled}}$$

$$g = \frac{8-12}{2.244} = 1.8$$

$$g = \frac{9-12}{2.244} = 1.3,$$

where

$$\hat{\sigma}_{Pooled} = \sqrt{\frac{85.333 + 50.667}{3(10-1)}} = 2.244.$$

According to Cohen's guidelines for interpreting d-like measures of effect size in Section 10.6, both of the contrasts represent large effects. This suggests that the difference between diets a_1 and a_3 and between diets a_2 and a_3 is large enough to be of practical value. This conclusion is consistent with our intuition that a weight-loss difference of 3 or 4 pounds after dieting for one month is a worthwhile difference.

Assumptions Associated With a Randomized Block Design

The assumptions for the simplest ANOVA design, the completely randomized design, were described in detail in Section 14.4. The randomized block design shares several of the assumptions, as the following list shows.

1. The model equation $X_{ij} = \mu + \alpha_j + \pi_i + \epsilon_{ij}$ reflects all the sources of variation that affect X_{ij}.
2. The blocks represent a random sample from a population of blocks. The block effects, π_i, within each block population are normally distributed, and the variances of the block populations, σ_π^2, are homogeneous. Furthermore, the block effects are independent of one another and other effects in the model equation.
3. The population variances of differences for all pairs of treatment levels, $\sigma_{a_j}^2 + \sigma_{a_{j'}}^2 - 2\sigma_{a_j a_{j'}}$, are homogeneous; $\sigma_{a_j a_{j'}}$ is the covariance (see Section 5.3) of treatment levels a_j and $a_{j'}$.
4. The error effects, ϵ_{ij}, are normally distributed and the variances of the error effects, σ_ϵ^2, are homogeneous. Furthermore, the error effects are independent of one another and other effects in the model equation.

Assumptions 1 and 4 are discussed in Section 14.4 in connection with a completely randomized design; assumptions 2 and 3 are new. Assumption 2 states, among other things, that the blocks in an experiment are a random sample from a population of blocks. In many experiments, a researcher does not actually obtain a random sample of blocks. In such cases, the conclusions from the experiment are restricted to the population represented by the blocks in the experiment. Recall that blocks represent a nuisance variable whose effects we want to control. In the weight-loss experiment, the blocks represented 10 levels of initial obesity and were not randomly sampled from a population of levels of initial obesity. Instead, 30 volunteers who wanted to lose weight were recruited. The specific values of initial obesity were determined by the initial weights of the 30 girls. The researcher was not interested in the specific levels of obesity, but instead, in controlling for the effects of initial obesity. Although a random sample of blocks was not obtained, a population of girls must exist that would have produced the blocks in the experiment if a random sample had been obtained. The results of the experiment apply to this hypothetical population of blocks. To the extent that the blocks in an experiment are representative of a population of interest, the results may generalize to that population. However, in the absence of random sampling, generalizations to other block populations involve a leap of faith.

Assumption 3 states that the population variances of differences for all pairs of treatment levels are homogeneous. For the weight-loss data, this means that

$$\sigma_{a_1}^2 + \sigma_{a_2}^2 - 2\sigma_{a_1 a_2} = \sigma_{a_1}^2 + \sigma_{a_3}^2 - 2\sigma_{a_1 a_3} = \sigma_{a_2}^2 + \sigma_{a_3}^2 - 2\sigma_{a_2 a_3}.$$

Violation of this assumption, which is called the *sphericity condition,* can seriously affect the probability of making a type I error and the power of the F test. Procedures for testing the assumption and adjustments to compensate for observed violations are complicated and beyond the scope of this book. The interested reader is referred to Kirk (1995, pp. 274–282).

The model equation and associated assumptions that have been described are called a *mixed model* and underlie most randomized block designs. For a discussion of other models, the reader can consult Howell (1997, pp. 452–453), Keppel (1991, pp. 350–353), Kirk (1995, pp. 265–268), and Maxwell and Delaney (1990, pp. 463–471).

CHECK YOUR UNDERSTANDING OF SECTION 15.2

5. Fill in the missing values in the following table.

Source	SS	df	MS	F
1. Treatment A	51.765	3	( )	[1/3] ( )**
2. Blocks	( )	20	( )	[2/3] ( )*
3. Residual	271.500	( )	( )	
4. Total	484.765	( )		

* $p < ($)
** $p < ($)

6. Brain-damaged patients are expected to score lower on the Willner Unusual Meanings Vocabulary Test (*WUMV*), which measures knowledge of unusual meanings of familiar words, and the Willner-Sheerer Analogy Test (*WSA*) than on the vocabulary items of the Wechsler Adult Intelligence Scale (*WAIS*). A random sample of 12 brain-damaged patients took all three tests. The order of administration of the tests was randomized independently for each patient. The dependent variable was the participant's standard score on each test. According to the test manual, all three tests have a mean of 10 and a standard deviation of 3. The following data were obtained. (Experiment suggested by Willner, W. [1965]. Impairment of knowledge of

unusual meanings of familiar words in brain damage and schizophrenia. *Journal of Abnormal Psychology, 70,* 405–411.)

	a_1 WAIS	a_2 WUMV	a_3 WSA
s_1	15	12	11
s_2	10	11	8
s_3	6	4	3
s_4	7	7	5
s_5	9	6	6
s_6	16	14	10
s_7	11	10	7
s_8	13	9	4
s_9	12	10	8
s_{10}	10	8	7
s_{11}	11	9	9
s_{12}	14	11	10

a. Construct stacked box plots for the data. Are the sample distributions relatively symmetrical? Do the data contain outliers?

b. Compute descriptive statistics, $\overline{X}_{.j}$'s and $\hat{\sigma}_j$'s, for the data, and construct a table similar to Table 14.3-1.

c. What do the descriptive statistics in (b) tell you?

d. Test the null hypothesis that $\mu_{.1} = \mu_{.2} = \mu_{.3}$. Let $\alpha = .05$.

e. Estimate the proportion of the population variance in the dependent variable that is accounted for by treatment A and interpret the result.

f. Use the Fisher-Hayter statistic to determine which population means differ.

g. Use Hedges's g statistic to measure the effect size for the three pairwise contrasts and interpret the results.

h. According to the description of the experiment, the researcher was specifically interested in testing two a priori one-sided hypotheses. What were these hypotheses? Use the Dunn-Šidàk statistic to test these hypotheses by computing one-sided confidence intervals. Graph the confidence intervals.

i. Ignore the blocking variable and analyze the data as if the randomization plan for a CR-3 design had been used. Compare the results of the two analyses by constructing a figure similar to Figure 15.2-1. Was the blocking procedure effective? Explain.

7. Term to remember

a. Partial omega squared

15.3 COMPLETELY RANDOMIZED FACTORIAL DESIGN

Introduction to Factorial Designs

The two ANOVA designs discussed thus far involve one treatment, but often a researcher wants to test hypotheses about two or more treatments. This can be accomplished by performing two or more separate experiments, but this is inefficient. An alternative approach is to use a factorial ANOVA design to simultaneously test hypotheses about two or more treatments in a single experiment.

A **factorial design** is distinguished from other ANOVA designs in that it has two or more treatments and the levels of each treatment are investigated in combination with those of other treatments.

For example, a participant's performance on a learning task might be observed for the combined conditions of large monetary reward for good performance (one level of treatment *A*) and absence of distractions in the learning environment (one level of treatment *B*). A participant in a factorial design is always simultaneously exposed to one level each of two or more treatments. The combination of conditions to which a participant is simultaneously exposed is called a **treatment combination.**

The levels of the treatments in a factorial design can be **completely crossed,** meaning that each level of one treatment occurs once with each level of the other treatments and vice versa, or **partially crossed,** meaning that each level of one treatment occurs with some of the levels of the other treatments but not with all of them. A completely randomized factorial design, the simplest factorial design, is constructed by completely crossing the treatment levels contained in two or more completely randomized designs. The resulting design with two treatments, say, *A* and *B*, is designated by the letters CRF-*pq*, where *p* denotes the number of levels of treatment *A* and *q*, the number of levels of treatment *B*.[1] Perhaps the following example will clarify the main features of a CRF-*pq* design.

Consider an experiment to investigate the effects of treatments *A* and *B* on reading speed. Suppose that treatment *A* consists of two levels of room illumination: a_1 is 15 foot-candles and a_2 is 30 foot-candles. Treatment *B* consists of three levels of type size: b_1 is 6-point type, b_2 is 12-point type, and b_3 is 18-point type. Each level of *A* is combined with all levels of *B* to form $2 \times 3 = 6$ treatment combinations: $a_1b_1, a_1b_2, a_1b_3, \ldots, a_2b_3$. The layout for this CRF-23 design with five participants in each treatment combination is shown in Figure 15.3-1.

The randomization plan for the design is as follows. We will assume that 30 participants are available. The participants are randomly assigned to $p \times q =$

---

[1] Some writers refer to this design as a *two-way* or *two-factor ANOVA,* but these designations are imprecise because they could refer to any one of 10 different kinds of factorial designs. This point is discussed by Kirk (1995, pp. 43–46).

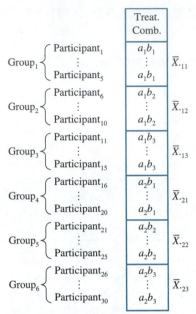

Figure 15.3-1. **Layout for a CRF-23 design. Thirty participants were randomly assigned to the 2 × 3 = 6 combinations of treatments *A* and *B*.**

2 × 3 = 6 treatment combinations with the restriction that five participants are assigned to each combination.

Linear Model Equation for a Score

A participant's score in a CRF-*pq* design is represented by X_{ijk}, where i denotes one of the n participants, j denotes one of the p levels of treatment A, and k denotes one of the q levels of treatment B. As in all ANOVA designs, the score X_{ijk} is composite. It is equal to the sum of five parameters of the linear model equation. The values of the parameters are unknown, but data from a sample can be used to estimate them as follows:

Parameters of the linear model equation

$$X_{ijk} = \mu + \alpha_j + \beta_k + (\alpha\beta)_{jk} + \epsilon_{ijk}$$

Estimators of the parameters

$$X_{ijk} = \overline{X}_{...} + (\overline{X}_{.j.} - \overline{X}_{...}) + (\overline{X}_{..k} - \overline{X}_{...}) + (\overline{X}_{.jk} - \overline{X}_{.j.} - \overline{X}_{..k} + \overline{X}_{...}) + (X_{ijk} - \overline{X}_{.jk})$$

| Score | Grand Mean | *A* Treatment Effect | *B* Treatment Effect | *AB* Interaction Effect | Within-Cell Error Effect |

This model equation allows us to partition the total sum of squares and total degrees of freedom $(npq - 1)$ into four parts as follows:

$$SS\ TOTAL = SSA + SSB + SSAB + SS\ WCELL$$
$$npq - 1 = p - 1 + q - 1 + (p - 1)(q - 1) + pq(n - 1)$$

The following null hypotheses can be tested.

$H_0: \mu_{1.} = \mu_{2.} = \cdots = \mu_{p.}$ (Treatment A population means are equal)

$H_0: \mu_{.1} = \mu_{.2} = \cdots = \mu_{.q}$ (Treatment B population means are equal)

$H_0:$ All $(\alpha\beta)_{jk}$ interaction effects $= 0$ (Treatments A and B do not interact)[2]

The first two null hypotheses are familiar; the third null hypothesis is new. We will have more to say about the interaction hypothesis later.

Computational Procedures for CRF-23 Design

Descriptive summaries of the data for the reading-speed experiment are presented in Figure 15.3-2 and Table 15.3-1. Reading speed appears to be fastest for the 30 foot-candle condition and the larger type sizes. The standard deviations appear to

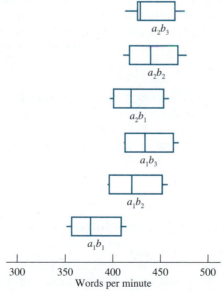

Figure 15.3-2. **With the exception of treatment combination a_2b_3, the distributions are relatively symmetrical. The data do not contain outliers.**

---

[2] The interaction null hypothesis can be expressed in a variety of ways. Two of the more common ways are as follows: (1) $(\alpha\beta)_{jk} = 0$ for all j and k and (2) $\mu_{jk} - \mu_{j'k} - \mu_{jk'} + \mu_{j'k'} = 0$ for all j, j', k, k'. For a discussion of these hypotheses, see Kirk (1995, pp. 370–372).

TABLE 15.3-1. Descriptive Summary of the Reading-Speed Data (Means and Standard Deviations Expressed in Words per Minute)

Illumination Level		$b_1 = 6\text{-}pt$	*Type Size* $b_2 = 12\text{-}pt$	$b_3 = 18\text{-}pt$	$\overline{X}_{\cdot j \cdot}$	$\hat{\sigma}_{j \cdot}$
	$\overline{X}_{\cdot jk} =$	382	423	436		
$a_1 = 15$ ft-c					413.7	35.1
	$\hat{\sigma}_{jk} =$	28.2	29.1	26.2		
	$\overline{X}_{\cdot jk} =$	423	442	441		
$a_2 = 30$ ft-c					435.3	27.8
	$\hat{\sigma}_{jk} =$	28.4	29.6	27.0		
	$\overline{X}_{\cdot \cdot k} =$	402.5	432.5	438.5		
	$\hat{\sigma}_{\cdot k} =$	34.3	29.4	25.2		

be fairly homogeneous. Descriptive summaries of the data should always precede the presentation of inferential statistics. The preparation of such summaries may uncover suspicious outliers, unsuspected promising lines of investigation, or assumptions of the design that do not appear to be tenable.

The computational procedures for the two-treatment completely randomized factorial design are shown in Table 15.3-2. The .05 level of significance is adopted. The results of the analysis are summarized in Table 15.3-3. It is apparent from Table 15.3-3 that the null hypotheses for treatments A and B can be rejected. We know from the significant test of treatment A and the means in Table 15.3-1 that reading speed is faster under 30 foot-candles of illumination than under 15 foot-candles. A researcher probably would be interested in determining which type-size means are unequal. Before addressing this question using the Fisher-Hayter multiple comparison procedure, we will describe the nature and interpretation of an interaction.

Interpreting Interactions

The test of the AB interaction in Table 15.3-3 is not significant. This tells us that there is no reason for believing that the difference between the population means for treatment A is unequal across the three levels of treatment B. Similarly, there is no reason for believing that the differences among the population means for treatment B are not the same at each level of treatment A. To put it another way, if we graphed the population means for a_1 and a_2 at each level of treatment B, lines connecting the means would be parallel. Consider the graph of the sample means in

TABLE 15.3-2. Computational Procedures for CRF-23 Design

(i) Data and notation [X_{ijk} denotes a score for participant i in treatment combination jk; $i = 1, \ldots, n$ participants (s_i); $j = 1, \ldots, p$ levels of treatment A (a_j); $k = 1, \ldots, q$ levels of treatment B (b_k)]

ABS Summary Table[a]
Table entry is X_{ijk}

	a_1 b_1	a_1 b_2	a_1 b_3	a_2 b_1	a_2 b_2	a_2 b_3
	378	454	432	415	439	426
	408	394	411	396	467	428
	357	452	466	451	477	464
	353	396	411	455	410	412
	414	419	460	398	417	475
$\sum\limits_{i=1}^{n} X_{ijk} = $	1910	2115	2180	2115	2210	2205

AB Summary Table
Table entry is $\sum\limits_{i=1}^{n} X_{ijk}$

	b_1	b_2	b_3	$\sum\limits_{i=1}^{n}\sum\limits_{k=1}^{q} X_{ijk}$
a_1	1910	2115	2180	6205
a_2	2115	2210	2205	6530
$\sum\limits_{i=1}^{n}\sum\limits_{j=1}^{p} X_{ijk} = $	4025	4325	4385	

(ii) Computational symbols

$$\sum_{i=1}^{n}\sum_{j=1}^{p}\sum_{k=1}^{q} X_{ijk} = 378 + 408 + \cdots + 475 = 12{,}735.000$$

$$\sum_{i=1}^{n}\sum_{j=1}^{p}\sum_{k=1}^{q} X_{ijk}^{2} = [ABS] = (378)^2 + (408)^2 + \cdots + (475)^2 = 5{,}437{,}581.000$$

$$\frac{\left(\sum\limits_{i=1}^{n}\sum\limits_{j=1}^{p}\sum\limits_{k=1}^{q} X_{ijk}\right)^2}{npq} = [X] = \frac{(12{,}735)^2}{(5)(2)(3)} = 5{,}406{,}007.500$$

$$\sum_{j=1}^{p}\frac{\left(\sum\limits_{i=1}^{n}\sum\limits_{k=1}^{q} X_{ijk}\right)^2}{nq} = [A] = \frac{(6{,}205)^2}{(5)(3)} + \frac{(6{,}530)^2}{(5)(3)} = 5{,}409{,}528.333$$

(continued)

TABLE 15.3-2. Computational Procedures for CRF-23 Design (*Continued*)

$$\sum_{k=1}^{q} \frac{\left(\sum_{i=1}^{n}\sum_{j=1}^{p} X_{ijk}\right)^2}{np} = [B] = \frac{(4{,}025)^2}{(5)(2)} + \cdots + \frac{(4{,}385)^2}{(5)(2)} = 5{,}413{,}447.500$$

$$\sum_{j=1}^{p}\sum_{k=1}^{q} \frac{\left(\sum_{i=1}^{n} X_{ijk}\right)^2}{n} = [AB] = \frac{(1{,}910)^2}{(5)} + \cdots + \frac{(2{,}205)^2}{(5)} = 5{,}418{,}615.000$$

(iii) Computational formulas

$$SSTO = [ABS] - [X] = 5{,}437{,}581.000 - 5{,}406{,}007.500 = 31{,}573.500$$

$$SSA = [A] - [X] = 5{,}409{,}528.333 - 5{,}406{,}007.500 = 3{,}520.833$$

$$SSB = [B] - [X] = 5{,}413{,}447.500 - 5{,}406{,}007.500 = 7{,}440.000$$

$$\begin{aligned}SSAB &= [AB] - [A] - [B] + [X]\\ &= 5{,}418{,}615.000 - 5{,}409{,}528.333 - 413{,}447.500 + 5{,}406{,}007.500\\ &= 1{,}646.667\end{aligned}$$

$$SSWCELL = [ABS] - [AB] = 5{,}437{,}581.000 - 5{,}418{,}615.000 = 18{,}966.000$$

[a] *A* denotes treatment *A*, *B* denotes treatment *B*, and *S* denotes participants or subjects; the table is so named because it reflects variation attributable to treatments *A* and *B* and subjects (*S*).

Figure 15.3-3. The lines for the sample data are not parallel. The nonsignificant interaction, however, tells us that the departure from parallelism in Figure 15.3-3 can be attributed to chance.

An interaction test is unique to factorial designs. Two treatments are said to **interact** if differences in performance under the levels of one treatment are different at two or more levels of the other treatment.

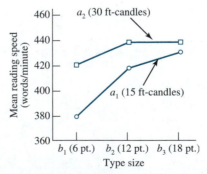

Figure 15.3-3. **Graph of the interaction between treatment *A* (level of illumination) and treatment *B* (size of type) for the data in Table 15.3-1.**

TABLE 15.3-3. ANOVA Table for CRF-23 Design

Source	SS	df	MS	F
1. Treatment A (illumination level)	3520.883	$p - 1 = 1$	3520.000	$[^1\!/_4]$ 4.46*
2. Treatment B (size of type)	7440.000	$q - 1 = 2$	3720.000	$[^2\!/_4]$ 4.71*
3. AB Interaction	1646.667	$(p - 1)(q - 1) = 2$	823.334	$[^3\!/_4]$ 1.04
4. Within Cell	18966.000	$pq(n - 1) = 24$	790.250	
5. Total	31573.500	$npq - 1 = 29$		

*$p < .05$; $[^1\!/_4]$ indicates that the F was obtained by dividing MSA in row 1 by $MSWCELL$ in row 4, and so on.

A significant interaction is always a signal that the interpretation of tests of treatments A and B must be qualified. Consider the population means in Table 15.3-4. The means for the two levels of treatment A are equal, as are those for treatment B. An analysis of variance performed on sample data from these populations undoubtedly would support this conclusion and also detect the interaction between the two treatments. A graph of the interaction is given in Figure 15.3-4(a). As expected, the lines connecting the means are anything but parallel. Also, we can see how misleading are the nonsignificant tests for treatments A and B. Clearly, there is a difference between the A means at b_1 as well as at b_2, and between the B means at a_1 as well as at a_2.

If an F test indicates that two treatments interact, a graph like those in Figures 15.3-3 and 15.3-4 is helpful in interpreting the interaction. We know that the graph will reveal at least two nonparallel lines between at least two levels of a treatment. A significant interaction doesn't mean that all lines throughout their length are nonparallel. Such a case is shown in Figure 15.3-4(b). In this figure the value of the contrast between a_1 and a_2 at b_1 $(30 - 12 = 18)$ is different from its value at b_2 $(25 - 21 = 4)$, but the value of the contrast is the same at b_2 $(25 - 21 = 4)$ and b_3

TABLE 15.3-4. Population Means for Treatments A and B

			Treatment B		
			b_1	b_2	$\mu_{j.}$
Treatment A	a_1	$\mu_{jk} =$	10	20	15
	a_2	$\mu_{jk} =$	20	10	15
		$\mu_{jk} =$	15	15	

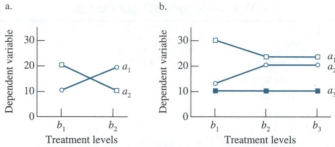

Figure 15.3-4. **Part (a) illustrates the interaction between treatment *A* and treatment *B* for the data in Table 15.3-4. Part (b) illustrates interaction between treatment *A* and treatment *B* for a hypothetical set of data. Notice that a significant interaction does not mean that all lines throughout their length are nonparallel. A significant interaction does mean that there are at least two nonparallel lines between at least two levels of the other treatment.**

$(25 - 21 = 4)$. To put it another way, the lines are nonparallel over only a portion of their length. Before leaving the topic of interactions, two points should be emphasized: (1) The presence of an interaction is a signal that the interpretation of tests of the associated treatments is usually misleading and hence of little interest and (2) one of the most useful procedures for understanding and interpreting an interaction is to graph it.[3]

The ability to test interactions is an important feature of a factorial design. But the design has other features that help to account for its wide use. Before describing these features, we will illustrate the use of multiple comparison procedures to determine which population means differ.

Multiple Comparison Procedures

The *AB* interaction null hypothesis for the reading-speed data was not rejected, but null hypotheses for treatments *A* and *B* were rejected. After examining the three sample means for treatment *B*, a researcher might want to determine which pairwise population contrasts for treatment *B* are not equal to 0. The three a posteriori multiple comparison tests and confidence intervals discussed in Section 14.5 can be used for this purpose. Two modifications in the formulas are required: The error term, *MSWG,* in the denominator must be replaced with *MSWCELL,* the error term for a completely randomized factorial design, and *n* must be replaced with either *nq*

---

[3] Harris (1994) and Kirk (1995, pp. 377–389) discuss more advanced techniques for interpreting interactions.

or np, the sample sizes used to compute $\overline{X}_{\cdot j \cdot}$ and $\overline{X}_{\cdot\cdot k}$, respectively. In the following formulas, the number of levels of treatments A and B is denoted by p and q, respectively; the number of observations in each treatment combination is denoted by n; and the degrees of freedom for *MSWCELL* is $\nu = pq(n - 1)$.

The Tukey multiple comparison test statistics for treatments A and B are, respectively,

$$q = \frac{\overline{X}_{\cdot j \cdot} - \overline{X}_{\cdot j' \cdot}}{\sqrt{\dfrac{MSWCELL}{nq}}} \qquad q = \frac{\overline{X}_{\cdot\cdot k} - \overline{X}_{\cdot\cdot k'}}{\sqrt{\dfrac{MSWCELL}{nq}}}$$

The critical values for treatments A and B, $q_{\alpha;p,\nu}$ and $q_{\alpha;q,\nu}$, are obtained from Appendix Table D.10.

Two-sided $100(1 - \alpha)\%$ confidence intervals are

$$(\overline{X}_{\cdot j \cdot} - \overline{X}_{\cdot j' \cdot}) - \frac{q_{\alpha;p,\nu}\sqrt{MSWCELL}}{\sqrt{nq}} < \mu_{\cdot j \cdot} - \mu_{\cdot j' \cdot} < (\overline{X}_{\cdot j \cdot} - \overline{X}_{\cdot j' \cdot}) + \frac{q_{\alpha;p,\nu}\sqrt{MSWCELL}}{\sqrt{nq}}$$

$$(\overline{X}_{\cdot\cdot k} - \overline{X}_{\cdot\cdot k'}) - \frac{q_{\alpha;q,\nu}\sqrt{MSWCELL}}{\sqrt{np}} < \mu_{\cdot\cdot k} - \mu_{\cdot\cdot k'} < (\overline{X}_{\cdot\cdot k} - \overline{X}_{\cdot\cdot k'}) + \frac{q_{\alpha;q,\nu}\sqrt{MSWCELL}}{\sqrt{np}}.$$

The Fisher-Hayter multiple comparison test statistics for treatments A and B are, respectively,

$$qFH = \frac{\overline{X}_{\cdot j \cdot} - \overline{X}_{\cdot j' \cdot}}{\sqrt{\dfrac{MSWCELL}{nq}}} \qquad qFH = \frac{\overline{X}_{\cdot\cdot k} - \overline{X}_{\cdot\cdot k'}}{\sqrt{\dfrac{MSWCELL}{np}}}$$

The critical values for treatments A and B, $q_{\alpha;p-1,\nu}$ and $q_{\alpha;q-1,\nu}$, are obtained from Appendix Table D.10.

The Scheffé multiple comparison test statistic for treatments A and B are, respectively,

$$FS = \frac{(c_1\overline{X}_{\cdot 1 \cdot} + c_2\overline{X}_{\cdot 2 \cdot} + \cdots + c_p\overline{X}_{\cdot p \cdot})^2}{MSWCELL\left(\dfrac{c_1^2}{nq} + \dfrac{c_2^2}{nq} + \cdots + \dfrac{c_p^2}{nq}\right)}$$

$$FS = \frac{(c_1\overline{X}_{\cdot\cdot 1} + c_2\overline{X}_{\cdot\cdot 2} + \cdots + c_q\overline{X}_{\cdot\cdot q})^2}{MSWCELL\left(\dfrac{c_1^2}{np} + \dfrac{c_2^2}{np} + \cdots + \dfrac{c_q^2}{np}\right)}.$$

The $F_{\alpha;\nu_1,\nu_2}$ portion of the critical values for treatments A and B, $(p - 1)F_{\alpha;\nu_1,\nu_2}$ and $(q - 1)F_{\alpha;\nu_1,\nu_2}$ is obtained from Appendix Table D.5; $\nu_1 = (p - 1)$ for treatment A and $\nu_1 = (q - 1)$ for treatment B; and $\nu_2 = pq(n - 1)$.

Two-sided $100(1 - \alpha)\%$ confidence intervals are

$$\hat{\psi}_{i(A)} - \sqrt{(p-1)F_{\alpha; \nu_1, \nu_2}} \sqrt{MSWCELL \sum_{j=1}^{p} \frac{c_j^2}{nq}} < \psi_{i(A)}$$

$$< \hat{\psi}_{i(A)} + \sqrt{(p-1)F_{\alpha; \nu_1, \nu_2}} \sqrt{MSWCELL \sum_{j=1}^{p} \frac{c_j^2}{nq}}$$

$$\hat{\psi}_{i(B)} - \sqrt{(q-1)F_{\alpha; \nu_1, \nu_2}} \sqrt{MSWCELL \sum_{k=1}^{q} \frac{c_k^2}{np}} < \psi_{i(B)}$$

$$< \hat{\psi}_{i(B)} + \sqrt{(q-1)F_{\alpha; \nu_1, \nu_2}} \sqrt{MSWCELL \sum_{k=1}^{q} \frac{c_k^2}{np}},$$

where

$$\psi_{i(A)} = c_1 \mu_{1\cdot} + c_2 \mu_{2\cdot} + \cdots + c_p \mu_{p\cdot} \qquad \hat{\psi}_{i(A)} = c_1 \overline{X}_{\cdot 1\cdot} + c_2 \overline{X}_{\cdot 2\cdot} + \cdots + c_p \overline{X}_{\cdot p\cdot}$$

and

$$\psi_{i(B)} = c_1 \mu_{\cdot 1} + c_2 \mu_{\cdot 2} + \cdots + c_q \mu_{\cdot q} \qquad \hat{\psi}_{i(B)} = c_1 \overline{X}_{\cdot\cdot 1} + c_2 \overline{X}_{\cdot\cdot 2} + \cdots + c_q \overline{X}_{\cdot\cdot q}$$

The Dunn-Šidàk multiple comparison test statistics for treatments A and B are, respectively,

$$tDS = \frac{c_1 \overline{X}_{\cdot 1 \cdot} + c_2 \overline{X}_{\cdot 2 \cdot} + \cdots + c_p \overline{X}_{\cdot p \cdot}}{\sqrt{MSWCELL \left(\dfrac{c_1^2}{nq} + \dfrac{c_2^2}{nq} + \cdots + \dfrac{c_p^2}{nq} \right)}}$$

$$tDS = \frac{c_1 \overline{X}_{\cdot\cdot 1} + c_2 \overline{X}_{\cdot\cdot 2} + \cdots + c_q \overline{X}_{\cdot\cdot q}}{\sqrt{MSWCELL \left(\dfrac{c_1^2}{np} + \dfrac{c_2^2}{np} + \cdots + \dfrac{c_p^2}{np} \right)}}.$$

The critical value for treatments A and B, $tDS_{\alpha/2; C, \nu}$, is obtained from Appendix Table D.11; C is the number of a priori contrasts.

Two-sided $100(1 - \alpha)\%$ confidence intervals are

$$\hat{\psi}_{i(A)} - qDS_{\alpha/2; C, \nu} \sqrt{MSWCELL \sum_{j=1}^{p} \frac{c_j^2}{nq}} < \psi_{i(A)} < \hat{\psi}_{i(A)} + qDS_{\alpha/2; C, \nu} \sqrt{MSWCELL \sum_{j=1}^{p} \frac{c_j^2}{nq}}$$

$$\hat{\psi}_{i(B)} - qDS_{\alpha/2; C, \nu} \sqrt{MSWCELL \sum_{k=1}^{q} \frac{c_k^2}{np}} < \psi_{i(B)} < \hat{\psi}_{i(B)} + qDS_{\alpha/2; C, \nu} \sqrt{MSWCELL \sum_{k=1}^{q} \frac{c_k^2}{np}},$$

where the contrasts $\psi_{i(A)}$, $\hat{\psi}_{i(A)}$, $\psi_{i(B)}$, and $\hat{\psi}_{i(B)}$ are as defined for Scheffé's procedure. A one-sided $100(1 - \alpha)\%$ confidence interval for treatment A is

$$\hat{\psi}_{i(A)} - qDS_{\alpha; C, \nu} \sqrt{MSWCELL \sum_{j=1}^{p} \frac{c_j^2}{nq}} < \psi_{i(A)}$$

or

$$\psi_{i(A)} < \hat{\psi}_{i(A)} + qDS_{\alpha;C,\nu}\sqrt{MSWCELL\sum_{j=1}^{p}\frac{c_j^2}{nq}}.$$

A one-sided $100(1 - \alpha)\%$ confidence interval for treatment B is

$$\hat{\psi}_{i(B)} - qDS_{\alpha;C,\nu}\sqrt{MSWCELL\sum_{k=1}^{q}\frac{c_k^2}{np}} < \psi_{i(B)}$$

or

$$\psi_{i(B)} < \hat{\psi}_{i(B)} + qDS_{\alpha;C,\nu}\sqrt{MSWCELL\sum_{k=1}^{q}\frac{c_k^2}{np}}.$$

Computational Example for the Fisher-Hayter Multiple Comparison Procedure

We will now illustrate the use of the Fisher-Hayter multiple comparison procedure to test the null hypotheses $\mu_{.1} = \mu_{.2}$, $\mu_{.1} = \mu_{.3}$, and $\mu_{.2} = \mu_{.3}$. The reading-speed sample means are $\overline{X}_{..1} = 402.50$, $\overline{X}_{..2} = 432.50$, $\overline{X}_{..3} = 438.50$; $MSWCELL = 790.250$, $p = 2$, $q = 3$, and $n = 5$. Because the ANOVA F test for treatment B was significant, the next step is to test the three pairwise contrasts using

$$qFH = \frac{\overline{X}_{..k} - \overline{X}_{..k'}}{\sqrt{\dfrac{MSWCELL}{np}}}.$$

The test statistics are

$$qFH = \frac{402.50 - 432.50}{\sqrt{\dfrac{790.250}{(5)(2)}}} = -3.37 \qquad (\overline{X}_{..1} \text{ versus } \overline{X}_{..2})$$

$$qFH = \frac{402.50 - 438.50}{\sqrt{\dfrac{790.250}{(5)(2)}}} = -4.05 \qquad (\overline{X}_{..1} \text{ versus } \overline{X}_{..3})$$

$$qFH = \frac{432.50 - 438.50}{\sqrt{\dfrac{790.250}{(5)(2)}}} = -0.67 \qquad (\overline{X}_{..2} \text{ versus } \overline{X}_{..3})$$

To reject a null hypothesis, the absolute value $|qFH|$ must exceed or equal $q_{.05;3-1,24} = 2.92$. Because $|qFH(24)| = 3.37$ and 4.05 are greater than $q_{.05;3-1,24} = 2.92$, the null hypotheses for $\mu_{.1} = \mu_{.2}$ and $\mu_{.1} = \mu_{.3}$ are rejected. We can conclude that for the population of participants represented in the experiment and the levels of illumination employed, the use of 12- and 18-point type sizes (treatment levels b_2 and b_3) would result in faster reading speeds than the 6-point type (treatment level b_1). Based on the sample data given in Table 15.3-1, our best guess is that the use of 12-point type would result in reading 30 more words per minute than the 6-point type. The use of 18-point type would result in reading 36 more words per minute than the 6-point type.

As discussed in Section 14.5, computation of the Fisher-Hayter statistics is the second step of a two-step procedure. The first step is a test of the omnibus null hypothesis using an ANOVA F test. If the omnibus null hypothesis is not rejected, the Fisher-Hayter test is not used.

Practical Significance

We can use partial omega squared that was described in Section 15.2 to estimate the proportion of variance in the dependent variable for a CRF-pq design that is accounted for by each of the treatments and interaction. An estimate of the strength of association between the dependent variable X and treatment A while ignoring treatment B and the AB interaction is given by

$$\hat{\omega}^2_{X|A \cdot B, AB} = \frac{(p - 1)(F_A - 1)}{(p - 1)(F_A - 1) + npq} = \frac{(2 - 1)(4.46 - 1)}{(2 - 1)(4.46 - 1) + (5)(2)(3)} = .10,$$

where F_A denotes the value of the F statistic for treatment A. An estimate of the strength of association between the dependent variable X and treatment B while ignoring treatment A and the AB interaction is given by

$$\hat{\omega}^2_{X|B \cdot A, AB} = \frac{(q - 1)(F_B - 1)}{(q - 1)(F_B - 1) + npq} = \frac{(3 - 1)(4.71 - 1)}{(3 - 1)(4.71 - 1) + (5)(2)(3)} = .20,$$

where F_B denotes the value of the F statistic for treatment B. Treatment B accounts for more of the variance in reading speed than treatment A. According to Cohen's guidelines for interpreting partial omega squared, treatment A is a medium-size association; treatment B is a large association. If the AB interaction had been significant, we would want to estimate the strength of association between the dependent variable X and the AB interaction while ignoring treatments A and B. This estimate is given by

$$\hat{\omega}^2_{\overline{X}|AB \cdot A, B} = \frac{(p-1)(q-1)(F_{AB}-1)}{(p-1)(q-1)(F_{AB}-1)+npq},$$

where F_{AB} denotes the value of the F statistic for the AB interaction.

Hedges's g statistic, described in Section 12.4, can be used to measure the effect size of contrasts among the means for treatments A and B. The g statistic for treatment A is

$$g = \frac{|\overline{X}_{\cdot j \cdot} - \overline{X}_{\cdot j' \cdot}|}{\hat{\sigma}_{Pooled}} = \frac{|413.667 - 435.333|}{28.111} = \frac{21.666}{28.111} = 0.77,$$

where $\hat{\sigma}_{Pooled} = \sqrt{MSWCELL} = \sqrt{790.250} = 28.111$. The g statistic for treatment B is

$$g = \frac{|\overline{X}_{\cdot \cdot k} - \overline{X}_{\cdot \cdot k'}|}{\hat{\sigma}_{Pooled}}.$$

The effect sizes for the two significant contrasts, $\overline{X}_{\cdot \cdot 1} - \overline{X}_{\cdot \cdot 2}$ and $\overline{X}_{\cdot \cdot 1} - \overline{X}_{\cdot \cdot 3}$, are

$$g = \frac{|\overline{X}_{\cdot \cdot 1} - \overline{X}_{\cdot \cdot 2}|}{\hat{\sigma}_{Pooled}} = \frac{|402.50 - 432.50|}{28.111} = \frac{30.00}{28.111} = 1.07$$

$$g = \frac{|\overline{X}_{\cdot \cdot 1} - \overline{X}_{\cdot \cdot 3}|}{\hat{\sigma}_{Pooled}} = \frac{|402.50 - 438.50|}{28.111} = \frac{36.00}{28.111} = 1.28.$$

According to Cohen's guidelines for interpreting d-like measures of effect size in Section 10.6, the contrast for treatment A is a medium-size effect; those for treatment B are both large effects. These results are consistent with our intuition that the mean reading-rate difference of 21.7 words per minute for treatment A is large enough to be of interest. Furthermore, the reading-rate differences of 30 and 36 words per minute for treatment B are quite large.

Relative Merits of Factorial Designs

A two-treatment, completely randomized factorial design is the simplest of the factorial designs.[4] It also is one of the more widely used designs. There are good reasons for its popularity. First, the design permits us to test hypotheses about

---

[4] A completely randomized factorial design can be used with any number of treatments. A discussion of the analysis procedures for designs with three or more treatments is beyond the scope of this book. The interested reader is referred to books by Howell (1997), Hays (1994), Keppel (1991), Kirk (1995), and Maxwell and Delaney (1990).

interactions, as we have just seen. Second, the design makes efficient use of participants. For example, the CRF-23 design described previously uses all 30 participants simultaneously in evaluating the effects of treatments *A* and *B*. If treatment *A* were evaluated by using a CR-2 design and treatment *B*, by a separate CR-3 design, 60 participants—30 in each experiment—would be required to achieve the power of the CRF-23 design. In view of these two advantages, it is easy to understand the popularity of factorial designs. But the design has some disadvantages.

1. If numerous treatments are included in an experiment, the number of participants required may be prohibitive. For example, a four-treatment CRF-2433 design has $2 \times 4 \times 3 \times 3 = 72$ treatment combinations. If each combination were assigned to only two participants, the experiment would require $72 \times 2 = 144$ participants.
2. The interpretation of the analysis is not straightforward if the test of the interaction is significant. The presence of significant interaction effects always calls for some qualification of the test of the associated treatments.
3. The use of a factorial design commits a researcher to a relatively large experiment. Small one-treatment exploratory experiments may indicate much more promising lines of investigation than those originally envisioned. Relatively small experiments permit greater freedom in the pursuit of serendipity.

Assumptions Associated With a Completely Randomized Factorial Design

The assumptions for a two-treatment completely randomized factorial design represent extensions of the assumptions for a completely randomized design. These assumptions, which are discussed in Section 14.4, can be summarized as follows:

1. The model equation $X_{ijk} = \mu + \alpha_j + \beta_k + (\alpha\beta)_{jk} + \epsilon_{ijk}$ reflects all the sources of variation that affect X_{ijk}.
2. Participants are random samples from the respective populations, or the participants have been randomly assigned to the treatment combinations.
3. The population for each of the pq treatment combinations is normally distributed.
4. The variances of each of the pq treatment combinations are equal.

As discussed in Section 14.4, the *F* test is robust with respect to violation of assumption 3. However, violation of the other assumptions can undermine the interpretation of the results of an experiment and seriously affect the probability of making type I and II errors. The reader should refer to the detailed discussion of the assumptions in Section 14.4.

CHECK YOUR UNDERSTANDING OF SECTION 15.3

8. List the treatment combinations for the following completely randomized factorial designs.
   a. CRF-22 design   b. CRF-32 design   c. CRF-33 design
9. How many participants are required for the following completely randomized factorial designs? Assume that n is equal to 4.
   a. CRF-24 design   b. CRF-43 design   c. CRF-33 design
10. Fill in the missing values in the following table.

Source	SS	df	MS	F
1. Treatment A	273.000	4	( )	$[1/4]$ ( )**
2. Treatment B	263.550	2	( )	$[2/4]$ ( )***
3. AB Interaction	302.400	( )	( )	$[3/4]$ ( )*
4. Within Cell	( )	( )	( )	
5. Total	2413.950	74		

* $p < ($)
** $p < ($)
*** $p < ($)

11. It was hypothesized that people who are required to evaluate someone they have just hurt tend to denigrate the victim as a means of justifying the harmful act. To investigate this hypothesis, white male college students were required to give a series of either painful or mild electric shocks (treatment A) as feedback for errors made by a confederate who was learning a task in another room. Shocks were not actually delivered to the confederate, but he acted as if he were being shocked. The participants were told that the confederate was either white or black (treatment B). Each participant had a brief telephone conversation with the confederate at the start of the experiment. Prior to and after administering the shocks, the participants rated the confederate in terms of likability, intelligence, and personal adjustment. The dependent variable was the change in ratings from the pretest to the posttest. The participants were randomly assigned to the four treatment combinations with five participants in each combination. The following data were obtained. The constant 20 has been added to each score to avoid negative numbers. (Experiment suggested by Katz, I., Glass, D. C., & Cohn, S. [1973]. Ambivalence, guilt, and the scapegoating of minority group victims. *Journal of Experimental Social Psychology, 9,* 423–436.)

a_1	a_1	a_2	a_2
b_1	b_2	b_1	b_2
34	20	14	29
30	12	18	13
22	16	10	25
18	28	2	21
26	24	6	17

a_1 = mild shock
a_2 = strong shock
b_1 = black confederate
b_2 = white confederate

a. Construct stacked box plots for the four treatment combinations. Are the sample distributions relatively symmetrical? Do the data contain outliers?

b. Prepare descriptive statistics—means and standard deviations—for the data, and construct a table similar to Table 15.3-1.

c. What do the descriptive statistics in (b) tell you?

d. Test the following null hypotheses: $\mu_{1.} = \mu_{2.}$, $\mu_{.1} = \mu_{.2}$, and all $(\alpha\beta)_{jk}$ interaction effects = 0. Let α = .05.

e. Graph the AB interaction. Is the graph consistent with the test of the AB interaction?

f. Estimate the proportion of variance in the dependent variable that is accounted for by the AB interaction and interpret the result.

g. Analyze the data for treatments A and B separately, as if the randomization plan for a CR-2 design had been used. In analyzing treatment A, each level of A will have 10 participants instead of 5; the same is true for treatment B. The analysis of treatment A, for example, ignores the levels of treatment B. Compare the results of the two CR-2 designs with the CRF-22 design. Which of the designs is preferable? Explain.

12. Terms to remember
   a. Factorial design
   c. Completely crossed treatments
   e. Interaction
   b. Treatment combination
   d. Partially crossed treatments

15.4 SUMMARY

The simplest experimental design involves a single treatment with two treatment levels. If participants are randomly assigned to the treatment levels, the data can be analyzed using a t statistic for independent samples. Alternatively, blocks of two matched participants can be formed. The participants in each block are then randomly assigned to the treatment levels. The data for this design can be analyzed using a dependent-samples t test. These two simple t-test designs have ANOVA analogs—they are the completely randomized design and the randomized block design, respectively.

A randomized block design uses the blocking procedure to analyze data for experiments having one treatment with two or more levels. The blocking procedure isolates the effects of a nuisance variable and typically results in a more powerful test of a false null hypothesis than a completely randomized design. The effectiveness of the blocking procedure is determined by the size of the mean correlation among the treatment levels. The higher the mean correlation, the greater the power.

A completely randomized factorial design enables a researcher to test hypotheses about two or more treatments and associated interactions in a single experiment. For example, instead of testing hypotheses about treatments A and B in two separate experiments—a CR-3 design and a CR-4 design—a researcher can use one CRF-34 design. An interaction test is unique to factorial designs. Two treatments are said to interact if differences in performance under the levels of one treatment are different at two or more levels of the other treatment. The presence of significant interaction effects is a clear indication that the interpretation of tests of the treatments must be qualified. Inevitably such tests are misleading. A good way to understand an interaction is to graph it.

Throughout our discussion of analysis of variance designs, two ideas have been emphasized: (1) Each ANOVA design involves a unique randomization plan and statistical analysis and (2) each score is a composite that reflects all of the effects that influence the score. We formalized the latter idea by expressing a score as the sum of the parameters of a linear model equation. Associated with each model equation is a set of assumptions. As we saw, ANOVA is robust with respect to violation of some assumptions. However, recent research suggests that ANOVA is not as robust with respect to violations of other assumptions, such as the homogeneity of variance assumption, as was once thought. Violation of these assumptions can seriously affect the probability of making a type I error and the power of the F test. Fortunately, there are robust alternatives that can be used when the tenability of the assumptions is suspect.[5]

REVIEW EXERCISES FOR CHAPTER 15

1. In a study to investigate the effects of three student-teacher ratios on reading performance of second-grade students, the researcher wanted to control the nuisance variable of IQ. Describe the simplest way to accomplish this. Assume that IQ scores are available for all of the children in the study.

---

[5] Wilcox (1996) describes many of these procedures.

2. Fill in the missing values in the following table.

Source	SS	df	MS	F
1. Treatment A	( )	4	( )	[$^1/_3$] 4.12**
2. Blocks	( )	7	41.053	[$^2/_3$] ( )*
3. Residual	( )	( )	16.825	
4. Total	( )	( )		

*$p < ($ $)$
**$p < ($ $)$

3. The effect of strenuous to exhaustive physical exercise on the performance of a discrimination task was investigated. Seven men performed a line-matching task while jogging at various speeds on a motor-driven treadmill. A new set of lines was presented immediately following the participant's response, making the task self-paced. The dependent variable was the number of responses made during a 3-minute period. The periods consisted of a pretest resting stage (level a_1), 2.5 mph exercise at 12% grade (level a_2), 3.4 mph exercise at 14% grade (level a_3), 4.2 mph exercise at 16% grade (level a_4), 5.0 mph exercise at 18% grade (level a_5), and posttest resting stage (level a_6). The order of administration of the conditions, with the exception of the pretest and posttest conditions, was randomized independently for each participant. The following data were obtained. (Experiment suggested by McGlynn, G. H., Laughlin, N. T., & Bender, V. L. [1977]. Effect of strenuous to exhaustive exercise on a discrimination task. *Perceptual and Motor Skills, 44,* 1139–1147.)

	a_1 Pretest	a_2 2.5 mph	a_3 3.4 mph	a_4 4.2 mph	a_5 5.0 mph	a_6 Posttest
s_1	45	47	48	50	51	44
s_2	48	50	58	54	61	51
s_3	46	54	51	57	56	48
s_4	40	37	44	40	45	34
s_5	34	41	38	48	41	38
s_6	42	45	46	43	48	41
s_7	55	58	54	60	57	55

a. Construct stacked box plots for the data. Are the sample distributions relatively symmetrical? Do the data contain outliers?
b. Compute descriptive statistics, $\bar{X}_{.j}$'s and $\hat{\sigma}_j$'s, for the data, and construct a table similar to Table 14.3-1.
c. What do the descriptive statistics in (b) tell you?

d. Test the null hypothesis that $\mu_{.1} = \mu_{.2} = \cdots = \mu_{.6}$. Let $\alpha = .05$.

e. Use the Fisher-Hayter statistic to determine which population means differ.

f. Use Hedges's g statistic to assess the effect size of those contrasts for which the Fisher-Hayter statistic is significant, and interpret the results.

g. Ignore the blocking variable and analyze the data as if the randomization plan for a CR-6 design had been used. Compare the results of the two analyses by constructing a figure similar to Figure 15.2-1. Was the blocking procedure effective? Explain.

4. List the treatment combinations for the following completely randomized factorial designs.
   a. CRF-23 design   b. CRF-42 design   c. CRF-24 design

5. How many participants are required for the following completely randomized factorial designs? Assume that n is equal to 5.
   a. CRF-34 design   b. CRF-35 design   c. CRF-44 design

6. Fill in the missing values in the following tables.

Source	SS	df	MS	F
1. Treatment A	( )	( )	22.100	$[1/4]$ ( )**
2. Treatment B	( )	3	( )	$[2/4]$ 3.30*
3. AB Interaction	( )	6	( )	$[3/4]$ 3.20**
4. Within Cell	( )	( )	4.250	
5. Total	( )	71		

*$p < ($)
**$p < ($)

7. It was hypothesized that focusing on helping others versus focusing on accomplishing a task (treatment A) and instructions designed to vary the perceived need to hurry (treatment B) would affect the likelihood of a person behaving as a "good Samaritan." To test this hypothesis, 30 seminary students were asked to prepare and record a short message describing their work and the satisfactions of their profession. Half of the students, the task-relevant group, received no other instructions. The other half, the helping-relevant group, were given the same instructions and, in addition, had their attention directed to the parable of the Good Samaritan from the Revised Standard Version of the Bible (Luke 10:29−37). In the process of telling the students how to get to the recording studio that was in another building, one-third were told to hurry because they were running late, one-third were told to go right on over to the studio, and one-third were told that it would be a few minutes until the recording session but they

might as well go on to the studio. The seminary students were randomly assigned to the six treatment combinations with five students in each combination. On the way to the recording studio the students passed the "victim" sitting in a doorway, head down, coughing and groaning. If a student offered help, the victim mumbled a prepared statement about pills, a condition, and resting. The dependent variable was the victim's rating of the helping behavior that was offered: 0 = failed to notice, . . . , 5 = stopped to render aid and refused to leave the victim or offered to take him to the infirmary. The following data were obtained. (Experiment suggested by Darley, J. M., & Batson, C. D. [1973]. From Jerusalem to Jerico: A study of situational and dispositional variables in helping behavior. *Journal of Personality and Social Psychology, 27,* 100–108.)

a_1 b_1	a_1 b_2	a_1 b_3	a_2 b_1	a_2 b_2	a_2 b_3
4	1	0	0	1	0
4	5	0	4	0	0
5	1	4	1	2	0
1	0	0	1	5	2
5	2	2	4	1	0

a_1 = helping-relevant group
a_2 = task-relevant group
b_1 = no-rush instruction
b_2 = go-on-over instruction
b_3 = hurry instruction

a. Visually inspect the treatment-combination distributions. Do they appear to be symmetrical?
b. Prepare descriptive statistics—means and standard deviations—for the data, and construct a table similar to Table 15.3-1.
c. What do the descriptive statistics in (b) tell you?
d. Test the following null hypotheses: $\mu_1. = \mu_2.$, $\mu_{.1} = \mu_{.2} = \mu_{.3}$, and all $(\alpha\beta)_{jk}$ interaction effects = 0. Let $\alpha = .05$.
e. Graph the *AB* interaction. Is the graph consistent with the test of the *AB* interaction?
f. Estimate the proportion of variance in the dependent variable that is accounted for by treatment *B* and interpret the result.
g. Use the Fisher-Hayter statistic to determine which population means for treatment *B* differ.
h. Use Hedges's *g* statistic to assess the effect size of those contrasts for which the Fisher-Hayter statistic is significant.
i. Analyze the data for treatments *A* and *B* separately as if the randomization plan for a CR-2 design and a CR-3 design had been

used. In analyzing treatment A, each level of A will have 15 participants instead of 5; in analyzing treatment B, each level of B will
have 10 participants. The analysis of treatment A, for example, ignores the levels of treatment B. Compare the results of the two CR-p
designs with the CRF-23 design. Which of the designs is preferable?
Explain.

Chapter 16

Statistical Inference for Frequency Data

16.1 THREE APPLICATIONS OF PEARSON'S CHI-SQUARE STATISTIC

So far our discussion has been limited to test statistics that are appropriate for measured characteristics such as IQ, reaction time, blood pressure, weight of 2-year-olds, and time to learn a list of nonsense syllables. Instead of measuring a variable, we may choose to count the number of observations in two or more mutually exclusive categories of the variable, in which case the data are a set of frequencies. A statistic for testing hypotheses about frequency data was developed by Karl Pearson in 1900. It is called **Pearson's chi-square statistic** because the statistic is approximately distributed as the chi-square distribution.[1] We will describe three applications of the statistic: testing goodness of fit, testing independence, and testing the equality of c population proportions. The three applications are often confused because they all use the same Pearson test statistic and involve similar statistical analyses. However, once you know what to look for, it is easy to distinguish the experimental designs for the three applications because they involve distinct randomization plans. The major features of the three applications are as follows:

1. *Testing goodness of fit.* Pearson's chi-square statistic can be used to determine whether the population distribution estimated by a single random sample containing n independent observations is identical to some hypothesized or expected population distribution. Depending on the researcher's interests, expectations may be based on one of the theoretical distributions (such as the normal distribution) or on the results of an earlier empirical investigation. Pearson's chi-square statistic is used to test the null hypothesis that the observed frequencies $O_1, O_2, \ldots, O_k$ in k mutually exclusive categories of a population are equal to a set of expected frequencies $E_1, E_2, \ldots, E_k$. The randomization plan consists of obtaining one random sample of n elements and classifying each element in terms of membership in one of the k mutually exclusive categories.

2. *Testing independence.* Another use of Pearson's chi-square statistic is in determining whether two variables are statistically independent. This is accomplished by classifying each of n independent observations for a single random sample in terms of two variables, denoted by A and B. Recall from Section 7.3 that A and B are statistically independent if the conditional probability of A given B, $p(A|B)$, is equal to the probability of A, $p(A)$. For example, variable A might represent a person's gender and variable B, his or her political affiliation (Democrat, Republican, independent, or other). The variables are independent if $p(\text{Man}|\text{Democrat}) = p(\text{Man})$, $p(\text{Man}|\text{Republican}) = p(\text{Man})$, and

---

[1] Pearson's chi-square statistic is not related to $\chi^2 = (n - 1)\, \hat{\sigma}^2/\sigma_0^2$, which is discussed in Section 11.3, although both are referred to the chi-square distribution.

TABLE 16.1-1.   Comparison of Tests That Use Pearson's Chi-Square Statistic

Purpose	Null hypothesis	Randomization Plan
1. Testing goodness of fit	$H_0: O_{Pop_1} = E_{Pop_1}, O_{Pop_2} = E_{Pop_2}, \ldots, O_{Pop_k} = E_{Pop_k}$	One random sample of n elements; each element is classified in terms of membership in one of k mutually exclusive categories.
2. Testing independence	$H_0: p(A \text{ and } B) = p(A)p(B)$	One random sample of n elements; each element is classified in terms of two variables, denoted by A and B, where each variable has two or more categories.
3a. Testing equality of proportions	$H_0: p_1 = p_2 = \cdots = p_c$	c random samples, where $c \geq 2$; for each sample the elements are classified in terms of membership in one of $r = 2$ mutually exclusive categories.
3b. Testing homogeneity of proportions	$H_0: \begin{vmatrix} P_{a_1\|b_1} = P_{a_1\|b_2} = \cdots = P_{a_1\|b_c} \\ P_{a_2\|b_1} = P_{a_2\|b_2} = \cdots = P_{a_2\|b_c} \\ \vdots \\ P_{a_r\|b_1} = P_{a_r\|b_2} = \cdots = P_{a_r\|b_c} \end{vmatrix}$	c random samples, where $c \geq 2$; for each sample the elements are classified in terms of membership in one of $r > 2$ mutually exclusive categories.

so on, which means that a knowledge of political affiliation indicates nothing about the individual's gender and vice versa. The randomization plan for testing independence consists of obtaining one random sample of n elements and classifying each element in terms of two variables, where each variable has two or more categories.

3. *Testing equality of $c \geq 2$ population proportions.* A final use of Pearson's chi-square statistic is to test the null hypothesis that c population proportions are equal, that is,[2] $p_1 = p_2 = \cdots = p_c$. The randomization plan consists of obtaining c random samples from c populations where $c \geq 2$ and for each sample classifying the elements in terms of membership in one of $r = 2$ mutually exclusive categories. When r, the number of categories, is greater than 2, the test is referred to as a *test of homogeneity of proportions.*

The distinguishing characteristics of the three applications of Pearson's chi-square statistic are summarized in Table 16.1-1.

---

[2] The letter p is used to denote a proportion as well as a probability. The meaning of the letter will be stated if it isn't clear from the context.

16.2   TESTING GOODNESS OF FIT

The goodness-of-fit test was developed to test the hypothesis that a population distribution estimated by a random sample is identical to a hypothesized or expected distribution. Let O_1, O_2, . . . , O_k represent observed frequencies and E_1, E_2, . . . , E_k represent expected frequencies. The null hypothesis of equality of the observed and expected frequencies is rejected if Pearson's statistic,

$$\chi^2 = \sum_{j=1}^{k} \frac{(O_j - E_j)^2}{E_j},$$

exceeds or equals the critical value, $\chi^2_{\alpha,\nu}$, at α level of significance for $\nu = k - 1$ degrees of freedom.

Critical values of chi-square are given in Appendix Table D.4. The test is approximate because it uses the continuous chi-square distribution to estimate a probability for a discrete sampling distribution.[3] If the expected frequencies are sufficiently large, the approximate test is quite accurate. An alternative exact test can be used. When k is equal to 2, the exact test is based on the binomial distribution; when k is greater than 2, the exact test is based on the multinomial distribution. Exact tests usually require a prohibitive amount of computation and should be performed with a computer.

Computational Example

Suppose we want to know whether the distribution of academic potential for this year's graduate school applicants, as measured by the Graduate Record Examination (GRE), is the same as that for past years. Data for previous applicants are given in Table 16.2-1. The statistical hypotheses for Pearson's test usually are stated in terms of proportions, although the test statistic uses frequencies. This is perfectly consistent because frequencies are readily converted into proportions and vice versa. An observed proportion in the jth category is denoted by $\hat{p}_j$ and the expected proportion, by p'_j. Proportions can be computed from frequencies by

$$\hat{p}_j = O_j/n \qquad \text{and} \qquad p'_j = E_j/n,$$

where O_j denotes an observed frequency, E_j denotes an expected frequency, and n is the sample size. If proportions are known, the frequencies are given by

$$O_j = n\hat{p}_j \qquad \text{and} \qquad E_j = np'_j.$$

---

[3] For the case in which k is equal to 2, an alternative approximate test is based on the normal distribution. A comparison of this test and Pearson's test that is based on the chi-square distribution is presented in Supplementary Note 16.7-1.

TABLE 16.2-1. Proportion of Former Applicants With Various Graduate Record Examination (GRE) Scores ($n = 200$)

GRE Score	p'_j
1400–1499	.04
1300–1399	.14
1200–1299	.20
1100–1199	.32
1000–1099	.22
900–999	.08

The null and alternative hypotheses for the data in Table 16.2-1 are as follows; p_j denotes a population proportion.

$$H_0: \ p_1 = .08, p_2 = .22, p_3 = .32, p_4 = .20, p_5 = .14, p_6 = .04$$

$$H_1: \ p_j \neq p_{j'} \text{ for one or more of the } j = 1, \ldots, k \text{ categories}$$

The hypotheses also can be expressed in terms of $O_{Pop\,j}$'s and $E_{Pop\,j}$'s, as follows:

$$H_0: \ O_{Pop\,1} = 16, O_{Pop\,2} = 44, O_{Pop\,3} = 64, O_{Pop\,4} = 40, O_{Pop\,5} = 28, O_{Pop\,6} = 8$$

$$H_1: \ O_{Pop\,j} \neq E_{Pop\,j} \text{ for one or more of the } j = 1, \ldots, k \text{ categories}$$

The values of $E_{Pop\,j} = np'_j$ are given by $E_{Pop\,1} = (200)(.08) = 16$, $E_{Pop\,2} = (200)(.22) = 44$, and so on.

We want to know whether the proportions in the six categories for the population represented by the sample differ from the proportions for the population of previous applicants. We are faced with a minor interpretation problem—this year's applicants were not obtained by random sampling. We circumvent the problem by assuming that there is a population for which random sampling could have produced the sample we obtained. Conclusions about equality of the proportions apply only to this population.

The observed frequencies for the 200 students who applied to graduate school this year, along with expected frequencies based on data for previous years' applicants, are given in Table 16.2-2. The computation of Pearson's statistic is illustrated in the table. The degrees of freedom equal one less than the number of categories, $k - 1 = 6 - 1 = 5$. If the .05 level of significance is adopted, the critical value of $\chi^2_{.05,5}$ is 11.070. Although the null hypothesis is nondirectional, the critical region always lies in the upper tail of the sampling distribution of χ^2. This seems reasonable when we recall that all $O_j - E_j$ discrepancies are squared; consequently, the test statistic is insensitive to the direction of the discrepancies. Large discrepancies can produce only large values of the test statistic. An examination of the chi-square table reveals that the upper tail contains the larger values. According to Table 16.2-2, the computed chi square with 5 degrees of freedom, $\chi^2(5) = 12.484$, exceeds the critical value, $\chi^2_{.05,5} = 11.070$. Hence, the null hypothesis is rejected, and it is

TABLE 16.2-2. Computation of Pearson's Chi-Square Statistic for 200 Graduate School Applicants

GRE Score	O_j	$np_j' = E_j$	$O_j - E_j$	$\dfrac{(O_j - E_j)^2}{E_j}$
1400–1499	13	$200(.04)^a = 8$	5	3.125
1300–1399	35	$200(.14) = 28$	7	1.750
1200–1299	49	$200(.20) = 40$	9	2.025
1100–1199	57	$200(.32) = 64$	-7	0.766
1000–1099	38	$200(.22) = 44$	-6	0.818
900–999	8	$200(.08) = 16$	$\underline{-8}$	$\underline{4.000}$
			0^b	$\chi^2(5) = 12.484$
				$\chi^2_{.05,5} = 11.070$

[a] Values of p_j' are obtained from Table 16.2-1.
[b] Computational check: $\Sigma(O_j - E_j)$ should equal 0.

concluded that the frequencies in one or more of the population categories are not equal to the corresponding expected frequencies.[4]

Characteristics of Pearson's Statistic

An examination of the formula $\sum_{j=1}^k (O_j - E_j)^2/E_j$ for Pearson's statistic reveals the following:

1. The statistic is never negative because all $O_j - E_j$ discrepancies are squared. Because the statistic makes no distinction between positive and negative discrepancies, the hypothesis tested is nondirectional. This is true even though the critical region of the sampling distribution of χ^2 is always in the upper tail.
2. The only way the statistic can equal 0 is for each observed frequency to equal the corresponding expected frequency.
3. The larger the $O_j - E_j$ discrepancies, the larger χ^2. However, the contribution of a discrepancy to χ^2 is affected by the size of E_j because $(O_j - E_j)^2$ is divided by E_j. This seems reasonable. If we tossed 10 coins and observed nine heads where the expected number is five, the discrepancy of four would lead us to question the fairness of the coins. If the discrepancy of four occurred when 100 coins were tossed, where the expected frequency is 50, we wouldn't be surprised. A discrepancy of four is viewed one way when E is

[4] Procedures for determining which observed and expected frequencies are not equal are described by Marascuilo (1971, pp. 380–382) and Marascuilo and McSweeney (1977).

equal to 5 and a different way when E is equal to 50. The formula takes this into account by expressing the size of the discrepancy relative to the magnitude of the expected frequency.

4. The larger the number of categories, the larger the degrees of freedom and the computed χ^2. As the number of degrees of freedom increases, the chi-square value required for significance also increases. Thus, the test procedure takes the number of categories into account.

Degrees of Freedom When E_j's Are Based on a Theoretical Distribution

A modification of the goodness-of-fit test is required if parameters of a theoretical distribution must be estimated in computing the expected frequencies. In the previous example, the expected frequencies, E_j's, were computed from past years' data. Hence, no distribution parameters were estimated. For this case, $\nu = k - 1$, where k is the number of categories. Suppose, however, that we compared a frequency distribution with that predicted by, say, the normal distribution. We would have to use sample data to estimate two parameters of the normal distribution, μ and σ, to compute the expected frequencies. For each parameter estimated from sample data, the degrees of freedom are reduced by one. The formula for degrees of freedom is $\nu = k - 1 - e$, where e is the number of distribution parameters estimated from sample data. Except for this modification, the test procedure is the same as that described previously.

Practical Significance

As with any null hypothesis significance test, it is important to know whether the result is practically significant. Cohen (1988, p. 216) has described a statistic that can help a researcher or consumer of statistics make this judgment. The statistic, which is a measure of effect size, is

$$\hat{w} = \sqrt{\sum_{j=1}^{k} \frac{(\hat{p}_j - p'_j)^2}{p'_j}},$$

where $\hat{p}_j$ is the observed proportion in the jth category and p'_j is the expected proportion. Cohen has suggested the following guidelines for interpreting w, the population effect size:

.1 is a small effect.
.3 is a medium effect.
.5 is a large effect.

TABLE 16.2-3. Computation of Effect Size

(i) Data ($\hat{p}_j$ is the observed proportion in the *j*th category, p'_j is the expected proportion)

GRE Score	$\hat{p}_j = 0_j / 200$	p'_j	$\hat{p}_j - p'_j$	$\dfrac{(\hat{p}_j - p'_j)^2}{p'_j}$
1400–1499	13/200 = .065	.04	.025	.01563
1300–1399	35/200 = .175	.14	.035	.00875
1200–1299	49/200 = .245	.20	.045	.01013
1100–1199	57/200 = .285	.32	−.035	.00383
1000–1099	38/200 = .190	.22	−.030	.00409
900–999	8/200 = .040	.08	−.040	.00200
			0^a	.04443

(ii) Computation of effect size

$$\hat{w} = \sqrt{\sum_{j=1}^{k} \frac{(\hat{p}_j - p'_j)^2}{p'_j}} = \sqrt{.04443} = 0.21$$

[a] Computational check: $\Sigma(\hat{p}_j - p'_j)$ should equal 0.

The computation of $\hat{w}$ for the graduate school data in Table 16.2-2 is illustrated in Table 16.2-3. The value of $\hat{w}$ for these data is 0.21. According to Cohen's guidelines, 0.21 is a small effect. Thus, although the difference between this year's applicants for graduate school and previous applicants is statistically significant, the effect is small. A comparison of the observed proportions, $\hat{p}_j$, and expected proportions p'_j, in Table 16.2-3 supports this conclusion.

Assumptions of the Goodness-of-Fit Test

The goodness-of-fit test can be used for any population distribution, provided the distribution is discrete or can be grouped into a manageable number of categories. The assumptions of the test are minimal: (1) Every sample observation must fall in one and only one category, (2) the observations must be independent, and (3) the sample *n* must be large.

How large is large? This is difficult to specify because the adequacy of Pearson's chi-square statistic in approximating an exact multinomial probability depends on (1) *n*, (2) the true proportion in the *k* categories, and (3) the number of degrees of freedom, among other things. Furthermore, Pearson's statistic is not exactly distributed as the chi-square distribution unless *n* is infinitely large. A conservative rule of thumb states that the approximation to the exact multinomial probability is satisfactory if, when the degrees of freedom equal 1, each expected frequency is at least 10. When the degrees of freedom are greater than 1, each expected frequency should be at least 5. One remedy if k is greater than 2 and expected frequencies are below the minimum is to combine categories where it is reasonable to do so until all expected frequencies are at least 5.[5]

When the test has one degree of freedom, **Yates' correction for continuity**[6] can be applied to make the sampling distribution of the test statistic, which is discrete, more consistent with the chi-square distribution, which is continuous. Recall from Section 1.4 that a continuous variable can assume any value in an interval. Such is not the case for a discrete variable. For example, the number of children in a family can assume only one value in the interval 2.5–3.5, namely, 3; values such as 2.5, 2.7, or 3.2 are not possible. The continuity problem arises whenever we use a continuous distribution to obtain probabilities for a discrete distribution. The continuity correction for the chi-square goodness-of-fit statistic consists of reducing the absolute value of each difference $O_j - E_j$ by 0.5. The correction can be included in the test statistic as follows:

$$\chi^2 = \sum_{j=1}^{k} \frac{(|O_j - E_j| - 0.5)^2}{E_j}.$$

It is good practice to apply the correction when the degrees of freedom equal 1 and any expected frequency is not appreciably greater than 10.

CHECK YOUR UNDERSTANDING OF SECTIONS 16.1 AND 16.2

1. What are the distinguishing features of the tests for goodness of fit, independence, and equality of proportions?
2. If the critical value for a test for goodness of fit in which socioeconomic indices for this year are compared with those for last year is $\chi^2_{.05,6} = 12.592$, how many mutually exclusive categories were used?
3. A random sample of students was asked whether they favor a change from the semester system to the quarter system. Thirty-three said yes; 17 said no.
   a. List the steps you would follow in testing the null hypothesis that opinion is equally divided on the issue. Let $\alpha = .05$.
   b. Do the data suggest that opinion is not equally divided on this issue?
   c. If appropriate, compute the size of the effect and interpret the result.

---

[5] An alternative approach is to use the Kolmogorov-Smirnov goodness-of-fit test. This test, which has greater power than Pearson's test, is discussed by Hays (1994, pp. 854–855).

[6] Proposed by Frank Yates, a British statistician.

4. According to the most recent public opinion poll in Johnson County, 71 eligible voters were Democrats, 52 were Republicans, and 33 belonged to other parties. Traditionally, the ratio of Democrats to Republicans to others has been 4:3:2. Does the poll suggest a change in party affiliation? Let $\alpha = .05$.

5. A student in a statistics class tossed a die 300 times and obtained the results shown in the table. Is the die fair? Let $\alpha = .05$.

Outcome	1	2	3	4	5	6
Frequency	53	41	60	47	38	61

6. Terms to remember
   a. Approximate and exact tests
   b. Yates' correction for continuity

16.3 TESTING INDEPENDENCE

Pearson's statistic,

$$\chi^2 = \sum_{i=1}^{r} \sum_{j=1}^{c} \frac{(O_{ij} - E_{ij})^2}{E_{ij}},$$

can be used to obtain an approximate test of the null hypothesis that two variables, say, A and B, are statistically independent. Recall from Section 7.3 that A and B are statistically independent if the probability of, say, A occurring is unaffected by the occurrence of B. The first step in computing Pearson's chi-square test is to classify each of n independent observations for a single random sample in terms of variable A with $i = 1, \ldots, r$ rows and variable B with $j = 1, \ldots, c$ columns.

Computational Example

Suppose that a random sample of 200 high school students has been obtained and that each student has been classified in terms of gender, variable A, and use or nonuse of marijuana, variable B. A table representing the classification of each of n elements in terms of two or more variables is called a **contingency table.** A contingency table for the 200 high school students has $i = 2$ rows for variable A and $j = 2$ columns for variable B. A partial summary of the gender and marijuana data is given in Table 16.3-1. If the two variables in the population are independent,

TABLE 16.3-1. Partial Summary of Gender and Marijuana Data

	Nonuser, b_1	User, b_2	
Man, a_1			$n_{a_1} = 40; p(a_1) = \dfrac{40}{200} = .20$
Woman, a_2			$n_{a_2} = 160; p(a_2) = \dfrac{160}{200} = .80$
	$n_{b_1} = 72$	$n_{b_2} = 128$	$n = 200$
	$p(b_1) = \dfrac{72}{200}$	$p(b_2) = \dfrac{128}{200}$	
	$= .36$	$= .64$	

what frequencies should be in the cells of the contingency table? We know from Section 7.3 that if two variables are independent, $p(A|B) = p(A)$, in which case $p(A \text{ and } B) = p(A)p(B)$. Typically, the population proportions are unknown, but we can use the sample marginal proportions, $p(a_1)$, $p(a_2)$, and so on, in Table 16.3-1 to estimate the expected cell frequencies, denoted by $E_{a_i \text{ and } b_j}$. Using the relationship

$$E_{a_i \text{ and } b_j} = np(a_i \text{ and } b_j) = np(a_i) \, p(b_j),$$

we can estimate each of the expected cell values, as follows:

$$E_{a_1 \text{ and } b_1} = np(a_1) \, p(b_1) = 200(.20)(.36) = 14.4$$
$$E_{a_1 \text{ and } b_2} = np(a_1) \, p(b_2) = 200(.20)(.64) = 25.6$$
$$E_{a_2 \text{ and } b_1} = np(a_2) \, p(b_1) = 200(.80)(.36) = 57.6$$
$$E_{a_2 \text{ and } b_2} = np(a_2) \, p(b_2) = 200(.80)(.64) = 102.4$$

These are the cell frequencies you would obtain if variables A and B were independent. The expected cell frequencies also can be computed directly from the marginal frequencies by the formula

$$E_{a_i \text{ and } b_j} = \frac{n_{a_i} n_{b_j}}{n}$$

because $E_{a_i \text{ and } b_j} = np(a_i)p(b_j) = n_{a_i} n_{b_j}/n$. For example, $E_{a_1 \text{ and } b_1} = (40)(72)/200 = 14.4$. The expected cell frequencies, along with the observed cell frequencies, are given in Table 16.3-2. The computation of the chi-square statistic is illustrated in the table.[7]

[7] A simpler computational formula for a 2×2 contingency table is given in Supplementary Note 16.7-2.

TABLE 16.3-2.   Gender and Marijuana Data

(i) Data (O_{ij} and E_{ij} denote observed and expected frequencies for the $i = 1$, . . . , r rows of variable A and $j = 1, \ldots, c$ columns of variable B)

	Nonuser, b_1	User, b_2	
Man, a_1	$O_{11} = 8$ $E_{11} = 14.4$	$O_{12} = 32$ $E_{12} = 25.6$	$n_{a_1} = 40$
Woman, a_2	$O_{21} = 64$ $E_{21} = 57.6$	$O_{22} = 96$ $E_{22} = 102.4$	$n_{a_2} = 160$
	$n_{b_1} = 72$	$n_{b_2} = 128$	$n = 200$

(ii) Computation of chi-square statistic

O_{ij}	E_{ij}	$O_{ij} - E_{ij}$	$\dfrac{(O_{ij} - E_{ij})^2}{E_{ij}}$
8	14.4	−6.4	2.844
64	57.6	6.4	0.711
32	25.6	6.4	1.600
96	102.4	−6.4	0.400
		0^a	$\chi^2(1) = 5.555$
			$\chi^2_{.05,1} = 3.841$

[a] Computational check: $\Sigma (O_{ij} - E_{ij})$ should equal 0.

The advisability of using Yates' correction for a 2×2 contingency table is the subject of continuing debate among statisticians (Conover, 1974a, 1974b; Grizzle, 1967; Mantel, 1974; Miettinen, 1974; Plackett, 1964; Starmer, Grizzle, & Sen, 1974) and therefore is not illustrated in Table 16.3-2. If the correction is desired, it can be incorporated in the chi-square formula as follows:

$$\chi^2 = \sum_{i=1}^{r} \sum_{j=1}^{c} \frac{(|O_{ij} - E_{ij}| - 0.5)^2}{E_{ij}}$$

Degrees of Freedom for a Contingency Table

How many degrees of freedom are associated with the chi-square statistic for testing independence? For the goodness-of-fit test, we saw that the degrees of freedom are $k - 1 - e$, where e is the number of distribution parameters that is estimated from sample data. A 2×2 table is a special case of an $r \times c$ contingency table where r and c equal 2. We will develop the degrees-of-freedom formula for the more general case in which r or c is greater than 2.

If we denote the number of rows by r and the number of columns by c, an $r \times c$ contingency table has $k = rc$ categories. Because there are r categories for variable A, we must estimate only $r - 1$ of the expected row frequencies for this variable. Once we have estimated $r - 1$ of the expected row frequencies, the remaining one can be obtained by subtracting the $r - 1$ expected frequencies from n, the total number of frequencies. This follows because the sum of the r expected row frequencies must equal n. By the same line of reasoning it follows that we must estimate only $c - 1$ expected column frequencies for variable B. In all, we must make $e = (r - 1) + (c - 1)$ estimates. Thus, the number of degrees of freedom for an $r \times c$ contingency table is

$$df = k - 1 - e$$
$$= rc - 1 - [(r - 1) + (c - 1)]$$
$$= rc - 1 - r + 1 - c + 1$$
$$= rc - r - c + 1$$
$$= (r - 1)(c - 1).$$

For a 2×2 contingency table, the degrees of freedom are $(2 - 1)(2 - 1) = 1$.

Statistical Hypotheses

The statistical hypotheses that we want to test using the data in Table 16.3-2 are

$$H_0: p(A \text{ and } B) = p(A)p(B)$$
$$H_1: p(A \text{ and } B) \neq p(A)p(B).$$

The hypothesis of statistical independence is rejected if the computed χ^2 exceeds or equals the critical value at α level of significance for $\nu = (r - 1)(c - 1)$ degrees of freedom. For the data in Table 16.3-2, the computed chi-square with 1 degree of freedom, $\chi^2(1) = 5.555$, exceeds the critical value, $\chi^2_{.05,1} = 3.841$. Hence, the null hypothesis is rejected, and we conclude that gender and marijuana usage are not independent.

Knowing that two variables are related is useful, but it would be even more useful to know the strength of the association and whether the association is practically significant. Before describing indices of association and practical significance, we will see how to apply a test of independence to contingency tables with more than two rows or columns.

Contingency Tables With Three or More Rows or Columns

The test for independence can be extended to the case in which the row variable A has $r > 2$ mutually exclusive categories, $a_1, a_2, \ldots, a_i, \ldots, a_r$, and the

TABLE 16.3-3.   University Size and Starting Salaries of Graduates

(i) Data (O_{ij} and E_{ij} denote observed and expected frequencies for the
   $i = 1, \ldots, r$ rows of variable A and $j = 1, \ldots, c$ columns of variable B)

	Less Than $20,000, b_1	$20,000–30,000 b_2	Greater Than $30,000, b_3	
Small University, a_1	$O_{11} = 13$ $E_{11} = 10.08$	$O_{12} = 13$ $E_{12} = 34.44$	$O_{13} = 15$ $E_{13} = 11.48$	$n_{a_1} = 56$
Medium-Size University, a_2	$O_{21} = 11$ $E_{21} = 13.14$	$O_{22} = 40$ $E_{22} = 44.90$	$O_{23} = 22$ $E_{23} = 14.96$	$n_{a_2} = 73$
Large University, a_3	$O_{31} = 12$ $E_{31} = 12.78$	$O_{32} = 55$ $E_{32} = 43.66$	$O_{33} = 4$ $E_{33} = 14.56$	$n_{a_3} = 71$
	$n_{b_1} = 36$	$n_{b_2} = 123$	$n_{b_3} = 41$	$n = 200$

(ii) Computation of chi-square statistic

O_{ij}	E_{ij}	$O_{ij} - E_{ij}$	$\dfrac{(O_{ij} - E_{ij})^2}{E_{ij}}$
13	10.08	2.92	0.846
11	13.14	−2.14	0.349
12	12.78	−0.78	0.048
28	34.44	−6.44	1.204
40	44.09	−4.90	0.535
55	43.66	11.34	2.945
15	11.48	3.52	1.079
22	14.96	7.04	3.313
4	14.56	−10.56	7.659
		0^a	$\chi^2(4) = 17.978$
			$\chi^2_{.05,4} = 9.488$

[a] Computational check: $\Sigma (O_{ij} - E_{ij})$ should equal 0.

column variable B has $c > 2$ mutually exclusive categories, $b_1, b_2, \ldots, b_j,$
$\ldots, b_c$.

   Suppose we want to know whether a college graduate's starting salary is independent of the size of the university from which he or she graduated. Data for a random sample of 200 graduates are given in Table 16.3-3. The expected frequencies
are computed from

$$E_{a_i \text{ and } b_j} = \frac{n_{a_i} n_{b_j}}{n}.$$

The degrees of freedom are $(r - 1)(c - 1) = (3 - 1)(3 - 1) = 4$. For a test at the .05 level of significance, the value of $\chi^2_{.05,4}$ is 9.488. Because $\chi^2(4) = 17.978$ is greater than $\chi^2_{.05,4} = 9.488$, the null hypothesis is rejected. It is concluded that starting salary and university size are not independent.

Finding a significant χ^2 often is only the first step in analyzing data. To better understand the data, it is helpful to look for large discrepancies between observed and expected frequencies in the contingency table. From an inspection of Table 16.3-3, it appears that graduates of large universities are less likely than expected to have starting salaries over \$30,000, whereas the converse is true for those from medium and small universities. Such hypotheses must be regarded as tentative because they are not based on the outcome of significance tests.[8] The significant chi-square test statistic applies to the data taken as a whole and provides no clue as to which cells are responsible for significance.

In the following section we will describe several statistics that can help a researcher assess the practical significance of an association between row and column variables.

Practical Significance

If the null hypothesis $p(A \text{ and } B) = p(A)p(B)$ is rejected, we know that the variables are correlated. Several correlation coefficients were discussed in Chapter 5 (r, r_s, and η^2), but none of them is appropriate for unordered qualitative variables. One coefficient that is appropriate is *Cramér's measure of association,* denoted by V.

The formula for computing an estimate, $\hat{V}$, of Cramér's measure of association is

$$\hat{V} = \frac{\sqrt{\hat{\phi}^2_{\text{observed}}}}{\sqrt{\hat{\phi}^2_{\text{maximum}}}} = \frac{\sqrt{\chi^2/n}}{\sqrt{s - 1}} = \sqrt{\frac{\chi^2}{n(s - 1)}},$$

where s is the smaller of the number of rows and columns.[9]

If $p(A \text{ and } B) = p(A)p(B)$, the parameter ϕ, which is estimated by $\hat{\phi}^2_{\text{observed}} = \sqrt{\chi^2/n}$, is equal to 0. When there is perfect association, $\phi = s - 1$, which is its maximum value. Cramér's statistic is a relative measure because it is the ratio of an observed statistic to its maximum possible value. The statistic can range from 0

---

[8] Procedures for determining the contribution to the overall chi-square statistic of a portion of the contingency table are described by Bresnahan and Shapiro (1966), Castellan (1965), Marascuilo (1966), and Marascuilo and McSweeney (1977).

[9] For a 2 × 2 contingency table, $\hat{V} = \sqrt{\chi^2/n}$ because $s - 1 = 1$. In this special case, $\hat{V}$ is identical to another measure of strength of association called the *phi coefficient,* $\hat{\phi}$. Both $\hat{V}$ and $\hat{\phi}$ are related to the Pearson product-moment correlation coefficient. Suppose that the two categories of variables A and B are considered to be ordered and are assigned scores of 0 and 1, where 1 is assigned to the higher category. Under these conditions, the formula for r is algebraically equivalent to that for $\hat{V}$ and $\hat{\phi}$ (Hays, 1994, pp. 866–869).

(indicating complete independence) to 1 (indicating complete dependence, or perfect correlation).

Cramér's statistic is computed only when the chi-square test is significant. A nonsignificant chi-square test suggests that any $\hat{V}$ greater than 0 is due to chance. Put another way, a test of the null hypothesis $p(A \ and \ B) = p(A)p(B)$ is equivalent to a test of the null hypothesis $V = 0$. Thus, if the null hypothesis isn't rejected, it is meaningless to proceed further and compute $\hat{V}$. Unfortunately, Cramér's statistic does not have a simple, intuitively useful interpretation as, say, the proportion of explained variance between two variables. It can be thought of only as reflecting magnitude of association on a scale of 0 to 1; the larger the number, the stronger the association. Cramér's statistic for the data in Tables 16.3-2 and 16.3-3 is, respectively,

$$\hat{V} = \sqrt{\frac{5.555}{200(2 - 1)}} = .17 \quad \text{and} \quad \hat{V} = \sqrt{\frac{17.978}{200(3 - 1)}} = .21.$$

We know from Tables 16.3-2 and 16.3-3 that the chi square statistics for the marijuana data and the salary data are both statistically significant, but are they practically significant? Cohen's $\hat{w}$, which was introduced in Section 16.2, can help a researcher make this assessment.

The $\hat{w}$ statistic can be computed using the formula

$$\hat{w} = \sqrt{\sum_{i=1}^{r} \sum_{j=1}^{c} \frac{(\hat{p}_{ij} - p'_{ij})^2}{p'_{ij}}},$$

where $\hat{p}_{ij}$ is the observed proportion in the ijth cell and p'_{ij} is the expected proportion. For data in a contingency table, the formula for $\hat{w}$ simplifies to

$$\hat{w} = \hat{V} \sqrt{s - 1},$$

where $\hat{V}$ is an estimate of Cramér's V and s is the smaller of the number of rows and columns in the contingency table.

Cohen's $\hat{w}$ for the data in Tables 16.3-2 and 16.3-3 is, respectively,

$$\hat{w} = .167 \sqrt{2 - 1} = .17 \quad \text{and} \quad \hat{w} = .212 \sqrt{3 - 1} = .30.$$

Recall from Section 16.2 that $w = .1$ is a small effect, $w = .3$ is a medium effect, and $w = .5$ is a large effect. Thus, the effect size for the gender and marijuana data is small. The effect size for the university size and starting salaries data is medium. These examples illustrate the maxim that statistical significance and practical significance address different questions. The chi-square test statistic for the variables of university size and starting salaries of graduates, for example, is large enough to be significant beyond the .002 level. However, the strength of the association and effect size are barely medium ($\hat{V} = .21$ and $\hat{w} = .30$). The point cannot be made too often that statistical significance means only that chance is an unlikely explanation for an observed result. Other procedures must be used to assess the usefulness or practical significance of the result.

Assumptions of the Independence Test

The assumptions associated with the test for independence and the estimation of strength of association and effect size are as follows: (1) Every observation must fall in one and only one cell of the contingency table. (2) The observations must be independent. One situation in which this assumption is likely to be violated occurs when an individual is represented more than once in a cell or in more than one cell. (3) The sample n should be large enough so that every expected frequency is at least 10 when there is one degree of freedom and at least 5 when there is more than one degree of freedom.[10]

CHECK YOUR UNDERSTANDING OF SECTION 16.3

7. List the similarities and differences between Pearson's product-moment correlation coefficient and Cramér's measure of association.
8. Two hundred women between the ages of 19 and 25 were asked whether they favored the use of birth-control pills. The women were classified according to attitude and religious preference.

	Protestants	Roman Catholics	Non-Christians	Sum
Favor	58	30	28	116
Oppose	8	23	5	36
Undecided	10	15	23	48
Sum	76	68	56	200

a. For the data in the table, list the steps you would use in testing the null hypothesis of independence. Let $\alpha = .001$.
b. What is your decision concerning the null hypothesis?
c. If the null hypothesis is rejected, compute Cramér's statistic.
d. If appropriate, compute the size of the effect and interpret the result.

---

[10] Fisher's exact test for a 2×2 contingency table can be used to test independence when n is small and expected cell frequencies are less than 10. The test is described by Hays (1994, pp. 863–865). A comparison of p-values obtained with Pearson's chi-square test and Fisher's exact test for the data in Table 16.3-2 is given in Section 16.5.

9. A random sample of 200 college students was classified according to class year and political conservatism as follows:

	Conservative	Neutral	Liberal	Sum
Freshman	38	22	6	66
Sophomore	22	24	5	51
Junior	11	12	19	42
Senior	7	13	21	41
Sum	78	71	51	200

   a. Are the variables independent? Let $\alpha = .05$.
   b. If the null hypothesis is rejected, compute Cramér's statistic.
   c. If appropriate, compute the size of the effect and interpret the results.

10. Use the table of random numbers in Appendix Table D.1 to draw a random sample without replacement of 40 students from the Student Database in Appendix E.
   a. List the Participant Number, Gender, and Course Grade for each participant in your sample.
   b. For the variables of Gender (*A*) and Course Grade (*B*), construct a contingency table.
   c. Test the hypothesis that the two variables are independent. Let $\alpha = .05$.
   d. If the null hypothesis is rejected, compute Cramér's $\hat{V}$.
   e. If the null hypothesis is rejected, compute the size of the effect.
   f. Write a paragraph summarizing the results of your analyses and your conclusions.

11. Term to remember
   a. Contingency table

16.4 TESTING EQUALITY OF $c \geq 2$ PROPORTIONS

The last application of Pearson's chi-square statistic that will be described is testing the equality of $c \geq 2$ population proportions.

If a random sample is obtained from each of $j = 1, \ldots, c$ binomially distributed populations, the sample proportions $\hat{p}_1, \hat{p}_2, \ldots, \hat{p}_c$ can be used to test the null hypothesis

$$H_0: p_1 = p_2 = \cdots = p_c$$

versus

$$H_1: p_j \neq p_{j'} \text{ for some } j \text{ and } j' \text{ where } j \neq j'.$$

The null hypothesis is rejected if $\chi^2 = \sum_{i=1}^{r} \sum_{j=1}^{c} (O_{ij} - E_{ij})^2/E_{ij}$ exceeds or equals the critical value $\chi^2_{\alpha,\nu}$, at α level of significance for $\nu = c - 1$ degrees of freedom.

Rejection of the null hypothesis means that some population proportions are not equal. It doesn't mean that they are all unequal; perhaps only one is discrepant. This test, like the two described earlier, is approximate because the continuous chi-square distribution is used to estimate a probability for a discrete sampling distribution. The proportions $\hat{p}_1, \hat{p}_2, \ldots, \hat{p}_c$, which may be based on unequal sample sizes, are assumed to represent independent observations for c independent binomially distributed random variables. Like all binomial experiments, each trial must result in one of two outcomes. Later, we will see that the test can be extended to the multinomial case in which each trial can result in one of three or more outcomes.

Computational Example

Suppose we surveyed older people living in public housing in Borborygme, Texas, to determine whether satisfaction with living conditions is related to age heterogeneity of people in their neighborhood. Neighborhoods were categorized as high, medium, or low in heterogeneity of residents' ages. Random samples of 100 elderly women from each category were interviewed (equal sample n's are not required) and asked, among other things, "Are you satisfied with your living conditions?" The answers were classified as "satisfied" or "not satisfied." It was anticipated that satisfaction would be different for the three neighborhood categories. Responses to the question are given in Table 16.4-1. The computation of Pearson's chi-square statistic is shown in the table; the procedure is identical to that for an $r \times c$ contingency table for testing independence (see Section 16.3). The degrees of freedom are equal to $c - 1 = 2$, the number of age-heterogeneity categories minus one. Alternatively, the degrees of freedom can be computed from $(r - 1)(c - 1) = (2 - 1)(3 - 1) = 2$. For a test at the .05 level of significance, the critical value of $\chi^2_{.05,2}$ is 5.991. This value is obtained from Appendix Table D.4. The computed chi-square with two degrees of freedom, $\chi^2(2) = 9.708$, exceeds the critical value, $\chi^2_{.05,2} = 5.991$. Hence, the null hypothesis is rejected. The researcher can conclude that at least two of the population proportions are not equal.[11]

Comparison of Designs for Testing Independence and Equality of Proportions

The experimental design for the test of equality of $c \geq 2$ proportions and the experimental design for the test of independence use the same Pearson test statistic and

[11] Marascuilo and McSweeney (1977, pp. 141–147) describe a procedure for determining which population proportions are unequal. The procedure is based on Scheffé's method, which is described in Section 14.5.

TABLE 16.4-1   Satisfaction and Age Heterogeneity

(i) Data (O_{ij} and E_{ij} denote observed and expected frequencies for the $i = 1$, . . . , r rows of variable A and $j = 1$, . . . , c columns of variable B)

	Age Heterogeneity				
	Low, b_1	Medium, b_2	High, b_3		
Satisfied, a_1	$O_{11} = 56$ $E_{11} = 50.67$	$O_{12} = 58$ $E_{12} = 50.67$	$O_{13} = 38$ $E_{13} = 50.67$	$n_{a_1} = 152$
Not Satisfied, a_2	$O_{21} = 44$ $E_{21} = 49.33$	$O_{22} = 42$ $E_{22} = 49.33$	$O_{23} = 62$ $E_{23} = 49.33$	$n_{a_2} = 148$
	$n_{b_1} = 100$	$n_{b_2} = 100$	$n_{b_3} = 100$	$n = 300$

(ii) Computation of chi-square statistic

O_{ij}	E_{ij}	$O_{ij} - E_{ij}$	$\dfrac{(O_{ij} - E_{ij})^2}{E_{ij}}$
56	50.67	5.33	0.561
44	49.33	− 5.33	0.576
58	50.67	7.33	1.060
42	49.33	− 7.33	1.089
38	50.67	− 12.67	3.168
62	49.33	12.67	3.254
		0^a	$\chi^2(2) = 9.708$
			$\chi^2_{.05,2} = 5.991$

[a] Computational check: $\sum (O_{ij} - E_{ij})$ should equal 0.

the same formula for computing degrees of freedom, and both are approximately distributed as the chi-square distribution. It is not surprising, then, that the two designs are often confused. There is no reason for confusion if you know what to look for.

The key differences between the two designs are the randomization plan and the way the sample elements are classified. In the design for testing independence, (1) a single random sample is obtained from a population and (2) the elements are classified in terms of two variables, where each variable has two or more categories. In the design for testing equality of proportions, (1) c random samples are obtained and (2) for each sample, the elements are classified in terms of membership in one of $r = 2$ mutually exclusive categories, such as satisfied versus not satisfied. The important distinction is that each element's status with respect to the second variable, say, degree of neighborhood heterogeneity, has been predetermined by sampling from the appropriate population. In the design for testing independence, the status of the sample elements is not predetermined for either variable. Because of differences in the randomization plans and classification procedures, the hypotheses tested by the two designs are different—$p(A \text{ and } B) = p(A)p(B)$ for the test of independence and $p_1 = p_2 = \cdots = p_c$ for the test of equality of Proportions.

Extension of the Test of Equality of Proportions to More Than Two Response Categories

The test illustrated in Table 16.4-1 can be extended to the case in which variable A has r greater than two row categories: for example, very satisfied, somewhat satisfied, somewhat dissatisfied, very dissatisfied. When the number of rows is greater than 2, the test is referred to as a *test of homogeneity of proportions*. A proportion in row i and column j, denoted by $p_{a_i|b_j}$, is assumed to represent an observation for an independent multinomial random variable instead of a binomial random variable. The statistical hypotheses can be expressed as follows:

$$H_0: \begin{bmatrix} p_{a_1|b_1} = p_{a_1|b_2} = \cdots = p_{a_1|b_c} \\ p_{a_2|b_1} = p_{a_2|b_2} = \cdots = p_{a_2|b_c} \\ \vdots \\ p_{a_r|b_1} = p_{a_r|b_2} = \cdots = p_{a_r|b_c} \end{bmatrix}$$

$H_1: p_{a_i|b_j} \neq p_{a_i|b_{j'}}$ in at least one row for columns j and j'.

In words, the null hypothesis states that the proportions in the first row are equal across the c columns, the proportions in the second row are equal across the c columns, and so on . If the null hypothesis is rejected, we know that at least two proportions in at least one row are not equal. That is, there is some row for which the jth and j'th proportions are not equal. Ordinarily, numerical values are not specified in the null hypothesis; but if they were, a null hypothesis for $i = 1, \ldots, 4$ rows and $j = 1, \ldots, 3$ columns might look like

$$H_0: \begin{bmatrix} .20 = .20 = .20 \\ .40 = .40 = .40 \\ .30 = .30 = .30 \\ .10 = .10 = .10 \end{bmatrix}.$$

At the risk of telling you more than you wanted to know about writing null hypotheses, let me contrast the above hypotheses for the multinomial case with that for a test of equality of proportions for the binomial case. If variable A has only two categories, the null hypothesis can be written as

$$H_0: p_{a_1|b_1} = p_{a_1|b_2} = \cdots = p_{a_1|b_c},$$

or, simply,

$$H_0: p_1 = p_2 = \cdots = p_c.$$

For this binomial case, the null hypothesis does not need a second row of proportions because q, the proportion in the second category, is equal to $1 - p$. It follows that if $p_1 = p_2 = \cdots = p_c$, then $q_1 = q_2 = \cdots = q_c$.

The computation of Pearson's statistic for testing homogeneity of proportions is the same as that for testing equality of proportions. The number of degrees of freedom for the homogeneity test is equal to $(r - 1)(c - 1)$. The general assumptions discussed in connection with an $r \times c$ contingency table apply as well to the homogeneity test.

CHECK YOUR UNDERSTANDING OF SECTION 16.4

12. Company executives were classified as smokers or nonsmokers. Random samples from the two populations were obtained and tested for the presence of lung cancer. The following data were obtained:

	Smoker	Nonsmoker	Sum
Cancer present	16	5	21
Cancer absent	14	25	39
Sum	30	30	60

   a. State the statistical hypotheses.
   b. Test the null hypothesis. Let $\alpha = .01$.

13. State in words the meaning of the hypothesis

$$H_0: \begin{bmatrix} .30 = .30 = .30 \\ .60 = .60 = .60 \\ .10 = .10 = .10 \end{bmatrix}.$$

14. New employees on an assembly line were randomly assigned to one of four groups and given different amounts of training. After two weeks on the job, their performance was rated by their supervisor as follows:

Rating	Amount of Training (Days)				Sum
	1	2	5	10	
Excellent	4	4	6	6	20
Good	5	3	10	11	29
Fair	9	9	5	8	31
Poor	7	9	4	0	20
Sum	25	25	25	25	100

   a. State the statistical hypotheses.
   b. Test the null hypothesis. Let $\alpha = .05$.

15. A program of home-care services designed to enable the elderly to postpone the need for long-term institutional care is available to all residents of Manitoba, Canada. Differences in terms of perceived health between the elderly in Manitoba who use these services and those who do not was investigated using a structured interview. A random sample of 400 community residents age 65 or older was obtained from each of the populations. A portion of the data are as follows. (Experiment suggested by Chappell, N. L. [1985]. Social support and the receipt of home-care services. *The Gerontologist, 25,* 47–54.)

Perceived Health	Home-Care User	Non-Home-Care User	Sum
High	26	112	138
Medium	129	187	316
Low	233	97	330
Sum	388*	396*	784

* Numbers do not equal 400 because of missing data.

   a. State the statistical hypotheses.
   b. Test the null hypothesis. Let $\alpha = .05$.

16. Use the table of random numbers in Appendix D to draw a random sample without replacement of 20 men and 20 women students from the Student Database in Appendix E.
   a. List the Participant Number, Gender, and Stat Grade (use only letter grades A = 4, B+ = 3.5, B = 3, . . . , F = 0) for each participant in your sample.
   b. For the variables of Gender (*A*) and Stat Grade (*B*), construct a contingency table.
   c. Test the hypothesis that the proportion of A's, B's, and so on in the population are equal for men and women. Let $\alpha = .05$.
   d. State the statistical hypotheses.
   e. Write a paragraph summarizing the results of your analysis and your conclusions.

†16.5 PRINTOUTS FOR THREE MICROCOMPUTER PACKAGES

JMP

JMP was used to compute a chi-square statistic for the gender and marijuana data in Table 16.3-2. A JMP data table is shown in Figure 16.5-1. By default, the columns

† This and similarly marked sections can be omitted without loss of continuity.

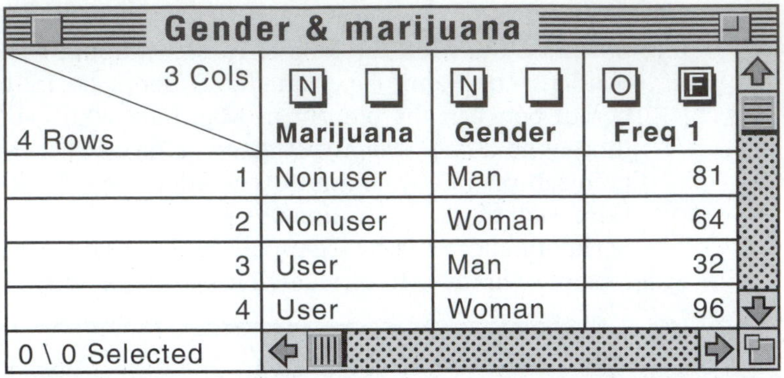

Gender & marijuana			
3 Cols **4 Rows**	[N] [ ] **Marijuana**	[N] [ ] **Gender**	[O] [F] **Freq 1**
1	Nonuser	Man	81
2	Nonuser	Woman	64
3	User	Man	32
4	User	Woman	96

0 \ 0 Selected

Figure 16.5-1.   **JMP data table for the gender and marijuana data in Table 16.3-2. Column names can contain up to 32 characters. Long names are accommodated by dragging the column boundaries. By default, the data type for the columns is "numeric." The data type for the marijuana and gender columns was changed to "character" and the modeling type was changed to "nominal," denoted by [N] . The modeling type for the frequency column was changed to "ordinal," denoted by [O] .**

in a data table are assumed to contain numeric data. Clicking on the top of the **Marijuana** and **Gender** columns brought up a dialog box in which **Data Type** was changed to **Character** and **Modeling Type** was changed to **Nominal.** The **Modeling Type** for the third column, **Freq,** was changed to **Ordinal.** After the data were entered in the data table, the selection of the **Analyze** command in the menu bar followed by the pull-down command **Fit Y by X** brought up another dialog box in which Marijuana was identified as the **X** (column) variable, Gender was identified as the **Y** (row) variable, and Freq was identified as the **Freq** variable. Clicking on **OK** produced the mosaic plot shown in Figure 16.5-2 and the crosstabs and tests displays shown in Figure 16.5-3.

JMP performed three tests for the gender and marijuana data: the likelihood ratio test and Fisher's exact test, which are discussed in advanced textbooks, and the Pearson chi-square test. The *p*-value for the chi-square test, .0184, is close to that for Fisher's exact test, .0261.

SPSS

SPSS was used to compute a chi-square statistic for the gender and marijuana data in Table 16.3-2. An SPSS data table is shown in Figure 16.5-4. To weight the four cells by the corresponding frequencies, the **Data** command was selected in the menu bar followed by the pull-down command called **Weight Cases . . . . Freq** was identified as the frequency (weighting) variable. Then the **Statistics** command in

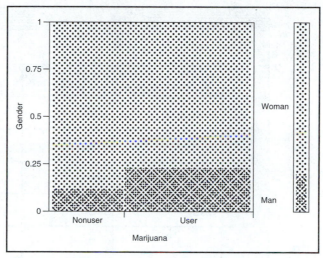

Figure 16.5-2. **JMP produced a mosaic plot for the gender and marijuana data in Table 16.3-2. The display graphically compares the proportions of marijuana nonusers and users among men and women.**

Crosstabs ▶

Gender	Count	Nonuser	User	
	Man	8	32	40
	Woman	64	96	160
		72	128	200

(Marijuana)

Tests

Source	DF	–LogLikelihood	RSquare (U)
Model	1	2.98568	0.0298
Error	198	97.09481	
C Total	199	100.08048	
Total Count	200		

Test	ChiSquare	Prob>ChiSq
Likelihood Ratio	5.971	0.0145
Pearson	5.556	0.0184

Fisher's Exact Test	Prob
Left	0.0129
Right	0.9957
2-Tail	0.0261

Figure 16.5-3. **The JMP contingency table in the crosstabs display mirrors the gender and marijuana data in Table 16.3-2. The JMP program produced three tests: the likelihood ratio test and Fisher's exact test, which are discussed in more advanced textbooks, and Pearson's chi-square test, which is the subject of this chapter. The *p*-value for Pearson's test, which uses the chi-square distribution to approximate the exact probability, is quite close to the *p*-value given by Fisher's two-tailed exact test.**

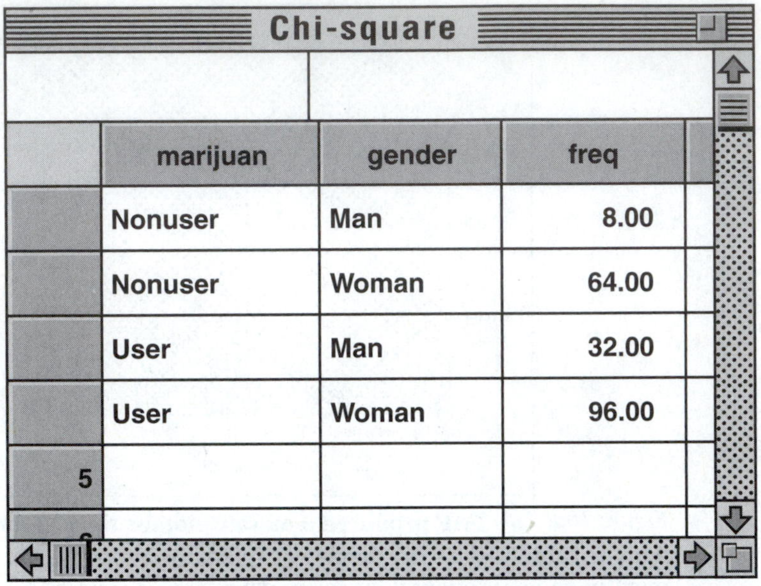

	marijuan	gender	freq
	Nonuser	Man	8.00
	Nonuser	Woman	64.00
	User	Man	32.00
	User	Woman	96.00
5			

Figure 16.5-4. **SPSS data table for the gender and marijuana data in Table 16.3-2 (Variable names are limited to 8 characters).**

the menu bar was selected followed by the pull-down commands called **Summarize** and **Crosstabs . . . .** The selection of **Crosstabs . . .** brought up the dialog box shown in Figure 16.5-5. **Gender** was identified as the row variable and **marijuan** was identified as the column variable. Clicking on the **Statistics** button brought up a dialog box in which **Chi-square** was checked. Clicking on the **Cells** button brought up a dialog box in which the **Observed** and **Expected** boxes were checked. Finally, clicking on **OK** produced the output in Figure 16.5-6. The SPSS output provided a chi-square test with and without a correction for continuity and the likelihood ratio test, which is discussed in advanced textbooks.

SYSTAT

SYSTAT was used to compute a chi-square statistic for the gender and marijuana data in Table 16.3-2. The data were entered in the data table shown in Figure 16.5-7. Then the **Preferences . . .** pull-down command under **Edit** in the menu bar was selected. From the **Preferences . . .** dialog box, **Extended** in the **Statistics** pop-up box was requested. The number of decimal places was set to 4 in the **Analysis** and **Editor** sections. Next, the **Weight . . .** pull-down command under **Data** in the menu bar was selected. **Freq** was identified as the weighting variable. The selection of the **Tabulate . . .** pull-down

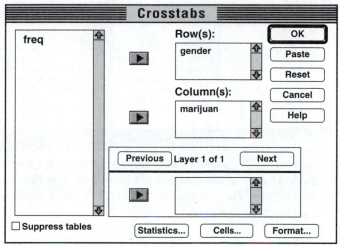

Figure 16.5-5. **This dialog box in SPSS was used to identify the row and column variables: gender and marijuan, respectively. The Statistics... button was used to request the chi-square statistic. The Cells... button was used to request both observed and expected cell frequencies. Clicking on OK produced the output in Table 16.5-6.**

```
GENDER by MARIJUAN

                    MARIJUAN  Page 1 of 1

           Count
           Exp Val                               Row
                        Nonuser    User          Total
   GENDER  ─────────────────────────────────
           Man             8        32            40
                          14.4      25.6         20.0%

           Woman          64        96           160
                          57.6     102.4         80.0%

           Column         72       128           200
           Total         36.0%     64.0%        100.0%


   Chi-Square              Value      DF      Significance
   ───────────            ─────      ──      ──────────
   Pearson                5.55556     1        .01842
   Continuity correction  4.72141     1        .02979
   Likelihood Ratio       5.97135     1        .01454

   Minimum Expected Frequency − 14.400


   Number of Missing Observations:  0
```

Figure 16.5-6. **The SPSS output for the gender and marijuana data in Table 16.5-4 contains a contingency table with observed and expected cell frequencies, Pearson's chi-square with and without a correction for continuity, and the likelihood ratio test.**

SYSTAT Data Editor

	MARIJUAN$	GENDER$	FREQ
1	Nonuser	Man	8.000
2	Nonuser	Woman	64.000
3	User	Man	32.000
4	User	Woman	96.000

Figure 16.5-7. **SYSTAT data table for the gender and marijuana data in Table 16.3-2. Variable names are limited to eight characters and must begin with a letter. The $ sign after MARIJUAN and GENDER indicate that these are character variables.**

```
TABLE OF   GENDER$   (ROWS)  BY  MARIJUAN$   (COLUMNS)

FREQUENCIES

              Nonuser    User        TOTAL
           -----------------------
Man               8        32          40

Woman            64        96         160
           -----------------------
TOTAL            72       128         200


TEST STATISTIC                              VALUE        DF      PROB
  PEARSON CHI-SQUARE                       5.5556         1    0.0184
  LIKELIHOOD RATIO CHI-SQUARE              5.9714         1    0.0145
  MCNEMAR SYMMETRY CHI-SQUARE             10.6667         1    0.0011
  YATES CORRECTED CHI-SQUARE               4.7214         1    0.0298
  FISHER EXACT TEST (TWO-TAIL)                                 0.0261

COEFFICIENT                                 VALUE   ASYMPTOTIC STD ERROR
  PHI                                     -0.1667
  CONTINGENCY                              0.1644
  GOODMAN-KRUSKAL GAMMA                   -0.4545         0.1694
  KENDALL TAU-B                           -0.1667         0.0621
  STUART TAU-C                            -0.1280         0.0494
  YULE Q                                  -0.4545         0.1694
  YULE Y                                  -0.2404         0.1006
  COHEN KAPPA                             -0.1538         0.0582
  SPEARMAN RHO                            -0.1667         0.0621
  SOMMERS D      (COLUMN  DEPENDENT)      -0.2000         0.0742
  LAMBDA         (COLUMN  DEPENDENT)       0.0000         0.0000
  UNCERTAINTY    (COLUMN  DEPENDENT)       0.0228         0.0178
```

Figure 16.5-8. **The SYSTAT output for the gender and marijuana data in Table 16.5-7 gives Pearson chi-square statistics with and without Yates' correction for continuity and three other test statistics that are discussed in advanced textbooks. In addition, a variety of measures of association are provided. For the 2 × 2 contingency table, the Phi coefficient is identical to Cramér's $\hat{V}$.**

command under **Tables** in the menu bar brought up a dialog box in which GENDER was selected from the left column of variables and MARIJUAN from the right column of variables. Clicking on [**OK**] produced the output in Figure 16.5-8. SYSTAT produced four tests and a variety of measures of association. For the 2×2 contingency table, the Phi coefficient is identical to Cramér's $\hat{V}$.

16.6 SUMMARY

Pearson's chi-square test statistic is one of a limited number that is appropriate for frequency data. It provides an approximate test when an exact test based on the binomial or multinomial distributions would require a prohibitive amount of computation. The statistic is versatile. The three applications we have described are testing goodness of fit, independence, and equality of proportions. These applications are summarized in Table 16.6-1. In each application, a set of observed frequencies is compared with a set of expected frequencies. However, the apparent simplicity of the statistic $\Sigma(O - E)^2/E$ is deceptive. Its use involves important assumptions that are often overlooked or misunderstood by the novice researcher. The problem is compounded because all three applications use the same statistic for testing different hypotheses. The main points to consider in using Pearson's chi-square statistic are the following:

1. A single random sample is used in testing goodness of fit and independence; more than one random sample is used in testing equality of population proportions.
2. Each observation must be assigned to one and only one category or one cell of a contingency table.
3. Each participant or observational element should be represented only once. Multiple observations on the same participant almost always result in violation of the assumption of independence of observations.
4. The Pearson chi-square approximation to exact binomial or multinomial probabilities is generally unsatisfactory for very small samples. As a conservative rule of thumb, if the degrees of freedom are equal to 1, all expected frequencies should be at least 10; if the degrees of freedom are greater than 1, all expected frequencies should be at least 5.
5. If the chi-square test statistic is not significant for an $r \times c$ contingency table, no further analyses such as Cramér's $\hat{V}$ or Cohen's $\hat{w}$ should be performed.
6. The hypothesis tested by Pearson's statistic is nondirectional even though the region for rejection always lies in the upper tail of the sampling distribution.

TABLE 16.6-1   Applications of Pearson's Chi-Square Statistic

Purpose	Null Hypothesis	Degrees of Freedom	Requirements
1. Testing goodness of fit	$H_0: p_1 = p_1', \ldots, p_k = p_k'$ or $O_{Pop_1} = E_{Pop_1}, O_{Pop_2} = E_{Pop_2}, \ldots, O_{Pop_k} = E_{Pop_k}$	$k - 1 - e$	1. One random sample 2. If $\nu = 1$, every expected frequency should exceed 10. If $\nu > 1$, every expected frequency should exceed 5. 3. Random variable is binomially distributed for $k = 2$ and multinomially distributed for $k > 2$.
2. Testing independence	$H_0: p(A \text{ and } B) = p(A)p(B)$	$(r - 1)(c - 1)$	1. One random sample 2. If $\nu = 1$, every expected frequency should exceed 10. If $\nu > 1$, every expected frequency should exceed 5. 3. Random variable is binomially distributed when A and B have two categories and is multinomially distributed otherwise.
3a. Testing equality of proportions	$H_0: p_1 = p_2 = \cdots = p_c$	$c - 1$	1. $c \geq 2$ random samples 2. If $\nu = 1$, every expected frequency should exceed 10. If $\nu > 1$, every expected frequency should exceed 5. 3. Random variable is binomially distributed.
3b. Testing homogeneity of proportions	$H_0:$ $\begin{bmatrix} p_{a_1\|b_1} = p_{a_1\|b_2} = \cdots = p_{a_1\|b_c} \\ p_{a_2\|b_1} = p_{a_2\|b_2} = \cdots = p_{a_2\|b_c} \\ \vdots \\ p_{a_r\|b_1} = p_{a_r\|b_2} = \cdots = p_{a_r\|b_c} \end{bmatrix}$	$(r - 1)(c - 1)$	1. c random samples, where $c \geq 2$; for each sample, the elements are classified in terms of one of $r > 2$ mutually exclusive categories. 2. Every expected frequency should exceed 5. 3. Random variable is multinomially distributed.

REVIEW EXERCISES FOR CHAPTER 16

1. Why is the hypothesis tested by Pearson's statistic always nondirectional?

2. College students ($n = 197$) voted at a student-center booth for a

beauty queen from among six photographs equivalent in physical attractiveness as determined by rankings of 35 students at a nearby university. The pictures were randomly assigned names that the 35 students had previously judged to be desirable (Kathy, Jennifer, Christine) or undesirable (Ethel, Harriet, Gertrude). The total number of votes for the photographs having the desirable names was 158; the number for the photographs having the undesirable names was 39. (Experiment suggested by Garwood, S. C., Cox, L., Kaplan, V., Wasserman, N., & Sulzer, Jefferson L. [1980]. Beauty is only "name" deep: The effect of first name on ratings of physical attraction. *Journal of Applied Social Psychology, 10,* 431–435.)

a. List the steps you would follow in testing the null hypothesis that for the population represented by the sample of students who voted, the number of votes is evenly divided between the photographs assigned the attractive and unattractive names. Let $\alpha = .01$.

b. Is it necessary to apply Yates' correction? Why?

c. Perform the test and make a decision.

d. If appropriate, compute the size of the effect and interpret the result.

3. The dean believes that students in M−W−F classes are more likely to be absent on Monday and Friday than on Wednesday. A random sample of 200 students revealed that 68 were absent on Monday, 48 on Wednesday, and 84 on Friday.

a. List the steps you would follow in testing the hypothesis that the ratio of absences is M: W: F = 3:2:3. Let $\alpha = .05$.

b. Perform the test and make a decision.

4. A random sample of 300 music majors took a test of creativity. Their scores and the expected number of scores based on the normal distribution are as follows:

Test Score	O_j	E_j
140 and above	0	5.0
130–139	32	20.2
120–129	48	54.2
110–119	76	83.8
100–109	90	78.4
90–99	36	42.4
80–89	18	13.4
Less than 80	0	2.7

a. Test the hypothesis that the scores are normally distributed. Let $\alpha = .01$. The E_j column in the table presents expected frequencies,

given that the null hypothesis is true; the O_j column presents the observed frequencies.
   b. How many degrees of freedom does the test have?
   c. If appropriate, compute the size of the effect and interpret the result.
5. What is Yates' correction and why is it used?
6. State in your own words the meaning of the null hypothesis $p(A \text{ and } B) = p(A)p(B)$. If the null hypothesis is rejected, what do you know about the variables?
7. Why is Cramér's measure of association computed only when the null hypothesis $p(A \text{ and } B) = p(A)p(B)$ is rejected?
8. Three hundred divorced men were classified by age at time of first marriage and duration of first marriage as follows:

Age at Marriage	Duration of Marriage (Years)				
	< 5	$5-9$	$10-14$	≥ 15	Sum
< 19	41	31	15	15	102
$19-24$	30	27	22	21	100
$25-34$	11	7	16	16	50
≥ 35	13	14	9	12	48
Sum	95	79	62	64	300

   a. List the steps you would use in testing the null hypothesis that the two variables are independent. Let $\alpha = .05$.
   b. Perform the test and make a decision.
   c. If the null hypothesis is rejected, compute Cramér's statistic.
   d. If appropriate, compute the size of the effect and interpret the result.
9. Hip fractures in elderly patients are known to be associated with a high incidence of mortality. Data for 225 elderly patients who had undergone hip surgery were collected. The following variables were measured: mortality, number of previous hip injuries (antecedents), and patient's age. (Experiment suggested by Banna, S. E., Raynal, L., & Gerebzof, A. [1984]. Fractures of the hip and medico-social considerations. *Archives of Gerontology and Geriatrics, 3,* 311–319.)

Medical Antecedents	Died	Survived	Sum
No antecedent	8	27	35
1 antecedents	20	62	82
2 antecedents	21	25	46
3 antecedents	13	23	36
≥ 4 antecedents	20	5	25
Sum	82	142	224*

(table continued on following page)

Age			
56–65	2	12	14
66–75	10	32	42
76–85	40	64	104
86–95	30	20	50
Sum	82	128	210*

* n does not equal 225 because of missing data.

    a. For the data in the table, test the hypotheses that mortality is independent of the number of antecedents and age. Let $\alpha = .05$.
    b. If the null hypothesis is rejected, compute Cramér's statistic.
    c. If appropriate, compute the size of the effect for number of antecedents and age and interpret the results.

10. An analysis was performed on federal court cases in which a complainant charged that the Age Discrimination in Employment Act of 1967 and subsequent amendments had been violated. Data for 120 cases were examined in terms of the outcome of the discrimination suit and the gender of the complainant. (Experiment suggested by Schuster, M., & Miller, C. S. [1984]. An empirical assessment of the age discrimination in employment act. *Industrial and Labor Relations Review, 38,* 64–74.)

	Outcome of Suit		
Gender	Won	Lost	Sum
Man	19	15	34
Woman	21	65	86
Sum	40	80	120

    a. Test the null hypothesis that the variables of gender and suit outcome are independent. Let $\alpha = .05$.
    b. If the null hypothesis is rejected, compute Cramér's statistic.
    c. If appropriate, compute the size of the effect and interpret the results.

11. The equality of proportions chi-square test and the independence chi-square test are applicable to an $r \times c$ contingency table, and both use the same test statistic. How do they differ?

12. Students were given a choice of writing or not writing a paper for extra credit. Half of the students, selected randomly, were made to feel coerced; the other half received no pressure. The number who chose to write or not to write a paper is as follows:

	Coerced	Not Coerced	Sum
Wrote paper	13	9	22
Didn't write paper	17	21	38
Sum	30	30	60

a. List the steps you would use to test the null hypothesis. Let $\alpha = .05$.

b. Did the conditions affect paper writing?

13. State in words the meaning of the hypothesis

$$H_0: \begin{bmatrix} .20 = .20 = .20 \\ .30 = .30 = .30 \\ .50 = .50 = .50 \end{bmatrix}$$

14. Random samples of seventh-, eighth-, and ninth-grade students were interviewed following one year of busing. They were asked, "Did black and white students mix more than, the same as, or less than last year?" The following data were obtained:

	Grade			
Response	7	8	9	Sum
More	26	12	4	42
Same	18	25	35	78
Less	6	13	11	30
Sum	50	50	50	150

a. State the statistical hypotheses.

b. Test the null hypothesis. Let $\alpha = .05$.

15. Use the table of random numbers in Appendix D to draw a random sample without replacement of 20 men and 20 women students from the Student Database in Appendix E.

a. List the Participant Number, Gender, and Math Test score for each participant in your sample.

b. For the variables of Gender (A) and Math Test score (B), construct a contingency table. Assign the Math Test scores to one of the following class intervals: 0–9, 10–19, 20–29, 30–39, 40–48.

c. Test the hypothesis that the population proportion in each of the five class intervals is equal for men and women. Let $\alpha = .05$.

    d. Write the null and alternative hypotheses.

    e. Write a paragraph summarizing the results of your analysis and your conclusions.

†16.7 SUPPLEMENTARY NOTES

16.7-1 Two Ways to Test the Hypothesis That $p = p'$ (or $p = p_0$)

A goodness-of-fit test with one degree of freedom is formally equivalent to the large-sample z test for a proportion described in Section 11.4. We will show by an example that

$$z = \frac{\hat{p} - p_0}{\sqrt{p_0 q_0 / n}}$$

leads to the same decision about the population proportion, p, as Pearson's χ^2 statistic and, in addition, that the absolute value of z is equal to $\sqrt{\chi^2}$.

    In Section 11.4 we tested the null hypothesis that the proportion of substandard dwelling units in a survey was equal to the proportion found in an earlier survey. The proportion in the earlier survey was .30. The proportion in the later survey was .34 and was based on a random sample of 900 dwelling units. To test the null hypothesis, $p = .30$, that the proportion of substandard units had not changed, the z test statistic was computed:

$$z = \frac{\hat{p} - p_0}{\sqrt{p_0 q_0 / n}} = \frac{.34 - .30}{\sqrt{(.30)(.70)/900}} = 2.619.$$

The computed z statistic, $z = 2.62$, exceeded the critical value, $z_{.05/2} = 1.96$, required to reject the null hypothesis at the .05 level. Hence, we concluded that the proportion of substandard dwelling units was not equal to .30 and, in fact, had increased.

    The same decision is reached if the data are analyzed by Pearson's chi-square statistic. The computation is shown in Table 16.7-1. The critical value of χ^2 for $\nu = 1$ degree of freedom at the .05 level of significance is $\chi^2_{.05,1} = 3.841$. Because the computed chi square, $\chi^2(1) = 6.857$, exceeds the critical value, $\chi^2_{.05,1} = 3.841$, the null hypothesis is rejected. We note also that both the absolute value of the z test statistic and the square root of the chi-square test statistic are equal—that is, $|z| = \sqrt{\chi^2} = 2.619$.

---

† These supplementary notes can be omitted without loss of continuity.

TABLE 16.7-1. Computation of Pearson's Chi-Square Statistic for $k = 2$ Categories

(i) Computation of observed (O_j) and expected (E_j) frequencies (Observed proportions: $\hat{p} = .34$, $1 - \hat{p} = .66$. Expected proportions according to the null hypothesis: $p' = .30$, $1 - p' = .70$.)

$$O_1 = n\hat{p} = 900(.34) = 306$$

$$O_2 = n(1 - \hat{p}) = 900(.66) = 594$$

$$E_1 = np' = 900(.30) = 270$$

$$E_2 = n(1 - p') = 900(.70) = 630$$

(ii) Computation of chi-square statistic

O_j	E_j	$O_j - E_j$	$\dfrac{(O_j - E_j)^2}{E_j}$
306	270	36	$(36)^2/270 = 4.800$
594	630	−36	$(-36)^2/630 = 2.057$
		0^a	$\chi^2(1) = 6.857$
			$\chi^2_{.05,\,1} = 3.841$

[a] Computational check: $\Sigma(O_j - E_j)$ should equal 0.

16.7-2 Special Computational Procedure for a 2 × 2 Contingency Table

A simpler procedure for computing Pearson's chi-square statistic can be used when a contingency table has 2 rows and 2 columns—a 2 × 2 contingency table. This procedure has the advantage of not requiring the computation of expected frequencies. Consider the following 2 × 2 table in which observed frequencies are denoted

	Variable 2		
Variable 1	a	b	$a + b$
	c	d	$c + d$
	$a + c$	$b + d$	

by the letters a, b, c, and d. The formula for Pearson's statistic using only observed cell frequencies is

$$\chi^2 = \frac{n(ad - bc)^2}{(a + b)(c + d)(a + c)(b + d)}.$$

For the data in Table 16.3-2, the formula yields

$$\chi^2 = \frac{200[(8)(96) - (32)(64)]^2}{(8 + 32)(64 + 96)(8 + 64)(32 + 96)} = 5.555,$$

which is identical to the answer obtained using the conventional formula. If desired, Yates' correction for continuity can be included in the formula as follows:

$$\chi^2 = \frac{n(|ad - bc| - n/2)^2}{(a + b)(c + d)(a + c)(b + d)}.$$

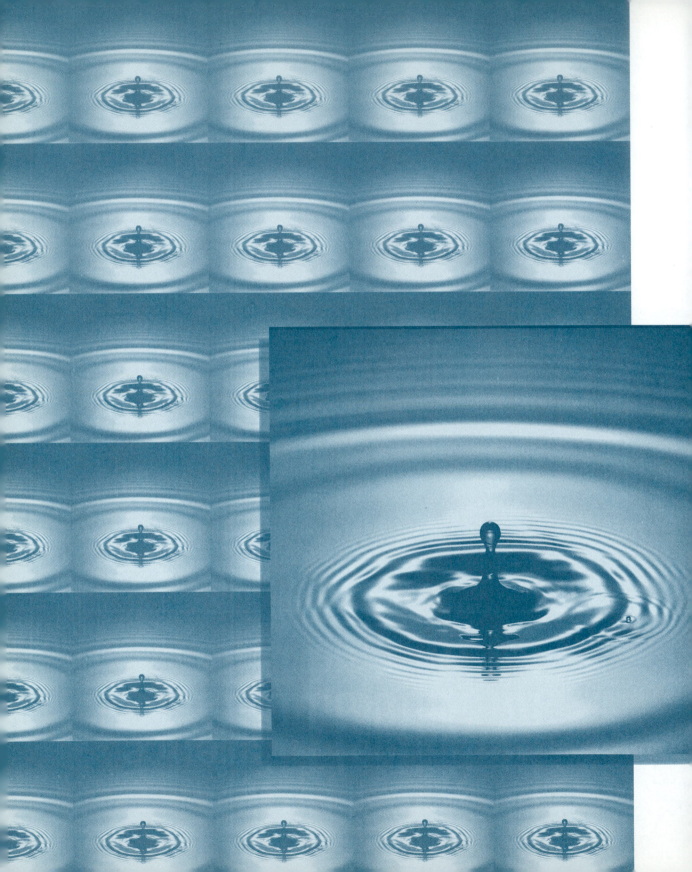

Chapter 17

Statistical Inference for Ranked Data

589

17.1 INTRODUCTION TO ASSUMPTION-FREER TESTS[1]

So far we have presented procedures for testing hypotheses about a variety of population parameters. In each case it was necessary to assume that the sampled population had a probability distribution of a particular shape—usually normal or binomial. For many variables, such an assumption seems warranted. For other variables, however, we may not know the shape of the underlying population distribution and may be unwilling to make an assumption about it. The procedures we have presented also required other assumptions. For example, the independent-samples t statistic for testing the null hypothesis that $\mu_1 - \mu_2 = 0$ assumes that the population variances are equal. To avoid having to make such assumptions, nonparametric and distribution-free tests have been developed that are assumption freer—that is, they require less stringent assumptions. Before describing the tests, let's review the three kinds of distributions about which assumptions are made: (1) the sampled population (for example, the population of the observation statistic X), (2) the sampling distribution of the descriptive statistic used in the test (for example, $\overline{X}$), and (3) the sampling distribution of the test statistic (for example, t). Nonparametric and distribution-free tests are assumption freer with respect to the distribution of the sampled population.

> A statistical test is **nonparametric** if it does not test a hypothesis about one of the parameters of the sampled population. It is **distribution-free** if it makes no assumptions about the shape of the sampled population.

Most distribution-free tests, however, do assume that the sampled population is continuous. Although the distinction between nonparametric and distribution-free tests seems clear enough, in practice the distinction is frequently blurred. Consequently, many statisticians use the terms interchangeably. We will follow Ury's (1967) lead and denote both kinds of tests by the more descriptive label *assumption-freer tests.*

Several assumption-freer tests have already been described. The chi-square tests in Chapter 16, for example, are assumption-freer tests for frequency data. The two tests to be described in this chapter are assumption-freer tests for ranked data (ordered qualitative variables).

Assumption-freer tests differ from parametric tests in a number of important respects. We will mention one difference now and defer a complete discussion until Section 17.4. Parametric tests utilize the magnitude information contained in observations (scores), but assumption-freer tests ignore this information. Instead, they use either the frequency with which observations occur, as in the case of chi-square, or their rank (original position), as in the case of the tests in this chapter. One ad-

---

[1] For a more detailed introduction, see Bradley (in Kirk, 1972). Sections of this chapter were influenced by Bradley's article.

vantage of focusing on either the categorical or ordinal information contained in observations has already been mentioned: We can avoid having to make assumptions regarding the shape of the sampled population. But as we will see, this freedom is bought at a price. Assumption-freer tests tend to be less efficient than parametric tests when the assumptions of the parametric tests are fulfilled.

Another advantage of assumption-freer tests is that they require less sophisticated measurement procedures. One of the simplest measurement procedures is ranking people or objects with respect to some characteristic. We observe, for example, that John is a better quarterback than Fred, who is better than Elmer; this piece of pie looks better than that one; or Jane is more resourceful than Dennis. It is convenient to use numbers to denote rank order. For example, John is 1; Fred is 2; and Elmer is 3. However, the numbers don't reflect the magnitude of differences in quarterbacking skill or whether the difference between John and Fred is the same as that between Fred and Elmer. Presumably, measuring instruments could be devised that would assign numbers that reflect the magnitude of differences in quarterbacking skill, pie attractiveness, and resourcefulness. This has been done in the area of intellectual assessment: The measuring instrument is an intelligence test. But such instruments are not easy to develop, which is why researchers frequently resort to counting or ranking.

Two test statistics that utilize only the ordinal information contained in observations are described in Sections 17.2 and 17.3. They are regarded as assumption-freer alternatives to the independent and dependent two-sample *t* tests for means. There are many other assumption-freer tests. The interested reader is referred to Marascuilo and McSweeney (1977).

17.2 MANN-WHITNEY *U* TEST FOR TWO INDEPENDENT SAMPLES

The Mann-Whitney *U* test[2] is used to test the hypothesis that two population distributions are identical. It assumes that the populations are continuous and that random samples have been drawn from each or that participants have been randomly assigned to two conditions. The test statistic is based on the ranks of observations rather than on their numerical values, and hence it is appropriate for most data in the behavioral sciences and education. Because of the *U* test's modest assumptions, it is used widely as an assumption-freer alternative to the two-sample *t* test for independent samples.

---

[2] The test was originally developed by Frank Wilcoxon in 1945 and called the Wilcoxon rank-sum test. Since then, various forms of the test have appeared—a form, by Festinger in 1946, the Mann-Whitney form in 1947, and a form by White in 1952. The Wilcoxon rank-sum test should not be confused with the Wilcoxon matched-pairs signed ranks test that is discussed in Section 17.3.

Computational Procedure for Small Samples

The computational procedures described here for the Mann-Whitney U statistic can be used when both sample sizes are 20 or less. When either of the samples contains more than 20 scores, a z statistic described later can be used.

Suppose an experiment was performed to determine whether the amount of aggressive behavior exhibited by children is affected by observing aggression on TV. A sample of $N = 21$ six-year-old girls was randomly assigned to one of two conditions: viewing a television program containing numerous aggressive acts, the experimental condition, and viewing a program without aggression, the control condition. Following the television viewing, each girl was observed at play, and her aggressive acts were counted.

The data are given in Table 17.2-1 along with the computational procedures for the U statistic. The first step in the analysis is to rank order the scores. In assigning ranks to the scores, the data for the experimental and control groups are treated as one sample. The scores, frequency of aggressive acts for each girl, are ordered from the smallest to the largest. The first n positive integers are then substituted for the scores, with the smallest score receiving a rank of 1 and the largest, a rank of N. For example, one of the girls exhibited 0 aggressive acts, which is the fewest number. This 0 is assigned the rank of 1. Another girl exhibited 1 aggressive act, the next fewest number. This 1 is assigned the rank of 2, and so on. If two or more observations have the same value (tied scores), they are assigned the mean of the ranks they would have occupied. For example, two girls exhibited 13 aggressive acts. These two 13s would occupy ranks 12 and 13. So each 13 is assigned the mean of ranks 12 and 13, which is 12.5. The ranks associated with the experimental and control groups are added separately. The Mann-Whitney test statistic, U, is based on the sum of ranks as indicated in part (iii) of Table 17.2-1.

No assumptions regarding the shape of the populations are required because the test statistic is based not on scores but on ranks. The null hypothesis states that the distribution of aggressive acts for girls in the experimental population is identical to that for girls in the control population. The statistical hypotheses are as follows:[3]

H_0: Population distributions for the experimental and control groups are identical.

H_1: Population distributions are not identical.

The .05 level of significance is adopted. To be significant at the .05 level, the computed value of the test statistic, $U(n_1, n_2)$, must be *less than* or *equal to* the critical value, $U_{.05/2;n_1,n_2}$, obtained from Appendix Table D.12. For the data in Table 17.2-1, the computed value of the Mann-Whitney statistic, $U(10, 11) = 18.5$, is less than the critical value, $U_{.05/2;10,11} = 26$. Hence, we can conclude that the two populations

---

[3] If it can be assumed that the two population distributions are symmetrical, the Mann-Whitney U test is a test of the hypothesis that the population medians are equal.

TABLE 17.2-1. Computational Procedure for Mann-Whitney U Test

(i) Data ($N = 21$ girls were randomly assigned to two conditions. The two samples were treated as one combined sample, and the scores were ranked from 1 to N, with the smallest score receiving a rank of 1 and the largest, a rank of 21. Two or more scores with the same value (tied scores) were assigned the mean of the ranks they would have received. For example, the two scores of 13 would have received ranks of 12 and 13; instead, they both received the mean rank of 12.5.)

Number of Aggressive Acts for Experimental Group	Rank, R_1	Number of Aggressive Acts for Control Group	Rank, R_2
2	3	8	8
19	17	1	2
13	12.5	0	1
9	9	10	10
17	15	20	18
18	16	5	6
24	21	11	11
15	14	7	7
22	20	3	4
21	19	13	12.5
		4	5
$n_1 = 10$	$\Sigma R_1 = 146.5$	$n_2 = 11$	$\Sigma R_2 = 84.5$

(ii) Computational check

$$\Sigma R_1 + \Sigma R_2 = \frac{N(N + 1)}{2}, \text{ where } N = n_1 + n_2$$

$$146.5 + 84.5 = \frac{21(21 + 1)}{2} = 231$$

(iii) Computation of U

$$U(n_1, n_2) = \text{Smaller of} \left[\begin{array}{c} n_1 n_2 + \dfrac{n_1(n_1 + 1)}{2} - \Sigma R_1 \\ n_1 n_2 + \dfrac{n_2(n_2 + 1)}{2} - \Sigma R_2 \end{array} \right]$$

$$U(10, 11) = \text{Smaller of} \left[\begin{array}{c} (10)(11) + \dfrac{10(10 + 1)}{2} - 146.5 = 18.5 \\ (10)(11) + \dfrac{11(11 + 1)}{2} - 84.5 = 91.5 \end{array} \right] = 18.5$$

To be significant at α level of significance, the computed $U(10, 11)$ must be less than or equal to the critical value $U_{\alpha/2;n_1, n_2}$ in Appendix Table D.12. This value is $U_{.05/2;10,11} = 26$. Because $U(10, 11) = 18.5$ is less than $U_{.05/2;10,11} = 26$, the null hypothesis is rejected.

are not identical. Inspection of the data indicates that the girls who watched a television program containing aggression engaged in more aggressive acts than those who didn't.

The Mann-Whitney U test also can be used to test directional hypotheses if the population distributions are symmetrical. The test statistic U is computed as before. However, U must be less than or equal to the one-tailed critical value from Appendix Table D.12. In addition, the relative position of the sample distributions must be consistent with the alternative hypothesis. For example, if the alternative hypothesis states that the population distribution for the experimental group is displaced (shifted) above that for the control group, the sample distributions must exhibit a similar displacement.

Computational Procedures When One or Both *n*'s Exceed 20

Table D.12 in Appendix D provides critical values of U for n_1 and n_2 from 3 to 20. When either of the samples contains more than 20 scores, a z statistic that is approximately normally distributed can be used. The approximate procedure is satisfactory if both n's are greater than 10. The z test statistic is

$$z = \frac{(U + c) - E(U)}{\sigma_U} = \frac{(U + c) - n_1 n_2 / 2}{\sqrt{(n_1 n_2)(n_1 + n_2 + 1)/12}},$$

where U is defined in Table 17.2-1 and n_1 and n_2 are the two sample sizes. The c term in the formula is a correction for continuity and is equal to 0.5. The decision rule for the z test is as follows: Reject the null hypothesis if z falls in the critical region of the normal distribution; otherwise, don't reject the null hypothesis. Because of the way U is defined, the computed value of z will always be negative, regardless of whether the test is one-tailed or two-tailed. To be significant, the absolute value of the z test statistic must be greater than or equal to $z_{\alpha/2}$ for a two-tailed test or greater than or equal to z_α for a one-tailed test.

As noted earlier, if two or more observations have the same value (tied scores), they are assigned the mean of the ranks they would have occupied. The denominator, σ_U, of the z statistic can be corrected for ties; the corrected formula is

$$\sigma_U = \sqrt{\frac{(n_1 n_2)(n_1 + n_2 + 1)}{12} \left[1 - \frac{\Sigma(t_i^3 - t_i)}{(n_1 + n_2)^3 - (n_1 + n_2)}\right]},$$

where t_i is the number of tied observations in a particular set. The term $(t_i^3 - t_i)$ is computed for each set and then is summed for the sets. In Table 17.2-1, there is one set of two tied scores. The two tied scores are 13 and 13. For this set, $t_i^3 - t_i = 2^3 - 2 = 6$. If $n_1 + n_2$ is large and the number of ties is small, the correction can be ignored.

The computation of the z statistic will be shown using the data in Table 17.2-1.

The test statistic is

$$z = \frac{(U + c) - n_1 n_2/2}{\sqrt{\frac{(n_1 n_2)(n_1 + n_2 + 1)}{12}\left[1 - \frac{\Sigma(t_i^3 - t_i)}{(n_1 + n_2)^3 - (n_1 + n_2)}\right]}}$$

$$= \frac{(18.5 + 0.5) - (10)(11)/2}{\sqrt{\frac{(10)(11)(10 + 11 + 1)}{12}\left[1 - \frac{2^3 - 2}{(10 + 11)^3 - (10 + 11)}\right]}}$$

$$= \frac{-36.00}{\sqrt{201.667(0.999)}} = -2.54.$$

The critical value of z for a two-tailed test at the $\alpha = .05$ level of significance is $z_{.05/2} = 1.96$. Because the absolute value of the computed test statistic, $|z| = 2.54$, is greater than the critical value, $z_{.05/2} = 1.96$, the null hypothesis is rejected. The absolute value of the z test statistic is large enough to be significant at the .02 level. A similar conclusion would be reached using the small-sample exact test procedure. As expected, the correction for ties, which is $\sqrt{0.999}$, had virtually no effect on the test.

Earlier, we mentioned that assumption-freer tests tend to be less efficient than parametric tests when the assumptions of the parametric tests are fulfilled. Several statistics can be used to compare the relative efficiency of two tests. A simple relative index called *power efficiency* is described next.

Measures of Relative Efficiency

We saw in Section 10.4 that power is determined by four factors: (1) level of significance, (2) sample size, (3) population dispersion, and (4) magnitude of the difference between the true and hypothesized parameters. Furthermore, any desired power can be achieved for a given significance level and true alternative hypothesis by obtaining a sufficiently large sample. If one test statistic requires a smaller sample size to achieve a desired power than does another statistic, it is said to be more efficient.

One index for comparing the efficiency of two test statistics when both are used to test the same null hypothesis at α significance level against the same alternative hypothesis is called **power efficiency.** It is given by

$$Power\ efficiency = \frac{100(n_S)}{n_L},$$

where n_L is the sample size required by test L to equal the power of the more efficient test S, based on n_S observations.

Suppose, for example, that test S requires 40 participants to reject the null hypothesis in favor of the alternative hypothesis at α significance level with power equal to .90, and that test L requires 80 participants. The power efficiency, PE, of test L relative to S is

$$\text{PE} = \frac{100(40)}{80} = 50\%.$$

The PE index has a drawback. Its value is determined by the particular values of α, power, H_0, H_1, and the sample size of the more efficient comparison test statistic. Statisticians prefer another index called **asymptotic relative efficiency,** or ARE, that doesn't depend on qualifying conditions that vary from one situation to the next. A description of the index is beyond the scope of this book. It turns out that when the two indexes, PE and ARE, are used to rank order various test statistics in terms of efficiency, the results are almost identical.

Relative Efficiency of the Mann-Whitney U Test

In general, when the assumptions of parametric tests are met, they are more efficient than assumption-freer tests. This is true for the two-sample t test for independent samples when compared with the Mann-Whitney U test. The two provide tests of the same hypothesis if observations are randomly sampled from a normal population because in that case, the population mean is equal to the population median. The efficiency of the U test relative to that of the t test is 95.5%. When the distribution assumptions of the t test are violated, the relative efficiency of the U test can exceed that for t. Thus, the U test is an excellent alternative to the t test. It has two important advantages: It is applicable to ranked data and it assumes only random assignment or random sampling from continuous populations.

CHECK YOUR UNDERSTANDING OF SECTIONS 17.1 AND 17.2

1. Compare the assumptions of the Mann-Whitney U test with those for the two-sample t test for independent samples. What are the relative merits of the tests?
2. The effect of administering a noxious stimulus (an electric shock) at random intervals on the exploratory behavior of gerbils during infancy was investigated. Animals were randomly assigned to the experimental condition (shock) or the control condition (nonshock). The dependent variable (duration in minutes of exploratory behavior during one day) was measured when the animals were six months old. For the data in the table, test the hypothesis that the experimental and control populations are identical. Let $\alpha = .05$.

Control Group				Experimental Group		
40	42	25	30	32	26	30
33	31	34		16	24	20

3. The effect on motor skill development of playing with educational toys for six months was investigated. The participants were 4- and 5-year-olds. Half of the participants were randomly assigned to the play group; the remaining half didn't play with the toys. For the following data, test the hypothesis that the two populations are identical. Let $\alpha = .01$. Perform the test with and without a correction for ties.

Motor Skill Scores for Play Group				Motor Skill Scores for Control Group			
28	22	19	15	27	18	17	13
26	21	18	14	25	18	17	10
25	20	18	12	23	18	16	8
24	19	17	11	21	17	16	7
23	19	16	9	20	17	16	6

4. What are the qualifying conditions associated with the PE index?
5. Under what conditions can the z test be used instead of the U test?
6. Suppose that the two-sample t test required 82 participants to reject the nondirectional null hypothesis at the .01 level of significance with power equal to .80, and the Mann-Whitney U test required 86 participants. (a) What is the PE of the Mann-Whitney test? (b) What are the qualifying conditions associated with your estimate?
7. Terms to remember
   a. Nonparametric tests
   b. Distribution-free tests
   c. Assumption-freer tests
   d. Power efficiency
   e. Asymptotic relative efficiency

17.3 WILCOXON T TEST FOR DEPENDENT SAMPLES

The Wilcoxon matched-pairs signed-ranks test is used to test the hypothesis that two population distributions are identical. It is appropriate for dependent samples. Such samples can result from (1) obtaining repeated measures on the same participants, (2) using participants matched on a variable that is known to be correlated with the dependent variable, (3) using identical twins or littermates, or (4) obtaining pairs of participants who are matched by mutual selection.[4] The Wilcoxon test assumes that the populations are continuous and that a random sample of paired elements has been obtained or that the paired elements have been randomly assigned to the conditions. Its efficiency relative to that of the two-sample *t* test for dependent samples is 95.5% when the latter test's assumptions are met. When the *t* test's assumptions are not met, Wilcoxon's relative efficiency can equal or exceed that for the *t* test. Thus, Wilcoxon's test is an excellent alternative to the *t* test for dependent samples.

The Wilcoxon test statistic, denoted by *T*, is based on the rank of the absolute difference between paired observations rather than on the numerical value of the difference. Consequently, the test is appropriate for observations that represent ordinal information.

Computational Procedure for Small Samples

The computational procedure described here for the Wilcoxon *T* statistic can be used when the sample contains 50 or fewer pairs of scores. When the sample contains more than 50 pairs of scores, a *z* statistic described later can be used.

Suppose that a test of assertiveness was administered to female college students and the scores were used to form 16 pairs of women matched on assertiveness. One woman in each pair was randomly assigned to participate in an assertiveness-training group; the other member of the pair participated in a psychology seminar, the control condition. It was hypothesized that women in the assertiveness-training group would become more assertive relative to those in the control group. The statistical hypotheses are as follows:

H_0: The population distributions of assertiveness scores are identical for the two groups.

H_1: The population distribution of scores for women in the training group is displaced (shifted) above that for the control group.

The alternative hypothesis calls for a one-tailed test in which the sample distribution for the training group is displaced above that for the control group. The .05 level of significance is adopted. The data are given in Table 17.3-1, along with the computational procedures.

The computations in Table 17.3-1 for Wilcoxon's *T* test are easy to perform. First, the magnitude of the difference between each pair of observations is determined (see column 4). These differences are rank ordered in column 5 in terms of their absolute size; that is, their signs are ignored. The smallest difference receives a rank of 1; the largest, a rank of *n*. Finally, two columns, 6 and 7, containing the ranks, respectively, for the positive and negative differences are formed. The test

---

[4] Procedures for obtaining dependent samples are discussed in Section 12.5.

TABLE 17.3-1.   Computational Procedure for Wilcoxon *T* Test

(i) Data ($n = 16$ pairs of women matched on assertiveness were formed. The women in each matched pair were randomly assigned to the training and control groups.)

(1) Pair	(2) Training Group	(3) Control Group	(4) Difference	(5) Rank of Difference, Ignoring Sign	(6) Rank Associated with Positive Difference, R_+	(7) Rank Associated with Negative Difference, R_-
1	34	32	2	6.5	6.5	
2	36	26	10	16.0	16.0	
3	31	28	3	8.5	8.5	
4	42	41	1	4.0	4.0	
5	47	47	0	1.5		-1.5^a
6	32	33	−1	4.0		−4.0
7	33	29	4	10.0	10.0	
8	39	41	−2	6.5		−6.5
9	31	26	5	11.0	11.0	
10	34	28	6	12.0	12.0	
11	32	29	3	8.5	8.5	
12	41	41	0	1.5	1.5	
13	35	28	7	13.0	13.0	
14	45	44	1	4.0	4.0	
15	31	23	8	14.0	14.0	
16	33	24	9	15.0	15.0	
	$\sum X_T = 576$	$\sum X_C = 520$			$\sum R_+ = 124.0$	$|\sum R_-| = 12.0$

(ii) Computational check

$$\sum R_+ + |\sum R_-| = \frac{n(n + 1)}{2}$$

$$124 + 12 = \frac{16(16 + 1)}{2} = 136$$

(iii) Test statistic

$$T(16) = (\text{Smaller of } \sum R_+ \text{ and } |\sum R_-|) = 12.0$$

To be significant at α level of significance, the computed $T(16)$ must be less than or equal to the one-tailed critical value, $T_{.05,16}$, in Appendix Table D.13 and the training group must be displaced above the control group. Because $T(16) = 12.0 < T_{.05,16} = 36$ and the training group is displaced above the control group, the null hypothesis is rejected.

^{a} See text for explanation of why this zero difference is assigned a negative sign.

statistic T is the smaller of the sum of the positive ranks and the absolute value of the sum of the negative ranks.

The presence of zero differences requires a computational adjustment. If the number of zero differences is even, each zero difference is assigned the average rank for the set, and then half are arbitrarily given a positive sign and half, a negative sign. If an odd number of zero differences occurs, one randomly selected difference is discarded, and the procedure for an even number of zero differences is followed. When a score is discarded, the sample size, n, is reduced by one.

To be significant, the computed $T(n)$ for the data in Table 17.3-1 must be *less than* or *equal to* the one-tailed critical value $T_{\alpha,n}$ in Appendix Table D.13, and the training group must be displaced above the control group. Inspection of the data indicates that the latter condition is satisfied. The computed value of the Wilcoxon statistic in Table 17.3-1, $T(16) = 12$, is less than the critical value, $T_{.05,16} = 35$. Hence, we can conclude that the two populations are not identical; the training group is displaced above the control group.

Computational Procedures When n Is Greater Than 50

Table D.13 in Appendix D provides critical values of Wilcoxon's T for n from 5 to 50. When the sample n is greater than 50, a z statistic that is approximately normally distributed can be used. The approximate procedure is satisfactory for n's as small as 10. The z statistic is

$$z = \frac{(T + c) - E(T)}{\sigma_T} = \frac{(T + c) - n(n + 1)/4}{\sqrt{n(n + 1)(2n + 1)/24}},$$

where T is defined in Table 17.3-1 and n is the number of pairs of scores. The c term in the formula is a correction for continuity and is equal to 0.5. The decision rule for the z test is as follows: Reject the null hypothesis if the absolute value of z is greater than or equal to z_α; otherwise, don't reject the hypothesis. Because of the way T is defined, the computed value of z will always be negative, whether the test is one-tailed or two-tailed.

If two or more ranks have the same value, they are assigned the mean of the ranks they would have occupied. The denominator σ_T of the z statistic can be corrected for ties; the formula with the correction is

$$\sigma_T = \sqrt{\frac{n(n + 1)(2n + 1)}{24} - \frac{\Sigma(t_i^3 - t)}{48}},$$

where t_i is the number of tied observations in a particular set. The term $(t_i^3 - t_i)$ is computed for each set and then summed for the sets. If n is large and the number of ties is small, the correction can be ignored.

The z test will be illustrated using the data in Table 17.3-1. The procedure provides a satisfactory approximation when n is greater than or equal to 10. The test statistic is

$$z = \frac{(T + c) - n(n + 1)/4}{\sqrt{\dfrac{n(n + 1)(2n + 1)}{24} - \dfrac{\Sigma(t_i^3 - t)}{48}}}$$

$$z = \frac{(12 + 0.5) - \dfrac{16(16 + 1)}{4}}{\sqrt{\dfrac{16(16 + 1)[(2)(16) + 1]}{24} - \dfrac{(2^3 - 2) + (2^3 - 2) + (2^3 - 2)}{48}}}$$

$$= \frac{- 55.5}{\sqrt{374 - 0.375}} = - 2.87.$$

The critical value of z for a one-tailed test at $\alpha = .05$ level of significance is 1.645. Because $|z| = 2.87$ is greater than $z_{.05} = 1.645$ and the training group is displaced above the control group, the null hypothesis is rejected. The absolute value of the z test statistic is large enough to be significant at the .003 level. The table of critical values for T doesn't have significance levels beyond .005, but the computed T is small enough to have been significant at this level.

CHECK YOUR UNDERSTANDING OF SECTION 17.3

8. The effect on one's sense of well-being of participating in a transactional analysis group was investigated. Participants completed a questionnaire before and after participating in the group. For the data in the table, test the hypothesis that the two populations are identical. Let $\alpha = .05$. The higher the score, the higher the individual's sense of well-being.

Participant	Score Before Participation	Score After Participation	Participant	Score Before Participation	Score After Participation
1	50	56	8	36	40
2	46	50	9	35	34
3	45	50	10	35	34
4	43	48	11	34	34
5	40	44	12	34	32
6	37	40	13	33	33
7	36	38	14	31	31

9. The absolute threshold for a 1000-Hertz tone was investigated under the effects of a hallucinogen, hashish, and a placebo. The order of administration of the conditions was randomized independently for each participant. For the data in the table, test the hypothesis that

the two populations are identical versus the alternative that the placebo population is displaced above the hallucinogen population. Let $\alpha = .05$. Scores are dB re. 0.0002 dyne/cm².

Participant	Hashish	Placebo	Participant	Hashish	Placebo
1	4	6	9	0	0
2	0	0	10	5	8
3	1	1	11	−1	−2
4	0	−1	12	6	7
5	0	1	13	2	2
6	1	2	14	1	1
7	3	3	15	4	5
8	−1	0	16	2	4

10. It has been claimed that college students' grades improve following marriage. To test the hypothesis, the variables of college aptitude, gender, and size of high school attended were used to form matched pairs of students: One student of a pair had been married for at least two semesters, and the other was unmarried. For the data in the table, test the hypothesis that the populations are identical versus the alternative that the married population is displaced above the unmarried population. Use the z statistic to analyze the data. Let $\alpha = .05$. Don't use the correction for ties.

Pair	Married	Unmarried	Pair	Married	Unmarried
1	3.7	3.8	19	3.1	3.1
2	3.4	3.2	20	3.8	3.6
3	2.9	3.1	21	3.6	3.3
4	2.9	2.7	22	3.6	3.8
5	3.0	2.8	23	3.5	3.1
6	2.2	2.3	24	3.1	3.0
7	3.1	2.7	25	2.8	2.9
8	3.2	2.7	26	2.6	2.8
9	3.4	3.4	27	2.5	2.3
10	3.5	3.4	28	3.6	3.4
11	3.3	2.6	29	3.5	3.0
12	2.7	3.1	30	3.4	3.5
13	3.2	3.1	31	3.3	3.6
14	1.8	2.3	32	3.2	3.0
15	3.4	3.0	33	3.5	2.2
16	3.9	3.4	34	3.4	2.6
17	3.3	3.2	35	2.0	2.4
18	3.2	2.6			

11. Use the z statistic to analyze the data in Exercise 9. Use the correction for ties. Let $\alpha = .05$.

12. Suppose the two-sample t test required 122 participants to reject the nondirectional null hypothesis at the .01 level of significance with power equal to .95, and the Wilcoxon T test required 128 participants. (a) What is the PE of the Wilcoxon test? (b) What are the qualifying conditions associated with your estimate?

17.4 COMPARISON OF PARAMETRIC TESTS AND ASSUMPTION-FREER TESTS FOR RANKED DATA

When assumption-freer tests first appeared, they were regarded as no more than quick and dirty substitutes for parametric tests because their power efficiency was thought to be inferior. Now we have a clearer understanding of the differences between the two kinds of tests, which mainly involve (1) their assumptions, (2) the level of mathematics necessary to understand their rationale, (3) their computational simplicity, and (4) the nature of the hypothesis they test. These differences will now be examined.

Most parametric test statistics assume that (1) population elements are randomly sampled or that the elements are randomly assigned to experimental conditions, (2) the population is normally distributed, and (3) the null hypothesis is true. Of course, the null hypothesis is advanced provisionally in the hope that it can be rejected. A fourth assumption is required by some test statistics if the null hypothesis concerns two or more populations—that the population variances are equal.

Assumption-freer test statistics make fewer assumptions and hence can be used in situations for which parametric methods are not appropriate. Most assumption-freer procedures assume that (1) the population elements are randomly sampled or that the elements are randomly assigned to experimental conditions, (2) the sampled population is continuous, which implies that no two population elements have the same value (that is, no tied values)[5], and (3) the null hypothesis is true. It is relatively easy to determine whether the assumptions of assumption-freer tests are satisfied. For example, a sampling procedure is under a researcher's control—the researcher knows whether it is random. And one can decide on logical grounds whether or not the population is continuous.

On the other hand, the parametric assumptions of normality and equal variances are more difficult to check, because in any practical situation the population is not available for examination. Statistical tests can be applied to sample data to test these assumptions. However, for the small samples typically used in the behavioral

---

[5] This follows because the probability of randomly drawing the same value twice in a finite sample from a continuous population is 0. However, even if the population is continuous, the same sample value may occur more than once because the measuring instrument is calibrated in discrete units.

sciences, health sciences, and education, the tests may lack the power necessary to detect departures from normality and equal variances.

If all the assumptions of parametric tests are met, these tests are more efficient than or as efficient as their assumption-freer counterparts. If, however, the assumptions of parametric tests aren't met, they do not provide as precise control of the probability of making a type I error as do assumption-freer tests. When their assumptions aren't met, parametric tests are only approximate and the probability of making a type I error can be considerably larger than α. Fortunately, some parametric tests are relatively insensitive to violation of some of their assumptions.[6] Nevertheless, one may prefer to use an assumption-freer test for which the probability of making a type I error is known rather than relying on an inexact parametric test.

The second major way in which parametric and assumption-freer tests differ is in the level of mathematics necessary to understand their rationale. The derivation of parametric tests involves mathematics beyond the training of most researchers in the behavioral sciences and education. Many assumption-freer tests, however, can be derived using high-school algebra and elementary probability and counting rules. This is a real plus because most researchers want to understand the rationale for the procedures they use rather than having to accept their validity and appropriateness on faith.

Third, assumption-freer tests differ from parametric tests in being easier to apply. For example, the chi-square tests discussed in Chapter 16 use the simplest kind of measurement—counting the number of observations in categories—and a test statistic that is easy to compute. The tests in the present chapter also use a simple measuring procedure—ranking—and statistics that are easy to compute.

The fourth difference is in the nature of the hypothesis tested. Two-sample parametric procedures, for example, test hypotheses about particular population parameters; most assumption-freer methods test hypotheses about equality of population distributions. As we have seen, populations can differ in a number of ways, such as central tendency, dispersion, skewness, and kurtosis. To test the null hypothesis $\mu_1 - \mu_2 = 0$ using a t statistic, one must assume that the populations have equal variances and are symmetrical and mesokurtic. Thus, to test a hypothesis about one population parameter, we must be willing to make assumptions about other parameters. Assumption-freer tests don't require such assumptions and, accordingly, are much less specific in what they tell us.

†17.5 PRINTOUTS FOR THREE MICROCOMPUTER PACKAGES

JMP

JMP was used to perform a Mann-Whitney U test for the aggressive-behavior data in Table 17.2-1. As noted in footnote 2, the test is known by different names be-

---

[6] This point is discussed in Sections 11.2, 11.3, 12.4, 13.1, 14.4, and 15.3.

† This and similarly marked sections can be omitted without loss of continuity.

Mann-Whitney		
2 Cols	N ☐ Group	C ☐ Score
21 Rows		
1	E	2
2	E	19
3	E	13
4	E	9
5	E	17
6	E	18
7	E	24
8	E	15
9	E	22
10	E	21
11	C	8
12	C	1
0 \ 0 Selected		

Figure 17.5-1. **Portion of the JMP data table for the aggressive-behavior data in Table 17.2-1. The data type for Group was changed from the default of numeric to "character" and the modeling type to "nominal." The letters E and C denote, respectively, girls assigned to the experimental and control conditions.**

cause it was independently developed by different researchers. JMP refers to the test as the *Wilcoxon rank sum test* after Frank Wilcoxon, who originally developed the test in 1945. A portion of the aggressive-behavior data from Table 17.2-1 is shown in the JMP data table in Figure 17.5-1. The girls assigned to the experimental group are denoted by the letter E; those in the control group, by the letter C. The Wilcoxon rank sum test can be thought of as an assumption-freer analogue of the independent samples *t* test. For this reason, JMP uses the series of commands for the independent samples *t* test to obtain the Wilcoxon rank sum test. The selection of the **Analysis** command in the menu bar followed by the pull-down command **Fit Y by X** brought up a dialog box in which **Group** was identified as the **X** variable and **Score** as the **Y** variable. Clicking on OK produced the display in Figure 17.5-2. The **Analysis** ▶ button at the bottom of the figure provided access to an option called **Nonpar-Wilcoxon** that produced the output shown in Figure 17.5-3.

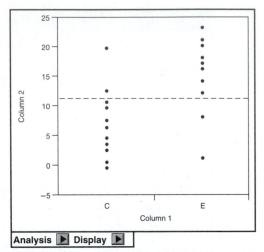

Figure 17.5-2.   **The aggressive-behavior scores for the girls assigned to the control, C, and experimental, E, conditions are represented by dots. The Analysis ▶ button was used to access the pull-down command Nonpar-Wilcoxon that produced the output in Figure 17.5-3.**

Wilcoxon / Kruskal-Wallis Tests (Rank Sums)				
Level	**Count**	**Score Sum**	**Score Mean**	**(Mean-Mean0)/Std0**
C	11	84.5	7.6818	−2.536
E	10	146.5	14.6500	2.536

2-Sample Test, Normal Approximation

S	**Z**	**Prob>|Z|**
146.5	2.53587	0.0112

1-way Test, Chi-Square Approximation

ChiSquare	**DF**	**Prob>ChiSq**
6.6105	1	0.0101

Figure 17.5-3.   **JMP output for the aggressive-behavior data in Figure 17.5-1. The Score Sum corresponds to $\Sigma R_2 = 84.5$ and $\Sigma R_1 = 146.5$ in Table 17.2-1. The value of U can be computed from**

$$U = n_1 n_2 + \frac{n_1(n_1 + 1)}{2} - \Sigma R_1 = (10)(11) + \frac{10(10 + 1)}{2} - 146.5 = 18.5.$$

If both n's (count) are 10 or less, the exact U test should be used. If both n's are greater than 10, the two-tailed z statistic, 2.53587, and associated p-value, .0112, are sufficiently accurate. The z statistic provided a normal distribution approximation to the exact p-value. The Kruskal-Wallis statistic, 6.6105, with 1 degree of freedom, yielded a p-value of 0.0101. The Kruskal-Wallis statistic is approximately distributed as chi-square and is appropriate for two or more independent samples. It can be regarded as an extension of the Wilcoxon rank-sum test (Mann-Whitney test).

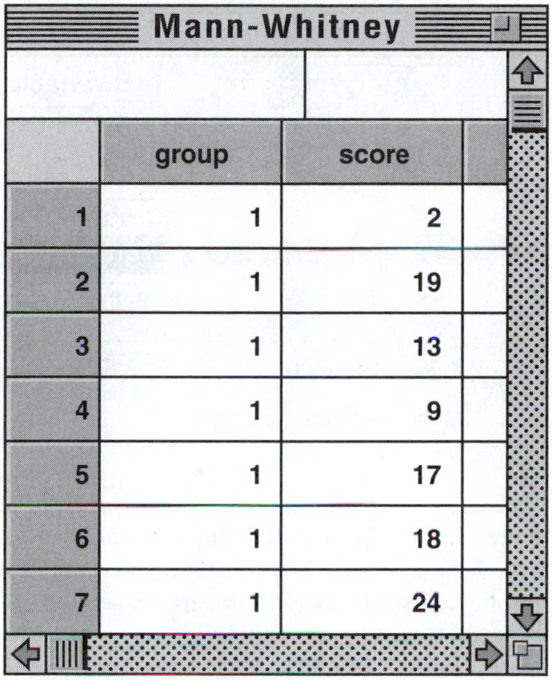

	group	score	
1	1	2	
2	1	19	
3	1	13	
4	1	9	
5	1	17	
6	1	18	
7	1	24	

Figure 17.5-4. **Portion of the SPSS data table for the aggressive-behavior data in Table 17.2-1. The numbers 1 and 2 were used to identify the experimental and control groups, respectively.**

If the **Group** variable in Figure 17.5-1 had had more than two categories, JMP would have produced a Kruskal Wallis test, which is an assumption-freer analog of a completely randomized analysis of variance design.

SPSS

SPSS was used to compute a Mann-Whitney U statistic for the aggressive-behavior data in Table 17.2-1. The data were entered in a SPSS data table like that in Figure 17.5-4. The selection of the **Statistics** command in the menu bar followed by the pull-down command called **Nonparametric Tests** and the selection of **2 Independent-Samples . . .** brought up the dialog box in Figure 17.5-5 in which **Score** was identified as the test variable and **Group** was identified as the

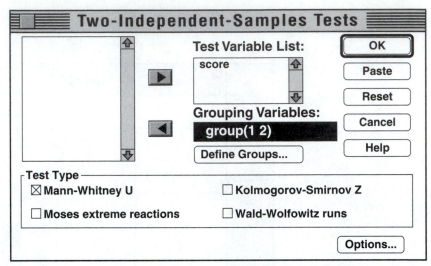

Figure 17.5-5.   **The SPSS dialog box was used to identify `Score` as the test variable and `Group` as the grouping variable. The `Define Groups ...` button was used to identify the groups as 1 and 2. Clicking on** `OK` **produced the output in Table 17.5-6.**

```
-------- Mann-Whitney U – Wilcoxon Rank Sum W Test

     SCORE
by GROUP



   Mean Rank    Cases

      14.65       10     GROUP = 1
       7.68       11     GROUP = 2
                  --
                  21     Total

                                    Exact     Corrected for ties
        U              W         2-Tailed P     Z      2-tailed P
       18.5          146.5         .0079     −2.5711     .0101
```

Figure 17.5-6.   **The SPSS output contains the Mann-Whitney U statistic, Wilcoxon rank-sum W statistic (which corresponds to $\Sigma R_1 = 146.5$ in Table 17.2-1), exact two-tailed p-value, and two-tailed z statistic, which provided a normal distribution approximation to the exact p-value.**

grouping variable. Then the **Define Groups . . .** button was selected and the groups were identified as **1** and **2**. The SPSS output is shown in Figure 17.5-6.

SYSTAT

SYSTAT was used to compute the Kruskal-Wallis statistic for the aggressive-behavior data in Table 17.2-1. As mentioned earlier, the Kruskal-Wallis test is an assumption-freer analog of a completely randomized analysis of variance design for *k* independent samples. When there are only two samples, the Kruskal-Wallis test is equivalent to the Mann-Whitney *U* test. The aggressive-behavior data were entered in a SYSTAT data table like that in Figure 17.5-7. The $ sign after the word GROUP indicates that this is a character variable. The two values of the character variable are E for experimental group and C for control group. The dialog box in Figure 17.5-8 was obtained by selecting the **Stats** command in the menu bar followed by the pull-down command called **Npar** and selecting **Kruskal-Wallis . . . .** **SCORE** was identified as the dependent variable and **GROUP$** was identified as the grouping variable. Clicking on **OK** produced the SYSTAT output in Figure 17.5-9.

	GROUP$	SCORE
SYSTAT Data Editor		
1	E	2.0000
2	E	19.0000
3	E	13.0000
4	E	9.0000
5	E	17.0000
6	E	18.0000
7	E	24.0000
8	E	15.0000
9	E	22.0000
10	E	21.0000
11	C	8.0000
12	C	1.0000

Figure 17.5-7. **Portion of the SYSTAT data table. The letters E and C denote, respectively, the experimental and control groups. The $ sign after GROUP identifies this as a character variable.**

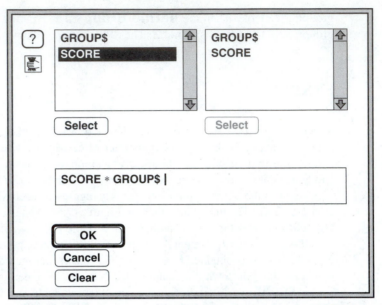

Figure 17.5-8.   **The SYSTAT dialog box was used to identify SCORE in the left box as the dependent variable and Group\$ in the right box as the grouping variable.**

```
KRUSKAL-WALLIS ONE-WAY ANALYSIS OF VARIANCE FOR  21  CASES
   DEPENDENT VARIABLE IS     SCORE
   GROUPING VARIABLE IS      GROUP$

   GROUP       COUNT     RANK SUM

E                10        146.5000
C                11         84.5000


MANN-WHITNEY U TEST STATISTIC =        91.5000
PROBABILITY IS           0.0101
CHI-SQUARE APPROXIMATION =          6.6105  WITH  1 DF
```

Figure 17.5-9.   **SYSTAT used the Kruskal-Wallis statistic to obtain the values of $\Sigma R_1 = 146.5$ and $\Sigma R_2 = 84.5$ for the aggressive-behavior data in Table 17.5-7. The Kruskal-Wallis statistic is approximately distributed as the chi-square distribution with $k - 1$ degrees of freedom, where k is the number of independent categories for GROUP. The Mann-Whitney U statistic with two independent categories can be considered a special case of the Kruskal-Wallis statistic. SYSTAT defines U as the larger of**

$$n_1 n_2 + \frac{n_1(n_1 + 1)}{2} - \Sigma R_1 = 18.5 \text{ and } n_1 n_2 + \frac{n_2(n_2 + 1)}{2} - \Sigma R_2 = 91.5.$$

17.6   SUMMARY

Test statistics are often classified according to whether they are parametric, non-parametric, or distribution-free. The classification scheme is not entirely satisfactory because some tests fall into more than one category. A test is parametric if it tests a hypothesis concerning one of the parameters of the sampled population and if it requires stringent assumptions regarding the shape of the sampled population; if not, it is nonparametric. A test is distribution-free if it makes no assumptions about the shape of the sampled population. The Mann-Whitney U test and the Wilcoxon T test can be classified as distribution-free and nonparametric because they don't require assumptions about the shape of the sampled population nor do they test hypotheses about parameters of the sampled population. Certainly, a classification scheme is less useful if its categories are not mutually exclusive. Even the parametric-distribution-free distinction becomes blurred under some conditions. For example, many parametric tests that assume that the sampled population is normally distributed are approximately distribution-free for very large samples. Little is gained by trying to distinguish between nonparametric and distribution-free tests; it is more useful to label the two categories collectively as assumption freer.

The Mann-Whitney U test is used to test the hypothesis that two population distributions are identical. It is an excellent alternative to the two-sample t test for independent samples because its relative efficiency is 95.5%. The Wilcoxon T test often is used in place of the two-sample t test for dependent samples when the assumptions of the latter aren't tenable. Although it involves less stringent assumptions, Wilcoxon's T is nearly as efficient as the two-sample t—its relative efficiency is 95.5%. Like the U test, it tests the hypothesis that two population distributions are identical.

The major differences between assumption-freer and parametric tests can be summarized as follows: The assumption-freer methods based on ranks (1) require less stringent assumptions, (2) involve assumptions that are easier to verify, (3) are usually less powerful when the assumptions of corresponding parametric tests are satisfied, (4) are easier to compute, (5) require simpler mathematical procedures for their derivation and understanding, (6) usually test hypotheses about population distributions instead of parameters, and (7) utilize information regarding rank order instead of the numerical value of individual observations.

REVIEW EXERCISES FOR CHAPTER 17

1. Recognizing that in practice the distinction between nonparametric and distribution-free tests is often blurred, indicate the principle differences between them. How do these tests differ from parametric tests?

2. A paired-associates learning task is one in which participants are presented with stimulus-response paired items and must learn to

give the second item in each pair when the first is presented. The effect on learning of having as the stimulus item a dirty word versus a neutral word was investigated. Participants were randomly assigned to the conditions. For the recall scores listed in the table, test the hypothesis that the populations are identical. Let $\alpha = .05$.

Dirty Stimulus Item				Neutral Stimulus Item			
12	14	16	13	11	10	7	5
10	18	19		8	13	9	

3. The effect on motor skill development of playing with educational toys for six months was investigated. The participants were 8- and 9-year-olds. Half of the participants were randomly assigned to the play group; the remaining half didn't play with the toys. For the data in the table, test the hypothesis that the two populations are identical. Let $\alpha = .05$. Perform the test with and without a correction for ties.

Motor Skill Scores for Play Group				Motor Skill Scores for Control Group			
47	36	43	32	36	23	26	16
46	35	39	31	34	21	25	15
44	34	37	30	32	20	25	14
45	33	37	29	29	19	24	11
44	32	26	27	27	18	24	12
48							

4. To measure the effect of time of day on test performance, a multiple-choice general knowledge test was administered to a sample of 24 college students. Half of the students were tested at 7:30 A.M. on Saturday; the other half were tested at 4:00 P.M. on the same day. The participants were randomly assigned to the two testing times, with the restriction that the number of students assigned to each time was equal. The following data representing number of correct answers on the test were obtained. (Suggested by Hughey, Arron Wilson. [1982]. Effects of scheduling test administration on the academic performance of college students. *Psychological Reports, 50,* 1346.)

7:30 A.M. Group				4:00 P.M. Group			
90	80	89	94	88	91	85	80
90	97	92	95	96	88	86	77
93	82	87	83	84	79	81	78

a. Compute the medians for the two samples.
b. Use the Mann-Whitney U statistic to test the hypothesis that the two population medians are equal. Let $\alpha = .05$.
c. What assumption must be tenable to use the Mann-Whitney U statistic to test the hypothesis of equal medians?

5. Suppose the two-sample t test required 101 participants to reject the nondirectional null hypothesis at the .05 level of significance with power equal to .90, and the Mann-Whitney U test required 106 participants. (a) What is the PE of the Mann-Whitney test? (b) What are the qualifying conditions associated with your estimate?

6. Compare the assumptions of the Wilcoxon T test with those for the two-sample t test for dependent samples. What are the relative merits of the tests?

7. An experiment was performed to determine the effects of sustained physical activity on hand steadiness. For the data in the table, test the hypothesis that the two populations are identical. Let $\alpha = .01$.

Participant	Steadiness Before Activity	Steadiness After Activity	Participant	Steadiness Before Activity	Steadiness After Activity
1	14	12	9	13	9
2	12	11	10	11	10
3	16	13	11	14	12
4	6	6	12	13	11
5	13	14	13	9	6
6	15	10	14	11	9
7	14	10	15	13	12
8	12	12			

8. Use the z statistic to analyze the data in Exercise 7. Use the correction for ties. Let $\alpha = .01$.

9. Suppose the two-sample t test required 57 participants to reject the nondirectional null hypothesis at the .05 level of significance with power equal to .80, and the Wilcoxon T test required 60 participants. (a) What is the PE of the Wilcoxon test? (b) What are the qualifying conditions associated with your estimate?

10. Briefly describe the four major ways in which assumption-freer tests differ from parametric tests.

Appendix A

Review of Basic Mathematics

This appendix provides a brief review of selected arithmetic and algebraic concepts. You have, no doubt, been exposed to this material in the past, but chances are you have forgotten some of it. If so, this review should help refresh your memory.

The following test is designed to appraise your knowledge of basic mathematics and help you pinpoint concepts that you should review. Answers are given at the end of the test, along with references to relevant review sections.

A.1 TEST OF MATHEMATICAL SKILLS

Round the following numbers to three digits.

1. 2.576 _____   2. 100.4 _____

3. 1.645 _____   4. 2.328 _____

5. 15.35 _____   6. 16.25 _____

Perform the following basic operations.

7. $|-3| + |3|$ = _____

8. $-5 + 2$ = _____

9. $3 - 2 + 4 - 8$ = _____

10. $-6 - 3$ = _____

11. $5 - (-1)$ = _____

12. $-9 - (-4)$ = _____

13. $(-2)(-6)$ = _____

14. $10/(-2)$ = _____

15. $0/6$ = _____

16. $9/0$ = _____

17. $(a/b)(n/n)$ = _____

18. $(a/b)^2$ = _____

19. $(2/5)(3/6)$ = _____

20. $(^3/_4)/2$ = _____

21. $3/(^4/_2)$ = _____

22. 2^0 = _____

23. $(X)(X^2)$ = _____

24. $(X^2)^3$ = _____

25. 2^{-1} = $\underline{(\quad)/(\quad)}$

26. 3^{-2} = $\underline{(\quad)/(\quad)^{(\quad)}}$

27. $3^2/3^4$ = $\underline{(\quad)^{(\quad)}\quad}$

28. $3\sqrt{15}$ = $\underline{\sqrt{(\quad)}15}$

29. Factor $X^2 - 2XY + Y^2$ = _____

30. Factor $pn - p$ = _____

31. $3!$ = _____

32. $0!$ = _____

Remove the parentheses.

33. $X + (Y - Z)$ _____   34. $X - (Y + C)$ _____

35. $nS(1 - R^2)$ _____   36. $(X - Y)S + M$ _____

Solve the equations and inequalities.

37. $3X - 6 = 12$ $X =$ _____   38. $2\,a/3 = 6$ $a =$ _____

39. $X = \dfrac{a + b}{n}$ $a =$ _____   40. $z = (X - Y)/S$ $X =$ _____

41. $Y = a + bX$ $X =$ _____   42. $S = R/\sqrt{2n}$ $R =$ _____

43. $S = a\sqrt{1 - b^2}$ $b =$ _____   44. $X = [(n - 1)S]/b$ $S =$ _____

45. $2X - 1 < 3$ $X <$ _____   46. $-3 < \dfrac{16 - X}{7} < 5$ ___$< X <$___

47. $-z < \dfrac{X - M}{S} < z$ ___$< M <$___

48. $[(n - 1)S]/b \le X$ $\underline{b \ge}$ _____

A.2 ANSWERS TO TEST OF MATHEMATICAL SKILLS

The answers to the skills test follow. The numbers in parentheses refer to the review sections that discuss the principles involved.

Principles discussed in Section A.3 (Rounding Numbers)

1. 2.58 (1)   2. 100 (2)   3. 1.64 (3)
4. 2.33 (1)   5. 15.4 (3)   6. 16.2 (3)

Principles discussed in Section A.4 (Basic Operations)

7. 6 (5b, 6a)   8. -3 (6b)   9. -3 (6c)
10. -9 (7)   11. 6 (7)   12. -5 (7)
13. 12 (8)   14. -5 (8)   15. 0 (9c)
16. Undefined (9d)   17. a/b (10c-iii)   18. a^2/b^2 (10c-iv)
19. $6/30$ (10c-i)   20. $3/8$ (10d-i)   21. $6/4$ (10d-ii)
22. 1 (11d)   23. X^3 (11b-i)   24. X^6 (11b-ii)
25. $\frac{1}{2}$ or 0.5 (11c-i)   26. $1/3^2$ (11c-i)   27. 3^{-2} (11c-iv)
28. $\sqrt{9}(15)$ (12c)   29. $(X - Y)^2$ (13)   30. $p(n - 1)$ (13)
31. 6 (14a)   32. 1 (14b)

Principles discussed in Section A.5 (Order of Performing Operations)

33. $X + Y - Z$ (17a)   34. $X - Y - C$ (17b)
35. $nS - nSR^2$ (17c)   36. $XS - YS + M$ (17c)

Principles discussed in Section A.6 (Equations)

37. 6   (19c, 20, 21, 22)   38. 9   (19c, 20, 22)
39. $nX - b$ (19c, 20, 21, 22)   40. $zS + Y$ (19c, 20, 21, 22)
41. $(Y - a)/b$ (19c, 20, 21, 22) 42. $S/\sqrt{2n}$ (19c, 20, 22)
43. $\sqrt{1 - S^2/d^2}$ (19c, 20, 21, 22)   44. $Xb/(n - 1)$ (19c, 20, 22)

Principles discussed in Section A.7 (Inequalities)

45. 2   (25)   46. $-19 < X < 37$ (25, 26)
47. $X - zS < M < X + zS$ (25, 26)   48. $[(n - 1)S]/X$ (25, 27)

A.3 ROUNDING NUMBERS

The number of significant digits in a number (all digits except 0 when it is used only to position the decimal point) should reflect the precision of a measurement. Therefore, numbers should be rounded to give a correct impression of the measurement precision actually achieved. Rounding involves dropping digits if they are to the right of the decimal or replacing them by 0 if they are to the left of the decimal.

1. When the digit to be dropped is greater than 5 or is a 5 with nonzero digits to the right, the digit to the left of it is increased by 1.

    Examples   246.36 rounded to four significant digits becomes 246.4
                 386 rounded to two significant digits becomes 390
                 0.0068 rounded to one significant digit becomes 0.007
                 6.51 rounded to one significant digit becomes 7

2. When the digit to be dropped is less than 5, no change is made in the digit to the left of it.

    Examples   246.31 rounded to four significant digits becomes 246.3
                 384 rounded to two significant digits becomes 380
                 0.0063 rounded to one significant digit becomes 0.006

3. When the digit to be dropped is 5 or is 5 with only zeros to the right, the digit to the left of 5 is increased by 1 if it is odd and is not changed if it is even. (Not all handheld calculators follow this convention; some always increase the digit to the left of 5.)

Examples   75 rounded to one significant digit becomes 80
935.35 rounded to four significant digits becomes 935.4
674.5 rounded to three significant digits becomes 674
912.5 rounded to three significant digits becomes 912

4. If the final result of a computation is to be rounded to s digits to the right of the decimal, at least $s + 1$ digits to the right should be retained in intermediate computational steps.

Example $(115 - 110)/(14/\sqrt{26}) = 5/(14/5.099) = 5/2.746 = 1.82$

A.4 BASIC OPERATIONS

5. Numbers
   a. A signed number, for example, 4, -2, 9, -11, indicates (1) direction and (2) size. The sign, $+$ or $-$, indicates the direction of movement away from a starting point, 0. Zero has no direction. The number part of the signed number indicates the extent or size of movement away from 0.

   Example   The size and direction of movement for -2 and 4 are shown here.

   b. The absolute value of a number, denoted by $|\ |$, indicates size but not direction. The absolute value is always positive for nonzero numbers. The general rule is

   $$|a| = \begin{cases} a \text{ if } a \geq 0 \\ -a \text{ if } a < 0. \end{cases}$$

   The second part of the rule appears contradictory but isn't. If a is less than 0, it is a negative number, and a minus sign in front of a negative number makes it positive.

   Examples $|3| = 3$; $|-3| = 3$; $|0| = 0$; $|-1.96| = 1.96$;
   $|X| = X$ if X is a positive number, and $|X| = -X$ if X is a negative number.

6. Addition
   a. Two numbers of like sign: add the absolute values of the numbers and attach the common sign to the sum.

   Examples $3 + 2 = 5$; $-3 + (-2) = -5$

b. Two numbers of unlike sign: determine the difference between their absolute values and attach the sign of the larger number.

Examples $3 + (-2) = 1$; $-3 + 2 = -1$

c. More than two numbers with unlike signs: add the absolute values of the positive numbers, as in Rule 6a, and do the same for the negative numbers; then determine the difference between their absolute values and attach the sign of the larger of the two, as in Rule 6b.

Example $3 + 2 + (-5) + (-3) + (-1) = 5 + (-9) = -4$

7. Subtraction

To subtract one number from another, change the sign of the number to be subtracted and proceed as in addition.

Examples
$$3 - (2) = \quad 3 + (-2) = \quad 1$$
$$3 - (-2) = \qquad 3 + 2 = \quad 5$$
$$-3 - (2) = -3 + (-2) = -5$$
$$-3 - (-2) = \qquad -3 + 2 = -1$$

8. Multiplication and division

Multiplying two numbers results in another number called a *product;* dividing one number by another results in another number called a *quotient.* When two numbers have like signs, their product and quotient are positive; when they have unlike signs, their product and quotient are negative.

Examples
$$(6)(3) = \quad 18 \qquad 6/3 = \quad 2$$
$$(6)(-3) = -18 \qquad 6/-3 = -2$$
$$(-6)(3) = -18 \qquad -6/3 = -2$$
$$(-6)(-3) = \quad 18 \qquad -6/-3 = \quad 2$$

9. Operations with zero

a. If 0 is added to or subtracted from any number, the result is the number itself.

Examples $3 + 0 = 3$; $9 - 0 = 9$

b. The product of 0 and any other number is equal to 0.

Examples $(3)(0) = 0$; $(2)(3)(0) = 0$

c. $0/a = 0$ for all nonzero values of a.

Examples $0/3 = 0$; $0/7 = 0$

d. The use of 0 as a divisor results in a fraction that cannot be evaluated.

Example $5/0$ is undefined.

10. Fractions
   a. A fraction, for example, 6/2 or *a*/*b*, is the result of dividing one number or expression by another. The upper part of the fraction is called the *numerator;* the lower part (the divisor) is called the *denominator.*
   b. Addition and subtraction
      i. To add or subtract fractions with the same denominator, perform the indicated operation on the numerator and leave the denominator unchanged.

$$\text{Examples}\quad \frac{a}{c} + \frac{b}{c} = \frac{a+b}{c}; \quad \frac{a}{c} - \frac{b}{c} = \frac{a-b}{c}; \quad \frac{2}{3} + \frac{4}{3} = \frac{6}{3};$$

$$\frac{2}{3} - \frac{4}{3} = \frac{-2}{3}$$

   ii. To add or subtract fractions with different denominators, find a common denominator, change all fractions accordingly, and proceed as above. Some multiple of all the original denominators is selected as the common denominator; each new numerator is formed by multiplying the original numerator by the number of times the original denominator divides into the common denominator.

$$\text{Examples}\quad \frac{a}{b} + \frac{c}{d} = \frac{ad}{bd} + \frac{bc}{bd} = \frac{ad+bc}{bd};$$

$$\frac{1}{2} + \frac{3}{4} = \frac{4}{8} + \frac{6}{8} = \frac{10}{8}$$

   iii. In general, if the same quantity is added to or subtracted from both the numerator and the denominator, the value of the fraction is changed.

$$\text{Examples}\quad \frac{a}{b} \neq \frac{a+n}{b+n} \text{ unless } a = b \text{ or } n = 0;$$

$$\frac{3}{4} \neq \frac{3+2}{4+2} = \frac{5}{6}$$

   c. Multiplication
      i. To multiply two or more fractions, multiply their numerators together and their denominators together to obtain, respectively, the numerator and the denominator of the product.

$$\text{Examples}\quad \left(\frac{a}{b}\right)\left(\frac{c}{d}\right) = \frac{ac}{bd}; \quad \left(\frac{2}{3}\right)\left(\frac{3}{4}\right) = \frac{(2)(3)}{(3)(4)} = \frac{6}{12}$$

   ii. Multiplying anything by 1 leaves its value unchanged.

$$\text{Examples}\quad \frac{a}{b}(1) = \frac{a}{b}; \quad \frac{3}{2}(1) = \frac{3}{2}$$

iii. Multiplying both the numerator and the denominator of a fraction by the same quantity other than 0 does not change its value.

$$\text{Examples} \quad \left(\frac{a}{b}\right)\left(\frac{n}{n}\right) = \frac{an}{bn} = \frac{a}{b}; \quad \left(\frac{3}{4}\right)\left(\frac{2}{2}\right) = \frac{(3)(2)}{(4)(2)} = \frac{3}{4}$$

iv. In general, squaring a fraction or taking its square root changes its value.

$$\text{Examples} \quad \frac{a}{b} \neq \left(\frac{a}{b}\right)^2 \text{ and } \frac{a}{b} \neq \frac{\sqrt{a}}{\sqrt{b}} \text{ unless } a = b;$$

$$\frac{4}{9} \neq \left(\frac{4}{9}\right)^2 = \frac{16}{81} \text{ and } \frac{4}{9} \neq \frac{\sqrt{4}}{\sqrt{9}} = \frac{2}{3}$$

d. Division

i. To divide a fraction by a quantity, multiply the denominator of the fraction by that quantity.

$$\text{Examples} \quad \frac{a/b}{c} = \frac{a}{bc}; \quad \frac{2/3}{4} = \frac{2}{(3)(4)} = \frac{2}{12}$$

ii. To divide a quantity by a fraction, invert the fraction and multiply.

$$\text{Examples} \quad \frac{a}{b/c} = a\frac{c}{b} = \frac{ac}{b}; \quad \frac{2}{3/4} = 2\left(\frac{4}{3}\right) = \frac{8}{3}$$

iii. To divide a fraction by another fraction, invert the second fraction and multiply.

$$\text{Examples} \quad \frac{a/b}{c/d} = \left(\frac{a}{b}\right)\left(\frac{d}{c}\right) = \frac{ad}{bc}; \quad \frac{2/3}{4/5} = \left(\frac{2}{3}\right)\left(\frac{5}{4}\right) = \frac{10}{12}$$

iv. Any quantity (other than 0) divided by itself equals 1.

$$\text{Examples} \quad a/a = 1 \text{ if } a \neq 0; \quad 3/3 = 1$$

v. Dividing any quantity by 1 leaves its value unchanged.

$$\text{Examples} \quad \frac{a/b}{1} = \frac{a}{b}; \quad \frac{3/2}{1} = \frac{3}{2}$$

11. Exponents

a. The number of times a number, the *base,* is multiplied by itself is denoted by a superscript, the *exponent.*

$$\text{Examples} \quad a^1 = a; a^2 = (a)(a); \quad a^3 = (a)(a)(a)$$

b. Laws of positive exponents

i. $a^n a^m = a^{n+m}$ *Example* $(2)^2(2)^3 = 2^{2+3} = 2^5$

ii. $(a^n)^m = a^{nm}$ *Example* $(2^2)^3 = 2^{(2)(3)} = 2^6$

iii. $a^n b^n = (ab)^n$ *Example* $(2)^2(4)^2 = [(2)(4)]^2 = 8^2$

c. Laws of negative exponents and mixed exponents

    i. $a^{-1} = \dfrac{1}{a}$ *Example* $2^{-1} = \dfrac{1}{2}$

       $a^{-2} = \dfrac{1}{a^2}$ *Example* $2^{-2} = \dfrac{1}{2^2}$

       $a^{-n} = \dfrac{1}{a^n}$

    ii. $(a^n)^{-1} = (a^{-1})^n = a^{(-1)(n)} = a^{-n}$

       Example $(2^3)^{-1} = 2^{(3)(-1)} = 2^{-3}$

    iii. $\left(\dfrac{a}{b}\right)^n = a^n\left(\dfrac{1}{b}\right)^n = a^n(b^{-1})^n = a^n b^{-n} = \dfrac{a^n}{b^n}$

       Example $\left(\dfrac{2}{4}\right)^2 = \dfrac{(2)^2}{(4)^2}$

    iv. $\dfrac{a^n}{b^m} = a^n a^{-m} = a^{n-m}$

       Example $\dfrac{(2)^2}{(2)^3} = 2^{2-3} = 2^{-1}$

d. A number not equal to 0 with a zero exponent, a^0, is equal to 1. This follows, because according to 11c-iv, $a^n/a^n = a^{n-n} = a^0$, and according to 10d-iv, $a^n/a^n = 1$; therefore $a^0 = 1$.

    Examples $a^0 = 1$ for $a \neq 0$; $2^0 = 1, 5^0 = 1$

e. Do not confuse exponents and coefficients. When multiplying terms with coefficients and exponents, add exponents and multiply coefficients.

    Examples $(3X^2)(2X^3) = 6X^5$; $(3X)(5X^2) = 15X^3$

12. Radicals
    a. A radical is used to indicate a specific root of a quantity, as, for example, in the expression $b = \sqrt[n]{a}$; b is said to be the nth root of a, $\sqrt{}$ is a radical sign, n is the index of the radical, and a is the radicand. If n is not specified, it is understood to equal 2, in which case $b = \sqrt{a}$ is called the square root of a.
    b. To multiply two radicals with the same index where both radicands are positive, multiply their radicands under one radical. Similarly, to divide one radical by another, divide (under one radical) the radicand of the first by the radicand of the second.

       Examples $\sqrt{a}\sqrt{b} = \sqrt{ab}$; $\sqrt{2}\sqrt{3} = \sqrt{(2)(3)}$
                   $\sqrt{a}/\sqrt{b} = \sqrt{a/b}$; $\sqrt{2}/\sqrt{3} = \sqrt{2/3}$

c. To multiply or divide a radical of the *n*th order by a number *a* not equal to 0, place the number raised to the *n*th power under the radical and multiply or divide the radicand by it.

Examples $a\sqrt{b} = \sqrt{a^2b};$ $2\sqrt{3} = \sqrt{2^2(3)};$ $2\sqrt[3]{3} = \sqrt[3]{2^3(3)}$

$$\sqrt{a/c} = \sqrt{a/c^2};   \sqrt{3/2} = \sqrt{3/2^2}$$

d. Note that the *n*th root of a sum is not equal to the sum of the respective *n*th roots.

Examples $\sqrt{a^2 + b^2} \neq \sqrt{a^2} + \sqrt{b^2};$ $\sqrt{3^2 + 4^2} = 5 \neq \sqrt{3^2} + \sqrt{4^2} = 7$

13. Factoring
Factoring an expression consists of dividing it into smaller terms or expressions that, when multiplied, will yield the original expression.

Examples $ab - a = a(b - 1);$
$a^2 - b^2 = (a + b)(a - b);$
$a^2 - 5a - 6 = (a + 1)(a - 6);$
$a^2 - 5a + 6 = (a - 2)(a - 3)$

14. Factorials
a. The product of the first *n* natural numbers (positive integers) is called *n factorial* and is denoted by *n*!, which equals $n(n - 1)(n - 2) \cdots (3)(2)(1)$.

Example $4! = 4(4 - 1)(4 - 2)(4 - 3) = (4)(3)(2)(1) = 24$

b. For $n = 0$, 0! is defined as 1.

A.5 ORDER OF PERFORMING OPERATIONS

15. The order in which numbers are added does not affect the result.

Examples $a + b = b + a;$ $2 + 3 = 3 + 2 = 5;$
$(a + b) + c = a + (b + c);$ $(2 + 3) + 5 = 2 + (3 + 5) = 10$

$a + b = b + a$ illustrates the *commutative law of addition.*
$(a + b) + c = a + (b + c)$ *illustrates the associative law of addition.*

16. The order in which numbers are multiplied does not affect the result.

Examples $ab = ba;$ $(2)(3) = (3)(2) = 6;$ $(ab)c = a(bc);$
$[(2)(3)]5 = 2[(3)(5)] = 30$

$ab = ba$ illustrates the *commutative law of multiplication.*
$(a\,b)c = a(bc)$ illustrates the *associative law of multiplication.*

17. Parentheses ( ), braces { }, brackets [ ], and the radical sign $\sqrt{}$ indicate that the enclosed expression is to be treated as a single number. The bar of a

fraction has a similar effect: the numerator and the denominator are treated as single numbers.

Examples $10(16 - 14) = 10(2) = 20;$ $(3 - 1)4.21 = (2)4.21 = 8.42;$

$$\frac{2 + 4}{3 - 1} = \frac{6}{2} = 3$$

a. When a plus sign (+) precedes parentheses, the parentheses may be removed without changing the signs of terms within the parentheses.

Examples $a + (b + c) = a + b + c;$ $2 + (3 + 5) = 2 + 3 + 5 = 10$

b. If a minus sign (−) precedes parentheses and the parentheses are removed, the sign of every term within the parentheses must be changed.

Examples $(a + b) - (c + d) = a + b - c - d;$
$2 - (3 + 5) = 2 - 3 - 5 = -6$

c. When a quantity within parentheses is to be multiplied by a number, each term within the parentheses must be so multiplied.

Examples $a(b + c) = ab + ac;$
$10(16 - 14) = 10(16) - 10(14) = 160 - 140 = 20;$

$$10\left(\frac{1}{20} + \frac{6}{24}\right) = \frac{10}{20} + \frac{60}{24} = \frac{1}{2} + \frac{5}{2} = 3$$

$a(b + c) = ab + ac$ illustrates the *distributive law.*

18. Unless specifically altered, for example by parentheses, the order for performing operations is as follows: first, exponentiation (raising a number to a power); next, multiplication and division; and last, addition and subtraction.

Examples $Mdn = 44.5 + 10\left(\dfrac{30/2 - 14}{3}\right) = 44.5 + 10\left(\dfrac{15 - 14}{3}\right)$

$$= 44.5 + 10\left(\frac{1}{3}\right) = 44.5 + 3.33 + 47.8;$$

$$S = \sqrt{\frac{10(32) - (16)^2}{(10)^2}} = \sqrt{\frac{320 - 256}{100}} = \sqrt{\frac{64}{100}} = 0.8;$$

$$F = \frac{320/(3 - 1)}{1350/[3(10) - 3]} = \frac{320/2}{1350/27} = \frac{160}{50} = 3.2$$

A.6 EQUATIONS

19. An equation is a statement asserting that what is on the left side of the equal sign is equal to what is on the right.

Examples $2 + 4 = 6$ is an example of an *arithmetic equation,* because it contains only numbers.

$2X - 5 = 7$ is an example of an *algebraic equation,* because it contains a symbol.

a. An equation in which both sides have the same numerical value or one that is true for all values of the variables employed is called an *identity.*

Examples $2 + 4 = 6$; $3a + 4a = 7a$

One that is true only when certain values are substituted for variables is called a *conditional equation.*

Examples $2X = 6$; $3X - 4 = X + 6$

b. To solve for an unknown in an algebraic equation, find the set of values (called *roots*) that, when substituted for the unknown, makes the two sides of the equation numerically equal. For $2X - 5 = 7$, the root is 6, because $2(6) - 5 = 7$—that is, $7 = 7$.

c. To find the roots of an equation, perform a series of manipulations that place the unknown alone on the left side (see Rules 20–23).

Example

$$2X - 5 = 7$$

$$2X - 5 + 5 = 7 + 5 \qquad \text{Add 5 to both sides (see Rule 21)}$$

$$\frac{2X}{2} = \frac{7 + 5}{2} \qquad \text{Divide both sides by 2 (see Rule 22)}$$

$$X = \frac{12}{2}$$

$$X = 6$$

20. An operation performed on one side of an equation must also be performed on the other. The condition of equality is not affected by
    a. Adding the same quantity to both sides
    b. Subtracting the same quantity from both sides
    c. Multiplying both sides by the same quantity
    d. Dividing both sides by the same nonzero quantity
    e. Raising both sides to the same power if both sides have the same sign
    f. Taking the same root of both sides if both sides have the same sign.

21. Any term on one side of an equation may be transposed to the other side by changing its sign. In essence, the term to be transposed is either added to or subtracted from both sides of the equation.

Example   Solving for *a*:

$$a + b = c$$

$$a + b - b = c - b$$

$$a = c - b$$

22. A quantity that multiplies one side of an equation may be transposed to divide the other side or vice versa. In essence, both sides of the equation are subjected to the same operation—either multiplication or division.

Examples   Solving for *a*:   Solving for *X*:

$$ab = c \qquad\qquad \left(\frac{X - a}{S}\right)b + c = z$$

$$\frac{ab}{b} = \frac{c}{b} \qquad\qquad \left(\frac{X - a}{S}\right)b = z - c$$

$$a = \frac{c}{b} \qquad\qquad \frac{X - a}{S} = \frac{z - c}{b}$$

$$X - a = \left(\frac{z - c}{b}\right)S$$

$$X = \left(\frac{z - c}{b}\right)S + a$$

23. When each side of an equation consists of a fraction, the fractions can be removed by cross-multiplying as follows.

Example $\dfrac{a}{b} = \dfrac{c}{d}$

$$ad = bc$$

A.7 INEQUALITIES

24. Two or more expressions connected by one of the ordering symbols $<$, $>$, $\leq$, or $\geq$ is an *inequality*.

Examples $a \leq b$; $-1.96 < t < 1.96$; $z > 2.576$

25. The solutions to an inequality are not affected by the following operations:
    a. Adding the same quantity to both sides
    b. Subtracting the same quantity from both sides
    c. Multiplying both sides by a positive quantity
    d. Dividing both sides by a positive quantity.

    Example $4X + 2 \geq 10$
    $$4X \geq 10 - 2$$
    $$X \geq 2$$

26. If both sides of an inequality are multiplied or divided by the same negative number, a new inequality is formed, with direction opposite to that of the original.

Examples $-a < b$ $-3 < 2$

$-1\,(-a < b)$ $-1\,(-3 < 2)$

$a > -b$ $3 > -2$

Find μ if $-3 \le \dfrac{2 - \mu}{5} \le 8$.

$-3(5) \le 2 - \mu \le 8(5)$ Multiply each member by 5

$-15 - 2 \le -\mu \le 40 - 2$ Subtract 2 from each member

$-1\,(-17 \le -\mu \le 38)$ Multiply by -1

$17 \ge \mu \ge -38$

$-38 \le \mu \le 17$ Rearrange terms

27. Taking the reciprocal of, or inverting, all expressions in an inequality results in a new inequality with direction opposite to that of the original.

Examples $a > b$ implies that $\dfrac{1}{a} < \dfrac{1}{b}$ if $ab > 0$;

$$a < \frac{(n-1)b}{c} < d \quad \text{implies that} \quad \frac{1}{a} > \frac{c}{(n-1)b} > \frac{1}{d}$$

$$\text{if } a \text{ times } \frac{(n-1)b}{c} > 0 \quad \text{and} \quad \frac{(n-1)b}{c} \text{ times } d > 0$$

Glossary of Symbols

MATHEMATICAL SYMBOLS

Symbol	Example	Meaning[1]
$+$	$X + Y$	X and Y are added (**A.4**)
$-$	$X - Y$	Y is subtracted from X (**A.4**)
$(\ )(\ )$, $\times$	$(X)(Y)$, $X \times Y$, or XY	X and Y are multiplied (**A.4**)
$/$, $\div$	X/Y or $X \div Y$	X is divided by Y (**A.4**)
$=$	$X = Y$	X is equal to Y (**A.6**)
$\neq$	$X \neq Y$	X is not equal to Y
$\cong$	$X \cong Y$	X is approximately equal to Y (**2.2**)
$>$	$X > Y$	X is greater than Y (**A.7**)
$\geq$	$X \geq Y$	X is greater than or equal to Y (**A.7**)
$<$	$X < Y$	X is less than Y (**A.7**)
$\leq$	$X \leq Y$	X is less than or equal to Y (**A.7**)
$<\ <$	$W < X < Y$	X is greater than W and less than Y (**A.7**)
$\leq\ \leq$	$W \leq X \leq Y$	X is greater than or equal to W and less than or equal to Y (**A.7**)
$\sum\limits_{i=1}^{n}$	$\sum\limits_{i=1}^{n} X_i$	Sum of X_i, letting i equal $1, \ldots, n$ (**3.3, 3.8**)
$\ldots$	$1, 2, 3, \ldots, 6$	Continue the pattern—that is, 1, 2, 3, 4, 5, 6 in this case
$\vert\ \ \vert$	$\vert X \vert$	Absolute value of X; for $X = 0$, $\vert X \vert = 0$, and for $X \neq 0$, $\vert X \vert$ is equal to the positive member of the couple X, $-X$ (**A.4**)
$\sqrt{\ }$	$\sqrt{X}$	Square root of X (**A.4**)
$!$	$n!$	n factorial, $n(n - 1)(n - 2) \cdots (3)(2)(1)$ (**A.4**)

GREEK LETTERS

Symbol	Meaning
α (alpha)	Significance level (**10.2**); probability of a type I error (**10.4**)
β (beta)	Probability of a type II error (**10.4**)

[1] The letter or number in parentheses refers to the section in which the symbol is discussed. The letter A denotes Appendix A.

α_j	Treatment effect for the jth population (**14.2**)
β_k	Treatment effect for the kth population (**15.3**)
$(\alpha\beta)_{jk}$	Interaction effect for the jkth population treatment combination (**15.3**)
δ_0 (delta)	Value of the difference between two population parameters specified by the null hypothesis (**12.2**)
ϵ_{ij} (epsilon)	Error effect for subject i in treatment level j (**14.2**)
η^2 (eta)	Correlation ratio (**5.6**)
θ (theta)	Population parameter (**9.3**); a caret over the symbol, $\hat{\theta}$, denotes an estimator of θ (**9.3**)
μ (mu)	Population mean (**3.3**)
$\mu_j, \mu_{j'}$	Means for populations j and j', $j \neq j'$ (**14.1, 14.5**)
μ_0	Value of the population mean specified by the null hypothesis (**9.3**)
$\mu_{\bar{X}}$	Mean of means (**9.3**)
ν (nu)	Degrees of freedom (**11.2**)
π (pi)	Ratio of the circumference of a circle to the diameter, approximately 3.1416 (**9.1**)
ρ (rho)	Pearson product-moment population correlation parameter (**5.2**)
$\sum$ (sigma)	Summation (**3.3**)
$\sum f_a$	Number of scores above the upper limit of the class interval that contains the median (**3.4**)
$\sum f_b$	Number of scores below the lower limit of the class interval that contains the median (**3.4**)
$\sum R_1$ and $\sum R_2$	Sum of ranks, respectively, for variables 1 and 2 (**17.2**)
$\sum R_+$ and $\sum R_-$	Sum, respectively, of positive and negative ranks (**17.3**)
σ (*sigma*)	Population standard deviation (**4.2**); a caret over the symbol, $\hat{\sigma}$, denotes an estimator of σ (**4.2**)
σ_r	Standard error of a correlation coefficient (**9.3**)
σ_S	Standard error of a standard deviation (**9.3**)
σ_T	Standard error of T (**17.3**)
σ_U	Standard error of U (**17.2**)
$\sigma_{\bar{X}}$	Standard error of a mean (**9.3**); a caret over the symbol, $\hat{\sigma}_{\bar{X}}$, denotes an estimator of $\sigma_{\bar{X}}$ (**11.2**)
$\hat{\sigma}_{\bar{X}_D}$	Estimator of the standard error of the mean of difference scores (**12.5**)
$\sigma_{\bar{X}_1 - \bar{X}_2}$	Standard error of the difference between means (**12.2**); a caret over the symbol, $\hat{\sigma}_{\bar{X}_1 - \bar{X}_2}$, denotes an estimator of $\sigma_{\bar{X}_1 - \bar{X}_2}$ (**12.4**)
$\hat{\sigma}_{Y \cdot X}$	Estimator of the population standard error of estimate (**6.3**)
σ^2	Population variance (**4.2**); a caret over the symbol, $\hat{\sigma}^2$, denotes an estimator of σ^2 (**4.2**)

σ_0^2	Value of the population variance specified by the null hypothesis (**11.3**)
σ_ϵ^2	Population error variance (**14.2**)
$\hat{\sigma}_{est}^2$	Estimator of the population variance (**9.5**)
$\hat{\sigma}_{Pooled}^2, \hat{\sigma}_{Pd}^2$	Weighted estimator of the population variance (**12.4**)
ϕ' (phi)	Cramér's measure of association; also denoted by V (**16.3**); a caret over the symbol, $\hat{\phi}'$, denotes an estimator of ϕ' (**16.3**)
χ^2 (chi)	Chi-square random variable (**11.3**); Pearson's chi-square random variable (**16.2**)
$\chi_{\alpha,\nu}^2$ and $\chi_{1-\alpha,\nu}^2$	Values that cut off, respectively, the upper and lower α regions of the sampling distribution of χ^2 for ν degrees of freedom (**11.3**)
ψ (psi)	Contrast among population means (**14.5**); a caret over the symbol, $\hat{\psi}$, denotes an estimator of ψ (**14.5**)
$\hat{\omega}^2$ (omega squared)	Strength of association for the ANOVA F test (**14.6**)
$\hat{\omega}_{X|A\cdot BL}^2$	Partial omega squared (**15.2**)

ENGLISH LETTERS

Letter	*Meaning*
ANOVA	Analysis of variance (**14.1**)
ARE	Asymptotic relative efficiency (**17.2**)
a_j	Level j of treatment A (**14.2**)
$a_{Y\cdot X}$	Y intercept of a line (**6.2**)
b_k	Level k of treatment B (**15.3**)
$b_{Y\cdot X}$	Sample coefficient of linear regression of Y on X (**6.2**)
b_1	Expected change in Y when X_1 changes one unit and X_2 remains constant (**6.5**); level 1 of treatment B (**15.3**)
b_2	Expected change in Y when X_2 changes one unit and X_1 remains constant (**6.5**); level 2 of treatment B (**15.3**)
C	Number of contrasts among means (**14.5**)
CR-p	Completely randomized ANOVA design (**14.3**)
CRF-pq	Completely randomized factorial ANOVA design (**15.3**)
CV	Coefficient of variation (**4.2**)
Cum f	Cumulative frequency (**2.2**)
Cum prop. f	Cumulative proportionate frequency (**2.2**)
Cum % f	Cumulative percentage frequency (**2.2**)
$_nC_r$	Combination of n objects taken r at a time (**7.4**)
c	A constant (**3.8**); number of qualitative categories (**4.2**, **16.4**); correction for continuity (**17.2**)
c_j	Coefficient of a linear contrast (**15.3**)

D	Index of dispersion (**4.2**)
DP	Number of distinguishable pairs (**4.2**)
DP_{max}	Number of distinguishable pairs when observations are equally divided among categories (**4.2**)
D_i	Difference between scores for the ith pair of elements (**12.5**)
d	Effect size (**10.4**)
df	Degrees of freedom; also denoted by ν (**11.2**)
$E(MSBG)$ and $E(MSWG)$	Expected value of $MSBG$ and $MSWG$ (**14.2**)
$E(S^2)$	Expected value of S^2 (**9.5**)
$E(T)$	Expected value of T in the Wilcoxon T statistic (**17.3**)
$E(U)$	Expected value of U in the Mann-Whitney U statistic (**17.2**)
$E(X)$	Expected value of X (**8.2**)
E_i	ith event (**7.2**); sample point for the ith event (**7.2**)
E_j	Expected frequency in the jth category (**16.2**)
$E(\hat{\theta})$	Expected value of an estimator (**9.3**)
$E(\hat{\sigma}^2)$	Expected value of $\hat{\sigma}^2$ (**9.5**)
$E(\chi_\nu^2)$	Expected value of a chi-square random variable (**11.3**)
e	Base of the system of natural logarithms, approximately 2.7183 (**9.1**); number of distribution parameters estimated (**16.2**)
e_i	Prediction error for the ith element; difference between the observed and predicted scores (**6.2**)
F	F random variable (**13.1**)
FS	Scheffé's multiple comparison test statistic (**14.5**)
$F_{\alpha;\nu_1,\nu_2}$ and $F_{1-\alpha;\nu_1,\nu_2}$	Values that cut off, respectively, the upper and lower α regions of the sampling distribution of F (**13.1**)
f_a and f_b	Number of scores, respectively, above the real upper limit of a class interval and below the real lower limit of a class interval (**3.4**)
f, f_j	Frequency of a measurement or event class (**2.2**); frequency of scores in the jth class interval (**3.3**); number of scores in the class interval containing the median (**3.4**)
f_i	Number of scores in the class interval containing a particular statistic such as the median (**3.4**)
$\%f$	Percentage frequency (**2.2**)
g	Effect size (**12.4**)
H_0	Null hypothesis (**10.1**)
H_1	Alternative hypothesis (**10.1**)
i	Class interval size (**2.2**); index of summation (**3.3**); an unspecified level of blocks (**15.2**)
j	An unspecified level of treatment A (**14.2**)
Kur	Kurtosis index (**4.6**)

k	Number of class intervals in a frequency distribution (**3.3**); an unspecified level of treatment B (**15.3**)
k^2	Coefficient of nondetermination (**5.4**)
L_1 and L_2	Lower and upper endpoints, respectively, of a confidence interval (**10.5**)
MSA, MSB	Treatment A (**15.2**) or treatment B (**15.3**) mean of squares
$MSBG$	Between-groups mean squares (**14.2**)
$MSBL$	Blocks mean squares (**15.2**)
$MSRES$	Residual mean squares (**15.2**)
$MSWCELL$	Within-cell mean squares (**15.3**)
$MSWG$	Within-groups mean squares (**14.2**)
Mdn	Sample median (**3.4**)
Mo	Sample mode (**3.2**)
n	Number of observations in a sample (**2.2**); number of trials in a binomial experiment (**8.3**)
$n!$	n factorial (**7.4**)
n_A	Number of equally likely events favoring A (**7.1**)
n_L and n_S	Sample size of tests L and S (**17.2**)
n_S	Total number of equally likely events (**7.1**)
n_{Pop}	Number of elements in a population (**11.4**)
O_j	Number of observations in the jth category (**16.2**)
PE	Power efficiency (**17.2**)
Prop f	Proportionate frequency (**2.2**)
P_R	Percentile rank (**4.2**)
$P_\%$	Percentile point (**4.2**)
$_nP_n$	Permutation of n objects taken n at a time (**7.4**)
$_nP_r$	Permutation of n objects taken r at a time (**7.4**)
$_nP_{r_1, r_2, \ldots, r_k}$	Permutation of n objects in which r_1, r_2, . . . , r_k are alike (**7.4**)
p	Probability of a success (**8.3**); population proportion (**11.4**); a caret over the symbol, $\hat{p}$, denotes an estimator of p (**11.4**); number of levels of treatment A (**14.2**)
p_j	Population proportion of observations in the jth category (**16.1**); a caret over the symbol, $\hat{p}_j$, denotes an estimator of p_j (**16.2**)
p_j'	Value of the population proportion specified by the null hypothesis (**16.2**)
p_0	Value of the population proportion specified by the null hypothesis (**11.4**)
$\hat{p}_{Pooled}$, $\hat{p}_{Pd}$	Weighted mean of two population proportion estimators (**13.3**)
$p(A)$	Probability of event A (**7.1**)
$p(A|B)$	Conditional probability of A given B (**7.3**)
$p(A$ and $B)$	Probability of the intersection of events A and B (**7.3**)

$p(A \text{ or } B)$	Probability of the union of events A and B **(7.3)**
$p(E_i)$	Probability of event E_i **(7.2)**
$p(X = r)$	Probability that X is equal to r **(8.3)**
Q	Semi-interquartile range **(4.2)**
Q_1, Q_2, Q_3	First, second, and third quartile points, respectively **(4.2)**
q	Probability of a failure **(8.3)**; Tukey's multiple comparison test statistic **(14.5)**; number of levels of treatment B **(15.3)**
qFH	Fisher-Hayter multiple comparison test statistic **(14.5)**
q_0	Value of the population proportion specified by the null hypothesis **(11.4)**
$q_{\alpha;p,v}$	Value that cuts off the $\alpha/2$ region of the sampling distribution of q for p treatment levels and v degrees of freedom **(14.5)**
R	Sample range **(4.2)**
$RB - p$	Randomized block ANOVA design **(15.2)**
$R_{Y \cdot X_1 X_2, \ldots, X_k}$	Coefficient of multiple correlation **(6.5)**
R_X and R_Y	Ranks, respectively, on variables X and Y **(5.7)**
$R^2_{Y \cdot X_1 X_2, \ldots, X_k}$	Coefficient of multiple determination **(6.5)**
r	Sample Pearson product-moment correlation coefficient **(5.2)**; number of successes in a binomial experiment **(8.3)**
r_s	Spearman rank correlation coefficient for a sample **(5.7)**
r^2	Sample coefficient of determination **(5.4)**
S	Sample standard deviation **(4.2)**
S^2	Sample variance **(4.2)**
S'	Desired sample standard deviation **(9.2)**
SSA, SSB	Treatment A **(15.2)** or treatment B **(15.3)** sum of squares
$SSBG$	Between-groups sum of squares **(14.2)**
$SSBL$	Blocks sum of squares **(15.2)**
$SSRES$	Residual sum of squares **(15.2)**
$SSTO$	Total sum of squares **(14.2)**
$SSWCELL$	Within-cell sum of squares **(15.3)**
$SSWG$	Within-groups sum of squares **(14.2)**
S_{cX}	Standard deviation that has been altered by multiplying each score by a constant **(4.2)**
S_X and S_Y	Sample standard deviations, respectively, of X and Y **(5.3)**
S^2_X and S^2_Y	Sample variances, respectively, of X and Y **(5.4)**
S_{X+c}	Standard deviation that has been altered by adding a constant to each score **(4.2)**
S_{XY}	Sample covariance **(5.3)**

$S_{Y \cdot X}$	Standard error of estimate for predicting Y from X (**6.3**)
Sk	Skewness index (**4.6**)
T	Wilcoxon's T random variable (**17.3**)
$T_{\alpha,n}$ and $T_{\alpha/2,n}$	Values that cut off, respectively, the α and $\alpha/2$ regions of the sampling distribution of Wilcoxon's T for n pairs of observations (**17.3**)
t	Student's t random variable (**11.2**)
tDS	Dunn-Šidàk multiple comparison test statistic (**14.5**)
$tDS_{\alpha;C,\nu}$ and $tDS_{\alpha/2;C,\nu}$	Values that cut off, respectively, the α and $\alpha/2$ regions of the sampling distribution of tDS for C a priori contrasts and ν degrees of freedom (**14.5**)
t_i	Number of tied observations in a set (**17.2**)
$t_{\alpha;\nu}$ and $t_{\alpha/2,\nu}$	Values that cut off, respectively, the α and $\alpha/2$ regions of the sampling distribution of t for ν degrees of freedom (**11.2**)
U	Mann-Whitney U random variable (**17.2**)
$U_{\alpha;n_1,n_2}$ and $U_{\alpha/2;n_1,n_2}$	Values that cut off, respectively, the α and $\alpha/2$ regions of the sampling distribution of U for n_1 and n_2 observations in samples 1 and 2 (**17.2**)
V	A variable (**3.8**); Cramér's measure of association, also denoted by ϕ' (**16.3**); a caret over the symbol, $\hat{V}$, denotes an estimator of V (**16.3**)
$Var(Mdn)$	Variance of sample medians (**9.3**)
$Var(\bar{X})$	Variance of sample means (**9.3**)
$Var(t)$	Variance of Student's t random variable (**11.2**)
$Var(\chi_\nu^2)$	Variance of a chi-square random variable (**11.3**)
$Var(\hat{\sigma}^2)$	Variance of $\hat{\sigma}^2$ (**9.5**)
$Var(\hat{\sigma}_{est}^2)$	Variance of $\hat{\sigma}_{est}^2$ (**9.5**)
W	A variable (**3.8**)
$\hat{w}$	Effect size (**16.2**)
X	A score (**1.4**); the independent variable in an experiment (**5.1**)
X_i	A score for the ith measurement or event class (**3.3**)
X_n	A score for the nth measurement or event class (**3.3**)
X_{ij}	A score for the ith subject in the jth treatment condition (**14.2**)
X_{ijk}	A score for the ith subject in the jkth treatment combination (**15.3**)
X_j	Value of the jth class interval (**3.3**)
X_{ll}	Real lower limit of a class interval (**3.4**) or score (**4.2**)
X_{ul}	Real upper limit of a class interval (**3.4**) or score (**4.2**)
$\bar{X}$	Sample arithmetic mean (**3.3**)
$\bar{X}_D$	Mean of difference scores (**12.5**)
$\bar{X}'$	Desired sample mean (**9.2**)
$\bar{X}_i.$	Arithmetic mean of the ith level of blocks (**15.2**)

$\overline{X}..$ and $\overline{X}...$	Arithmetic mean of all scores, grand mean **(14.2, 15.3)**
$\overline{X}_{.j}$ and $\overline{X}_{.j.}$	Arithmetic mean of the jth level of treatment A **(14.2, 15.3)**
$\overline{X}_{..k}$	Arithmetic mean of the kth level of treatment B **(15.3)**
$\overline{X}_{.jk}$	Arithmetic mean of the jkth treatment combination **(15.3)**
$\overline{X}_W$	Weighted mean of two or more sample means **(3.7)**
Y	A score **(1.4)**; the dependent variable in an experiment **(5.1)**
Y'_i	A predicted Y score **(6.2)**
$\overline{Y}$	Sample arithmetic mean **(3.3)**
Z'	Fisher's transformation of r **(11.5)**
Z'_0	Value of population Z' specified by the null hypothesis **(11.5)**
z	Standard score **(9.1)**; z random variable **(10.2)**
z_α and $z_{\alpha/2}$	Values that cut off, respectively, the upper α and $\alpha/2$ regions of the sampling distribution of z **(10.4)**

Appendix C

Answers to Check Your Understanding

CHAPTER 1

1. a. Those who must be able to understand statistical presentations in their fields; those who select, apply, and interpret statistical procedures in their work; applied statisticians; and mathematical statisticians.
2. a. white women students in this university, a woman student, a measure of career ambivalence
   b. all drivers in Tequila Tech students' age group, a driver in that age group, the number of automobile accidents for that driver
   c. homes in Chickasha, Oklahoma; a home in Chickasha, Oklahoma; presence or absence of a color TV in the home
   d. students at Ginebra University, a student at Ginebra University, grade point average of that student
   e. American men between the ages of 27 and 39, an American man, presence or absence of the AIDS virus
   f. women high school students, a woman high school student, whether or not the student performed a community service in the past two years
3. one and all but one of the population elements
4. a. R   b. NR   c. R   d. NR
5. See Sections 1.1–1.3 for meaning of terms.
6. a. D   b. U   c. C   d. O
7. a. E   b. E   c. A   d. E
8. a. D   b. U   c. D   d. O
9. a. ratio   b. nominal   c. Between ordinal and interval   d. ordinal
10. nominal: one-to-one substitution; ordinal: monotonic; interval: positive linear; ratio: multiplication by a positive constant

11. a. ratio   b. between ordinal and interval
12. Although the person couldn't answer any questions on the test, easier items may exist that the individual could answer, which would indicate that the individual does know something about the subject.
13. A change of three points on the measurement scale represents the same empirical change from 62 to 65 as from 68 to 71 and from 71 to 74.
14. See Section 1.4 for meaning of terms.
15. national statistics, probability theory, and experimental statistics
16. national statistics: enumerative in character; probability theory: developing rules for determining the probability associated with events; experimental statistics: determining how to design and analyze experiments
17. The modern era uses exact inductive procedures appropriate for both large and small samples; the previous period relied on large-sample procedures.
18. See Section 1.5 for meaning of terms.

CHAPTER 2

1.

X	f	X	f
13	1	6	2
12	0	5	4
11	0	4	6
10	1	3	3
9	1	2	2
8	0	1	1
7	1	0	1

$n = 23$

2.

X	f	X	f
25	1	13	1
24	0	12	1
23	0	11	4
22	1	10	4
21	1	9	5
20	0	8	8
19	0	7	7
18	0	6	6
17	1	5	4
16	0	4	3
15	2	3	1
14	0		

$n = 50$

3. See the list in Section 2.2.
4. a. 49.5–54.5, 5   b. 73.5–74.5, 1   c. 17.95–19.95, 2
5. a. 16, 3, 21–23   b. 11, 15, 105–119   c. 17, 10, 90–99

6.

X	f	X	f
95–99	1	60–64	2
90–94	1	55–59	4
85–89	4	50–54	5
80–84	5	45–49	3
75–79	4	40–44	2
70–74	2	35–39	1
65–69	1		

$n = 35$

7. a.

X	f	X	f
210–212	1	192–194	3
207–209	0	189–191	5
204–206	1	186–188	6
201–203	2	183–185	4
198–200	2	180–182	1
195–197	2		

$n = 27$

X	f	X	f
210–211	1	194–195	1
208–209	0	192–193	3
206–207	0	190–191	3
204–205	1	188–189	4
202–203	2	186–187	4
200–201	0	184–185	4
198–199	2	182–183	0
196–197	1	180–181	1

$n = 27$

b. The distribution with $i = 3$ is better than the one with $i = 2$. The larger class interval size provides a clearer picture of the distribution of scores because the number of scores is relatively small.

8.

X	Prop f	X	Prop f
95–99	.03	60–64	.06
90–94	.03	55–59	.11
85–89	.11	50–54	.14
80–84	.14	45–49	.09
75–79	.11	40–44	.06
70–74	.06	35–39	.03
65–69	.03		

9.

X	f	Cum f	X	f	Cum f
16	1	32	10	7	17
15	0	31	9	4	10
14	1	31	8	3	6
13	2	30	7	2	3
12	5	28	6	1	1
11	6	23			

$n = 32$

10.

X	f	Cum f	Cum prop f	X	f	Cum f	Cum prop f
13	1	23	1.00	6	2	19	.83
12	0	22	.96	5	4	17	.74
11	0	22	.96	4	6	13	.57
10	1	22	.96	3	3	7	.30
9	1	21	.91	2	2	4	.17
8	0	20	.87	1	1	2	.09
7	1	20	.87	0	1	1	.04

$$n = 23$$

11.

X	f
Graduate	1
Senior	8
Junior	10
Sophomore	6
Freshman	4

$$n = 29$$

12. When the order of the class intervals is arbitrarily determined, it is meaningless to construct a cumulative frequency distribution.

13. See Section 2.2 for meaning of terms.

14.

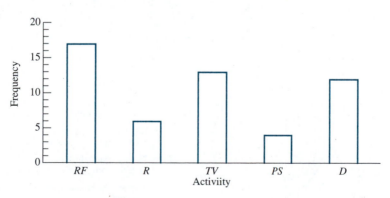

15.

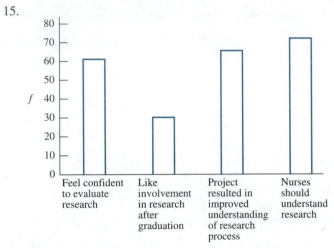

Attitudes toward research

16.

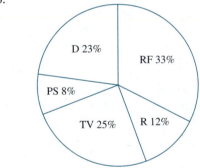

Favorite leisure time activity of college students

17.

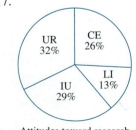

Attitudes toward research

CE = Feel confident to
evaluate research

LI = Like involvement in
research after graduation

IU = Project resulted in improved
understanding of research process

UR = Nurses should understand
research

18. See Section 2.4 for meaning of terms.

19.

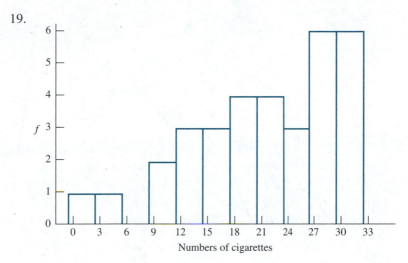

Histogram for number of cigarettes smoked per day by mothers whose first babies were stillborn.

20.

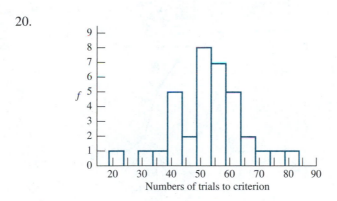

Histogram for number of trials required by rats to reach the criterion of eight consecutive correct responses.

21. a. 22   b. 9.5   c. 132.5   d. 22

22.

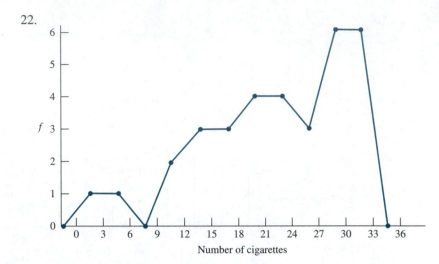

Frequency polygon for number of cigarettes smoked by mothers whose first babies were stillborn.

23.

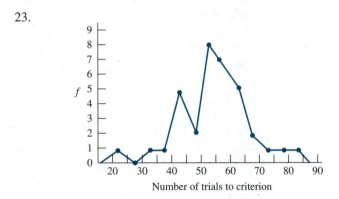

Frequency polygon for number of trials required by rats to reach the criterion of eight consecutive correct responses.

24.

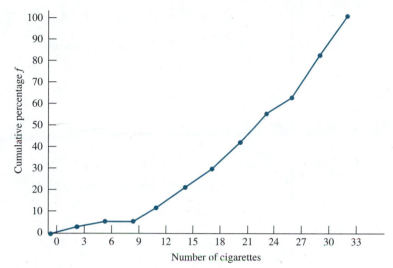

Cumulative percentage frequency polygon for number of cigarettes
smoked per day by mothers whose first babies were stillborn.

25. A cumulative polygon will have an S shape if there are more scores in the
middle of the corresponding frequency distribution than at the extremes.

26. ────────────────

Stems (Class Intervals)	Leaves (Scores)
0–2	0
3–5	3
6–8	
9–11	90
12–14	234
15–17	566
18–20	8990
21–23	1123
24–26	556
27–29	777889
30–32	000112

27. See Section 2.5 for meaning of terms.
28. a. true   b. true   c. false   d. true   e. false

29. a.

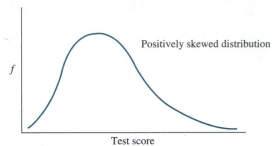

Positively skewed distribution

f

Test score

b.

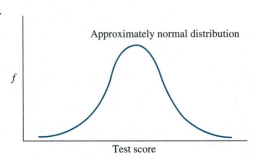

Approximately normal distribution

f

Test score

c.

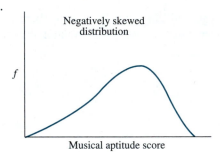

Negatively skewed distribution

f

Musical aptitude score

d.

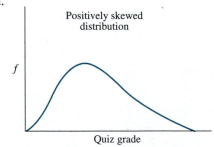

Positively skewed distribution

f

Quiz grade

30. See Section 2.6 for meaning of terms.

31.

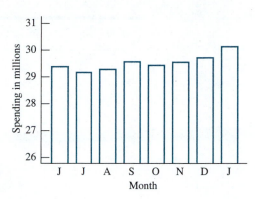

32. See Section 2.7 for meaning of term.

CHAPTER 3

1. a. $Mo = S$　　b. ordered qualitative variable
2. a. The distribution is bimodal; the maximum values occur at 1 and 3.
   b. unordered qualitative variable
3. The value of the mode computed from a grouped frequency distribution depends on the scheme used to group the data.
4. a. X score for element one　　b. X score for element i
   c. mean of population one　　d. X score for element j
5. a. $X_1 + X_2 + \cdots + X_n$　　b. $(f_1X_1 + f_2X_2 + \cdots + f_kX_k)/n$
   c. $(Z_1 + Z_2 + Z_4)/3$
6. $\bar{X} = 78/17 = 4.59$
7. $\bar{X} = 340/36 = 9.44$
8.

X_j	f_j	f_jX_j
9	1	9
8	0	0
7	2	14
6	2	12
5	4	20
4	3	12
3	2	6
2	2	4
1	1	1

$$n = 17 \quad \sum_{j=1}^{k} f_jX_j = 78$$

$$\bar{X} = 78/17 = 4.59$$

9.

X_j	f_j	f_jX_j
22	1	22
21	0	0
20	0	0
19	0	0
18	0	0
17	0	0
16	1	16
15	0	0
14	2	28
13	1	13
12	3	36
11	4	44
10	6	60
9	5	45
8	5	40
7	3	21
6	0	0
5	2	10
4	0	0
3	1	3
2	1	2
1	0	0
0	1	0

$$n = 36 \quad \sum_{j=1}^{k} f_jX_j = 340$$
$$\overline{X} = 340/36 = 9.44$$

10. See Section 3.3 for meaning of terms.
11. a. 9   b. 18   c. 3.25   d. 3.75

12.

X_j	f_j	$Cum\ f$
22	1	36
21	0	35
20	0	35
19	0	35
18	0	35
17	0	35
16	1	35
15	0	34
14	2	34
13	1	32
12	3	31
11	4	28
10	6	24
9	5	18
8	5	13
7	3	8
6	0	5
5	2	5
4	0	3
3	1	3
2	1	2
1	0	1
0	1	1

$$n = 36$$

$$Mdn = 8.5 + 1[(18 - 13)/5] = 9.5$$

13. X_{ul} = real upper limit of class interval containing the median, i = class interval size, n = number of scores, Σf_a = number of scores above X_{ul}, f_i = number of scores in the class interval containing the median.

14. $Mdn = 8.5 - 1[(4 - 2)/3] = 7.83$

15. a. Compute the mean because the data are quantitative and the distribution is relatively symmetrical.
    b. Compute the mean because the data are quantitative and the distribution is relatively symmetrical.
    c. Compute the median because the data contain an extreme score, $X = 23$.

16. a. $\bar{X} = 1, Mdn = 2, Mo = 3$ b. Only the Mo is appropriate.

17. See Section 3.5 for meaning of terms.

18. a. positively skewed   b. positively skewed   c. bimodal
    d. symmetrical   e. negatively skewed   f. multimodal

19. a. 43.33   b. 26.25

20. a. $X_1 + X_2 + X_3$　　　　　　b. $Y_1 + Y_2 + Y_3 + Y_4$
　　c. $f_1X_1 + f_2X_2 + f_3X_3$　　　d. $f_1X_1 + f_2X_2 + \cdots + f_kX_k$
　　e. $aX_1 + aX_2 + aX_3 = a(X_1 + X_2 + X_3)$
　　f. $(X_1 + a) + (X_2 + a) + \cdots + (X_n + a) = (X_1 + X_2 + \cdots + X_n) + na$

21. a. $3(2) = 6$　　b. $4(3) = 12$　　c. 9
　　d. 16　　　　　e. 5　　　　　　f. $2(2 + 3 + 4) = 18$
　　g. $(2 + 3 + 4) + 3(2) = 15$　　h. $(1 + 2 + 4 + 9) + 4(2) - 4(3) = 12$
　　i. $(2 + 3) + 2(2) = 9$

22. a. $\displaystyle\sum_{i=1}^{n}(X_i + c) = \sum_{i=1}^{n}X_i + \sum_{i=1}^{n}c$ 　　　Rules 3.8-4 and 3.8-2

　　　　　　$\displaystyle = \sum_{i=1}^{n}X_i + nc$ 　　　Rule 3.8-1

　　b. $\displaystyle\sum_{i=1}^{n}(cX_i) = c\sum_{i=1}^{n}X_i$ 　　　Rule 3.8-3

CHAPTER 4

1. a. 16　　b. 16　　c. 10　　d. 14
2. The range is determined only by the two most extreme scores.
3. a. $Mdn = 27.33, Q = 1.33$　　b. $P_{10} = 24.70, P_{90} = 30.30$
　　c.

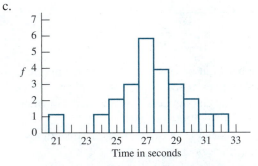

**Time in seconds required to notice the
onset of a warning light during the
performance of a simulated driving test**

4. $P_R = 87.50$
5. a. $\overline{X} = 2.467, S = 1.258$　　b. $CV = 100(1.258/2.467) = 50.99$
6. a. $\sqrt{[115 - (37)^2/15]/15} = 1.258$
　　b. CV for the data in Exercise 3 is equal to $100(2.306/27.375) = 8.42$. CV for
　　the data in Exercise 5 is equal to $100(1.258/2.467) = 50.99$. The data in
　　Exercise 5 have the largest relative dispersion.

7. a. Mo = moderately desire career, D = .97

    b.

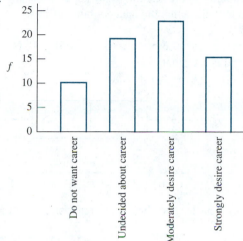

8. a. $\sum_{i=1}^{n}(X_i + c)/n = \sum_{i=1}^{n}X_i/n + \sum_{i=1}^{n}c/n$ Rule 3.8-4

    $\sum_{i=1}^{n}c/n = nc/n$ Rule 3.8-1

    b. $\sum_{i=1}^{n}cX_i/n = c\sum_{i=1}^{n}X_i/n$ Rule 3.8-3

    $\sum_{i=1}^{n}c^2(X_i - \overline{X})^2 = c^2\sum_{i=1}^{n}(X_i - \overline{X})^2$ Rule 3.8-3

9. a. Approximately 68% of the scores fall between 85 and 115.
    b. Approximately 50% of the scores fall between 58 and 82.
    c. A range of four includes all of the scores; the most frequent score is 16.
    d. The number of distinguishable pairs of categories is 25% of the maximum number; the most frequent category is Pizza Inn pizza.

10. See Section 4.2 for meaning of terms.

11. a. Compute the mean and the standard deviation because the variable is quantitative and the distribution is relatively symmetrical.
    b. Compute the median and the semi-interquartile range because the distribution is skewed.
    c. Compute the mode and the index of dispersion because the variable is qualitative.
    d. Compute the mode and index of dispersion because the variable is qualitative.

12. a. 84.13%   b. 99.73%   c. 97.72   d. 15.87

13. a. 3.37   b. 20

14. S_{min} = 3, S_{max} = 15

15. a. correct   b. incorrect, S_{max} = 17.5   c. correct

16. See Section 4.4 for meaning of term.

17. a. $Mdn \pm 2(Q_3 - Q_1) = 5.0 \pm 2(6.5 - 3.5) = 5.0 \pm 6.0 = 0$ and 11. Note, a socioeconomic score cannot be negative and is set equal to zero. There is no reason to believe that the data contain outliers.

   b. $Mdn = 5.0$
   $Q_1 - 1.5(Q_3 - Q_1) = 3.5 - 1.5(6.5 - 3.5) = 0$. Note, the value cannot be negative and is set equal to zero.
   $Q_3 + 1.5(Q_3 - Q_1) = 6.5 + 1.5(6.5 - 3.5) = 11.0$

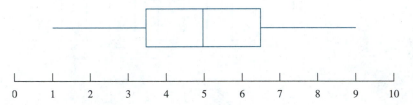

0	1	2	3	4	5	6	7	8	9	10

The two criteria lead to the same conclusion that the data do not contain outliers.

18. a. $Mdn \pm 2(Q_3 - Q_1) = 27.33 \pm 2(28.83 - 26.17) = 22.0$ and 32.6. There is reason to believe that $X = 21$ is an outlier.

   b. $\bar{X} \pm 2.5S = 27.375 \pm 2.5(2.306) = 21.6$ and 33.1. This criterion leads to the same decision as the criterion in (a).

   c. $Mdn = 27.33$
   $Q_1 - 1.5(Q_3 - Q_1) = 26.17 - 1.5(28.83 - 26.17) = 22.18$
   $Q_3 + 1.5(Q_3 - Q_1) = 28.83 + 1.5(28.83 - 26.17) = 32.82$

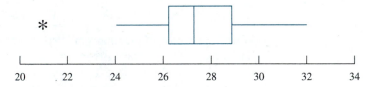

20	22	24	26	28	30	32	34

All of the criteria lead to the same conclusion: $X = 21$ is an outlier.

19. See Section 4.5 for meaning of term.

20. a. $Sk = -1.02$; distribution is negatively skewed.

b.

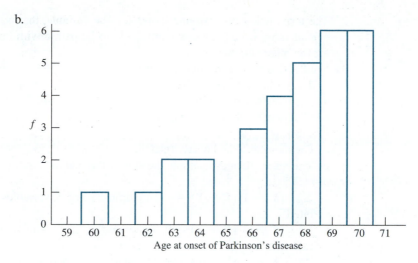

Age at onset of Parkinson's disease

c. yes

21. a. Because $Kur = -0.04$, the data do not support the prediction.
  b. The data are slightly negatively skewed; $Sk = -0.09$.
22. $Kur = 0.23$; distribution is leptokurtic.
23. See Section 4.6 for meaning of terms.

CHAPTER 5

1. a.

Test A	Test B									
	30	31	32	33	34	35	36	37	38	39
33										1
32										1
31								1		
30									1	
29							1	1		
28					1	1				
27				1	1	1				
26			1		2	1	1			
25				1	2		1			
24			1		1					
23			1							
22				1						
21			1							
20	1									

b. linear

2. The term means that extreme scores for one variable, that is, scores that differ considerably from their mean, are likely to be paired with less extreme scores for the other variable.

3. See Section 5.1 for meaning of terms.

4. a. 1   b. 0   c. -1 d. .4   e. $-.9$

5. a. positive   b. positive   c. zero   d. positive

6. See Section 5.2 for meaning of terms.

7. $r = .86$

8. a. Data appear to be linearly related.   b. $r = -.53$
    c. The faster the music tempo, the slower the rate of sipping.

9. $r = .90$

10. a. $\Sigma_{i=1}^{n} (X_i - \overline{X})(Y_i - \overline{Y}) = 18$, quadrants 1 and 3, variables are positively related.
     b. $\Sigma_{i=1}^{n} (X_i - \overline{X})(Y_i - \overline{Y}) = 0$, quadrants 1, 2, 3, and 4, variables are not related.
     c. $\Sigma_{i=1}^{n} (X_i - \overline{X})(Y_i - \overline{Y}) = -15$, quadrants 2 and 4, variables are inversely related.
     d. $\Sigma_{i=1}^{n} (X_i - \overline{X})(Y_i - \overline{Y}) = 13$, quadrants 1 and 3, variables are positively related.

11. a.

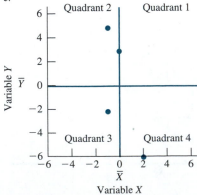

   b.

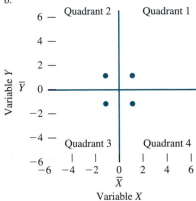

   c.

   d.

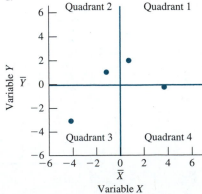

12. a. $r = .95$ b. $r = .0$ c. $r = -.71$ d. $r = .60$
13. a. The cross product reflects both the nature and the degree of relationship between X and Y.
     b. By dividing the cross product by n, you obtain a measure that is independent of the number of pairs of scores.
14. The largest possible value of S_{XY} is 30.
15. a. The possible values of r are 1 and -1. If both scores are equal to the mean of either X or Y, the correlation coefficient is undefined because $S_X S_Y = 0$.

b.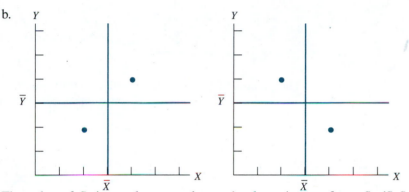

16. The value of S_X is equal to zero, hence the denominator of $r = S_{XY}/S_X S_Y$ is equal to zero and the ratio is undefined.
17. See Section 5.3 for meaning of terms.
18. a. The proportion of variance in English grades explained by variation in grades in bowling is .048; the proportion that is not explained is .952.

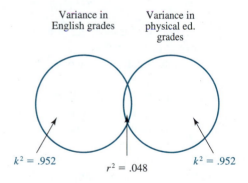

Variance in English grades   Variance in physical ed. grades

$k^2 = .952$ $r^2 = .048$ $k^2 = .952$

b. The proportion of variance in family cohesion explained by men's marital satisfaction is .314; the proportion that is not explained is .686.

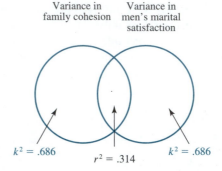

Variance in family cohesion Variance in men's marital satisfaction

$k^2 = .686$ $k^2 = .686$
$r^2 = .314$

c. The proportion of variance in social security numbers explained by total fiber consumed is .001; the proportion that is not explained is .999.

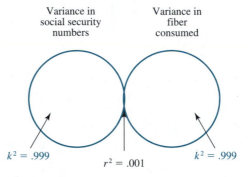

Variance in social security numbers   Variance in fiber consumed

$k^2 = .999$ $k^2 = .999$
$r^2 = .001$

19. See Section 5.4 for meaning of terms.
20. a. Correct interpretation
    b. This interpretation is incorrect because it uses an arbitrary descriptive label, medium, to denote r's between .30 and .69.
    c. This interpretation is incorrect because a .15 unit increase from 0 to .15 does not represent the same increase in correlation as that from .15 to .30.
    d. This interpretation is incorrect because a nonzero correlation indicates a concomitant relationship but not a causal relationship.
21. The mean IQ should increase because of regression toward the mean.
22. See Section 5.5 for meaning of terms.

23. a. *r* underestimates the magnitude of the relationship.

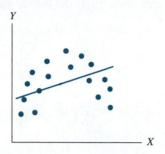

b. The combined *r* overestimates the magnitude of the relationship for either group.

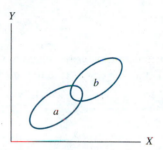

c. The combined *r* underestimates the magnitude of the relationship for either group.

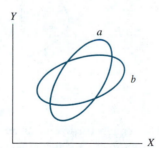

d. *r* underestimates the magnitude of the relationship for small values of *X* and large values of *Y*; the converse is true for large values of *X* and small values of *Y*.

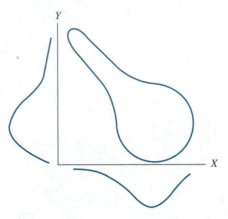

e. *r* underestimates the magnitude of the relationship for large values of *X* and *Y*; the converse is true for small values of *X* and *Y*.

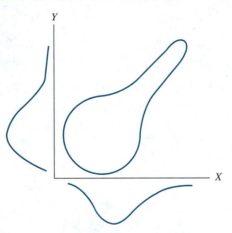

f. The combined *r* overestimates the magnitude of the relationship for *a* and underestimates the magnitude of the relationship for *b*.

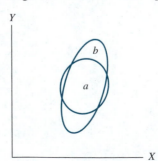

g. The combined r is negative although the r for both a and b is positive.

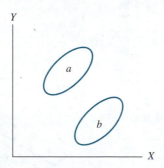

h. r underestimates the value of the relationship.

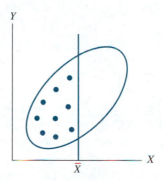

24. The correlation between IQ and creativity for the sample of highly creative individuals may be misleadingly low because the range of creativity is truncated.
25. See Section 5.6 for meaning of the terms.
26. $r_s = .76$
27. An estimate of r_s using the Pearson product-moment correlation formula is $-.30$.
28. a. strictly monotonic   b. nonmonotonic
    c. strictly monotonic   d. strictly monotonic
29. See Section 5.7 for meaning of the terms.

CHAPTER 6

1. The primary purpose of a regression analysis is to predict the value of a dependent variable from the value of an independent variable.

2. a. $b_{Y\cdot X} = 2/4 = 0.5$

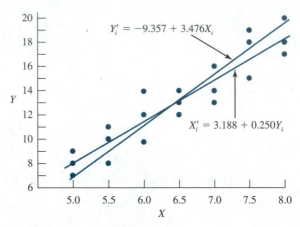

The data appear to be linearly related.

b. $a_{Y\cdot X} = -9.357$ $\qquad b_{Y\cdot X} = 3.476$ $\qquad Y'_i = -9.357 + 3.476X_i$
   $r = 3.476(1.000/3.728) = .93$

c. $a_{X\cdot Y} = 3.188$ $\qquad b_{X\cdot Y} = 0.250$ $\qquad X'_i = 3.188 + 0.250Y_i$
   The slope $b_{Y\cdot X} = 3.476$ is steepest. $\qquad r = 0.250(3.728/1.000) = .93$

d. $r = \sqrt{(3.476)(0.250)} = .93$; yes

e. Estimate based on the regression equation is 11.5; estimate based on the line of best fit is 11.5.

3. It is a best fitting line in the sense that it minimizes the sum of the squared prediction errors.

4. The regression lines are identical when $|r|$ is equal to one.

5. $b_{Y\cdot X} = \dfrac{\Sigma(X_i - \bar{X})(Y_i - \bar{Y})}{\Sigma(X_i - \bar{X})^2} = \dfrac{\Sigma(X_iY_i - X_i\bar{Y} - Y_i\bar{X} + \bar{X}\bar{Y})}{\Sigma(X_i^2 - 2X_i\bar{X} + \bar{X}^2)}$

$= \dfrac{\Sigma X_iY_i - \bar{Y}\Sigma X_i - \bar{X}\Sigma Y_i + n\bar{X}\bar{Y}}{\Sigma X_i^2 - 2\bar{X}\Sigma X_i + n\bar{X}^2}$

$= \dfrac{\Sigma X_iY_i - \dfrac{\Sigma Y_i}{n}\Sigma X_i - \dfrac{\Sigma X_i}{n}\Sigma Y_i + n\dfrac{\Sigma X_i}{n}\dfrac{\Sigma Y_i}{n}}{\Sigma X_i^2 - 2\dfrac{\Sigma X_i}{n}\Sigma X_i + n\dfrac{(\Sigma X_i)^2}{n^2}}$

$= \dfrac{\Sigma X_iY_i - 2\dfrac{\Sigma X_i\Sigma Y_i}{n} + \dfrac{\Sigma X_i\Sigma Y_i}{n}}{\Sigma X_i^2 - 2\dfrac{(\Sigma X_i)^2}{n} + \dfrac{(\Sigma X_i)^2}{n}}$

$= \dfrac{\Sigma X_iY_i - \dfrac{\Sigma X_i\Sigma Y_i}{n}}{\Sigma X_i^2 - \dfrac{(\Sigma X_i)^2}{n}}$

6. Predict that $Y_i = \bar{Y}$ for all i.

7. You know that r is equal to zero.

8. See Sections 6.1 and 6.2 for meaning of terms.

9. a. $S_{Y \cdot X} = 1.42$

   b. $13.2 \pm 1.42 = 11.78$ and 14.62

   c. For $r = 0$, the maximum value of $S_{Y \cdot X} = 2.97$; for $r = 1$, the minimum value of $S_{Y \cdot X} = 0$. The observed value of $S_{Y \cdot X} = 1.42$ is somewhere in between.

10. The larger $S_{Y \cdot X}$, the larger the average prediction error. The minimum value of $S_{Y \cdot X}$ is 0; the maximum value of S_Y is 3.728.

11. See Sections 6.3 and 6.4 for meaning of terms.

12. a. (i) $R^2_{Y \cdot X_1 X_2} = \dfrac{(.20)^2 + (.30)^2 - 2(.20)(.30)(.60)}{1 - (.60)^2} = .091$

   (ii) $R^2_{Y \cdot X_1 X_2} = \dfrac{(.60)^2 + (.50)^2 - 2(.60)(.50)(.30)}{1 - (.30)^2} = .473$

   (iii) $R^2_{Y \cdot X_1 X_2} = \dfrac{(.60)^2 + (-.50)^2 - 2(.60)(-.50)(-.10)}{1 - (-.10)^2} = .556$

   b. (i) $R^2_{Y \cdot X_1 X_2} - r^2_{Y X_2} = .091 - .090 = .001$

   (ii) $R^2_{Y \cdot X_1 X_2} - r^2_{Y X_1} = .473 - .360 = .113$

   (iii) $R^2_{Y \cdot X_1 X_2} - r^2_{Y X_1} = .556 - .360 = .196$

13. a. $R^2_{Y \cdot X_1 X_2} = \dfrac{(.773)^2 + (.681)^2 - 2(.773)(.681)(.544)}{1 - (.544)^2} = .694$

   $R^2_{Y \cdot X_1 X_3} = \dfrac{(.773)^2 + (.289)^2 - 2(.773)(.289)(.065)}{1 - (.065)^2} = .655$

   $R^2_{Y \cdot X_2 X_3} = \dfrac{(.681)^2 + (.289)^2 - 2(.681)(.289)(.083)}{1 - (.083)^2} = .518$

   $R^2_{Y \cdot X_1 X_2 X_3} - R^2_{Y \cdot X_1 X_2} = .743 - .694 = .049$

   b. $Y'_3 = 1.069 + 0.742(3.6) + 0.496(0) + 0.323(0) = 3.74$; the predicted letter grade is B+.

   $Y'_{16} = 1.069 + 0.742(2.8) + 0.496(1) + 0.323(1) = 3.97$; the predicted letter grade is A.

   $Y'_{21} = 1.069 + 0.742(3.1) + 0.496(1) + 0.323(0) = 3.87$, the predicted letter grade is A.

   $Y'_{34} = 1.069 + 0.742(2.3) + 0.496(1) + 0.323(0) = 3.27$, the predicted letter grade is B.

14. See Section 6.5 for meaning of terms.

CHAPTER 7

1. a. $p(odd\ number) = \frac{3}{6} = \frac{1}{2}$
    b. It is assumed that there are six possible outcomes, they are equally likely, and the number of outcomes favoring an odd number is three.
2. a. $p(queen\ of\ spades) = \frac{1}{52}$
    b. It is assumed that there are 52 possible outcomes, they are equally likely, and only one of them is a queen of spades.
3. a. $p(head) = 52/100 = .52$ b. $p(head) = .5$
4. a. $p(H) = .5005$ b. $p(T) = 1 - p(H) = 1 - .5005 = .4995$
5. a.

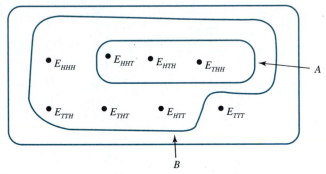

    b. $p(A) = 3/8$ c. $p(B) = 7/8$
6. a.

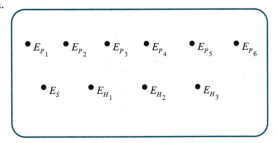

    b. $p(psychology\ major) = 6/10 = 3/5$
    c. $p(psychology\ or\ sociology\ major) = 7/10$
7. a. $p(psychologist) = 3/10$ b. $p(win\ a\ car) = 6/10,000 = 3/5,000$

8. a.

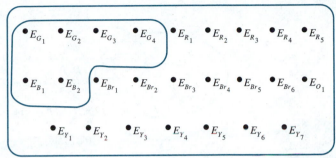

b. 6/25
9. See Section 7.2 for meaning of terms.
10. a. $p(ace) = 4/52 = 1/13$ b. $p(heart) = 13/52 = 1/4$
  c. $p(ace\ or\ heart) = 16/52 = 4/13$ d. $p(heart\ or\ spade) = 26/52 = 1/2$
  e. $p(face\ card) = 12/52 = 3/13$ f. $p(card < 5) = 16/52 = 4/13$
  g. $p(Not\ ace) = 1 - 4/52 = 48/52 = 12/13$
11. a. $p(A\ or\ B) = 2/3$ b. $p(A\ or\ B\ or\ C) = 3/3 = 1$
  c. $p(Not\ A) = 1 - 1/3 = 2/3$ d. $p[Not(A\ or\ B)] = 1 - 2/3 = 1/3$
12. a. $p(A\ and\ B) = p(A)\ p(B) = (.6)(.8) = .48$
  b. $p(Not\ A\ and\ Not\ B) = [1 - p(A)][1 - p(B)] = (1 - .6)(1 - .8) = (.4)(.2) = .08$
  c. $p(A\ or\ B) = p(A) + p(B) - p(A\ and\ B) = .6 + .8 - .48 = .92$
13. a.

	Fatal, F	Nonfatal, $Not\ F$	
Drunken driver, D	$p(D\ and\ F) = .002$	$p(D\ and\ Not\ F) = .098$	$p(D) = .100$
Other cause, O	$p(O\ and\ F) = .002$	$p(O\ and\ Not\ F) = .898$	$p(O) = .900$
	$p(F) = .004$	$p(Not\ F) = .996$	

b. $p(D\ and\ F) = .002$
14. $p(M) = .98, p(Not\ D|M) = .15; p(M\ and\ Not\ D) = (.98)(.15) = .147$
15. a. $p(G) = 4/25$ b. $p(R\ or\ Y) = 12/25$ c. $p(Not\ G) = 1 - 4/25 = 21/25$
  d. $p(Not\ G\ or\ R\ or\ Br\ or\ O\ or\ B\ or\ Y) = 1 - 25/25 = 0$
  e. $p(B\ and\ O) = (2/25)(1/24) = 2/600 = 1/300$
  f. $p[B\ and\ (O\ or\ Br)] = (2/25)(7/24) = 14/600 = 7/300$

16. a.

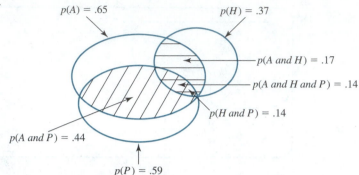

$$p(A) = .65 \qquad p(H) = .37$$

$p(A \text{ and } H) = .17$

$p(A \text{ and } H \text{ and } P) = .14$

$p(H \text{ and } P) = .14$

$p(A \text{ and } P) = .44$

$p(P) = .59$

b. $p(A \text{ and } H \text{ and } P) = p(A) \, p(H|A) \, p(P|A \text{ and } H)$
$= (.65)(.17/.65)(.14/.17) = .14$

c. $p(A \text{ and Not } P) = p(A) - p(A \text{ and } P) = .65 - .44 = .21$, because $p(A) = p(A \text{ and } P) + p(A \text{ and Not } P)$

d. $p(H \text{ and Not } A) = p(H) - p(A \text{ and } H) = .37 - .17 = .20$

e. $p(P \text{ and Not } A \text{ and Not } H) = p(P) - p(A \text{ and } P) - p(H \text{ and } P) + p(A \text{ and } H \text{ and } P) = .59 - .44 - .14 + .14 = .15$

17. See Section 7.3 for meaning of terms.

18. a. $n_1 n_2 n_3 = (2)(2)(2) = 8$ b. $n_1 n_2 n_3 n_4 = (6)(6)(6)(6) = 1296$
c. $n_1 n_2 = (2)(6) = 12$

19. $n_1 n_2 = (3)(5) = 15$

20. $n! = 4! = (4)(3)(2)(1) = 24$

21. $_{10}P_4 = 10!/(10 - 4)! = 5040$

22. $_{10}P_{33121} = 10!/(3! \, 3! \, 1! \, 2! \, 1!) = 50400$

23. a. $n_1 n_2 = (9)(8) = 72$ b. $n \times {_8P_2} = 9[8!/(8 - 2)!] = 504$
c. $n \times {_8C_2} = 9\{8!/[2!(8 - 2)!]\} = 252$

24. See Section 7.4 for meaning of terms.

CHAPTER 8

1. Identify the population, decide whether to sample with or without replacement, and select elements using a random sampling procedure.

2. The two problems are obtaining an accurate list of the population elements and securing their participation once they have been selected.

3. a. $_{50}C_5 = 50!/[5!(50 - 5)!] = 2{,}118{,}760$ b. $n^r = (50)^5 = 312{,}500{,}000$

4. a. $_8C_4 = 8!/[4!(8 - 4)!] = 70$ b. $1/_8C_4 = 1/\{8!/[4!(8 - 4)!]\} = .0143$
   c. $n^r = (8)^4 = 4096$

5. See the section titled Using a Table of Random Numbers for a description of how to use the table.

6. See Section 8.1 for meaning of terms.

7. a.

r	$p(X = r)$
0	.0625
1	.2500
2	.3750
3	.2500
4	.0625

   b.

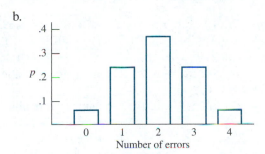

Number of errors

8. a. $p(X \le 2) = .93$ b. $p(X \ge 3) = .07$ c. $p(1 \le X \le 2) = .77$
   d. $E(X) = .16(0) + .54(1) + \cdots + .01(5) = 1.24$
   e. $\sigma = \sqrt{.16(0 - 1.24)^2 + .54(1 - 1.24)^2 + \cdots + .01(5 - 1.24)^2} = 0.88$

9. $E(X) = .6(30) + .4(10) = 22$. The maximum you should be willing to pay is $22.

10. a. $E(X) = 0(0) + 2/5(1) + \cdots + 1/5(4) = 2.20$
    b. $\sigma = \sqrt{0(0 - 2.2)^2 + 2/5(1 - 2.2)^2 + \cdots + 1/5(4 - 2.2)^2} = 1.17$

11. a. $p(W) = 1/1000$
    b. $E(X) = (1/1000)[750 + (- 1.00)] + (999/1000)(- 1.00) = - .25$
    c. no
    d. The maximum you should be willing to pay for a ticket is an amount such that the expected value is equal to zero, that is,

$$E(X) = (1/1000)[750 + (- T)] + (999/1000)(- T) = 0.$$

   Solving for T gives

$$.75 - \frac{T}{1000} - \frac{999\,T}{1000} = 0$$
$$T = .75$$

12. See Section 8.2 for meaning of terms.

13. The probability is .2 that the value of X is equal to 3.

14. A trial can result in one of three outcomes. The probability of success remains constant from trial to trial. The outcomes of successive trials are independent.

15. a. $p(X = 0) = .16, p(X = 1) = .48, p(X = 2) = .36$

    b.

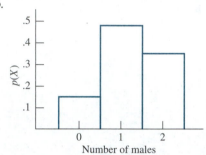

Number of males

   c. $E(X) = np = 2(.6) = 1.2, \sigma = \sqrt{npq} = \sqrt{2(.6)(.4)} = 0.693$

16. a. $p(X \leq 1) = {}_{10}C_0(.3)^0(.7)^{10} + {}_{10}C_1(.3)^1(.7)^9 = .028 + .121 = .149$

    b. $E(X) = np = 10(.3) = 3, \sigma = \sqrt{npq} = \sqrt{10(.3)(.7)} = 1.45$

17. a. $p(3 \; girls) = {}_5C_3(.5)^3(.5)^2 = .3125$. The number of families with three girls is $.3125(800) = 250$.

    b. $p(5 \; boys) = {}_5C_0(.5)^0(.5)^5 = .0312$. The number of families with five boys is $.0312(800) = 25$.

    c. $p(2 \; girls) = {}_5C_2(.5)^2(.5)^3 = .3125; p(2 \; or \; 3 \; girls) = .3125 + .3125 = .625$. The number of families with two or three girls is $.625(800) = 500$.

18. $p(X_N = 6 \text{ and } X_D = 3 \text{ and } X_Q = 1) = \dfrac{10!}{6! \; 3! \; 1!} (.5)^6(.3)^3(.2)^1 = .071$

19. $p(X_N = 6 \text{ and } X_D = 3 \text{ and } X_Q = 1) = \dfrac{({}_{10}C_6)({}_6C_3)({}_4C_1)}{{}_{20}C_{10}} = .091$

20. See Section 8.3 for meaning of terms.

CHAPTER 9

1. The standard normal distribution has a $\mu = 0$ and $\sigma = 1$; this is not necessarily true for other normal distributions.

2. a. normal   b. normal   c.   d. normal

Income

e.   f.

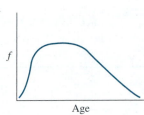

Age

Arrival time

3. a. 2   b. -1.6 c. -1 d. 1.4   e. 0
4. a. .0668   b. .0228   c. .4987   d. .1359   e. .8400
   f. .1574
5. a. .6826   b. .9000   c. .9500   d. .9902   e. .9990
6. a. 190   b. 120   c. 212   d. 150   e. 160
7. a. 0   b. 1.645   c. 0.25   d. -0.53 e. -1.645
8. $z = (2.2 - 2.8)/0.24 = -2.50$, $z = (2.5 - 2.8)/0.24 = -1.25$. The area between z's of -2.50 and -1.25 is .0994. If the university raises its minimum entrance GPA to 2.5, the percentage of eligible junior college students will decrease by 9.94%.
9. a. $E(X) = np = 20(.5) = 10$, $\sigma = \sqrt{npq} = \sqrt{20(.5)(.5)} = 2.24$. $z = (11.5 - 10)/2.24 = .67$; the area beyond $z = .67$ is approximately .25.
   b. $E(X) = np = 40(.5) = 20$, $\sigma = \sqrt{npq} = \sqrt{40(.5)(.5)} = 3.16$. $z = (23.5 - 20)/3.16 = 1.11$; the area beyond $z = 1.11$ is approximately .13.
10. a. $E(X) = np = 400(.1) = 40$, $\sigma = \sqrt{npq} = \sqrt{400(.1)(.9)} = 6.0$. $z = (30.5 - 40)/6.0 = -1.58$; the area beyond $z = -1.58$ is approximately .06.
    b. $z = (29.5 - 40)/6.0 = -1.75$, $z = (50.5 - 40)/6.0 = 1.75$; the area between the two z's is approximately .92.
    c. $z = (49.5 - 40)/6.0 = 1.58$; the area beyond $z = 1.58$ is approximately .06.
11. See Section 9.1 for meaning of terms.
12. $z_1 = (72 - 60)/11 = 1.09$, $z_2 = (61 - 44)/17 = 1.0$, $z_3 = (63 - 53)/8 = 1.25$. Performance on test 3 was best, and performance on test 2 was poorest.
13. $z = (99 - 82)/14 = 1.21$; the area beyond $z = 1.21$ is .11. A score of 99 is in the top 11.3% of test scores, hence you get an A.
14. a. $z = [(18 - 22)/5]15 + 100 = 88$ b. $z = [(18 - 22)/5]10 + 50 = 42$
    c. $z = [(18 - 22)/5]2 + 10 = 8.4$

15. a.

Sample No.	Sample Values	$\overline{X}_j$	Sample No.	Sample Values	$\overline{X}_j$
1	0, 0	0.0	9	2, 0	1.0
2	0, 1	0.5	10	2, 1	1.5
3	0, 2	1.0	11	2, 2	2.0
4	0, 3	1.5	12	2, 3	2.5
5	1, 0	0.5	13	3, 0	1.5
6	1, 1	1.0	14	3, 1	2.0
7	1, 2	1.5	15	3, 2	2.5
8	1, 3	2.0	16	3, 3	3.0

    b. $\mu = \Sigma_{i=1}^{N} X_i/N = 6/4 = 1.5, \sigma_{\overline{X}} = \sigma/\sqrt{n} = 1.11803/\sqrt{2} = 0.7906$

    c. $\mu_{\overline{X}} = \Sigma_{j=1}^{k} \overline{X}_j/k = 24/16 = 1.5, \sigma_{\overline{X}} = \sqrt{\Sigma_{j=1}^{k}(\overline{X}_j - \mu_{\overline{X}})^2/k} = 0.7906$

16. a.

Sample No.	Sample Values	$\overline{X}_j$
1	0, 1	0.5
2	0, 2	1.0
3	0, 3	1.5
4	1, 2	1.5
5	1, 3	2.0
6	2, 3	2.5

    b. $\mu = \Sigma_{i=1}^{N} X_i/N = 6/4 = 1.5, \sigma_{\overline{X}} = \sigma/\sqrt{n} = 1.11803/\sqrt{2} = 0.7906$

    c. $\mu_{\overline{X}} = \Sigma_{j=1}^{k} \overline{X}_j/k = 9/6 = 1.5, \sigma_{\overline{X}} = \sqrt{\Sigma_{j=1}^{k}(\overline{X}_j - \mu_{\overline{X}})^2/k} = 0.6455$

    d. $\sigma_{\overline{X}} = \sigma/\sqrt{n} \sqrt{(N - n)/(N - 1)} = .7906 \sqrt{(4 - 2)/(4 - 1)} = 0.6455$

    e. Consider a population with $N = 340$. A sample of $n = 17$ yields $17/340 = .05$. The correction for a finite population is $\sqrt{(340 - 17)/(340 - 1)} = .9761$. Applying this correction would have little affect on $\sigma_{\overline{X}}$.

17. The larger the value of σ and the smaller the value of n, the greater is the dispersion of a sampling distribution.

18. a. $\sigma_{\overline{X}} = 10/\sqrt{2} = 7.07$ b. $\sigma_{\overline{X}} = 10/\sqrt{4} = 5.00$

    c. $\sigma_{\overline{X}} = 10/\sqrt{8} = 3.54$ d. $\sigma_{\overline{X}} = 10/\sqrt{16} = 2.50$

19. $(115 - 120)/(10/\sqrt{25}) = -2.5$; the probability of obtaining a mean of 115 or lower if the mean is really 120 is .0062.

20. See Section 9.3 for meaning of terms.

CHAPTER 10

1. a. scientific hypothesis   b. scientific hypothesis
   c. not a scientific hypothesis   d. scientific hypothesis
2. a. yes   b. no   c. yes   d. no   e. yes   f. no
   g. yes   h. no   i. yes   j. yes
3. a. alternative hypothesis   b. null hypothesis
4. $H_0: \mu \leq 8, H_1: \mu > 8$
5. $H_0: \mu \leq 14, H_1: \mu > 14$
6. See Section 10.1 for meaning of terms.
7. a. State the null and alternative hypotheses: $H_0: \mu \leq 45, H_1: \mu > 45.$
   Specify the test statistic: $z = (\bar{X} - \mu_0)/(\sigma/\sqrt{n})$ because we want to test $\mu \leq 45$, σ is known, and we assume the population distribution of X is approximately normal.

   Specify the sample size: $n = 100,$
   and the sampling distribution: standard normal distribution.
   Specify the level of significance: $\alpha = .05.$
   Obtain a random sample of size n,
   compute z, and make a decision.

   b. Reject the null hypothesis if z falls in the upper 5% of the sampling distribution of z; otherwise do not reject the null hypothesis. If the null hypothesis is rejected, conclude that the new program is superior to the old program; if the null hypothesis is not rejected, do not draw this conclusion.

8.

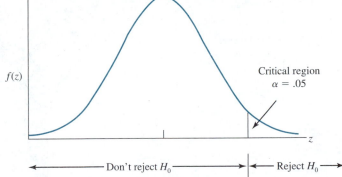

9. a. $H_0: \mu \leq 15$ b. $H_1: \mu > 15$
10. H_1 determines the location of the critical region and α determines its size.
11. See Section 10.2 for meaning of terms.
12. When the population distribution of X is normal or n is very large and H_0 is true.

13. a. State the null and alternative hypotheses: $H_0: \mu \le 50, H_1: \mu > 50.$
    Specify the test statistic: $z = (\bar{X} - \mu_0)/(\sigma/\sqrt{n})$ because we want to test $\mu \le 50$, σ is known, and we assume the population distribution of X is approximately normal.

    Specify the sample size: $n = 30,$
    and the sampling distribution: standard normal distribution.
    Specify the level of significance: $\alpha = .05.$
    Obtain a random sample of size n,
    compute z, and make a decision.

    b. Reject the null hypothesis if z falls in the upper 5% of the sampling distribution of z; otherwise do not reject the null hypothesis. If the null hypothesis is rejected, conclude that habitual criminals have higher Pd scores than noncriminals; if the null hypothesis is not rejected, do not draw this conclusion.

14. a. $z = (55.1667 - 50)/(10/\sqrt{30}) = 2.83$
    b. Because $z = 2.83 > z_{.05} = 1.645$, the null hypothesis is rejected. Conclude that habitual criminals have higher Pd scores than noncriminals.

15. The null hypothesis would not have been rejected because $z = 2.83 < z_{.001} = 3.08$. Do not conclude that habitual criminals have higher Pd scores than noncriminals.

16. a. $z = (54.8276 - 50)/(10/\sqrt{29}) = 2.60$
    b. Because $z = 2.60 > z_{.05} = 1.645$, the null hypothesis is rejected. Conclude that habitual criminals have higher Pd scores than noncriminals.

17. a.

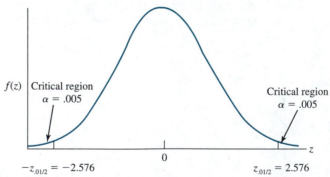

b.

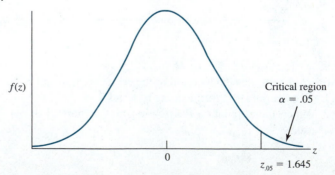

c.

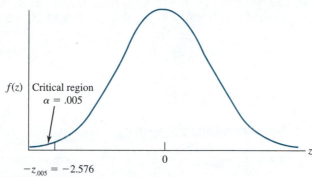

$-z_{.005} = -2.576$

18. a. nondirectional   b. directional
    c. directional
19. a. type I error   b. type II error
    c. correct rejection   d. correct acceptance
    e. correct rejection   f. type I error
20. a. $z_\beta = (117.01 - 118)/(15/\sqrt{150}) = -.81$; power is equal to $1 - \beta = 1 - .2090 = .79$.
    b. $z_\alpha = (117.47 - 115)/(15/\sqrt{150}) = 2.02$; the p-value would have changed from .05 to .0217.
    c. $n = [1.645 - (-1.28)]^2/[(118 - 115)^2/(15)^2] = 214$
21.

<table>
<thead>
<tr><th></th><th colspan="2">True Situation</th></tr>
<tr><th></th><th>$\mu = 115$</th><th>$\mu = 118$</th></tr>
</thead>
<tbody>
<tr><td>$\mu \le 115$</td><td>Correct acceptance
$1 - \alpha = .95$</td><td>Type II error
$\beta = .21$</td></tr>
<tr><td>$\mu > 115$</td><td>Type I error
$\alpha = .05$</td><td>Correct rejection
$1 - \beta = .79$</td></tr>
</tbody>
</table>

Researcher's Decision

22. See Section 10.4 for meaning of terms.
23. Random sampling, normal population, population variance is known.
24. A confidence interval specifies an estimate of the population parameter and the error variation qualifying that estimate. Any null hypothesis can be tested by examining the confidence interval.
25. a. $50 - 1.645(15)/\sqrt{100} < \mu$
       $47.53 < \mu$
    b. $H_0: \mu \le \mu_0$, where $\mu_0 \le 47.53$
    c. $d = (50 - 45)/15 = .33$. According to Cohen's guidelines, the effect is small.
26. a. $\mu < 55.1667 + 1.645(10)/\sqrt{30}$
       $\mu < 58.17$
    b. $H_0: \mu \ge \mu_0$, where $\mu_0 \ge 58.17$
    c. $d = (55.1667 - 50)/10 = .52$. According to Cohen's guidelines, the effect is of medium size.

d. $Mdn = 55.17$, $Q_1 = 51.00$, $Q_3 = 60.75$, calculation for whiskers: $51.00 - 1.5(60.75 - 51.00) = 36.38$, $60.75 + 1.5(60.75 - 51.00) = 75.38$

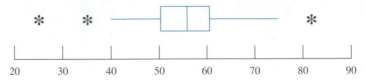

The data contain three outliers: 25, 35, and 82. The sample distribution is relatively symmetrical.

27. a. $7.2 - 2.576(0.42)/\sqrt{29} < \mu < 7.2 + 2.576(0.42)/\sqrt{29}$
$$7.0 < \mu < 7.4$$
b. Yes
c. $d = (7.2 - 8.0)/0.42 = 1.9$. According to Cohen's guidelines, the effect is large.

28. a. I   b. C   c. I   d. C   e. C   f. I
29. a. The larger σ, the larger the interval.
b. The larger n, the smaller the interval.
c. The larger $1 - \alpha$, the larger the interval.
31. See Sections 10.5 and 10.6 for meaning of terms.

CHAPTER 11

1. The sampling distributions of t and z have a mean of zero, are symmetrical, and are unimodal. The sampling distribution of t is more leptokurtic and has a larger variance than that for z when ν is less than ∞.
2. a. State the statistical hypotheses—H_0: $\mu \geq 320$, H_1: $\mu < 320$. Specify the test statistic—$t = (\overline{X} - \mu_0)/(\hat{\sigma}/\sqrt{n})$ because we want to test $\mu \geq 320$, σ is unknown, the sample is random, and we assume the population distribution of X is approximately normal. Specify the sample size—$n = 65$, and the sampling distribution—t distribution with $\nu = 64$. Specify the significance level—$\alpha = .05$. Obtain a sample of size 65, compute t, and make a decision. Reject the null hypothesis if t falls in the lower 5% of the sampling distribution of t; otherwise do not reject the null hypothesis. If the null hypothesis is rejected, conclude that the look-say program resulted in a decrease in the time required to translate the French passage; if the null hypothesis is not rejected, do not draw this conclusion.
b. $t = (302 - 320)/(56/\sqrt{65}) = -2.591$. Reject the null hypothesis because $t(64) = -2.591 < t_{.05,64} = -1.671$. The look-say program resulted in a decrease in the time required to translate the French passage.
c. The p-value is less than .01 ($p = .006$).

   d. Assign participants to a control group following the same procedure used to assign participants to the experimental group. Use the conventional teaching procedure with the students in the control group, but in all other ways treat them as if they were getting a special program like the students in the experimental group.

   e. According to Appendix Table D.9, a sample size equal to 45 would be adequate. Thus, a smaller sample could have been used.

   f. $\mu < 302 + 1.669(56)/\sqrt{65}$
      $\mu < 313.59$

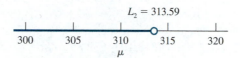

   g. $H_0: \mu \geq \mu_0$, where $\mu_0 \geq 313.59$

   h. $d = |302 - 320|/56 = 0.32$. The size of the difference between the mean translation time for the look-say program and the conventional program is a small effect.

3. $$\text{Prob}(-t_{\alpha/2,\nu} < t < t_{\alpha/2,\nu}) = 1 - \alpha.$$

Replace t with its formula, $t = (\overline{X} - \mu)/(\hat{\sigma}/\sqrt{n})$.

$$\text{Prob}\left(-t_{\alpha/2,\nu} < \frac{\overline{X} - \mu}{\hat{\sigma}/\sqrt{n}} < t_{\alpha/2,\nu}\right) = 1 - \alpha.$$

Multiply each term in the inequalities by $\hat{\sigma}/\sqrt{n}$.

$$\text{Prob}\left(\frac{-t_{\alpha/2,\nu}\hat{\sigma}}{\sqrt{n}} < \overline{X} - \mu < \frac{t_{\alpha/2,\nu}\hat{\sigma}}{\sqrt{n}}\right) = 1 - \alpha.$$

Subtract $\overline{X}$ from each term.

$$\text{Prob}\left(-\overline{X} - \frac{t_{\alpha/2,\nu}\hat{\sigma}}{\sqrt{n}} < -\mu < -\overline{X} + \frac{t_{\alpha/2,\nu}\hat{\sigma}}{\sqrt{n}}\right) = 1 - \alpha.$$

Multiply each term by -1.

$$\text{Prob}\left(\overline{X} + \frac{t_{\alpha/2,\nu}\hat{\sigma}}{\sqrt{n}} > \mu > \overline{X} - \frac{t_{\alpha/2,\nu}\hat{\sigma}}{\sqrt{n}}\right) = 1 - \alpha.$$

Rearrange the terms in the inequality.

$$\text{Prob}\left(\overline{X} - \frac{t_{\alpha/2,\nu}\hat{\sigma}}{\sqrt{n}} < \mu < \overline{X} + \frac{t_{\alpha/2,\nu}\hat{\sigma}}{\sqrt{n}}\right) = 1 - \alpha.$$

4. See Section 11.2 for meaning of terms.

5. a. $\hat{\sigma}^2 = 313.1024$

   b. State the statistical hypotheses—$H_0: \sigma^2 = 306.1$, $H_1: \sigma^2 \neq 306.1$. Specify the test statistic—$\chi^2 = (n - 1)\hat{\sigma}^2/\sigma_0^2$ because we want to test $\sigma^2 = 306.1$, the sample is random, and we assume the population distribution of X is approximately normal. Specify the sample size—$n = 20$, and the sampling distribution—χ^2 distribution with $\nu = 19$. Specify the significance level—$\alpha = .05$. Obtain a random sample of size 20, compute χ^2, and make a decision. Reject the null hypothesis if χ^2 falls in the lower 2.5% or the upper 2.5% of the sampling distribution of χ^2; otherwise do not reject the null hypothesis. If the null hypothesis is rejected, conclude that the dispersion of applicants for KTI is not equal to the dispersion of last year's applicants; if the null hypothesis is not rejected, do not draw this conclusion.

c. $\chi^2 = (20 - 1)(313.1024)/306.1 = 19.435$. Do not reject H_0 because $\chi^2(19) = 19.345 < \chi^2_{1-.05/2,19} = 32.852$.

d. The p-value is less than .70. ($p = .57$)

e. $(20 - 1)(313.1024)/32.852 < \sigma^2 < (20 - 1)(313.1024)/8.907$
$$181.08 < \sigma^2 < 667.90$$

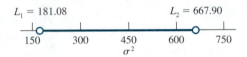

$L_1 = 181.08 \qquad\qquad L_2 = 667.90$

150　　300　　450　　600　　750
σ^2

f. $H_0\colon \sigma^2 \leq 181.08$ or $\sigma^2 \geq 667.90$

6. a. State the statistical hypotheses—$H_0\colon \sigma^2 = 1.69$, $H_1\colon \sigma^2 \neq 1.69$. Specify the test statistic—$\chi^2 = (n - 1)\hat{\sigma}^2/\sigma_0^2$ because we want to test $\sigma^2 = 1.69$, the sample is random, and we assume the population distribution of X is approximately normal. Specify the sample size—$n = 31$, and the sampling distribution—χ^2 distribution with $\nu = 30$. Specify the significance level—$\alpha = .05$. Obtain a random sample of size 31, compute χ^2, and make a decision. Reject the null hypothesis if χ^2 falls in the lower 2.5% or the upper 2.5% of the sampling distribution of χ^2; otherwise do not reject the null hypothesis. If the null hypothesis is rejected, conclude that the dispersion of the movie attendance distribution for boys appearing in the Houston juvenile court is different from that for the nation at large; if the null hypothesis is not rejected, do not draw this conclusion.

b. $\chi^2 = (31 - 1)(2.56)/1.69 = 45.444$. Do not reject H_0 because $\chi^2_{1-.05/2,30} = 16.791 < \chi^2(30) = 45.444 < \chi^2_{.05/2,30} = 46.979$.

c. The p-value is less than .10. ($p = .0702$)

d. $(31 - 1)(2.56)/46.979 < \sigma^2 < (31 - 1)(2.56)/16.791$
$$1.63 < \sigma^2 < 4.57$$

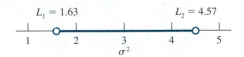

$L_1 = 1.63 \qquad\qquad L_2 = 4.57$

1　　2　　3　　4　　5
σ^2

e. $H_0\colon \sigma^2 \leq 1.63$ or $\sigma^2 \geq 4.57$

7. The n should be at least 26 because in that case both $n(.20)$ and $n(1 - .20)$ are greater than 5.

8. a. State the statistical hypotheses—$H_0: p = .50$, $H_1: p \neq .50$. Specify the test statistic—$z = (\hat{p} - p_0)/\sqrt{p_0 q_0/n}$ because we want to test $p = .50$, the sample is random, and both np_0 and $n(1 - p_0)$ are greater than 5. Specify the sample size—$n = 1000$, and the sampling distribution—z distribution. Specify the significance level—$\alpha = .01$. Obtain a random sample of size 1000, compute z, and make a decision. Reject the null hypothesis if z falls in the lower 0.5% or the upper 0.5% of the sampling distribution of z; otherwise do not reject the null hypothesis. If the null hypothesis is rejected, conclude that the population proportion is not equal to .50; if the null hypothesis is not rejected, do not draw this conclusion.

   b. $z = (.55 - .50)/\sqrt{(.50)(.50)/1000} = 3.16$. Reject the null hypothesis because $z = 3.16 > z_{.01/2} = 2.576$.

   c. Mr. Mander wanted to avoid making a type I error.

   d. $p = .0016$.

   e. $.55 - 2.576\sqrt{(.55)(.45)/1000} < p < .55 + 2.576\sqrt{(.55)(.45)/1000}$
   $$.51 < p < .59$$

   f. $H_0: p \leq .51$ or $p \geq .59$
   Mr. Mander's decision to forego the Hawaii vacation was not a good one.

9. a. State the statistical hypotheses—$H_0: p = .50$, $H_1: p \neq .50$. Specify the test statistic—$z = [(\hat{p} \pm c/n) - p_0]/\sqrt{p_0 q_0/n}$ because we want to test $p = .50$, the sample is random, the sample n is small, and both np_0 and $n(1 - p_0)$ are greater than 5. Specify the sample size—$n = 20$, and the sampling distribution—z distribution. Specify the significance level—$\alpha = .05$. Obtain a random sample of size 20, compute z, and make a decision. Reject the null hypothesis if z falls in the lower 2.5% or the upper 2.5% of the sampling distribution of z; otherwise do not reject the null hypothesis. If the null hypothesis is rejected, conclude that babies have a color preference; if the null hypothesis is not rejected, do not draw this conclusion.

   b. $z = [(.60 - .5/20) - .50]/\sqrt{(.50)(.50)/20} = 0.67$. Do not reject the null hypothesis because $z = 0.67 < z_{.05/2} = 1.96$. There is no reason to believe that the babies have a color preference.

   c. $p = .5028$.

   d. $(.6 - .5/20) - 1.96\sqrt{(.60)(.40)/20} < p$
   $$< (.6 + .5/20) + 1.96\sqrt{(.60)(.40)/20}$$
   $$.36 < p < .84$$

   e. $H_0: p \leq .36$ or $p \geq .84$

10. a. State the statistical hypotheses—$H_0: p = .37$, $H_1: p \neq .37$. Specify the test statistic—$z = (\hat{p} - p_0)/\sqrt{p_0 q_0/n}$ because we want to test $p = .37$, the sample is random, and both np_0 and $n(1 - p_0)$ are greater than 5. Specify the sample size—$n = 200$, and the sampling distribution—z distribution. Specify the significance level—$\alpha = .01$. Obtain a random sample of size 200, compute z, and make a decision. Reject the null hypothesis if z falls in the lower 0.5% or the upper 0.5% of the sampling distribution of z; otherwise do not reject the null hypothesis. If the null hypothesis is rejected, conclude that the population proportion is not equal to .37; if the null hypothesis is not rejected, do not draw this conclusion.

 b. $z = (.46 - .37)/\sqrt{(.37)(.63)/300} = 3.23$. Reject the null hypothesis because $z = 3.23 > z_{.01/2} = 2.576$.

 c. $p = .0012$.

 d. $.46 - 2.576\sqrt{(.46)(.54)/300} < p < .46 + 2.576\sqrt{(.46)(.54)/300}$
 $$.39 < p < .53$$

$$L_1 = .39 \qquad L_2 = .53$$
$$\underset{.30 \qquad .40 \qquad .50 \qquad .60}{\vdash\!\!\!\!\!-\!\!\!\!\!-\!\!\!\!\!\circ\!\!\!\!\!-\!\!\!\!\!-\!\!\!\!\!-\!\!\!\!\!-\!\!\!\!\!\circ\!\!\!\!\!-\!\!\!\!\!\dashv}$$
$$p$$

 e. $H_0: p \leq .39$ or $p \geq .53$

11. a. State the statistical hypotheses—$H_0: p = .10$, $H_1: p \neq .10$. Specify the test statistic—$z = [(\hat{p} \pm c/n) - p_0]/\sqrt{p_0 q_0/n}$ because we want to test $p = .10$, the sample is random, and both np_0 and $n(1 - p_0)$ are greater than 5. Specify the sample size—$n = 100$, and the sampling distribution—z distribution. Specify the significance level—$\alpha = .05$. Obtain a random sample of size 100, compute z, and make a decision. Reject the null hypothesis if z falls in the lower 2.5% or the upper 2.5% of the sampling distribution of z; otherwise do not reject the null hypothesis. If the null hypothesis is rejected, conclude that the proportion of men who had a second heart attack after participating in the supervised physical fitness program is not equal to that for men who didn't participate; if the null hypothesis is not rejected, do not draw this conclusion.

 b. $z = [(.07 + .5/100) - .10]/\sqrt{(.10)(.90)/100} = -0.83$. Do not reject the null hypothesis because $|z| = 0.83 < z_{.05/2} = 1.96$. There is no reason to believe that the supervised physical fitness program affected the chances of a man having a second heart attack.

 c. $p = .4066$.

 d. $(.07 - .5/100) - 1.96\sqrt{(.07)(.93)/100} < p$
 $$< (.07 + .5/100) + 1.96\sqrt{(.07)(.93)/100}$$
 $$.015 < p < .125$$

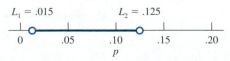
$$L_1 = .015 \qquad\qquad L_2 = .125$$
$$\underset{0 \qquad .05 \qquad .10 \qquad .15 \qquad .20}{\vdash\!\!\!\!\!-\!\!\!\!\!\circ\!\!\!\!\!-\!\!\!\!\!-\!\!\!\!\!-\!\!\!\!\!-\!\!\!\!\!\circ\!\!\!\!\!-\!\!\!\!\!\dashv}$$
$$p$$

 e. $H_0: p \leq .015$ or $p \geq .125$

12. See Section 11.4 for meaning of term.
13. a. 0.497   b. -0.234
    c. -1.946 d. .151
14. a. .500   b. $-.190$
    c. .240   d. $-.850$
15. a. State the statistical hypotheses—$H_0: \rho = 0, H_1: \rho \neq 0$. Specify the test statistic—$t = (r\sqrt{n-2})/\sqrt{1-r^2}$ because we want to test $\rho = 0$, the sample is random, and the population is assumed to be bivariate normal. Specify the sample size—$n = 26$, and the sampling distribution—t distribution. Specify the significance level—$\alpha = .05$. Obtain a random sample of size 26, compute t, and make a decision. Reject the null hypothesis if t falls in the lower 2.5% or the upper 2.5% of the sampling distribution of t; otherwise do not reject the null hypothesis. If the null hypothesis is rejected, conclude that the correlation between the scores of truck drivers on the realistic and artistic scales of the Career Assessment Inventory (CAI) is not zero; if the null hypothesis is not rejected, do not draw this conclusion.
    b. $t = (.09\sqrt{26-2})/\sqrt{1-(.09)^2} = 0.44$. Do not reject the null hypothesis because $t(24) = 0.44 < t_{.05/2;24} = 2.064$.
    c. The p-value is greater than .50. ($p = .66$)
    d. According to Appendix Table D.6, a correlation of .374 is required to reject the null hypothesis that $\rho = 0$.
    e. $.09 - 1.96\sqrt{1/(26-3)} < Z'_{Pop} < .09 + 1.96\sqrt{1/(26-3)}$
    $$-.319 < Z'_{Pop} < .499$$
    $$-.31 < \rho < .46$$

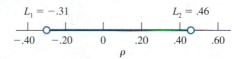

f. $H_0: \rho \leq -.31$ or $\rho \geq .46$
    g. The effect size, $r = .09$, is just below Cohen's criterion of a small effect.
16. a. State the statistical hypotheses—$H_0: \rho = .61, H_1: p \neq .61$. Specify the test statistic—$z = (Z' - Z'_0)/\sqrt{1/(n-3)}$ because we want to test $\rho = .61$, the sample is random, the sample n is moderately large, and the population is assumed to be bivariate normal. Specify the sample size—$n = 100$, and the sampling distribution—z distribution. Specify the significance level—$\alpha = .05$. Obtain a random sample of size 100, compute z, and make a decision. Reject the null hypothesis if z falls in the lower 2.5% or the upper 2.5% of the sampling distribution of z; otherwise do not reject the null hypothesis. If the null hypothesis is rejected, conclude that correlation between the scores on the TAC and grade point average is different from that for last year.
    b. $z = (.604 - .709)/\sqrt{1/(100-3)} = -1.03$. Do not reject the null hypothesis because $|z| = 1.03 < z_{.05/2} = 1.96$.
    c. $p = .30$.

d. $.604 - 1.96\sqrt{1/(100-3)} < Z'_{Pop} < .604 + 1.96\sqrt{1/(100-3)}$

$.405 < Z'_{Pop} < .803$

$.38 < \rho < .67$

$L_1 = .38 \qquad L_2 = .67$

0	.20	.40	.60	.80

ρ

e. $H_0: \rho \leq .38$ or $\rho \geq .67$

17. See Section 11.5 for meaning of terms.

CHAPTER 12

1. When the null hypothesis is stated as $\mu_1 = \mu_2$, it indicates that $\delta_0 = 0$.

2. State the statistical hypotheses—$H_0: \mu_1 - \mu_2 \leq 0$, $H_1: \mu_1 - \mu_2 > 0$. Specify the test statistic—$z = (\overline{X}_1 - \overline{X}_2)/\sigma_{\overline{X}_1 - \overline{X}_2}$ because we want to test $\mu_1 - \mu_2 \leq 0$, σ_1^2 and σ_2^2 are known, the samples are random, and we assume the population distributions of X_1 and X_2 are approximately normal. Specify the sample sizes—$n_1 = 50$ and $n_2 = 52$, and the sampling distribution—standard normal distribution. Specify the level of significance—$\alpha = .05$. Obtain random samples of size $n_1 = 50$ and $n_2 = 52$, compute z, and make a decision. Reject the null hypothesis if z falls in the upper 5% of the sampling distribution of z; otherwise do not reject the null hypothesis. If the null hypothesis is rejected, conclude that fraternity members have higher GPAs than nonmembers; if the null hypothesis is not rejected, do not draw this conclusion.

3. a. $z = (2.91 - 2.72)/\sqrt{(0.5)^2/50 + (0.4)^2/52} = 2.114$. $\qquad z = 2.114 > z_{.05} = 1.645$. Reject the null hypothesis.

   b. $p = .0173$.

4. See Section 12.2 for meaning of term.

5. a. The researchers' recommendation is not appropriate.

   b. The researchers did not randomly assign the workers to the two conditions. It is possible that the workers who opted to use the stereo headsets would have had higher scores on the dependent measures if they had not used the headsets. Also, it is possible that the attention associated with receiving the headsets created a positive attitude toward the company. As a result, the workers were motivated to perform better and the improvement was not related to listening to the music. It also is possible that the workers who did not receive the headsets felt shortchanged and expressed these feelings by lowering their performance level.

6. You know nothing about the size of the difference, only that chance is an unlikely explanation for the difference.

7. All conditions except the independent variable must be held constant.
8. a. random assignment   b. random sampling
   c. random sampling   d. random assignment
9. See Section 12.3 for meaning of terms.
10. Pooling $\hat{\sigma}_1^2$ and $\hat{\sigma}_2^2$ is appropriate when it is reasonable to believe that the population variances are equal.
11. a.

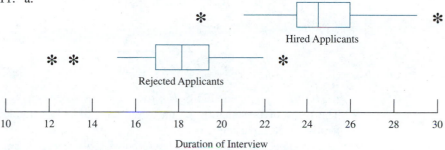

   The data for the hired and rejected applicants contain outliers. The sample distributions appear to be relatively symmetrical.
   b. $t = (24.731 - 18.000)/0.712 = 9.45$; $t(47) = 9.45 > t_{.05,47} = 1.678$. The data support the researcher's scientific hypothesis.
   c. $p < .0005$.
   d. $g = 2.7$; the effect is large.
   e. The sample size is adequate. The minimum sample size is $21 + 21 = 42$.
   f. $5.54 < \mu_1 - \mu_2$

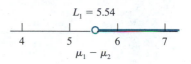

   g. $H_0: \mu_1 - \mu_2 \leq 5.54$
12. a.

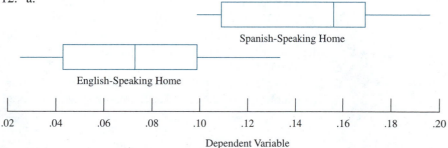

   Neither distribution contains outliers. The sample distribution for infants raised in the Spanish-speaking homes is negatively skewed, the distribution for English-speaking homes is relatively symmetrical.

b. $t = (0.0728 - 0.1482)/0.0133 = -5.67$; $|t(26)| = |-5.67| > t_{.001/2,26} =$ 3.707. Reject the null hypothesis and conclude that early language experience in Spanish-speaking homes resulted in better discrimination of the Spanish contrasts.

c. The *p*-value is less than .0001.

d. $g = |0.0728 - 0.1482|/0.0352 = 2.1$; the effect is large.

e. $-0.125 < \mu_1 - \mu_2 < -0.026$

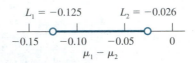

f. $H_0: \mu_1 - \mu_2 \leq -0.125$ or $H_0: \mu_1 - \mu_2 \geq -0.026$

14. The order of presentation of the conditions should be randomized independently for each participant.

15. a. The larger the positive correlation between samples, the smaller is the standard error of the difference between means.

b. The larger the positive correlation, the higher is the probability of rejecting a false null hypothesis.

16. a.

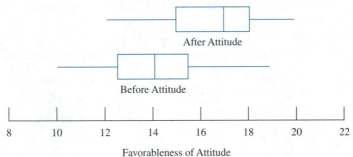

The data do not contain outliers. The "before attitudes" appear to be negatively skewed. The "after attitudes" are fairly symmetrical.

b. $t = -2.1875/0.2772 = -7.891$; $t(15) = -7.891 < -t_{.05,15} = -1.753$. Reject the null hypothesis; viewing the film does result in more favorable attitudes toward legalization of marijuana.

c. $p < .0005$.

d. $g = |14.1875 - 16.3750|/2.5046 = 0\ 87$; the effect is large.

e. The sample size is adequate. The minimum sample size is 11.

f. $\mu_1 - \mu_2 < -1.70$

g. $H_0: \mu_1 - \mu_2 \geq -1.70$

17. a.

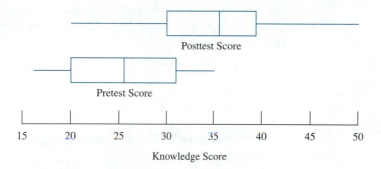

The data do not contain outliers. The pretest scores are relatively symmetrical; the posttest scores are negatively skewed.

b. $t = -9.3182/1.2916 = -7.214$; $|t(21)| = |-7.214| > t_{.01/2,21} = 2.831$. Reject the null hypothesis.

c. $p < .001$.

d. $g = |25.6818 - 35.0000|/6.3710 = 1.5$; the effect is large.

e. The sample size is adequate. The minimum sample size is 20.

f. $-12.97 < \mu_1 - \mu_2 < -5.66$

$$L_1 = -12.97 \quad L_2 = -5.66$$

$$\mu_1 - \mu_2$$

g. $H_0: \mu_1 - \mu_2 \leq -12.97$ or $H_0: \mu_1 - \mu_2 \geq -5.66$

h. For independent samples, $t = -9.3182/1.9209 = -4.851$; $|t(42)| = |-4.851| > t_{.01/2,42} = 2.698$. Reject the null hypothesis. The use of repeated measures was an effective experimental design strategy because the absolute value of the dependent samples t statistic is approximately 2.5 times larger than the critical value; the independent samples t statistic is only 1.8 times larger than the critical value.

i. In the present experiment the difference $\overline{X}_1 - \overline{X}_2$ reflects the effects of the 10-day workshop as well as other effects, such as (1) improved test-taking skills due to taking the pretest, (2) increased sensitivity during the workshop to the kinds of material on the test due to taking the pretest, and (3) acquisition of cancer knowledge from sources other than the workshop such as professional journals and colleagues. The following design, with participants randomly divided into experimental and control groups, would enable the researcher to measure the effects of the workshop and acquisition of course knowledge from other sources.

	Pretest	Workshop	Posttest
Experimental group	X	W	X
Control group	X		X

The use of two experimental and two control groups as follows would enable the researcher to measure the effects of the workshop and the effects 1, 2, and 3 above.

	Pretest	Workshop	Posttest
Experimental group 1	X	W	X
Experimental group 2		W	X
Control group 1	X		X
Control group 2			X

18. a. $n_1 + n_2 = 100$ b. $n_1 + n_2 = 1492$ c. $n_1 + n_2 = 84$
    d. $n = 21$ e. $n = 225$ f. $n = 22$

19. See Section 12.5 for meaning of terms.

CHAPTER 13

1. No, the form of the test statistic is a ratio that doesn't provide for values other than 1.

2. Because you want to detect situations in which the t test is not appropriate, the use of $\alpha = .15$ or $.20$ provides greater power for the F test. In such situations, a type II error is considered to be more serious than a type I error.

3. a.

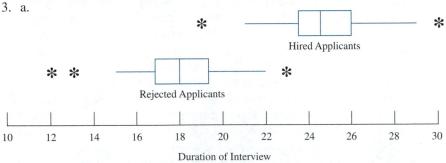

The data for the hired and rejected applicants contain outliers. The sample distributions appear to be relatively symmetrical.

b. $F_{(22, 25)} = 1.11 < F_{.05/2;22,25} = 2.269$. Do not reject the null hypothesis.

c. $0.49 < \sigma_2^2/\sigma_1^2 < 2.58$

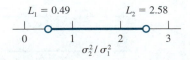

d. Because the confidence interval includes 1, it is consistent with the null hypothesis significance test.

4. a.

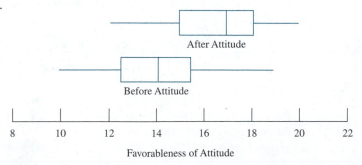

Neither distribution contains outliers. The sample distribution for infants raised in the Spanish-speaking homes is negatively skewed, the distribution for English-speaking homes is relatively symmetrical.

b. $F(13, 13) = 0.99 > F_{1-.05;13,13} = 0.388$. Do not reject the null hypothesis.

c. $\sigma_1^2/\sigma_2^2 < 2.55$

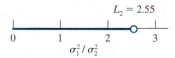

d. Because the confidence interval includes 1, it is consistent with the null hypothesis significance test.

5. a. $F(37, 34) = 2.174 > F_{.05/2;37,34} = 1.962$. Reject the null hypothesis.

b. $1.11 < \sigma_1^2/\sigma_2^2 < 4.22$

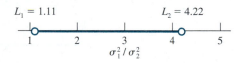

c. Because the confidence interval does not include 1, it is consistent with the null hypothesis significance test.

d. $H_0: \sigma_1^2/\sigma_2^2 \leq 1.11$ and $H_0: \sigma_1^2/\sigma_2^2 \geq 4.22$

6. a.

The data do not contain outliers. The after attitudes appear to be negatively skewed. The before attitudes are fairly symmetrical.

b. $t(14) = -0.718$; $|t(14)| = 0.718 < t_{.05/2,14} = 2.145$. Do not reject the null hypothesis.

c. $-4.071 < \sigma_1^2 - \sigma_2^2 < 2.029$

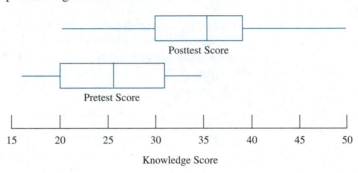

d. Because the confidence interval includes 0, it is consistent with the null hypothesis significance test.

7. a.

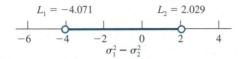

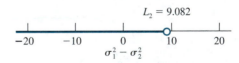

The data do not contain outliers. Both sample distributions are fairly symmetrical.

b. $t(20) = -1.109 < -t_{.05,20} = -1.725$. Do not reject the null hypothesis.

c. $\sigma_1^2 - \sigma_2^2 < 9.082$

d. Because the confidence interval includes 0, it is consistent with the null hypothesis significance test.

8. a. $z = -2.66$; $|z| = 2.66 > z_{.05/2} = 1.96$. Reject the null hypothesis.

b. $-.122 < p_1 - p_2 < -.018$

c. Because the confidence interval does not include 0, it is consistent with the null hypothesis significance test.

d. $H_0 : p_1 - p_2 \leq -.122$ and $H_0 : p_1 - p_2 \geq -.018$

9. a. $z = 3.33 > z_{.05/2} = 1.96$. Reject the null hypothesis.
    b. $.033 < p_1 - p_2 < .127$

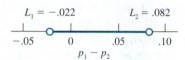

    c. Because the confidence interval does not include 0, it is consistent with the null hypothesis significance test.
    d. $H_0: p_1 - p_2 \leq .033$ and $H_0: p_1 - p_2 \geq .127$
10. a. $z = -1.90; |z| = 1.90 < z_{.05/2} = 1.96$. Do not reject the null hypothesis.
    b. $-.022 < p_1 - p_2 < .082$

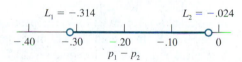

    c. Because the confidence interval includes .08, it is consistent with the null hypothesis significance test.
11. a. $p_1 = .446, p_2 = .614$
    b. $z = -2.21; |z| = 2.21 > z_{.05/2} = 1.96$. Reject the null hypothesis.
    c. $-.314 < p_1 - p_2 < -.024$

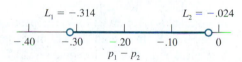

    d. Because the confidence interval does not include 0, it is consistent with the null hypothesis significance test.
    e. $H_0: p_1 - p_2 \leq -.314$ and $H_0: p_1 - p_2 \geq -.024$

CHAPTER 14

1. a. $H_0: \mu_1 = \mu_2 = \mu_3 = \mu_4$
    b. $4(4 - 1)/2 = 6$
    c. Probability of a type I error using ANOVA is .01; probability using multiple t tests is less than $1 - (1 - .01)^6 = .06$.

d. The researcher knows that at least one of the following alternative hypotheses is probably true.

$$H_1: \mu_j \neq \mu_{j'} \qquad \text{for some } j\text{'s}$$

$$H_1: \mu_j \neq \frac{\mu_{j'} + \mu_{j''}}{2} \qquad \text{for some } j\text{'s}$$

$$H_1: \mu_j \neq \frac{\mu_{j'} + \mu_{j''} + \mu_{j'''}}{3} \qquad \text{for some } j\text{'s}$$

$$H_1: \frac{\mu_j + \mu_{j'}}{2} \neq \frac{\mu_{j''} + \mu_{j'''}}{2} \qquad \text{for some } j\text{'s}$$

2. The advantage of ANOVA is that it controls the probability of a type I error at α for the omnibus null hypothesis. The multiple t approach allows the probability of a type I error to exceed α for the collection of tests.

3. Factors that might affect the score include the a_2 exercise program, diet during the preceding month, time of day that the measurement was made, and variation in the measurement procedures.

4. a. treatment level 2
   b. score for participant 2 in treatment level 4
   c. score for participant 16 in treatment level 1
   d. mean of treatment level 4
   e. grand mean
   f. linear model equation for participant 7 in treatment level 3
   g. population 2 treatment effect
   h. population error effect for participant 1 in treatment level 3

5. a. Subtract $\overline{X}..$ from both sides of the equation
   b. Square both sides of the equation
   c. Sum the squared deviations for $j = 1, \ldots, p$ and $i = i, \ldots, n$
   d. Perform the square of the term on the right side of the equation
   e. Distribute the summation operators
   f. Delete the middle term on the right because $\sum_{i=1}^{n} (X_{ij} - \overline{X}_{.j}) = 0$ (see Section 3.9)

6. a. correct   b. incorrect
   c. incorrect   d. incorrect
   e. correct

7. a. $X_{83} = \overline{X}.. + (\overline{X}_{.3} - \overline{X}..) + (X_{83} - \overline{X}_{.3})$
   b. $X_{52} = \overline{X}.. + (\overline{X}_{.2} - \overline{X}..) + (X_{52} - \overline{X}_{.2})$
   c. $X_{24} = \overline{X}.. + (\overline{X}_{.4} - \overline{X}..) + (X_{24} - \overline{X}_{.4})$

8. a. $df_{TO} = 83, df_{BG} = 3, df_{WG} = 80$ b. $df_{TO} = 54, df_{BG} = 4, df_{WG} = 50$
   c. $df_{TO} = 31, df_{BG} = 3, df_{WG} = 28$ d. $df_{TO} = 16, df_{BG} = 2, df_{WG} = 14$

9. a. Both $MSBG$ and $MSWG$ estimate σ_ϵ^2 when random samples are drawn from normally distributed populations having equal means and equal variances.
   b. $MSBG$ should be bigger than $MSWG$ when any of the treatment effects, α_j, are not equal to 0.

10. See Section 14.2 for meaning of the terms.

11. a. Square $(\overline{X}_{.j} - \overline{X}..)$
    b. Distribute the summation operator

c. Replace $\bar{X}_{j\cdot}^2$, $\bar{X}_{\cdot\cdot}$, $\bar{X}_{\cdot j}$, and $\bar{X}_{\cdot\cdot}^2$ with their formulas

d. Multiply $n \sum\limits_{j=1}^{p} \dfrac{\left(\sum\limits_{i=1}^{n} X_{ij}\right)^2}{n^2}$ by $\dfrac{1}{n} / \dfrac{1}{n}$, multiply $2n \dfrac{\sum\limits_{j=1}^{p}\sum\limits_{i=1}^{n} X_{ij}}{np}$ by $\dfrac{\sum\limits_{j=1}^{p}\sum\limits_{i=1}^{n} X_{ij}}{n}$,

and multiply $np \dfrac{\left(\sum\limits_{j=1}^{p}\sum\limits_{i=1}^{n} X_{ij}\right)^2}{n^2 p^2}$ by $\dfrac{1}{np} / \dfrac{1}{np}$

e. Add $-2 \dfrac{\left(\sum\limits_{j=1}^{p}\sum\limits_{i=1}^{n} X_{ij}\right)^2}{np}$ and $\dfrac{\left(\sum\limits_{j=1}^{p}\sum\limits_{i=1}^{n} X_{ij}\right)^2}{np}$

12. a.

Source	SS	df	M_S	F
Between groups	168.000	3	56.000	3.50
Within groups	1216.000	76	16.000	
Total	1384.000	79		

b. $p < .05$

13. a.

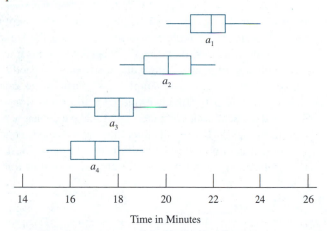

The sample distributions are relatively symmetrical. The data do not contain outliers.

b. **Descriptive Statistics for Time Required to Learn Nonsense Syllables**

	Association Value of Nonsense Syllables			
	25%	50%	75%	100%
	a_1	a_2	a_3	a_4
$\bar{X}_{\cdot j}$	21.875	20.000	17.875	17.000
$\hat{\sigma}_j$	1.246	1.309	1.246	1.309

c. Yes

d. **Analysis of Variance Table for Time Required to Learn Nonsense Syllables**

Source	SS	df	MS	F
1 Between groups (association value)	115.1250	3	38.3750	[½] 23.49*
2 Within groups	45.7500	28	1.6339	
3 Total	160.8750	31		

*$p < .0001$

Reject the null hypothesis.

e. According to the ANOVA and descriptive statistics, the learning-time population means for the four levels of association value are not all equal, $F(3, 28) = 23.49$, $p < .0001$. It appears that there is an inverse relationship between association value and time required to learn nonsense syllables.

14. State the statistical hypotheses—H_0: $\mu_1 = \mu_2 = \mu_3 = \mu_4$, H_1: $\mu_j \neq \mu_{j'}$, for some j and j'. Specify the test statistic—$F = MSBG/MSWG$ because we want to test $\mu_1 = \mu_2 = \mu_3 = \mu_4$, random sampling was used, and we assume that the four populations are approximately normally distributed with equal variances. Specify the sample size—$pn = 32$, and the sampling distribution—F distribution with $\nu_1 = 3$ and $\nu_2 = 28$ because we assume that the three populations are approximately normally distributed. Specify the level of significance—$\alpha = .05$. Obtain a sample of 32 participants, randomly assign the participants to the p treatment levels with the restriction that n participants are assigned to each level, compute F, and make a decision. Reject the null hypothesis if $F \geq 2.95$. If the null hypothesis is rejected, conclude that the time to learn the lists of nonsense syllables is not the same for the four association values; if the null hypothesis is not rejected, do not draw this conclusion.

15. a.

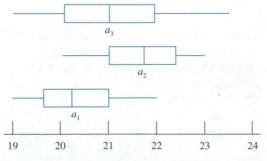

Reaction Time (Hundredths of a Second)

The sample distributions are relatively symmetrical. The data do not contain outliers.

b. **Descriptive Statistics for Reaction Time in Hundredths of a Second to Three Colors of Warning Lights**

	Yellow a_1	Red a_2	Green a_3
		Color of Warning Light	
$\overline{X}_{\cdot j}$	20.300	21.700	21.000
$\hat{\sigma}_j$	0.949	0.949	1.183

c. Yes
d. **Analysis of Variance Table for Reaction Time to Warning Lights**

Source	SS	df	MS	F
Between groups (color of light)	9.8000	2	4.9000	[$^1/_2$] 4.54*
Within groups	30.2000	28	1.0786	
Total	40.0000	30		

*$p < .05$
Reject the null hypothesis.

e. According to the ANOVA, the reaction-time population means for the three colors of instrument panel warning lights are not equal, $F(2, 28) = 4.54$, $p < .05$.

16. State the statistical hypotheses—H_0: $\mu_1 = \mu_2 = \mu_3$, H_1: $\mu_j \neq \mu_{j'}$, for some j and j'. Specify the test statistic—$F = MSBG/MSWG$ because we want to test $\mu_1 = \mu_2 = \mu_3$, random sampling was used, and we assume that the three populations are approximately normally distributed with equal variances. Specify the sample size—$n_1 + n_2 + n_3 = 31$, and the sampling distribution—F distribution with $\nu_1 = 2$ and $\nu_2 = 28$ because we assume that the three populations are approximately normally distributed. Specify the level of significance—$\alpha = .05$. Obtain a sample of 31 participants, randomly assign the participants to the p treatment levels with the restriction that approximately the same number of participants receive each level, compute F, and make a decision. Reject the null hypothesis if $F \geq 3.34$. If the null hypothesis is rejected, conclude that reaction time is not the same for the three colors of instrument-panel warning lights; if the null hypothesis is not rejected, do not draw this conclusion.

17. The F test is robust if the treatment populations all have the same shape, for example all positively skewed or all leptokurtic.

18. a.

	a_1	a_2	a_3	a_4
	f	f	f	f
24	I			
23	I			
22	III	I		
21	II	II		
20	I	II	I	
19		II	I	I
18		I	III	II
17			II	II
16			I	II
15				I

The distributions are relatively symmetrical. There is no reason to believe that the populations are not symmetrical.

b.

	a_1	a_2	a_3
X	f	f	f
23		II	I
22	I	IIII	III
21	III	III	III
20	III	I	III
19	II		I

The distributions are relatively symmetrical. There is no reason to believe that the populations are not symmetrical.

19. This assumption states that the $j = 1, \ldots, p$ population variances are equal to σ_ϵ^2.

20. See Section 14.4 for meaning of term.

21. a. $1, -1, 0, 0$ b. $0, 1, 0, -1$ c. $1, -\frac{1}{2}, -\frac{1}{2}, 0$

    d. $1, -\frac{1}{3}, -\frac{1}{3}, -\frac{1}{3}$ e. $\frac{1}{2}, \frac{1}{2}, -\frac{1}{2}, -\frac{1}{2}$ f. $1, -\frac{2}{3}, -\frac{1}{3}, 0$

22. a. contrast   b. contrast   c. not a contrast

    d. contrast   e. contrast   f. contrast

23. a. satisfies   b. doesn't satisfy   c. doesn't satisfy

    d. doesn't satisfy   e. doesn't satisfy   f. satisfies

24. a. $q_{.01;4,40} = 4.70$ b. $q_{.05;5,60} = 3.98$ c. $q_{.05;3,15} = 3.67$

25. a. $q_{.01;4-1,40} = 4.45$ b. $q_{.05;5-1,60} = 3.74$ c. $q_{.05;3-1,15} = 3.01$
26. a. $(4 - 1)F_{.01;3,40} = (4 - 1)4.31 = 12.93$
    b. $(5 - 1)F_{.05;4,60} = (5 - 1)2.53 = 10.12$
    c. $(3 - 1)F_{.05;2,18} = (3 - 1)3.55 = 7.10$
27. a. $tDS_{.01/2;6,40} = 3.370$ b. $tDS_{.01/2;4,40} = 3.225$ c. $tDS_{.05/2;10,60} = 2.906$
28. a. $tDS_{.05;2,40} = 2.009$ b. $tDS_{.05;3,30} = 2.215$ c. $tDS_{.05;4,60} = 2.283$
29. a. $qFH = -0.02/0.02 = -1.00$, $qFH = -0.10/0.02 = -5.00^*$, $qFH = -0.08/0.02 = -4.00^*$; $q_{.05;3-1,12} = 3.08$. Reject the null hypothesis for $\psi_2 = \mu_1 - \mu_3$ and $\psi_3 = \mu_2 - \mu_3$.
    b. For $\hat{\psi}_2$, $g = 2.24$ For $\hat{\psi}_3$, $g = 1.79$
    The two effects sizes are large.
30. a. $FS = 0.49/0.80 = .61$, $FS = 12.96/0.80 = 16.20^*$, $FS = 8.41/0.80 = 10.51^*$, $FS = 10.56/.60 = 17.60^*$; $(3 - 1) F_{.01;2,120} = 9.58$. Reject the null hypothesis for $\psi_2 = \mu_1 - \mu_3$, $\psi_3 = \mu_2 - \mu_3$, and $\psi_4 = (\mu_1 + \mu_2)/2 - \mu_3$.
    b. $-3.47 < \psi_1 < 2.07$
    $-6.37 < \psi_2 < -0.83$
    $-5.67 < \psi_3 < -0.13$
    $-5.65 < \psi_4 < -0.85$

$L_1 = -3.47$ $L_2 = 2.07$

$\mu_1 - \mu_2$

$L_1 = -6.37$ $L_2 = -0.83$

$\mu_1 - \mu_3$

$L_1 = -5.67$ $L_2 = -0.13$

$\mu_2 - \mu_3$

$L_1 = -5.65$ $L_2 = -0.85$

$(\mu_1 - \mu_2) - \mu_3$

    c. For $\hat{\psi}_2$, $g = .89$ For $\hat{\psi}_3$, $g = .72$ For $\hat{\psi}_4$, $g = .80$
    The three effects sizes are large.
    d. $tDS = -.70/.894 = -.78$, $tDS = -3.60/.894 = -4.02^*$, $tDS = -2.90/.894 = -3.24^*$, $tDS = -3.25/.7746 = -4.20^*$; $tDS_{.01/2;4,120} = 3.087$. Reject $\psi_2 = \mu_1 - \mu_3 = 0$, $\psi_3 = \mu_2 - \mu_3 = 0$, and $\psi_4 = (\mu_1 + \mu_2)/2 - \mu_3 = 0$. The two multiple comparison procedures lead to the same decisions regarding the null hypotheses.
31. a. $\hat{\omega}^2 = \dfrac{110.223}{162.509} = .68$

    The strength of association is large; the independent variable accounts for 68% of the variance in the dependent variable.
    b. For $\psi_1 = \mu_1 - \mu_2$, $qFH = 4.15^*$ For $\psi_2 = \mu_1 - \mu_3$, $qFH = 8.85^*$
    For $\psi_3 = \mu_1 - \mu_4$, $qFH = 10.79^*$ For $\psi_4 = \mu_2 - \mu_3$, $qFH = 4.70^*$
    For $\psi_5 = \mu_2 - \mu_4$, $qFH = 6.63^*$ For $\psi_6 = \mu_3 - \mu_4$, $qFH = 1.94$
    $qFH_{.05;4-1,28} = 3.50$; reject the null hypothesis for all contrasts except ψ_6.
32. See Sections 14.5 and 14.6 for meaning of terms.

CHAPTER 15

1. Nuisance variables are undesired sources of variation that increase the variance of the error effects. They can be controlled or minimized by holding them constant, assigning experimental units randomly to the treatment levels, and including the nuisance variable as one of the factors in the experiment.
2. Any variable that is positively correlated with the dependent variable is a potential blocking variable.
3. a. The independent variable is kind of instruction; the dependent variable is rating of amount of help offered.
   b. Nuisance variables that were held constant included the student's grade (first grade) and the student's gender (boy).
   c. Idiosyncratic characteristics of the boys such as shyness, aggressiveness, and so forth.
   d. The test scores could be used to form 16 blocks of three boys each, such that the boys in a block are matched with respect to their conforming-compulsive scores.
4. See Section 15.1 for meaning of the terms.

5. ### Analysis of Variance Table

Source	SS	df	Ms	F
1. Treatment A	51.765	3	17.255	[$\frac{1}{3}$] 3.81*
2. Blocks	161.500	20	8.075	[$\frac{2}{3}$] 1.78*
3. Residual	271.500	60	4.525	
4. Total	484.765	83		

* $p < .05$

6. a.

The a_2 and a_3 sample distributions are relatively symmetrical; the a_1 distribution is slightly positively skewed. The data do not contain outliers.

b. **Means and Standard Deviations for Three Psychological Tests**

	a_1 WAIS	a_2 WUMV	a_3 WSA
$\bar{X}_{\cdot j}$	11.17	9.25	7.33
$\hat{\sigma}_j$	3.04	2.73	2.50

c. The means are consistent with the researcher's expectations; that is, the means for the WUMV and WSA tests are lower than the mean for the WAIS test. The WAIS standard deviation is close to the national norm value of 3; the WUMV and WSA standard deviations are smaller than the national norm values. The standard deviations are quite homogeneous.

d. **Analysis of Variance Table for Psychological Test Data**

Source	SS	df	MS	F
1. Treatment A (tests)	88.1667	2	44.0834	[$1/3$] 31.80*
2. Blocks	222.0833	11	20.1894	[$2/3$] 14.56*
3. Residual	30.5000	22	1.3864	
4. Total	340.7500	35		

*$p < .0001$

Reject the null hypothesis that the population means for the three tests are equal.

e. $\hat{\omega}^2_{X|A \cdot BL} = .63$. The strength of association is large. Treatment A accounts for 63% of the variance in the dependent variable.

f. $qFH = 1.9167/0.3399 = 5.64^*$ for μ_1 versus μ_2, $3.8334/0.3399 = 11.28^*$ for μ_1 versus μ_3, and $q = 1.9167/0.3399 = 5.64^*$ for μ_2 versus μ_3; $q_{.05;3-1,22} = 2.94$. Reject the null hypothesis for all pairwise contrasts among the three population means.

g. $g = 0.69$ The effect size for μ_1 versus μ_2 is a medium size effect.
   $g = 1.39$ The effect size for μ_1 versus μ_3 is a large size effect.
   $g = 0.69$ The effect size for μ_2 versus μ_3 is a medium size effect.

h. The two hypotheses of interests were $H_0: \mu_1 - \mu_2 \geq 0$ versus $H_1: \mu_1 - \mu_2 < 0$, and $H_0: \mu_1 - \mu_3 \geq 0$ versus $H_1: \mu_1 - \mu_3 < 0$, where the subscripts 1,

2, and 3, denote, respectively, the *WAIS, MUMV,* and *WSA* tests. The Dunn-Šidàk confidence intervals for $\psi_1 = \mu_1 - \mu_2$ and $\psi_2 = \mu_1 - \mu_3$, are respectively, $0.925 < \psi_1$ and $2.842 < \psi_2$.

Reject both null hypotheses.

i.

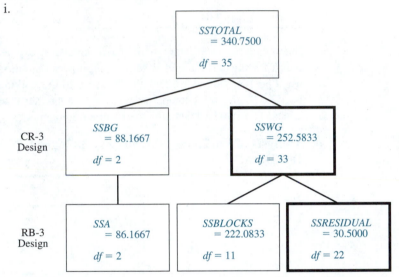

The blocking procedure was effective. When the block source of variation is removed from *SSWG*, a much smaller error term *(MS RESIDUAL)* results. The *F* statistic for the CR-3 design is $(88.1667/2)/(252.5833/33) = 5.81$; the *F* statistic for the RB-3 design is $(88.1667/2)/(30.5000/22) = 31.80$.

7. See Section 15.2 for meaning of term.
8. a. $a_1b_1, a_1b_2, a_2b_1, a_2b_2$
   b. $a_1b_1, a_1b_2, a_2b_1, a_2b_2, a_3b_1, a_3b_2$
   c. $a_1b_1, a_1b_2, a_1b_3, a_2b_1, a_2b_2, a_2b_3, a_3b_1, a_3b_2, a_3b_3$
9. a. $N = 32$ b. $N = 48$ c. $N = 36$

10. **Analysis of Variance Table**

Source	SS	df	MS	F
1. Treatment *A*	273.000	4	68.250	[$^{1}\!/_{4}$] 2.60**
2. Treatment *B*	263.550	2	131.775	[$^{2}\!/_{4}$] 5.02***
3. *AB* Interaction	302.400	8	37.800	[$^{3}\!/_{4}$] 1.44*
4. Within cell	1575.000	60	26.250	
5. Total	2413.950	74		

$*p < .25$ $**p < .05$ $***p < .01$

11. a.

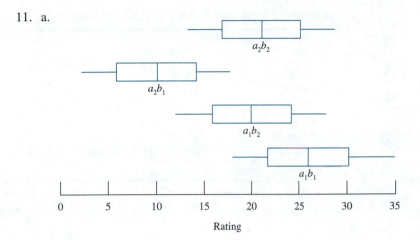

The sample distributions are symmetrical. The data do not contain outliers.

b. **Means and Standard Deviations for Ratings Data**

		Race of confederate		$\overline{X}_{\cdot j \cdot}$	$\hat{\sigma}_{j \cdot}$
		$b_1 = black$	$b_2 = white$		
	$\overline{X}_{\cdot 1k} =$	26.00	20.00		
$a_1 = $ mild shock				23.00	6.75
	$\hat{\sigma}_{1k} =$	6.32	6.32		
	$\overline{X}_{\cdot 2k} =$	10.0	21.00		
$a_2 = $ strong shock				15.50	8.32
	$\hat{\sigma}_{2k} =$	6.32	6.32		
	$\overline{X}_{\cdot \cdot k} =$	18.00	20.50		
	$\hat{\sigma}_{\cdot k} =$	10.33	5.99		

c. The participants assigned to the mild shock condition rated the confederate higher in likability, intelligence, and personal adjustment than did the participants assigned to the strong shock condition. The cell means are such as to suggest that shock level interacts with the race of the confederate. The cell standard deviations are homogeneous.

d. **Analysis of Variance Table for Ratings Data**

Source	SS	df	MS	F
1. Treatment A (shock level)	281.250	1	281.250	$[^{1}/_{4}]$ 7.03*
2. Treatment B (race of confederate)	31.250	1	31.250	$[^{2}/_{4}]$ 0.78
3. AB Interaction	361.250	1	361.250	$[^{3}/_{4}]$ 9.03**
4. Within cell	640.000	16	40.000	
5. Total	1313.750	19		

*$p < .05$ **$p < .01$

Reject the null hypothesis for treatment A and the AB interaction.

e.

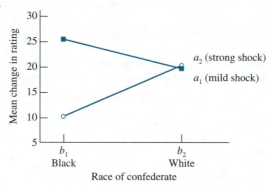

a_2 (strong shock)

a_1 (mild shock)

The graph is consistent with the AB interaction test.

f. $\hat{\omega}^2_{Y|AB \cdot A,B} = .29$. The strength of association is large. The AB interaction accounts for 29% of the variance in the dependent variable.

g. **Analysis of Variance Table for Treatment A and Treatment B**

Source	SS	df	MS	F
	Treatment A			
1. Treatment A (shock level)	281.2500	1	281.250	$[^{1}/_{2}]$ 4.90*
2. Within cell	1032.5000	18	57.3611	
3. Total	1313.7500	19		
	Treatment B			
4. Treatment B (race of confederate)	31.2500	1	31.2500	$[^{4}/_{5}]$ 0.44
5. Within cell	1282.5000	18	71.2500	
6. Total	1313.7500	19		

*$p < .05$

The CRF-22 design is preferable because it provides more powerful tests of treatments A and B than do the separate CR-2 designs. This occurs because sources of variation not specifically identified and isolated in the analysis are included in the error term. For example, the error sum of squares for testing treatment A, $SSWG = 1032.5000$, is equal to $SSB + SSAB + SSW\text{-}CELL = 31.250 + 361.250 + 640.000 = 1032.500$ from the ANOVA table in part (d). The CRF-22 design also is preferable because it enables a researcher to determine if the two treatments interact.

12. See Section 15.3 for meaning of terms.

CHAPTER 16

1. The tests for goodness of fit and independence both use one random sample. However, the test for goodness of fit classifies the elements of the sample into k mutually exclusive categories. The test for independence classifies each elements in terms of two variables. The test for equality uses c random samples and classifies each element in terms of one of two mutually exclusive categories.

2. Seven mutually exclusive socioeconomic categories were used.

3. a. State the statistical hypotheses—H_0: $p_1 = .50$, H_1: $p_1 \neq .50$. Specify the test statistic—$\chi^2 = \Sigma(O_j - E_j)^2/E_j$. Specify the sample size—$n = 50$, and the sampling distribution—chi-square distribution. Specify the level of significance—$\alpha = .05$. Obtain a random sample of size 50, compute χ^2, and make a decision.

   b. $\chi^2 = (33 - 25)^2/25 + (17 - 25)^2/25 = 5.12;$ $\chi^2(1) = 5.12 > \chi^2_{.05,1} = 3.841$.

   Reject the null hypothesis; the data suggest that opinion is not equally divided on the issue.

   c. $\hat{w} = \sqrt{\dfrac{(.66 - .50)^2}{.50} + \dfrac{(.34 - .50)^2}{.50}} = 0.32$. The effect size is medium.

4. $\chi^2 = (71 - 69.3333)^2/69.3333 + (52 - 52)^2/52 + (33 - 34.6667)^2/34.6667 = 0.120;$ $\chi^2(2) = 0.120 < \chi^2_{.05,2} = 5.991$. The data do not suggest that there has been a change in party affiliation.

5. $\chi^2 = (53 - 50)^2/50 + (41 - 50)^2/50 + \cdots + (61 - 50)^2/50 = 9.280;$ $\chi^2(5) = 9.280 < \chi^2_{.05,5} = 11.070$. The data do not suggest that the die is not fair.

6. See Section 16.2 for meaning of terms.

7. Both r and $\hat{V}$ are measures of association, but, unlike r, $\hat{V}$ is appropriate for unordered qualitative variables and ranges over the values 0 to 1. Furthermore,

$\hat{V}$ does not have a simple interpretation in terms of proportion of explained variance.

8. a. State the statistical hypotheses—H_0: $p(A \text{ and } B) = p(A)p(B)$, H_1: $p(A \text{ and } B) \neq p(A)p(B)$. Specify the test statistic—$\chi^2 = \Sigma\Sigma(O_{ij} - E_{ij})^2/E_{ij}$. Specify the sample size—$n = 200$, and the sampling distribution—chi-square distribution. Specify the level of significance—$\alpha = .001$. Obtain a random sample of size 200, compute χ^2 and make a decision.
   b. $\chi^2 = (58 - 44.08)^2/44.08 + (30 - 39.44)^2/39.44 + \cdots + (23 - 13.44)^2/13.44 = 32.28$; $\chi^2(4) = 32.28 > \chi^2_{.001, 4} = 18.467$. Reject the null hypothesis; the variables are not independent.
   c. $\hat{V} = \sqrt{32.28 / [200(3 - 1)]} = .284$
   d. $\hat{w} = .284\sqrt{3 - 1} = 0.40$. The effect size is medium.
9. a. $\chi^2 = (38 - 25.740)^2/25.740 + \cdots + (21 - 10.455)^2/10.455 = 44.574$; $\chi^2(6) = 44.574 > \chi^2_{.05,6} = 12.592$. Reject the null hypothesis; the variables are not independent.
   b. $\hat{V} = \sqrt{44.574 / [200(3 - 1)]} = .334$
   c. $\hat{w} = .334\sqrt{3 - 1} = 0.687$. The effect size is large.
10. See Section 16.3 for meaning of the term.
11. a. H_0: $p_1 = p_2$, H_1: $p_1 \neq p_2$
    b. $\chi^2 = (16 - 10.5)^2/10.5 + \cdots + (25 - 19.5)^2/19.5 = 8.864$; $\chi^2(1) = 8.864 > \chi^2_{.01,1} = 6.635$. Reject the null hypothesis.
12. The population proportions in the three categories of variable A (.30, .60, .10) are equal across the three categories of variable B.
13. a.
$$H_0: \begin{bmatrix} p_{a_1|b_1} = p_{a_1|b_2} = p_{a_1|b_3} = p_{a_1|b_4} \\ p_{a_2|b_1} = p_{a_2|b_2} = p_{a_2|b_3} = p_{a_2|b_4} \\ p_{a_3|b_1} = p_{a_3|b_2} = p_{a_3|b_3} = p_{a_3|b_4} \\ p_{a_4|b_1} = p_{a_4|b_2} = p_{a_4|b_3} = p_{a_4|b_4} \end{bmatrix}$$

H_1: $p_{a_i|b_j} \neq p_{a_i|b_{j'}}$ in at least one row for some j and j'
    b. $\chi^2 = (4 - 5)^2/5 + \cdots + (0 - 5)^2/5 = 17.560$; $\chi^2(9) = 17.560 > \chi^2_{.05,9} = 16.919$. Reject the null hypothesis.
14. a.
$$H_0: \begin{bmatrix} p_{a_1|b_1} = p_{a_1|b_2} = p_{a_1|b_3} \\ p_{a_2|b_1} = p_{a_2|b_2} = p_{a_2|b_3} \\ p_{a_3|b_1} = p_{a_3|b_2} = p_{a_3|b_3} \end{bmatrix}$$

H_1: $p_{a_i|b_j} \neq p_{a_i|b_{j'}}$ in at least one row for some j and j'
    b. $\chi^2 = (26 - 68.295918)^2/68.295918 + \cdots + (97 - 166.683674)^2/ 166.683674 = 120.219$; $\chi^2(2) = 120.219 > \chi^2_{.05,2} = 5.991$. Reject the null hypothesis.

15. d.

$$H_0: \begin{bmatrix} p_{a_1|b_1} = p_{a_1|b_2} \\ p_{a_2|b_1} = p_{a_2|b_2} \\ p_{a_3|b_1} = p_{a_3|b_2} \\ p_{a_4|b_1} = p_{a_4|b_2} \\ p_{a_5|b_1} = p_{a_5|b_2} \\ p_{a_6|b_1} = p_{a_6|b_2} \\ p_{a_7|b_1} = p_{a_7|b_2} \end{bmatrix}$$

H_1: $p_{a_i|b_1} \neq p_{a_i|b_2}$ in at least one row

CHAPTER 17

1. The Mann-Whitney U test assumes that the populations are continuous, the samples are independent, and either random sampling or random assignment has been used. The t test assumes random sampling or random assignment, normality, equal variances, and independent samples. The Mann-Whitney U test can be used with rank data and is almost as efficient as the t test.

2. $U(7, 6) = 42 + 28 - 64.5 = 5.5$; $U(7, 6) = 5.5 < U_{.05/2;7,6} = 6$. Reject the null hypothesis that the populations are identical.

3. Without the correction for ties,

$$z = \frac{(148.5 + 0.5) - 200}{\sqrt{\frac{400}{12}(41)}} = \frac{-51}{36.9685} = -1.3796;$$

$|z| = 1.3796 < z_{.01/2} = 2.576$. Do not reject the null hypothesis. With the correction,

$$z = \frac{(148.5 + 0.5) - 200}{\sqrt{\frac{400}{12}(41)(1 - 0.0044)}} = \frac{-51}{36.8869} = -1.3826;$$

$|z| = 1.3826 < z_{.01/2} = 2.576$. Do not reject the null hypothesis.

4. The value of PE is dependent on α, $1 - \beta$, H_0, and H_1, and the sample size of the more efficient comparison test statistic.

5. The approximate z test can be used when either n_1 or n_2 is greater that 20. The test is satisfactory if both n's are greater than 10.

6. a. 95%
   b. $\alpha = .01$, $1 - \beta = .80$, H_0 and H_1 are nondirectional, and $n_S = 82$.

7. See Sections 17.1 and 17.2 for meaning of terms.

8. $T(14) = 14.5 < T_{.05/2,14} = 21$; reject the null hypothesis.

9. $T(16) = 30.5 < T_{.05,16} = 35$; reject the null hypothesis.

10. $z = \dfrac{(175 + 0.5) - 35(35 + 1)/4}{\sqrt{\dfrac{35(35 + 1)[2(35) + 1]}{24}}} = -2.285$;

$|z| = 2.285 > z_{.05} = 1.645$. Reject the null hypothesis.

11. $z = \dfrac{(30.5 + 0.5) - 16(16 + 1)/4}{\sqrt{\dfrac{16(16 + 1)[2(16) + 1]}{24} - \dfrac{(6^3 - 6) + (7^3 - 7) + (2^3 - 2)}{48}}}$

$= \dfrac{-37.0000}{19.0394} = -1.943$;

$|z| = 1.943 > z_{.05} = 1.645$. Reject the null hypothesis.

12. a. 95%

b. $\alpha = .01$, $1 - \beta = .95$, H_0 and H_1 are nondirectional, and $n_S = 122$.

Appendix D

Tables

TABLE D.1. Random Numbers[a]

	1	2	3	4	5	6	7	8	9	10	11	12	13	14	15	16	17	18	19	20	21	22	23	24	25
1	10	27	53	96	23	71	50	54	36	23	54	31	04	82	98	04	14	12	15	09	26	78	25	47	47
2	28	41	50	61	88	64	85	27	20	18	83	36	36	05	56	39	71	65	09	62	94	76	62	11	89
3	34	21	42	57	02	59	19	18	97	48	80	30	03	30	98	05	24	67	70	07	84	97	50	87	46
4	61	81	77	23	23	82	82	11	54	08	53	28	70	58	96	44	07	39	55	43	42	34	43	39	28
5	61	15	18	13	54	16	86	20	26	88	90	74	80	55	09	14	53	90	51	17	52	01	63	01	59
6	91	76	21	64	64	44	91	13	32	97	75	31	62	66	54	84	80	32	75	77	56	08	25	70	29
7	00	97	79	08	06	37	30	28	59	85	53	56	68	53	40	01	74	39	59	73	30	19	99	85	48
8	36	46	18	34	94	75	20	80	27	77	78	91	69	16	00	08	43	18	73	68	67	69	61	34	25
9	88	98	99	60	50	65	95	79	42	94	93	62	40	89	96	43	56	47	71	66	46	76	29	67	02
10	04	37	59	87	21	05	02	03	24	17	47	97	81	56	51	92	34	86	01	82	55	51	33	12	91
11	63	62	06	34	41	94	21	78	55	09	72	76	45	16	94	29	95	81	83	83	79	88	01	97	30
12	78	47	23	53	90	34	41	92	45	71	09	23	70	70	07	12	38	92	79	43	14	85	11	47	23
13	87	68	62	15	43	53	14	36	59	25	54	47	33	70	15	59	24	48	40	35	50	03	42	99	36
14	47	60	92	10	77	88	59	53	11	52	66	25	69	07	04	48	68	64	71	06	61	65	70	22	12
15	56	88	87	59	41	65	28	04	67	53	95	79	88	37	31	50	41	06	94	76	81	83	17	16	33
16	02	57	45	86	67	73	43	07	34	48	44	26	87	93	29	77	09	61	67	84	06	69	44	77	75
17	31	54	14	13	17	48	62	11	90	60	68	12	93	64	28	46	24	79	16	76	14	60	25	51	01
18	28	50	16	43	36	28	97	85	58	99	67	22	52	76	23	24	70	36	54	54	59	28	61	71	96
19	63	29	62	66	50	02	63	45	52	38	67	63	47	54	75	83	24	78	43	20	92	63	13	47	48
20	45	65	58	26	51	76	96	59	38	72	86	57	45	71	46	44	67	76	14	55	44	88	01	62	12
21	39	65	36	63	70	77	45	85	50	51	74	13	39	35	22	30	53	36	02	95	49	34	88	73	61
22	73	71	98	16	04	29	18	94	51	23	76	51	94	84	86	79	93	96	38	63	08	58	25	58	94
23	72	20	56	20	11	72	65	71	08	86	79	57	95	13	91	97	48	72	66	48	09	71	17	24	89
24	75	17	26	99	76	89	37	20	70	01	77	31	61	95	46	26	97	05	73	51	53	33	18	72	87
25	37	48	60	82	29	81	30	15	39	14	48	38	75	93	29	06	87	37	78	48	45	56	00	84	47
26	68	08	02	80	72	83	71	46	30	49	89	17	95	88	29	02	39	56	03	46	97	74	06	56	17
27	14	23	98	61	67	70	52	85	01	50	01	84	02	78	43	10	62	98	19	41	18	83	99	47	99
28	49	08	96	21	44	25	27	99	41	28	07	41	08	34	66	19	42	74	39	91	41	96	53	78	72
29	78	37	06	08	43	63	61	62	42	29	39	68	95	10	96	09	24	23	00	62	56	12	80	73	16
30	37	21	34	17	68	68	96	83	23	56	32	84	60	15	31	44	73	67	34	77	91	15	79	74	58
31	14	29	09	34	04	87	83	07	55	07	76	58	30	83	64	87	29	25	58	84	86	50	60	00	25
32	58	43	28	06	36	49	52	83	51	14	47	56	91	29	34	05	87	31	06	95	12	45	57	09	09
33	10	43	67	29	70	80	62	80	03	42	10	80	21	38	84	90	56	35	03	09	43	12	74	49	14
34	44	38	88	39	54	86	97	37	44	22	00	95	01	31	76	17	16	29	56	63	38	78	94	49	81
35	90	69	59	19	51	85	39	52	85	13	07	28	37	07	61	11	16	36	27	03	78	86	72	04	95
36	47	47	10	25	62	97	05	31	03	61	20	26	36	31	62	68	69	86	95	44	84	95	48	46	45
37	91	94	14	63	19	75	89	11	47	11	31	56	34	19	09	79	57	92	36	59	14	93	87	81	40
38	80	06	54	18	66	09	18	94	06	19	98	40	07	17	81	22	45	44	84	11	24	62	20	42	31
39	67	72	77	63	48	84	08	31	55	58	24	33	45	77	58	80	45	67	93	82	75	70	16	08	24
40	59	40	24	13	27	79	26	88	86	30	01	31	60	10	39	53	58	47	70	93	85	81	56	39	38
41	05	90	35	89	95	01	61	16	96	94	50	78	13	69	36	37	68	53	37	31	71	26	35	03	71
42	44	43	80	69	98	46	68	05	14	82	90	78	50	05	62	77	79	13	57	44	59	60	10	39	66
43	61	81	31	96	82	00	57	25	60	59	46	72	60	18	77	55	66	12	62	11	08	99	55	64	57
44	42	88	07	10	05	24	98	65	63	21	47	21	61	88	32	27	80	30	21	60	10	92	35	36	12
45	77	94	30	05	39	28	10	99	00	27	12	73	73	99	12	49	99	57	94	82	96	88	57	17	91
46	78	83	19	76	16	94	11	68	84	26	23	54	20	86	85	23	86	66	99	07	36	37	34	92	09
47	87	76	59	61	81	43	63	64	61	61	65	76	36	95	90	18	48	27	45	68	27	23	65	30	72
48	91	43	05	96	47	55	78	99	95	24	37	55	85	78	78	01	48	41	19	10	35	19	54	07	73
49	84	97	77	72	73	09	62	06	65	72	87	12	49	03	60	41	15	20	76	27	50	47	02	29	16
50	87	41	60	76	83	44	88	96	07	80	83	05	83	38	96	73	70	66	81	90	30	56	10	48	59

Table D.1 is taken from Table XXXIII of Fisher and Yates: *Statistical Tables for Biological, Agricultural and Medical Research,* published by Longman Group Ltd., London (previously published by Oliver & Boyd, Edinburgh), and reprinted by permission of the authors and publishers.
[a]Discussed in Section 8.1

TABLE D.1. *(Continued)*

	1	2	3	4	5	6	7	8	9	10	11	12	13	14	15	16	17	18	19	20	21	22	23	24	25
1	22	17	68	65	84	68	95	23	92	35	87	02	22	57	51	61	09	43	95	06	58	24	82	03	47
2	19	36	27	59	46	13	79	93	37	55	39	77	32	77	09	85	52	05	30	62	47	83	51	62	74
3	16	77	23	02	77	09	61	87	25	21	28	06	24	25	93	16	71	13	59	78	23	05	47	47	25
4	78	43	76	71	61	20	44	90	32	64	97	67	63	99	61	46	38	03	93	22	69	81	21	99	21
5	03	28	28	26	08	73	37	32	04	05	69	30	16	09	05	88	69	58	28	99	35	07	44	75	47
6	93	22	53	64	39	07	10	63	76	35	87	03	04	79	88	08	13	13	85	51	55	34	57	72	69
7	78	76	58	54	74	92	38	70	96	92	52	06	79	79	45	82	63	18	27	44	69	66	92	19	09
8	23	68	35	26	00	99	53	93	61	28	52	70	05	48	34	56	65	05	61	86	90	92	10	70	80
9	15	39	25	70	99	93	86	52	77	65	15	33	59	05	28	22	87	26	07	47	86	96	98	29	06
10	58	71	96	30	24	18	46	23	34	27	85	13	99	24	44	49	18	09	79	49	74	16	32	23	02
11	57	35	27	33	72	24	53	63	94	09	41	10	76	47	91	44	04	95	49	66	39	60	04	59	81
12	48	50	86	54	48	22	06	34	72	52	82	21	15	65	20	33	29	94	71	11	15	91	29	12	03
13	61	96	48	95	03	07	16	39	33	66	98	56	10	56	79	77	21	30	27	12	90	49	22	23	62
14	36	93	89	41	26	29	70	83	63	51	99	74	20	52	36	87	09	41	15	09	98	60	16	03	03
15	18	87	00	42	31	57	90	12	02	07	23	47	37	17	31	54	08	01	88	63	39	41	88	92	10
16	88	56	53	27	59	33	35	72	67	47	77	34	55	45	70	08	18	27	38	90	16	95	86	70	75
17	09	72	95	84	29	49	41	31	06	70	42	38	06	45	18	64	84	73	31	65	52	53	37	97	15
18	12	96	88	17	31	65	19	69	02	83	60	75	86	90	68	24	64	19	35	51	56	61	87	39	12
19	85	94	57	24	16	92	09	84	38	76	22	00	27	69	85	29	81	94	78	70	21	94	47	90	12
20	38	64	43	59	98	98	77	87	68	07	91	51	67	62	44	40	98	05	93	78	23	32	65	41	18
21	53	44	09	42	72	00	41	86	79	79	68	47	22	00	20	35	55	31	51	51	00	83	63	22	55
22	40	76	66	26	84	57	99	99	90	37	36	63	32	08	58	37	40	13	68	97	87	64	81	07	83
23	02	17	79	18	05	12	59	52	57	02	22	07	90	47	03	28	14	11	30	79	20	69	22	40	98
24	95	17	82	06	53	31	51	10	96	46	92	06	88	07	77	56	11	50	81	69	40	23	72	51	39
25	35	76	22	42	92	96	11	83	44	80	34	68	35	48	77	33	42	40	90	60	73	96	53	97	86
26	26	29	13	56	41	85	47	04	66	08	34	72	57	59	13	82	43	80	46	15	38	26	61	70	04
27	77	80	20	75	82	72	82	32	99	90	63	95	73	76	63	89	73	44	99	05	48	67	26	43	18
28	46	40	66	44	52	91	36	74	43	53	30	82	13	54	00	78	45	63	98	35	55	03	36	67	68
29	37	56	08	18	09	77	53	84	46	47	31	91	18	95	58	24	16	74	11	53	44	10	13	85	57
30	61	65	61	68	66	37	27	47	39	19	84	83	70	07	48	53	21	40	06	71	95	06	79	88	54
31	93	43	69	64	07	34	18	04	52	35	56	27	09	24	86	61	85	53	83	45	19	90	70	99	00
32	21	96	60	12	99	11	20	99	45	18	48	13	93	55	34	18	37	79	49	90	65	97	38	20	46
33	95	20	47	97	97	27	37	83	28	71	00	06	41	41	74	45	89	09	39	84	51	67	11	52	49
34	97	86	21	78	73	10	65	81	92	59	58	76	17	14	97	04	76	62	16	17	17	95	70	45	80
35	69	92	06	34	13	59	71	74	17	32	27	55	10	24	19	23	71	82	13	74	63	52	52	01	41
36	04	31	17	21	56	33	73	99	19	87	26	72	39	27	67	53	77	57	68	93	60	61	97	22	61
37	61	06	98	03	91	87	14	77	43	96	43	00	65	98	50	45	60	33	01	07	98	99	46	50	47
38	85	93	85	86	88	72	87	08	62	40	16	06	10	89	20	23	21	34	74	97	76	38	03	29	63
39	21	74	32	47	45	73	96	07	94	52	09	65	90	77	47	25	76	16	19	33	53	05	70	53	30
40	15	69	53	82	80	79	96	23	53	10	65	39	07	16	29	45	33	02	43	70	02	87	40	41	45
41	02	89	08	04	49	20	21	14	68	86	87	63	93	95	17	11	29	01	95	80	35	14	97	35	33
42	87	18	15	89	79	85	43	01	72	73	08	61	74	51	69	89	74	39	82	15	94	51	33	41	67
43	98	83	71	94	22	59	97	50	99	52	08	52	85	08	40	87	80	61	65	31	91	51	80	32	44
44	10	08	58	21	66	72	68	49	29	31	89	85	84	46	06	59	73	19	85	23	65	09	29	75	63
45	47	90	56	10	08	88	02	84	27	83	42	29	72	23	19	66	56	45	65	79	20	71	53	20	25
46	22	85	61	68	90	49	64	92	85	44	16	40	12	89	88	50	14	49	81	06	01	82	77	45	12
47	67	80	43	79	33	12	83	11	41	16	25	58	19	68	70	77	02	54	00	52	53	43	37	15	26
48	27	62	50	96	72	79	44	61	40	15	14	53	40	65	39	27	31	58	50	28	11	39	03	34	25
49	33	78	80	87	15	38	30	06	38	21	14	47	47	07	26	54	96	87	53	32	40	36	40	96	76
50	13	13	92	66	99	47	24	49	57	74	32	25	43	62	17	10	97	11	69	84	99	63	22	32	98

TABLE D.2.   Areas Under the Standard Normal Distribution[a]

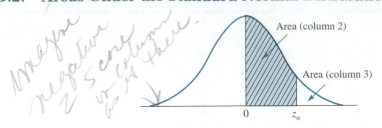

Area (column 2)

Area (column 3)

0 z_α

(1)	(2) Area Between Mean and	(3) Area Above	(1)	(2) Area Between Mean and	(3) Area Above	(1)	(2) Area Between Mean and	(3) Area Above
z_α	z_α	z_α	z_α	z_α	z_α	z_α	z_α	z_α
0.00	0.0000	0.5000	0.30	0.1179	0.3821	0.60	0.2257	0.2743
0.01	0.0040	0.4960	0.31	0.1217	0.3783	0.61	0.2291	0.2709
0.02	0.0080	0.4920	0.32	0.1255	0.3745	0.62	0.2324	0.2676
0.03	0.0120	0.4880	0.33	0.1293	0.3707	0.63	0.2357	0.2643
0.04	0.0160	0.4840	0.34	0.1331	0.3669	0.64	0.2389	0.2611
0.05	0.0199	0.4801	0.35	0.1368	0.3632	0.65	0.2422	0.2578
0.06	0.0239	0.4761	0.36	0.1406	0.3594	0.66	0.2454	0.2546
0.07	0.0279	0.4721	0.37	0.1443	0.3557	0.67	0.2486	0.2514
0.08	0.0319	0.4681	0.38	0.1480	0.3520	0.68	0.2517	0.2483
0.09	0.0359	0.4641	0.39	0.1517	0.3483	0.69	0.2549	0.2451
0.10	0.0398	0.4602	0.40	0.1554	0.3446	0.70	0.2580	0.2420
0.11	0.0438	0.4562	0.41	0.1591	0.3409	0.71	0.2611	0.2389
0.12	0.0478	0.4522	0.42	0.1628	0.3372	0.72	0.2642	0.2358
0.13	0.0517	0.4483	0.43	0.1664	0.3336	0.73	0.2673	0.2327
0.14	0.0557	0.4443	0.44	0.1700	0.3300	0.74	0.2704	0.2296
0.15	0.0596	0.4404	0.45	0.1736	0.3264	0.75	0.2734	0.2266
0.16	0.0636	0.4364	0.46	0.1772	0.3228	0.76	0.2764	0.2236
0.17	0.0675	0.4325	0.47	0.1808	0.3192	0.77	0.2794	0.2206
0.18	0.0714	0.4286	0.48	0.1844	0.3156	0.78	0.2823	0.2177
0.19	0.0753	0.4247	0.49	0.1879	0.3121	0.79	0.2852	0.2148
0.20	0.0793	0.4207	0.50	0.1915	0.3085	0.80	0.2881	0.2119
0.21	0.0832	0.4168	0.51	0.1950	0.3050	0.81	0.2910	0.2090
0.22	0.0871	0.4129	0.52	0.1985	0.3015	0.82	0.2939	0.2061
0.23	0.0910	0.4090	0.53	0.2019	0.2981	0.83	0.2967	0.2033
0.24	0.0948	0.4052	0.54	0.2054	0.2946	0.84	0.2995	0.2005
0.25	0.0987	0.4013	0.55	0.2088	0.2912	0.85	0.3023	0.1977
0.26	0.1026	0.3974	0.56	0.2123	0.2877	0.86	0.3051	0.1949
0.27	0.1064	0.3936	0.57	0.2157	0.2843	0.87	0.3078	0.1922
0.28	0.1103	0.3897	0.58	0.2190	0.2810	0.88	0.3106	0.1894
0.29	0.1141	0.3859	0.59	0.2224	0.2776	0.89	0.3133	0.1867

Table D.2 is abridged from Table IIi of Fisher and Yates: *Statistical Tables for Biological, Agricultural and Medical Research*, published by Longman Group Ltd., London (previously published by Oliver & Boyd, Edinburgh), and reprinted by permission of the authors and publishers.
[a]Discussed in Section 9.1.

TABLE D.2. (Continued)

(1) z_α	(2) Area Between Mean and z_α	(3) Area Above z_α	(1) z_α	(2) Area Between Mean and z_α	(3) Area Above z_α	(1) z_α	(2) Area Between Mean and z_α	(3) Area Above z_α
0.90	0.3159	0.1841	1.30	0.4032	0.0968	1.70	0.4554	0.0446
0.91	0.3186	0.1814	1.31	0.4049	0.0951	1.71	0.4564	0.0436
0.92	0.3212	0.1788	1.32	0.4066	0.0934	1.72	0.4573	0.0427
0.93	0.3238	0.1762	1.33	0.4082	0.0918	1.73	0.4582	0.0418
0.94	0.3264	0.1736	1.34	0.4099	0.0901	1.74	0.4591	0.0409
0.95	0.3289	0.1711	1.35	0.4115	0.0885	1.75	0.4599	0.0401
0.96	0.3315	0.1685	1.36	0.4131	0.0869	1.76	0.4608	0.0392
0.97	0.3340	0.1660	1.37	0.4147	0.0853	1.77	0.4616	0.0384
0.98	0.3365	0.1635	1.38	0.4162	0.0838	1.78	0.4625	0.0375
0.99	0.3389	0.1611	1.39	0.4177	0.0823	1.79	0.4633	0.0367
1.00	0.3413	0.1587	1.40	0.4192	0.0808	1.80	0.4641	0.0359
1.01	0.3438	0.1562	1.41	0.4207	0.0793	1.81	0.4649	0.0351
1.02	0.3461	0.1539	1.42	0.4222	0.0778	1.82	0.4656	0.0344
1.03	0.3485	0.1515	1.43	0.4236	0.0764	1.83	0.4664	0.0336
1.04	0.3508	0.1492	1.44	0.4251	0.0749	1.84	0.4671	0.0329
1.05	0.3531	0.1469	1.45	0.4265	0.0735	1.85	0.4678	0.0322
1.06	0.3554	0.1446	1.46	0.4279	0.0721	1.86	0.4686	0.0314
1.07	0.3577	0.1423	1.47	0.4292	0.0708	1.87	0.4693	0.0307
1.08	0.3599	0.1401	1.48	0.4306	0.0694	1.88	0.4699	0.0301
1.09	0.3621	0.1379	1.49	0.4319	0.0681	1.89	0.4706	0.0294
1.10	0.3643	0.1357	1.50	0.4332	0.0668	1.90	0.4713	0.0287
1.11	0.3665	0.1335	1.51	0.4345	0.0655	1.91	0.4719	0.0281
1.12	0.3686	0.1314	1.52	0.4357	0.0643	1.92	0.4726	0.0274
1.13	0.3708	0.1292	1.53	0.4370	0.0630	1.93	0.4732	0.0268
1.14	0.3729	0.1271	1.54	0.4382	0.0618	1.94	0.4738	0.0262
1.15	0.3749	0.1251	1.55	0.4394	0.0606	1.95	0.4744	0.0256
1.16	0.3770	0.1230	1.56	0.4406	0.0594	1.96	0.4750	0.0250
1.17	0.3790	0.1210	1.57	0.4418	0.0582	1.97	0.4756	0.0244
1.18	0.3810	0.1190	1.58	0.4429	0.0571	1.98	0.4761	0.0239
1.19	0.3830	0.1170	1.59	0.4441	0.0559	1.99	0.4767	0.0233
1.20	0.3849	0.1151	1.60	0.4452	0.0548	2.00	0.4772	0.0228
1.21	0.3869	0.1131	1.61	0.4463	0.0537	2.01	0.4778	0.0222
1.22	0.3888	0.1112	1.62	0.4474	0.0526	2.02	0.4783	0.0217
1.23	0.3907	0.1093	1.63	0.4484	0.0516	2.03	0.4788	0.0212
1.24	0.3925	0.1075	1.64	0.4495	0.0505	2.04	0.4793	0.0207
			1.645	0.4500	0.0500			
1.25	0.3944	0.1056	1.65	0.4505	0.0495	2.05	0.4798	0.0202
1.26	0.3962	0.1038	1.66	0.4515	0.0485	2.06	0.4803	0.0197
1.27	0.3980	0.1020	1.67	0.4525	0.0475	2.07	0.4808	0.0192
1.28	0.3997	0.1003	1.68	0.4535	0.0465	2.08	0.4812	0.0188
1.29	0.4015	0.0985	1.69	0.4545	0.0455	2.09	0.4817	0.0183

TABLE D.2. *(Continued)*

(1) z_α	*(2)* Area Between Mean and z_α	*(3)* Area Above z_α	*(1)* z_α	*(2)* Area Between Mean and z_α	*(3)* Area Above z_α	*(1)* z_α	*(2)* Area Between Mean and z_α	*(3)* Area Above z_α
2.10	0.4821	0.0179	2.45	0.4929	0.0071	2.80	0.4974	0.0026
2.11	0.4826	0.0174	2.46	0.4931	0.0069	2.81	0.4975	0.0025
2.12	0.4830	0.0170	2.47	0.4932	0.0068	2.82	0.4976	0.0024
2.13	0.4834	0.0166	2.48	0.4934	0.0066	2.83	0.4977	0.0023
2.14	0.4838	0.0162	2.49	0.4936	0.0064	2.84	0.4977	0.0023
2.15	0.4842	0.0158	2.50	0.4938	0.0062	2.85	0.4978	0.0022
2.16	0.4846	0.0154	2.51	0.4940	0.0060	2.86	0.4979	0.0021
2.17	0.4850	0.0150	2.52	0.4941	0.0059	2.87	0.4979	0.0021
2.18	0.4854	0.0146	2.53	0.4943	0.0057	2.88	0.4980	0.0020
2.19	0.4857	0.0143	2.54	0.4945	0.0055	2.89	0.4981	0.0019
2.20	0.4861	0.0139	2.55	0.4946	0.0054	2.90	0.4981	0.0019
2.21	0.4864	0.0136	2.56	0.4948	0.0052	2.91	0.4982	0.0018
2.22	0.4868	0.0132	2.57	0.4949	0.0051	2.92	0.4982	0.0018
2.23	0.4871	0.0129	2.576	0.4950	0.0050	2.93	0.4983	0.0017
2.24	0.4875	0.0125	2.58	0.4951	0.0049	2.94	0.4984	0.0016
			2.59	0.4952	0.0048			
2.25	0.4878	0.0122	2.60	0.4953	0.0047	2.95	0.4984	0.0016
2.26	0.4881	0.0119	2.61	0.4955	0.0045	2.96	0.4985	0.0015
2.27	0.4884	0.0116	2.62	0.4956	0.0044	2.97	0.4985	0.0015
2.28	0.4887	0.0113	2.63	0.4957	0.0043	2.98	0.4986	0.0014
2.29	0.4890	0.0110	2.64	0.4959	0.0041	2.99	0.4986	0.0014
2.30	0.4893	0.0107	2.65	0.4960	0.0040	3.00	0.4987	0.0013
2.31	0.4896	0.0104	2.66	0.4961	0.0039	3.01	0.4987	0.0013
2.32	0.4898	0.0102	2.67	0.4962	0.0038	3.02	0.4987	0.0013
2.33	0.4901	0.0099	2.68	0.4963	0.0037	3.03	0.4988	0.0012
2.34	0.4904	0.0096	2.69	0.4964	0.0036	3.04	0.4988	0.0012
2.35	0.4906	0.0094	2.70	0.4965	0.0035	3.05	0.4989	0.0011
2.36	0.4909	0.0091	2.71	0.4966	0.0034	3.06	0.4989	0.0011
2.37	0.4911	0.0089	2.72	0.4967	0.0033	3.07	0.4989	0.0011
2.38	0.4913	0.0087	2.73	0.4968	0.0032	3.08	0.4990	0.0010
2.39	0.4916	0.0084	2.74	0.4969	0.0031	3.09	0.4990	0.0010
2.40	0.4918	0.0082	2.75	0.4970	0.0030	3.10	0.4990	0.0010
2.41	0.4920	0.0080	2.76	0.4971	0.0029	3.11	0.4991	0.0009
2.42	0.4922	0.0078	2.77	0.4972	0.0028	3.12	0.4991	0.0009
2.43	0.4925	0.0075	2.78	0.4973	0.0027	3.13	0.4991	0.0009
2.44	0.4927	0.0073	2.79	0.4974	0.0026	3.14	0.4992	0.0008

TABLE D.2. *(Continued)*

(1)	*(2)* Area Between Mean and	*(3)* Area Above	*(1)*	*(2)* Area Between Mean and	*(3)* Area Above
z_α	z_α	z_α	z_α	z_α	z_α
3.15	0.4992	0.0008	3.25	0.4994	0.0006
3.16	0.4992	0.0008	3.30	0.4995	0.0005
3.17	0.4992	0.0008	3.35	0.4996	0.0004
3.18	0.4993	0.0007	3.40	0.4997	0.0003
3.19	0.4993	0.0007	3.45	0.4997	0.0003
3.20	0.4993	0.0007	3.50	0.4998	0.0002
3.21	0.4993	0.0007	3.60	0.4998	0.0002
3.22	0.4994	0.0006	3.70	0.4999	0.0001
3.23	0.4994	0.0006	3.80	0.4999	0.0001
3.24	0.4994	0.0006	3.90	0.49995	0.00005
			4.00	0.49997	0.00003

TABLE D.3.   Percentage Points of Student's *t* Distribution[a]

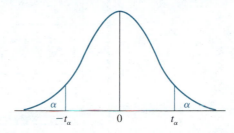

Degrees of Freedom, v	Level of Significance for a One-Tailed Test								
	.25	.20	.15	.10	.05	.025	.01	.005	.0005
	Level of Significance for a Two-Tailed Test								
	.50	.40	.30	.20	.10	.05	.02	.01	.001
1	1.000	1.376	1.963	3.078	6.314	12.706	31.821	63.657	636.619
2	.816	1.061	1.386	1.886	2.920	4.303	6.965	9.925	31.598
3	.765	.978	1.250	1.638	2.353	3.182	4.541	5.841	12.924
4	.741	.941	1.190	1.533	2.132	2.776	3.747	4.604	8.610
5	.727	.920	1.156	1.476	2.015	2.571	3.365	4.032	6.869
6	.718	.906	1.134	1.440	1.943	2.447	3.143	3.707	5.959
7	.711	.896	1.119	1.415	1.895	2.365	2.998	3.499	5.408
8	.706	.889	1.108	1.397	1.860	2.306	2.896	3.355	5.041
9	.703	.883	1.100	1.383	1.833	2.262	2.821	3.250	4.781
10	.700	.879	1.093	1.372	1.812	2.228	2.764	3.169	4.587
11	.697	.876	1.088	1.363	1.796	2.201	2.718	3.106	4.437
12	.695	.873	1.083	1.356	1.782	2.179	2.681	3.055	4.318
13	.694	.870	1.079	1.350	1.771	2.160	2.650	3.012	4.221
14	.692	.868	1.076	1.345	1.761	2.145	2.624	2.977	4.140
15	.691	.866	1.074	1.341	1.753	2.131	2.602	2.947	4.073
16	.690	.865	1.071	1.337	1.746	2.120	2.583	2.921	4.015
17	.689	.863	1.069	1.333	1.740	2.110	2.567	2.898	3.965
18	.688	.862	1.067	1.330	1.734	2.101	2.552	2.878	3.922
19	.688	.861	1.066	1.328	1.729	2.093	2.539	2.861	3.883
20	.687	.860	1.064	1.325	1.725	2.086	2.528	2.845	3.850
21	.686	.859	1.063	1.323	1.721	2.080	2.518	2.831	3.819
22	.686	.858	1.061	1.321	1.717	2.074	2.508	2.819	3.792
23	.685	.858	1.060	1.319	1.714	2.069	2.500	2.807	3.767
24	.685	.857	1.059	1.318	1.711	2.064	2.492	2.797	3.745
25	.684	.856	1.058	1.316	1.708	2.060	2.485	2.787	3.725
26	.684	.856	1.058	1.315	1.706	2.056	2.479	2.779	3.707
27	.684	.855	1.057	1.314	1.703	2.052	2.473	2.771	3.690
28	.683	.855	1.056	1.313	1.701	2.048	2.467	2.763	3.674
29	.683	.854	1.055	1.311	1.699	2.045	2.462	2.756	3.659
30	.683	.854	1.055	1.310	1.697	2.042	2.457	2.750	3.646
40	.681	.851	1.050	1.303	1.684	2.021	2.423	2.704	3.551
60	.679	.848	1.046	1.296	1.671	2.000	2.390	2.660	3.460
120	.677	.845	1.041	1.289	1.658	1.980	2.358	2.617	3.373
∞	.674	.842	1.036	1.282	1.645	1.960	2.326	2.576	3.291

Table D.3 is taken from Table III of Fisher and Yates: *Statistical Tables for Biological, Agricultural and Medical Research,* published by Longman Group Ltd., London (previously published by Oliver & Boyd, Edinburgh), and reprinted by permission of the authors and publishers.
[a]Discussed in Section 11.2

TABLE D.4. Upper Percentage Points of the Chi-Square Distribution[a]

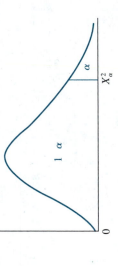

ν[b]	.99	.975	.95	.90	.80	.70	.50	.30	.20	.10	.05	.025	.01	.005
1	$.0^3157$	$.0^3982$	$.0^2393$	.0158	.0642	.148	.455	1.074	1.642	2.706	3.841	5.024	6.635	7.879
2	.0201	.0506	.103	.211	.446	.713	1.386	2.408	3.219	4.605	5.991	7.378	9.210	10.597
3	.115	.216	.352	.584	1.005	1.424	2.366	3.665	4.642	6.251	7.815	9.348	11.345	12.838
4	.297	.484	.711	1.064	1.649	2.195	3.357	4.878	5.989	7.779	9.488	11.143	13.277	14.860
5	.554	.831	1.145	1.610	2.343	3.000	4.351	6.064	7.289	9.236	11.070	12.832	15.086	16.750
6	.872	1.237	1.635	2.204	3.070	3.828	5.348	7.231	8.558	10.645	12.592	14.449	16.812	18.548
7	1.239	1.690	2.167	2.833	3.822	4.671	6.346	8.383	9.803	12.017	14.067	16.013	18.475	20.278
8	1.646	2.180	2.733	3.490	4.594	5.527	7.344	9.524	11.030	13.362	15.507	17.535	20.090	21.955
9	2.088	2.700	3.325	4.168	5.380	6.393	8.343	10.656	12.242	14.684	16.919	19.023	21.666	23.589
10	2.558	3.247	3.940	4.865	6.179	7.267	9.342	11.781	13.442	15.987	18.307	20.483	23.209	25.188
11	3.053	3.816	4.575	5.578	6.989	8.148	10.341	12.899	14.631	17.275	19.675	21.920	24.725	26.757
12	3.571	4.404	5.226	6.304	7.807	9.034	11.340	14.011	15.812	18.549	21.026	23.337	26.217	28.300
13	4.107	5.009	5.892	7.042	8.634	9.926	12.340	15.119	16.985	19.812	22.362	24.736	27.688	29.819
14	4.660	5.629	6.571	7.790	9.467	10.821	13.339	16.222	18.151	21.064	23.685	26.119	29.141	31.319
15	5.229	6.262	7.261	8.547	10.307	11.721	14.339	17.322	19.311	22.307	24.996	27.488	30.578	32.801
16	5.812	6.908	7.962	9.312	11.152	12.624	15.338	18.418	20.465	23.542	26.296	28.845	32.000	34.267
17	6.408	7.564	8.672	10.085	12.002	13.531	16.338	19.511	21.615	24.769	27.587	30.191	33.409	35.718
18	7.015	8.231	9.390	10.865	12.857	14.440	17.338	20.601	22.760	25.989	28.869	31.526	34.805	37.156
19	7.633	8.907	10.117	11.651	13.716	15.352	18.338	21.689	23.900	27.204	30.144	32.852	36.191	38.582
20	8.260	9.591	10.851	12.443	14.578	16.266	19.337	22.775	25.038	28.412	31.410	34.170	37.566	39.997

21	8.897	10.283	11.591	13.240	15.445	17.182	20.337	23.858	26.171	29.615	32.671	35.479	38.932	41.401
22	9.542	10.982	12.338	14.041	16.314	18.101	21.337	24.939	27.301	30.813	33.924	36.781	40.289	42.796
23	10.196	11.689	13.091	14.848	17.187	19.021	22.337	26.018	28.429	32.007	35.172	38.076	41.638	44.181
24	10.856	12.401	13.848	15.659	18.062	19.943	23.337	27.096	29.553	33.196	36.415	39.364	42.980	45.558
25	11.524	13.120	14.611	16.473	18.940	20.867	24.337	28.172	30.675	34.382	37.652	40.646	44.314	46.928
26	12.198	13.844	15.379	17.292	19.820	21.792	25.336	29.246	31.795	35.563	38.885	41.923	45.642	48.290
27	12.879	14.573	16.151	18.114	20.703	22.719	26.336	30.319	32.912	36.741	40.113	43.195	46.963	49.645
28	13.565	15.308	16.928	18.939	21.588	23.647	27.336	31.391	34.027	37.916	41.337	44.461	48.278	50.994
29	14.256	16.047	17.708	19.768	22.475	24.577	28.336	32.461	35.139	39.087	42.557	45.722	49.588	52.335
30	14.953	16.791	18.493	20.599	23.364	25.508	29.336	33.530	36.250	40.256	43.773	46.979	50.892	53.672
31	15.655	17.539	19.281	21.434	24.255	26.440	30.336	34.598	37.359	41.422	44.985	48.232	52.191	55.002
32	16.362	18.291	20.072	22.271	25.148	27.373	31.336	35.665	38.466	42.585	46.194	49.480	53.486	56.328
34	17.789	19.806	21.664	23.952	26.938	29.242	33.336	37.795	40.676	44.903	48.602	51.966	56.061	58.964
36	19.233	21.336	23.269	25.643	28.735	31.115	35.336	39.922	42.879	47.212	50.998	54.437	58.619	61.581
38	20.691	22.878	24.884	27.343	30.537	32.992	37.335	42.045	45.076	49.513	53.384	56.895	61.162	64.181
40	22.164	24.433	26.509	29.051	32.345	34.872	39.335	44.165	47.269	51.805	55.758	59.342	63.691	66.766
42	23.650	25.999	28.144	30.765	34.157	36.755	41.335	46.282	49.456	54.090	58.124	61.777	66.206	69.336
44	25.148	27.575	29.787	32.487	35.974	38.641	43.335	48.396	51.639	56.369	60.481	64.201	68.710	71.892
47	27.416	29.956	32.268	35.081	38.708	41.474	46.335	51.562	54.906	59.774	64.001	67.821	72.443	75.704
50	29.707	32.357	34.764	37.689	41.449	44.313	49.335	54.723	58.164	63.167	67.505	71.420	76.154	79.490

[a] Discussed in Section 11.3.

[b] For $\nu > 30$, the expression $\sqrt{2\chi^2} - \sqrt{2\nu - 1}$ may be referred to the standard normal distribution, Table D.2.

TABLE D.5. Upper Percentage Points of the F Distribution[a]

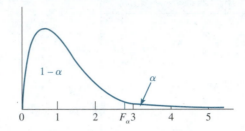

Degrees of Freedom for Denominator, v_2	α	\multicolumn{12}{c}{Degrees of Freedom for Numerator, v_1}
		1	*2*	*3*	*4*	*5*	*6*	*7*	*8*	*9*	*10*	*11*	*12*
1	.25	5.83	7.50	8.20	8.58	8.82	8.98	9.10	9.19	9.26	9.32	9.36	9.41
	.10	39.9	49.5	53.6	55.8	57.2	58.2	58.9	59.4	59.9	60.2	60.5	60.7
	.05	161	200	216	225	230	234	237	239	241	242	243	244
2	.25	2.57	3.00	3.15	3.23	3.28	3.31	3.34	3.35	3.37	3.38	3.39	3.39
	.10	8.53	9.00	9.16	9.24	9.29	9.33	9.35	9.37	9.38	9.39	9.40	9.41
	.05	18.5	19.0	19.2	19.2	19.3	19.3	19.4	19.4	19.4	19.4	19.4	19.4
	.01	98.5	99.0	99.2	99.2	99.3	99.3	99.4	99.4	99.4	99.4	99.4	99.4
3	.25	2.02	2.28	2.36	2.39	2.41	2.42	2.43	2.44	2.44	2.44	2.45	2.45
	.10	5.54	5.46	5.39	5.34	5.31	5.28	5.27	5.25	5.24	5.23	5.22	5.22
	.05	10.1	9.55	9.28	9.12	9.01	8.94	8.89	8.85	8.81	8.79	8.76	8.74
	.01	34.1	30.8	29.5	28.7	28.2	27.9	27.7	27.5	27.3	27.2	27.1	27.1
4	.25	1.81	2.00	2.05	2.06	2.07	2.08	2.08	2.08	2.08	2.08	2.08	2.08
	.10	4.54	4.32	4.19	4.11	4.05	4.01	3.98	3.95	3.94	3.92	3.91	3.90
	.05	7.71	6.94	6.59	6.39	6.26	6.16	6.09	6.04	6.00	5.96	5.94	5.91
	.01	21.2	18.0	16.7	16.0	15.5	15.2	15.0	14.8	14.7	14.5	14.4	14.4
5	.25	1.69	1.85	1.88	1.89	1.89	1.89	1.89	1.89	1.89	1.89	1.89	1.89
	.10	4.06	3.78	3.62	3.52	3.45	3.40	3.37	3.34	3.32	3.30	3.28	3.27
	.05	6.61	5.79	5.41	5.19	5.05	4.95	4.88	4.82	4.77	4.74	4.71	4.68
	.01	16.3	13.3	12.1	11.4	11.0	10.7	10.5	10.3	10.2	10.1	9.96	9.89
6	.25	1.62	1.76	1.78	1.79	1.79	1.78	1.78	1.78	1.77	1.77	1.77	1.77
	.10	3.78	3.46	3.29	3.18	3.11	3.05	3.01	2.98	2.96	2.94	2.92	2.90
	.05	5.99	5.14	4.76	4.53	4.39	4.28	4.21	4.15	4.10	4.06	4.03	4.00
	.01	13.7	10.9	9.78	9.15	8.75	8.47	8.26	8.10	7.98	7.87	7.79	7.72
7	.25	1.57	1.70	1.72	1.72	1.71	1.71	1.70	1.70	1.69	1.69	1.69	1.68
	.10	3.59	3.26	3.07	2.96	2.88	2.83	2.78	2.75	2.72	2.70	2.68	2.67
	.05	5.59	4.74	4.35	4.12	3.97	3.87	3.79	3.73	3.68	3.64	3.60	3.57
	.01	12.2	9.55	8.45	7.85	7.46	7.19	6.99	6.84	6.72	6.62	6.54	6.47

Abridged from Table 18 in *Biometrika Tables for Statisticians*, Vol. 1 (3rd ed.), E. S. Pearson and H. O. Hartley (Eds.). Reprinted by permission of the Biometrika Trustees.
[a]Discussed in Section 13.1.

				Degrees of Freedom for Numerator, v_1									Degrees of Freedom for Denominator,
15	20	24	30	40	50	60	100	120	200	500	∞	α	v_2
9.49	9.58	9.63	9.67	9.71	9.74	9.76	9.78	9.80	9.82	9.84	9.85	.25	
61.2	61.7	62.0	62.3	62.5	62.7	62.8	63.0	63.1	63.2	63.3	63.3	.10	1
246	248	249	250	251	252	252	253	253	254	254	254	.05	
3.41	3.43	3.43	3.44	3.45	3.45	3.46	3.47	3.47	3.48	3.48	3.48	.25	
9.42	9.44	9.45	9.46	9.47	9.47	9.47	9.48	9.48	9.49	9.49	9.49	.10	2
19.4	19.4	19.5	19.5	19.5	19.5	19.5	19.5	19.5	19.5	19.5	19.5	.05	
99.4	99.4	99.5	99.5	99.5	99.5	99.5	99.5	99.5	99.5	99.5	99.5	.01	
2.46	2.46	2.46	2.47	2.47	2.47	2.47	2.47	2.47	2.47	2.47	2.47	.25	
5.20	5.18	5.18	5.17	5.16	5.15	5.15	5.14	5.14	5.14	5.14	5.13	.10	3
8.70	8.66	8.64	8.62	8.59	8.58	8.57	8.55	8.55	8.54	8.53	8.53	.05	
26.9	26.7	26.6	26.5	26.4	26.4	26.3	26.2	26.2	26.2	26.1	26.1	.01	
2.08	2.08	2.08	2.08	2.08	2.08	2.08	2.08	2.08	2.08	2.08	2.08	.25	
3.87	3.84	3.83	3.82	3.80	3.80	3.79	3.78	3.78	3.77	3.76	3.76	.10	4
5.86	5.80	5.77	5.75	5.72	5.70	5.69	5.66	5.66	5.65	5.64	5.63	.05	
14.2	14.0	13.9	13.8	13.7	13.7	13.7	13.6	13.6	13.5	13.5	13.5	.01	
1.89	1.88	1.88	1.88	1.88	1.88	1.87	1.87	1.87	1.87	1.87	1.87	.25	
3.24	3.21	3.19	3.17	3.16	3.15	3.14	3.13	3.12	3.12	3.11	3.10	.10	5
4.62	4.56	4.53	4.50	4.46	4.44	4.43	4.41	4.40	4.39	4.37	4.36	.05	
9.72	9.55	9.47	9.38	9.29	9.24	9.20	9.13	9.11	9.08	9.04	9.02	.01	
1.76	1.76	1.75	1.75	1.75	1.75	1.74	1.74	1.74	1.74	1.74	1.74	.25	
2.87	2.84	2.82	2.80	2.78	2.77	2.76	2.75	2.74	2.73	2.73	2.72	.10	6
3.94	3.87	3.84	3.81	3.77	3.75	3.74	3.71	3.70	3.69	3.68	3.67	.05	
7.56	7.40	7.31	7.23	7.14	7.09	7.06	6.99	6.97	6.93	6.90	6.88	.01	
1.68	1.67	1.67	1.66	1.66	1.66	1.65	1.65	1.65	1.65	1.65	1.65	.25	
2.63	2.59	2.58	2.56	2.54	2.52	2.51	2.50	2.49	2.48	2.48	2.47	.10	7
3.51	3.44	3.41	3.38	3.34	3.32	3.30	3.27	3.27	3.25	3.24	3.23	.05	
6.31	6.16	6.07	5.99	5.91	5.86	5.82	5.75	5.74	5.70	5.67	5.65	.01	

TABLE D.5   *(Continued)*

Degrees of Freedom for Denominator, v_2	α	Degrees of Freedom for Numerator, v_1											
		1	2	3	4	5	6	7	8	9	10	11	12
8	.25	1.54	1.66	1.67	1.66	1.66	1.65	1.64	1.64	1.63	1.63	1.63	1.62
	.10	3.46	3.11	2.92	2.81	2.73	2.67	2.62	2.59	2.56	2.54	2.52	2.50
	.05	5.32	4.46	4.07	3.84	3.69	3.58	3.50	3.44	3.39	3.35	3.31	3.28
	.01	11.3	8.65	7.59	7.01	6.63	6.37	6.18	6.03	5.91	5.81	5.73	5.67
9	.25	1.51	1.62	1.63	1.63	1.62	1.61	1.60	1.60	1.59	1.59	1.58	1.58
	.10	3.36	3.01	2.81	2.69	2.61	2.55	2.51	2.47	2.44	2.42	2.40	2.38
	.05	5.12	4.26	3.86	3.63	3.48	3.37	3.29	3.23	3.18	3.14	3.10	3.07
	.01	10.6	8.02	6.99	6.42	6.06	5.80	5.61	5.47	5.35	5.26	5.18	5.11
10	.25	1.49	1.60	1.60	1.59	1.59	1.58	1.57	1.56	1.56	1.55	1.55	1.54
	.10	3.29	2.92	2.73	2.61	2.52	2.46	2.41	2.38	2.35	2.32	2.30	2.28
	.05	4.96	4.10	3.71	3.48	3.33	3.22	3.14	3.07	3.02	2.98	2.94	2.91
	.01	10.0	7.56	6.55	5.99	5.64	5.39	5.20	5.06	4.94	4.85	4.77	4.71
11	.25	1.47	1.58	1.58	1.57	1.56	1.55	1.54	1.53	1.53	1.52	1.52	1.51
	.10	3.23	2.86	2.66	2.54	2.45	2.39	2.34	2.30	2.27	2.25	2.23	2.21
	.05	4.84	3.98	3.59	3.36	3.20	3.09	3.01	2.95	2.90	2.85	2.82	2.79
	.01	9.65	7.21	6.22	5.67	5.32	5.07	4.89	4.74	4.63	4.54	4.46	4.40
12	.25	1.46	1.56	1.56	1.55	1.54	1.53	1.52	1.51	1.51	1.50	1.50	1.49
	.10	3.18	2.81	2.61	2.48	2.39	2.33	2.28	2.24	2.21	2.19	2.17	2.15
	.05	4.75	3.89	3.49	3.26	3.11	3.00	2.91	2.85	2.80	2.75	2.72	2.69
	.01	9.33	6.93	5.95	5.41	5.06	4.82	4.64	4.50	4.39	4.30	4.22	4.16
13	.25	1.45	1.55	1.55	1.53	1.52	1.51	1.50	1.49	1.49	1.48	1.47	1.47
	.10	3.14	2.76	2.56	2.43	2.35	2.28	2.23	2.20	2.16	2.14	2.12	2.10
	.05	4.67	3.81	3.41	3.18	3.03	2.92	2.83	2.77	2.71	2.67	2.63	2.60
	.01	9.07	6.70	5.74	5.21	4.86	4.62	4.44	4.30	4.19	4.10	4.02	3.96
14	.25	1.44	1.53	1.53	1.52	1.51	1.50	1.49	1.48	1.47	1.46	1.46	1.45
	.10	3.10	2.73	2.52	2.39	2.31	2.24	2.19	2.15	2.12	2.10	2.08	2.05
	.05	4.60	3.74	3.34	3.11	2.96	2.85	2.76	2.70	2.65	2.60	2.57	2.53
	.01	8.86	6.51	5.56	5.04	4.69	4.46	4.28	4.14	4.03	3.94	3.86	3.80
15	.25	1.43	1.52	1.52	1.51	1.49	1.48	1.47	1.46	1.46	1.45	1.44	1.44
	.10	3.07	2.70	2.49	2.36	2.27	2.21	2.16	2.12	2.09	2.06	2.04	2.02
	.05	4.54	3.68	3.29	3.06	2.90	2.79	2.71	2.64	2.59	2.54	2.51	2.48
	.01	8.68	6.36	5.42	4.89	4.56	4.32	4.14	4.00	3.89	3.80	3.73	3.67
16	.25	1.42	1.51	1.51	1.50	1.48	1.47	1.46	1.45	1.44	1.44	1.44	1.43
	.10	3.05	2.67	2.46	2.33	2.24	2.18	2.13	2.09	2.06	2.03	2.01	1.99
	.05	4.49	3.63	3.24	3.01	2.85	2.74	2.66	2.59	2.54	2.49	2.46	2.42
	.01	8.53	6.23	5.29	4.77	4.44	4.20	4.03	3.89	3.78	3.69	3.62	3.55

15	20	24	30	40	50	60	100	120	200	500	∞	α	Degrees of Freedom for Denominator, v_2
1.62	1.61	1.60	1.60	1.59	1.59	1.59	1.58	1.58	1.58	1.58	1.58	.25	
2.46	2.42	2.40	2.38	2.36	2.35	2.34	2.32	2.32	2.31	2.30	2.29	.10	8
3.22	3.15	3.12	3.08	3.04	3.02	3.01	2.97	2.97	2.95	2.94	2.93	.05	
5.52	5.36	5.28	5.20	5.12	5.07	5.03	4.96	4.95	4.91	4.88	4.86	.01	
1.57	1.56	1.56	1.55	1.55	1.54	1.54	1.53	1.53	1.53	1.53	1.53	.25	
2.34	2.30	2.28	2.25	2.23	2.22	2.21	2.19	2.18	2.17	2.17	2.16	.10	9
3.01	2.94	2.90	2.86	2.83	2.80	2.79	2.76	2.75	2.73	2.72	2.71	.05	
4.96	4.81	4.73	4.65	4.57	4.52	4.48	4.42	4.40	4.36	4.33	4.31	.01	
1.53	1.52	1.52	1.51	1.51	1.50	1.50	1.49	1.49	1.49	1.48	1.48	.25	
2.24	2.20	2.18	2.16	2.13	2.12	2.11	2.09	2.08	2.07	2.06	2.06	.10	10
2.85	2.77	2.74	2.70	2.66	2.64	2.62	2.59	2.58	2.56	2.55	2.54	.05	
4.56	4.41	4.33	4.25	4.17	4.12	4.08	4.01	4.00	3.96	3.93	3.91	.01	
1.50	1.49	1.49	1.48	1.47	1.47	1.47	1.46	1.46	1.46	1.45	1.45	.25	
2.17	2.12	2.10	2.08	2.05	2.04	2.03	2.00	2.00	1.99	1.98	1.97	.10	11
2.72	2.65	2.61	2.57	2.53	2.51	2.49	2.46	2.45	2.43	2.42	2.40	.05	
4.25	4.10	4.02	3.94	3.86	3.81	3.78	3.71	3.69	3.66	3.62	3.60	.01	
1.48	1.47	1.46	1.45	1.45	1.44	1.44	1.43	1.43	1.43	1.42	1.42	.25	
2.10	2.06	2.04	2.01	1.99	1.97	1.96	1.94	1.93	1.92	1.91	1.90	.10	12
2.62	2.54	2.51	2.47	2.43	2.40	2.38	2.35	2.34	2.32	2.31	2.30	.05	
4.01	3.86	3.78	3.70	3.62	3.57	3.54	3.47	3.45	3.41	3.38	3.36	.01	
1.46	1.45	1.44	1.43	1.42	1.42	1.42	1.41	1.41	1.40	1.40	1.40	.25	
2.05	2.01	1.98	1.96	1.93	1.92	1.90	1.88	1.88	1.86	1.85	1.85	.10	13
2.53	2.46	2.42	2.38	2.34	2.31	2.30	2.26	2.25	2.23	2.22	2.21	.05	
3.82	3.66	3.59	3.51	3.43	3.38	3.34	3.27	3.25	3.22	3.19	3.17	.01	
1.44	1.43	1.42	1.41	1.41	1.40	1.40	1.39	1.39	1.39	1.38	1.38	.25	
2.01	1.96	1.94	1.91	1.89	1.87	1.86	1.83	1.83	1.82	1.80	1.80	.10	14
2.46	2.39	2.35	2.31	2.27	2.24	2.22	2.19	2.18	2.16	2.14	2.13	.05	
3.66	3.51	3.43	3.35	3.27	3.22	3.18	3.11	3.09	3.06	3.03	3.00	.01	
1.43	1.41	1.41	1.40	1.39	1.39	1.38	1.38	1.37	1.37	1.36	1.36	.25	
1.97	1.92	1.90	1.87	1.85	1.83	1.82	1.79	1.79	1.77	1.76	1.76	.10	15
2.40	2.33	2.29	2.25	2.20	2.18	2.16	2.12	2.11	2.10	2.08	2.07	.05	
3.52	3.37	3.29	3.21	3.13	3.08	3.05	2.98	2.96	2.92	2.89	2.87	.01	
1.41	1.40	1.39	1.38	1.37	1.37	1.36	1.36	1.35	1.35	1.34	1.34	.25	
1.94	1.89	1.87	1.84	1.81	1.79	1.78	1.76	1.75	1.74	1.73	1.72	.10	16
2.35	2.28	2.24	2.19	2.15	2.12	2.11	2.07	2.06	2.04	2.02	2.01	.05	
3.41	3.26	3.18	3.10	3.02	2.97	2.93	2.86	2.84	2.81	2.78	2.75	.01	

Degrees of Freedom for Numerator, v_1

TABLE D.5   *(Continued)*

Degrees of Freedom for Denominator, v_2	α	Degrees of Freedom for Numerator, v_1											
		1	2	3	4	5	6	7	8	9	10	11	12
17	.25	1.42	1.51	1.50	1.49	1.47	1.46	1.45	1.44	1.43	1.43	1.42	1.41
	.10	3.03	2.64	2.44	2.31	2.22	2.15	2.10	2.06	2.03	2.00	1.98	1.96
	.05	4.45	3.59	3.20	2.96	2.81	2.70	2.61	2.55	2.49	2.45	2.41	2.38
	.01	8.40	6.11	5.18	4.67	4.34	4.10	3.93	3.79	3.68	3.59	3.52	3.46
18	.25	1.41	1.50	1.49	1.48	1.46	1.45	1.44	1.43	1.42	1.42	1.41	1.40
	.10	3.01	2.62	2.42	2.29	2.20	2.13	2.08	2.04	2.00	1.98	1.96	1.93
	.05	4.41	3.55	3.16	2.93	2.77	2.66	2.58	2.51	2.46	2.41	2.37	2.34
	.01	8.29	6.01	5.09	4.58	4.25	4.01	3.84	3.71	3.60	3.51	3.43	3.37
19	.25	1.41	1.49	1.49	1.47	1.46	1.44	1.43	1.42	1.41	1.41	1.40	1.40
	.10	2.99	2.61	2.40	2.27	2.18	2.11	2.06	2.02	1.98	1.96	1.94	1.91
	.05	4.38	3.52	3.13	2.90	2.74	2.63	2.54	2.48	2.42	2.38	2.34	2.31
	.01	8.18	5.93	5.01	4.50	4.17	3.94	3.77	3.63	3.52	3.43	3.36	3.30
20	.25	1.40	1.49	1.48	1.46	1.45	1.44	1.43	1.42	1.41	1.40	1.39	1.39
	.10	2.97	2.59	2.38	2.25	2.16	2.09	2.04	2.00	1.96	1.94	1.92	1.89
	.05	4.35	3.49	3.10	2.87	2.71	2.60	2.51	2.45	2.39	2.35	2.31	2.28
	.01	8.10	5.85	4.94	4.43	4.10	3.87	3.70	3.56	3.46	3.37	3.29	3.23
22	.25	1.40	1.48	1.47	1.45	1.44	1.42	1.41	1.40	1.39	1.39	1.38	1.37
	.10	2.95	2.56	2.35	2.22	2.13	2.06	2.01	1.97	1.93	1.90	1.88	1.86
	.05	4.30	3.44	3.05	2.82	2.66	2.55	2.46	2.40	2.34	2.30	2.26	2.23
	.01	7.95	5.72	4.82	4.31	3.99	3.76	3.59	3.45	3.35	3.26	3.18	3.12
24	.25	1.39	1.47	1.46	1.44	1.43	1.41	1.40	1.39	1.38	1.38	1.37	1.36
	.10	2.93	2.54	2.33	2.19	2.10	2.04	1.98	1.94	1.91	1.88	1.85	1.83
	.05	4.26	3.40	3.01	2.78	2.62	2.51	2.42	2.36	2.30	2.25	2.21	2.18
	.01	7.82	5.61	4.72	4.22	3.90	3.67	3.50	3.36	3.26	3.17	3.09	3.03
26	.25	1.38	1.46	1.45	1.44	1.42	1.41	1.39	1.38	1.37	1.37	1.36	1.35
	.10	2.91	2.52	2.31	2.17	2.08	2.01	1.96	1.92	1.88	1.86	1.84	1.81
	.05	4.23	3.37	2.98	2.74	2.59	2.47	2.39	2.32	2.27	2.22	2.18	2.15
	.01	7.72	5.53	4.64	4.14	3.82	3.59	3.42	3.29	3.18	3.09	3.02	2.96
28	.25	1.38	1.46	1.45	1.43	1.41	1.40	1.39	1.38	1.37	1.36	1.35	1.34
	.10	2.89	2.50	2.29	2.16	2.06	2.00	1.94	1.90	1.87	1.84	1.81	1.79
	.05	4.20	3.34	2.95	2.71	2.56	2.45	2.36	2.29	2.24	2.19	2.15	2.12
	.01	7.64	5.45	4.57	4.07	3.75	3.53	3.36	3.23	3.12	3.03	2.96	2.90
30	.25	1.38	1.45	1.44	1.42	1.41	1.39	1.38	1.37	1.36	1.35	1.35	1.34
	.10	2.88	2.49	2.28	2.14	2.05	1.98	1.93	1.88	1.85	1.82	1.79	1.77
	.05	4.17	3.32	2.92	2.69	2.53	2.42	2.33	2.27	2.21	2.16	2.13	2.09
	.01	7.56	5.39	4.51	4.02	3.70	3.47	3.30	3.17	3.07	2.98	2.91	2.84

				Degrees of Freedom for Numerator, v_1									Degrees of Freedom for Denominator, v_2
15	20	24	30	40	50	60	100	120	200	500	∞	α	
1.40	1.39	1.38	1.37	1.36	1.35	1.35	1.34	1.34	1.34	1.33	1.33	.25	
1.91	1.86	1.84	1.81	1.78	1.76	1.75	1.73	1.72	1.71	1.69	1.69	.10	17
2.31	2.23	2.19	2.15	2.10	2.08	2.06	2.02	2.01	1.99	1.97	1.96	.05	
3.31	3.16	3.08	3.00	2.92	2.87	2.83	2.76	2.75	2.71	2.68	2.65	.01	
1.39	1.38	1.37	1.36	1.35	1.34	1.34	1.33	1.33	1.32	1.32	1.32	.25	
1.89	1.84	1.81	1.78	1.75	1.74	1.72	1.70	1.69	1.68	1.67	1.66	.10	18
2.27	2.19	2.15	2.11	2.06	2.04	2.02	1.98	1.97	1.95	1.93	1.92	.05	
3.23	3.08	3.00	2.92	2.84	2.78	2.75	2.68	2.66	2.62	2.59	2.57	.01	
1.38	1.37	1.36	1.35	1.34	1.33	1.33	1.32	1.32	1.31	1.31	1.30	.25	
1.86	1.81	1.79	1.76	1.73	1.71	1.70	1.67	1.67	1.65	1.64	1.63	.10	19
2.23	2.16	2.11	2.07	2.03	2.00	1.98	1.94	1.93	1.91	1.89	1.88	.05	
3.15	3.00	2.92	2.84	2.76	2.71	2.67	2.60	2.58	2.55	2.51	2.49	.01	
1.37	1.36	1.35	1.34	1.33	1.33	1.32	1.31	1.31	1.30	1.30	1.29	.25	
1.84	1.79	1.77	1.74	1.71	1.69	1.68	1.65	1.64	1.63	1.62	1.61	.10	20
2.20	2.12	2.08	2.04	1.99	1.97	1.95	1.91	1.90	1.88	1.86	1.84	.05	
3.09	2.94	2.86	2.78	2.69	2.64	2.61	2.54	2.52	2.48	2.44	2.42	.01	
1.36	1.34	1.33	1.32	1.31	1.31	1.30	1.30	1.30	1.29	1.29	1.28	.25	
1.81	1.76	1.73	1.70	1.67	1.65	1.64	1.61	1.60	1.59	1.58	1.57	.10	22
2.15	2.07	2.03	1.98	1.94	1.91	1.89	1.85	1.84	1.82	1.80	1.78	.05	
2.98	2.83	2.75	2.67	2.58	2.53	2.50	2.42	2.40	2.36	2.33	2.31	.01	
1.35	1.33	1.32	1.31	1.30	1.29	1.29	1.28	1.28	1.27	1.27	1.26	.25	
1.78	1.73	1.70	1.67	1.64	1.62	1.61	1.58	1.57	1.56	1.54	1.53	.10	24
2.11	2.03	1.98	1.94	1.89	1.86	1.84	1.80	1.79	1.77	1.75	1.73	.05	
2.89	2.74	2.66	2.58	2.49	2.44	2.40	2.33	2.31	2.27	2.24	2.21	.01	
1.34	1.32	1.31	1.30	1.29	1.28	1.28	1.26	1.26	1.26	1.25	1.25	.25	
1.76	1.71	1.68	1.65	1.61	1.59	1.58	1.55	1.54	1.53	1.51	1.50	.10	26
2.07	1.99	1.95	1.90	1.85	1.82	1.80	1.76	1.75	1.73	1.71	1.69	.05	
2.81	2.66	2.58	2.50	2.42	2.36	2.33	2.25	2.23	2.19	2.16	2.13	.01	
1.33	1.31	1.30	1.29	1.28	1.27	1.27	1.26	1.25	1.25	1.24	1.24	.25	
1.74	1.69	1.66	1.63	1.59	1.57	1.56	1.53	1.52	1.50	1.49	1.48	.10	28
2.04	1.96	1.91	1.87	1.82	1.79	1.77	1.73	1.71	1.69	1.67	1.65	.05	
2.75	2.60	2.52	2.44	2.35	2.30	2.26	2.19	2.17	2.13	2.09	2.06	.01	
1.32	1.30	1.29	1.28	1.27	1.26	1.26	1.25	1.24	1.24	1.23	1.23	.25	
1.72	1.67	1.64	1.61	1.57	1.55	1.54	1.51	1.50	1.48	1.47	1.46	.10	30
2.01	1.93	1.89	1.84	1.79	1.76	1.74	1.70	1.68	1.66	1.64	1.62	.05	
2.70	2.55	2.47	2.39	2.30	2.25	2.21	2.13	2.11	2.07	2.03	2.01	.01	

TABLE D.5   *(Continued)*

Degrees of Freedom for Denominator, v_2	α	Degrees of Freedom for Numerator, v_1											
		1	*2*	*3*	*4*	*5*	*6*	*7*	*8*	*9*	*10*	*11*	*12*
40	.25	1.36	1.44	1.42	1.40	1.39	1.37	1.36	1.35	1.34	1.33	1.32	1.31
	.10	2.84	2.44	2.23	2.09	2.00	1.93	1.87	1.83	1.79	1.76	1.73	1.71
	.05	4.08	3.23	2.84	2.61	2.45	2.34	2.25	2.18	2.12	2.08	2.04	2.00
	.01	7.31	5.18	4.31	3.83	3.51	3.29	3.12	2.99	2.89	2.80	2.73	2.66
60	.25	1.35	1.42	1.41	1.38	1.37	1.35	1.33	1.32	1.31	1.30	1.29	1.29
	.10	2.79	2.39	2.18	2.04	1.95	1.87	1.82	1.77	1.74	1.71	1.68	1.66
	.05	4.00	3.15	2.76	2.53	2.37	2.25	2.17	2.10	2.04	1.99	1.95	1.92
	.01	7.08	4.98	4.13	3.65	3.34	3.12	2.95	2.82	2.72	2.63	2.56	2.50
120	.25	1.34	1.40	1.39	1.37	1.35	1.33	1.31	1.30	1.29	1.28	1.27	1.26
	.10	2.75	2.35	2.13	1.99	1.90	1.82	1.77	1.72	1.68	1.65	1.62	1.60
	.05	3.92	3.07	2.68	2.45	2.29	2.17	2.09	2.02	1.96	1.91	1.87	1.83
	.01	6.85	4.79	3.95	3.48	3.17	2.96	2.79	2.66	2.56	2.47	2.40	2.34
200	.25	1.33	1.39	1.38	1.36	1.34	1.32	1.31	1.29	1.28	1.27	1.26	1.25
	.10	2.73	2.33	2.11	1.97	1.88	1.80	1.75	1.70	1.66	1.63	1.60	1.57
	.05	3.89	3.04	2.65	2.42	2.26	2.14	2.06	1.98	1.93	1.88	1.84	1.80
	.01	6.76	4.71	3.88	3.41	3.11	2.89	2.73	2.60	2.50	2.41	2.34	2.27
∞	.25	1.32	1.39	1.37	1.35	1.33	1.31	1.29	1.28	1.27	1.25	1.24	1.24
	.10	2.71	2.30	2.08	1.94	1.85	1.77	1.72	1.67	1.63	1.60	1.57	1.55
	.05	3.84	3.00	2.60	2.37	2.21	2.10	2.01	1.94	1.88	1.83	1.79	1.75
	.01	6.63	4.61	3.78	3.32	3.02	2.80	2.64	2.51	2.41	2.32	2.25	2.18

			Degrees of Freedom for Numerator, v_1										Degrees of Freedom for Denominator,
15	20	24	30	40	50	60	100	120	200	500	∞	α	v_2
1.30	1.28	1.26	1.25	1.24	1.23	1.22	1.21	1.21	1.20	1.19	1.19	.25	
1.66	1.61	1.57	1.54	1.51	1.48	1.47	1.43	1.42	1.41	1.39	1.38	.10	40
1.92	1.84	1.79	1.74	1.69	1.66	1.64	1.59	1.58	1.55	1.53	1.51	.05	
2.52	2.37	2.29	2.20	2.11	2.06	2.02	1.94	1.92	1.87	1.83	1.80	.01	
1.27	1.25	1.24	1.22	1.21	1.20	1.19	1.17	1.17	1.16	1.15	1.15	.25	
1.60	1.54	1.51	1.48	1.44	1.41	1.40	1.36	1.35	1.33	1.31	1.29	.10	60
1.84	1.75	1.70	1.65	1.59	1.56	1.53	1.48	1.47	1.44	1.41	1.39	.05	
2.35	2.20	2.12	2.03	1.94	1.88	1.84	1.75	1.73	1.68	1.63	1.60	.01	
1.24	1.22	1.21	1.19	1.18	1.17	1.16	1.14	1.13	1.12	1.11	1.10	.25	
1.55	1.48	1.45	1.41	1.37	1.34	1.32	1.27	1.26	1.24	1.21	1.19	.10	120
1.75	1.66	1.61	1.55	1.50	1.46	1.43	1.37	1.35	1.32	1.28	1.25	.05	
2.19	2.03	1.95	1.86	1.76	1.70	1.66	1.56	1.53	1.48	1.42	1.38	.01	
1.23	1.21	1.20	1.18	1.16	1.14	1.12	1.11	1.10	1.09	1.08	1.06	.25	
1.52	1.46	1.42	1.38	1.34	1.31	1.28	1.24	1.22	1.20	1.17	1.14	.10	200
1.72	1.62	1.57	1.52	1.46	1.41	1.39	1.32	1.29	1.26	1.22	1.19	.05	
2.13	1.97	1.89	1.79	1.69	1.63	1.58	1.48	1.44	1.39	1.33	1.28	.01	
1.22	1.19	1.18	1.16	1.14	1.13	1.12	1.09	1.08	1.07	1.04	1.00	.25	
1.49	1.42	1.38	1.34	1.30	1.26	1.24	1.18	1.17	1.13	1.08	1.00	.10	∞
1.67	1.57	1.52	1.46	1.39	1.35	1.32	1.24	1.22	1.17	1.11	1.00	.05	
2.04	1.88	1.79	1.70	1.59	1.52	1.47	1.36	1.32	1.25	1.15	1.00	.01	

TABLE D.6.   Critical Values of the Pearson r^a

	Level of Significance for a One-Tailed Test			
Degrees of Freedom, $v = n - 2^b$	.05	.025	.01	.005
	Level of Significance for a Two-Tailed Test			
	.10	.05	.02	.01
1	0.988	0.997	0.9995	0.9999
2	0.900	0.950	0.980	0.990
3	0.805	0.878	0.934	0.959
4	0.729	0.811	0.882	0.917
5	0.669	0.754	0.833	0.874
6	0.622	0.707	0.789	0.834
7	0.582	0.666	0.750	0.798
8	0.549	0.632	0.716	0.765
9	0.521	0.602	0.685	0.735
10	0.497	0.576	0.658	0.708
11	0.476	0.553	0.634	0.684
12	0.458	0.532	0.612	0.661
13	0.441	0.514	0.592	0.641
14	0.426	0.497	0.574	0.623
15	0.412	0.482	0.558	0.606
16	0.400	0.468	0.542	0.590
17	0.389	0.456	0.528	0.575
18	0.378	0.444	0.516	0.561
19	0.369	0.433	0.503	0.549
20	0.360	0.423	0.492	0.537
21	0.352	0.413	0.482	0.526
22	0.344	0.404	0.472	0.515
23	0.337	0.396	0.462	0.505
24	0.330	0.388	0.453	0.496
25	0.323	0.381	0.445	0.487
26	0.317	0.374	0.437	0.479
27	0.311	0.367	0.430	0.471
28	0.306	0.361	0.423	0.463
29	0.301	0.355	0.416	0.456
30	0.296	0.349	0.409	0.449
35	0.275	0.325	0.381	0.418
40	0.257	0.304	0.358	0.393
45	0.243	0.288	0.338	0.372
50	0.231	0.273	0.322	0.354
60	0.211	0.250	0.295	0.325
70	0.195	0.232	0.274	0.302
80	0.183	0.217	0.256	0.283
90	0.173	0.205	0.242	0.267
100	0.164	0.195	0.230	0.254
120	0.150	0.178	0.210	0.232
150	0.134	0.159	0.189	0.208
200	0.116	0.138	0.164	0.181
300	0.095	0.113	0.134	0.148
400	0.082	0.098	0.116	0.128
500	0.073	0.088	0.104	0.115

Table D.6 is taken from Table VII of Fisher and Yates: *Statistical Tables for Biological, Agricultural and Medical Research,* published by Longman Group Ltd., London (previously published by Oliver & Boyd, Edinburgh), and reprinted by permission of the authors and publishers.

[a] Discussed in Section 11.5.

[b] n is the number of pairs.

TABLE D.7. Critical Values of r_s (Spearman Rank Correlation Coefficient)[a]

Number of Pairs, n	Level of Significance for a One-Tailed Test			
	.05	.025	.01	.005
	Level of Significance for a Two-Tailed Test			
	.10	.05	.02	.01
5	.900	1.000	1.000	
6	.829	.886	.943	1.000
7	.714	.786	.893	.929
8	.643	.738	.833	.881
9	.600	.700	.783	.833
10	.564	.648	.745	.794
11	.536	.618	.709	.755
12	.503	.587	.671	.727
13	.484	.560	.648	.703
14	.464	.538	.622	.675
15	.443	.521	.604	.654
16	.429	.503	.582	.635
17	.414	.485	.566	.615
18	.401	.472	.550	.600
19	.391	.460	.535	.584
20	.380	.447	.520	.570
21	.370	.435	.508	.556
22	.361	.425	.496	.544
23	.353	.415	.486	.532
24	.344	.406	.476	.521
25	.337	.398	.466	.511
26	.331	.390	.457	.501
27	.324	.382	.448	.491
28	.317	.375	.440	.483
29	.312	.368	.433	.475
30	.306	.362	.425	.467
32	.296	.350	.412	.452
34	.287	.340	.399	.439
36	.279	.330	.388	.427
38	.271	.321	.378	.415
40	.264	.313	.368	.405
42	.257	.305	.359	.395
44	.251	.298	.351	.386
46	.246	.291	.343	.378
48	.240	.285	.336	.370
50	.235	.279	.329	.363
52	.231	.274	.323	.356
54	.226	.268	.317	.349
56	.222	.264	.311	.343
58	.218	.259	.306	.337
60	.214	.255	.300	.331
70	.198	.235	.278	.307
80	.185	.220	.260	.287
90	.174	.207	.245	.271
100	.165	.197	.233	.257

Abridged from "Significance Testing of the Spearman Rank Correlation Coefficient" by J. H. Zar, *Journal of the American Statistical Association*, 1972, *67*, 578–580.
[a] Discussed in Section 11.5.

TABLE D.8.   Transformation of r to Z' [a]

r	Z'	r	Z'	r	Z'	r	Z'	r	Z'
0.000	0.000	0.200	0.203	0.400	0.424	0.600	0.693	0.800	1.099
0.005	0.005	0.205	0.208	0.405	0.430	0.605	0.701	0.805	1.113
0.010	0.010	0.210	0.213	0.410	0.436	0.610	0.709	0.810	1.127
0.015	0.015	0.215	0.218	0.415	0.442	0.615	0.717	0.815	1.142
0.020	0.020	0.220	0.224	0.420	0.448	0.620	0.725	0.820	1.157
0.025	0.025	0.225	0.229	0.425	0.454	0.625	0.733	0.825	1.172
0.030	0.030	0.230	0.234	0.430	0.460	0.630	0.741	0.830	1.188
0.035	0.035	0.235	0.239	0.435	0.466	0.635	0.750	0.835	1.204
0.040	0.040	0.240	0.245	0.440	0.472	0.640	0.758	0.840	1.221
0.045	0.045	0.245	0.250	0.445	0.478	0.645	0.767	0.845	1.238
0.050	0.050	0.250	0.255	0.450	0.485	0.650	0.775	0.850	1.256
0.055	0.055	0.255	0.261	0.455	0.491	0.655	0.784	0.855	1.274
0.060	0.060	0.260	0.266	0.460	0.497	0.660	0.793	0.860	1.293
0.065	0.065	0.265	0.271	0.465	0.504	0.665	0.802	0.865	1.313
0.070	0.070	0.270	0.277	0.470	0.510	0.670	0.811	0.870	1.333
0.075	0.075	0.275	0.282	0.475	0.517	0.675	0.820	0.875	1.354
0.080	0.080	0.280	0.288	0.480	0.523	0.680	0.829	0.880	1.376
0.085	0.085	0.285	0.293	0.485	0.530	0.685	0.838	0.885	1.398
0.090	0.090	0.290	0.299	0.490	0.536	0.690	0.848	0.890	1.422
0.095	0.095	0.295	0.304	0.495	0.543	0.695	0.858	0.895	1.447
0.100	0.100	0.300	0.310	0.500	0.549	0.700	0.867	0.900	1.472
0.105	0.105	0.305	0.315	0.505	0.556	0.705	0.877	0.905	1.499
0.110	0.110	0.310	0.321	0.510	0.563	0.710	0.887	0.910	1.528
0.115	0.116	0.315	0.326	0.515	0.570	0.715	0.897	0.915	1.557
0.120	0.121	0.320	0.332	0.520	0.576	0.720	0.908	0.920	1.589
0.125	0.126	0.325	0.337	0.525	0.583	0.725	0.918	0.925	1.623
0.130	0.131	0.330	0.343	0.530	0.590	0.730	0.929	0.930	1.658
0.135	0.136	0.335	0.348	0.535	0.597	0.735	0.940	0.935	1.697
0.140	0.141	0.340	0.354	0.540	0.604	0.740	0.950	0.940	1.738
0.145	0.146	0.345	0.360	0.545	0.611	0.745	0.962	0.945	1.783
0.150	0.151	0.350	0.365	0.550	0.618	0.750	0.973	0.950	1.832
0.155	0.156	0.355	0.371	0.555	0.626	0.755	0.984	0.955	1.886
0.160	0.161	0.360	0.377	0.560	0.633	0.760	0.996	0.960	1.946
0.165	0.167	0.365	0.383	0.565	0.640	0.765	1.008	0.965	2.014
0.170	0.172	0.370	0.388	0.570	0.648	0.770	1.020	0.970	2.092
0.175	0.177	0.375	0.394	0.575	0.655	0.775	1.033	0.975	2.185
0.180	0.182	0.380	0.400	0.580	0.662	0.780	1.045	0.980	2.298
0.185	0.187	0.385	0.406	0.585	0.670	0.785	1.058	0.985	2.443
0.190	0.192	0.390	0.412	0.590	0.678	0.790	1.071	0.990	2.647
0.195	0.198	0.395	0.418	0.595	0.685	0.795	1.085	0.995	2.994

Table D.8 is taken from Table VIIi of Fisher and Yates: *Statistical Tables for Biological, Agricultural and Medical Research,* published by Longman Group Ltd., London (previously published by Oliver & Boyd, Edinburgh), and reprinted by permission of the authors and publishers.
[a] Discussed in Section 11.5.

TABLE D.9. Approximate *n* Required for Testing Hypotheses About Means[a]

		One-Sample Test					
		One-Sided Hypothesis, $1-\beta$			Two-Sided Hypothesis, $1-\beta$		
Effect Size, d	α	.80	.90	.95	.80	.90	.95
0.2	.05	156	215	272	198	264	326
	.01	253	328	396	294	374	447
0.5	.05	27	36	45	34	44	54
	.01	43	55	66	51	63	75
0.8	.05	12	15	19	15	19	22
	.01	19	24	28	22	27	32

Effect Size, d	α	Two-Sample Test (Independent Samples)					
0.2	.05	310	429	542	393	526	651
	.01	503	652	790	586	746	892
0.5	.05	50	69	87	64	85	105
	.01	82	105	128	95	120	144
0.8	.05	21	27	35	26	34	42
	.01	33	42	51	38	48	57

Effect Size, d	α	Two-Sample Test (Dependent Samples)						
		ρ						
0.2	.05	0.4	187	258	326	237	317	391
		0.5	156	215	272	198	264	326
		0.6	125	172	218	159	212	261
		0.7	94	130	164	119	159	197
		0.8	63	87	109	80	107	131
		0.9	32	44	55	41	54	66

[a]Discussed in Sections 11.2, 12.4, and 12.5. For the two-sample test (independent samples), it is assumed that $\sigma_1^2 = \sigma_2^2$ and $n_1 = n_2$; the values in the table are for each of the samples. If dependent samples are used, the values in the table are for the number of pairs of dependent elements.

TABLE D.9. *(Continued)*

			One-Sided Hypothesis, $1-\beta$			Two-Sided Hypothesis, $1-\beta$		
Effect Size, d	α		.80	.90	.95	.80	.90	.95
		ρ						
0.2	.01	0.4	303	393	475	353	449	537
		0.5	253	328	396	294	374	447
		0.6	203	262	317	236	300	358
		0.7	153	197	239	177	225	269
		0.8	102	132	160	119	151	180
		0.9	52	67	81	60	76	91
0.5	.05	0.4	31	42	53	39	52	63
		0.5	26	35	44	33	44	53
		0.6	21	29	36	27	35	43
		0.7	16	22	27	20	27	33
		0.8	11	15	19	14	18	22
		0.9	6	8	10	8	10	12
	.01	0.4	50	65	78	58	73	88
		0.5	42	54	65	49	62	73
		0.6	34	44	52	39	50	59
		0.7	26	33	40	30	38	45
		0.8	18	23	27	21	26	31
		0.9	10	12	15	11	14	16
0.8	.05	0.4	13	17	21	16	21	26
		0.5	11	15	18	13	18	22
		0.6	9	12	15	11	15	18
		0.7	7	9	11	9	11	14
		0.8	5	7	8	6	8	10
		0.9	3	4	5	4	5	6
	.01	0.4	21	26	32	24	30	35
		0.5	18	22	27	20	25	30
		0.6	15	18	22	17	21	24
		0.7	11	14	17	13	16	19
		0.8	8	10	12	9	11	13
		0.9	5	6	7	6	7	8

Two-Sample Test (Dependent Samples)

TABLE D.10. Percentage Points of the Studentized Range Distribution[a]

Error df	α	Number of Means (p)									
		2	3	4	5	6	7	8	9	10	11
2	.05	6.08	8.33	9.80	10.9	11.7	12.4	13.0	13.5	14.0	14.4
	.01	14.0	19.0	22.3	24.7	26.6	28.2	29.5	30.7	31.7	32.6
3	.05	4.50	5.91	6.82	7.50	8.04	8.48	8.85	9.18	9.46	9.72
	.01	8.26	10.6	12.2	13.3	14.2	15.0	15.6	16.2	16.7	17.8
4	.05	3.93	5.04	5.76	6.29	6.71	7.05	7.35	7.60	7.83	8.03
	.01	6.51	8.12	9.17	9.96	10.6	11.1	11.5	11.9	12.3	12.6
5	.05	3.64	4.60	5.22	5.67	6.03	6.33	6.58	6.80	6.99	7.17
	.01	5.70	6.98	7.80	8.42	8.91	9.32	9.67	9.97	10.24	10.48
6	.05	3.46	4.34	4.90	5.30	5.63	5.90	6.12	6.32	6.49	6.65
	.01	5.24	6.33	7.03	7.56	7.97	8.32	8.61	8.87	9.10	9.30
7	.05	3.34	4.16	4.68	5.06	5.36	5.61	5.82	6.00	6.16	6.30
	.01	4.95	5.92	6.54	7.01	7.37	7.68	7.94	8.17	8.37	8.55
8	.05	3.26	4.04	4.53	4.89	5.17	5.40	5.60	5.77	5.92	6.05
	.01	4.75	5.64	6.20	6.62	6.96	7.24	7.47	7.68	7.86	8.03
9	.05	3.20	3.95	4.41	4.76	5.02	5.24	5.43	5.59	5.74	5.87
	.01	4.60	5.43	5.96	6.35	6.66	6.91	7.13	7.33	7.49	7.65
10	.05	3.15	3.88	4.33	4.65	4.91	5.12	5.30	5.46	5.60	5.72
	.01	4.48	5.27	5.77	6.14	6.43	6.67	6.87	7.05	7.21	7.36
11	.05	3.11	3.82	4.26	4.57	4.82	5.03	5.20	5.35	5.49	5.61
	.01	4.39	5.15	5.62	5.97	6.25	6.48	6.67	6.84	6.99	7.13
12	.05	3.08	3.77	4.20	4.51	4.75	4.95	5.12	5.27	5.39	5.51
	.01	4.32	5.05	5.50	5.84	6.10	6.32	6.51	6.67	6.81	6.94
13	.05	3.06	3.73	4.15	4.45	4.69	4.88	5.05	5.19	5.32	5.43
	.01	4.26	4.96	5.40	5.73	5.98	6.19	6.37	6.53	6.67	6.79
14	.05	3.03	3.70	4.11	4.41	4.64	4.83	4.99	5.13	5.25	5.36
	.01	4.21	4.89	5.32	5.63	5.88	6.08	6.26	6.41	6.54	6.66
15	.05	3.01	3.67	4.08	4.37	4.59	4.78	4.94	5.08	5.20	5.31
	.01	4.17	4.84	5.25	5.56	5.80	5.99	6.16	6.31	6.44	6.55
16	.05	3.00	3.65	4.05	4.33	4.56	4.74	4.90	5.03	5.15	5.26
	.01	4.13	4.79	5.19	5.49	5.72	5.92	6.08	6.22	6.35	6.46
17	.05	2.98	3.63	4.02	4.30	4.52	4.70	4.86	4.99	5.11	5.21
	.01	4.10	4.74	5.14	5.43	5.66	5.85	6.01	6.15	6.27	6.38
18	.05	2.97	3.61	4.00	4.28	4.49	4.67	4.82	4.96	5.07	5.17
	.01	4.07	4.70	5.09	5.38	5.60	5.79	5.94	6.08	6.20	6.31
19	.05	2.96	3.59	3.98	4.25	4.47	4.65	4.79	4.92	5.04	5.14
	.01	4.05	4.67	5.05	5.33	5.55	5.73	5.89	6.02	6.14	6.25
20	.05	2.95	3.58	3.96	4.23	4.45	4.62	4.77	4.90	5.01	5.11
	.01	4.02	4.64	5.02	5.29	5.51	5.69	5.84	5.97	6.09	6.19
24	.05	2.92	3.53	3.90	4.17	4.37	4.54	4.68	4.81	4.92	5.01
	.01	3.96	4.55	4.91	5.17	5.37	5.54	5.69	5.81	5.92	6.02
30	.05	2.89	3.49	3.85	4.10	4.30	4.46	4.60	4.72	4.82	4.92
	.01	3.89	4.45	4.80	5.05	5.24	5.40	5.54	5.65	5.76	5.85
40	.05	2.86	3.44	3.79	4.04	4.23	4.39	4.52	4.63	4.73	4.82
	.01	3.82	4.37	4.70	4.93	5.11	5.26	5.39	5.50	5.60	5.69
60	.05	2.83	3.40	3.74	3.98	4.16	4.31	4.44	4.55	4.65	4.73
	.01	3.76	4.28	4.59	4.82	4.99	5.13	5.25	5.36	5.45	5.53
120	.05	2.80	3.36	3.68	3.92	4.10	4.24	4.36	4.47	4.56	4.64
	.01	3.70	4.20	4.50	4.71	4.87	5.01	5.12	5.21	5.30	5.37
∞	.05	2.77	3.31	3.63	3.86	4.03	4.17	4.29	4.39	4.47	4.55
	.01	3.64	4.12	4.40	4.60	4.76	4.88	4.99	5.08	5.16	5.23

[a]Discussed in Section 14.5.

TABLE D.10.   *(Continued)*

12	13	14	15	16	17	18	19	20	α	Error df
				Number of Means (p)						
14.7	15.1	15.4	15.7	15.9	16.1	16.4	16.6	16.8	.05	2
33.4	34.1	34.8	35.4	36.0	36.5	37.0	37.5	37.9	.01	
9.72	10.2	10.3	10.5	10.7	10.8	11.0	11.1	11.2	.05	3
17.5	17.9	18.2	18.5	18.8	19.1	19.3	19.5	19.8	.01	
8.21	8.37	8.52	8.66	8.79	8.91	9.03	9.13	9.23	.05	4
12.8	13.1	13.3	13.5	13.7	13.9	14.1	14.2	14.4	.01	
7.32	7.47	7.60	7.72	7.83	7.93	8.03	8.12	8.21	.05	5
10.70	10.89	11.08	11.24	11.40	11.55	11.68	11.81	11.93	.01	
6.79	6.92	7.03	7.14	7.24	7.34	7.43	7.51	7.59	.05	6
9.48	9.65	9.81	9.95	10.08	10.21	10.32	10.43	10.54	.01	
6.43	6.55	6.66	6.76	6.85	6.94	7.02	7.10	7.17	.05	7
8.71	8.86	9.00	9.12	9.24	9.35	9.46	9.55	9.65	.01	
6.18	6.29	6.39	6.48	6.57	6.65	6.73	6.80	6.87	.05	8
8.18	8.31	8.44	8.55	8.66	8.76	8.85	8.94	9.03	.01	
5.98	6.09	6.19	6.28	6.36	6.44	6.51	6.58	6.64	.05	9
7.78	7.91	8.03	8.13	8.23	8.33	8.41	8.49	8.57	.01	
5.83	5.93	6.03	6.11	6.19	6.27	6.34	6.40	6.47	.05	10
7.49	7.60	7.71	7.81	7.91	7.99	8.08	8.15	8.23	.01	
5.71	5.81	5.90	5.98	6.06	6.13	6.20	6.27	6.33	.05	11
7.25	7.36	7.46	7.56	7.65	7.73	7.81	7.88	7.95	.01	
5.61	5.71	5.80	5.88	5.95	6.02	6.09	6.15	6.21	.05	12
7.06	7.17	7.26	7.36	7.44	7.52	7.59	7.66	7.73	.01	
5.53	5.63	5.71	5.79	5.86	5.93	5.99	6.05	6.11	.05	13
6.90	7.01	7.10	7.19	7.27	7.35	7.42	7.48	7.55	.01	
5.46	5.55	5.64	5.71	5.79	5.85	5.91	5.97	6.03	.05	14
6.77	6.87	6.96	7.05	7.13	7.20	7.27	7.33	7.39	.01	
5.40	5.49	5.57	5.65	5.72	5.78	5.85	5.90	5.96	.05	15
6.66	6.76	6.84	6.93	7.00	7.07	7.14	7.20	7.26	.01	
5.35	5.44	5.52	5.59	5.66	5.73	5.79	5.84	5.90	.05	16
6.56	6.66	6.74	6.82	6.90	6.97	7.03	7.09	7.15	.01	
5.31	5.39	5.47	5.54	5.61	5.67	5.73	5.79	5.84	.05	17
6.48	6.57	6.66	6.73	6.81	6.87	6.94	7.00	7.05	.01	
5.27	5.35	5.43	5.50	5.57	5.63	5.69	5.74	5.79	.05	18
6.41	6.50	6.58	6.65	6.73	6.79	6.85	6.91	6.97	.01	
5.23	5.31	5.39	5.46	5.53	5.59	5.65	5.70	5.75	.05	19
6.34	6.43	6.51	6.58	6.65	6.72	6.78	6.84	6.89	.01	
5.20	5.28	5.36	5.43	5.49	5.55	5.61	5.66	5.71	.05	20
6.28	6.37	6.45	6.52	6.59	6.65	6.71	6.77	6.82	.01	
5.10	5.18	5.25	5.32	5.38	5.44	5.49	5.55	5.59	.05	24
6.11	6.19	6.26	6.33	6.39	6.45	6.51	6.56	6.61	.01	
5.00	5.08	5.15	5.21	5.27	5.33	5.38	5.43	5.47	.05	30
5.93	6.01	6.08	6.14	6.20	6.26	6.31	6.36	6.41	.01	
4.90	4.98	5.04	5.11	5.16	5.22	5.27	5.31	5.36	.05	40
5.76	5.83	5.90	5.96	6.02	6.07	6.12	6.16	6.21	.01	
4.81	4.88	4.94	5.00	5.06	5.11	5.15	5.20	5.24	.05	60
5.60	5.67	5.73	5.78	5.84	5.89	5.93	5.97	6.01	.01	
4.71	4.78	4.84	4.90	4.95	5.00	5.04	5.09	5.13	.05	120
5.44	5.50	5.56	5.61	5.66	5.71	5.75	5.79	5.83	.01	
4.62	4.68	4.74	4.80	4.85	4.89	4.93	4.97	5.01	.05	∞
5.29	5.35	5.40	5.45	5.49	5.54	5.57	5.61	5.65	.01	

TABLE D.11. Percentage Points of Dunn-Šidák's tDS[a]

	One-Tailed Test α	Two-Tailed Test α	Number of Comparisons (C)												
Error df			2	3	4	5	6	7	8	9	10	15	20	25	30
2	.05	.10	4.243	5.243	6.081	6.816	7.480	8.090	8.656	9.188	9.691	11.890	13.741	15.371	16.845
	.025	.05	6.164	7.582	8.774	9.823	10.769	11.639	12.449	13.208	13.927	17.072	19.721	22.054	24.163
	.005	.01	14.071	17.248	19.925	22.282	24.413	26.372	28.196	29.908	31.528	38.620	44.598	49.865	54.626
3	.05	.10	3.149	3.690	4.115	4.471	4.780	5.055	5.304	5.532	5.744	6.627	7.326	7.914	8.427
	.025	.05	4.156	4.826	5.355	5.799	6.185	6.529	6.842	7.128	7.394	8.505	9.387	10.129	10.778
	.005	.01	7.447	8.565	9.453	10.201	10.853	11.436	11.966	12.453	12.904	14.796	16.300	17.569	18.678
4	.05	.10	2.751	3.150	3.452	3.699	3.909	4.093	4.257	4.406	4.542	5.097	5.521	5.870	6.169
	.025	.05	3.481	3.941	4.290	4.577	4.822	5.036	5.228	5.402	5.562	6.214	6.714	7.127	7.480
	.005	.01	5.594	6.248	6.751	7.166	7.520	7.832	8.112	8.367	8.600	9.556	10.294	10.902	11.424
5	.05	.10	2.549	2.882	3.129	3.327	3.493	3.638	3.765	3.880	3.985	4.403	4.718	4.972	5.187
	.025	.05	3.152	3.518	3.791	4.012	4.197	4.358	4.501	4.630	4.747	5.219	5.573	5.861	6.105
	.005	.01	4.771	5.243	5.599	5.888	6.133	6.346	6.535	6.706	6.862	7.491	7.968	8.355	8.684
6	.05	.10	2.428	2.723	2.939	3.110	3.253	3.376	3.484	3.580	3.668	4.015	4.272	4.477	4.649
	.025	.05	2.959	3.274	3.505	3.690	3.845	3.978	4.095	4.200	4.296	4.675	4.956	5.182	5.372
	.005	.01	4.315	4.695	4.977	5.203	5.394	5.559	5.704	5.835	5.954	6.428	6.782	7.068	7.308
7	.05	.10	2.347	2.618	2.814	2.969	3.097	3.206	3.302	3.388	3.465	3.768	3.990	4.167	4.314
	.025	.05	2.832	3.115	3.321	3.484	3.620	3.736	3.838	3.929	4.011	4.336	4.574	4.764	4.923
	.005	.01	4.027	4.353	4.591	4.782	4.941	5.078	5.198	5.306	5.404	5.791	6.077	6.306	6.497
8	.05	.10	2.289	2.544	2.726	2.869	2.987	3.088	3.176	3.254	3.324	3.598	3.798	3.955	4.086
	.025	.05	2.743	3.005	3.193	3.342	3.464	3.569	3.661	3.743	3.816	4.105	4.316	4.482	4.621
	.005	.01	3.831	4.120	4.331	4.498	4.637	4.756	4.860	4.953	5.038	5.370	5.613	5.807	5.969
9	.05	.10	2.246	2.488	2.661	2.796	2.907	3.001	3.083	3.155	3.221	3.474	3.658	3.802	3.921
	.025	.05	2.677	2.923	3.099	3.237	3.351	3.448	3.532	3.607	3.675	3.938	4.129	4.280	4.405
	.005	.01	3.688	3.952	4.143	4.294	4.419	4.526	4.619	4.703	4.778	5.072	5.287	5.457	5.598

Table D.11 is abridged from Table 1 in An improved t table for simultaneous control on g contrasts. *Journal of the American Statistical Association*, 1977, 72, 531–534, with permission of the author, P. A. Games, and the editor.
[a]Discussed in Section 14.5.

TABLE D.11.   *(Continued)*

Number of Comparisons (C)

Error df	One-Tailed Test α	Two-Tailed Test α	2	3	4	5	6	7	8	9	10	15	20	25	30
10	.05	.10	2.213	2.446	2.611	2.739	2.845	2.934	3.012	3.080	3.142	3.380	3.552	3.686	3.796
	.025	.05	2.626	2.860	3.027	3.157	3.264	3.355	3.434	3.505	3.568	3.813	3.989	4.128	4.243
	.005	.01	3.580	3.825	4.002	4.141	4.256	4.354	4.439	4.515	4.584	4.852	5.046	5.199	5.326
11	.05	.10	2.186	2.412	2.571	2.695	2.796	2.881	2.955	3.021	3.079	3.306	3.468	3.595	3.699
	.025	.05	2.586	2.811	2.970	3.094	3.196	3.283	3.358	3.424	3.484	3.715	3.880	4.010	4.117
	.005	.01	3.495	3.726	3.892	4.022	4.129	4.221	4.300	4.371	4.434	4.682	4.860	5.001	5.117
12	.05	.10	2.164	2.384	2.539	2.658	2.756	2.838	2.910	2.973	3.029	3.247	3.402	3.522	3.621
	.025	.05	2.553	2.770	2.924	3.044	3.141	3.224	3.296	3.359	3.416	3.636	3.793	3.916	4.017
	.005	.01	3.427	3.647	3.804	3.927	4.029	4.114	4.189	4.256	4.315	4.547	4.714	4.845	4.953
13	.05	.10	2.146	2.361	2.512	2.628	2.723	2.803	2.872	2.933	2.988	3.198	3.347	3.463	3.557
	.025	.05	2.526	2.737	2.886	3.002	3.096	3.176	3.245	3.306	3.361	3.571	3.722	3.839	3.935
	.005	.01	3.371	3.582	3.733	3.850	3.946	4.028	4.099	4.162	4.218	4.438	4.595	4.718	4.819
14	.05	.10	2.131	2.342	2.489	2.603	2.696	2.774	2.841	2.900	2.953	3.157	3.301	3.413	3.504
	.025	.05	2.503	2.709	2.854	2.967	3.058	3.135	3.202	3.261	3.314	3.518	3.662	3.775	3.867
	.005	.01	3.324	3.528	3.673	3.785	3.878	3.956	4.024	4.084	4.138	4.347	4.497	4.614	4.710
15	.05	.10	2.118	2.325	2.470	2.582	2.672	2.748	2.814	2.872	2.924	3.122	3.262	3.370	3.459
	.025	.05	2.483	2.685	2.827	2.937	3.026	3.101	3.166	3.224	3.275	3.472	3.612	3.721	3.810
	.005	.01	3.285	3.482	3.622	3.731	3.820	3.895	3.961	4.019	4.071	4.271	4.414	4.526	4.618
16	.05	.10	2.106	2.311	2.453	2.563	2.652	2.726	2.791	2.848	2.898	3.092	3.228	3.334	3.420
	.025	.05	2.467	2.665	2.804	2.911	2.998	3.072	3.135	3.191	3.241	3.433	3.569	3.675	3.761
	.005	.01	3.251	3.443	3.579	3.684	3.771	3.844	3.907	3.963	4.013	4.206	4.344	4.451	4.540

df															
18	.05	.10	2.088	2.287	2.426	2.532	2.619	2.691	2.753	2.808	2.857	3.043	3.174	3.275	3.358
	.025	.05	2.439	2.631	2.766	2.869	2.953	3.024	3.085	3.138	3.186	3.370	3.499	3.599	3.681
	.005	.01	3.195	3.379	3.508	3.609	3.691	3.760	3.820	3.872	3.920	4.102	4.231	4.332	4.414
20	.05	.10	2.073	2.269	2.405	2.508	2.593	2.663	2.724	2.777	2.824	3.005	3.132	3.229	3.309
	.025	.05	2.417	2.605	2.736	2.836	2.918	2.986	3.045	3.097	3.143	3.320	3.445	3.541	3.620
	.005	.01	3.152	3.329	3.454	3.550	3.629	3.695	3.752	3.802	3.848	4.021	4.144	4.239	4.317
25	.05	.10	2.047	2.236	2.367	2.466	2.547	2.614	2.672	2.722	2.767	2.938	3.058	3.149	3.224
	.025	.05	2.379	2.558	2.683	2.779	2.856	2.921	2.976	3.025	3.069	3.235	3.351	3.440	3.513
	.005	.01	3.077	3.243	3.359	3.449	3.521	3.583	3.635	3.682	3.723	3.882	3.995	4.081	4.152
30	.05	.10	2.030	2.215	2.342	2.439	2.517	2.582	2.638	2.687	2.731	2.895	3.010	3.098	3.169
	.025	.05	2.354	2.528	2.649	2.742	2.816	2.878	2.932	2.979	3.021	3.180	3.291	3.376	3.445
	.005	.01	3.029	3.188	3.298	3.384	3.453	3.511	3.561	3.605	3.644	3.794	3.900	3.981	4.048
40	.05	.10	2.009	2.189	2.312	2.406	2.481	2.544	2.597	2.644	2.686	2.843	2.952	3.036	3.103
	.025	.05	2.323	2.492	2.608	2.696	2.768	2.827	2.878	2.923	2.963	3.113	3.218	3.298	3.363
	.005	.01	2.970	3.121	3.225	3.305	3.370	3.425	3.472	3.513	3.549	3.689	3.787	3.862	3.923
60	.05	.10	1.989	2.163	2.283	2.373	2.446	2.506	2.558	2.603	2.643	2.793	2.897	2.976	3.040
	.025	.05	2.294	2.456	2.568	2.653	2.721	2.777	2.826	2.869	2.906	3.049	3.148	3.223	3.284
	.005	.01	2.914	3.056	3.155	3.230	3.291	3.342	3.386	3.425	3.459	3.589	3.679	3.749	3.805
120	.05	.10	1.968	2.138	2.254	2.342	2.411	2.469	2.519	2.562	2.600	2.744	2.843	2.918	2.978
	.025	.05	2.265	2.422	2.529	2.610	2.675	2.729	2.776	2.816	2.852	2.987	3.081	3.152	3.209
	.005	.01	2.859	2.994	3.087	3.158	3.215	3.263	3.304	3.340	3.372	3.493	3.577	3.641	3.693
∞	.05	.10	1.949	2.114	2.226	2.311	2.378	2.434	2.482	2.523	2.560	2.697	2.791	2.862	2.920
	.025	.05	2.237	2.388	2.491	2.569	2.631	2.683	2.727	2.766	2.800	2.928	3.016	3.083	3.137
	.005	.01	2.806	2.934	3.022	3.089	3.143	3.188	3.226	3.260	3.289	3.402	3.480	3.539	3.587

TABLE D.12.   Critical Values of Mann-Whitney's U^a

For a one-tailed test at $\alpha = .01$ (roman type) and $\alpha = .005$ (boldface type) and for a two-tailed test at $\alpha = 0.2$ (roman type) and $\alpha = .01$ (boldface type)

n_2 \ n_1	1	2	3	4	5	6	7	8	9	10	11	12	13	14	15	16	17	18	19	20
1	—b	—	—	—	—	—	—	—	—	—	—	—	—	—	—	—	—	—	—	—
2	—	—	—	—	—	—	—	—	—	—	—	—	0	0	0	0	0	0	1	1
													—	—	—	—	—	—	**0**	**0**
3	—	—	—	—	—	—	0	0	1	1	1	2	2	2	3	3	4	4	4	5
							—	—	**0**	**0**	**0**	**1**	**1**	**1**	**2**	**2**	**2**	**2**	**3**	**3**
4	—	—	—	—	0	1	1	2	3	3	4	5	5	6	7	7	8	9	9	10
					—	**0**	**0**	**1**	**1**	**2**	**2**	**3**	**3**	**4**	**5**	**5**	**6**	**6**	**7**	**8**
5	—	—	—	0	1	2	3	4	5	6	7	8	9	10	11	12	13	14	15	16
				—	**0**	**1**	**1**	**2**	**3**	**4**	**5**	**6**	**7**	**7**	**8**	**9**	**10**	**11**	**12**	**13**
6	—	—	—	1	2	3	4	6	7	8	9	11	12	13	15	16	18	19	20	22
				0	**1**	**2**	**3**	**4**	**5**	**6**	**7**	**9**	**10**	**11**	**12**	**13**	**15**	**16**	**17**	**18**
7	—	—	0	1	3	4	6	7	9	11	12	14	16	17	19	21	23	24	26	28
			—	**0**	**1**	**3**	**4**	**6**	**7**	**9**	**10**	**12**	**13**	**15**	**16**	**18**	**19**	**21**	**22**	**24**
8	—	—	0	2	4	6	7	9	11	13	15	17	20	22	24	26	28	30	32	34
			—	**1**	**2**	**4**	**6**	**7**	**9**	**11**	**13**	**15**	**17**	**18**	**20**	**22**	**24**	**26**	**28**	**30**
9	—	—	1	3	5	7	9	11	14	16	18	21	23	26	28	31	33	36	38	40
			0	**1**	**3**	**5**	**7**	**9**	**11**	**13**	**16**	**18**	**20**	**22**	**24**	**27**	**29**	**31**	**33**	**36**
10	—	—	1	3	6	8	11	13	16	19	22	24	27	30	33	36	38	41	44	47
			0	**2**	**4**	**6**	**9**	**11**	**13**	**16**	**18**	**21**	**24**	**26**	**29**	**31**	**34**	**37**	**39**	**42**
11	—	—	1	4	7	9	12	15	18	22	25	28	31	34	37	41	44	47	50	53
			0	**2**	**5**	**7**	**10**	**13**	**16**	**18**	**21**	**24**	**27**	**30**	**33**	**36**	**39**	**42**	**45**	**48**
12	—	—	2	5	8	11	14	17	21	24	28	31	35	38	42	46	49	53	56	60
			1	**3**	**6**	**9**	**12**	**15**	**18**	**21**	**24**	**27**	**31**	**34**	**37**	**41**	**44**	**47**	**51**	**54**
13	—	0	2	5	9	12	16	20	23	27	31	35	39	43	47	51	55	59	63	67
		—	**1**	**3**	**7**	**10**	**13**	**17**	**20**	**24**	**27**	**31**	**34**	**38**	**42**	**45**	**49**	**53**	**56**	**60**
14	—	0	2	6	10	13	17	22	26	30	34	38	43	47	51	56	60	65	69	73
		—	**1**	**4**	**7**	**11**	**15**	**18**	**22**	**26**	**30**	**34**	**38**	**42**	**46**	**50**	**54**	**58**	**63**	**67**
15	—	0	3	7	11	15	19	24	28	33	37	42	47	51	56	61	66	70	75	80
		—	**2**	**5**	**8**	**12**	**16**	**20**	**24**	**29**	**33**	**37**	**42**	**46**	**51**	**55**	**60**	**64**	**69**	**73**
16	—	0	3	7	12	16	21	26	31	36	41	46	51	56	61	66	71	76	82	87
		—	**2**	**5**	**9**	**13**	**18**	**22**	**27**	**31**	**36**	**41**	**45**	**50**	**55**	**60**	**65**	**70**	**74**	**79**
17	—	0	4	8	13	18	23	28	33	38	44	49	55	60	66	71	77	82	88	93
		—	**2**	**6**	**10**	**15**	**19**	**24**	**29**	**34**	**39**	**44**	**49**	**54**	**60**	**65**	**70**	**75**	**81**	**86**
18	—	0	4	9	14	19	24	30	36	41	47	53	59	65	70	76	82	88	94	100
		—	**2**	**6**	**11**	**16**	**21**	**26**	**31**	**37**	**42**	**47**	**53**	**58**	**64**	**70**	**75**	**81**	**87**	**92**
19	—	1	4	9	15	20	26	32	38	44	50	56	63	69	75	82	88	94	101	107
		0	**3**	**7**	**12**	**17**	**22**	**28**	**33**	**39**	**45**	**51**	**56**	**63**	**69**	**74**	**81**	**87**	**93**	**99**
20	—	1	5	10	16	22	28	34	40	47	53	60	67	73	80	87	93	100	107	114
		0	**3**	**8**	**13**	**18**	**24**	**30**	**36**	**42**	**48**	**54**	**60**	**67**	**73**	**79**	**86**	**92**	**99**	**105**

[a] Discussed in Section 17.2. To be significant for any given n_1 and n_2, the obtained U must be *equal to* or *less than* the value shown in the table.
[b] Dashes in the body of the table indicate that no decision is possible at the stated level of significance.

TABLE D.12.   *(Continued)*

Critical values for a one-tailed test at $\alpha = .05$ (roman type) and $\alpha = .025$ (boldface type) and for a two-tailed test at $\alpha = .10$ (roman type) and $\alpha = .05$ (boldface type)

n_2 \ n_1	1	2	3	4	5	6	7	8	9	10	11	12	13	14	15	16	17	18	19	20
1	—	—	—	—	—	—	—	—	—	—	—	—	—	—	—	—	—	—	0	0
																			—	—
2	—	—	—	—	0	0	0	1	1	1	1	2	2	2	3	3	3	4	4	4
								0	**0**	**0**	**0**	**1**	**1**	**1**	**1**	**1**	**2**	**2**	**2**	**2**
3	—	—	0	0	1	2	2	3	3	4	5	5	6	7	7	8	9	9	10	11
	—	—	—	—	**0**	**1**	**1**	**2**	**2**	**3**	**3**	**4**	**4**	**5**	**5**	**6**	**6**	**7**	**7**	**8**
4	—	—	0	1	2	3	4	5	6	7	8	9	10	11	12	14	15	16	17	18
	—	—	—	**0**	**1**	**2**	**3**	**4**	**4**	**5**	**6**	**7**	**8**	**9**	**10**	**11**	**11**	**12**	**13**	**13**
5	—	0	1	2	4	5	6	8	9	11	12	13	15	16	18	19	20	22	23	25
	—	—	**0**	**1**	**2**	**3**	**5**	**6**	**7**	**8**	**9**	**11**	**12**	**13**	**14**	**15**	**17**	**18**	**19**	**20**
6	—	0	2	3	5	7	8	10	12	14	16	17	19	21	23	25	26	28	30	32
	—	—	**1**	**2**	**3**	**5**	**6**	**8**	**10**	**11**	**13**	**14**	**16**	**17**	**19**	**21**	**22**	**24**	**25**	**27**
7	—	0	2	4	6	8	11	13	15	17	19	21	24	26	28	30	33	35	37	39
	—	—	**1**	**3**	**5**	**6**	**8**	**10**	**12**	**14**	**16**	**18**	**20**	**22**	**24**	**26**	**28**	**30**	**32**	**34**
8	—	1	3	5	8	10	13	15	18	20	23	26	28	31	33	36	39	41	44	47
	—	**0**	**2**	**4**	**6**	**8**	**10**	**13**	**15**	**17**	**19**	**22**	**24**	**26**	**29**	**31**	**34**	**36**	**38**	**41**
9	—	1	3	6	9	12	15	18	21	24	27	30	33	36	39	42	45	48	51	54
	—	**0**	**2**	**4**	**7**	**10**	**12**	**15**	**17**	**20**	**23**	**26**	**28**	**31**	**34**	**37**	**39**	**42**	**45**	**48**
10	—	1	4	7	11	14	17	20	24	27	31	34	37	41	44	48	51	55	58	62
	—	**0**	**3**	**5**	**8**	**11**	**14**	**17**	**20**	**23**	**26**	**29**	**33**	**36**	**39**	**42**	**45**	**48**	**52**	**55**
11	—	1	5	8	12	16	19	23	27	31	34	38	42	46	50	54	57	61	65	69
	—	**0**	**3**	**6**	**9**	**13**	**16**	**19**	**23**	**26**	**30**	**33**	**37**	**40**	**44**	**47**	**51**	**55**	**58**	**62**
12	—	2	5	9	13	17	21	26	30	34	38	42	47	51	55	60	64	68	72	77
	—	**1**	**4**	**7**	**11**	**14**	**18**	**22**	**26**	**29**	**33**	**37**	**41**	**45**	**49**	**53**	**57**	**61**	**65**	**69**
13	—	2	6	10	15	19	24	28	33	37	42	47	51	56	61	65	70	75	80	84
	—	**1**	**4**	**8**	**12**	**16**	**20**	**24**	**28**	**33**	**37**	**41**	**45**	**50**	**54**	**59**	**63**	**67**	**72**	**76**
14	—	2	7	11	16	21	26	31	36	41	46	51	56	61	66	71	77	82	87	92
	—	**1**	**5**	**9**	**13**	**17**	**22**	**26**	**31**	**36**	**40**	**45**	**50**	**55**	**59**	**64**	**67**	**74**	**78**	**83**
15	—	3	7	12	18	23	28	33	39	44	50	55	61	66	72	77	83	88	94	100
	—	**1**	**5**	**10**	**14**	**19**	**24**	**29**	**34**	**39**	**44**	**49**	**54**	**59**	**64**	**70**	**75**	**80**	**85**	**90**
16	—	3	8	14	19	25	30	36	42	48	54	60	65	71	77	83	89	95	101	107
	—	**1**	**6**	**11**	**15**	**21**	**26**	**31**	**37**	**42**	**47**	**53**	**59**	**64**	**70**	**75**	**81**	**86**	**92**	**98**
17	—	3	9	15	20	26	33	39	45	51	57	64	70	77	83	89	96	102	109	115
	—	**2**	**6**	**11**	**17**	**22**	**28**	**34**	**39**	**45**	**51**	**57**	**63**	**67**	**75**	**81**	**87**	**93**	**99**	**105**
18	—	4	9	16	22	28	35	41	48	55	61	68	75	82	88	95	102	109	116	123
	—	**2**	**7**	**12**	**18**	**24**	**30**	**36**	**42**	**48**	**55**	**61**	**67**	**74**	**80**	**86**	**93**	**99**	**106**	**112**
19	0	4	10	17	23	30	37	44	51	58	65	72	80	87	94	101	109	116	123	130
	—	**2**	**7**	**13**	**19**	**25**	**32**	**38**	**45**	**52**	**58**	**65**	**72**	**78**	**85**	**92**	**99**	**106**	**113**	**119**
20	0	4	11	18	25	32	39	47	54	62	69	77	84	92	100	107	115	123	130	138
	—	**2**	**8**	**13**	**20**	**27**	**34**	**41**	**48**	**55**	**62**	**69**	**76**	**83**	**90**	**98**	**105**	**112**	**119**	**127**

TABLE D.13.   Critical Values of Wilcoxon's T^a

n	Level of Significance for a One-Tailed Test				n	Level of Significance for a One-Tailed Test			
	.05	.025	.01	.005		.05	.025	.01	.005
	Level of Significance for a Two-Tailed Test					Level of Significance for a Two-Tailed Test			
n	.10	.05	.02	.01	n	.10	.05	.02	.01
5	0	—	—	—	28	130	116	101	91
6	2	0	—	—	29	140	126	110	100
7	3	2	0	—	30	151	137	120	109
8	5	3	1	0	31	163	147	130	118
9	8	5	3	1	32	175	159	140	128
10	10	8	5	3	33	187	170	151	138
11	13	10	7	5	34	200	182	162	148
12	17	13	9	7	35	213	195	173	159
13	21	17	12	9	36	227	208	185	171
14	25	21	15	12	37	241	221	198	182
15	30	25	19	15	38	256	235	211	194
16	35	29	23	19	39	271	249	224	207
17	41	34	27	23	40	286	264	238	220
18	47	40	32	27	41	302	279	252	233
19	53	46	37	32	42	319	294	266	247
20	60	52	43	37	43	336	310	281	261
21	67	58	49	42	44	353	327	296	276
22	75	65	55	48	45	371	343	312	291
23	83	73	62	54	46	389	361	328	307
24	91	81	69	61	47	407	378	345	322
25	100	89	76	68	48	426	396	362	339
26	110	98	84	75	49	446	415	379	355
27	119	107	92	83	50	466	434	397	373

[a]Discussed in Section 17.3. The symbol T denotes the smaller sum of ranks associated with differences that are all of the same sign. For any given n (number of ranked differences), the obtained T is significant at a given level if it is *equal to* or *less than* the value shown in the table.

Appendix E

Student Database

DESCRIPTION OF DATABASE

Over the years I have collected data about students who enroll in my introductory statistics course. These data have been organized so that they can be updated from semester to semester and analyzed in a variety of ways. Such an organization of data is called a *database*. A portion of this database is reproduced in Table E.1. The following information is contained in the table.

Column 1: Student identification number (ID No.)
        Range = 1–461
Column 2: Student identification number by gender (ID No. by Gen)
        Men = 1–180   Women = 181–461
Column 3: Student's gender (Gender)
        M = Man   W = Woman
Column 4: Major in college (Major)
        BIO = Biology   CHE = Chemistry
        CSI = Computer science   ENG = English
        HIS = History   LAW = Pre-law
        MATH = Mathematics   MED = Pre-medicine
        NURS = Nursing   OPT = Pre-optometry
        PSY = Psychology   PT = Physical Therapy
        REL = Religion   SPATH = Speech pathology
        UNDE = Undecided
Column 5: Number of previous psychology courses (No. Psy)
        Range = 0–11
Column 6: Number of previous mathematics courses (No. Math)
        Range = 0–6
Column 7: Overall grade point average (GPA)
Column 8: Score on the Test of Mathematical Skills in Appendix A (Math Test)
Column 9: Grade in introductory statistics course (Stat Grade)
        4 = A   3.5 = B+   3 = B
        2.5 = C+   2 = C   1 = D
        0 = F   I = Incomplete   W = Withdrew
Missing information is indicated by a period.

TABLE E.1.   Student Database

(1) ID No.	(2) ID No. by Gen	(3) Gender	(4) Major	(5) No. Psy	(6) No. Math	(7) GPA	(8) Math Test	(9) Stat Grade
1	1	M	PSY	3	2	2.84	29	2
2	2	M	PSY	6	1	3.30	17	2
3	3	M	PSY	1	2	3.46	37	4
4	4	M	PSY	3	3	3.34	45	2
5	5	M	PSY	2	1	3.22	25	3
6	6	M	PSY	4	3	2.35	16	2
7	7	M	PSY	3	3	2.04	34	W
8	8	M	PSY	8	2	3.38	39	3
9	9	M	PSY	1	1	3.33	20	3.5
10	10	M	PSY	4	2	2.41	31	2
11	11	M	MED	1	3	3.42	39	3
12	12	M	MATH	1	4	2.66	38	3
13	13	M	PSY	4	1	2.01	25	1
14	14	M	PSY	3	3	2.42	38	2
15	15	M	PSY	3	2	3.22	36	2.5
16	16	M	PSY	2	2	2.29	41	I
17	17	M	PSY	4	3	3.32	38	4
18	18	M	PSY	1	2	2.72	41	3
19	19	M	MED	2	2	3.76	37	4
20	20	M	PT	3	1	3.23	34	2.5
21	21	M	PSY	11	1	3.40	30	0
22	22	M	PSY	1	1	3.75	37	4
23	23	M	MED	1	2	3.26	35	3.5
24	24	M	PSY	4	1	3.76	40	4
25	25	M	PSY	4	1	3.23	26	2.5
26	26	M	PSY	1	3	3.87	39	4
27	27	M	PSY	5	1	2.32	26	2
28	28	M	PSY	7	3	2.79	41	2
29	29	M	PSY	8	1	3.13	37	3
30	30	M	PT	2	2	3.68	30	4
31	31	M	PSY	4	1	2.65	26	1
32	32	M	PSY	1	1	2.91	42	3
33	33	M	PSY	4	2	2.27	17	I
34	34	M	PSY	8	1	2.53	35	I
35	35	M	PSY	5	4	2.72	40	2
36	36	M	PSY	3	1	3.32	29	3.5
37	37	M	PSY	3	2	3.73	43	4
38	38	M	PSY	5	2	3.24	26	3
39	39	M	MED	2	4	3.72	41	3.5
40	40	M	PSY	2	2	3.01	34	3

TABLE E.1. *Continued*

(1) ID No.	(2) ID No. by Gen	(3) Gender	(4) Major	(5) No. Psy	(6) No. Math	(7) GPA	(8) Math Test	(9) Stat Grade
41	41	M	.	2	5	3.74	44	4
42	42	M	PSY	4	1	3.27	31	4
43	43	M	PSY	.	.	2.82	22	2
44	44	M	PSY	1	2	3.52	29	3
45	45	M	PSY	1	2	3.79	40	4
46	46	M	PSY	.	.	3.71	32	3.5
47	47	M	PSY	3	1	2.31	28	2
48	48	M	PSY	5	1	2.25	16	1
49	49	M	PSY	4	1	3.06	27	3
50	50	M	MED	2	4	3.79	43	4
51	51	M	PSY	4	1	3.65	18	4
52	52	M	PSY	2	1	3.04	35	2.5
53	53	M	PSY	6	1	2.16	31	1
54	54	M	PSY	1	2	3.01	25	4
55	55	M	PSY	5	1	2.70	17	2
56	56	M	PSY	3	.	2.91	31	2
57	57	M	PSY	8	3	3.35	39	3
58	58	M	PSY	7	2	3.23	37	4
59	59	M	MED	1	1	2.94	35	3
60	60	M	PSY	1	5	3.79	40	4
61	61	M	PSY	5	4	2.32	34	2
62	62	M	PSY	2	1	2.96	29	2
63	63	M	PSY	.	1	2.51	37	3
64	64	M	.	2	2	2.42	43	2
65	65	M	PSY	1	1	4.00	40	4
66	66	M	PSY	4	2	1.01	17	0
67	67	M	PSY	1	4	2.71	45	W
68	68	M	.	1	2	2.86	37	3
69	69	M	BIO	2	2	3.71	39	3.5
70	70	M	PSY	2	3	2.94	35	I
71	71	M	PSY	3	1	2.80	18	2
72	72	M	PSY	1	1	2.55	25	2
73	73	M	LAW	3	1	2.29	39	2
74	74	M	PSY	2	2	3.44	40	3
75	75	M	PSY	4	2	2.26	37	2
76	76	M	PSY	2	2	2.89	33	2
77	77	M	PSY	2	0	2.95	14	2
78	78	M	PSY	2	2	3.31	39	3
79	79	M	PSY	2	2	2.32	31	3
80	80	M	PSY	3	2	3.11	45	2

TABLE E.1. *Continued*

(1) ID No.	(2) ID No. by Gen	(3) Gender	(4) Major	(5) No. Psy	(6) No. Math	(7) GPA	(8) Math Test	(9) Stat Grade
81	81	M	PSY	1	2	3.02	37	4
82	82	M	PSY	2	0	2.16	25	0
83	83	M	PSY	4	4	3.87	43	4
84	84	M	PSY	2	3	3.03	34	3
85	85	M	PSY	3	3	3.21	36	4
86	86	M	CSI	1	1	1.00	37	I
87	87	M	PSY	4	2	3.39	29	3
88	88	M	PSY	3	1	3.42	18	4
89	89	M	PSY	8	0	3.21	20	2
90	90	M	PSY	1	3	3.24	31	3.5
91	91	M	PSY	4	2	3.60	38	4
92	92	M	PT	7	2	2.13	34	1
93	93	M	PSY	5	0	2.22	14	1
94	94	M	PSY	7	2	2.81	23	2
95	95	M	PSY	4	1	3.25	28	4
96	96	M	PSY	5	2	2.32	24	1
97	97	M	MED	2	4	2.82	42	2.5
98	98	M	MED	1	4	2.93	40	3.5
99	99	M	PSY	6	2	3.36	24	4
100	100	M	PSY	3	1	3.45	40	4
101	101	M	PT	3	1	2.51	25	2
102	102	M	PSY	6	3	2.65	45	1
103	103	M	PSY	2	1	3.24	19	4
104	104	M	PSY	8	1	2.60	19	1
105	105	M	PSY	6	0	2.37	19	0
106	106	M	PSY	0	1	2.24	25	2
107	107	M	PSY	2	2	2.72	38	3
108	108	M	PSY	.	1	2.24	25	W
109	109	M	PSY	2	2	3.14	44	3
110	110	M	PSY	4	2	2.43	33	1
111	111	M	PSY	2	2	3.35	30	3
112	112	M	PSY	5	1	2.90	41	2
113	113	M	PSY	3	3	3.95	43	4
114	114	M	BIO	2	3	3.71	42	3
115	115	M	PSY	4	1	2.65	41	2
116	116	M	PSY	3	3	3.00	35	4
117	117	M	PSY	2	1	2.51	23	2
118	118	M	OPT	.	1	3.32	39	4
119	119	M	PSY	2	1	2.62	31	1
120	120	M	PSY	3	2	2.97	38	3

TABLE E.1. *Continued*

(1) ID No.	(2) ID No. by Gen	(3) Gender	(4) Major	(5) No. Psy	(6) No. Math	(7) GPA	(8) Math Test	(9) Stat Grade
121	121	M	PSY	3	2	2.83	41	3
122	122	M	PSY	1	2	2.99	25	3
123	123	M	PSY	1	3	3.21	39	4
124	124	M	PSY	2	1	2.32	26	2
125	125	M	PSY	7	3	2.79	41	2
126	126	M	PT	1	1	2.85	24	2
127	127	M	PSY	3	1	2.65	45	1
128	128	M	PSY	3	1	3.24	19	2
129	129	M	PSY	8	1	2.60	19	1
130	130	M	PSY	6	0	2.36	19	0
131	131	M	PSY	0	1	2.24	25	2
132	132	M	PSY	1	3	2.73	37	3
133	133	M	PSY	8	1	3.13	37	3
134	134	M	PT	1	2	3.87	31	4
135	135	M	PSY	1	2	2.29	41	I
136	136	M	PSY	4	3	3.32	38	4
137	137	M	PSY	1	3	2.72	43	3
138	138	M	MED	2	2	3.76	37	4
139	139	M	PT	3	1	2.76	34	2.5
140	140	M	PSY	1	3	2.37	15	2
141	141	M	PSY	4	2	2.04	34	W
142	142	M	PSY	8	2	3.38	39	3
143	143	M	PSY	3	2	3.31	23	3.5
144	144	M	PSY	1	1	2.51	30	2
145	145	M	PSY	1	1	2.09	28	2
146	146	M	PSY	1	3	2.30	41	2
147	147	M	PSY	4	1	3.31	28	2
148	148	M	PSY	8	2	2.90	44	.
149	149	M	MED	6	3	1.93	24	2
150	150	M	PSY	6	4	2.08	33	2
151	151	M	PSY	3	0	2.66	16	2
152	152	M	PSY	3	1	2.78	34	3
153	153	M	PSY	4	0	2.42	23	2
154	154	M	PSY	4	2	2.13	42	2
155	155	M	PSY	4	1	2.51	24	2
156	156	M	LAW	3	2	3.07	39	3
157	157	M	MED	2	2	3.90	46	4
158	158	M	PSY	3	0	2.55	27	2
159	159	M	MED	2	1	2.44	34	2
160	160	M	PSY	2	0	2.81	24	1

TABLE E.1. *Continued*

(1) ID No.	(2) ID No. by Gen	(3) Gender	(4) Major	(5) No. Psy	(6) No. Math	(7) GPA	(8) Math Test	(9) Stat Grade
161	161	M	PSY	5	1	2.39	30	2
162	162	M	PSY	7	3	3.39	43	4
163	163	M	PSY	4	1	2.17	27	0
164	164	M	PSY	3	1	3.77	37	4
165	165	M	PSY	3	4	3.42	29	3
166	166	M	PSY	2	1	3.11	32	3.5
167	167	M	PSY	4	2	2.92	34	2.5
168	168	M	PSY	1	3	2.14	41	3
169	169	M	PSY	6	2	3.46	38	W
170	170	M	PSY	7	2	2.59	21	2
171	171	M	PSY	2	2	3.36	42	3.5
172	172	M	PSY	2	1	3.69	39	3.5
173	173	M	PSY	2	1	2.26	25	W
174	174	M	PSY	1	3	3.24	36	2.5
175	175	M	PSY	4	3	3.45	39	3
176	176	M	PSY	2	0	2.56	16	2
177	177	M	PSY	4	2	3.44	36	4
178	178	M	MED	5	2	3.00	33	4
179	179	M	PSY	2	1	3.47	31	3
180	180	M	CHE	1	3	3.10	44	3.5
181	1	W	PSY	2	1	3.23	26	2
182	2	W	PSY	1	4	2.85	39	4
183	3	W	PT	2	1	3.02	40	3
184	4	W	BIO	2	3	3.66	41	3
185	5	W	PSY	5	2	3.16	42	3
186	6	W	PT	1	2	3.46	34	2.5
187	7	W	BIO	1	2	3.51	45	4
188	8	W	PSY	1	1	2.83	17	3
189	9	W	PSY	3	4	3.31	45	4
190	10	W	PT	2	2	2.67	38	3
191	11	W	NURS	1	0	2.75	10	2
192	12	W	PSY	2	1	2.96	35	2.5
193	13	W	MED	3	2	3.07	33	W
194	14	W	PSY	3	2	3.84	42	4
195	15	W	PSY	4	3	2.97	30	3
196	16	W	PSY	6	2	3.18	37	3.5
197	17	W	MED	3	1	2.44	38	2
198	18	W	PSY	2	4	3.40	38	3
199	19	W	PSY	4	2	2.11	33	2
200	20	W	PSY	2	1	2.97	10	2

TABLE E.1. *Continued*

(1) ID No.	(2) ID No. by Gen	(3) Gender	(4) Major	(5) No. Psy	(6) No. Math	(7) GPA	(8) Math Test	(9) Stat Grade
201	21	W	PSY	4	0	2.02	23	0
202	22	W	ENG	2	1	3.44	24	3
203	23	W	MED	2	3	3.16	38	3.5
204	24	W	PSY	2	0	3.93	10	4
205	25	W	PT	2	2	3.07	34	2
206	26	W	PSY	.	.	2.82	29	2
207	27	W	PSY	5	0	2.67	18	2
208	28	W	PSY	10	1	2.82	20	2
209	29	W	PSY	4	3	3.31	40	3
210	30	W	PSY	4	1	3.10	33	2
211	31	W	PSY	3	2	3.26	43	4
212	32	W	PSY	3	1	2.64	21	2
213	33	W	PSY	2	2	2.93	43	4
214	34	W	PSY	3	6	2.81	39	3
215	35	W	NURS	2	1	3.19	27	2
216	36	W	PSY	3	3	3.37	30	4
217	37	W	PT	3	2	3.31	28	1
218	38	W	PT	4	2	2.90	28	2
219	39	W	PSY	4	0	1.90	19	0
220	40	W	PSY	4	4	3.10	34	3
221	41	W	PSY	.	.	3.19	42	2.5
222	42	W	PSY	2	.	3.58	38	3.5
223	43	W	PSY	2	4	3.66	38	4
224	44	W	PSY	4	1	2.61	30	2
225	45	W	PT	1	1	3.09	37	2
226	46	W	PSY	6	1	2.48	18	2
227	47	W	PT	3	1	3.57	44	4
228	48	W	PSY	4	1	3.33	35	4
229	49	W	PSY	7	1	3.78	42	4
230	50	W	PSY	.	1	3.40	21	3
231	51	W	PT	1	1	2.64	43	2.5
232	52	W	PSY	3	1	3.09	38	3
233	53	W	PSY	.	1	2.93	39	2
234	54	W	PT	4	2	2.92	29	2
235	55	W	.	2	3	3.47	43	4
236	56	W	PSY	10	0	3.47	8	3
237	57	W	PSY	4	0	1.88	17	0
238	58	W	PSY	3	0	2.01	.	1
239	59	W	PSY	2	3	3.67	32	4
240	60	W	PSY	3	3	3.75	39	4

TABLE E.1. *Continued*

(1) ID No.	(2) ID No. by Gen	(3) Gender	(4) Major	(5) No. Psy	(6) No. Math	(7) GPA	(8) Math Test	(9) Stat Grade
241	61	W	PSY	4	1	2.90	35	2
242	62	W	PSY	6	0	3.38	32	4
243	63	W	BIO	2	2	3.42	41	2
244	64	W	PSY	2	1	3.40	34	3
245	65	W	PSY	3	1	2.35	20	2
246	66	W	PSY	4	1	2.68	12	I
247	67	W	SPATH	2	1	3.89	26	4
248	68	W	PSY	2	1	2.33	30	W
249	69	W	PT	2	3	2.95	44	4
250	70	W	PSY	7	0	2.69	35	2
251	71	W	PSY	2	1	3.26	27	2
252	72	W	.	4	2	3.39	40	2
253	73	W	BIO	2	2	3.39	42	2
254	74	W	PSY	5	1	2.39	35	2
255	75	W	PSY	3	1	3.71	35	4
256	76	W	PSY	2	4	3.81	41	3.5
257	77	W	PSY	4	0	2.77	16	2
258	78	W	MED	3	2	3.65	41	4
259	79	W	PSY	10	1	2.47	36	4
260	80	W	PSY	3	3	3.32	40	4
261	81	W	PSY	2	3	3.68	31	4
262	82	W	PSY	4	2	3.41	23	3
263	83	W	PSY	2	1	2.90	8	3
264	84	W	PSY	8	1	3.72	32	4
265	85	W	UNDE	2	2	2.34	23	2.5
266	86	W	HIS	3	2	2.87	30	4
267	87	W	BIO	2	3	3.01	40	2
268	88	W	PT	1	1	2.75	39	3
269	89	W	PSY	2	3	3.58	33	3
270	90	W	PT	2	1	3.54	34	3
271	91	W	PT	1	1	3.64	39	4
272	92	W	PSY	2	3	3.33	42	3.5
273	93	W	PSY	2	2	2.83	41	2.5
274	94	W	MED	3	3	3.30	35	4
275	95	W	PSY	2	4	3.71	35	3
276	96	W	PSY	5	1	2.66	31	1
277	97	W	PSY	2	3	3.63	31	4
278	98	W	SPATH	4	2	3.45	20	2
279	99	W	PSY	4	1	2.31	37	2
280	100	W	PSY	4	2	3.54	35	4

TABLE E.1. *Continued*

(1) ID No.	(2) ID No. by Gen	(3) Gender	(4) Major	(5) No. Psy	(6) No. Math	(7) GPA	(8) Math Test	(9) Stat Grade
281	101	W	PSY	3	2	3.38	44	4
282	102	W	PSY	5	2	2.70	45	3
283	103	W	PSY	3	3	3.62	39	4
284	104	W	PSY	2	2	2.42	25	2
285	105	W	PSY	5	3	2.53	37	2
286	106	W	PT	1	1	2.74	31	2
287	107	W	PSY	3	0	3.58	41	4
288	108	W	PSY	4	2	2.63	25	2
289	109	W	.	3	4	4.00	43	4
290	110	W	PSY	3	1	2.54	30	1
291	111	W	PSY	3	1	3.86	30	4
292	112	W	PT	4	1	3.75	37	4
293	113	W	PSY	7	1	2.28	21	1
294	114	W	BIO	3	3	2.91	42	3
295	115	W	PSY	5	1	2.43	28	2
296	116	W	NURS	4	2	2.16	36	2.5
297	117	W	PSY	2	4	3.22	43	4
298	118	W	PSY	2	1	3.89	34	3.5
299	119	W	PSY	1	1	2.62	42	2
300	120	W	PSY	2	2	2.95	27	I
301	121	W	PT	2	1	3.54	37	3.5
302	122	W	PSY	4	2	3.71	38	3
303	123	W	NURS	2	0	2.95	34	2
304	124	W	PSY	2	3	2.89	34	3
305	125	W	PT	.	.	3.84	40	4
306	126	W	PT	1	2	3.48	39	3.5
307	127	W	PSY	.	.	2.13	18	.
308	128	W	PSY	3	3	3.66	43	4
309	129	W	MED	3	1	2.55	33	2.5
310	130	W	PSY	5	2	2.01	30	2
311	131	W	PT	1	1	2.35	43	2
312	132	W	PSY	4	1	2.28	20	2
313	133	W	.	4	1	3.18	29	2
314	134	W	PSY	3	1	3.01	33	2
315	135	W	PSY	4	0	3.83	43	4
316	136	W	PSY	2	4	3.87	36	4
317	137	W	PSY	4	1	3.21	17	3
318	138	W	NURS	2	2	3.10	20	4
319	139	W	PSY	2	4	2.96	40	3
320	140	W	PSY	3	2	3.49	27	4

TABLE E.1. *Continued*

(1) ID No.	(2) ID No. by Gen	(3) Gender	(4) Major	(5) No. Psy	(6) No. Math	(7) GPA	(8) Math Test	(9) Stat Grade
321	141	W	PSY	4	3	3.21	41	2.5
322	142	W	PT	2	2	3.75	43	4
323	143	W	PSY	2	5	3.60	41	4
324	144	W	PSY	6	1	3.08	43	2.5
325	145	W	PT	1	1	3.49	30	4
326	146	W	PSY	1	1	2.64	37	4
327	147	W	PSY	6	4	3.08	39	3
328	148	W	PSY	4	1	3.54	42	4
329	149	W	PSY	5	1	3.23	41	3
330	150	W	MED	3	3	3.65	39	4
331	151	W	PSY	4	3	3.44	45	4
332	152	W	PT	4	1	3.43	41	4
333	153	W	PSY	4	0	4.00	16	4
334	154	W	.	4	0	2.54	21	2
335	155	W	PT	2	4	3.82	33	4
336	156	W	PSY	3	1	3.58	30	4
337	157	W	PSY	6	1	3.32	27	3
338	158	W	PSY	1	.	2.88	31	2.5
339	159	W	PSY	3	3	3.38	40	2
340	160	W	PSY	4	1	2.91	23	2
341	161	W	PSY	3	2	2.51	36	2
342	162	W	PSY	4	1	3.48	28	W
343	163	W	PSY	2	1	3.43	33	3
344	164	W	PSY	1	0	2.38	22	3
345	165	W	PSY	2	0	3.84	35	4
346	166	W	PSY	1	1	2.73	30	2
347	167	W	PSY	4	2	2.29	21	1
348	168	W	PSY	1	3	3.98	38	4
349	169	W	PSY	5	1	2.63	28	3
350	170	W	PT	3	2	2.61	40	3
351	171	W	PSY	2	1	3.23	26	2
352	172	W	PSY	2	3	2.85	39	4
353	173	W	PT	2	1	3.02	40	3
354	174	W	BIO	2	2	3.66	41	3
355	175	W	PSY	5	2	3.16	42	3
356	176	W	PT	1	2	3.46	34	2.5
357	177	W	PSY	5	0	2.02	23	0
358	178	W	ENG	1	2	3.44	24	3
359	179	W	MED	2	3	3.16	38	3.5
360	180	W	PSY	2	0	3.93	10	4

TABLE E.1. *Continued*

(1) ID No.	(2) ID No. by Gen	(3) Gender	(4) Major	(5) No. Psy	(6) No. Math	(7) GPA	(8) Math Test	(9) Stat Grade
361	181	W	PSY	3	1	3.19	42	2.5
362	182	W	PSY	1	.	3.58	38	3.5
363	183	W	PSY	2	3	3.75	39	4
364	184	W	PSY	4	2	2.90	35	2
365	185	W	PSY	6	0	3.38	32	4
366	186	W	MED	3	3	3.65	39	4
367	187	W	PSY	4	3	3.44	45	4
368	188	W	PT	4	1	3.43	41	4
369	189	W	PSY	5	0	4.00	16	4
370	190	W	PSY	4	2	2.54	21	.
371	191	W	PSY	4	2	2.40	26	2
372	192	W	PSY	3	1	3.40	34	3
373	193	W	PSY	5	3	3.66	38	4
374	194	W	PSY	4	1	2.91	23	2
375	195	W	PSY	4	2	2.51	36	2
376	196	W	PSY	3	1	3.48	28	W
377	197	W	PSY	4	2	3.43	33	3
378	198	W	PSY	1	0	2.38	22	3
379	199	W	PSY	5	1	2.61	30	2
380	200	W	MED	2	2	2.34	38	2
381	201	W	PT	2	2	3.50	46	3
382	202	W	PSY	5	1	2.58	21	2
383	203	W	PSY	2	2	2.79	40	2
384	204	W	MED	2	2	2.03	26	2
385	205	W	PT	1	1	3.80	36	4
386	206	W	PSY	3	2	3.51	41	3.5
387	207	W	MED	2	2	3.04	38	3
388	208	W	PSY	3	2	2.48	34	2
389	209	W	PSY	3	3	3.55	42	4
390	210	W	PSY	2	1	2.45	33	2
391	211	W	PSY	3	0	.	28	W
392	212	W	PSY	2	2	2.71	43	2
393	213	W	PSY	1	0	2.03	34	W
394	214	W	PSY	3	1	3.18	38	2
395	215	W	PSY	3	3	3.50	39	3.5
396	216	W	PSY	2	0	2.40	14	0
397	217	W	PSY	2	1	3.52	39	3
398	218	W	PSY	3	1	3.46	27	W
399	219	W	LAW	2	2	2.31	40	2.5
400	220	W	PSY	2	1	2.42	29	2

TABLE E.1.   *Continued*

(1) ID No.	(2) ID No. by Gen	(3) Gender	(4) Major	(5) No. Psy	(6) No. Math	(7) GPA	(8) Math Test	(9) Stat Grade
401	221	W	REL	3	1	2.92	21	2
402	222	W	PSY	3	1	2.88	36	2
403	223	W	PSY	2	0	3.26	26	2
404	224	W	PSY	1	1	3.13	34	2
405	225	W	PSY	6	0	1.81	15	0
406	226	W	PSY	2	1	3.62	43	4
407	227	W	PSY	8	1	3.04	30	4
408	228	W	PSY	2	0	2.36	13	1
409	229	W	PT	2	2	3.37	39	4
410	230	W	MATH	1	1	3.91	47	4
411	231	W	PSY	2	1	2.44	40	1
412	232	W	PSY	2	1	2.64	36	2
413	233	W	PSY	2	1	2.49	33	2
414	234	W	LAW	2	1	3.75	41	4
415	235	W	PSY	3	1	3.33	35	2
416	236	W	MED	2	2	2.51	30	2
417	237	W	BIO	1	1	3.68	47	4
418	238	W	PSY	1	2	3.40	23	4
419	239	W	PSY	3	2	3.21	28	2
420	240	W	PSY	2	0	3.06	22	2.5
421	241	W	PSY	3	1	3.49	28	3
422	242	W	PSY	1	1	2.96	16	2
423	243	W	PSY	1	0	3.25	27	2
424	244	W	PSY	2	5	2.19	37	2
425	245	W	PT	1	1	3.56	44	4
426	246	W	PSY	4	0	2.98	20	2
427	247	W	BIO	1	4	3.38	45	4
428	248	W	PSY	1	0	3.23	45	3.5
429	249	W	PSY	1	1	1.20	30	1
430	250	W	PSY	5	2	3.78	38	4
431	251	W	PSY	1	3	2.80	38	3
432	252	W	PSY	6	1	3.10	22	2
433	253	W	PSY	1	0	3.44	44	2
434	254	W	PSY	2	1	2.64	40	2
435	255	W	PSY	2	1	1.83	32	0
436	256	W	PSY	4	1	3.68	27	3.5
437	257	W	PSY	2	1	2.87	33	3.5
438	258	W	MED	2	2	2.99	33	2.5
439	259	W	PSY	3	2	3.50	38	4
440	260	W	PSY	2	1	2.73	32	2

TABLE E.1. *Continued*

(1) ID No.	(2) ID No. by Gen	(3) Gender	(4) Major	(5) No. Psy	(6) No. Math	(7) GPA	(8) Math Test	(9) Stat Grade
441	261	W	PSY	2	2	2.12	38	I
442	262	W	PSY	3	0	2.27	18	1
443	263	W	PSY	5	1	3.45	22	2
444	264	W	PSY	6	1	2.98	32	4
445	265	W	PSY	5	1	2.96	30	2
446	266	W	PSY	3	1	1.82	15	0
447	267	W	PSY	2	1	2.89	30	3
448	268	W	PSY	3	2	3.66	46	4
449	269	W	PSY	2	0	3.49	45	3.5
450	270	W	PSY	2	1	2.62	35	2
451	271	W	MED	4	2	3.78	40	3
452	272	W	PSY	3	1	2.88	34	2
453	273	W	PSY	1	1	3.30	40	2
454	274	W	PSY	2	1	3.01	40	2
455	275	W	PSY	2	1	3.14	36	2
456	276	W	PSY	2	0	3.52	22	3.5
457	277	W	PSY	4	1	2.61	30	2
458	278	W	PSY	1	0	2.70	27	I
459	279	W	PSY	13	1	3.63	34	3.5
460	280	W	PSY	4	2	2.66	35	I
461	281	W	PSY	3	2	2.83	33	2

References

American Statistical Association. *Careers in statistics.* Washington, DC: Author. [3]*

American Statistical Association. *Statistics as a career: Women at work.* Washington, DC: Author. [3]

Anderson, N. H. (1961). Scales and statistics: Parametric and nonparametric. *Psychological Bulletin, 58,* 305–316. [20]

Arken, A., & Colton, R. (1938). *Graphs: How to make and use them* (2nd ed.). New York: Harper. [42]

Bakan, D. (1966). The test of significance in psychological research. *Psychological Bulletin, 66,* 423–437. [324]

Binder, A. (1963). Further considerations on testing the null hypothesis and the strategy and tactics of investigating theoretical models. *Psychological Review, 70,* 107–115. [302]

Boneau, C. A. (1960). The effects of violations of assumptions underlying the *t* test. *Psychological Bulletin, 57,* 49–64. [351]

Boneau, C. A. (1961). A note on measurement scales and statistical tests. *American Psychologist, 16,* 160–161. [20]

Boneau, C. A., & Pennypacker, H. S. (1961). Group matching as research strategy: How not to get significant results. *Psychological Reports, 8,* 143–147. [409]

Box, G. E. P. (1954). Some theorems on quadratic forms applied in the study of analysis of variance problems, I. Effect of inequality of variance in the one-way classification. *Annals of Mathematical Statistics, 25,* 290–302. [480]

Bresnahan, J. L., & Shapiro, M. M. (1966). A general equation and technique for the exact partitioning of chi-square contingency tables. *Psychological Bulletin, 66,* 252–262. [565]

* Page on which reference is cited.

Campbell, D. T. (1957). Factors relevant to the validity of experiments in social settings. *Psychological Bulletin, 54,* 297–312. [350, 479]

Castellan, N. J., Jr. (1965). On the partitioning of contingency tables. *Psychological Bulletin, 64,* 330–338. [565]

Chissom, B. S. (1970). Interpretation of the kurtosis statistic. *American Statistician, 24,* 19–22. [130]

Cleveland, W. S. (1985). *The elements of graphing data.* Monterey, CA: Wadsworth. [42]

Clinch, J. J., & Keselman, H. J. (1982). Parametric alternatives to the analysis of variance. *Journal of Educational Statistics, 7,* 207–214. [479, 480]

Cohen, J. (1988). *Statistical power analysis for the behavioral sciences* (2nd ed.). Hillsdale, NJ: Lawrence Erlbaum. [322, 334, 351, 362, 368, 372, 472, 495, 557]

Cohen, J., & Cohen, P. (1983). *Applied multiple regression/correlation analysis for the behavioral sciences* (2nd ed.). Hillsdale, NJ: Lawrence Erlbaum. [204]

Conover, W. J. (1974a). Rejoinder on "Some reasons for not using the Yates continuity correction on 2×2 contingency tables" by W. J. Conover. *Journal of the American Statistical Association, 69,* 382. [562]

Conover, W. J. (1974b). Some reasons for not using the Yates continuity correction on 2×2 contingency tables. *Journal of the American Statistical Association, 69,* 374–376. [562]

Cook, T. D., and Campbell, D. T. (1979). *Quasi-experimentation: Design and analysis issues for field settings.* Chicago: Rand McNally. [479]

Darlington, R. B. (1970). Is kurtosis really "peakedness?" *American Statistician, 24,* 19–22. [130]

Dudycha, A. L., & Dudycha, L. W. (1972). Behavioral statistics: An historical perspective. In R. E. Kirk (Ed.), *Statistical issues* (pp. 1–25). Monterey, CA: Brooks/Cole. [22, 300]

Edgington, E. S. (1966). Statistical inference and nonrandom samples. *Psychological Bulletin, 66,* 485–487. [391]

Edwards, W. (1965). Tactical note on the relation between scientific and statistical hypotheses. *Psychological Bulletin, 63,* 400–402. [302]

Fisher, R. A., & Yates, F. (1974). *Statistical tables for biological, agricultural and medical research.* London: Longman. Previously, Edinburgh: Oliver & Boyd, 1963. [v, 700, 702, 707, 718, 720]

Gaito, J. (1960). Scale classification and statistics. *Psychological Review, 67,* 277–278. [20]

Galton, F. (1889). *Natural inheritance.* London and New York: Macmillan. [146]

Games, P. (1977). An improved *t* table for simultaneous control on *g* contrasts. *Journal of the American Statistical Association, 72,* 531–534. [725]

Gardner, P. L. (1975). Scales and statistics. *Review of Educational Research, 45,* 43–57. [20]

Glass, G. V., & Hopkins, K. D. (1996). *Statistical methods in education and psychology* (3rd ed.). Boston, MA: Allyn and Bacon. [174]

Grant, D. A. (1962). Testing the null hypothesis and the strategy and tactics of investigating theoretical models. *Psychological Review, 69,* 54–61. [302]

Grizzle, J. E. (1967). Continuity correction in the χ^2 test for 2×2 tables. *American Statistician, 21,* 28–32. [562]

Halperin, M., Hartley, H. O., & Hoel, P. G. (1965). Recommended standards for statistical symbols and notation. *American Statistician, 19,* 12–14. [72]

Harris, R. J. (1994). *ANOVA: An analysis of variance primer.* Itasca, IL: Peacock. [536]

Hays, W. L. (1994). *Statistics* (5th ed.). New York: Holt, Rinehart and Winston. [162, 174, 218, 257, 261, 262, 393, 541, 559, 565, 567]

Hedges, L. V. (1981). Distributional theory for Glass's estimator of effect size and related estimators. *Journal of Educational Statistics, 6,* 107–128. [397]

Hooke, R., & Liles, J. M. (1983). *How to tell the liars from the statisticians.* New York: Marcel Dekker. [2]

Howell, D. C. (1997). *Statistical methods for psychology* (4th ed.). Boston: Duxbury Press. [174, 393, 527, 541]

Huff, D. (1954). *How to lie with statistics.* New York: Norton. [55]

Jaffe, A. J., & Spirer, H. F. (1986). *Misused statistics: Straight talk for twisted numbers.* New York: Marcel Dekker. [2]

Keppel, G. (1991). *Design and analysis: A researcher's handbook.* Englewood Cliffs, NJ: Prentice-Hall. [527, 541]

Kirk, R. E. (Ed.). (1972). *Statistical issues.* Monterey, CA: Brooks/Cole. [20, 300, 302, 317, 350, 391, 409, 479, 590]

Kirk, R. E. (1978). *Introductory statistics.* Monterey, CA: Brooks/Cole. [116, 125, 150, 157, 170, 197, 321]

Kirk, R. E. (1994). Choosing a multiple comparison procedure. In B. Thompson (Ed.), *Advances in social science methodology* (pp. 77–121). Greenwich, CT: JAI Press. [483]

Kirk, R. E. (1995). *Experimental design: Procedures for the behavioral sciences* (3rd ed.). Monterey, CA: Brooks/Cole. [147, 393, 457, 466, 470, 472, 486, 490, 527, 529, 531, 536, 541]

Kirk, R. E. (1996). Practical significance: A concept whose time has come. *Educational and Psychological Measurement, 56,* 746–759. [334]

Kraemer, H. C., & Thiemann, S. (1987). *How many subjects?* Newbury Park, CA: Sage Publications. [351, 362, 368]

Mantel, N. (1974). Comment and suggestion. *Journal of the American Statistical Association, 69,* 378–380. [562]

Marascuilo, L. A. (1966). Large sample multiple comparisons. *Psychological Bulletin, 65,* 280–290. [565]

Marascuilo, L. A. (1971). *Statistical methods for behavioral science research.* New York: McGraw-Hill. [556]

Marascuilo, L. A., & McSweeney, M. (1977). *Nonparametric and distribution-free methods for the social sciences.* Monterey, CA: Brooks/Cole. [556, 565, 569, 591]

Marcus-Roberts, H. M., & Roberts, F. S. (1987). Meaningless statistics. *Journal of Educational Statistics, 12,* 383–394. [20]

Mauro, J. (1992). *Statistical deception at work.* Hillsdale, NJ: Lawrence Erlbaum. [2]

Maxwell, S. E., & Delaney, H. D. (1990). *Designing experiments and analyzing data.* Belmont, CA: Wadsworth. [527, 541]

McGee, V. E. (1971). *Principles of statistics.* New York: Appleton-Century-Crofts. [218]

McNemar, Q. (1947). Note on the sampling error of the difference between correlated proportions or percentages. *Psychometrika, 12,* 153–157. [444]

Micceri, T. (1989). The unicorn, the normal curve, and other improbable creatures. *Psychological Bulletin, 105,* 156–166. [347, 352]

Miettinen, O. S. (1974). Comment on "Some reasons for not using the Yates continuity correction on 2 × 2 contingency tables" by W. J. Conover. *Journal of the American Statistical Association, 69,* 380–382. [562]

Neter, J., Wasserman, W., & Kutner, M. H. (1990). *Linear statistical models.* Homewood, IL: Irwin. [204]

Novick, M. R., & Jackson, P. H. (1974). *Statistical methods for educational and psychological research.* New York: McGraw-Hill. [218]

Nunnally, J. (1960). The place of statistics in psychology. *Educational and Psychological Measurement, 20,* 641–650. [324]

Pearson, E. S., & Hartley, H. O. (1966). *Biometrika tables for statisticians* (Vol. 1, 3rd ed.). New York: Cambridge. [v, 710, 723]

Pedhazur, E. J. (1982). *Multiple regression in behavioral research* (2nd ed.). New York: Holt, Rinehart and Winston. [204]

Plackett, R. L. (1964). The continuity correction in 2 × 2 tables. *Biometrika, 51,* 327–337. [562]

Robinson, F. P. (1946). *Effective Study.* New York: Harper & Brothers. [4]

Rosnow, R., & Rosenthal, R. (1989). Statistical procedures and the justification of knowledge in psychological science. *American Psychologist, 44,* 1276–1284. [327]

Rozeboom, W. W. (1960). The fallacy of the null-hypothesis significance test. *Psychological Bulletin, 57,* 416–428. [324]

Senders, V. L. (1958). *Measurement and statistics.* New York: Oxford. [18]

Siegel, S. (1956). *Nonparametric statistics for the behavioral sciences.* New York: McGraw-Hill. [18]

Starmer, C. J., Grizzle, J. E., & Sen, P. K. (1974). Comment on "Some reasons for not using the Yates continuity correction on 2 × 2 contingency tables" by W. J. Conover. *Journal of the American Statistical Association, 69,* 376–378. [562]

Stevens, S. S. (1946). On the theory of scales of measurement. *Science, 103,* 667–680. [14, 18]

Stevens, S. S. (1951). Mathematics, measurement, and psychophysics. In S. S. Stevens (Ed.), *Handbook of experimental psychology* (pp. 1–49). New York: Wiley. [18]

Stevens, S. S. (1968). Measurement, statistics, and the schemapiric view. *Science, 161,* 849–856. [20]

Tan, W. Y. (1982). Sampling distributions and robustness of *t*, *F* and variance-ratio in two samples and ANOVA models with respect to departure from normality. *Communications in Statistics—Theory and Methods, 11,* 486–511. [479]

Tippett, L. H. C. (1925). On the extreme individuals and the range of samples from a population. *Biometrika, 17,* 386. [125]

Tufte, E. R. (1983). *The visual display of quantitative information.* Cheshire, CT: Graphics Press. [42, 55]

Tukey, J. W. (1977). *Exploratory data analysis.* Reading, MA: Addison-Wesley. [48, 127]

Tukey, J. W. (1991). The philosophy of multiple comparison. *Statistical Science, 6,* 100–116. [324, 327]

Ury, H. (1967). In response to Noether's letter, "Needed—a new name." *American Statistician, 21,* 53. [590]

Wainer, H. (1976). Estimating coefficients in linear models: It don't make no nevermind. *Psychological Bulletin, 83,* 213–217. [20]

Wilcox, R. R. (1996). *Statistics for the social sciences.* San Diego, CA: Academic Press. [174, 347, 480, 486, 545]

Wilson, W. R., & Miller, H. (1964). A note on the inconclusiveness of accepting the null hypothesis. *Psychological Review, 71,* 238–242. [302]

Wilson, W., Miller, H. L., & Lower, J. S. (1967). Much ado about the null hypothesis. *Psychological Bulletin, 67,* 188–196. [302]

Zar, J. H. (1972). Significance testing of the Spearman rank correlation coefficient. *Journal of the American Statistical Association, 67,* 578–580. [719]

Index

Descriptive Statistics
Quick Reference

*2.2 Proportionate frequency, Prop $f = \dfrac{f}{n}$

2.2 Percentage frequency, $\%f = \dfrac{f}{n} \times 100$

3.3 Mean, $\bar{X} = \dfrac{\Sigma X_i}{n}$

3.4 Median, $Mdn = X_{ll} + i\left(\dfrac{n/2 - \Sigma f_b}{f_i}\right)$

3.7 Weighted mean,

$$\bar{X}_W = \dfrac{n_1\bar{X}_1 + n_2\bar{X}_2 + \cdots + n_n\bar{X}_n}{n_1 + n_2 + \cdots + n_n}$$

4.2 Range, $R = X_{ul(largest\ score)} - X_{ll(smallest\ score)}$

4.2 Semi-interquartile range, $Q = \dfrac{Q_3 - Q_1}{2}$

4.2 Percentile point,

$$P_\% = X_{ll} + i\left(\dfrac{n(P_R/100) - \Sigma f_b}{f_i}\right)$$

4.2 Percentile rank,

$$P_R = \dfrac{100}{n}\left[\Sigma f_b + \dfrac{f_i\,(P_\% - X_{ll})}{i}\right]$$

4.2 Standard deviation, $S = \sqrt{\dfrac{\Sigma X_i^2 - \dfrac{(\Sigma X_i)^2}{n}}{n}}$

4.2 Coefficient of variation, $CV = 100(S/\bar{X})$

4.2 Index of dispersion, $D = \dfrac{c\left(n^2 - \sum\limits_{j=1}^{c} n_j^2\right)}{n^2(c - 1)}$

4.6 Skewness, $Sk = \dfrac{\dfrac{\Sigma(X_i - \bar{X})^3}{n}}{S^3}$

4.6 Kurtosis, $Kur = \dfrac{\dfrac{\Sigma(X_i - \bar{X})^4}{n}}{S^4} - 3$

5.3 Pearson correlation,

$$r = \dfrac{\Sigma X_i Y_i - \dfrac{(\Sigma X_i)\,(\Sigma Y_i)}{n}}{\sqrt{\left[\Sigma X_i^2 - \dfrac{(\Sigma X_i)^2}{n}\right]\left[\Sigma Y_i^2 - \dfrac{(\Sigma Y_i)^2}{n}\right]}}$$

5.7 Spearman correlation, $r_s = 1 - \dfrac{6\Sigma(R_{X_i} - R_{Y_i})^2}{n(n^2 - 1)}$

6.2 Regression, $Y_i' = a_{Y\cdot X} + b_{Y\cdot X}\,X_i$

6.3 Standard error of estimate, $S_{X\cdot Y} = S_Y\sqrt{1 - r^2}$

6.5 Multiple correlation,

$$R_{Y\cdot X_1 X_2} = \sqrt{\dfrac{r_{YX_1}^2 + r_{YX_2}^2 - 2r_{YX_1}\,r_{YX_2}\,r_{X_1 X_2}}{1 - r_{X_1 X_2}^2}}$$

7.1 Probability of A, $p(A) = n_A/n_S$

7.3 Prob of A or B, $p(A\ or\ B) = p(A) + p(B) - p(A\ and\ B)$

7.3 Prob of A and B, $p(A\ and\ B) = p(A)p(B|A)$

7.4 Permutation, $_nP_n = n! = n(n - 1)(n - 2) \cdots$ (1)

7.4 Permutation, $_nP_r = \dfrac{n!}{(n - r)!}$

7.4 Combination, $_nC_r = \dfrac{n!}{r!\,(n - r)!}$

8.2 Expected value, $E(X) = \Sigma p(X_i)X_i$

9.1 z score, $z = \dfrac{X - \bar{X}}{S}$

10.6 Cohen's effect size, $d = \dfrac{|\bar{X} - \mu_0|}{\sigma}$

12.4 Hedges' effect size, $g = \dfrac{|\bar{X}_1 - \bar{X}_2|}{\hat{\sigma}_{Pooled}}$

14.6 Omega squared, $\hat{\omega}^2 = \dfrac{SSBG - (p - 1)MSWG}{SSTO + MSWG}$

16.2 Cohen's effect size, $\hat{w} = \sqrt{\Sigma\dfrac{(\hat{p}_j - p_j')^2}{p_j'}}$

16.3 Cramér's correlation, $\hat{V} = \sqrt{\dfrac{\chi^2}{n(s - 1)}}$

*Section where statistic is described

Inferential Statistics
Selection Guide
(TS = Test Statistic, CI = Confidence Interval)

Number of Samples	Nature of Variable		
	Unordered Qualitative Variable	Ordered Qualitative Variable	Quantitative Variable
One-sample	z TS & CI for p, 11.4* χ^2 TS for goodness of fit, 16.2 χ^2 TS for independence, 16.3	z TS & CI for p, 11.4 χ^2 TS for goodness of fit, 16.2 χ^2 TS for independence, 16.3	z TS for μ, 10.3 z CI for μ, 10.5 t TS & CI for μ, 11.2 χ^2 TS & CI for σ^2, 11.3 t TS for ρ, 11.5 z TS & CI for ρ, 11.5
Two independent samples	z TS & CI for $p_1 - p_2$, 13.3	z TS & CI for $p_1 - p_2$, 13.3 Mann-Whitney U TS, 17.2	z TS for $\mu_1 - \mu_2$, 12.2 t TS & CI for $\mu_1 - \mu_2$, 12.4 F TS & CI for σ_1^2/σ_2^2, 13.1
Two dependent samples	z TS & CI for $p_1 - p_2$, 13.4	z TS & CI for $p_1 - p_2$, 13.4 Wilcoxon T TS, 17.3	z TS for $\mu_1 - \mu_2$, 12.5 t TS & CI for $\mu_1 - \mu_2$, 12.5 t TS & CI for $\sigma_1^2 - \sigma_2^2$, 13.2
Multiple independent samples	χ^2 TS for equality of p's, 16.4 χ^2 TS for homogeneity of p's, 16.4	χ^2 TS for equality of p's, 16.4 χ^2 TS for homogeneity of p's, 16.4	Completely randomized ANOVA design, 14.3 Dunn-Šidàk TS & CI for μ's, 14.5 Fisher-Hayter TS for μ's, 14.5 Scheffé TS & CI for μ's, 14.5 Tukey TS & CI for μ's, 14.5 Completely randomized factorial ANOVA design, 15.3 Dunn-Šidàk TS & CI for μ's, 15.3 Fisher-Hayter TS for μ's, 15.3 Scheffé TS & CI for μ's, 15.3 Tukey TS & CI for μ's, 15.3
Multiple dependent samples			Randomized block ANOVA design, 15.2 Dunn-Šidàk TS & CI for μ's, 15.2 Fisher-Hayter TS for μ's, 15.2 Scheffé TS & CI for μ's, 15.2 Tukey TS & CI for μ's, 15.2

*Section where statistic is described

DATE DUE

FEB 1 3 2004	

VIRAL DISEASES

Disease	Virus	Reservoir	Disease	Virus	Reservoir
bronchitis, rhinitis	parainfluenza	humans, some other mammals	influenza	influenza	swine, humans (type A)
					humans (type B)
Burkitt's lymphoma	Epstein-Barr	humans			humans (type C)
chickenpox	varicella-zoster	humans			
coryza (common cold)	rhinovirus	humans	Lassa fever	arenavirus	rodents
	coronavirus	humans	measles (rubeola)	measles	humans
cytomegalic inclusion disease	cytomegalovirus	humans	meningoencephalitis	herpes	humans
Dengue fever	Dengue	humans	molluscum contagiosum	poxvirus group	humans
encephalitis	Colorado tick fever	mammals			
	Eastern equine encephalitis	birds	mumps	paramyxovirus	humans
	St. Louis encephalitis	birds	pneumonia	adenoviruses, respiratory syncytial virus	humans
	Venezuelan equine encephalitis	rodents	poliomyelitis	poliovirus	humans
	Western equine encephalitis	birds	rabies	rabies	all warm-blooded animals
epidemic keratoconjunctivitis	adenovirus	humans	respiratory infections	adenovirus	humans
hantavirus pulmonary syndrome	bunyavirus	rodents		paramyxoviruses	none
			Rift Valley fever	bunyavirus (phlebovirus)	humans, sheep, cattle
hemorrhagic fever, Bolivian	arenavirus	rodents and humans	rubella (German measles)	rubella	humans
hemorrhagic fever, Korean	bunyavirus (Hantaan)	rodents	shingles	varicella-zoster	humans
hemorrhagic fever	Ebola virus (filovirus)	humans (?)	smallpox	variola (major and minor)	humans
	Marburg virus (filovirus)	humans (?)	viral enteritis	rotavirus	humans
hepatitis A (infectious hepatitis)	hepatitis A	humans	warts, common (papillomas)	human papillomavirus	humans
hepatitis B (serum hepatitis)	hepatitis B	humans	yellow fever	yellow fever	monkeys, humans, mosquitoes
hepatitis C (non-A, non-B)	hepatitis C	humans			
hepatitis D (delta hepatitis)	hepatitis D	humans			
hepatitis E (enterically transmitted non-A, non-B, non-C)	hepatitis E	humans			
herpes, oral	usually herpes simplex type 1, sometimes type 2	humans			
herpes, genital	usually herpes simplex type 2, sometimes type 1	humans			
HIV disease, AIDS	human immunodeficiency virus (HIV)	humans			
infectious mononucleosis	Epstein-Barr	humans			

The tables of fungal and protozoal diseases appear on the back cover endpapers

DISCARD

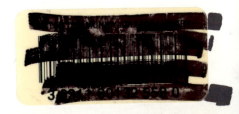